The **Rough Guide** to

The Philippines

written and researched by

David Dalton

NEW YORK · LONDON · DELHI

www.roughguides.com

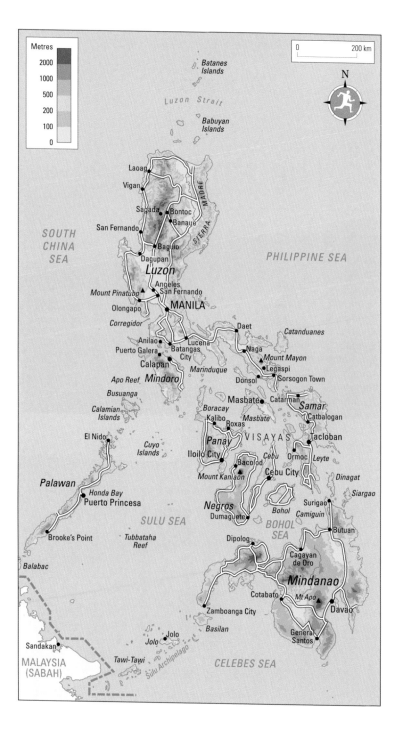

Contents

Diving colour section
following p.216

Music colour section
following p.328

◀◀ White Beach, Boracay

Introduction to

The Philippines

With more than seven thousand islands, sixty percent of them uninhabited, it's hardly surprising that most tourists visit the Philippines for sand and sea, for secluded tropical islets where you might be the only visitor and for world-class scuba diving among dazzling marine life. This is a diverse country in a small package, where a day's travel will take you from the unearthly tribal villages of the north to the idyllic islands of the Visayas. Landscapes range from sweeping rice plains to jungled peaks, from razor-sharp cliffs enclosing

placid lagoons to shining ribbons of sand. If you're ready to explore – and willing to cope with some eccentric infrastructure and a very laidback attitude to time – you're in for a rewarding trip.

The country is broadly divided into three main areas: **Luzon**, where the frenetic capital Manila is located; the scattered islands of the **Visayas**; and massive **Mindanao**. Luzon's two great mountain ranges, the Cordilleras and the Sierra Madre, both run north–south and act as natural impediments to travel, with the few roads that do penetrate the mountains in poor condition. Nowhere in the country are there any sweeping motorways or freeways, but the good news is that, as well as a decent domestic plane network, there's an intricate tracery of **ferry routes** that links the clamorous cities with the most far-flung little islands. Many of these ferries don't run to a tight schedule, and some are badly equipped and poorly maintained, but whichever island you want to visit, there will be a boat that can take you there.

5

◀ Philippines beach life

Fact file

- The Philippines consists of 7107 **islands** covering 300,000 square kilometres (slightly larger than Arizona) and with a coastline longer than America's. There are 73 provinces and 61 cities.

- The **population** is 85 million, 83 percent of which is Roman Catholic, 9 percent Protestant, 5 percent Muslim and 3 percent Buddhist, animist and other religions. The bulk of the population – more than ninety percent – is of the same stock as the Malays of Malaysia, with a small minority of Chinese.

- There are more than 150 **languages** and dialects. The main languages are Tagalog, English, Cebuano (spoken in Cebu), Ilocano (northern Luzon), Ilonggo (around Iloilo), Bicol (the Bicol region), Waray (Leyte), Pampango and Pangasinense (both Luzon).

- The country is a **republic**, modelled on the US system of government, with separation of powers between the executive presidency, bicameral legislature and an independent judiciary.

- Major **industries** are textiles, pharmaceuticals, chemicals, wood products, food processing, electronics assembly, petroleum refining and fishing. Agricultural products include rice, coconuts, corn, sugar cane, bananas, pineapples and mangoes. The most important sectors of the economy are farming and light industries such as food processing, textiles and garments, electronics and car parts.

▼ Roxas Boulevard at sunset, Manila

This is a country rich in **flora** and **fauna** – a thousand kinds of orchid, and forests that are home to macaques, spotted deer, boars, giant bats, pythons and cobras. There are so many types of butterfly and bird that they haven't all been documented, but you're likely to see bleeding-heart pigeons, green kingfishers darting through rainforest greenery, stately whistling herons with their melodious call and, circling above the jungle canopy, a dozen sorts of raptors, including the tiny Philippine falconet. The world's smallest fish, the *pondoka pygmaea*, inhabits the surrounding waters, as does the largest, the whale shark.

Diversity also characterizes the **people**, who speak more than 150 language and dialects and are variously descended from early Malay settlers, Muslim Sufis from the Middle East, Spanish conquistadors and friars, Mongoloid tribes from China who arrived 15,000 years ago and later Chinese traders. Indeed, it's the unaffected and gregarious inhabitants that often provide a visitor's enduring memory of the country. It's a hoary old cliché, but

Beauty pageants

It's somehow fitting that Imelda Marcos began her rise to power by winning a beauty pageant. Thousands of young Filipinas see these pageants – held in every city, town and barrio around the country – as a similar opportunity to make a fortune, without the prohibitive expense of struggling through school and college. The biggest nationwide contest is the annual Binibining Pilipinas (Binibining is the formal Tagalog for "Miss"). The winner is guaranteed advertising contracts, her face glowing from billboards around the country advertising shampoo, soap and skin-whitening lotion. After that, if she's got the nous, it's TV work and big-peso movie deals. Sometimes success comes in reverse, with expatriate Filipinas winning competitions in the US or Canada and using their success as an introduction to the showbiz circuit back home. Take Joyce Jimenez, who won a contest in the late nineties in Los Angeles and promptly headed to Manila, deciding she'd rather be a big fish in a small pond than struggle for fame in America. She has now become the Philippines' leading soft-porn star, with her own range of lingerie to boot.

largely true: Filipinos take pride in making visitors welcome, even in the most rustic barrio home. Equally important is the culture of entertaining, evident in the hundreds of colourful **fiestas** that are held throughout the country, most of them essentially religious in nature – this is, after all, the only predominantly Roman Catholic country in Asia – but with a lively secular element of pageantry, street dancing and singing.

Even the politics is rich in showmanship and pizzazz, masking a deplorable lack of substance. From Ferdinand and Imelda Marcos to the "housewife President" Cory Aquino and tough-guy movie actor Joseph Estrada,

▲ Jeepney

the country's leaders have never been short on charisma, but all have conspicuously failed to help the country shed its **developing-nation** status. Grinding poverty, visible everywhere you go in the shanty towns and rickety barrios, can be traced as far back as Spanish rule, when friars appropriated farmland, leaving locals with nothing. Inequality of land ownership still exists, but these days it's also the economy's inability to grow that perpetuates poverty.

Ordinary people, however, somehow remain stoical in the face of these problems, infectiously optimistic and upbeat. This determination to enjoy life is a national characteristic, encapsulated in the common Tagalog phrase *bahala na* – "what will be will be". For Filipinos, there's simply no excuse not to have fun.

The Philippine eagle

If you see a Philippine eagle in the wild, count yourself extremely lucky. This beautiful endangered bird (Pithecophaga jefferyi) is the second largest in the world and has the longest wingspan, up to two-and-a-half metres, making it a majestic sight in flight. But its most noticeable feature is its highly arched, powerful bill, longer and sharper than a butcher's knife, which it uses to rip apart snakes, hornbills, civet cats, flying lemurs and monkeys – the reason it is also called monkey-eating eagle. Sadly, this magnificent creature has been on the critical list since the 1960s, when a Filipino biologist alerted the world that it was in serious danger of extinction. Today, only a handful of birds – between 100 and 300 – are said to exist on Leyte, Samar and Mindanao. From every other island in the archipelago, they have disappeared due to deforestation. The bird's only hope, it seems, is the captive-breeding programme at the Philippine Eagle Foundation near Davao, where twenty eaglets have hatched. Sixteen have survived and are slowly being reintroduced to the wild.

Where to go

Most flights to the Philippines arrive in **Manila**, the crazy, chaotic capital which, despite first impressions, is worth a day or two of your time. The city's major historical attraction is the old Spanish walled city of **Intramuros**, while nearby in Malate – the best place to find budget accommodation – there's some of Asia's wildest nightlife. There are also some worthwhile day-trips from the city; top of the list is the island of **Corregidor** in Manila Bay, which was fought over bitterly during World War II and, with its now-silent guns and ruins, is a poignant place to soak up the history of the conflict. Another easy day out takes you to the agricultural province of **Laguna**, known for its therapeutic hot springs and some excellent trekking and climbing on peaks such as Makiling, a dormant volcano.

Within easy striking distance of Manila – about two hours south by road – the province of **Batangas** features rolling, verdant countryside and a number of attractions that make it worth an overnight trip. Around the small coastal town of **Anilao** you'll find the best scuba diving in the province, while near the busy little city of Tagaytay you

9

can explore **Lake Taal** and climb **Taal Volcano**, one of the smallest in the world, but still active. Continue south from here through the **Bicol** region and you'll reach perhaps the best-known of Philippine volcanoes, **Mayon**, an almost perfect cone that towers over the city of Legaspi and is a strenuous four- or five-day climb. The whole of Bicol, though off the usual tourist trail, is full of natural wonders and terrific adventure opportunities. Around **Donsol** you can swim with whale sharks, and in **Bulusan Volcano National Park** trek through lush rainforest to waterfalls, hot springs and volcanic craters. Even further off the tourist trail, there are two rural islands in the region: **Catanduanes**, where there's excellent surfing; and **Marinduque**, a pastoral backwater that only ever gets touristy for the annual Moriones festival, held at Easter.

For most visitors, the myriad islands and islets of the **Visayas**, right at the heart of the archipelago, are top of the agenda. The beautiful little island of **Boracay**, with its pristine beach, is on almost everyone's itinerary. There are plenty of other tropical idylls throughout the Visayas, most offering a combination of scuba diving and lively nightlife. If Boracay's a little too touristy for you, try **Panglao Island** off Bohol, the dazzling beaches and waters of **Malapascua** off the northern top of Cebu island or tiny **Apo Island** near Negros, a marine reserve where the only accommodation is in rustic cottages. If you get sick of sea and sand, there's plenty of exploring to do elsewhere around the Visayas. Head for **Mount Kanlaon National Park** on Negros, which has some extreme trekking and climbing in one of the country's finest wilderness areas. The largest city in the Visayas, **Cebu City**, is the arrival point for a limited number of international flights – as well as being served by regular domestic flights – making it a good alternative base to Manila. It's friendly, affordable and has a buzzing nightlife scene, with great restaurants and live music.

The text revolution

The Philippines leads the world in the use of text messaging – pervasive largely because it is cheap, and also because many rural areas don't have reliable landlines, but do have mobile phones. Texting crops up in the unlikeliest of situations. During a lull in hostilities, Muslim insurgents in Mindanao once sent insults to government soldiers by text – and the soldiers texted insults right back. Politically motivated texting is a major feature in Philippine presidential election campaigns. In the run-up to polls, each mobile-phone user will receive hundreds of political text messages both for and against the major candidates. Texting is also an important form of entertainment. Thousands of star-struck fans text their favourite actresses on a regular basis and receive replies through a special star-texting service. Indeed, texting has become so popular that the Catholic Church recently had to ban confessions by text.

Island hopping in the Bacuit Archipelago

If you're looking for some serious diving, head for **Puerto Galera** on the northern coast of **Mindoro Island**. "PG" has got everything – gentle drift dives along coral reefs and deep dives among sharks. It also boasts some excellent beaches, and trekking through the jungled interior to tribal communities. There's more world-class diving off the west coast of Mindoro at **Apo Reef**, although you'll have to hire a liveaboard boat to get here.

To the west of the archipelago, out in the northern Sulu Sea, is the stunning island of **Palawan**. Again, many visitors come here for the superb scuba diving, especially on the sunken World War II wrecks around **Busuanga**, one of the **Calamian Islands** to the north of Palawan. Palawan itself is also home to the seaside town of **El Nido** and the **Bacuit archipelago**, hundreds of gem-like limestone islands with sugar-white beaches and lagoons. From **Puerto Princesa**, Palawan's capital, strike out for the laidback beach town of **Port Barton** or, by boat, to **Tubbataha Reef Marine Park**, where you can dive among manta rays and sharks.

In the far south of the country, the large island of **Mindanao** is a place of great contrasts, ranging from the powdery beaches and secret lagoons of **Siargao Island** in the north to the tribal homelands of the T'boli people around **Lake Sebu** in the south. Off the island's northern coast, one of the area's major attractions is the wonderfully friendly and scenic island of **Camiguin**. Mindanao's capital is **Davao**, from where you can head inland to **Mount Apo**, the tallest mountain in the archipelago and a tough ascent even for experienced climbers. (Note that western Mindanao, including

▼ San Agustin Church

the Sulu archipelago, is off-limits because of continuing Muslim separatist unrest.)

It often comes after the Visayas and Palawan on visitors' priority list, but it's worth making time for the unique attractions and dramatic mountain scenery of **northern Luzon**. From the mountain city of **Baguio**, it's a rough but memorable trip north along winding roads to tribal communities such as **Sagada**, known for its hanging coffins, and **Banaue**, where you can trek through spectacular rice-terrace countryside. Off Luzon's northern tip are the dazzling islands of **Batanes**, one of the country's greatest secrets, while along Luzon's west coast you can surf around San Fernando or explore the atmospheric colonial town of **Vigan**, a UNESCO World Heritage site. Still in northern Luzon, but closer to Manila, there's island-hopping in the **One Hundred Islands** and trekking on **Mount Pinatubo**.

When to go

The Philippines has a tropical marine climate characterized by two distinct seasons: the **wet season** (southwest monsoon, or *habagat*) from May to October and the **dry season** (northeast monsoon, or *amihan*) from November to April.

Obviously the **best time** to visit is during the dry season, although even during the wet season it doesn't always rain torrentially and days can be hot and sunny, with short, intense downpours at dusk. And the dry season isn't dry everywhere. Areas facing northeast – Siargao in Mindanao is a good example – have no clear-cut dry season and see their heaviest rains between November and March, while most of the rest of the country basks in hot sunshine. The biggest threat during the wet season is from **typhoons**: the country is hit by five or six and affected by an average of fifteen during the wet season, with flights sometimes cancelled and roads impassable. The first typhoon can hit as early as May, although typically it is June or July before the rains really start, with July and August the wettest months. The southern Visayas and Palawan are less prone to this danger, and Mindanao sees less rain during the wet season and no typhoons.

Temperatures remain fairly high throughout the year, except in the mountains, but excessive heat is rare. The worst feature of the climate, apart from the occasional typhoon, is the high humidity and clouds during the rainy season. January and February are the coolest months and good for travelling, while March, April and May are very hot: expect sunshine all day and temperatures to peak at a broiling 36°C.

▼ Intramuros, Manila

▼ Fruit market

Weather bulletins are issued by the Philippine Atmospheric, Geophysical and Astronomical Service in Quezon City, known by the abbreviation PAGASA, which also means "hope". Storm warnings range from one up to four. When storm warning two or above is issued all schools and many offices shut down and ferries stop sailing.

Average temperatures and rainfall

	Jan	Feb	Mar	Apr	May	Jun	Jul	Aug	Sep	Oct	Nov	Dec
Manila												
Temp. °C	25	27	28.5	31.5	31	29	28.5	27.6	28	28.5	28	26.9
Temp. °F	77	80.6	83.3	88.7	87.8	84.2	83.2	81.7	82.4	83.3	82.4	80.4
Rainfall (mm)	0.74	0.46	0.58	1.1	4.2	8.5	13.9	13.6	11.8	6.2	4.8	2.1
Iloilo City												
Temp. °C	25.5	27	29	30.5	31.5	29.5	29	28.5	28	28	27.5	26.5
Temp. °F	77.9	80.6	84.2	86.9	88.7	85.1	84.2	83.3	82.4	82.4	81.5	79.7
Rainfall (mm)	2.06	1.6	1.1	1.4	5	8.8	14.4	12.4	10.5	8.6	7	3.8
Baguio												
Temp. °C	17	19	20.5	23.5	23	21	20.5	19.5	20	20.5	20	18.5
Temp. °F	62.6	66.2	68.9	74.3	73.4	69.8	68.9	67.1	68	68.9	68	65.3
Rainfall (mm)	0.74	1.2	1.1	1.4	4.8	10.2	14.8	14.2	12.6	8.4	6.6	3.2
Siargao												
Temp. °C	25.5	26	26	27	27	27	27	27	27	27	26	26.5
Temp. °F	77.9	78.8	78.8	80.6	80.6	80.6	80.6	80.6	80.6	80.6	78.8	79.7
Rainfall (mm)	17.5	13.4	16.3	8.4	5	4.2	5.7	4.1	5.6	8.8	14.2	20

things not to miss

It's not possible to see everything the Philippines has to offer in one trip – and we don't suggest you try. What follows is a selective taste of the country's highlights: idyllic beaches, spectacular hikes and fascinating tribal villages. They're arranged in five colour-coded categories, in no particular order, which you can browse through to find the very best things to see and experience. All entries have a page reference to take you straight into the Guide, where you can find out more.

ACTIVITIES | CONSUME | EVENTS | NATURE | SIGHTS

| ACTIVITIES | CONSUME | EVENTS | NATURE | SIGHTS |

01 Boracay Beach Page **323** • Idyllic White Beach on picture-postcard Boracay Island is one of the country's major tourist draws.

03 **San Agustin Church** Page **94** •
Atmospheric San Agustin Church in Manila is the oldest stone church in the archipelago.

04 **Vigan** Page **440** •
Picturesque Vigan is an old Spanish trading post with cobblestone streets and horse-drawn carriages.

06 Batad Page **489** • It's a long hike but worth the effort to Batad, a remote and rustic Cordillera village high in a natural amphitheatre and surrounded by majestic rice-terrace scenery.

05 Apo Reef National Park Page **226** • The gin-clear waters of Apo Reef National Park off the west coast of Mindoro are a scuba diver's dream.

07 Mount Mayon Page **182** • The almost perfectly symmetrical cone of volcanic Mount Mayon, near Legaspi, makes for a challenging but rewarding climb.

08 Chocolate Hills Page **278** • According to local legend, Bohol's iconic Chocolate Hills are the calcified tears of a broken-hearted giant.

09 Taal Volcano
Page **154** • Taal Volcano, sitting in the middle of a lake, makes an ideal day-trip from the capital.

10
Seafood Page **39** • Fresh, plentiful and affordable, seafood is loved by Filipinos and appears on almost every menu.

11

Surfing
Page **440** • Avid surfers will find several locations where they can strut their stuff – such as at San Juan, northwest of Manila.

12 **Paoay Church** Page
451 • Built from huge coral blocks, stately Paoay Church, near Laoag in far northern Luzon, is a classic example of the Spanish Baroque style, common throughout the islands.

13

Trekking on Mount Pinatubo Page
424 • The lower slopes of Mount Pinatubo feature canyons formed by volcanic debris from the massive 1991 eruption.

14
Siargao
Page **386**
• A perfect retreat, with great surfing, sweeping beaches and lovely resorts.

15 **Malapascua** Page **269** • Pretty Malapascua Island boasts dazzling beaches, laid-back tropical nightlife and excellent diving.

16
Outdoor massage
Page **323** • An alfresco massage in Boracay is the perfect way to relax after a hard day on the beach.

17 **Swimming with whale sharks** Page **189** • Swimming alongside a giant but gentle whale shark off the coast of Sorsogon, in southern Luzon, is an unforgettable experience.

19 **Lanzones of Camiguin** Page **380** • The lanzones fruit is the major product of the little island of Camiguin, and the excuse every year for the colourful Lanzones festival.

18 **Underground River** Page 354 • The Underground River in Palawan, with eerie stalactites, stalagmites, caverns, chambers and pools, is said to be the longest subterranean river in the world.

20 Corregidor guns Page **133**
• The guns are silent now, but during World War II the tiny island of Corregidor in Manila Bay was the scene of fierce fighting.

21 Caveside coffins Page **483** • In the heart of the tribal north, Sagada's attractions include trekking, caves, waterfalls and ancient hanging coffins.

22 Puerto Galera
Page **209** • Only a few hours from the bustle of Manila, scenic Puerto Galera has everything — good accommodation, activities and nightlife.

23 Diving to a wreck Page **429** • With more than 7000 islands to choose from, it's hardly surprising the Philippines is one of the world's premier scuba diving destinations.

25 Rice terraces Page 487 •
The majestic rice terraces around Banaue offer superb trekking.

24 Manila nightlife Page 117 •
Cosmopolitan Manila has some of Asia's liveliest nightlife, much of it around J. Nakpil Street in Malate.

26 Ati-Atihan festival Page 312 •
At the annual Ati-Atihan festival in Kalibo, on Panay Island, everyone gets to dress up and dance.

29 **Island-hopping** Page **359** • The trusty banca (typically an outrigger) is the main form of transport for many Filipinos in rural areas, and a great way for tourists to go island-hopping.

28 **San Miguel beer** Page **42** • San Miguel beer is cheap, tastes good and is available everywhere, even at the smallest sari-sari store.

Basics

Basics

Getting there

There are some nonstop flights to the Philippines from the west coast of North America and from Australia; from Europe, the only nonstop flights are from Amsterdam. Otherwise, reaching the Philippines from outside Asia involves a stopover in East Asia or the Middle East; most major airlines in the region have regular flights to Manila, with a few also flying to Cebu. Hong Kong is the best gateway to the Philippines, served by frequent flights on Cathay Pacific, Philippine Airlines and Cebu Pacific.

High season for Philippines travel is November to April, though **airfares** vary relatively little with the season. This is because the low season for the Philippines (May–Oct) is the peak season in Europe and the US, so flights heading out of these regions to various hub airports are often full. Your best bet for a bargain is to fly on a route that has a lengthy layover somewhere; you can save money if you don't mind a night on an airport floor somewhere.

If the Philippines is only one stop on a longer journey, you might want to consider buying a **Round-the-World (RTW)** ticket. In addition, some agents also offer **Circle Pacific** tickets, which cover Australia, New Zealand, the west coast of North America and destinations in the Pacific. You can include Manila and/or Cebu on some of the itineraries.

Flights from the UK and Ireland

While there are no nonstop flights to Manila from the UK or the Republic of Ireland, there are routes involving only one stop on the way – in **East Asia**, in **Paris** or at a **Middle Eastern hub** such as Dubai or Doha. **From London**, the quickest journey is to fly to Hong Kong, from where there are numerous onward flights daily to Manila (total flying time is around 15hr, including the stopover), plus a Philippine Airlines/Cathay Pacific codeshare flight to Cebu. **From Manchester**, you can fly nonstop to Kuala Lumpur or Singapore to catch a connection to Manila (or Cebu from Kuala Lumpur, with Malaysia Airlines). Flying to Manila via the Middle East is an option if you're starting out in London, Manchester or Birmingham, and from London there's the

additional possibility of flying Qatar Airways to Cebu. Finally, if you're travelling from a major British airport or **from Ireland**, you could consider flying via Amsterdam to connect with KLM's nonstop service to Manila.

As for **fares**, flying via the Middle East can be significantly cheaper than going straight to Hong Kong. In August, low season in the Philippines, London–Manila on Qatar Airways, Emirates or Gulf Air costs around £560 return. At the more expensive end of the range, expect to pay £800–900 London–Manila return on Cathay Pacific. From the Republic of Ireland, the best fares are around €800 via the UK and the Middle East.

From the US and Canada

Philippine Airlines operate **nonstop** flights to Manila from Los Angeles, San Francisco, Las Vegas and Vancouver, charging US$800–1000 or Can$1100–1300 for the round trip. However, you can save around twenty percent on this fare if you travel on another airline via, say, South Korea, Taiwan or Japan.

From Los Angeles or San Francisco, the **flying time** to Manila is around eleven hours. From the east coast of North America, flying via the Pacific, the journey will take around twenty hours excluding any layover (allow at least 2hr extra) along the way. If you choose to fly from New York via Paris, say, expect the journey to take around 24 hours altogether.

From Australia and New Zealand

From Australia there are **nonstop** flights to Manila from **Sydney** and **Brisbane**, with connections from other cities such as **Perth** and **Melbourne**. A typical return fare from Sydney to Manila, a seven-hour trip, is A$1250. If you want to get to Cebu City, you can fly via Hong Kong or Kuala Lumpur, although it's probably easiest simply to change in Manila. From New Zealand there are no nonstop flights to the Philippines, so you'll have to go via Australia or a Southeast Asian hub such as Singapore or Hong Kong. A typical fare is NZ$1600 Auckland–Manila via Singapore, the journey taking 25 hours.

From South Africa

From South Africa you'll always make at least one stop en route to Manila, and often two. Depending on the length of the stop, the trip will take from 16 to 26 hours. Emirates has flights from around US$1100 return from Johannesburg that stop in Dubai. South African Airways and Cathay Pacific both have daily nonstop flights to Hong Kong from Johannesburg where you can connect with Cathay Pacific on to Manila; total return fare from around US$1350. It's also possible to go through Singapore with Singapore Airlines or Kuala Lumpur with Malaysia Airlines, although at around US$2000 return these routes are more expensive. Return flights from Cape Town with South African Airways and Cathay Pacific start from US$2000, the trip taking 20–22 hours with a stop in Hong Kong.

Airlines, agents and tour operators

Many discount travel websites offer you the opportunity to book flight tickets and holiday packages online, cutting out the costs of agents and middlemen; these are worth going for, as long as you don't mind the inflexibility of non-refundable, non-changeable deals. There are some bargains to be had on auction sites too, if you're prepared to bid keenly. Almost all airlines have their own websites, offering flight tickets that can sometimes be just as cheap, and are often more flexible.

The Philippines is not a major destination for **package tours**, most tour operators to the region preferring to stick to the Southeast Asian mainland. Those that do offer Philippines tours tend to focus on Manila, Cebu and Banaue, which means you don't have much flexibility in choosing where to go. You'll need to weigh the convenience of having accommodation, transport and excursions arranged for you against the fact that you'll pay significantly more than if you travel independently.

Boats to the Philippines

Many unlicensed **boats** ply back and forth between the Malaysian state of Sabah and the southern Philippines, but note that these craft are often overloaded and poorly maintained. There are a number of passenger ferries to **Zamboanga City** from Sandakan, Sabah. The M/V *Danica Joy* belonging to Aleson Shipping and Sampaguita Shipping's M/V *Sampaguita*, both serve this route, with departures twice a week. Both ferries offer cheap bunk-bed accommodation on-deck, as well as a limited number of cabins. SRN Fast Seacraft has small, but modern ferries that operate twice a week from Sandakan to Zamboanga, with stops in Jolo and Bongao, Tawi-Tawi.

A one-way ticket on the M/V *Sampaguita* is P900 (about US$17) for tourist class, which means a small bunk bed in communal quarters, or P1,680 (US$32) for a bunk bed in a cabin shared with three others. The trip takes 11 hours with one stop in Bongao.

Five passenger ferries sail from **Bitung** in northern Sulawesi, Indonesia, to **Davao** via General Santos. The biggest and fastest is Sampaguita Shipping's M/V *Sampaguita I*, which carries up to a thousand passengers and makes the twelve-hour trip once a week on Monday; one-way fares range from P990 to P1,650. The best accommodation is in small cabins shared by four, but the food on board is awful, so bring your own.

Online booking

Ⓦ www.expedia.co.uk (in the UK), Ⓦ www
.expedia.com (in the US), Ⓦ www.expedia.ca
(in Canada).
Ⓦ www.lastminute.com (in UK), Ⓦ www
.lastminute.com.au (in Australia), Ⓦ www
.lastminute.co.nz (in New Zealand).
Ⓦ www.opodo.co.uk (in UK).
Ⓦ www.orbitz.com (in US).
Ⓦ www.travelocity.co.uk (in UK), Ⓦ www
.travelocity.com (in US), Ⓦ www.travelocity.ca
(in Canada).
Ⓦ www.zuji.com.au (in Australia), Ⓦ www.zuji
.co.nz (in New Zealand).

Airlines

Air New Zealand Australia ☎ 13 24 76, New
Zealand ☎ 0800/737 000, Ⓦ www.airnz.co.nz.
Alaska Airlines US ☎ 1-800/252-7522, Ⓦ www
.alaskaair.com.
All Nippon Airways (ANA) US and Canada ☎ 1-
800/235-9262, Ⓦ www.anaskyweb.com.
Asiana Airlines US ☎ 1-800/227-4262, Ⓦ www
.flyasiana.com.
Cathay Pacific UK ☎ 020/8834 8888, Australia
☎ 13 17 47, New Zealand ☎ 09/379 0861, South
Africa ☎ 2711/700 8900 Ⓦ www.cathaypacific.com.
China Airlines US ☎ 917/368-2003, Ⓦ www
.china-airlines.com.
Continental Airlines US and Canada ☎ 1-
800/523-3273, Ⓦ www.continental.com.
Emirates UK ☎ 0870/243 2222, South Africa
☎ 12711/303 1951 Ⓦ www.emirates.com.
Etihad Airways UK ☎ 0870/241 7121, Ⓦ www
.etihadairways.com.
EVA Airways US and Canada ☎ 1-800/695-1188,
Ⓦ www.evaair.com.
Garuda Australia ☎ 1300/365 330 or 02/9334
9944, New Zealand ☎ 09/366 1862, Ⓦ www
.garuda-indonesia.com.
Gulf Air UK ☎ 0870/777 1717, Ireland ☎ 0818/272
818, Ⓦ www.gulfairco.com.
JAL Japan Airlines US and Canada ☎ 1-
800/525-3663, Ⓦ www.jal.com.
KLM UK ☎ 0870/507 4074, Ⓦ www.klm.com.
Korean Air US and Canada ☎ 1-800/438-5000,
Ⓦ www.koreanair.com.
Kuwait Airways UK ☎ 020/7412 0006, Ⓦ www
.kuwait-airways.com.
Lufthansa UK ☎ 0870/837 7747, Republic of
Ireland ☎ 01/844 5544, Ⓦ www.lufthansa.com.
Malaysia Airlines UK ☎ 0870/607 9090, Republic
of Ireland ☎ 01/676 2131, US and Canada ☎ 1-
800/552-9264, Australia ☎ 13 26 37, New Zealand
☎ 0800/777 747, South Africa ☎ 2711/880 9614,

Ⓦ www.malaysiaairlines.com.
Northwest/KLM ☎ 1-800/225-2525, Ⓦ www
.nwa.com.
Philippine Airlines (PAL) ☎ 1-800/FLY-PAL, UK
☎ 01293/596 680, Australia ☎ 1-300/888-PAL,
New Zealand ☎ 09/308-5206, Ⓦ www
.philippineairlines.com.
Qantas Australia ☎ 13 13 13, New Zealand ☎ 0800/
808 767 or 09/357 8900, Ⓦ www.qantas.com.
Qatar Airways UK ☎ 020/7896 3636, Ⓦ www.
qatarairways.com.
Royal Brunei UK ☎ 020/7584 6660, Australia
☎ 07/3017 5000, New Zealand ☎ 09/977 2240,
Ⓦ www.bruneiair.com.
Singapore Airlines UK ☎ 0844-800-2380,
Republic of Ireland ☎ 01/671 0722, US ☎ 1-
800/742-3333, Canada ☎ 1-800/ 663-3046,
Australia ☎ 13 10 11, New Zealand ☎ 0800/808-
909, South Africa ☎ 2721/674 0601, Ⓦ www
.singaporeair.com.
South African Airways South Africa
☎ 0861/359722, International ☎ 2711/978 5313,
Ⓦ www.flysaa.com.
Thai Airways UK ☎ 0870/606 0911, US
☎ 212/949-8424, Canada ☎ 416/971-5181,
Australia ☎ 1300 651 960, New Zealand ☎ 09/377
3886, Ⓦ www.thaiair.com.

Travel agents

ebookers UK ☎ 0800/082 3000, Republic of
Ireland ☎ 01/488 3507, Ⓦ www.ebookers.com.
Ⓦ www.ebookers.ie Low fares on an extensive
selection of scheduled flights and package deals.
North South Travel UK ☎ 01245/608 291,
Ⓦ www.northsouthtravel.co.uk. Friendly, competitive
travel agency, offering discounted fares worldwide.
Profits are used to support projects in the developing
world, especially the promotion of sustainable tourism.
Plan It Holidays Australia ☎ 03/9245 0747,
Ⓦ www.planit.com.au. Discounted airfares and
accommodation packages in Southeast Asia.
Trailfinders UK ☎ 0845/058 5858, Republic of
Ireland ☎ 01/677 7888, Australia ☎ 1300/780 212,
Ⓦ www.trailfinders.com. One of the best-informed
and most efficient agents for independent travellers.
STA Travel US ☎ 1-800/781-4040, UK ☎ 0871/230 0
040, Australia ☎ 134 STA, New Zealand ☎ 0800/474
400, SA ☎ 0861/781 781, Ⓦ www.statravel.com.
Worldwide specialists in independent travel; also student
IDs, travel insurance, car rental, rail passes, and more.
Good discounts for students and under-26s.

Tour operators

Absolute Asia US ☎ 1-800/736-8187, Ⓦ www.
absoluteasia.com. Luxury tours to the Philippines that

Fly less – stay longer! Travel and climate change

Climate change is the single biggest issue facing our planet. It is caused by a build-up in the atmosphere of carbon dioxide and other greenhouse gases, which are emitted by many sources – including planes. Already, flights account for around 3–4% of human-induced global warming: that figure may sound small, but it is rising year on year and threatens to counteract the progress made by reducing greenhouse emissions in other areas.

Rough Guides regard travel, overall, as a global benefit, and feel strongly that the advantages to developing economies are important, as are the opportunities for greater contact and awareness among peoples. But we all have a responsibility to limit our personal "carbon footprint". That means giving thought to how often we fly and what we can do to redress the harm that our trips create.

Flying and climate change

Pretty much every form of motorized travel generates CO_2, but planes are particularly bad offenders, releasing large volumes of greenhouse gases at altitudes where their impact is far more harmful. Flying also allows us to travel much further than we would contemplate doing by road or rail, so the emissions attributable to each passenger are greater. For example, one person taking a return flight between Europe and California produces the equivalent impact of 2.5 tonnes of CO_2 – similar to the yearly output of the average UK car.

Less harmful planes may evolve but it will be decades before they replace the current fleet – which could be too late for avoiding climate chaos. In the meantime, there are limited options for concerned travellers: to reduce the amount we travel by air (take fewer trips, stay longer!), to avoid night flights (when plane contrails trap heat from Earth but can't reflect sunlight back to space), and to make the trips we do take "climate neutral" via a carbon offset scheme.

Carbon offset schemes

Offset schemes run by **climatecare.org**, **carbonneutral.com** and others allow you to "neutralize" the greenhouse gases that you are responsible for releasing. Their websites have simple calculators that let you work out the impact of any flight. Once that's done, you can pay to fund projects that will reduce future carbon emissions by an equivalent amount (such as the distribution of low-energy lightbulbs and cooking stoves in developing countries). Please take the time to visit our website and make your trip climate neutral.

www.roughguides.com/climatechange

---

can be combined with other destinations in Southeast Asia. The fourteen-day Highlights of the Philippines tour includes Manila, Banaue, Sagada, Baguio, Bohol and Cebu City, for $3900, excluding international flights.
Allways Dive Expeditions Australia ☏ 1800/338 239 or 03/9885 8863, ⊛ www.allwaysdive.com. au. All-inclusive dive packages to prime locations in Southeast Asia and elsewhere. Destinations in the Philippines include Coron and El Nido in Palawan, and Sangat Island Resort and Puerto Galera in Mindoro.
Dive Worldwide UK ☏ 01243/870616, ⊛ www. diveworldwide.com. Specialist dive operator offering trips to a number of destinations in the Philippines, including Palawan, Bohol, Dumaguete and Puerto Galera. A typical one-week trip to Puerto Galera including domestic transfers, twenty dives and

accommodation at the *Atlantis Beach Resort* – one of the best establishments in the area – starts at £1225; one week on Coron Town from £665.
Philippine Island Connections UK ☏ 020/7404 8877, ⊛ www.pic-uk.com. Philippines specialist offering flights to the Philippines, plus hotel bookings, holiday packages and tours. They also offer domestic flight reservations, though it's often cheaper to book once you're in the Philippines.
Swagman Travel Australia ☏ 07/5591 1968, Philippines ☏ 02/523 8541, ⊛ www.swaggy. com. Australian company with offices throughout the Philippines, offering everything from flights, cheap accommodation, diving, sailing, golf tours and domestic transport.

Getting around

The large number of flights and ferry services between major destinations makes it easy to cover the archipelago, even on a tight budget. There are dozens of flights every day from Manila to destinations such as Palawan, Cebu City and Boracay. Domestic airlines also serve secondary destinations such as Leyte and Mindanao. Long-distance road transport largely comprises buses and jeepneys – the utilitarian passenger vehicles modelled on American World War II jeeps. Throughout the provinces, and in some areas of cities, tricycles – motorbikes with steel sidecars – are commonly used for short journeys.

Airlines and major bus and ferry companies operate to timetables and have published **fares**, but for smaller ferries, jeepneys and tricycles, it's often a question of asking other passengers how much to pay in order to avoid being surcharged as a tourist.

Note that **holiday weekends** are bad times to travel, with buses full and roads jammed – cities start to empty on Friday afternoon and the exodus continues into the night, with a mass return on Sunday evening and Monday morning. Travelling is a particular hassle at Christmas, New Year and Easter with buses and ferries full (sometimes illegally overloaded), airports chaotic and resorts charging more than usual. Almost everyone seems to be on the move at these times of year, particularly heading out of big cities to the provinces, and the transport system can become strained. If you have to travel at these times, book tickets in advance or turn up at bus stations and ferry piers early and be prepared to wait.

By air

Air travel is a godsend for island-hoppers in the Philippines, with a number of airlines, large and small, linking Manila with most of the country's major destinations. **Philippine Airlines** (PAL; ⓦwww.philippineairlines.com) has a comprehensive domestic schedule, while two of the newer airlines, **Air Philippines** (ⓦwww.airphils.com) and **Cebu Pacific** (ⓦwww.cebupacificair.com), are catching up fast and offering competitive fares, particularly if you book some way in advance. There are two good smaller airlines – **Asian Spirit** (ⓦwww.asianspirit.com) and

Seair (ⓦwww.flyseair.com) – serving a number of popular routes. Asian Spirit's network includes Batanes, Baguio, Caticlan, Cebu City, Masbate, Virac, Busuanga and Surigao. Seair flies to, among other places, Busuanga, El Nido, Puerto Princesa, Clark, Caticlan, Surigao and Tawi-Tawi. Both these airlines serve some destinations from Cebu City, saving you the effort of backtracking to Manila if you're travelling within the south of the country – you can, for instance, fly straight from Cebu City to Caticlan (for Boracay) and Siargao. On the popular Manila-Caticlan route (for Boracay) Seair uses quicker aircraft that cut the flight time from the usual one hour with Asian Spirit to 35 minutes.

Fares

The three major airlines have various fare classes, depending mostly on how far in advance you book your ticket. Tickets booked at the last minute – usually no more than two days before departure – are ten percent cheaper than those booked some time in advance, but are valid for three months instead of six or twelve. Fares on Seair and Asian Spirit don't depend on how far in advance you book, though both airlines do offer promotional fares during low season.

There's not a great deal of variation in domestic **air fares** offered by the three main carriers. But note that the low prices you see quoted on airline websites and in advertisements are only half the story. Taxes can double the advertised fare. For example, Cebu Pacific's advertised net fare on the

Manila-Cebu-Manila route is P1136, but on top of that there's tax of P2102, for a total of P3238. The cheapest Philippine Airlines fare on this route is also P3238; with Air Philippines it's P3878.

By ferry

Ferries and **bancas** – wooden outrigger boats – are the bread and butter of Philippine travel. Throughout the thousands of islands comprising the Visayas, where sea travel is most crucial, there's hardly a coastal barrio that doesn't have some sort of ferry service, however irregular. There's a hierarchy of vessels, with proper ferries at the top; so-called **big bancas**, taking around fifty passengers, in the middle; and ordinary bancas at the bottom. The smaller bancas are often poorly equipped, with little shelter from the elements, while even many of the larger vessels have been bought second-hand from Japan or Europe and are well past their prime. Ferries of all sizes are frequently crowded.

A number of large ferry lines operate large ships between major ports in the Philippines. They are: **WG&A** (@www.superferry.com.ph), **Negros Navigation** (@www.negrosnavigation.ph), **Sulpicio Lines** (@www.sulpiciolines.com), **Cebu Ferries** (@www.cebuferries.com), **Supercat** (part of WG&A) (@www.supercat.com.ph), **Montenegro Lines** (@www.montenegrolines.com.ph), **Cokaliong** (@www.cokaliongshipping.com) and **TransAsia** (www.transasiashipping.com). These companies have regular sailings on routes between Manila and major cities throughout the Visayas and Mindanao, or on secondary routes within the Visayas. Most post schedules and fares on their websites. On less popular routes you might have to take your chances with smaller companies, which rarely operate to published timetables. In rural areas you may have to ask around at the harbour or wharf as to what boats are leaving, for where and when.

Tickets are available in a number of different categories, depending on the operator and the vessel. From Manila to Coron Town, for example, a one-way ticket with WG&A for a bunk in an air-conditioned dorm is P1893 and for a comfortable bed in a good-sized cabin with shower and toilet, P2455. Tickets can be bought at the pier up until departure, though it's often more convenient to avoid the long queues and buy in advance: travel agents sell ferry tickets, and the larger ferry companies have ticket offices in cities and towns. You can get significant discounts if you buy at the last minute – a ticket bought less than two days before your journey with WG&A can be almost P1000 cheaper than a ticket bought weeks ahead. In the case of WG&A, Supercat and Cebu Ferries, Aboitiz Express outlets are an additional source of tickets, while WG&A also offers online ticketing.

The cheapest **accommodation** is in bunk beds in cavernous dorms either below deck or on a semi-open deck, with shared toilets and showers that are often unpleasant. Most of the larger ferries have cabins, though the standard of these varies according to the age of the vessel and from one company to another. Older ships might have just a handful of cramped cabins sharing a tiny shower and toilet. The major operators generally have newer ships with a range of accommodation that includes dorms, straw mats in an air-conditioned area, shared cabins (usually for four) with bathroom, and in some cases staterooms and suites for two. These ferries usually also have a bar, karaoke lounge and a canteen, though the food that's served is often greasy and unappetizing.

Even in the dry season the open ocean can get surprisingly rough, so think carefully about whether you want to chance a ride on a small boat that looks ill-equipped or overcrowded. Safety regulations are being tightened, but ferry **accidents** remain common in the Philippines, so common that only the ones involving huge loss of life are worthy of mention on the front pages.

By bus

Hundreds of bus routes spread out like a web from Manila and every other town and city; even the most isolated barrios have occasional creaky old buses making trips to the closest hub. The largest bus companies have fleets of reasonably new air-conditioned buses on longer routes, although these don't come close to offering the kind of space or comfort you'd get with, say, Greyhound in the US. Otherwise, most buses are utilitarian vehicles which rarely have toilets and never serve food on board, although most will have a television playing Tagalog movies at full blast throughout the trip. On shorter routes many buses are dilapidated contraptions with no air-conditioning and, in some cases, no glass in the windows.

Fares are low; around P310 from Manila to Banaue and P380 from Manila to Baguio. A one-way ticket for the 48-hour Manila to Davao trip costs around P1500, but journeys can take longer than you'd expect. Roads can be poor, and even when the distances involved aren't great, the buses will make numerous stops along the way. Some bus companies advertise **express** services, but in reality a bus that goes from A to B without stopping is unheard of. Buses that have a "derecho" sign (meaning "straight" or "direct") in the window usually make the fewest stops.

Many travellers on long trips prefer to make these epic journeys at night, when traffic is light. On the longer hauls, buses stop every three or four hours to give passengers a chance to stretch their legs and buy some food. The meals sold at rest stops, however, have often been lying around a long time, and the range of snacks on sale is often not especially appetizing, so you might want to bring your own supplies.

Published **timetables** for most bus companies are non-existent, but departures on popular routes such as Manila to Baguio or Manila to Vigan usually happen every hour or half-hour. The **larger operators** – Victory Liner (Ⓦwww.victoryliner.com) BLTB, JAM Transit, Philtranco (Ⓦwww.philtranco.com) and Philippine Rabbit – allow you to **book seats** in advance, either by telephone (be warned, the lines are often engaged) or at the terminal. It isn't usually necessary to book tickets in advance though – as long as it's not a holiday weekend when you can get trampled in the rush back to the provinces, it's fine to buy your ticket at the terminal an hour before the bus leaves. For a list of bus companies with offices in Manila, see box on p.130; smaller regional operators are mentioned in the text as they arise.

By jeepneys, FX taxis and tricycles

The **jeepney** is the ultimate Philippine icon, admired and reviled in equal measure, and stubbornly enduring. The original jeepneys, cannibalized from vehicles left behind by departing Americans at the end of World War II, have evolved over the past five decades into the mass-produced mobile confections that you see on the streets today, impressively hung with chrome trinkets, gewgaws and sundry additions. Inside are strings of blinking fairy lights, velour seats and cheap speakers thudding out disco music at the kind of volume that makes it difficult to make yourself heard. Many have galloping stallions stuck to the bonnet, supposedly indicative of the number of mistresses the driver has. All this frippery is known as *bongga*, a form of flamboyant decoration that underlines the driver's machismo and shows his optimism in the face of adversity.

Reams of prose have been produced about the jeepney's pre-eminence, its status as a proudly working-class, utilitarian incarnation of Filipino creativity. Depending on where you stand, it's either a work of art that should be celebrated or a pestilent jalopy that should be eradicated from the nation's roads. The truth is, despite the number of jeepneys gradually falling due to the availability of reasonably priced substitutes like the Toyota FX vehicles (see p.34), millions of ordinary Filipinos depend on jeepneys to get to school and the office, or to transport chickens and hogs to market. Jeepneys are able to operate where roads are too narrow for buses, and though city authorities, especially in Manila, periodically try to regulate jeepneys in an effort to reduce congestion, the drivers have a powerful union and have so far been able to resist major changes.

In Manila, Cebu City, Davao and Baguio, jeepneys are important for **city transport**, with frequent services between important locations in each city. In the provinces jeepneys connect isolated barrios to nearby towns and towns to cities, but they might run only two or three times a day, depending on demand, the weather and the mood of the driver. There are absolutely no timetables.

Routes are painted on the side or on a signboard in the window. Even so, using jeepneys takes a little local knowledge because they make numerous stops and deviations to drop off and pick up passengers. There's no such thing as a designated jeepney stop, so people wait in the shade at the side of the road and flag one down. Remarkably, no one seems to mind when passengers wait a matter of yards apart from each other, forcing the driver to stop and start a dozen times in the space of a couple of blocks.

The vehicles are **cramped** and incredibly uncomfortable, usually holding about twenty passengers inside and any number of extras clinging to the back or sitting precariously on top. It can be a hassle to get **luggage** on and off – small items might end up on the floor, but larger items will go on the roof. At least jeepneys are a great social equalizer; you'll soon find yourself involved in jolly conversations with the rest of the passengers about your nationality, destination and marital status.

Fares are low: in the provinces they start at P4 for a trip of a few kilometres, rising to P40 for two- or three-hour drives. In the cities, a trip of a few hundred metres costs around P5, rising to P25 on longer routes. To pay, hand your money to the passenger next to you and say *bayad po* (pay please). If you're not sitting close to the driver, the fare will be passed down the line of passengers until it reaches him; he will then pass back any change. You can **charter** a jeepney for the day to take you on sightseeing trips or from one place to the next. The rate very much depends on your bargaining skills, but expect to pay at least P500 for a two-hour trip, P1000 for day hire.

FX taxis

Not unlike jeepneys in the way they operate, **FX taxis** are air-conditioned Toyota FX Tamaraw vans, with signs in the window indicating their destination. They made their debut in Manila in the late 90s, and now operate in other cities and on some popular intercity routes. However, routes are often not set, so it takes a little local knowledge to know where to catch the right vehicle. The vans can be a little claustrophobic – the driver won't even think about moving until he's got ten people on board, three more than the vehicle is designed for.

Tricycles

The cheapest form of shared transport in the country, **tricycles** are ubiquitous in the provinces to the point of being pestilential; their two-stroke engines emit a distinctive scream and they belch fumes with seeming impunity. In Manila and Cebu City they are prohibited from using certain roads, but almost everywhere else they go where they like, when they like and at speeds as high as their small engines are capable of. The sidecars are designed for four passengers – two facing forwards and two backwards – but it's not uncommon to see extras clinging on wherever they can, the only limiting factor being whether or not the machine can actually move under the weight of the extra bodies. Tricycles never follow fixed routes, so it's usually a question of flagging one down and telling the driver your destination.

Fares typically start at P4 per person for a short trip of a few hundred metres. Many tricycles charge a set rate per person for trips within town or city boundaries, usually around P5–8. If you want to use the tricycle as a private taxi you'll have to negotiate a price – P20 is reasonable for a trip of up to 2km. Anything further than that and the driver will ask for at least P50, though you can always try to bargain him down.

By train

The government-funded **Philippine National Railways (PNR)**, created in 1984 to provide the country with a national rail service, has been racked by debt and lack of investment. Consequently the rail network is in a sad state of disrepair, with only one operational line, the **Main Line South**, from Manila to Legaspi in Bicol (though the government has indicated it intends to start work on a line from Caloocan in Manila to the airport at Clark and on to San Fernando in La Union).

The trip from Manila to Legaspi takes ten hours by way of Calamba and Naga, about the same time as the bus. Trains are uncomfortable and at peak times, passengers actually sit on the carriage roofs, which are sloped to prevent trackside squatters throwing their rubbish on top. As with other modes of Philippine public transport, **fares** are low: a one-way ticket from Manila to Legaspi costs P300 in an

Addresses in the Philippines

For buildings, it is common to give the address as, for example, 122 Legaspi corner Velasco Streets, meaning the junction of Legaspi Street and Velasco Street. As for floors within buildings, G/F denotes street level, after which comes 2/F, 3/F and so on; "first floor" or 1/F isn't used. Some addresses include the name of a barangay, which is officially an electoral division for local elections, but is generally used to mean a village or, when mentioned in connection with a town, a neighbourhood or suburb. The word barangay isn't always written out in the address, although it's sometimes included in official correspondence and signposts, often abbreviated to "Brgy" or "Bgy". The term "National Highway" in an address doesn't necessarily refer to a vast motorway – on the smaller islands or in provincial areas, it could mean the coastal road or the main street in town. When it comes to discussing islands, Filipinos generally talk loosely in terms of the main island in the vicinity – so, for example, they would talk about visiting Panay when they actually mean offshore Pan de Azucar. We've adopted a similar approach in parts of the Guide, implicitly including small islands in coverage of the nearest large island.

air-conditioned carriage, P200 otherwise. Facilities on board are nonexistent apart from dirty toilets; there are no sleeper carriages.

By car

It's possible to rent a **self-drive** car in the Philippines – a standard saloon car costs about P2200 per day. The question is whether you'd want to. Not only is traffic in Manila and other cities often gridlocked, but most Filipino drivers have a very relaxed attitude towards the rules of the road. Swerving is common, as is changing lanes suddenly and driving with one hand permanently on the horn, particularly with bus and jeepney drivers.

If you do drive you'll require nerve and patience. Make sure you have an **international driving licence** and be prepared to show it if you get stopped. Police and "traffic enforcers" – uniformed men and women employed by local authorities to supplement the police – might try to elicit a bribe from you. If this happens it's best to play the dumb foreigner and hand over the "on-the-spot fine" of a few hundred pesos. If you take the moral high ground and refuse to play along, you'll probably end up having your licence confiscated or, in the worst case, your car towed away and impounded until you pay a fine to get it back.

Hiring a driver

For about P3000 you can hire a **car and driver** from some car rental agencies for 10

hours, the extra expense more than justified by the peace of mind a local driver brings. In fact some rental agencies won't let you have a car unless you also hire one of their drivers – this is Avis's policy throughout the Philippines, for example.

Hiring a car and driver through a rental agency is expensive. Most people strike a private deal with a car or van owner looking for extra work. A typical rate for their services is P1500 a day, although you'll need to negotiate. A good way to find someone with a vehicle is to ask at your accommodation; alternatively, locals with cars wait at many airports and ferry ports in the hope of making a bit of money driving arriving passengers into town. You can ask these drivers if they're available to be hired by the day.

Car rental agencies

The major rental agencies in the Philippines are Avis, Budget and the locally based Filcar (www.filcartransport.com), with smaller firms operating throughout the country, listed in the *Yellow Pages*.

Avis UK ☎ 0870/606 0100 (or ☎ 028/9024 0404 in Northern Ireland), Republic of Ireland ☎ 01/605 7500, US ☎ 1-800/331-1084, Canada ☎ 1-800/272-5871, Australia ☎ 13 63 33 or 02/9353 9000, New Zealand ☎ 09/526 2847 or 0800/655 111, www.avis.com.
Budget UK ☎ 0800/181 181, Republic of Ireland ☎ 0903/277 11, US ☎ 1-800/527-0700, Australia

☏ 1300/362 848, New Zealand ☏ 09/976 2222, ⓦ www.budget.com.
Dollar US ☏ 1-800/800-4000, Australia ☏ 02/9223 1444, ⓦ www.dollar.com.

Hertz UK ☏ 0870/844 8844, Republic of Ireland ☏ 01/676 7476, US ☏ 1-800/654-3001, Canada ☏ 1-800/263-0600, Australia ☏ 13 30 39 or 03/9698 2555, New Zealand ☏ 0800/654 321, ⓦ www.hertz.com.

Accommodation

The Philippines has accommodation to suit everyone, from international five-star hotels and swanky beach resorts to simple rooms – sometimes no more than a bamboo hut on a beach – and budget hotels that vary wildly in price and comfort.

Big cities have a good choice of hotels in all price brackets. The further you get from centres of population, the more utilitarian and inexpensive accommodation becomes. In rural areas the choice might be limited to a few beach huts or a tatty lodging, perhaps even without running water. Established tourist areas are, of course, a different matter: places like Boracay and some areas of Palawan, Cebu and Davao have much more choice.

The rule when looking for somewhere to stay is that if you can **compare**, do. Standards vary wildly, and in most of the main destinations you'll find a range of places clustered in the same area. A cheap budget room in some hotels might be better than a standard double in others. It can be worth checking that the air-conditioner, where available, isn't noisy. Rooms on lower floors overlooking main roads are best avoided as they can be hellishly noisy; always go for something high up or at the back (or both). If you plan on staying more than a few days, ask for a 25 percent discount and offer to pay cash upfront.

There are a number of **online booking** services for accommodation in the Philippines. Two of the best established are ⓦ www.asiatravel.com and ⓦ www.asiahotels.com. Asiatravel covers Manila, Cebu City, Bohol and Boracay, and offers packages which combine accommodation with a domestic flight to the resort's location. Asiahotels is less extensive, but includes Manila, Bohol, Davao and Palawan. However, it's generally not necessary to book in advance unless you are visiting at peak times – Easter, Christmas, New Year, or during a major local festival (see p.44). If you do want to book by phone, note that some hotels in out-of-the-way areas won't have a landline telephone on site, in which case they may have a mobile number and/or a booking office in a city (often Manila); details are given in the text as appropriate.

Hotels and beach resorts

The terms **hotel** and **beach resort** cover a multitude of sins in the Philippines. A hotel can mean anything from the most luxurious five-star establishment to dingy budget pensions or guesthouses that have bars on the windows and in reality are little more than flophouses. Beach resorts in turn range from sybaritic affairs on private atolls, with butlers and health spas, to dirt-cheap, rickety one-room cottages on a deserted island. Most resorts have a variety of accommodation, from double and twin rooms (with two single beds) to family cottages with rooms for four or five. It's worth remembering that in the Philippines people and travel agents do distinguish between a "hotel" and a "resort". The former usually refers to a concrete edifice that's not on the beach and the latter to an establishment with beach, gardens and accommodation in cottages instead of, or as well as, rooms. "Resort hotels" are a mid-range or top-range hybrid of the two,

Accommodation price codes

All accommodation in the guide has been categorized according to the following price codes, which represent the cost of the cheapest double or twin room – or beach hut sleeping two - in peak season, namely November to April. Prices during the May–October rainy season are usually about twenty percent lower. It's important to note that as a "walk-in" guest you'll usually be able to get a cheaper rate than the rack rate listed on hotel websites, especially in the off-season or in less touristy areas where occupancy rates are lower.

In the most popular beach areas such as Boracay, rates during the three major holidays - Christmas, New Year, Easter - can often rise by 20 percent or more above those during the rest of the November–April peak season. Our price codes do not reflect these local differences. Remember also that for these three holidays, you'll need to book in advance if you want to guarantee a room at a particular hotel.

These rates are for the room only, although in some cases hotels will include breakfast in the price. It's worth asking about this when you book.

An increasing number of hotels and dive resorts in the Philippines are introducing package rates that include diving, day trips and other activities. A room-rate only is used in our price codes.

Government tax of 12 percent and a service charge of 10 percent is sometimes included in the published rates, but not always. If you see a room advertised at P1000++ ("plus plus") it means you'll pay P1000 plus VAT plus service charge – a total of P1220. These additional charges have been factored into all our rates.

Where dormitory accommodation is available, we've given the price of a dorm bed in pesos.

① Under P500	④ P1000–1500	⑦ P2500–4000
② P500–700	⑤ P1500–2000	⑧ P4000–5000
③ P700–1000	⑥ P2000–2500	⑨ Over P5000

sometimes with their own area of private beach. Many hotels and beach resorts accept **credit cards**, although there are exceptions, such as in rural areas where electricity supply is not dependable and also in the cheapest budget accommodation, where you must pay cash.

In many provincial areas the **water supply** is temperamental, so in all but the best hotels water, when available, is stored in a tub for later use. Here you might have to flush the toilet using a *tabo* (scoop) to dispense water from the tub, and bathe the Filipino way, pouring water over yourself with the *tabo*.

Budget

Accommodation in this category (①–③) offers little more than a bed, four walls and a fan or small air-conditioning unit, although if you're by the beach, with a pleasant sea breeze blowing and the windows open, air-conditioning isn't really necessary. Budget places, especially at the low end of this range, can be badly maintained though. If you do get a private bathroom it will only have cold water, and the "shower" is sometimes little more than a tap sticking out of the wall producing a mere trickle of water. Breakfast is unlikely to be included in the rate, though there may be a canteen or coffee shop on the premises where you can buy food. At the higher end of the budget range, rooms are usually simple but can be reasonably spacious, perhaps – if they are on or near a beach – with a small balcony.

Mid-range

There are plenty of mid-range hotels (④–⑤), mostly in towns and cities. The rooms typically have air-conditioning and a private bathroom with hot water, but they may not boast a TV or other frills. Beach cottages in this bracket are usually quite spacious and will often have a decent-sized veranda too.

Most mid-range accommodation will feature a small coffee shop or restaurant with a choice of Filipino and Western **breakfasts** that may be included in the rate; If it's not expect to pay around P100–140.

Expensive

In big cities and the most popular beach destinations you can splash out on five-star comfort at hotels and beach resorts owned and operated by international chains (**❼–❾**). The cottages at the most expensive resorts are more like chic apartments, often with a separate living area. Many of these establishments include a buffet breakfast in the rate, and sports facilities and outdoor activities are on offer, though you'll have to pay extra to partake.

Campsites, hostels and homestays

Campsites are almost unknown in the Philippines. A small number of resorts allow you to pitch tents in their grounds for a negligible charge, but otherwise the only camping you're likely to do is if you go trekking or climbing and need to camp overnight in the wilderness – in which case note that rental outlets for equipment are few and far between, so you might need to bring your own gear from home.

There are very few **youth hostels** in the country, most of them in university cities where they may be booked up by students throughout term time. A Hostelling International (HI) card can in theory give you a tiny saving of around P25 a night at the handful of YMCAs and YWCAs in the big cities. The problem is that few staff have any idea what an HI card is.

There's no official **homestay** programme in the Philippines, but in rural areas where there may be no formal accommodation, you'll often find people willing to put you up in their home for a small charge, usually no more than P200 a night, including some food. If you enjoy the stay, it's best to offer some sort of tip when you leave, or a gift of soft drinks and sweets for the children. You can ask around at municipal halls if you're interested.

Food and drink

The high esteem in which Filipinos hold their food is encapsulated by the common greeting "Let's eat!" Admittedly, Filipino cuisine has not been accepted worldwide as Indian or Thai food have, perhaps because it has a reputation for being one of Asia's less adventurous cuisines. This reputation is to some extent warranted, with much of the staple diet revolving around readily available meat and rice with little variety or spice. The country's cuisine is slowly changing though, with young, entrepreneurial restaurateurs and chefs giving native dishes an increasingly sophisticated touch. It's also a good way for travellers to be inducted into the culture: visitors who are willing to eat balut (duck embryo) or bagoong (a smelly, salty fish paste) gain instant admiration.

Food is something of a comfort blanket for Filipinos and to be without it is cause for panic. Any Filipino who eats only three meals a day is considered either unwell or unbalanced. Sundry snacks – **merienda** – are eaten in between, and not to partake when offered can be considered rude. It's not unusual for breakfast to be eaten early, followed by merienda at 10am, lunch as early as 11am (especially in the provinces where many people are up at sunrise), more merienda at 2pm and 4pm, and dinner at 7pm. Meals are substantial, and even hassled office workers prefer to sit down at a table and make the meal last. Never be afraid to ask for a doggy bag, because everyone does.

Don't be confused by the absence of a knife from most table settings. It's normal to use just a **fork and spoon**, cutting any meat with the edge of the fork and using the spoon to put it in your mouth. This isn't as eccentric as it first seems. Most meat is served in small chunks, not steak-like slabs, so you usually don't have to cut it at all. Fish can be skewered with your fork and cut with the side of your spoon. And a spoon is so much easier for the local **staple**, steamed rice, than a knife and fork. That said, in some "native-style" restaurants food is served on banana leaves and you're expected to eat with your hands, combining the rice and food into mouthful-sized balls with your fingers – if you don't feel up to this it's fine to ask for cutlery.

Filipino cuisine

Filipino food (see p.537 for a food and drink **glossary**) is undergoing something of a nationalist revival, with intellectuals and cookery writers espousing the virtues of traditional home-and-hearth dishes. The cuisine is an intriguing mixture of the familiar, such as pork and rice, and the exotic – tamarind, screwpine and purple yam, for instance. Coconut, soy sauce, vinegar and *patis* (a brown fish sauce, more watery than *bagoong*) are widely used to add flavour. Colonization and migration have resulted in touches of Malay, Chinese, Spanish and, more recently, American, sometimes all part of the same meal. A typical spread for a special occasion will probably include noodles, dumplings, *sinigang* (a sour soup containing tamarind, vegetables and meat or fish), grilled or fried fish, *adobo*, paella, pizza and ice cream.

Meat dishes – notably of chicken and pork, both cheap and easily available – form the bulk of the diet. The national dish, if there is one, is **adobo**, which is chicken or pork (or both) cooked slowly in soy sauce and vinegar. *Baboy* (pig) is the basis of many coveted dishes such as *pata* (pig's knuckle) and *sisig* (chopped, fried pig's face). At special celebrations Filipinos are passionate about their *lechon*, pig stuffed with *pandan* (screwpine) leaves and roasted so the skin turns to crackling. Pork is also the basis of **Bicol Express** (the best known of very few spicy local dishes), consisting of pork ribs cooked in coconut milk, soy and vinegar, with chillies (a vegetable version also exists).

In the world's second largest archipelago, there's obviously a lot of **seafood** to enjoy. Much of this is fresher and tastier in the provinces than Manila, where it has to be brought by plane or boat from the richer and cleaner fishing grounds around the Visayas, Palawan and Mindanao. The king of Filipino fish is the *lapu-lapu*, a grouper that is cooked in dozens of different ways, but is best grilled over a fire and flavoured with *calamansi* (native limes). *Bangus* (milkfish, which is about the size of a trout and has soft brown flesh) is one of the staples of the diet and can be eaten for breakfast, lunch or dinner. Sometimes it's stuffed to make a seafood version of meatloaf, but more often it's slit down the middle, de-boned and fried, then served with a tangy dipping sauce of vinegar and garlic. While swordfish, tuna, blue marlin, crab and lobster are all on seafood-restaurant menus, Filipinos also love smaller, humbler fish such as *galunggong* (round scad), which is part of the everyday diet in the provinces.

Vegetables are not considered an integral part of the meal, but may well be mixed in with the meat or offered as a side dish. In restaurants serving Filipino food, one of the most common vegetable dishes is a version of Bicol Express with leafy vegetables such as *pechay* (aka pak choy) and *camote* tops (sweet potato leaves) in place of pork. Also popping up on many menus is a version of *chop suey*, here a vegetable stir-fry, often containing shrimp or small bits of pork.

Noodles (*pancit*) are frequently used in Filipino cooking and come in various forms. *Pancit canton* is ribbon-like, stir-fried rice noodles, while *sotanghon* refers to thin, vermicelli-like rice noodles.

The **cooking methods** are equally diverse. *Inihaw* refers to anything broiled over charcoal and is a popular way to prepare chicken, pork and fish. *Dinaing* refers to fish that has been cut open like a butterfly and fried or grilled, while *pinais* is food baked or steamed while wrapped in leaves (usually banana leaves, sometimes *pandan*) which aren't eaten but impart additional flavour. *Inadobo* refers to cooking with vinegar and spice (as in *adobo*). *Binuro* is anything that's been salted, such as fish, eggs or crabs.

Breakfast

At many hotels and resorts you'll be offered a Filipino **breakfast**, which typically consists of *longganisa* (garlic sausage), fried *bangus* fish, corned beef or beef *tapa* (beef marinated in vinegar), with a fried egg and garlic rice. If this sounds too much for you, there's usually fresh fruit and toast, though note that local **bread**, either of the sliced variety or in rolls known as *pan de sal*, is often slightly sweet (wholegrain or rye breads are unusual in all but a few big hotels). Another option is to ask for a couple of hot *pan de sal* with corned-beef filling, the beef taking away some of the bread's sweetness.

Desserts and snacks

The only difference between lunch and dinner is that the latter is more likely to be followed by a **dessert**. Traditionally this would be a sweet cake containing coconut, though these days dessert could mean fresh fruit, caramel custard, *halo-halo* (ice cream and jelly served with shaved ice and cream) or *brazos*, a cream-filled meringue log cake. Filipinos also eat a huge amount of **ice cream** in a challenging range of flavours, including *ube* (purple yam), jackfruit, corn, avocado and even cheese, most of them cloyingly sweet. Ice cream can be bought from street vendors, but may well be unhygienic; supermarkets sell ice-cream tubs from well-known manufacturers such as Magnolia and Nestlé.

Filipinos have a sweet tooth and even **snacks** are generally heavy on the sugar. Various cakes and even sweet spaghetti bolognese (with sugar in the sauce, served at many cafés) are all considered perfect for *merienda*, though in reality practically any food will do. For a snack in a packet, try salted dried fish like *dilis*, which can be bought in supermarkets and convenience stores. *Dilis* are a little like anchovies and are eaten whole, sometimes with a vinegar and garlic dip; they're often served along with other savouries (under the collective name *pulutan*) during drinking sessions. Salted dried *pusit* (squid) is also common and it's easy to sense when people are eating it – it stinks.

Where to eat

The choice of places to eat ranges from bewildering in Manila to extremely limited in the provinces. American influence has led to a proliferation of US franchise restaurants, ranging from the *Hard Rock Café* to *McDonald's* (there's one in almost every big town). The Philippines even has its own successful fast-food chain fashioned after the US giant, with four hundred branches of *Jollibee* throughout the country – indeed, its corpulent "jolly bee" mascot is more ubiquitous than Ronald McDonald. Expatriates and Filipinos returning from overseas have further expanded the range of food on offer, particularly in Manila, Cebu and Boracay.

In small **resorts**, however, the food will almost always consist of straightforward Filipino dishes such as grilled fish or chicken and rice followed by mango, for example. While the choice is limited, the food in the provinces is often incredibly fresh. If you're staying at a small resort in the provinces, the staff will often ask you in advance what you want for dinner and then buy it from the market or straight from a returning fisherman. As long as you don't mind simple fare, barrio food can beat the big city for taste hands down.

In provincial towns, dining seldom extends beyond local fast-food chains, the occasional Chinese restaurant or cheap **carinderias**, where you choose from a number of dishes placed on a counter in big aluminium pots. *Carinderia* fare includes *adobo*, *pancit* and **tapsilog**, a contraction formed from *tapa* (fried beef), *sinangag* (garlic fried rice) and *itlog* (egg) – which is exactly what you get, a bowl of rice with *tapa* and a fried egg on top. Other "combo" dishes include *tosilog* (with *tocino*, which is marinated fried pork) and *longsilog* (with *longganisa*). The only problem with *carinderias* is that the food has usually been standing around a while and is often served lukewarm.

Some provincial towns have their own modest fast-food outlets, where just P60 or less pays for a "rice topping", a serving of rice with *adobo* or some barbecue plonked on top. In many provincial cities, look out also for **ihaw-ihaw** (grill) restaurants, usually native-style bamboo structures where meat and fish are cooked over charcoal and served with hot rice and soup.

All cities and many towns have **shopping malls** which are packed with restaurants and food stalls, offering a surprisingly diverse cuisine, from hot dogs and pizza to Filipino, Thai, Italian and Greek; Western-style sandwich bars are starting to appear too. Most malls (and some commercial buildings in big cities) also have **food courts**, garish, noisy indoor marketplaces that bring together dozens of small stalls serving Filipino, Japanese, Chinese, Thai and Korean food. An adequate lunch at a food court costs less than P200 including a soft drink. Most food courts do not serve alcohol. It's also in urban areas that you find **seafood restaurants** displaying a range of seafood on ice; order by pointing at what you want and telling the waiter how you want it cooked.

There are some excellent French, Spanish and Italian restaurants in Manila and Cebu City, and dozens of casual European restaurants in Boracay. Prices depend on where you are. In areas of Manila, you can spend P2000 for a good three-course meal for two; in Boracay you could have a similar meal for half that. However, European cuisine on the coast tends to be a little less sophisticated, simply because it's hard to guarantee supplies of the necessary ingredients.

There are **Chinese** restaurants in every city and in many provincial towns. Don't expect modish Oriental cuisine though; most Chinese restaurants are inexpensive places offering straightforward, tasty food designed to be ordered in large portions and shared by a group. A good Chinese meal for two often costs no more than P500. Another of the Philippines' favourite cuisines is Japanese – there are Japanese restaurants in every city, ranging from fast-food noodle parlours to expensive restaurants serving sushi and tempura.

The final bill you get in a restaurant usually includes VAT of 12% and a service charge of 10%, adding 22% to the price shown on the menu.

Street food

Filipinos sometimes refer to street food as "ambulant food", as it's sold by **hawkers** who wander around with the ingredients in a container and a portable stove built ingeniously into a cart so it can be pushed home at the end of the trading day. Though not as common as it is in Thailand or India, street food still has a special place in the hearts (and stomachs) of Filipinos – compulsive snackers sing its praises, as much for its plain weirdness as for its culinary virtues.

The hawkers tend to appear in time for hungry office workers to pick up a snack for the journey home and hang around until about 8pm. Much of the food is grilled over charcoal and served on sticks kebab-style, or deep fried in a wok with oil that is poured into an old jam jar and re-used day after day. Highlights include deep-fried fishballs and squidballs (mashed fish or squid blended

Special diets

Committed **vegetarians and vegans** face a difficult mission to find suitable food in the Philippines. It's a poor country and many Filipinos have grown up on a diet of what's available locally, usually chicken and pork. If you ask for a plate of stir-fried vegetables it might come with slices of pork in it, or be served in a meat gravy. Fried rice always contains egg and meat.

Chinese and Japanese restaurants offer the best range of vegetable-based dishes, though you'll have to emphasize that you want absolutely no bits of meat added. In Manila, and to some extent in other cities, and in Boracay, pizzas are an option, or you could head to an upmarket restaurant and ask the chef to prepare something special. At least breakfast is straightforward – even in the most rural resorts, you can ask for a toast or pancakes and, if you're not vegan, an omelette or scrambled eggs.

It's much the same story for anyone looking for halal or kosher fare, except in Muslim areas of Mindanao where almost every *carinderia* and restaurant serves halal food. There are also one or two halal food outlets in the Ermita area of Manila.

with wheat flour), grilled pig intestines and *adidas* – chicken's feet, named after the sports-shoe manufacturer. Prices start from a few pesos a stick. Street vendors also supply the king of Filipino aphrodisiacs, **balut**, a half-formed duck embryo eaten with beak, feathers and all; sellers advertise their proximity with a distinctive baying cry. In business areas of the bigger cities you'll see people buying a quick lunch from a "jolly jeepney", a kitchen-on-wheels where simple and not especially appetizing rice-and-meat dishes are cooked over a portable stove in the back of a jeepney and served on plastic plates.

Drinking

The authorities in Manila claim **tap water** in many areas is safe for drinking, but it's not worth taking the chance. Bottled water is cheap though; good local brands such as Nestlé Pure Life, Viva and Hidden Spring cost P10–30 in convenience stores. **Fizzy soft drinks** such as Coca-Cola and Pepsi are available everywhere and cost around P20 a can in a 7-11.

At resorts and hotels, the "juice" which usually comes with breakfast is – irritatingly in a country rich in fresh fruit – often made from powder. Good fresh **juices**, usually available only in the more expensive restaurants, include watermelon, ripe mango, sour mango and papaya. Fresh *buko* (coconut) juice is a refreshing choice, especially on a hot day. In general, **sugar** is added to fresh juices and shakes unless you specify otherwise. You might well want sugar with the delightful soda made from *calamansi*, a small native lime.

Filipinos aren't big **tea** drinkers and except in the best hotels, the only tea on offer is usually made from Lipton's tea bags. **Coffee** is popular and can be ordered anywhere, but the quality varies widely. In Manila you're never far from a branch of *Starbucks* or *Figaro's*, the latter being a popular local café chain that serves a fancy range of coffees and various herbal teas. In the provinces, you'll usually be served Nescafé. Fresh milk is rare outside the cities so you'll often find yourself being offered tinned or powdered milk with coffee or tea. **Chocolate-eh**, a Spanish-style rich hot chocolate drink served in a small cup, is available in some city cafés.

Alcohol

The **beer** of choice in the Philippines is San Miguel, while for something stronger there are plenty of Philippine-made **spirits** such as Tanduay rum, San Miguel Ginebra (gin) and Fundador brandy. In street-corner convenience stores such as 7-11, San Miguel costs around P20 for a 320ml bottle and in a pub or ordinary bar P35 during happy hour if they have one, rising to P50 or P70 later in the evening. A large bottle of Tanduay rum will set you back less than P50 and gin costs about the same.

All restaurants, fast-food places excepted, serve alcohol, but **wine** is rarely drunk with Filipino food; a cold beer or fresh fruit juice is so much better. European restaurants usually have a limited wine list. For an average bottle of Australian Chardonnay or Merlot expect to pay at least P600. For something authentically native, try the strong and pungent *tapuy* (rice wine) or a speciality called *lambanog*, made from almost anything that can be fermented, including fruit. In the provinces both can be difficult to find because they're usually brewed privately for local consumption, though *lambanog* is now being bottled and branded, and can be found on some supermarket shelves in Manila and other cities.

The media

Filipinos are inordinately proud of their nation's status as the first democracy in Asia, a fact reflected in their love of a free press. Once Marcos was gone and martial law with him, the shackles truly came off and the Philippine media became one of the most vociferous and freewheeling in the world. A little too freewheeling perhaps: publish and be damned is the usual rallying call, politicians are maligned without substantiation and showbiz personalities become the subjects of endless streams of lurid gossip. Even the so-called quality press lets itself become a forum for rumour and counter-rumour, much of which is clearly untrue but is published anyway because it sells. As part of the battle for sales or viewers, most major newspapers and television networks rarely think twice about using distressing images of tragedies and corpses. If you're looking for news from home, most cities and tourist areas now have cable TV with CNN and possibly the BBC. Foreign news publications are harder to find. The best bet is to visit a five-star hotel, where lobby gift shops sometimes stock the *International Herald Tribune*, *Time*, *Newsweek* and *The Economist*.

Newspapers and magazines

Major English-language daily **broadsheet** newspapers include the *Philippine Daily Inquirer* (⬤www.inq7.net), the *Philippine Star* (⬤www.philstar.com) and *the Manila Times* (⬤www.manilatimes.net). These are among the country's most respected newspapers, but in reality the reporting is often slipshod and inaccurate. There are dozens of tabloids on the market, all of them lurid and often gruesome. Most of these are in Filipino, though *People's Tonight* is largely in English with Filipino thrown in where the vernacular better expresses the drama, such as in quotations from victims of crime and from the police.

Some of the most trusted reporting on the Philippines comes from the **Philippine Centre for Investigative Journalism** (⬤www.pcij.org), an independent, non-profit agency founded in 1989 by nine Filipino journalists who wanted to go beyond the day-to-day razzmatazz and inanities of the mainstream press. The PCIJ functions as a domestic news agency and has had nearly two hundred major investigative reports published in Philippine newspapers and magazines, among them an exposé of former President Joseph Estrada's unexplained wealth, which led eventually to his downfall.

Television and radio

Terrestrial **television networks** include **GMA** (⬤www.gmanetwork.com) and **ABS-CBN** (⬤www.abs-cbn.com), offering a diet of histrionic soaps, chat shows and daytime game shows with sexy dancers. **Cable television** is now widely available in the Philippines, with the exception of some of the most undeveloped rural areas. Most providers carry BBC World, CNN and Australian ABC. At weekends during the season there's American football, baseball and English Premier League soccer on Star Sports or ESPN. Movie channels include HBO, Cinemax and Star Movies.

There are some 350 **radio** stations in the Philippines, more than ninety percent of which are privately owned; between them they present a mind-boggling mix of news, sport, music and chitchat. Radio news channels such as DZBB and RMN News AM tend to broadcast in Filipino, but there are dozens of anodyne FM pop stations that use English with a smattering of Filipino. The music they play isn't anything special, mostly mellow jazz and pop ballads by mainstream artists. Among the most popular FM stations are Klite (103.5MHz) and Crossover (105.1 MHz). A shortwave radio also gives access to the **BBC World Service** (🌐www.bbc.co. uk/worldservice), **Radio Canada** (🌐www. rcinet.ca), **Voice of America** (🌐www.voa. gov) and **Radio Australia** (🌐www.abc.net. au/ra), among other international broadcasters.

Festivals

Every community in the Philippines – from small barrio to busy metropolis – has at least a couple of festivals a year in honour of a patron saint, to give thanks for a good harvest, or to pay respects to a biblical character. It's well worth timing your visit to see one of the major events; the main fiesta months are from January to May, but exact dates often vary. Everyone is in a hospitable mood at these events. The beer flows, pigs are roasted, and there's dancing in the streets for days on end. Major mardi-gras-style festivals include the Ati-Atihan in January in Kalibo (see p.312), and the Sinulog in January in Cebu (see p.260). One of the biggest nationwide festivals is the Flores de Mayo, a religious parade held across the country throughout May in honour of the Virgin Mary.

More solemn fiestas, usually religious in nature, offer a mixture of devotion, drama, passion and reaffirmation of faith. The **crucifixions** held every Good Friday in Pampanga draw tourists who come to see penitents being flogged, then actually nailed to a cross for a few hours before being taken down, seemingly not much the worse for their ordeal.

A festivals calendar

Listing all Filipino festivals below is impossible. Those included here are larger ones that you might consider making a special trip for, at least if you happen to be in the area.

January and February

Feast of the Black Nazarene (Jan 9) Quiapo, Manila. Devotees gather in the plaza outside Quiapo Church to touch a miraculous image of Christ. See p.106 for more.
Coconut festival (Jan 11–15) San Pablo City, Laguna. Grand mardi-gras procession to pay homage to the area's most ubiquitous crop.
Sinulog (Third Sun in Jan) Cebu City. The second city's biggest annual event, in honour of the patron saint, Santo Niño. Huge street parade,

live music, plenty of food and drink. See p.260 for more.
Ati-Atihan (Variable, usually second week of Jan) Kalibo, Aklan province. Street dancing and wild costumes at arguably the biggest festival in the country, held to celebrate an ancient land pact between settlers and indigenous Atis. See p.312 for more.
Dinagyang (Fourth week of Jan) Iloilo. Relatively modern festival based on the Ati-Atihan and including a parade on the Iloilo River.
Bamboo Organ festival (Feb) Las Piñas City. The bamboo organ at St Joseph's Parish Church features live concerts by local and international artists.
Philippine Hot Air Balloon Fiesta (Feb) Clark Field, Pampanga. Balloon rides, microlight flying, skydiving and aerobatics displays.
Pamulinawen (First two weeks in Feb) Laoag City. City-wide fiesta in honour of St William the Hermit. Events include street parties, beauty pageants, concerts and religious parades.
Baguio Flower festival (Third week in Feb) Baguio City. The summer capital's largest annual event includes parades of floats beautifully decorated with flowers from the Cordillera region. There are also flower-related lectures and exhibitions.
Suman festival (Third week in Feb) Baler, Aurora. Another mardi-gras-style extravaganza featuring street parades, dancing and floats decorated with the native delicacy *suman*, sticky rice cake rolled in banana leaves.

March to May

Moriones (Easter weekend) Marinduque. A celebration of the life of the Roman centurion Longinus, who was blind in one eye. Legend says that when he pierced Christ's side with his spear, blood spurted into his eye and cured him. See p.164 for more.

Arya! Abra (First or second week of March) Bangued, Abra. Highlights include hair-raising bamboo-raft races along the frisky Abra River and gatherings of northern tribes.

Bangkero festival (First or second week of March) Pagsanjan, Laguna. Parade along the Pagsanjan River.

Kaamulan festival (First week of March) Malaybalay City, Bukidnon, Mindanao. Showcase of tribal culture and arts.

Pasayaw festival (Third week of March) Canlaon City, Negros. Thanksgiving festival to God and St Joseph, with twelve barangays competing for honours in an outdoor dancing competition. The final "dance-off" is held in the city gym.

International Dragon Boat Quest (April) Boracay. A local version of Hong Kong's dragon-boat races, featuring domestic and international teams competing in long wooden canoes on a course off White Beach.

Allaw Ta Apo Sandawa (Second week of April) Kidapawan City, North Cotabato. Gathering of highland tribes to pay respects to the sacred Mount Apo.

Turumba festival (April & May) Pakil, Laguna. Religious festival commemorating the seven sorrows of the Virgin Mary. The festival consists of seven novenas, one for each sorrow, held at weekends.

Flores de Mayo (Throughout May) Countrywide. Religious procession celebrating the coming of the rains, with girls dressed as the various "Accolades of our Lady", including Faith, Hope and Charity. Processions are sometimes held after dark and lit by candles, a lovely sight.

Carabao Carroza (May 3–4) Iloilo, Panay Island. Races held to celebrate the humble *carabao* (water buffalo), beast of burden for many a provincial farmer.

Carabao festival (May 14–15) Pulilian, Bulacan province and Angono, Rizal province. Thanksgiving for a good harvest, with *carabao* parades and races.

Pahiyas (May 15) Lucban, Quezon; also celebrated in the nearby towns of Candelaria, Tayabas, Sariaya, Tiaong and Lucena. Colourful harvest festival which sees houses gaily decorated with fruits and vegetables. It's held in honour of San Isidro Labrador, the patron saint of farmers. See p.160 for more.

Obando Fertility Rites (May 17–19) Obando, Bulacan. On the feast day of San Pascual, women gather in the churchyard to chant prayers asking for children. See p.141 for more.

June to September

Kadayawan sa Davao (Third week of Aug) Davao City. Week-long harvest festival with civic parades, military parades, street dances and horsefighting.

Peñafrancia Fluvial festival (Third Sat in Sept) Naga, Camarines Sur. A sacred statue of Our Lady of Peñafrancia, the patron saint of Bicol, is paraded through the streets, then sailed down the Bicol River back to its shrine. See p.173 for more.

October to December

Kansilay (Oct 19 or closest weekend) Silay. Modern festival commemorating Silay's charter day. Eating

All Saints' Day

It's the day for Catholic Filipinos to honour their dead, but All Saints' Day on November 1 is nothing to get maudlin about. Sometimes called **All Souls' Day**, it's when clans reunite at family graves and memorials, turning cemeteries throughout the country into fairgrounds. You don't pay your respects in the Philippines by being miserable, so All Saints' Day is a chance to show those who have gone before how much those who have been left behind are prospering. Filipinos approach All Saints' Day with the same gusto as Christmas, running from shop to shop at the last minute looking for candles to burn, food and offerings. The grave is painted, flowers are arranged and rosaries fervently prayed over, but once the ceremonial preliminaries are over, the fun begins. Guitars appear, capacious picnic hampers are opened and liquor flows freely. Many clans gather the night before and sleep in the cemetery. Some are so drunk at the end of the celebration that they stretch out on a convenient tomb to sleep it off and are still there the following morning.

With many family graves in the provinces, Manila empties fast the day before All Saints' Day, people leaving the city by anything on wheels. Needless to say, it's a bad time to travel.

and drinking contests, beauty pageants and an elaborate street parade.

Ibalong (Third week of Oct) Legaspi and throughout Bicol. Epic dances and street presentations portraying Bicol's mythical superheroes and gods.

Lanzones festival (Third week of Oct) Lambajao, Camiguin. Vibrant and good-natured outdoor party giving thanks for the island's crop of *lanzones* (a tropical fruit). See p.380 for more.

Masskara (Third week of Oct) Bacolod, Negros Occidental. Modern festival conceived in 1980 to promote the city. Festivities kick off with food fairs, mask-making contests, brass-band competitions, beauty and talent pageants, a windsurfing regatta and so forth. The climax is a mardi-gras parade where revellers don elaborate mask and costumes and dance to Latin rhythms Rio de Janeiro style. See p.291 for more.

Outdoor activities

There are some superb wilderness areas in the Philippines and dozens of volcanoes and mountains to be climbed, from the tallest in the country, Mount Apo (2954m), to more manageable peaks close to Manila in Batangas and Rizal provinces, some of which can be tackled in a day-trip. The country also offers opportunities for caving, white-water rafting, surfing and sailing.

But for a sizeable proportion of the two million tourists who visit the Philippines every year, the main attraction is the **scuba diving**. The abundance of exceptional dive sites in this nation of 7107 islands and the high standard of diving instruction available have made the archipelago one of the world's foremost diving destinations.

Scuba diving

Diving is one of the most popular activities in the Philippines and the main reason many tourists visit. It's possible year-round in the Philippines, with surface water temperatures in the 25–28°C range, the warmest conditions being from February to June. On deeper dives temperatures can drop to 22°C due to the upwelling of deeper, cooler water, so a wet suit is essential. During the typhoon season from June to November, be prepared for your plans to be disrupted if a major storm hits and dive boats are unable to venture out. Visibility depends on water temperature, the strength of the current and wind direction, but generally lies in 10–30m range, as good as anywhere in the world.

Every dive **costs** around P1100, including rental of the boat and equipment such as mask, booties, wetsuit, fins, weight belt and air tanks. For night dives and more demanding technical dives, expect to pay around P500 extra. If you've booked a package, two dives a day will normally be included in the cost.

See the *Diving in the Philippines* colour section for more.

Courses

All PADI-accredited resorts offer a range of courses run by qualified professional instructors. If you haven't been diving before and aren't sure if you'll take to it, try a gentle twenty-minute "discovery dive", guided by an instructor, for about P1500. The obligatory course for all beginners is the **Open Water Diver Course** (costing around P8500), on which your instructor will talk you through the theory, give you some written tests, then take you through a series of exercises in a controlled environment, usually a swimming pool or a sheltered area of the sea. This is followed by the most enjoyable part of the four-day course, a **checkout dive** in the ocean, when you get to show the instructor just how good you are. He or she will want to be sure that you understand the equipment and the basic rules of pressure, and that you know what to do in emergencies such as running out of air or your mask falling off.

You might want to consider doing a **referral course** with PADI at home. This involves doing pool sessions and written tests before you travel, then doing the checkout dives at a PADI resort in the Philippines. It saves time and means you don't have to slave over homework in the tropical heat. If you choose this option, make sure you bring your PADI referral documents with you.

Once you've learned the ropes and been given your coveted certification card or **"C-Card"**, you are free to dive not just anywhere in the Philippines, but anywhere in the world. You might also want to take another step up the diving ladder by enrolling in a more **advanced** course. There are many to choose from, including Advanced Open Water Diver, Medic First Aid, which is also suitable for non-divers, Underwater Navigation, and Search and Recovery.

Liveaboards

There are two great advantages to diving from a liveaboard – you can get to places that are inaccessible by banca and once you're there you can linger for a night or two. Liveaboards allow you to explore terrific destinations such as Apo Reef off the coast of Mindoro and Tubbataha in the Sulu Sea, arguably the best dive spot in the country. For $450 you can buy a four-night package, including all meals and dives. Most of the boats used have air-conditioned en-suite cabins for two. Packages often include unlimited diving and are always full board. In the listings below, M/Y stands for "marine yacht" and M/V refers to a bigger "marine vessel".

M/Y Isla ⓦ www.victorydivers.com. Overnight trips from Boracay to Maniguin Island, Apo Reef and Panagatan Keys, where there are whale sharks, sharks, rays and turtles.
M/Y Maribeth ⓦ www.abcdive.com. Operated out of Coron Town, Palawan, the *Maribeth* accommodates only eight people, making it ideal for small groups. Owner Heinz, from Switzerland, acts as captain and divemaster, and his partner Vera cooks excellent onboard meals. Destinations include Apo Reef and Tubbataha, or you can simply pay by the day to potter around the dive sites of Busuanga. The daily rate is €100 per person, including meals, hot drinks,

unlimited diving, tanks and weights. Discounts for non-divers.
M/V Oceanic Explorer and M/Y Apo Explorer ⓦ www.expeditionfleet.com. Trips to Apo Reef and around the Coron area in northern Palawan. Rates for a four-night trip to Apo start from US$770 with unlimited diving.
M/Y Stella Maris Explorer ⓦ www.divingworld .co.uk. Two twin a/c cabins each with en-suite toilet and shower. Ten-day packages from the UK to Busuanga, including flights and three dives a day from £1528.
M/V Tristar ⓦ atlantishotel.com. Thirty metres long with six twin cabins and one four-berth cabin. Trips to Puerto Galera, Apo Reef, Malapascua, Boracay, Balicasag and Apo Island.
M/Y Vasco ⓦ divephil.com. Trips out of Puerto Princesa to Tubbataha. Accommodation for 22 passengers in eight a/c cabins with four toilets and showers. Good food including the chef's home-made bread.

Recompression chambers

There are five recompression chambers (aka hyperbaric chambers) in the Philippines to treat recompression sickness. All offer a 24-hour emergency service. You might also want to check that your dive operator is aware of the nearest facility. If he's not, go somewhere else.

Manila AFP Medical Center, V. Luna Rd, Quezon City ⓣ 02/920 7183.
Batangas City St Patrick's Hospital, Lopez Jaena St ⓣ 043/ 723 8388.
Cebu City Camp Lapu-Lapu, Lahug ⓣ 032/232 2464-8.
Subic Bay Subic Bay Freeport Zone ⓣ 252 2743.
Cavite City Armed Forces of the Philippines Base ⓣ 032/833 7546.

Diving resources

Asian Diver ⓦ www.asiandiver.com. Online edition of the diving magazine with lots of general Asia information as well as some articles about the Philippines.
Asia Divers ⓦ www.asiadivers.com. Thoroughly professional dive outfit with an office in Manila and a dive centre and accommodation in Puerto Galera. Good people to learn with.
Divephil ⓦ www.divephil.com. Useful guide to scuba diving in the Philippines, plus information about destinations and accommodation.
Philippine Diver ⓦ www.diver.com.ph. Comprehensive overview of diving around the world, but with links to some Philippines sites.

Seaquest ⓦwww.seaquestdivecenter.net. Long established operator with centres in Bohol and Cebu, offering general diving advice, safaris, courses and accommodation.

Tubbataha.com ⓦwww.tubbataha.com. Dive portal with links to Philippines dive sites, dive operators and liveaboards.

Diving dos and don'ts

Divers can cause damage to reefs, sometimes inadvertently. Be aware of your fins because they can break off coral heads that take years to re-grow. Don't grab coral to steady yourself and always maintain good buoyancy control – colliding with a reef can be destructive. Don't kick up sediment, which can choke and kill corals. For more information about reef conservation efforts in the Philippines, check out ⓦwww.ocean-heritage.com.ph, the website of the Ocean Heritage Foundation, a local environmentalist group. Below is a list of additional do's and don'ts:

Collecting aquatic life Resist the temptation to take home corals or shells, and never take souvenirs from wreck dives or remove anything dead or alive – except rubbish – from the ocean.

Riding aquatic life Hard to credit, but some divers still think it's a great lark to hang onto the back of a turtle or manta ray. Simply put, there are no circumstances in which this is right.

Spear-fishing This has been outlawed in the Philippines, and environmental groups are increasingly reporting spear-fishers to the authorities for prosecution.

Touching and handling aquatic life For many organisms this is a terrifying and injurious experience. Handling marine life is best left to people who have experience with the creatures concerned.

Trekking and climbing

The Philippines offer plenty of opportunities to explore fecund, often pristine wilderness areas. **Luzon**, for example, has the Sierra Madre and the Balbalasang-Balbalan National Park in Kalinga, both rarely visited by tourists and offering exhilarating trekking through dense rainforest and across dizzying peaks. In **Bicol** there are some terrific **volcano** climbs (Mount Mayon and Mount Isarog, for instance), while Mindoro, Palawan and the Visayas between them have dozens of national parks, heritage areas, wildlife

sanctuaries and volcanoes. **Mount Kanlaon**, an active volcano in **Negros**, is one of the country's more risky climbs, while the nearby **Northern Negros Forest Reserve** is a raw, mesmerizing landscape of peaks, waterfalls and fumaroles, typical of wilderness areas throughout the archipelago.

The country actually has 38 national parks and protected areas, but because funds for their management are scarce, you won't find the kind of **infrastructure** that exists in national parks in the West. While the most popular climbs – **Mount Apo** in Mindanao and **Mount Pulag** in Mountain province, for example – have **trails** that are relatively easy to find and follow, it's important to realize that trails are generally poorly maintained and hardly marked, if they're marked at all. There are seldom more than a few badly paid wardens or rangers responsible for huge tracts of land. Where **accommodation** exists, it will be extremely basic. Some national parks have administrative buildings where you might be able to get a bed in a dorm for the night, or where you can roll out a mattress or sleeping bag on the floor. They may also have basic cooking facilities, but the closest you'll get to a shower is filling a bucket and washing outside. Deep within park territory, the best you can hope for is a wooden shack to shelter in for the night.

This lack of facilities means you'll need to hire a reliable **guide**. Often, the place to make contact with guides is the municipal hall in the barangay or town closest to the trailhead. The usual fee is P500–800 per day, plus food and water, which you'll have to bring with you as it's unlikely you'll come across anywhere to buy anything once you're on the trail.

There are some outdoor shops in big cities – mainly Manila (see p.129 for details) – where you can buy a basic frame-tent for P3000 and a sleeping bag for P1500. Other essentials such as cooking equipment, lanterns and backpacks are also available, and you may be able to rent some items, though the range of gear on offer is limited even in the best shops.

A good place to read up about trekking and climbing is the Bundok Philippines website ⓦwww.geocities.com/Yosemite/3712. This detailed and well-maintained site has sample itineraries for major climbs and a long list of **climbing clubs** in the country. You can also try the National Mountaineering Federation of the Philippines (𝔚www.mfpi.org), an umbrella group that can offer general information about routes and practicalities.

Among the more active trekking groups are the Association of Philippine Mountaineers (℡02/922 5760), the Metropolitan Mountaineering Society (𝔚www.metropolitanms.org, ℡02/850 3337) and Tropang Kubaw (℡02/800 4062). On the easier treks they may well be willing to take you along at short notice, though you might need to take a basic survival course to be allowed on the more challenging expeditions. An organized trek will probably reveal that climbing is very much a group activity in the Philippines, with "evening socials" at which climbers swap life stories and indulge in communal singing in front of the campfire. Foreigners might be granted special dispensation not to participate, but it's always better to try to join in.

Other activities

A number of adventure tour companies offer **white-water rafting** trips along the Chico River and the Cagayan River, both in northern Luzon. Two of the country's most experienced rafting and kayaking operators, Adventure and Expeditions Philippines, and

Chico River Quest, also offer packages around Tuguegarao (see p.459).

Surfing is also becoming popular, with good waves in eastern Bicol, Catanduanes, eastern Mindanao (especially Siargao Island and Tandag), and around San Fernando in La Union. There are also any number of hard-to-reach areas in the archipelago that are visited only by a handful of diehard surfers, such as Baler in northern Luzon (see p.464), or around Borongan (see p.238) in eastern Samar.

It's hardly surprising that **caving** – spelunking as it's known in the Philippines – is a growth industry, as there are caves to explore throughout the country. The largest cave systems are in northern Luzon – in Sagada (see p.483) and in Cagayan province near Tuguegarao, where the Peñablanca Protected Area (see p.460) has three hundred caves, many deep, dangerous and not yet fully explored. The other exciting caving area is the Sohoton Natural Bridge National Park in Samar (see p.238).

Recreational **sailing** is beyond the means of most Filipinos, but there are still a number of active yacht clubs in the country, foremost among them Manila Yacht Club, Taal Yacht Club and Puerto Galera Yacht Club. The website 𝔚www.sailphi.org.ph, run by a keen expat yachtsman, is a good place for information.

Spectator sport

Basketball and boxing are among the biggest passions in the Philippines, with pool enjoying a significant increase in popularity in the last decade because of a number of high-profile Filipino successes on the international circuit. Badminton has also seen something of a boom in recent years with a handful of new centers springing up, mostly in Manila. One of the problems the Philippines face in nurturing a sporting culture is the lack of facilities. In Manila there are a couple of decent basketball arenas and a few shabby athletic tracks, but not much else. This means most Filipinos are brought up on sports that can be played in a relatively confined space, or even on the street.

Basketball

The Filipinos embraced basketball as they did everything else American, from pizza to popcorn. Every barrio and town has a basketball court, even if all it consists of are a couple of makeshift baskets nailed to wooden poles in the church plaza. The major league – the equivalent of the NBA – is the **Philippine Basketball Association** (PBA; Ⓦwww.pba.com.ph). Twelve teams compete for honours, all of them sponsored by a major corporation and taking their sponsors' name. So you might find yourself watching Coca-Cola Tigers play Purefoods Hotdogs, or San Miguel Beermen take on Red Bull Thunder. PBA games are all played in Manila; see the box on p.124 for details.

The players are household names to most Filipinos; Jolly Escobar, Boybits Victoria and Dondon Hontiveros command huge attention. Each team is allowed two foreign players, many of whom are Filipino Americans (known as Fil-Ams).

Boxing

Ferdinand Marcos capitalized on the nation's love of boxing by using government money to finance the "Thrilla in Manila" in 1975, a notoriously brutal fight between Muhammad Ali and Joe Frazier, fought at the Araneta Coliseum in Quezon City. The beneficent Marcos even stumped up the cash for the fight's multi-million dollar purse. Filipinos themselves aren't big enough to make it in the high-profile heavyweight game, but in the **lighter divisions** they've excelled. In recent years, one name stands out in particular: **Manny "the Pacman" Pacquiao**, the poor boy from the boondocks of Mindanao who became world **super featherweight champion**, made a movie, made millions and is now rumoured to be considering a career in politics. Other well-known Filipino boxers currently fighting, all with the obligatory nickname, include Dindo "Diesel" Castanares, Rey "Boom-Boom" Bautista and Malcolm "Eagle Eye" Tunacao. There are fights almost every week, with major venues in Caloocan (Manila), Cebu City, Mandaluyong (Manila), Tagaytay City, Victoria (Negros) and Taytay in the Luzon province of Rizal. **Tickets** are cheap and often sell out; whenever there's a bout of any significance Filipinos gather around every available television set in the same way Americans do for the Superbowl. You can check schedules for fights at Ⓦwww.philboxing.com.

Pool

Every town and city in the country has some sort of **billiards hall**, even if it's just a few old tables on the pavement, where games are played by kerosene lamps, between locals, for the price of a few San Miguels. The sport has always been popular – it's cheap and reasonably accessible – but has boomed over the past decade because of the success of **Efren Reyes** and **Francisco Bustamante**. Reyes, sometimes called "The Magician", is one of the pool world's great characters; a diminutive fellow with a toothy grin, he picked up the nickname "Bata" ("The Kid") while helping out in his uncle's pool halls in Manila as a child. He was born in Pampanga province, to the north of Manila, and can still occasionally be found on a Friday or Saturday night shooting pool in his hometown bars around Clark, good naturedly scalping unsuspecting tourists' drinks. In 2006, Reyes and Francisco "Django" Bustamante represented their country as "Team Philippines" and won the inaugural **World Cup of Pool** in the UK – a victory of major significance for a country with few global sporting heroes.

Cockfighting

National hero José Rizal, martyred by the Spanish in 1896, once pointed out that the average Filipino loves his rooster more than he does his children. The national sport of the common man, cockfighting (**sabong**) has given rise to other wry observations: if your house catches fire, save the rooster, then your wife. Wallace Stegner, an American writer, wrote: "You don't know Filipinos until you have seen some little fellow who has trained a chicken for months put it into the ring against another's rooster. He bets everything he owns on it, steals his wife's savings, sells his children's shirts to raise a peso. If he wins, glorious; if in one pass his rooster gets its throat cut, then you will see how a philosopher takes disaster."

The camaraderie that cockfighting nurtures is unashamedly macho, with women rarely having anything to do with it. The **cockpit** is the exclusive preserve of men, who see it as an egalitarian refuge from the world's woes, a place where class differences are temporarily put to one side and everyone wears flip-flops and vests.

Contrary to received wisdom, cockfighting was not introduced to the country by the Spanish. When conquistadors landed in Palawan shortly after the death of Magellan, they discovered native men already breeding domestic roosters to fight, putting them in shared cages and letting them scrap over small amounts of food.

Social scientists say cockfighting is popular in the Philippines because it reflects the national passion for brevity or a quick pay-off, the trait of **ningas cogon** (*cogon* being a wild grass that burns ferociously and quickly). Short the bouts may be, but they are also brutal. The fight begins when the two roosters are presented to each other in the pit. Both have a razor-sharp curved blade three inches long strapped to their leg. The fight is over in a burst of feathers in no more than a few minutes, when one rooster is too bloodied and wounded, or simply too dead, to peck back at its opponent when provoked. To make the evening last, most major cockfights feature seven contests.

No town fiesta is complete without a three-day **cocking festival**, with dozens of fights a day and big money wagered on the contestants. Part of the appeal is the **prize money**. For a P200 entrance fee, a struggling farmer from the backwoods could finish the day with P300,000 in his pocket, all thanks to a trusty rooster he has groomed and trained assiduously for months. In barrio hackfights, which are less formal than the big "Slasher Cups" in Manila, the owners of winning birds also get to keep the losing birds, which are cooked in a special dish called *talunan*, or "loser's feast".

The **betting** does not require chips or tickets and there are no guarantees or collateral. Word of honour and honesty are major elements in the cockpit's unwritten code of ethics. The bet-taker is known as the **Kristo**, because of the way he stands with his arms outstretched accepting bets from the audience in the gallery. The bets are shouted and the noise is deafening, yet the Kristo manages to remember who has wagered what on which rooster. If the two roosters are the same colour, one handler wears a hat and bets are taken on the one with the hat (*meron*) or the one without (*wala*).

Cockfighting remains a vivid and integral part of the culture in the Philippines, so much part of the grass-roots experience that no administration would dare outlaw it. To do so would instantly lose the government millions of votes and drive the sport and the betting underground.

Jai alai

Jai alai, a game that originated in the Basque area of Spain, was introduced to the Philippines more than a hundred years ago. It's a version of *pelota* (handball), involving two players using a *cesta* (wicker basket) tied to the right hand to hurl a rock-hard rubber ball, slightly smaller than a baseball, against a granite wall. The opponent must catch the ball in one motion and hurl it once more. **Points** are scored when a player fails to return a service, either by missing the ball entirely or mistakenly hurling it into the wrong zone of the court. It is the shattering **speed** at which the ball, made by hand at a cost of about US$150, is hurled and returned that makes the game so exciting – the ball has been clocked at speeds of more than 200km per hour. The only protection players wear is a helmet. Crowds wager money on their favourite player and during big matches the atmosphere can become as partisan as any football match.

The sport was played on an exclusively **professional** basis in the Philippines, in one location, namely Manila. But in 2000, then President Joseph Estrada suspended all games as part of a campaign against illegal gambling. President Arroyo has continued the ban and there is no sign yet that it is likely to be lifted. If official games do restart, they'll take place at the main Manila *fronton* (court), the **Jai Alai de Manila**, right next to Harrison Plaza, opposite the Rizal Memorial Stadium in Malate.

Culture and etiquette

Some travellers arriving in the Philippines are pleasantly surprised to find English spoken everywhere, young people dressed in jeans and familiar international stores in the malls. All the comfortable trappings of the West are there: franchised coffee shops selling iced cappuccinos, cinemas showing English-language films, supermarkets and fast-food chains. Combined with the approachability and sunny disposition of your average Filipino, this all makes for a trouble-free assimilation into the ways and values of the Philippines.

Or does it? In most other Asian countries the cultural differences are much more evident, in the religion, dress or language. In the Philippines the apparent familiarity initially invokes a false sense of security, which over time – as differences begin to surface – gives way to bewilderment and confusion. There are complex rules of engagement that govern behaviour among Filipinos, and failure to be sensitive to them can cast you unwittingly in the role of the ugly foreigner, ranting and raving with frustration at everyone from the bellhop to the bank teller.

One of the major controlling elements in Filipino society – undetected by most visitors – is **hiya**, a difficult word to define, though essentially it means a sense of shame. *Hiya* is a factor in almost all social situations. It is a sense of *hiya* that prevents someone asking a question, for fear he may look foolish. It is *hiya* that sees many Filipinos refuse to disagree openly, for fear they may cause offence. To not have *hiya* is a grave social sin. To be accused of being *walang-hiya* (to be shameless) is the ultimate insult. *Hiya* goes hand in hand with the preservation of **amor-propio** (the term literally means "love of self"), i.e. to avoid losing face. Filipinos feel uneasy if they are instrumental in making waves and exposing another person's fragile *amor-propio* to injury. If you ever wonder why a Filipino fails to broach awkward subjects with you, or to point out that your flies are undone, it is because *hiya* and *amor-propio* are at work.

If you are ever in doubt about how to behave in the Philippines, bring to mind the value of **pakikisama**, which in rough translation means "to get along". Don't flaunt your gauche liberal values and don't confront the waiter or bark insults if he gets your order wrong. This offends his sense of *amor-propio* and marks you out as being an obnoxious *walang-hiya* foreigner. Talk to him quietly and ask that the order be changed. The same rules apply with government officials, police, ticket agents, hotel receptionists and cashiers. If there's a problem, sort it out quietly and patiently. A sense of **delicadaza** is also important to Filipinos. This might be translated as "propriety", a simple sense of good behaviour, particularly in the presence of elders or ladies.

One of the root causes of frustration during social intercourse is the use of the word **yes**. In their desire to please, many Filipinos find it difficult to say no. So they say yes instead. Yes (actually *oo* in Tagalog, pronounced oh-oh, though most Filipinos would use the English word when talking to foreigners) can mean one of a multitude of things, from a plain and simple "yes" to "I'm not sure", "perhaps", "if you say so", or "sorry, I don't understand". A casual yes is never taken as binding. The concepts of *hiya* and *amor-propio* also filter through to the language in the form of a multitude of euphemisms for the word **no** (*hindi* in Tagalog). Instead of replying in the negative, in order not to upset you a Filipino will typically say "maybe" (*siguro nga*), "whatever" (*bahala na*) or "if you say so" (*kung sinabi mo ba e*). These subtleties of language are symptomatic of the unseen ebbs and flows of the tides that govern all social behaviour in the Philippines, few foreigners ever fully coming to terms with the eddies and whirls underneath.

Filipinos are **outgoing** people who don't consider it rude to ask personal questions. Prepare to be interrogated by everyone you meet, sometimes to the point of it seeming intrusive and a little tiresome. Filipinos will want to know where you are from, how old you are in the Philippines, how old you are, whether you are married, if not why not, and so on and so forth. They pride themselves on their hospitality and are always ready to share a meal or a few drinks. Don't offend them by refusing outright.

Colonization by America has left its mark on the national psyche, so don't be offended if everyone in the provinces thinks you are a '*Kano* (American, abbreviated from *Amerikano*). Protestations that you are from Britain, France or Australia will often be greeted with the response, "Is that in America?" It's still common for foreign men to be greeted by passers-by with calls of "Hey Joe!" This harks back to the GI Joes of World War II and American occupation.

Filipino time

Why do you never ask a Filipino to do something by the end of the week? He might think you're being pushy. The old joke still resonates for longtime residents of the Philippines. Even flying visitors often have reason to scoff at the Filipino concept of **time**, ingrained through generations by broiling heat and the Spanish ethic of *mañana*. There's an apocryphal story about a Spanish prime minister who, visiting the Philippines, supposedly asked a Filipino senator if there was a Tagalog equivalent of the word *mañana*. "There is," replied the senator, "but it doesn't convey quite the same sense of urgency."

Walk into a bank and you will often be asked to take a seat "for a while", only to be left there stewing while the person who's serving you disappears or does something else. In Benguet province in northern Luzon, they use the English phrase "by and by", defining a vague and flexible period that could range anywhere from a couple of minutes to a few days. When will the bus come? By and by. What time is the next jeepney? Oh, by and by.

In recent years, perhaps due to the number of young Filipinos returning home after an overseas education, the attitude towards **punctuality** has begun to change. For medical or work-related appointments you'll need to be on time, but for social gatherings turn up half an hour late: it is considered impolite to be on time for a party, for instance, simply because it makes you look like a glutton who wants to grab the food before everyone else gets their hands on it. The speed of service in the Philippines has also improved, but you should still expect your patience to occasionally be tested.

Gay and lesbian travellers

The Philippines is a Catholic and a generally conservative country, but attitudes towards sex are surprisingly liberal. The Catholic Church here does issue occasional diktats on contraception and abortion – former Manila archbishop Cardinal Jaime Sin organized a number of high-profile protests against condoms and the Pill – but it has never been rent by the kind of controversy the Anglican Church has suffered over homosexuality.

Few Filipinos, even the most pious, pay much heed to the Church on homosexuality, and the prevailing attitude is that people can carry on doing what's right for them. **Gay culture** in the Philippines is strong and largely unimpeded by narrow-mindedness, permeating the arts, business and every other walk of life with the possible exceptions of politics and the military, where heterosexuality is still considered correct. Even the most reserved and pious Filipinos accept homosexuality and are deeply troubled by the thought of gay-bashing or of spurning a loved one for being gay. Gays are respected as arbiters of fashion, beauty and art, and beauty parlours are often staffed by transsexuals. Jokes are told about gays, but they are rarely derogatory.

The word **bakla** is used generically by many Filipinos and visitors to the Philippines to refer to gays, but that would be inaccurate. A *bakla* considers himself a male with a female heart – a *pusong babae*. Most are not interested in a sex-change operation and consider themselves a "third sex", cross-dressing and becoming more female than many females in the way they sway their

The problem of prostitution

B

There are as many people working as prostitutes in the Philippines as there are in the country's manufacturing workforce, about 600,000. Most of these are adult women, but some are transvestites and others are children, both girls and boys. It's a pervasive problem that has been exacerbated by **sex tourism**. The Philippines is a favourite destination for paedophile tourists, customers paying $2000 for a tour on which the operator promises "you'll never sleep alone". According to the Coalition Against Trafficking in Women (🌐 www.catw-ap.org), a good source of information about human trafficking and prostitution in the Philippines as well as Asia in general, some fifteen thousand Australian men a year visit Angeles, north of Manila, on sex tours, and many of the girls they meet are under 16. Child Protection in the Philippines (🌐 www.childprotection.org.ph), a coalition of charitable organizations, says there are 1.5 million street children in the country and the number is increasing by more than 6000 a year. An estimated 60,000 of them engaged in prostitution (increasing by 3000 a year).

At the root of the problem, of course, is **poverty**. Syndicates within the Philippines lure illiterate young women from the provinces to Manila with promises of jobs as waitresses, only to force them to work as "exotic dancers" in miserable clubs. Filipino women have also been sold into prostitution in Japan. Some go willingly for a twelve-month stint as "hostesses", but others end up being held against their will and sold to Yakuza gangs for anything up to $18,000. Even many of the upmarket bars in P. Burgos Street in Makati are little more than fronts for prostitution (see box on p.120). It's not unknown for children to be drawn into prostitution just to obtain food and water.

Prostitution is **illegal** in the Philippines and so, since 2003, is the procuring of a prostitute. As such, prostitution often operates under the guise of entertainment: women are officially employed as singers, dancers, waitresses or guest relations officers (GROs) in clubs and bars where they are expected to leave with any client who pays a fee (usually for the purchase of "ladies' drinks"). Also in 2003, the Philippine government finally made human trafficking illegal, a crime not only for the perpetrators, but also for those who buy the trafficked person. Yet prosecutions for human trafficking or soliciting prostitutes are rare, with the exception in recent years of a limited number of high-profile cases against Western paedophiles.

hips. Not all *bakla* are attracted to men, and among those that are, most say they are attracted only to heterosexual men. A fellow *bakla* cannot become a boyfriend, and for a *bakla* to date a *bakla* would be the subject of much *tsismis* (gossip). Another category of male homosexual is known as **tunay ne lalake**, men who identify themselves publicly as heterosexual but have sex with other men. Homosexuals who aren't out permeate every stratum of Philippine society; rumours circulate almost daily of this-or-that tycoon or politician who is *tunay ne lalake*.

Lesbians are much more reticent about outing themselves than gay men, no doubt because there is still societal pressure for young women to become the quintessential Filipina lady – gracious, alluring and fulfilled by motherhood and the home, a concept known as **delicadaza** (propriety). Indeed, some Filipina lesbians complain that the more outspoken **tomboys** – lesbians are often referred to as tomboys – make the fight for women's rights even harder because they can come across as macho hardheads.

The **gay scene** is centred on the bars and clubs of Malate in Manila (see p.118), though there's no gay ghetto as such. The websites 🌐 www.utopia-asia.com and 🌐 www.fridae. com are useful sources of info on local gay life.

Women travellers

Women travellers rarely experience problems in the Philippines, either travelling alone or as part of a group. The culture, however, is a **macro** one and, especially in the provinces, foreign women may experience being stared at or the occasional catcall or lewd comment in Tagalog. In the barrios, Filipino men hold dear the oft-regurgitated image of themselves in local movies as gifted romancers, able to reduce any lady to jelly with a few choice words and the wink of an eye.

Reacting to this sort of joshing is the worst thing you can do. If you smile and remain good-natured but distant, your potential suitors will get the message and leave you alone. To shout back or to poke fun, particularly if Romeo is with his friends, will cause him serious loss of face and lead to resentment and the possibility that they will try to get back at you.

Modesty is essential to the behaviour of young Filipinas, especially in the provinces, and this should also be the case with visitors.

Shorts and T-shirts are fine for women anywhere, but bikinis are only for the beach, and even then, it's considered bad form to wander through a resort's restaurant or souvenir shop without covering up first (a sarong is perfect for this). Topless sunbathing is unheard of among Filipinos, and tourists in popular resorts such as Boracay who remove their clothes are likely to attract an amazed, gossiping crowd of locals. For some Filipino men this reinforces the stereotype that foreign women on holiday are game for anything.

It's safe to say the **women's movement** in the Philippines is slowly growing, but still marginal. A number of groups, many of them attached to universities, campaign for greater equality in the workplace and laws to prevent violence against women, but are stymied by a lack of funds.

Shopping

The Philippines isn't Asia's shopping mecca, though visitors are routinely surprised that every city has a number of shiny malls with stores offering much the same designer gear you can find in London or New York. The country's two main department-store chains are Rustan's and Shoemart (SM). Both are good for clothes and shoes, at slightly lower prices than in the West; children's clothes are especially inexpensive.

Electronic goods, particularly digital cameras, are often cheaper than back home, but top-end equipment is hard to find. **CDs** are a bargain in the Philippines, at around P500 apiece for legitimately produced items, though the choice is limited to mainstream Western artists and **OPM** ("original Pilipino music") from local stars. **DVDs** are also cheaper than in the West (P500–950 for legitimate releases), the range limited to Hollywood blockbusters and local movies. Note that **pirated** products are as common as the real McCoy, and are sold in many malls and on the street for a fraction of the price of genuine products. Some of these DVDs are actually filmed on video cameras in the cinemas, so all you see is a blurry image of the screen and the heads of the people sitting in front of the cameraman, with the soundtrack punctuated by the laughs, coughs and mobile phones of the audience. The best places to buy legitimate releases are in Manila (see p.126); elsewhere it's a case of scouting around in the malls to find local retailers.

Souvenirs

Typical Philippine souvenirs include models of jeepneys, wooden salad bowls, cotton linen and small items such as fridge magnets made

55

Bargaining

Prices are fixed in department stores and most retail outlets in malls, but in many antique shops and in markets, you're expected to haggle. Bargaining is always amicable and relaxed, never confrontational. Filipinos see it as something of a polite game, interjecting their offers and counter offers with friendly chit-chat about the weather, the state of the nation or, if you're a foreigner, where you come from and what you're doing in the Philippines.

Never play hardball and make a brusque "take it or leave it" offer because that's likely to cause embarrassment and offence. Start by offering fifty to sixty percent of the initial asking price and work your way up from there. Foreigners tend to get less of a discount than Filipinos, so if you're travelling with Filipino friends, ask them to do the haggling for you and hover in the background as if you're not interested.

of coconut shell or *carabao* horn. In department stores you can find cutlery sets made from *carabao* horn and bamboo and costing less than P2000. Woven placemats and coasters are inexpensive and easy to pack to take home. Filipino picture frames are eye-catching and affordable. Made from raw materials such as *carabao* horn and Manila hemp, they are available in most department stores. All towns have **markets** that sell cheap local goods such as sleeping mats (*banig*) which make colourful wall hangings, and earthernware water jars or cooking pots that make attractive additions to a kitchen.

For serious souvenir-hunting, you'll have to rummage around in small **antique shops**. There aren't many of these, and they're often tucked away in low-rent areas. The better shops in big cities are listed in the Guide; elsewhere, ask around at your hotel or look in the local *Yellow Pages* under "Antique dealers". Many of the items in these shops are religious artefacts, although you'll also find furniture, decorative vases, lamps, old paintings, mirrors and brassware.

Some souvenir stores and antique shops will **ship** goods home for you for an extra charge. Otherwise you could send bulky items home by regular post (see p.66) – which can be unreliable – or you can use a courier company: a 25kg box costs around US$200 to despatch to Europe, US$150 to the US, Australia or New Zealand.

Note that the trade in **coral** and **sea shells** as souvenirs in beach areas is decidedly unsound environmentally, as is the manufacture of decorative objects and jewellery from sea shells.

Tribal and religious artefacts

Not all tribal and religious artefacts are genuine, but even the imitations make good gifts. **Woven baskets and trays** of the kind used by Cordillera tribes are a bargain, starting from only a few hundred pesos. They come in a range of sizes and shapes, including circular trays woven from grass that are still used to sift rice, and baskets worn like a backpack for carrying provisions. The best are the original tribal baskets, which cost a little more than the reproductions, but have an appealing nut-brown timbre as a result of the many times they have been oiled. You can find them in antique shops around the country and also in markets in Banaue and Sagada.

Some exceptional home accessories and ornaments are produced by tribes in Mindanao, particularly in less touristy areas such as Marawi City and around Lake Sebu. Beautiful **brass jars**, some of them more than a metre tall, cost around P2000, while exquisite **wooden chests** inlaid with mother-of-pearl cost around P3000, inlaid serving trays P500.

Rice gods (*bulol*; see p.127), carved wooden deities sometimes with nightmarish facial expressions, are available largely in Manila and the Cordilleras. In Manila, they cost anything from a few hundred pesos for a small reproduction to P10,000–15,000 for a genuine figurine of modest size; they're much cheaper if you haggle for them in Banaue or Sagada. At markets in the Cordilleras, look out also for wooden bowls, various wooden wall carvings and fabric wall hangings.

Sari-sari stores

A Philippine institution, the humble sari-sari store – **sari-sari** means "various" or "a variety" – is often no more than a barrio shack or a hole-in-the-wall selling an eclectic but practical range of goods. If you're short of shampoo, body lotion, cigarettes, rum, beer or you've got a headache and need a painkiller, the local sari-sari store is the answer, especially in areas without supermarkets. All items are sold in the smallest quantities possible. Shampoo comes in packets half the size of a credit card, medicine can be bought by the pill and cigarettes are sold by the stick. You even get to use the lighter for free; it's normally hanging on a chain from the counter so it can't be stolen. Buy a soft drink or beer and you may be perplexed to see the store holder pour it into a plastic bag, from which you're expected to drink it through a straw. This is so they can keep the bottle and return it for the deposit of a few centavos. Most sari-sari stores are fiercely **familial**, their names – the Three Sisters, the Four Brothers or Emily and Jon-Jon's – reflecting their ownership.

The sari-sari store is also held dear by Filipinos as an **unofficial community centre**, where you can talk basketball and cockfighting or gently question the owners and other visitors about who's doing what to whom in the neighbourhood. Many sari-sari stores, especially in the provinces, have crude sitting areas outside, encouraging folk to linger in the shade and trade rumours and news.

The best place to look for **Catholic religious art** is in Manila (see p.127), though antique shops in other towns also have a selection. Wooden Catholic statues called **santos** (see box on p.127) and large wooden crucifixes are common. Cheaper religious souvenirs such as rosaries and icons of saints are sold by street vendors outside many of the more high-profile pilgrimage cathedrals and churches such as Quiapo in Manila and Santo Niño in Cebu.

Department stores everywhere have a good selection of Philippine **linen** products with delicate embroidery and lace flourishes. Some of these are handmade in Taal (see p.157); a good set of pillowcases and bedsheets will cost about P2000 in Taal's market, half the price in Rustan's or SM. In beach areas you'll find a good range of cotton **sarongs**, cheap (from P200), colourful and versatile – they can be used as tablecloths or throws.

Textiles

In markets such as Divisoria in Manila, Colon in Cebu and the Palitan barter centre in Marawi, Mindanao, you can find colourful raw cloth and finished **batik** products. Don't leave Mindanao without investing a couple of hundred pesos in a **malong**, a versatile tubelike garment of *piña* (pineapple fibre) that can be used as a skirt, housedress, blanket or bedsheet. Ceremonial *malong* are more ornate and expensive, from P3000 to P7000. Another native textile is **Manila hemp**, which comes from the trunk of a particular type of banana tree. Both *piña* and Manila hemp are used to make attractive home accessories sold in department stores, such as laundry baskets, lampshades and vases. The versatile and pliable native grass, **sikat**, is woven into everything from placemats to rugs.

Jewellery

The malls are full of stalls selling cheap jewellery, but you'll also find silver-plated earrings, replica tribal-style jewellery made with tin or brass, and attractive necklaces made from bone or polished coconut shell. In Mindanao – as well as in some malls in Manila, Cebu City and at souvenir stalls in Boracay – **pearl** jewellery is a bargain. Most of the pearls are cultivated on pearl farms in Mindanao and Palawan. White pearls are the most common, but you can also find pink and dove grey. They are made into earrings, necklaces and bracelets; simple earrings cost around P300 while a necklace can range from P1000 for a single string up to P10,000 for something more elaborate.

Clothing and shoe sizes

Women's dresses and skirts

American	4	6	8	10	12	14	16	18
British	8	10	12	14	16	18	20	22
Continental	38	40	42	44	46	48	50	52

Women's blouses and sweaters

American	6	8	10	12	14	16	18
British	30	32	34	36	38	40	42
Continental	40	42	44	46	48	50	52

Women's shoes

American	5	6	7	8	9	10	11
British	3	4	5	6	7	8	9
Continental	36	37	38	39	40	41	42

Men's suits

American	34	36	38	40	42	44	46	48
British	34	36	38	40	42	44	46	48
Continental	44	46	48	50	52	54	56	58

Men's shirts

American	14	15	15.5	16	16.5	17	17.5	18
British	14	15	15.5	16	16.5	17	17.5	18
Continental	36	38	39	41	42	43	44	45

Men's shoes

American	7	7.5	8	8.5	9.5	10	10.5	11	11.5
British	6	7	7.5	8	9	9.5	10	11	12
Continental	39	40	41	42	43	44	44	45	46

Musical instruments

In **Cebu**, and increasingly on the streets of Manila and Davao, you can pick up a locally made handcrafted guitar, *bandurria* (mandolin) or ukelele. Though the acoustic quality is nothing special, the finish may include mother-of-pearl inlays, and prices are low – a steel-string acoustic guitar will set you back P2000. Mindanao's markets – such as Aldevinco in Davao – are a good place to rummage for decorative drums and Muslim gongs.

Health

As long as you're careful about what you eat and drink and how long you spend in the sun, you shouldn't have any major health problems in the Philippines. Hospitals in cities and even in small towns are generally of a good standard, although health care is rudimentary in the remotest barrios. Anything potentially serious is best dealt with in Manila. Doctors and nurses almost always speak English, and doctors in major cities are likely to have received some training in the US or the UK, where many attend medical school.

We've listed **hospitals** in the accounts of cities and major towns in the Guide; for a full list of hospitals in the country and a searchable database of doctors by location and speciality, check ⓦ www.rxpinoy.com. There are **pharmacies** on almost every street corner where you can buy local and international brand medicines. Branches of Mercury, the country's biggest chain of pharmacies, are listed on ⓦ www.mercurydrug.com.

If you are **hospitalized**, you'll have to pay a deposit on your way in and settle the bill – either in person or through your insurance company – before you are discharged. The cost of a private room in a good city hospital (Manila, Cebu and Davao etc) is less than P2000 per day, but that's only a small percentage of what you'll pay out. If you have surgery there'll be the surgeon's and anaesthetist's fees, plus fees for tests, medication and surgical supplies – even plasters and gauze are charged back to you.

Food- and waterborne diseases are the most likely cause of illness in the Philippines. **Travellers' diarrhoea** can be caused by viruses, bacteria or parasites, which can contaminate food or water. There's also a risk of typhoid or cholera – occasional cases are reported in the Philippines, mostly in poor areas without adequate sanitation. Another potential threat is that of hepatitis A.

Travellers rarely suffer from these as long as they follow a few basic precautions. For starters, you should eat only thoroughly cooked food that hasn't been left lying around for hours, or fruits and vegetables you have peeled yourself. In the Philippines this is reasonably easy because food in most restaurants comprises well-cooked meat and fish dishes with steamed rice. **Tap water** is generally not safe to drink, so stick to bottled or boiled water (or carbonated drinks in cans or bottles); **ice** is also best avoided. If this is not possible, make water safer by both filtering through an "absolute 1-micron or less" filter (available from camping and outdoor supply stores) and adding iodine tablets to the filtered water.

Dengue fever, a debilitating and occasionally fatal viral disease, is on the increase across tropical Asia. Many cases are reported in the Philippines each year, mostly during or just after the wet season when the day-biting mosquito that carries the disease is most active. There is no vaccine against dengue. Initial symptoms – which develop five to eight days after being bitten – include a fever that subsides after a few days, often leaving the patient with a bad rash all over their body, headaches and fierce joint pain. The only treatment is rest, liquids and paracetamol or any other acetaminophen painkiller (not aspirin). Dengue can result in death, usually among the very young or very old, and serious cases call for hospitalization.

Malaria is a serious disease, though the risk of contracting it can be greatly reduced by starting a course of anti-malarial drugs before you enter a malarial zone, and by protecting yourself against mosquito bites. Thankfully, in the Philippines malaria is found only in isolated areas of southern Palawan and the Sulu archipelago, and few travellers bother with anti-malarials if they are sticking to the tourist trail. If you do take anti-malarials, note that some drugs are more effective in some parts of the world than others and that different drugs have different side effects, so consult your doctor before you travel. Note that resistance to chloroquine, one of the common anti-malarials, is a significant problem in Mindanao and Palawan.

Lymphatic filariasis, caused primarily by adult worms (filariae) that live in the human lymph system, can be spread by mosquitoes. Most infections show no symptoms at first, but the living adult worm causes progressive lymphatic vessel dilation and dysfunction, leading to swelling of the leg and other parts of the body. No vaccine is available, though cases are very rare in the Philippines; as ever, it pays to avoid being bitten by mosquitoes.

If you are travelling for long periods in the provinces between May and October (the rainy season), you may be at risk of contracting **Japanese encephalitis**, a viral inflammation of the brain spread by the *Culex* mosquito which breeds in rice fields. A vaccine is available, but the risk of catching the disease is very low.

To avoid mosquito bites, wear long-sleeved shirts, long trousers and a hat. Use an **insect repellent** that contains DEET (diethylmethyl-toluamide) and – unless you are staying in air-conditioned or well-screened accommodation – buy a **mosquito net** impregnated with the insecticide permethrin or deltamethrin. In the Philippines mosquito nets are hard to find, so buy one before you go. If you are unable to find a pretreated mosquito net you can buy one and spray it yourself.

If you're trekking through rainforest, especially in the rainy season, there's a good chance you'll encounter **leeches**, blood-sucking freshwater worms that attach themselves to your skin and can be tricky to remove. Their saliva contains an anaesthetic so the victim rarely notices any pain; it also contains an anticoagulant to stop the blood from coagulating. If you find a leech on your skin it's important not to pull it off because the mouth parts could be left behind and cause infection. Use an irritant like salt or heat from a cigarette or match to make the

leech let go, then treat the wound with antiseptic. You can guard against leeches in the first place by securing cuffs and trouser bottoms. Climbers in the Philippines say rubbing ordinary soap with a little water on your skin and clothes helps keep leeches at bay.

Stray and badly cared for dogs are everywhere in the Philippines, and **rabies** claims about eight hundred lives a year. The stereotype of rabid animals being deranged and foaming at the mouth is just that; some infected animals become lethargic and sleepy, so don't presume a docile dog is a safe one. If you are scratched or bitten by a stray dog, wash the wound immediately with soap and water, then get yourself to a hospital.

Medical resources for travellers

US and Canada

CDC ☎ 1-877/394-8747, ⓦ www.cdc.gov/travel. Official US government travel health site.
International Society for Travel Medicine ☎ 1-770/736-7060, ⓦ www.istm.org. Has a full list of travel health clinics.
Canadian Society for International Health ⓦ www.csih.org. Extensive list of travel health centres.

Australia, New Zealand and South Africa

Travellers' medical and Vaccination Centre ⓦ www.tmvc.com.au, ☎ 1300/658 844. Lists travel clinics in Australia, New Zealand and South Africa.

UK and Ireland

British Airways Travel Clinics ☎ 0845/600 2236, ⓦ www.britishairways.com/travel/healthclinintro/public/en_gb for nearest clinic.
Hospital for Tropical Diseases Travel Clinic ☎ 0845/155 5000 or ☎ 020/7387 4411, ⓦ www.thehtd.org.
MASTA (Medical Advisory Service for Travellers Abroad) ⓦ www.masta.org or ☎ 0870/606 2782 for the nearest clinic.
Travel Medicine Services ☎ 028/9031 5220.
Tropical Medical Bureau Republic of Ireland ☎ 1850/487 674, ⓦ www.tmb.ie.

Crime and personal safety

The Philippines has a reputation as a somewhat dangerous place to travel, but if you exercise discretion and common sense this really isn't the case. Yes, you'll find the same con artists and hustlers here as anywhere else, but there are very few tourist-related security incidents in the country. Politically though, the Philippines is a volatile place, with secessionist movements present in Mindanao and communist guerrillas active in a number of areas, especially Luzon. Insurgency rarely has an impact on tourists, but that's not to say you should be blasé. Keep up to date with travel advisories and avoid troublespots. Updated travel advisories are available on foreign office or state department websites including ⊛www.state.gov in the US and ⊛www.fco.gov.uk in the UK.

Most crime against visitors to the Philippines is carried out by people the visitor has befriended, usually in the form of men falling victim to petty theft from a new girlfriend who promptly disappears. There have been occasional reports of criminals holding up vehicles at traffic lights and removing mobiles and cash from passengers. If you're in a taxi, keep the windows closed and the doors locked, just to be safe.

A common scam is for foreigners in a touristy area to be approached by well-dressed young men or women who say they'll give you a lift back to your hotel. On the way they offer you a drink and the next day you wake up from a deep **drug-induced sleep** to find you have been relieved of your personal belongings. In the Malate area of Manila, the so-called Ativan Gang uses the drug lorazepam (Ativan is one of its proprietary names) to make their victims drowsy or put them to sleep. Similar cases have been reported in Baguio and Banaue, and it's best to be on your guard if you're approached out of the blue by people who seem unusually keen to offer you assistance. Also in the Malate area of Manila, so-called **kotong gangs** (*kotong* being street slang for extortion or rip-off) offer favourable rates to change money on the street, though they actually short-change you using sleight-of-hand and distraction techniques that would do a professional magician proud, disappearing before you realize what has happened. You can change money in safety in banks and moneychangers' shops, so there's no need to risk doing it on the street.

The 24-hour **emergency number** throughout the Philippines is ☏**166**. It's supplemented by ☏**757** nationwide for the fire service, and by a 24-hour hotline ☏**117** for the reporting of emergencies of all types in the capital (the service is due to be extended to Cebu and Davao and eventually to all major urban centres nationwide). In Manila you can report theft, lost property or overcharging by taxi drivers to the **Tourist Police** in the Department of Tourism Building (see p.69). Their personnel all speak good English and have been trained to act with less fuss and bureaucracy than the mainstream **Philippine National Police (PNP)**, which is not Asia's finest crime-fighting outfit. Successive governments have made some headway in cleaning up the PNP, but it is still plagued by accusations of corruption and an alleged willingness to shoot first and ask questions later.

There are a number of **insurgent groups** in the Philippines fighting for causes that range from an independent Muslim homeland in Mindanao to communist rule. The largest of these groups is the **Moro Islamic Liberation Front** (MILF), which was formed in 1981 and it wants independence for the Muslim population of an area it refers to as Moroland or Bangsamoro, which covers the southern portion of Mindanao, the Sulu archipelago, areas of Palawan, and Basilan. The struggle, say the MILF's leaders, is about political and social neglect.

Drugs offences

Drugs laws in the Philippines are stringent and the police are enthusiastic about catching offenders, urged on by a tough-talking president who has promised to "send all drug traffickers to hell". No one, foreigner or otherwise, caught in possession of hard or recreational drugs is likely to get much sympathy from the authorities. Carrying 500 grams or more of marijuana is deemed to be trafficking and carries the death penalty, while a lesser amount will usually result in a prison sentence.

Another group, the **Moro National Liberation Front** (MNLF), was formed in the 1960s and resorted to war in the 1970s in its fight for Muslim independence.

At the turn of the 21st century, the **Abu Sayyaf,** whose base is Basilan Island in Mindanao, became the most high-profile of the groups fighting for an independent Muslim homeland. Abu Sayyaf activities have largely been focused on southern Mindanao and have included bombings, assassinations, kidnappings and extortion. In 2001 the group, whose name means "father of the swordsman" in Arabic, took a number of hostages from the upmarket *Dos Palmas* beach resort in Honda Bay, central Palawan. One of the hostages, an American, was beheaded, and another killed in the crossfire when the military made a rescue attempt. In 2002, Abu Sayyaf took hostages from two resorts in Malaysia. Since then the Abu Sayyaf, which is said to have links to Al-Qaeda and has stated it wants to see a pan-Islamic superstate across southeast Asia, has been the target of a sustained military campaign, backed by the US, forcing it to retreat to the hinterland, its activities diminishing as a result. The group's most high-profile member, Abu Sabaya, was killed trying to evade the military in 2002. It's thought that its core membership is down to less than two hundred, though it isn't a spent force. Abu Sayyaf is still believed to be receiving funds from Al-Qaeda and there have been a number of incidents in recent years for which the group may have been responsible, including three bombs in various locations in Mindanao (General Santos City, Kidapawan City and Cotabato City), that killed seven people and injured at least 27 others in January 2007. In December 2006, the group was reported to have been planning a car bomb attack during the Association of Southeast Asian Nations (ASEAN) summit in Cebu. Police said the attack was foiled.

One more insurgent group to be aware of is the **New People's Army**, the military wing of the Communist Party of the Philippines (see box on p.171), whose members operate in fragmented, small pockets in Luzon and the Visayas. The NPA, whose founder Jose Maria Sison lives in the Netherlands in self-imposed exile, hasn't had a great impact on life in general, and your travel plans need not be affected by them unless there are specific warnings or travel advisories citing NPA activity.

Travelling with children

BASICS | Travelling with children • Travel essentials

Filipinos are extravagant in their generosity towards children, but because so much of the country lacks infrastructure, facilities specifically for them are often hard to find. Major hotels in big cities such as Manila and Cebu City have playrooms and babysitting services, but even in popular tourist destinations such as Boracay there are few special provisions in all but the most expensive resorts.

This doesn't mean travelling with children in the Philippines is a nightmare – far from it. Filipinos are very tolerant of children so you can take them almost anywhere without restriction, and children help to break the ice with strangers. They'll be fussed over, befriended and looked after every step of the way.

Supermarkets in towns and cities throughout the Philippines have well-stocked children's sections that sell fresh and formula milk, nappies and baby food. Department stores such as Rustan's and Shoemart sell baby clothes, bottles, sterilizing equipment and toys. And travelling with children in the Philippines needn't be a burden on your **budget**. Domestic airlines give a discount of around fifty percent for children under twelve and hotels and resorts offer family rooms,

extra beds for a minimal charge, or don't charge at all for a small child sharing the parents' bed. Most restaurants with buffet spreads will let a small child eat for free if he or she is simply taking nibbles from a parent's plate. Some restaurants offer children's menus, but not as many as should. Try asking for a special portion – the staff are usually happy to oblige.

One potential problem for young ones is the torpid **climate**. You'll need to go to extra lengths to protect them from the sun and to make sure they are hydrated. A hat and good sunblock are essential. If your child requires **medical attention** in the Philippines, there are good paediatricians at most major hospitals, in five-star hotels and many resorts. The fee for an initial consultation, not including medication, is P300–500.

Travel essentials

Airport Departure Tax

For international flights, the departure tax is P550 from Manila, P100 from Cebu City and Davao. For domestic flights it's P100 from Manila and Cebu City, P20–50 at other airports.

Costs

While upmarket resorts in the Philippines can be as expensive as anywhere else in

the world, for anyone with modest spending habits and tastes, the Philippines is inexpensive, thanks in part to the relative decline in the value of the peso since the Asian economic crisis of the late 1990s.

You can get by on a frugal budget of around **P700** per person (£7/US$13/€10) a day, but you might need to avoid the most popular tourist destinations such as Boracay (or visit during the off season), and you'll be limited to bare-bones cottages and pokey

63

rooms in basic hotels, usually without air-conditioning or hot water. On this budget you'd also have to confine your eating to local restaurants and *carinderias*, with little leeway for slap-up meals in nice restaurants. With domestic flights on main routes costing a minimum of P5000 return, you'd also have to limit yourself to buses and ferries, although that's not necessarily a bad thing because you can take your time and get to see places other travellers don't.

A budget of P1000 (£10/$19/€15) a day will take your standard of living up a few notches, allowing you to find reasonable beach cottage and hotel rooms and have enough left for modest eating out, drinking and domestic flights.

On P2500 (£26/$48) a day, you can afford to stay in solid, reasonably spacious cottages on the beach, usually with a veranda and air-conditioning, and have enough for domestic flights and good meals in local restaurants.

Electricity

Usually 220 volts, although you may come across 110 volts in some rural areas – it's best to ask before plugging in appliances. Plugs have two flat, rectangular pins. Power cuts (known locally as "brownouts") are common, especially in the provinces. If you use valuable electrical equipment in the Philippines – a laptop computer, for instance – always plug it into an automatic voltage regulator (AVR), a small appliance that ensures the voltage remains constant even if there is a sudden fluctuation or surge in the mains. AVRs are available in all department stores but they cost around P2000 apiece and they're heavy, so it's probably not worth buying one; ask your hotel if you can borrow one.

Entry requirements

Most tourists do not need a visa to enter the Philippines for up to 21 days, though a passport valid for at least six months and an onward plane or ship ticket to another country are required. Among notable exceptions, holders of Hong Kong Special Administrative Region passports and nationals of communist countries are granted a seven-day stay. Philippine passport holders living abroad are given a twelve-month visa-free stay on arrival (check with a Philippine embassy for details), a privilege which also applies to their spouse and minor unmarried children.

You can apply for a 59-day **visa** from a Philippine embassy or consulate before you travel. A single-entry visa, valid for three months from the date of issue, costs around $40, and a multiple-entry visa, valid for one year from the date of issue, around $80. Apart from a valid passport and a completed application form (downloadable from some Philippine embassy websites) you will have to present proof that you have enough money for the duration of your stay in the Philippines.

If you don't apply for a visa in advance, the 21-day stay you'll be granted on arrival can be **extended** by 38 days (giving a total stay of 59 days) at immigration offices in cities and towns (the key ones are listed in the Guide). The charge for this is around P1,700, and you may be asked if you want to pay a P500 Express Lane fee which is supposed to guarantee the application is dealt with within 24 hours, though this isn't reliable. If you don't pay the fee, the process can take at least a week. Note that it pays to be presentably dressed at immigration offices, as staff might refuse to serve you if you turn up wearing a vest, shorts or flip-flops.

The hassle-free way to get a visa extension is to use one of the **resorts** or **travel agents** that advertise this service; these companies can expedite the process. Many travel agents in tourist areas such as Malate in Manila and Boracay offer the service, for which they levy an all-in-one charge, including a service fee.

Whatever you do, don't be tempted to use one of the fixers that hang around immigration offices, particularly in Manila. The "visa" they get you is often a dud and you run the risk of being detained and fined when you try to leave the country.

After your first visa extension, **subsequent extensions** for two months at a time up to a maximum of one year are possible at the immigration office in Manila, Angeles or Cebu City. Once you're beyond six months the bureaucracy becomes an obstacle: besides a police clearance certificate from the National Bureau of Investigation in Ermita (for which you'll be photographed and finger-printed), you'll have to secure a Certificate of Temporary Residence (P710) and pay a legal search fee (another P710).

You'll be asked to fill in a **customs declaration** before landing in the Philippines, which you must hand to the customs officer at the airport. Visitors are allowed to bring in four hundred cigarettes, two tins of tobacco and two bottles of wine and spirits not exceeding one litre. Customs officers in the Philippines are occasionally accused of levying substantial and arbitrary "duties" on any items they suspect might be new, especially DVDs and cameras, so it's worth removing any original packaging from items when packing.

If you arrive with more than US$3000 in **cash** you are meant to declare it (in reality few people bother), and you won't be allowed to take out more than this sum in foreign currency on leaving. Note that not more than P1000 in local currency may be taken out of the country, though this is rarely, if ever, enforced.

Philippine embassies and consulates

For a full list of the Philippines' embassies and consulates, check the government's Department of Foreign Affairs website at Ⓦwww.dfa.gov.ph/posts/pemb.htm.

Australia 1 Moonah Placa, Yarralumla, Canberra ACT Ⓣ612/6273 2535 Ⓦwww.philembassy. au.com.
Canada 161 Eglinton Avenue East, Suite 800, Toronto, Ontario. Ⓣ416/922 7181, Ⓦwww .philcongen-toronto.com
New Zealand 50 Hobdon St, Thorndon, Wellington Ⓣ644/472 9848.
UK 9a Palace Green, London W8 4QE Ⓣ020/7361 4642, Ⓦwww.philemb.org.uk.
US 1600 Massachusetts Ave, NW, Washington DC Ⓣ202/467 9300, Ⓦwww.philippineembassy-usa .org.

Insurance

A typical travel insurance policy usually provides cover for the loss of baggage, tickets and cash or cheques, as well as cancellation or curtailment of your journey. When securing baggage cover, make sure that the per-article limit will cover your most valuable possession. Most policies exclude so-called dangerous sports unless an extra premium is paid: in the Philippines this can mean scuba diving, white-water rafting, windsurfing, trekking and kayaking.

If you need to make a **claim**, you should keep receipts for medicines and medical treatment, and in the event you have anything stolen, you must obtain an official statement from the police. In the Philippines this is sometimes a slow process that involves the police officer copying, by hand, the details of your loss into what is known as the police "blotter", or file. Once this has been signed by a superior officer you'll get an authorized copy.

Rough Guides has teamed up with Columbus Direct to offer you **travel insurance** that can be tailored to suit your needs. Products include a low-cost **backpacker** option for long stays; a **short break** option for city getaways; a typical **holiday package** option; and others. There are also annual **multi-trip** policies for those who travel regularly. Different sports and activities (trekking, skiing, etc) can usually be covered if required.

See our website (Ⓦwww.roughguidesinsurance.com) for eligibility and purchasing options. Alternatively, UK residents should call Ⓣ0870/033 9988; Australians should call Ⓣ1300/669 999 and New Zealanders should call Ⓣ0800/55 9911. All other nationalities should call Ⓣ+44 870/890 2843.

Internet

Major cities have dozens of **Internet cafés** and even in small towns and isolated resort areas you can usually find somewhere to log on and send email. The cost of getting online at an Internet café starts at around P50 for thirty minutes in the cities, while in the provinces it can be as cheap as P20 per hour. In the provinces a lot of Internet connections are via dial-up and can be slow, though in the cities many Internet cafés have leased lines for their traffic.

Laundry

There are no coin-operated launderettes in the Philippines, but there are laundries all over the place offering serviced washes for about P120 for an average load. Most of these places will iron clothes for you for an extra charge. It's also possible to get clothes washed at pretty much any guesthouse, resort or hotel.

Living and working in the Philippines

Opportunities to work in the Philippines are limited. There's no market for foreign English teachers as there is in other parts of Asia, and it's much the same for foreign au pairs, as most Filipino domestic helpers earn less than $100 a month, meaning the richest families can afford to employ two or three of them, along with yayas (nannies) for their children. There's really no way to get a job in the Philippines without specialist qualifications or experience, except possibly through working for a diving outfit. You can go from absolute beginner to divemaster – a "guide" who is allowed to accompany divers underwater, but isn't allowed to teach – in about four weeks. Rates of pay for divemasters and instructors are low, but board and lodging may be provided if you work for a good operator or resort in a busy area (Boracay or Puerto Galera, for instance). For more on learning to dive, see p.46. Some international organizations offer voluntary placements in the Philippines, though again opportunities are not plentiful.

Study opportunities are also limited. There are a number of language schools, mostly in Manila, where you can learn **Tagalog**; one of the biggest is Languages Internationale in Pasay Road (☎02/810 7971).

Useful resources

UK

Coral Cay Conservation ☎020/8545 7710, Ⓦwww.coralcay.org. Non-profit organization that trains volunteers to collect scientific data to aid conservation in sensitive environments around the world, particularly coral reefs and tropical forests. Projects in the Philippines are varied, and include reef-management projects in southern Leyte and forest conservation in Negros.
VSO (Voluntary Service Overseas) ☎020/8780 7200, Ⓦwww.vso.org.uk. Highly respected charity

that sends qualified professionals (in the fields of education, health, community and social work, engineering, information technology, law and media) to spend two years or more working for local wages on projects beneficial to developing countries. In the Philippines, VSO has a small number of volunteers working with disadvantaged rural groups in the fields of sustainable agriculture and aquaculture, or with displaced communities in Mindanao.

US

Peace Corps ☎1-800/424-8580, Ⓦwww. peacecorps.gov. Places people with specialist qualifications or skills in two-year postings in many developing countries, including the Philippines.

Australia

Australian Volunteers International ☎03/9279 1788, Ⓦwww.ozvol.org.au. Postings in the short term (at least six weeks) or lasting up to two years, in the Philippines and other countries. Volunteers have helped introduce sustainable fishing and marine conservation programmes, carried out research into gender and development, and campaigned for the rights of minority groups. Fundraising required on the part of volunteers.

Mail and couriers

Airmail letters from the Philippines take at least five days to reach other countries by air, though in many cases it's a lot longer, if they arrive at all. Ordinary domestic mail costs P5 for letters up to 20 grams. **Post offices** are open from 9am to 5pm, Monday to Friday.

If you have to post anything valuable, use registered mail or pay extra for a **courier**. DHL (Ⓦwww.dhl.com.ph), Fedex (Ⓦwww.fedex.com.ph), and the locally based LBC (Ⓦwww.lbcexpress.com) and 2Go (Ⓦwww.2go.com.ph) have offices throughout the country, listed on their websites, and can deliver stuff internationally. Sending documents to the US, Europe or Australia this way will cost up to P1000 and take three working days.

Maps

Many smaller towns and cities in the Philippines haven't been mapped, and if they have the result is a fuzzy black-and-white effort printed on low-grade paper. The best map the Philippine Department of Tourism (DoT) offers locally is the free *Tourist Map of the Philippines*, which includes a street map of Manila, contact numbers for all overseas and domestic DoT offices and listings of hotels, embassies and bus companies. Road maps and country maps can be bought at branches of the National Book Store in all major cities and towns, although supply is unreliable.

This is not to say that reasonable locally produced maps aren't available – United Tourist Promotions publishes a range of decent maps called **E-Z Map**, covering Manila and the country's regions, with each sheet featuring a combination of area and town maps. These are sold in many bookshops and Mercury pharmacies for P120.

If you want to seek out Philippines maps at home, you'll probably only find maps of Manila and Cebu City, in addition to country maps. **Nelles Verlag** publishes two good maps – a country map with a scale of 1:1,500,000 and a Manila city map, both of which are available in many of the map outlets listed below. They are sometimes available in Manila bookshops, but can be hard to track down. The 1:1,750,000 **Hema** map of the Philippines is another to look out for before you arrive.

For a more varied selection of **area maps** and **sea charts** of the Philippines, try the National Mapping and Resources Information Authority (⌖02/810 5466, ⌖www.namria. gov.ph) in Lawton Avenue, Fort Bonifacio, 10 minutes by taxi from Makati. Even here, however, the quality of maps is generally second-rate, and sometimes all they have is black and white photocopies.

Money

The Philippine currency is the peso. One peso is divided into 100 centavos, with bills in denominations of P20, 50, 100, 200, 500 and 1000. Coins come in values of 25 centavos, P1, P5 and P10. At the time of writing the exchange rate was P48 to US$1, P94 to £1 and a little less than P63 to the Euro. The only foreign currency that's likely to get you anywhere in the Philippines is the US dollar, as other currencies aren't widely accepted.

Traveller's cheques are safer to carry than cash, though note that you can only change them at a limited number of banks in Manila and in a few tourist haunts such as Malate and Boracay. It's best to bring US-dollar denominations from the major issuers – Thomas Cook, Visa or American Express.

Credit cards are a handy backup source of funds, and can be used either in ATMs or over the counter. Mastercard, Visa and American Express are accepted just about everywhere by most hotels and restaurants in cities and tourist areas, though the smaller hotels may levy a surcharge if you pay by card.

ATMs can be found in cities and tourist destinations all over the country, often in shopping malls, but not in less visited areas such as the interior of Mindanao, the northern mountains and many quieter areas of Palawan and the Visayas. It's best to use ATMs at major banks, and preferably in big cities, because these machines tend to be more reliable than provincial ones, which are often "offline" – because there's no cash in them, the computer has crashed or a power cut has affected their operation. Having money wired from home is never convenient or cheap, and should be considered a last resort. **Moneygram** has a few hundred agents throughout the country, usually local banks such as Bank of Commerce and Equitable PCI, while **Western Union** has its own branches in all major locations and many local agents such as Allied Bank, Metrobank, Banco de Oro and the M. Lhuillier chain of pawnshops.

Banks are open from 9am to 3pm, Monday to Friday and all major branches have ATMs and currency exchange. The best established local banks include **BPI** (Bank of the Philippine Islands), **UCPB** (United Coconut Planters Bank), **Metrobank** and **Equitable PCI**. Most banks only change **US dollars**, and though many hotels will change other currencies, they offer poor rates. It's easy to change dollars in Manila, where there are dozens of small **moneychangers' kiosks** in Malate and P. Burgos Street, Makati, offering better rates than the banks; ask around at a few places and compare. In rural areas there are few moneychangers and banks don't always change money, so if you're heading off the beaten track, be sure to take enough pesos to last the trip.

Opening hours and public holidays

Most government offices are open Monday to Friday from 8.30am to 5.30pm, but some close for an hour-long lunch break, usually starting at noon, so it's best to avoid the middle of the day. Businesses generally keep the same hours, with some also open on Saturday from 9am until noon. Banks are open Monday to Friday from 9am to 3pm and do not close for lunch, except for some of the smallest branches in rural areas. Shops in major malls open daily from 10am until 8pm or 9pm, later during the Christmas rush or "Midnight Madness" sales; the latter take place every two weeks, on the first Friday after each pay day. Churches are almost always open most of the day for worshippers and tourists alike. Typically, the first Mass of the day is at around 6am, the last at 6pm or 7pm.

Government offices and private businesses close on **public holidays**, though shops and most restaurants remain open except on Good Friday and Christmas Day. President Macapagal-Arroyo is in the habit of tinkering with the dates of some holidays, moving them to the closest Friday or Monday to their original date (given below), so that people in the cities can use the long weekend to get back to the provinces to spend a few days with their families. This moving of public holidays is done on an ad hoc basis and is announced in the press just a few weeks – sometimes only a few days – beforehand.

Phones

A **telephone charge card** from your phone company back home can be a convenient way to make calls from hotel, public and private phones while you're abroad, with the cost being charged to your account. Since most major charge cards are free to obtain, it's certainly worth getting one at least for emergencies, though enquire first if the Philippines is covered, and bear in mind that rates aren't necessarily cheaper than calling from a public phone.

The Philippines has embraced the **mobile-phone** age with vigour, partly because sending text messages is cheap and because mobile networks provide coverage in areas where landlines are limited. If you want to use a cellular phone bought abroad

Public holidays

January 1 New Year's Day
February 25 Anniversary of the Overthrow of Marcos
Maundy Thursday (variable)
Good Friday (variable)
April 9 Bataan Day (see p.142)
May 1 Labor Day
June 12 Independence Day
September/October (13 October in 2007, 2 October in 2008 and 21 September in 2009) Eid 'I Fitr, the end of Ramadan
November 1 All Saints' Day (see box on p.45)
November 30 Bonifacio Day (commemorating Andres Bonifacio; see p.498)
December 25 Christmas Day; the following day is also a holiday
December 30 Rizal Day, in honour of José Rizal (see p.404)

in the Philippines, you'll need a **GSM/Triband** phone and to have global roaming activated. Ask your service provider what the charges are for making and receiving calls when abroad. Another way of getting mobile access in the Philippines is to buy a local **SIM** (subscriber identity module) **card**, available at dozens of mobile-phone outlets in malls for any of the country's three mobile networks: Smart, Globe and Sun Cellular. Costing just P150–170, the card makes your home mobile a member of a local network, as long as your phone isn't locked to a network at home. Once you've inserted your local SIM card, you can buy **prepaid cards**, which come in units from P100 to P500, to make calls. Standard-rate domestic calls from mobiles cost from P6 a minute; there are no charges for receiving calls. There are card outlets and dispensing machines in malls and convenience stores and at airports.

Basic mobiles in the Philippines are inexpensive, starting at less than P3000, so it can be worth buying one if you plan to stay for any length of time and need to keep in touch. Unless you have a permanent address in the country for home billing, you'll be funding your calls with prepaid cards.

Useful numbers and codes

For emergency numbers, see p.61.

☏ **108** International operator

☏ **109** Assistance with long-distance domestic calls

☏ **112** To check an area code within the Philippines

☏ **114** Nationwide directory assistance

Calling abroad from the Philippines

To make international **collect calls** or to have an overseas call billed to your credit card, dial ☏ 105 plus the code for the country you want, and you'll be connected to the operator for that country. To make an IDD call, dial ☏ 00, then the relevant country code, area or city code and then the number. Note that the initial zero is omitted from the area code when dialling to the UK, Ireland, Australia and New Zealand from abroad.

Australia 61

New Zealand 64

Republic of Ireland 353

UK 44

USA and Canada 1

South Africa 27

Calling the Philippines from abroad

Dial your international access code, then **63** for the Philippines, then the number.

Texting has taken over from email as the foremost means of quick communication in the country, with two hundred million text messages sent a day, more than in any other country. Demonstrators used text messages to rally people against President Joseph Estrada in 2000 and television game shows give away tens of thousands of pesos looking for the fastest texters. In the Philippines it costs just P1 to send a text message from one local mobile to another.

Time

The Philippines is eight hours ahead of Universal Time (GMT) all year round.

Tipping

Keep your purse or wallet well stocked with P10 coins and P20 notes for tips. In cafés, bars and hotel coffee shops many Filipinos simply leave whatever coins they get in their change. For good service in restaurants and bars you should leave a tip of about ten percent. In more expensive restaurants where the bill could be a couple of thousand pesos, it's okay to leave a somewhat smaller tip in percentage terms

– P100 is a reasonable amount. Bellhops and porters get about P20 each and taxi drivers usually expect to keep the loose change.

Tourist information

The Philippine Department of Tourism (DoT; ⓦ www.wowphilippines.com.ph and ⓦ www.tourism.gov.ph) has a small number of overseas offices where you can pick up glossy brochures and get answers to general pre-trip questions about destinations, major hotels and domestic travel. These offices are not so helpful, however, when it comes to information about places off the beaten track. It's not their fault: there simply isn't much information about less well-known destinations in the first place.

The DoT has offices throughout the Philippines, but most of them have small budgets and very little in the way of reliable information or brochures. The best source of up-to-date information on travelling in the Philippines is guesthouses and hotels that cater to travellers, most of which have noticeboards where you can swap tips and ideas.

Tourist offices and government sites

Australian Department of Foreign Affairs
Ⓦ www.dfat.gov.au, Ⓦ www.smartraveller.gov.au.
British Foreign & Commonwealth Office
Ⓦ www.fco.gov.uk.
Canadian Department of Foreign Affairs
Ⓦ www.dfait-maeci.gc.ca.
Irish Department of Foreign Affairs
Ⓦ www.foreignaffairs.gov.ie.
New Zealand Ministry of Foreign Affairs
Ⓦ www.mft.govt.nz.
US State Department Ⓦ www.travel.state.gov.

Travellers with disabilities

The Philippines is a developing country and facilities for the disabled are rare except in the major cities. Taxis are cramped, while bancas are notoriously tricky even for the able-bodied. For wheelchair users the pavements represent a serious obstacle in themselves. Often dilapidated and potholed, they are frustrating at the best of times and simply impassable at the worst, when pedestrians are forced to pick their way along the gutter in the road, dodging cars and motorcycles.

In Manila, Cebu City, Davao and some other big cities, the most upmarket hotels cater to the disabled and so do malls, cinemas and restaurants. Elsewhere, the good news for disabled travellers is that Filipinos are generous when it comes to offering assistance. Even in the remotest barrio, people will go out of their way to help you board a boat or lift you up the stairs of a rickety pier. Time is no object. If you're finding it hard to board a small ferry, the ferry will wait while everyone rallies around to find the best way to help. Of course once you're on the ferry, facilities for the disabled are likely to be non-existent.

In the Philippines, the government agency the **National Council for the Welfare of Disabled Persons** (☎02/926 1165, Ⓦ www.ncwdp.gov.ph) doesn't have much practical advice for disabled travellers, though staff at the group's Quezon City office can give general pointers on transport and where to stay.

Water

Even in the rich enclaves of Manila, the water supply can be a problem. The authorities pump a limited amount of water into residential areas – many households save it in a purpose-built tank with a small electric pump attached so they can use it when they need it. Households without tanks often store water in a large plastic tub and take a bucketful when they need to shower or flush.

Guide

Guide

Manila and around

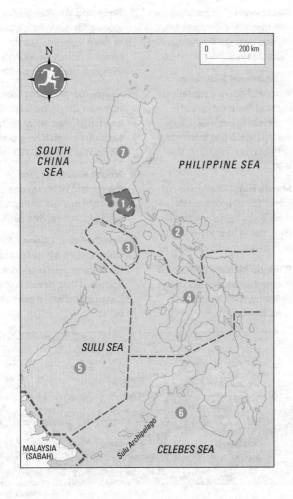

CHAPTER 1 # Highlights

✳ **Intramuros** The atmospheric old Spanish city, with cobbled streets and the beautiful San Agustin Church. See p.92

✳ **Rizal Shrine** This excellent little museum celebrates the life and death of the National Hero. See p.95

✳ **The National Museums** Two neighbouring museums housing the paintings of Filipino masters, relics from sunken ships and fascinating anthropology displays. See p.97

✳ **Manila Hotel** The grand old dame of Philippine hotels. Even if you're not staying here, come to enjoy a drink in the sparkling lobby. See p.97

✳ **Binondo** Manila's Chinatown means inexpensive jewellery, delicious and cheap street food. See p.101

✳ **Nightlife** From the outrageous to the sophisticated, there's a good night out to suit everyone in Malate. See p.117

✳ **Shopping** Whether you're looking for designer clothes or pearl jewellery, Manila remains one of the world's low-cost cities. See p.123

✳ **Corregidor** Intriguing island museum whose monuments and battle sites attest to the ferocious combat here during World War II. See p.133

✳ **Mount Makiling** Climb to the summit or tackle one of the trails that run through its jungle foothills. See p.1337

✳ **Fertility Rites, Obando** At which childless couples come to dance in the streets in the hope that their devotion will be rewarded with a baby. See p.141

△ Manila cityscape

1

Manila and around

ourteen cities and three municipalities make up what is officially known as **Metro Manila**, referred to by most residents and visitors simply as **MANILA**, a massive, clamorous conurbation that covers 636 square kilometres and is home to almost 10 million people. To add to the confusion the old part of Manila – the area near the old walled city of Intramuros – officially remains the capital and seat of the Philippine government. In practice, the seats of government are all around Metro Manila, with the executive, administrative and judicial branches in Manila, the Senate in Pasay City and Congress in Quezon City.

At first sight Manila (in this book, the word refers to the whole conurbation) is intimidating: noisy, unkempt and with appalling traffic. There are few open spaces and only a handful of remarkable buildings. Signposting has improved in recent years, but is still woefully inadequate or misleading. Finding your way around is made even more difficult by the absence of significant modern or historical landmarks – most of the buildings are low concrete structures built in a hurry since the end of World War II. Skyscrapers have gone up in some of the business districts, but none is as notable as Hong Kong's Bank of China or Kuala Lumpur's Petronas Towers.

Manila has no proper city centre. To some Manileños, the central business district of **Makati** is the city centre, to others it might be **Quezon City** or the **Roxas Boulevard/Manila Bay** area. Each is a city in its own right. Roads run everywhere like capillaries, and suburbs act as connecting tissue between new centres of population. It is this apparent lack of order, though, that imbues Manila with character. Its flaws are what make the city human, giving it an anarchic charm that sweeps you along. Manila is also a city of striking emotional counterpoint. Frothy mansions belonging to tycoons and politicians fight for space with squalid shantytowns built along railway tracks. One of the problems Manila faces is the unceasing influx of *provincianos*, people from the provinces who believe the streets are paved with gold, most of whom end up squatting illegally on any spare scrap of land they can find. The fight for space is intensified by the city's apparently insatiable appetite for shopping malls.

To understand Manila completely, to get under its skin, you need a grasp of its complex and sometimes tragi-burlesque history. It has been razed by an earthquake, bombed, occupied, bombed again and rebuilt. It has expanded inexorably, but public services have not kept pace. The result is a rakish megalopolis that lives on its wits and maintains a frenetic pace 24 hours a day just so it can get things done. The roads are always busy and the buses always full, but in Manila you learn to go with the flow, never worrying about whether you'll be late or whether your taxi is going the wrong way down a one-way street.

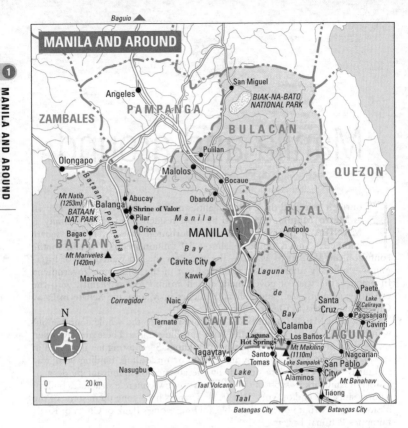

The Filipino maxim *bahala na* – what will be will be – applies as much to Manila as it does to life.

Despite its problems and troubled history, Manila is a sociable city, with a populace who take pride in their cultural affinities to the West and their embrace of all things American. Most tourists, however, use Manila as a transit point, a place to spend a day or two on the way to the islands and beaches of the south or the mountainous tribal areas of the north. A couple of days is all you really need to explore the key sights in and around **Intramuros**, the city's only notable historical enclave, its stone houses and grassy courtyards much as they were when the Spanish regime came to an end in the nineteenth century. If you've got a bit more time on your hands, take a wander through nearby **Binondo** – Chinatown – or head out of the city on a day-trip. There's plenty to see and do in the vicinity of the capital, from the Manila Bay island of **Corregidor**, a fascinating reminder of the horrors of war, to the rapids and waterfalls at **Pagsanjan**.

Manila also prides itself on the quality of its **nightlife** and the ability of its residents to kick up a good time. For many tourists, this will be their enduring memory of the place: funky bars and nightclubs in areas such as Malate and Makati whose attraction stems from their egalitarian nature. It doesn't matter who you are or what you are, you will have fun in Manila. All you have to do is take a deep breath and dive in.

Some history

Manila started life as a tiny settlement called **Maynila**, founded by the chieftain Rajah Soliman around the banks of the Pasig River; the name is believed to come from the words *may* ("there is") and *nilad*, a plant that grew near the Pasig. The growth of Manila into a metropolis is the result of almost four hundred years of colonial development: the village fell under **Spanish influence** in May 1570 when Miguel Lopez de Legaspi landed here. At that time it had a population of two thousand.

Spanish Augustinian and Franciscan **missionaries** subsequently established themselves in villages around Manila. The Jesuits arrived in 1581 and set up more missions, forming outlying centres of population – embryonic settlements that became the fourteen cities of today. Manila's central location in the archipelago, lying on the biggest island, Luzon, where the Pasig River flows into Manila Bay, made it the obvious choice as the **colonial capital**, and it became the hub from which the Spaniards effected the political, cultural and religious transformation of Philippine society. King Philip II of Spain called Manila "*insigne y siempre leal ciudad*" (distinguished and ever-loyal city). Images of the city in the eighteenth century show grand merchants' houses and schooners moored in the Pasig; the area around Chinatown, later to become Binondo, was alive with mercantile activity.

From the middle of the sixteenth century until the early nineteenth century, while the rest of the country remained economically stagnant, Manila prospered from the **galleon trade**. It is this lopsided development, continued out of self-interest under American rule, which accounts for the intense urbanization of the city today. Manila was the conduit through which modern ideas and institutions, as well as foreign capital, entered the Philippines. Refugees from the backward countryside were drawn to the capital, placing an immense burden on services and infrastructure that has only intensified.

At 7pm on June 3, 1863, a catastrophic event took place that changed the nature of Manila forever. An **earthquake** struck and large areas of the city crumbled, burying hundreds in the ruins. The new Manila that grew in its stead was thoroughly modern, with streetcars, steam trains and American-style public architecture. This was one of the most elegant and cosmopolitan cities in the Orient, with Otis elevators and Asia's first movie theatres, and connected by Pan-American Clipper seaplane services with the US West Coast. But this development had been brought about largely because of American colonialism, itself an indirect result of American intervention in Cuba, and the Spanish–American war of 1898. The Treaty of Paris that ended this conflict gave the United States control over the former Spanish colonies of Puerto Rico, Guam and the Philippines, with Manila now America's colonial seat of power in Asia. This colonial rule was to lead to the Filipino–American War in 1899, a brutal conflict in which some historians say as many as one million Filipino civilians died (for more on which see Contexts, p.499).

Manila suffered again during World War II. When the Japanese bombed Pearl Harbour, the then president of the Philippines, Manuel Quezon, vowed to stand by the US come what may. Hours later the Japanese bombed Baguio in the northern Philippines and on New Year's Day, 1942, Manileños woke to the news that the **Japanese Imperial Army** under General Homma was camped on the outskirts of the city. The Japanese marched into and occupied Manila until 1945, when it was liberated by the US at the **Battle of Manila**, lasting 29 days and claiming 1000 American lives, 16,000 Japanese lives and 100,000 Filipino lives, many of them civilians killed deliberately by the Japanese or accidentally by crossfire. Once again, Manila was a city in ruins,

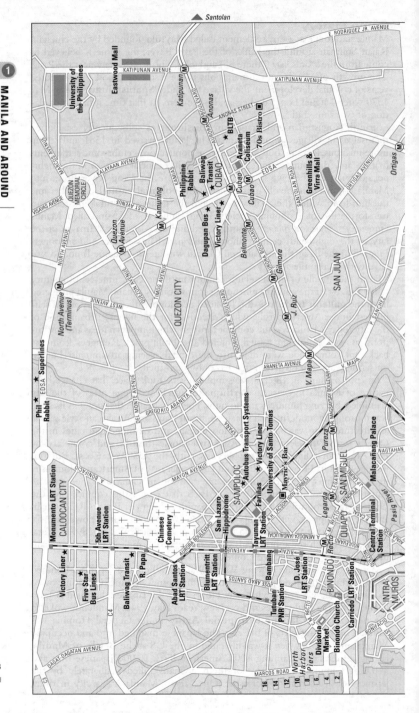

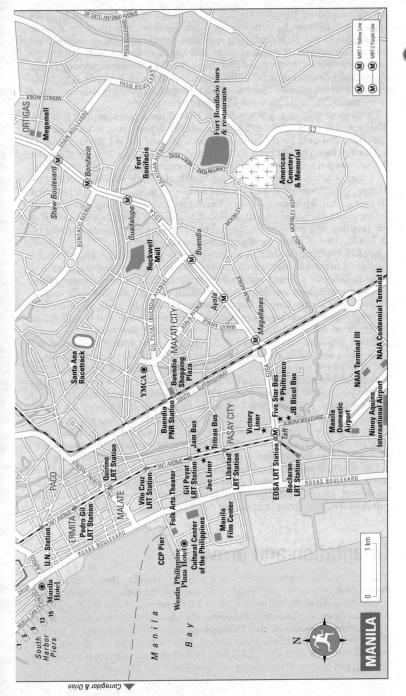

MANILA

MANILA AND AROUND

79

having undergone relentless shelling from American howitzers and been set alight by retreating Japanese troops. Only Warsaw suffered more damage during World War II. **Rebuilding** was slow and plagued by corruption and government inertia. Returning politicians coolly collected back pay for the years they weren't in office and racketeers opened crooked nightclubs, risqué shows and prostitution dens. In his biography of the city, *Manila My Manila*, the late Filipino poet and journalist Nick Joaquin wrote, "Everything seemed to be rotting as fast as the ruins all around us."

The rush to redevelop postwar Manila created more problems than it solved. The new mayor reorganized the police and fire departments, restored garbage collection and built neighbourhood latrines, but was vilified for his failure to reduce the high rate of **crime** in the city. Manila's residents were on the make. There was no return to normality because abnormality had become the pattern. In a sign of things to come, a popular stretch of greenery – Harrison Park in Malate – was destroyed at the behest of developers to make way for a hotel and shopping mall. Squatters took over Intramuros and defied City Hall for years before they were finally evicted in 1963. It was during these dissolute years that the **jeepney** first appeared on the streets, and *barongbarong* (shanties) sprang up in Tondo, close to where the main harbour is today.

In 1976, realizing that Manila was growing too rapidly for government to be contained in the old Manila area, President Marcos decreed that while the area around Intramuros would remain the capital city, the permanent seat of the national government would be Metro Manila – including new areas such as Makati and Quezon City. It was tacit recognition of the city's expansion and the problems it was bringing. **Imelda Marcos**, meanwhile, had been declared governor of Metro Manila and was busy exercising her "edifice complex", building a golden-domed mosque in Quiapo, the Cultural Center of the Philippines on Manila Bay and a number of five-star hotels along the bay. It can't be denied that she glamourized the city, at least for a short while, but because of her notoriously short attention span, it was never long before she moved on to some new construction project, leaving old ones to crumble.

Development continues pell-mell today, and the result is a giant city that is now beginning to devour neighbouring provinces. In the past few years two new mini-cities – Rockwell near Makati and Eastwood in Quezon City – have brought more changes to the skyline. The city fathers continue to fight congestion and pollution, and there is no doubt improvements have been made. The big question, however, has always been whether or not the old Manila area fronting the bay, the sentimental old heart of the city, will ever be restored to its former glory. Some progress is being made, with wide boardwalks for promenaders, new street lighting and street cafés introduced in recent years.

Orientation and arrival

The key tourist district is the area fronting **Manila Bay** along **Roxas Boulevard**, taking in the neighbourhoods of **Ermita** and **Malate**, and stretching north to the old walled city of **Intramuros** and over the Pasig River to **Chinatown**, also known as **Binondo**. On Manila Bay are landmarks such as the **Cultural Center of the Philippines** and, at the north end of the bay, **Rizal Park** and the *Manila Hotel*. Makati, 8km southeast of Manila Bay, is the **central business district** (**CBD**), built around the main thoroughfare of Ayala Avenue, and home to banks, insurance companies and five-star hotels.

The artery of Epifaño de los Santos Avenue, or **EDSA**, runs east of Makati stretching from Pasay in the south to Caloocan in the north. Up EDSA and beyond Makati is the commercial district of **Ortigas**, which is trying to outdo Makati with its hotels, malls and air-conditioned themed restaurants. Beyond that is **Quezon City**, which is off the beaten track for most visitors, though it has some lively nightlife catering to students of the nearby University of the Philippines.

For information about moving on from Manila see box on pp.130–131.

Arrival by air

Almost everyone visiting the Philippines arrives in Manila, **by air**. The international and domestic airports are in **Parañaque**, on the southern fringes of Manila. The roads around are narrow and quickly become gridlocked in heavy rain or at rush hour; it can take anything from twenty minutes to one hour to travel the 7km to the main tourist and budget accommodation area of Manila Bay. A shiny new terminal for international arrivals, Ninoy Aquino International Airport Terminal III, has been built at the northern end of the airport bordering Villamor Air Base, about 11km from Makati and 9km from Manila Bay. It is, however, another victim of corruption, and its launch has been delayed.

Until the new airport terminal is open – and it's impossible to say when that might be – most visitors will continue to arrive at the small, ageing **Ninoy Aquino International Airport** (or NAIA, named after the anti-Marcos politician who was assassinated here in 1983). Immigration and baggage reclaim are, most of the time, reasonably quick. All international flights except those of Philippine Airlines use the **main international terminal** here, whose arrivals hall has a small 24-hour **Department of Tourism** reception desk where you can pick up a Department of Tourism map of Manila that also contains some useful addresses such as hotels and embassies. The DoT also has a mobile number at the airport (⊕02/917 839 6242), but this isn't always reliable. There are three small **banks** near the baggage reclaim, one of which will be open when you arrive. Just beyond the customs desks, in the arrivals hall, are four more small banks. You can change money at any of these banks, but the rate will be a few pesos lower than in town. Philippine Airlines flights (including domestic services) use **NAIA Centennial Terminal II**, which is cleaner, better lit and more salubrious than the main international terminal next door. Centennial Terminal II has two small **banks**, open 24 hours. A third possibility, if you're on a domestic flight operated by another airline, is that you'll use the nearby **Domestic Airport** on Domestic Road.

Airport taxis and jeepneys

To head into the centre, the best thing is to take an official **airport taxi**; the fare to Manila Bay or Makati is P350. At the main international terminal and Terminal II the system for hiring an airport taxi is the same. You pay at the main booth (just outside the arrivals hall at both terminals) then present your receipt to the driver.

At the domestic airport you can get a **regular taxi** at the taxi stand right outside; you'll be given a ticket with the vehicle details as well as a number to call in the event that you're overcharged. No such provision exists at the NAIA terminals, where you might find a regular taxi, but it's hardly worth the bother. Many tourists are conned into paying much more than the metered rate. A common scam is for the driver to tell you he'll use his meter, which turns out to be a rate sheet that says it will cost you more than P1000 from the airport to your hotel. It's quicker, safer and less hassle to pay for the peace of mind an airport taxi brings. If someone offers you a taxi at NAIA and then starts leading you out of the arrivals area towards the car park, don't go, and nor should you get into a vehicle that is unmarked or has other people in it.

It is possible to take a **jeepney** from near any of the terminals, but again, it's hardly worth the trouble for the sake of saving a few dollars. You'll have to walk a long way to get outside the airport area to where the jeepneys stop on the closest main roads, and with luggage this is a real headache.

Arrival by ferry

There are two main harbour areas in Manila, the **North Harbor** along Marcos Road, a few kilometres north of Intramuros, and the **South Harbor** near the *Manila Hotel*. Nearly all inter-island **ferries** arrive at the North Harbor, from where a taxi to Ermita costs about P80. All WG&A passenger ferries leaving Manila use the new terminal at Pier 15, South Harbor, just north of the *Manila Hotel*.

The harbour area is busy and a little intimidating. You can hail a **taxi** inside the gates, but the drivers here try to rip off tired passengers, so make sure the driver uses his meter or you negotiate a rate first. You're less likely to be overcharged if you walk beyond the gates and hail a taxi outside, where there are also jeepneys running to Ermita (P20). Any jeepney with Mabini painted on the side or in the window will take you along A. Mabini Street in the tourist area.

Arrival by bus

Dozens of buses serve Manila from the provinces. As a general rule, if you're arriving from the south, you'll end up in the **Pasay** area of EDSA, in the south of the city, while if you're arriving from the north you'll find yourself at the northern end of EDSA in **Cubao**. From Pasay you can take the LRT (see p.84) north to the Malate area (get off at Pedro Gil station) or the MetroStar (see opposite) northeast to Makati and beyond. A taxi from the Pasay area to Malate costs less than P100. From most bus stations in Cubao it's a short walk to the Cubao MetroStar station; a taxi from Cubao to Makati costs P120–150. A small number of buses, mostly from Cavite province to the southwest, arrive in Intramuros or Baclaran. The "Moving on from Manila" box, pp.130–131, gives details of the various bus operators and terminals.

Arrival by train

The main **train station** is **Tutuban PNR station** in Dagupan Street, ten minutes' taxi ride north of Binondo. All trains to and from Tutuban also stop at **Buendia station** on the western edge of Makati, at the junction of South Superhighway and Buendia Avenue (also called Gil Puyat Avenue) on the southern edge of Makati. Buendia station is something of a no-man's land for public transport, though you should be able to flag down a passing taxi. The centre of Makati is a twenty-minute walk away.

Information

The **Department of Tourism** is in Room 106 of the Department of Tourism Building, T.M. Kalaw Street, Ermita (daily 24hr; ℡02/524 2257, 525 2000 or

524 2384), at the northern end of Rizal Park close to Taft Avenue. The entrance is not at the front beneath the grand Doric columns, but through a double door at the rear, where a guard will ask you to sign a visitors' book. Staff try to be helpful, but resources are thin on the ground. They have some general information and the useful *Travel Guide for Metro Manila* map, which has a very basic street map, and which also lists emergency numbers, airlines, embassies and all DoT offices in the Philippines. Staff can make hotel reservations, although it's usually better to do this yourself because you might be able to negotiate a discount. Opposite Room 106 is the **tourist police** office (T02/524 1728 or 1660), where you should report problems such as theft, lost property or overcharging by taxi drivers.

Many bookshops (see p.126) and hotels sell the E-Z Map range of folding **maps**, which cost around P120 and are reasonably up to date. The Manila map covers the whole of Metro Manila and contains smaller maps of Makati and Orgitas. They also publish separate maps of Manila's districts. Other maps are harder to find: the *National Auto Club Street Map of Manila* (P180) is a booklet mapping the entire Metro Manila area. The E-Z Map *Philippines Travel Atlas* (P599) combines all these maps into a 250-page book. It's useful if you're visiting multiple destinations; the downside is it's a little heavy to carry.

Daily newspapers such as the *Philippine Daily Inquirer* and the *Philippine Star* have entertainment sections with details of movies, concerts and arts events in Manila. Online, ClickTheCity (Wwww.clickthecity.com) has an events calendar, movie and gig guides and listings of restaurants and hotels.

City transport

Roads in the capital are in a perpetual state of chaos bordering on anarchy. There are so many vehicles fighting for every inch of road space that at peak times it can be a sweaty battle of nerves just to move a few hundred metres. **Walking** is usually out of the question, except for short distances, because **buses** and **jeepneys** belch smoke with impunity, turning the air around major thoroughfares into a poisonous miasma. Fortunately, Manila's **taxis** are not expensive and are mostly air-conditioned – many visitors use them all the time. The Metro Manila Development Authority (MMDA) employs an army of blue-shirted traffic enforcers to keep things moving, but theirs is a thankless task. They stand for hours under tropical sun or monsoon rains, trying to impose order but rarely getting much co-operation from road users themselves. Manila's two light railway lines, the **LRT** and the **MetroStar Express**, are cheap and reliable, but very cramped and uncomfortable during rush hour.

MetroStar Express

The **MetroStar Express** (daily 5.30am–9.30pm; every 5–10min; Wwww. dotcmrt3.gov.ph) runs the length of EDSA from Taft Avenue in Pasay City in the south to North Avenue, Quezon City in the north. Key stations for tourists are Taft, from where you can get a taxi, a jeepney or the LRT along Taft Avenue to Malate; Ayala, which is close to Makati's malls and hotels; Shaw Boulevard or Ortigas, which are both about the same distance from Megamall; and Cubao, for bus stations heading north. A single-journey **ticket** costs P10–15, or you could buy a multiple-journey ticket covering P200 worth of travel.

There are telephones and toilets at all stations and some have fast-food outlets such as *McDonald's* and *Jollibee*. The platforms are patrolled by armed security guards, but watch out for pickpockets and the more brazen "snatchers", who rip phones, bags and wallets from your hand and make a run for it. Police mugshots are posted at some of the stations, both as a deterrent to would-be felons and as a warning to passengers to be on their guard.

Manila Light Rail Transit (LRT)

The **LRT** (Ⓦ www.lrta.gov.ph) is an elevated railway system with two lines: the Yellow Line (LRT-1); and the Purple Line, which confusingly is known as MRT-2. The Yellow Line runs from Baclaran in the south (near the airport) to Monumento in Caloocan in the north. Plans have been announced to extend the line south, including a station at the airport, but this could take years. The more recent Purple Line runs from Santolan in Pasig City to Recto in Quiapo, close to the Yellow Line's Doroteo Jose station. Trains on both lines run frequently from 5.30am to 9pm and tickets are P12 for four stops or less and P15 for longer journeys. There are ticket booths at all stations, but if you have the correct change you can pay at the turnstiles.

In the Manila Bay area, the LRT Yellow Line runs above Taft Avenue, parallel to Roxas Boulevard. You can use it to get to Rizal Park and Intramuros (exit at United Nations station) and the Chinese Cemetery (José Abad Santos or Blumentritt station). Pedro Gil station is only a ten-minute walk from Ermita, while Quirino station is closest to Malate. Gil Puyat is a useful station for Pasay bus terminals. The Purple Line doesn't run through any tourist districts and isn't very useful for visitors. It has a stop in Cubao, from where you can reach a number of nearby bus stations, but otherwise it serves mostly traffic-clogged commuter areas away from the sights.

△ Jeepney

Jeepneys and FX taxis

Jeepneys are a cheap way to get around, and they run back and forth all over the city: fares start at P2.50 for the shorter journeys and increase by around P0.50 for each subsequent kilometre. A useful route runs the length of Taft Avenue from Baclaran in the south to Binondo in the north. From Baclaran there are also jeepneys to the bus terminals in Pasay. Jeepneys heading north from Pasay or Makati to Cubao will take you past a number of bus terminals at the northern end of EDSA.

Shared **FX taxis** – sometimes carrying a sign that says Megataxi – are a relatively recent phenomenon in Manila. Many FX drivers start their day by picking up office workers from the suburbs and taking them to the city. At lunchtime they hang around outside offices and whisk people back and forth to the closest mall, usually for P10. Prior to departure the driver will display a card showing the vehicle's destination.

Buses

Local **buses** in Manila bump and grind their way along all major thoroughfares, such as Taft, EDSA and Buendia Avenue, but are not allowed on most side streets. The destination is written on a sign in the front window. Most vehicles are ageing contraptions bought secondhand from Japan or Taiwan, and feature no particular colour scheme; it's a matter of luck whether any one bus has air-conditioning. There's no sophisticated swipe machinery for paying **fares**, which start at P8. Just hand your pesos to the conductor, who'll spend much of his time hanging dangerously from the open door trying to attract more custom – drivers and conductors get paid by the number of passengers they carry. The drivers work long hours and some are said to take drugs to stay awake. Some drivers are extraordinarily reckless, swerving from lane to lane and blocking busy junctions while they wait idly to pick up passengers. In the latest in a long line of desperate and usually unsuccessful measures to curb the excesses of city bus drivers, the authorities have painted a yellow bus lane on EDSA to keep buses out of the way of private vehicles.

Taxis

Manila **taxis** come in a confusing mix of models, colours and shapes, though it's relatively easy to use them to get around as long as you don't mind the occasional bout of wearisome haggling. Many taxi drivers are happy to turn on their meters, though others insist on starting even the shortest journey with a long negotiation. The metered rate is an initial P35 plus P2 for every 500m. If you have problems with a taxi driver, you can call the Department of Transport & Communications Action Center (℡7890) or the traffic police (℡02/819 3270 or 3271).

Accommodation

Most of Manila's budget accommodation is in the Manila Bay area, specifically in the enclaves of **Ermita** and **Malate**, which also have a high density of fashionable but affordable restaurants, bars and tourist services, and are also convenient for **Intramuros**. In recent years a number of affordable mid-range hotels have sprung up, as well as a number of five-star places along Manila Bay, including the historic *Manila Hotel*.

In the business district of **Makati**, there is some mid-range accommodation in and around P. Burgos Street at the northern end of Makati Avenue, beyond the *Mandarin Oriental Manila*. This is close to the red-light district, so if you want somewhere else in Makati try the anaemic but comfortable boutique hotels in Pasay Road (also called Arnaiz Avenue), behind the Greenbelt mall. Most of these hotels are aimed at travelling executives who don't want to fork out for a five-star, and are an affordable, safe option in a convenient location.

Ortigas is primarily a business area, a little out of the way if you want to be close to transport and nightlife, though it does have a number of decent mid-range hotels, many of which offer "mini-apartments" with a kitchen. The hotels in **Quezon City** are almost all around Timog Avenue and Tomas Morato Avenue, close to the nightlife, although not many tourists stay in this area.

Ermita, Malate and Paco Park

For the widest possible range of tourist accommodation in the smallest area, the twin Manila Bay enclaves of **Ermita** and **Malate** are by far your best bet. You can get here in less than 45 minutes from the airport and spend a while looking for the best deal by walking along A. Mabini Street in Ermita and the area around Adriatico Street in Malate. In terms of geography, Ermita is the area closest to Rizal Park, while Malate is the area around Remedios Circle. Both have their share of banks, shopping malls, travel agents and nightlife, and they're conveniently close to the sights of Intramuros and Rizal Park. If you want somewhere away from the bustle of Ermita and Malate but still reasonably close to restaurants and nightlife, there are a few reputable hotels by **Paco Park**, 1km southeast of the United Nations LRT station, that are well worth considering. The following hotels are all marked on the map opposite, unless otherwise stated.

Ermita

Best Western Hotel La Corona 1166 M.H. Del Pilar St corner Arquiza St ☏02/524 2631. Modern hotel with double a/c rooms. Good location and the rate includes a buffet breakfast for two. ④–⑤

City Garden Suites Hotel 1158 A. Mabini St ☏02/536 1541. Standard hotel with sparsely furnished but clean a/c rooms and a reasonable coffee shop in the lobby. You get a ten-percent discount if you stay fourteen days or longer. ④–⑤

Citystate Tower Hotel 1315 A. Mabini St ☏02/400 7351 to 7361. With its chandeliers and gold trimmings, the lobby deserves some sort of award for bad taste. All rooms have a/c and the choice includes singles, twins and standard doubles. The travel agent near the reception desk can arrange flights, visas and tours. ⑤–⑧

Ermita Tourist Inn 1549 A. Mabini St ☏02/521 8770 to 8771. Decent budget choice on the edge of Ermita close to Malate, with thirty relatively spacious a/c rooms with shower. There's a travel agent downstairs for flights and visas. ④–⑤

Iseya Hotel 1241 M.H. Del Pilar St ☏02/523 8166 to 8168. Dusty old pension house close to the noisy junction with Padre Faura and surrounded by money changers and halal *carinderias*. The rooms are austere and a little worn, but cheap. There's

also a 24-hour coffee shops and bar. ④–⑤

Mabini Pension 1337 A. Mabini St ☏02/523 3930. Convenient, friendly and well established; rooms are large and some have a/c, but all could do with a lick of paint. The tourist information desk arranges visa extensions and can make flight reservations. ④–⑤

Manila Hotel One Rizal Park ☏02/527 0011, ⓦwww.manila-hotel.com.ph. Esteemed establishment that is undoubtedly past its best but nevertheless reeks of history, at least in the old wing where General Douglas MacArthur stayed during World War II; if you've got $2000 to spare you can stay a night in his suite. The lobby is a grand affair with black-and-white tiled flooring and oxblood velvet sofas. The rooms, many in need of a revamp, remain stubbornly traditional, with dark wood and four-poster beds. Some of the public areas are also a little tired and the food in the *Ylang-Ylang Café* is average. Still, even if you don't stay here, it's nice to sip a drink in the lobby and watch Manila's rich and famous go by. Rooms start at around $200. ⑧

Richmond Pension 1165 Grey St ☏02/525 3864. Hard to find in a quiet side street that's also known as Jaycee Way, close to Arquiza St and the Sea Food Market. Quiet and simple family-run budget option, with plain but clean rooms. Dorm bed P200. ②–③

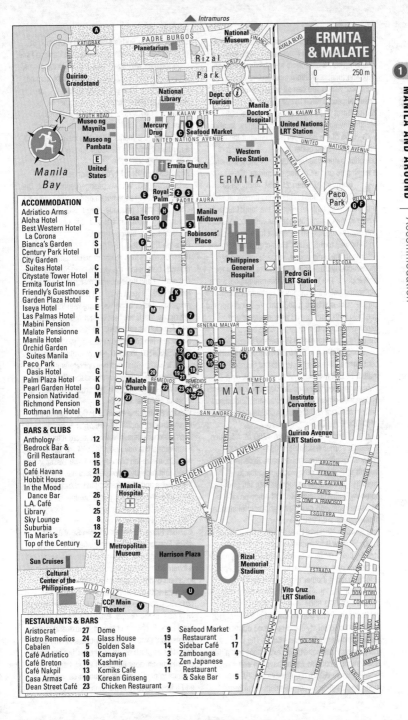

ERMITA & MALATE

0 — 250 m

ACCOMMODATION

Adriatico Arms	Q
Aloha Hotel	T
Best Western Hotel	
La Corona	D
Bianca's Garden	S
Century Park Hotel	U
City Garden	
Suites Hotel	C
Citystate Tower Hotel	H
Ermita Tourist Inn	J
Friendly's Guesthouse	P
Garden Plaza Hotel	F
Iseya Hotel	E
Las Palmas Hotel	L
Mabini Pension	I
Malate Pensionne	R
Manila Hotel	A
Orchid Garden	
Suites Manila	V
Paco Park	
Oasis Hotel	G
Palm Plaza Hotel	K
Pearl Garden Hotel	O
Pension Natividad	M
Richmond Pension	B
Rothman Inn Hotel	N

BARS & CLUBS

Anthology	12
Bedrock Bar &	
Grill Restaurant	18
Bed	15
Café Havana	21
Hobbit House	20
In the Mood	
Dance Bar	26
L.A. Café	6
Library	25
Sky Lounge	8
Suburbia	18
Tia Maria's	22
Top of the Century	U

RESTAURANTS & BARS

Aristocrat	27	Dome	9	Seafood Market	
Bistro Remedios	24	Glass House	19	Restaurant	1
Cabalen	5	Golden Sala	14	Sidebar Café	17
Café Adriatico	18	Kamayan	18	Zamboanga	4
Café Breton	16	Kashmir	2	Zen Japanese	
Café Nakpil	13	Komiks Café	11	Restaurant	
Casa Armas	10	Korean Ginseng		& Sake Bar	5
Dean Street Café	23	Chicken Restaurant	7		

87

Malate

Adriatico Arms 561 J. Nakpil St ☏ 02/521 0736. A pleasant refuge of a hotel in an unbeatable location. The 28 a/c rooms are smallish, but well kept and functional. Right next door is *Café Adriatico*, where you can sit and watch the beautiful people stroll by. ④–⑦

Aloha Hotel 2150 Roxas Blvd ☏ 02/526 8088. A Manila Bay stalwart, the *Aloha* is in a fine location with views of the bay from the front, but the rooms (all a/c) have seen better days – ask to see a selection before you hand over any money. There's a small café and a Chinese restaurant. ⑤–⑦

🏃 **Bianca's Garden** 2139 M. Adriatico St ☏ 02/526 0351. This idyllic provincial-style retreat on the southern edge of the tourist area bustle is understandably popular with backpackers and divers stopping off in Manila for a few nights on their way to the beach. Eleven quaint a/c rooms – some in the main house, some set around a garden courtyard – with stone floors and iron four-poster beds. The terrace and swimming pool are a big selling point and the small restaurant offers simple, well-prepared food. Staff are wonderful and can help with visas, travel arrangements and accommodation. ④–⑥

Century Park Hotel 599 P. Ocampo St ☏ 02/528 8888 or 528 5814 to 5816, ⓦ www.centurypark. com. Grand up-market hotel next to Harrison Plaza mall. It boasts five hundred guest rooms, gym, swimming pool, an expensive Japanese restaurant and various other bars and restaurants, including *Café in the Park* and the funky cocktail lounge *Top of the Century*. ⑧

🏃 **Friendly's Guesthouse** 1750 M. Adriatico St corner Nakpil St ☏ 0917 333 1418, ⓦ www.friendlysguesthouse.com. Excellent little budget option in a great location close to nightlife. Good range of rooms, both fan and a/c, some with shared showers and other private. Pleasant café with city views and helpful staff. A/c dorm beds are P250. ①–③

Las Palmas Hotel 1616 A. Mabini St ☏ 02/521 1000, ⓦ www.laspalmashotel.com.ph. Long-standing mid-range hotel with rather dowdy, musty a/c rooms and a coffee shop. Just about acceptable for a night if other places are full. ⑥–⑦

🏃 **Malate Pensionne** 1771 M. Adriatico St ☏ 02/523 8304, ⓦ www.mpensionne.com. ph. Well-run, rightly popular budget place furnished in Spanish colonial style and in a good position, a stone's throw from Remedios Circle. The in-house travel agency can handle visa extensions and airline reservations. Economy rooms have fan and shared facilities, while deluxe rooms have a/c, TV and fridge. Reservations recommended. Dorm beds P300, ②–⑤

Orchid Garden Suites Manila 620 P. Ocampo St ☏ 02/523 9870, ⓕ 523 9829. Opposite Harrison Plaza shopping mall. Mid-sized hotel with small a/c rooms, some with a bay view. There's a restaurant, bar and swimming pool. Rate includes breakfast. ⑥–⑧

Palm Plaza Hotel 526 Pedro Gil corner M. Adriatico St ☏ 02/522 1000 ⓦ www.palmplaza .com. Boutique hotel with a range of clean and comfortable a/c rooms. There's a travel agent and a car rental office in the lobby, plus a restaurant and a bar. ⑦–⑧

Pearl Garden Hotel 1700 M. Adriatico St ☏ 02/525 1000, ⓦ www.pearlgardenhotel.net. One of the best mid-range hotels on the block, with 83 clean and smart boutique-style rooms. There's a fashionably decorated bar and restaurant, and Starbucks-style coffee shop. ⑦

Pension Natividad 1690 M.H. Del Pilar St ☏ 02/521 0524. Choice of forty rooms in an old family house that was built before the war, but partially destroyed by bombing and subsequently restored. The pleasant terrace café serves a small but reasonably priced range of drinks and snacks. Along with the *Malate Pensionne*, this is the best budget accommodation in the area. Dorm beds P200; ②–⑤

Rothman Inn Hotel 1633 M. Adriatico St ☏ 02/523 4501 to 4510, ⓦ www.rothmanhotel .com. It has an unattractive concrete edifice, but the rooms are spacious and cheaper than many other mid-range hotels in the area. Good location close to nightlife. ⑤–⑧

Westin Philippine Plaza CCP Complex, Roxas Blvd; see map pp.78–79 ☏ 02/551 5555, ⓦ www .westin.com/manila. If you can afford it and want a room with a balcony and a view of the Manila Bay sunsets, this is the place to stay. The *Westin* is big, brash and recently renovated, and has a number of pricey bars and restaurants. First choice for many Japanese and Hong Kong tour groups. ⑧

Paco Park

Garden Plaza Hotel 1030 Belen St ☏ 02/522 4835. Congenial and well managed, the *Garden Plaza* is right next to Paco Park and has a/c rooms, a lovely little swimming pool on the roof and an excellent Swiss restaurant. ⑤–⑦

Paco Park Oasis Hotel 1032–1034 Belen St ☏ 02/521 2371 to 2375 ⓦ www.parkhotel.com.ph. Next door to the *Garden Plaza* outside the walls of Paco Park. Economy, standard, deluxe and superior rooms, some with four-poster bed and whirlpool bath. Not as plush as its neighbour, but the rooms are slightly cheaper and good value. Large swimming pool, pleasant terrace area, restaurant and a travel agency in the lobby. ⑤–⑦

Makati

The following hotels are shown on the main Makati map below or on the map of the area around P. Burgos Street on p.90, unless otherwise stated.

El Cielito Inn 804 Arnaiz Ave (also known as Pasay Rd) ☏02/815 8951 to 8954, ⓦwww .elcielitoinn.com. Small but clean glass-fronted boutique hotel close to Makati's malls, with

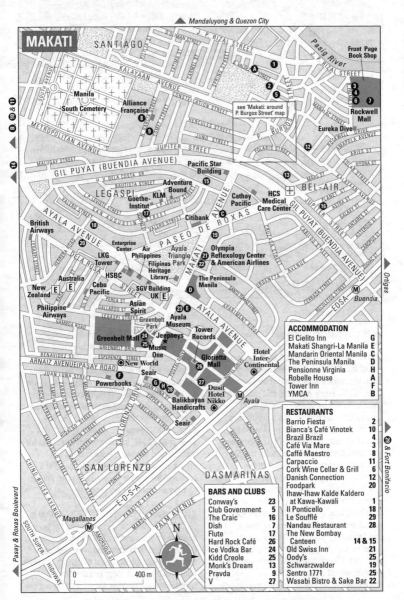

Mandaluyong & Quezon City

MAKATI

ACCOMMODATION

El Cielito Inn	G
Makati Shangri-La Manila	E
Mandarin Oriental Manila	C
The Peninsula Manila	D
Pensionne Virginia	H
Robelle House	A
Tower Inn	F
YMCA	B

RESTAURANTS

Barrio Fiesta	2
Bianca's Café Vinotek	10
Brazil Brazil	4
Café Via Mare	3
Caffé Maestro	8
Carpaccio	11
Cork Wine Cellar & Grill	6
Danish Connection	12
Foodpark	20
Ihaw-Ihaw Kalde Kaldero at Kawa-Kawali	1
Il Ponticello	18
Le Soufflé	29
Nandau Restaurant	28
The New Bombay Canteen	14 & 15
Old Swiss Inn	21
Oody's	25
Schwarzwalder	19
Sentro 1771	25
Wasabi Bistro & Sake Bar	22

BARS AND CLUBS

Conway's	23
Club Government	5
The Craic	16
Dish	7
Flute	17
Hard Rock Café	26
Ice Vodka Bar	24
Kidd Creole	25
Monk's Dream	13
Pravda	9
V	27

0   400 m

N

MAKATI: AROUND P. BURGOS STREET

RESTAURANTS	
Alba	6
Handlebar	7
Hossein's Persian Kebab	4
Next Door Noodles	3
North Park	1

ACCOMMODATION	
Citadel Inn Makati	F
City Garden Hotel Makati	A
Fersal Apartelle Tourist Inn	B
Jupiter Arms	G
Oxford Suites	E
Primetown Century Tower	C
Sunette Tower Hotel	D

BARS & CLUBS	
Heckle & Jeckle	8
Jools & Woodman's Head	2
Rogues	5

modern, carpeted a/c rooms and a coffee shop. ⑤–⑥

Makati Shangri-La Manila Ayala Ave, corner Makati Ave ☎02/813 8888, ⓦwww.shangri-la .com. Top-notch establishment in the heart of Makati with recently renovated chic rooms. The grand lobby is a convenient meeting place; *Conway's*, the bar upstairs, has a popular and affordable happy hour with some talented live bands and crooners; and there's a coffee shop with buffet food. Very close to shops, too. ⑧

Mandarin Oriental Manila Makati Ave ☎02/750 8888, ⓦwww.mandarin-oriental.com. Five-star establishment that serves as a good landmark in Makati, opposite Citibank and a short walk from the shops. Rooms are spacious, with all the comforts you'd expect from a five-star. The hotel's *Captain's Bar* is a popular venue for watching showbands, every night from 9pm. There's also a deli where you can buy sandwiches and salads. ⑧

The Peninsula Manila Ayala Ave, corner Makati Ave ☎02/887 2888, ⓦwww.manila.peninsula .com. Ostentatious five-star that takes up a city block and has a cheesily opulent lobby where people go to drink coffee and to see and be seen. There are no fewer than seven restaurants, running the gamut from Asian to French. Rooms are as you'd expect at this price, with soft furnishings and all mod cons. ⑧

Pensionne Virginia 816 Arnaiz Ave ☎02/844 5228 or 843 2546. In a convenient location at the business end of Makati, close to malls and offices; it's situated between ACA Video and a branch of the popular bakery, Goldilocks. Rooms all have a/c, cable TV, telephone and mini-bar. ⑤–⑥

Robelle House 4402 Valdez St ☎02/899 8209 to 8213. This rambling family-run pension has been in business for years and is still the most atmospheric Filipino budget accommodation in the business district. The location isn't great though: it's a good walk from the Makati shops in a desolate backstreet area. The floors are polished tile and the wooden staircases are authentically creaky, although the rooms are no more than serviceable. Ask for one on the first floor overlooking the small pool. ④–⑤

Tower Inn 1002 Arnaiz Ave ⊤ 02/888 5170, ⓦ www.towerinn.com.ph. Modern business hotel with 48 rooms, coffee shop and small Mediterranean restaurant. It's within walking distance of Makati's shops and restaurants. ④–⑥

YMCA 7 Sacred Heart Plaza, San Antonio Village; see map pp.78–79 ⊤ 02/899 6380 to 6382. Clean and fairly quiet budget accommodation 10 minutes by taxi from Makati's malls and 20 minutes from the Manila Bay area. It's in a chiefly residential area close to the big Manila South Cemetery. Beds in the fan-cooled dorm are cheapest, but there are also good en-suite rooms with fan or a/c for anything from two to six people. The food in the canteen is average, but very cheap. Dorm beds P200. ③–⑤

Around P. Burgos Street

Citadel Inn Makati 5007 P. Burgos St ⊤ 02/897 2370. Skyscraper in the heart of the P. Burgos tourist belt, with bars a few metres away. The rooms are in a somewhat sorry state and the place generally feels badly cared for; the only reason to stay here would be its proximity to the nightlife. There's a coffee shop downstairs with Internet access. ④–⑥

City Garden Hotel Makati 7870 Makati Ave corner Kalayaan Ave ⊤ 02/899 1111, ⓦ www .citygardenhotels.com. A comfortable, modern boutique hotel with spacious and well-maintained a/c rooms, small rooftop swimming pool and giddy views from the rooftop cafe. Good location, the staff are efficient and you can negotiate a discount off-season. ④–⑥

Fersal Apartelle Tourist Inn 107 Neptune St ⊤ 02/911 2161 or 897 9123. Functional a/c hotel in a relatively quiet side street off Makati Ave. ④–⑥

Jupiter Arms 102 Jupiter St corner Makati Ave, close to *McDonald's* ⊤ 02/890 5044, ⓦ www. jupiterarms.com. Offers spacious a/c singles and doubles, all en suite and with cable TV. Ask for a room at the back – those at the front overlook the busy street and you'll wake to the sound of jeepneys honking their horns at 5am. ④–⑥

Oxford Suites P. Burgos St corner Durban St ⊤ 02/899 7988. One of the best hotels on the P. Burgos strip, with 223 spacious rooms and suites, gymnasium, 24hr coffee shop and fourth-floor restaurant. Some rooms have kitchenette, living room and terrace. Buffet breakfast included. ⑤–⑦

Primetown Century Tower Kalayaan Ave corner Mercado St ⊤ 02/750 3010. New 35-storey hotel, offering a choice of studios and one- or two-bedroom suites, all with kitchens. ⑤–⑦

Sunette Tower Hotel Durban St ⊤ 02/897 1804 or 1806 ⓦ www.sunette.com.ph. This brown concrete tower is tucked away down a backstreet near off Makati Avenue and therefore has the advantage of being relatively quiet. Rooms are adequate for a night or two and have a/c, fridge and cable TV. ⑤–⑥

Ortigas

Very few tourists stay in **Ortigas**, a business district with five-star hotels and a handful of mid-range establishments catering to business travellers. However, it is convenient for Megamall, one of the largest indoor shopping centres in Asia. The following hotels are all marked on the map on p.109.

Discovery Suites 25 ADB Ave ⊤ 02/635 2222, ⓦ www.discoverysuites.com. Prim and well-kept rooms aimed at business travellers, and within walking distance of the Asian Development Bank, shops and nightlife. ⑦–⑧

Edsa Shangri-La 1 Garden Way, Ortigas Center ⊤ 02/633 8888, ⓦ www.shangri-la.com. The ritziest hotel in the area, with 658 guest rooms, seven restaurants, a gym, massage and the full range of five-star touches including a chocolate on your pillow at bedtime. ⑧

Holiday Inn Galleria Manila 1 ADB Ave, next to Robinson's Galleria ⊤ 02/633 7111. Imposing thirty-storey structure with 284 rooms aimed at business people, and boasting a gym, outdoor pool and deluxe rooms. A buffet breakfast is included in the rate. ⑧

Linden Suites 37 San Miguel Ave ⊤ 02/638 7878. Modern serviced apartments and rooms, all with a/c, cable TV and fridge, in a skyscraper close to the HQ of the corporation that brews San Miguel. All rooms are functional and spruce, and there's a lovely indoor pool. ⑦–⑧

Quezon City

Quezon City is convenient for public transport heading north. Most of the accommodation is within a short taxi ride of the main thoroughfare, Timog Avenue. The following hotels are all marked on the map on p.111.

Century Imperial Palace Suites Timog Ave corner T. Morato Ave ☎02/927 8001 to 8005. Impressive glass and metal monolith close to Quezon City's entertainment district and the offices of the ABS-CBN television channel. There are one-, two- and three-bedroom suites, each with its own kitchen. **⑦**–**⑧**

Danarra Hotel 120 Panay Ave ☎02/373 3601 ⓦwww.danarra.com. Rambling motel-style establishment with three swimming pools, a lobby lounge, two restaurants and 85 rooms ranging from a functional standard to an executive suite. Quiet and comfortable, with some of the best budget rooms in the area. **④**–**⑦**

Hotel Rembrandt 26 T. Morato Ave Extension ☎02/373 7466. Medium-sized, modern hotel with a/c rooms, a gymnasium, a cosy piano bar on the top floor with views of the metropolis and a branch of *TGI Friday's* on the ground floor. **⑤**–**⑦**

New Camelot Hotel 35 Mother Ignacia Ave ☎02/373 2101 to 2110. You can't miss it: look out for the mock Arthurian spires rising above one of Quezon City's shantytowns near the ABS-CBN television studios. The rooms are like a bad medieval dream with their imitation-silk sheets, plastic-flower arrangements and chairs carved with Gothic quatrefoils. There are suits of armour in the lobby, the coffee shop is called the *Winchester*, the ballroom the Great Hall of King Arthur and the nightclub (live bands Mon–Sat) the *Dungeon*. Need a present for someone special? Look no further than Lady Guinevere's Gift Shop. **⑤**–**⑦**

Sulo Hotel Matalino Rd, south of Quezon Memorial Circle ☎02/924 5051 to 5071. ⓦwww.sulohotel .com.ph. Well-run, mid-sized business person's hotel with Alpine chalet-style facade and lobby, and with a gym, massage, swimming pool, restaurants and bars. **⑥**–**⑦**

The City

Manila's reputation as an intimidating city for visitors stems partly from its size and apparent disorder. To see the major sights you will have to sweat it out in traffic and be prepared for delays, but at least the main attractions such as the old walled city of **Intramuros** and the nightlife of **Malate** are close to one another, grouped along the crescent sweep of Manila Bay and Roxas Boulevard, with the green oasis of **Rizal Park** close at hand too. **Makati** and **Ortigas** to the east are rather sterile business districts best known for their malls and restaurants. North of the Pasig River, near and beyond **Binondo** – Manila's Chinatown – are the museums at the **Malacañang Palace** and the **University of Santo Tomas**, and the gargantuan, morbidly interesting **Chinese Cemetery**. **Quezon City** on the city's northern edge is a little out of the way for most visitors, but it does boast some lively nightlife, most of it fuelled by students from the nearby University of the Philippines.

Intramuros

Intramuros, the old Spanish capital of Manila, is the one part of the metropolis where you get a real sense of history. It was begun in the 1570s and remains a monumental, if partially ruined, relic of the Spanish occupation, a city within a city, separated from the rest of Manila by its crumbling walls. You can walk from one end to the other in a matter of minutes. In fact, a good way to see it is by arranging a **walking tour** through the Philippine Convention and Visitors Bureau (☎02/525 1255) or the Intramuros Visitor Center (☎02/527 2961), which has a small office in the grounds of Fort Santiago. Rates start at $15 for

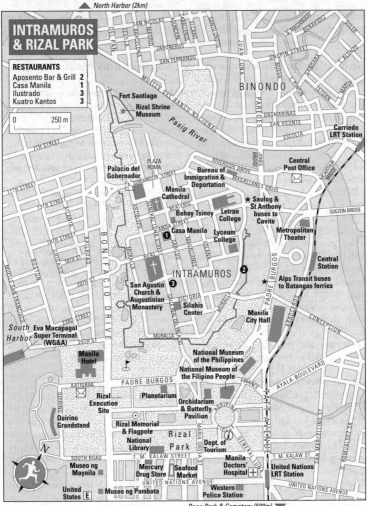

INTRAMUROS & RIZAL PARK

North Harbor (2km)

RESTAURANTS

Aposento Bar & Grill	2
Casa Manila	1
Ilustrado	3
Kuatro Kantos	3

0   250 m

Fort Santiago
Rizal Shrine Museum

Pasig River

BINONDO

Carriedo LRT Station

Palacio del Gobernador
Bureau of Immigration & Deportation
Central Post Office

Manila Cathedral
Saulog & St Anthony buses to Cavite

Bahay Tsinoy
Letran College
Casa Manila
Lyceum College

Metropolitan Theater

Central Station

INTRAMUROS
Alps Transit buses to Batangas ferries

San Agustin Church & Augustinian Monastery
Silahis Center
Manila City Hall

South Harbor
Eva Macapagal Super Terminal (WG&A)

Manila Hotel

PADRE BURGOS

National Museum of the Philippines
National Museum of the Filipino People

Rizal Execution Site
Planetarium
Orchidarium & Butterfly Pavilion

Quirino Grandstand
Rizal Memorial & Flagpole
National Library

Rizal Park

Dept. of Tourism

Museo ng Maynila
Mercury Drug Store
Seafood Market
Manila Doctors' Hospital
United Nations LRT Station

United States E
Museo ng Pambata
UNITED NATIONS AVENUE
Western Police Station

Paco Park & Cemetery (500m)

a half-day tour that includes a light-and-sound show and an opportunity for shopping.

This former seat of colonial power featured well-planned streets, plazas, the Governor's Palace, fifteen churches and six monasteries; it also had dozens of cannon that were used to keep the natives in their place. Many buildings were reduced to rubble in World War II, but Intramuros still lays claim to most of Manila's top tourist sights. The Romanesque **Manila Cathedral** (daily 6am–8pm; free), originally built in 1571, has been destroyed six times down the centuries by a combination of fire, typhoon, earthquake and war. It was comprehensively flattened during World War II, but the Vatican contributed funds to have it rebuilt. The present structure was completed in 1958, and is similar in style to the cathedral that stood here in the nineteenth century. It lacks the rich historical ambience of nearby San Agustin, but the interior is impressive in its simplicity, with a long aisle flanked by marble pillars, stained-glass rose windows and a central dome.

San Agustin Church and the Augustinian monastery

A few hundreds metres to the south of the cathedral on the west side of General Luna Street stands **San Agustin Church** (daily 9am–noon & 1–5pm; P25, including admission to the Augustinian monastery next door), with a magnificent Baroque interior, *trompe l'oeil* murals and a vaulted ceiling and dome. Dating back to 1587, it's the oldest stone church in the Philippines, and contains the modest tomb of Miguel Lopez de Legazpi, the founder of Manila (see p.77). The church and the monastery were the only structures in Intramuros to survive the devastation of World War II, an indication of just how badly Manila suffered under occupation.

Built around a quiet grassy plaza, the former **Augustinian monastery** (same hours as church) now houses a museum of icons and artefacts, along with an eighteenth-century Spanish pipe organ that was recently restored. The monastery was the centre of Augustinian power in the Philippines, and played host to illustrious guests such as the governor general and religious dignitaries from Europe, as well as being a centre of learning for artists and theologians, with its own printing press. The old vestry is where Governor General Fermin Jaudenes drafted the terms of surrender to the Americans in 1898. The refectory is now a mausoleum for Filipino families, containing a monument to the victims of Japanese occupation. If it's not being used for a wedding reception, take a stroll through **Father Blanco's Garden**, a neat area of tropical greenery with stone paths and gazebos. Father Blanco pioneered the study of medicinal plants in the Philippines and published his magnum opus on the subject, *Flora de Filipinas*, in 1883. Copies in English are on sale in the monastery gift shop.

Casa Manila and the Silahis Center

The splendid **Casa Manila**, a sympathetically restored colonial-era house (Tues–Sun 9am–6pm; P50), lies opposite San Agustin on General Luna Street in the Plaza San Luis Complex. Redolent of a grander age, the house contains an impressive *sala* (living room) where *tertulias* (soirees) and *bailes* (dances) were held. The upstairs family latrine is a two-seater, which allowed husband and wife to gossip out of earshot of the servants while simultaneously going about their business.

Beyond Casa Manila, at 744 Calle Real del Palacio, the **Silahis Center** is an emporium selling artefacts, antiques and cultural publications – you can purchase, if you wish, a pair of matching his and hers headstones from the Sulu archipelago. Across a pretty courtyard reached through the back door of the Silahis Center are the elegant *Ilustrado* restaurant (see p.113) and the atmospheric *Kuatro Kantos Bar* (see p.113). Either is worth dropping in on to take a break from sightseeing.

Fort Santiago

The ruins of **Fort Santiago** (daily 8am–9pm; P15) stand at the northwestern end of Intramuros, a five-minute walk from the cathedral on the opposite side of busy A. Soriano Jr. Street. The seat of the colonial powers of both Spain and the US, Fort Santiago was also a prison and torture chamber under the Spanish regime and the scene of countless military-police atrocities during the Japanese occupation. At the far end of the fort, overlooking the Pasig River, is the infamous dungeon where American and Filipino POWs were incarcerated and left to drown by the rising tide. There is a memorial to them nearby.

In the **Rizal Shrine Museum** inside the grounds (daily 8am–noon & 1–5pm; P15), you can see the room where the writer and revolutionary José Rizal spent the hours before his execution in Bagumbayan, the open space that has now become Rizal Park. The museum also houses the original copy of his valedictory poem, *Mi Ultimo Adios*, which was secreted in an oil lamp and smuggled to his family. The greatest, most poignant work of Filipino literature, it was written in Spanish. While even the best English translations fail to capture the felicity of the original, they do give a sense of the sacrifice Rizal was about to make and of his love of the country:

Farewell, my adored country, region beloved of the sun,
Pearl of the Orient Sea, our Eden lost,
Departing in happiness, to you I give the sad, withered remains of my life;
And had it been a life more brilliant, more fine, more fulfilled
I would have given it, willingly to you.

Bahay Tsinoy

Bahay Tsinoy (Tues–Sun 1pm–5pm; P50; ℡02/526 6798) lies at the heart of Intramuros, in the Kaisa-Angelo King Heritage Center on the corner of Anda and Cabildo streets. This small but interesting museum – the name means "house of the Filipino Chinese" – traces the crucial role of the Chinese in Philippine history from their first trade contact with the archipelago in the tenth century to the colonial Spanish period. Besides assorted artefacts and multimedia presentations, the displays include life-sized figures and authentic reproductions of objects related to Tsinoy history. Among the items of interest are a large replica of a Song dynasty junk and a charming diorama of the Parian ghetto (see box on pp.104–105). There's also a gallery of rare photographs and a martyrs hall dedicated to Tsinoys who formed guerilla units against Japanese occupation.

Around Intramuros

The area around Intramuros is the **City of Manila**, one of the fourteen cities within Metro Manila. There are a number of attractions here that can be seen on foot in a day. **Rizal Park** is the capital's best-known green space and the site of a number of contemporary and historical attractions, including the country's two most important museums, the **National Museum of the Philippines** and the **National Museum of the Filipino People**. Opposite on the other side of Roxas Boulevard is the sedate old **Manila Hotel**, whose grand lobby is an ideal place to stop for a drink. East of Rizal Park, **Paco Park** has historical resonance as the site of a cemetery for victims of cholera and original burial place of José Rizal.

Rizal Park and the national museums

Rizal ("rezal") **Park**, or the Luneta, is a ten-minute walk south of Intramuros across busy Padré Burgos Street. In a city notoriously short of greenery, the park was where the colonial-era glitterati used to promenade after church every Sunday. These days Rizal Park is an early-morning jogging circuit, a weekend playground for children and a refuge for couples and families escaping the clamour of the city. People take picnics and lie in the shade, or sit in an area known as Chess Plaza, gambling a few centavos on the outcome of a game. **Hawkers** sell everything from balloons and mangoes to plastic bags full of *chicheron*, deep-fried pig skin served with a little container of vinegar and chilli

△ Rizal Memorial, Rizal Park

for dipping. The park is often busy, with many distractions and activities, but few visitors report any problems with hustlers, pickpockets or what Filipinos generally refer to as "*scalawags*".

The park's sundry attractions include a run-down **planetarium** (4 shows daily 9am, 10.30am, 1.30pm & 3.30pm; P50), an amphitheatre where concerts are held every Sunday at 5pm, Chinese and Japanese gardens and a giant relief map of the Philippines. At the bay end of the park, close to the *Manila Hotel*, is the **Rizal Memorial** and the flagpole where Manuel Roxas, first President of the Republic, was sworn in on July 4, 1946. Rizal's execution site is near here, close to a memorial marking the execution site of three priests garrotted by the Spanish for alleged complicity in the uprising in Cavite in 1872. One of the park's newest features is the **Orchidarium & Butterfly Pavilion** (Tues–Sun 9am–5pm; P20; ℡02/527 6376), designed and operated by the Clean & Green Foundation, an environmental charity established by former First Lady Amelita Ramos. It contains dozens of species of butterfly, some remarkable tropical flora (not just orchids) and a pleasant restaurant that serves organic food.

The museums

Beyond the Orchidarium lie the country's two major museums, both under the auspices of the National Museum and both worth making time to visit. The **National Museum of the Philippines** (Tues–Sun 10am–4.30pm; free; ℡02/527 1215) is in what used to be the old Congress Building on the northern edge of the park. It houses paintings by Filipino masters including Juan Luna (1859–99), José Joya (1931–95) and Fernando Amorsolo (1892–1972), along with clearly labelled displays on geology, zoology, botany, crafts and weapons. The most famous painting on display is Luna's magnificent *Spolarium*, a thinly veiled attack in oils on the atrocities of the Spanish regime, portraying fallen gladiators being dragged onto a pile of corpses. If you're interested in tribes, the anthropology area has sections for many ethnic groups, including the Ibaloy, the Ifugao and the Tausug of Sulu. The excellent archeology section has relics from Philippine prehistory and a display of artefacts retrieved from the deep.

A short walk away on the opposite side of Rizal Park, close to the Department of Tourism, is the **National Museum of the Filipino People** (Tues–Sun 10am–4.30pm; P100). In what used to be the Government Finance Building, a grey edifice with Doric columns built by Americans in 1902, the museum includes treasures from the *San Diego*, which sank off the coast of Fortune island in Batangas in 1600. Not all the artefacts recovered from the wreck were intrinsically valuable: you'll see chicken bones and hazelnuts from the ship's store, as well as porcelain, rosaries and silver goblets. The well-labelled anthropology section upstairs is equally enthralling, with reburial jars from areas such as Palawan and Mindanao that date back to 5 BC. These jars were used to hold the bones of ancestors who were buried and then exhumed and stored for safekeeping.

The Manila Hotel

The **Manila Hotel**, grand old dame of Philippine hotels, though now a little careworn, stands near the bay end of Rizal Park. Here you can soak up some of the atmosphere of early twentieth-century Manila, those halcyon days when the city was at its cultural and social zenith; you can even stay (see p.86) in the General Douglas MacArthur Suite, residence from 1936 to 1941 of the man Filipinos called the Caesar of America. If even the standard rooms are beyond your means, you can at least sip a martini in the lobby while listening to a string quartet and watching the capital's elite strut by.

When the hotel opened in 1912 it represented the epitome of colonial class and luxury. In 1935 the first Pan-Am Trans-Pacific Clipper seaplane touched down in the bay outside, bringing mail from President Roosevelt to the President of the Commonwealth, Manuel Quezon. Glenn Miller crossed the Pacific on the clipper to play in the hotel's Fiesta Pavilion. The hotel was bombed during World War II, but reconstructed afterwards to resume its position as one of the most regal establishments in the Orient. Lavish dances known as **rigodon balls** were held every month in the Grand Ballroom, with high-society guests dancing the quadrille in traditional *ternos* (formal evening dresses) and dinner jackets. Rocky Marciano and Tyrone Power both used the hotel as their home away from home in the 1950s, while Bill Clinton did likewise in 1994 and Prince Charles in 1997.

The hotel has its own historical **archive**, which the concierge will open for you if you make arrangements in advance. It contains press clippings dating back to the opening, photographs of the hotel during World War II and signed photographs of illustrious guests, from Marlon Brando, looking young and slender in a native *barong* (formal shirt), to Ricky Martin and Jon Bon Jovi. A little further along from the hotel is the Quirino Grandstand where various official functions take place, including a military parade on Independence Day.

Paco Park and Cemetery

One of the loveliest spots in Manila, **Paco Park and Cemetery** is off a quiet street called San Marcellino, between Pedro Gil and UN Avenue LRT stations. It takes about fifteen minutes to get there on foot from Rizal Park – walk south to Padre Faura Street, then turn left.

A circular cemetery with an aged and beautiful garden dominated by a classical rotunda, Paco Park was built in 1820 for victims of a cholera epidemic, the coffins inserted into niches on the inner sides of the two surrounding walls. It was also here that **José Rizal** was buried by the Spanish in an unmarked grave. His sister, Narcisa Rizal-Lopez, combing the area around Luneta to discover what the Spanish had done with the remains of her martyred brother, saw a group of Civil Guards inside Paco's circular walls and was alerted. She went to the gate and the guards, seeing what they took to be a harmless woman, let her pass. Narcisa inspected the walls and saw no signs of a coffin having been put in recently, so she wandered the lawns and came across another group of guards standing beside a mound of freshly turned earth the length of a man. It could only be her brother's grave. She went away and had a small plaque made bearing Rizal's initials in reverse order, R.P.J. Returning to Paco, she prevailed upon the cemetery guardian to mark the site. Two years later, in August 1898, a few days after the Americans took Manila, Rizal's remains were exhumed. They were left in the custody of his family until 1911, when they were deposited beneath the Rizal Monument, built that year in Rizal Park. Paco Park is also the final resting place for Mario Gomez, José Burgos and Jacinto Zamora, the three priests who were garrotted by the Spanish in 1872 after being implicated in an abortive uprising.

The park's serenity has made it a favourite venue for weddings. It is also the setting every Friday at 5pm and 6pm for free **open-air concerts**, usually classical recitals by Filipino artists or students. It's worth timing your visit to take in one of these performances – they're rarely packed, and it's pleasant to sit amid the greenery at sundown listening to Chopin sonatas or a Monteverdi madrigal.

Along Manila Bay

When Manila was in its heyday, **Manila Bay** must have been a sight to behold, with its dreamy sunsets and sweeping panorama across the South China Sea. It's still fun to watch sunsets from the harbour wall or the outside bar at the *Westin Philippine Plaza*, but Manila Bay is really trading on its romantic past, the golden era before the war when this was one of the finest promenades in the world. The promenade has been souped-up in recent years, with some small cafés and snack bars, but the area still feels past its peak. Its buildings were bombed flat during the war and have been replaced with boxes made of concrete. Horse-drawn carriages (*calesas*) still tout for business, but the horses look exhausted and even the palm trees that line Roxas Boulevard are drooping from pollution.

A trip along the boulevard heading south from Rizal Park takes you past the **Museo ng Maynila** and the **Museo ng Pambata**, museums respectively devoted to the history of Manila and history for children. Proceeding along the western edge of Ermita and Malate, you'll come to the **Metropolitan Museum**. A few hundred metres south of here is the **Cultural Center of the Philippines** (CCP) complex, which includes a number of buildings constructed at the behest of Imelda Maros. Among them are the Cultural Center itself, the Manila Film Center and the Coconut Palace, built for a papal visit in 1981. Ferries for the one-hour journey to the fascinating island of **Corregidor** (see p.133) leave from near the CCP.

Museo ng Maynila and Museo ng Pambata

On Roxas Boulevard south of the *Manila Hotel*, the **Museo ng Maynila** (Tues–Sat 9am–6pm; P20) was once the Army & Navy Club, where American servicemen in the Philippines drank sundowners and shared the latest gossip from home. In 1997 the club was closed and converted into a museum dedicated to the history of Manila and its residents, including revolutionary heroes Andres Bonifacio and his wife Gregoria de Jesus, whose silk kimono is on display. The old photographs are fascinating, and the guides are friendly and knowledgeable, adding a great deal of extra information and trivia to the explanations of the exhibits. Next door is the **Museo ng Pambata** (Children's Museum; Tues–Sat 9am–5pm; Sun 1pm–6pm; P30 children, P50 adults), which has one hall where young children can get a feel for history using interactive displays – replicas of ships, churches and native Philippine homes.

Metropolitan Museum

One of Manila's best-maintained museums, the **Metropolitan Museum** (usually known as the Met; Mon–Sat 10am–6pm; P50 adults, P30 children; ⓦwww.metmuseum.org) is located at the Bangko Sentral ng Pilipinas Complex on Roxas Boulevard, opposite the Manila Yacht Club. This fine-arts museum, a Filipino mini-Guggenheim, houses an exciting and diverse range of exhibits and activities. The permanent collection is by far the best of its kind in the country, with contemporary and historic art from Asia, America, Europe, Africa and Egypt, plus regular displays of paintings, photographs and pottery from high-profile contemporary Filipino artists. Also showcased here is the Central Bank's collection of **prehistoric jewellery** and other permanent displays such as the Pottery Gallery, which contains prehistoric artefacts.

Cultural Center of the Philippines (CCP)

The **Cultural Center of the Philippines** was one of Imelda's grand plans for bringing world-class arts to the Philippines. The main building stands on reclaimed land on Roxas Boulevard, opposite the junction with Vito Cruz. Conceived during the early, promising years of her husband's presidency and opened on a night of great splendour in 1966, it's a slab-like construction typical of those built on Imelda's orders when she was suffering from her so-called "edifice complex". Various productions by Ballet Philippines and occasional Broadway-style hits such as *Miss Saigon* are staged in the main theatre, and there are a number of smaller theatres in the complex such as the **Folk Arts Theater**, which is the venue for occasional pop concerts, jazz and drama (see p.122 for more).

The Manila Film Center

If bricks could talk, those at the Manila Film Center would have a sinister story to tell. Back in the 1970s, Imelda Marcos wanted to stage an annual **film festival** that would rival Cannes and put Manila on the international cultural map. But the centre she commissioned for the purpose was jerry-built and a floor collapsed, allegedly burying workers under rubble and killing many. No one knows exactly how many, because most were poor labourers from the provinces and records were not kept of their names. Police were told to throw a cordon round the building so the press couldn't get to it, and work continued round the clock. The centre was completed in 1982, some say with dead workers still entombed inside, in time for the opening night of the Manila International Film Festival. Imelda celebrated by walking onto the stage to greet the audience in a black and emerald green *terno* (a formal Philippine gown) thick with layer upon layer of peacock feathers that were shipped specially from India.

In its heyday the centre housed six theatres, six preview rooms, a film archive and several offices, and staged the 1982 and 1983 Manila International Film Festivals. But the building had such a bad name – some say it was haunted and Imelda herself had it exorcized – that it soon had to make ends meet by showing soft-porn (*bomba*) films for the masses. It was briefly rehabilitated in the late 1980s when it was used as a centre for experimental film-making, but after an earthquake hit Manila in 1990 it was abandoned. The centre has now been partially renovated and holds transvestite song and dance extravaganzas organized by a group called Amazing Philippine Theater (☎02/834 8870).

Also part of the CCP Complex is the **Manila Film Center** (see box above) and the **Coconut Palace**, built on the orders of Imelda for the visit of Pope John Paul II in 1981. The pope gave her short shrift, saying he wouldn't stay in such an outrageous establishment while there was so much poverty on the streets of Manila, and suggested she spend her money more wisely. The palace, seventy percent of which was constructed from coconut and the rest from other native materials, was eventually opened by Brooke Shields. Today the seven private function rooms on the first floor are popular venues for posh but cheesy wedding receptions. Guided **tours** (Mon–Sat 9–11.30am & 1–4.30pm; P100) offer an intriguing close-up of yet another of Imelda's kitsch follies.

Ermita and Malate

Two of the city's oldest neighbourhoods, **Ermita** and **Malate**, nestle behind Roxas Boulevard within ten minutes' walk of Manila Bay. Ermita was infamous for its go-go bars and massage parlours up until the late 1980s, when tough-guy mayor Alfredo Lim came along and boarded up most of them, alleging that they were fronts for prostitution. Ermita and Malate are now a ragbag of budget hotels, choked streets and fast-food outlets, but both are good places to find travel agents, banks and nightlife. Major **malls** in the area include Robinson's Place, next to the *Manila Midtown Hotel* at the junction of Pedro Gil and M. Adriatico, and Harrison Plaza, opposite the Rizal Memorial Stadium at the southern end of M. Adriatico.

The area around **Remedios Circle** in Malate is known for its freewheeling nightlife. Most of it is centred on **J. Nakpil Street**, where a lively café society thrives and there are dozens of small, intimate clubs and restaurants. Modish nightspots have also started to open up in neighbouring **Maria Orosa Street**, and on Friday and Saturday nights this is the place to be seen. There are more cafés and bars in Remedios Circle itself and during the dry season dozens of (mostly free) live concerts take place on a stage erected at the centre of the circle. For more on Ermita and Malate nightlife, see p.117.

A five-minute walk towards the sea from Remedios brings you to the eye-catching Baroque-style **Malate Church** on M.H. Del Pilar Street, where British soldiers took refuge during Britain's brief occupation of the Philippines in 1762–63. The church, dedicated to Our Lady of Remedies and run by the Columbian Fathers, holds a special blessing for animals every first Sunday in October, attended by various cats, dogs, birds and reptiles. Outside the church, facing the sea, is a small square on whose south side is the popular, lively *Aristo-crat Restaurant* (see p.112).

Binondo and Quiapo

Manila's Chinatown, **Binondo**, exercises a curious, magnetic pull. This is city life in extremis, a rambunctious ghetto of people on the make, the streets full of merchants and middlemen flogging fake watches and herbs, sandalwood incense and gaudy jewellery. You can lose yourself for an afternoon wandering through its mercantile centre, snacking on dim sum at one of its many fan-cooled teahouses. A visit to the sepulchral **Binondo Church** will give you some idea of the area's historical significance. Nearby, is the district of **Quiapo**, whose **Quiapo Church** is said to be the most visited in the Philippines.

From Magellanes Drive on the northern edge of Intramuros you can walk to Binondo in fifteen minutes across **Jones Bridge**. The best **LRT station** for Binondo is Carriedo at Plaza Santa Cruz, only a short walk from the Ongpin Street Welcome Gate at the eastern end of Ongpin Street. There's also an MRT-2 station (Purple Line) in busy Recto avenue, a ten-minute walk north of Quiapo Church along Evangelista Street. There are plenty of **jeepneys** to Binondo from M. Adriatico in Malate and Ermita, and also from Taft Avenue marked for Divisoria; the Divisoria jeepneys take you right past Binondo Church. From Plaza Miranda, behind Quiapo Church, there are buses to Makati, and jeepneys and FX taxis to Quezon City, Ermita and Malate.

Once in Binondo, you can hire a **calesa** (horse-drawn carriage) – still used by Binondo residents instead of taxis – to take you from one place to the next; fares for short journeys should only cost P40, though you may need to haggle. A tour of the whole Binondo area should cost no more than P200 and should include the **Escolta** area, Binondo Church and the busiest thoroughfare in Binondo,

---

Chinatown's Fire Brigade

In the Philippines, the joke goes, you don't insure against fire, you insure against the fire service. Apocryphal stories abound of ill-equipped firemen arriving at the scene of a conflagration hours after they were summoned, or asking affluent householders for money before they turn their hoses on. Residents of Chinatown found a practical solution to the problem: in the early 1960s – when Binondo became so crowded that if a fire broke out it often spread quickly from one street to another – they started their own fire service. On the second floor of *Café Mezzanine* (Nueva St corner Ongpin St) there's a photo exhibit on the **Chinatown Volunteer Fire Brigade** (CVFB) in action; a percentage of profits from the café goes towards keeping the CVFB in business. The CVFB fire trucks you'll see parked on the streets of Chinatown are painted purple because they were bought with profits from the sale of Chinese mooncakes made with purple yam.

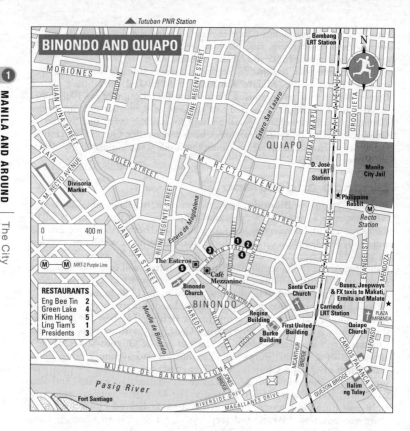

▲ Tutuban PNR Station

BINONDO AND QUIAPO

RESTAURANTS
Eng Bee Tin	2
Green Lake	4
Kim Hiong	5
Ling Tiam's	1
Presidents	3

Ongpin Street, site of a multitude of small noodle parlours, shops, apothecaries and restaurants.

Escolta

Escolta, a once prestigious shopping street named after the horse-mounted military escorts of the British commander-in-chief during the British invasion of 1762, is on the right immediately after you cross Jones Bridge. In the nineteenth century this was where Manila's elite promenaded and shopped, buying fine silk and trinkets from stores owned not only by Chinese, but by Spaniards, Americans, Japanese and Indians.

Escolta's dizzy days as a Champs Elysées of the Orient are long gone, but it's fascinating to wander around for a while, picking out the remnants of a glorious past. This is where the country's first movie theatres stood, all of them now gone. The **First United Building**, close to the Carriedo fountain at the eastern end of Escolta, is a pink and white Art Deco gem designed by the son of painter Juan Luna. Opposite is the **Regina Building** with its Art Nouveau cupolas, and next door to that is the **Burke Building**, which had the first elevator in the country; it has recently been restored, and is now office space for small enterprises.

Outside Carriedo station, **Santa Cruz Church** is an immense white Baroque structure that was originally built in the seventeenth century for the swelling ranks of Chinese in the area. It was most recently rebuilt in 1957 after damage from earthquakes and war.

Manila-based artist Carlos Celdran (℡02/484 4945, ℮celdrantour@hotmail .com) hosts entertaining and informative walking tours of the Escolta area; the tours cost P500 and take in many of these buildings, plus local markets and Quiapo Church.

Binondo Church
The Minor Basilica and the National Shrine of San Lorenzo Ruiz in Plaza de la Basco, at the western end of Ongpin Street, is commonly known simply as **Binondo Church**. It stands on the spot where the Dominican priests established their church when they first came to Binondo in the seventeenth century.

△ Binondo street scene

The Chinese in the Philippines

At the start of the twentieth century, ethnic Chinese comprised five percent of the Philippines' population. Today the proportion of **Tsinoys** – as the Chinese community is known here – is probably twice that, though no official statistics are available. It can be difficult to distinguish the Chinese from the rest of the population, as many Filipinos with Chinese ancestry do not speak Chinese and retain next to no Chinese customs, though surnames can be a giveaway: Tan, Dy and Go are all common among Tsinoys, as are combinations of Chinese names, such as Yuchengko and Gokongwei.

Chinese involvement with the Philippines goes back a long way. Chinese **traders** had been doing business in the archipelago for six hundred years before the coming of the West. Relations were not close, however, and few Chinese settled in Manila in pre-Hispanic times because they were wary of a petty kingdom that had no strong formal government. When the Spanish came to Manila they found only a few tens of Chinese living in Rajah Soliman's Kingdom of Maynila, the original camp on the banks of the Pasig. It wasn't until the 1560s, during which time Miguel Lopez de Legazpi landed in Bohol, that Chinese culture began to have an impact. Junks from China's eastern seaboard carried silks and luxury goods to Manila, returning to the Celestial Kingdom with Mexican silver that had been brought to the Philippines by galleon. The sailors spread word that Manila was rich, and Chinese tradesmen, artisans, farmers and fishermen poured in.

In 1581, Governor General Gonzalo Ronquillo, alarmed by the rapid growth of the Chinese community, decided to confine them to a ghetto that became known as the **Parian**, close to the location of Binondo today. The Parian has been called the Philippines' first mall and employment agency. At dawn the residents of Intramuros came to the Parian to do their shopping and to find hired help from among the **Sangley** (trader) folk. Here, it was possible to buy silk and porcelain, order a set of lacquered furniture or hire a carpenter, mason, scribe or printer. A visitor in 1590 noted that the goods on display were "so rare and curious that they merit the attention of the most civilized nations".

In the colonial tradition, the Chinese were made to pay for their success. Apart from mandatory tribute, City Hall collected all kinds of taxes from them. Many tried to avoid payment by converting to **Catholicism**, which made them exempt from tribute for ten years. Catholic Chinese could hold public office and marry Filipino women. Interracial marriages were common, explaining the "Chinito" look of many Filipinos today. Another way to escape paying tribute was to enlist in the **navy**. However, in October 1593, during a naval expedition from Manila to reclaim an area of Cavite from the Dutch, Chinese oarsmen mutinied and massacred the Spaniards, including the unfortunate leader of the party, Governor Gomez Peres Dasmarinas. His killing

The original building was destroyed by shelling in 1762 when the British invaded Manila and the Chinese were expelled. The Dominicans left with the Chinese but returned in 1842 and completed the church you see today, a solid granite structure with an octagonal bell tower, in 1854. Every Sunday, while Filipino parishioners hear Mass in the main church in Filipino, Chinese parishioners meet in the lobby of the San Lorenzo Academy next door to hear Mass in Mandarin (7am), Hokkien (the chief dialect of Fujian province in southeast China; 10am) and English (8am, 9am & 6pm).

The church was badly damaged by bombing during World War II and new features include the canopy at the entrance and the strikingly colourful murals on the ceilings. Depicting the life of Christ and the Assumption of the Virgin, these murals were not actually painted on the ceiling but were executed at ground level, then hoisted up and attached to the ceiling.

made Manila nervous about the Chinese multitudes. When three merchants arrived from Amoy (Xiamen) in 1602 looking for gold, the Spanish were in such a state of agitation they convinced themselves the merchants were part of a scouting party, gathering intelligence for an invasion. The Spanish began to add new battlements to Intramuros, which in turn led the Chinese in the Parian to believe they were about to be exterminated. Seizing the initiative, they marched on nearby Tondo, Quiapo and finally Intramuros itself, using ladders to storm the ramparts. This second "**Sangley uprising**" was a dismal failure. Four thousand Chinese were killed and 23,000 fled to Laguna where they were captured and duly slaughtered.

Trading fleets continued to arrive from Amoy, and thirty years after the uprising the Chinese population of Manila had reached 28,000. To decongest the Parian, hundreds of the Chinese were sent to work on haciendas owned by Spanish friars in the provinces. In 1639 these labourers revolted in Laguna and terrorized the province for a year before they surrendered – and were massacred. There was another move to resolve the Chinese problem in the 1650s when the King of Spain ordered a mass expulsion of Chinese from the colony, his fervent representatives in the colony herding hundreds onto boats bound for Amoy. Those Chinese merchants and artisans that Manila felt it needed were given a tract of land across the Pasig River from Intramuros. This land was strictly for Christian Chinese and was to become the district of **Binondo**, a Christian enclave where the Chinese were absorbed into Philippine culture. Descendants of the first immigrants from Amoy would later play their part in the revolution that saw Spain lose the Philippines forever.

During World War II many Tsinoys again showed loyalty to the flag in the face of oppression by supporting the anti-Japanese propaganda movement. Some even joined guerrilla units. In 1945, when the Americans returned to Manila, the Japanese tried to bomb as many buildings in Binondo as they could before fleeing. It was estimated that more than half the district was destroyed and hundreds of lives lost. After the war, rebuilding by the Chinese community was rapid and Binondo once again resumed its pre-eminence as a centre for trade and barter, its narrow streets crammed with noodle parlours, herbal apothecaries and rice dealers.

The Philippine Chinese still live largely in Manila, though they have a presence in other cities throughout the archipelago. Tsinoys play a significant role in society – the Chinese are known for their entrepreneurial flair, and many of the country's most high-profile tycoons are of Chinese descent. There is undoubtedly a certain amount of mild anti-Tsinoy sentiment, a lingering sense that Tsinoys are not really Filipino and carry with them an advantage because their families are presumed to be wealthy. Much the same is felt about the big Spanish-Filipino dynasties such as the Ayalas and the Lopezes.

The church is well known in the Philippines because it was where **San Lorenzo Ruiz** served as a sacristan. Of Filipino and Chinese parentage, Ruiz had a criminal record for quarrelling with a Spaniard. It was probably because of this that he was encouraged to go to Japan in 1636. There, he was arrested in Nagasaki in 1637 for spreading the Gospel of Christ, and was executed for refusing to renounce his faith. The Vatican canonized him in 1989.

Ongpin Street

Behind Binondo Church is **Ongpin Street**, which is about 2km long and runs eastwards to Santa Cruz Church. It was originally called Calle Sacristia but was renamed in 1915 after Roman Ongpin, a fervent nationalist who was said to be the first Chinese-Filipino to wear the *barong tagalog*, the formal shirt that became the national dress for men. Ongpin Street is at the heart of Chinatown, chock-full of restaurants, noodle parlours, apothecaries and shops selling goods imported from China. At the western end of the street is a row of hugely popular food stalls (see p.113).

Quiapo Church

Officially called the Basilica of St John the Baptist, **Quiapo Church** – as everyone in Manila calls it – houses the Black Nazarene, a supposedly miraculous wooden icon that came to the country on board a galleon from Spain in 1767. Every year on January 9, Plaza Miranda in front of the church is the venue for the **Feast of the Black Nazarene**, when 200,000 barefoot Catholic faithful from all over the Philippines come together to worship the image. The crowd is dense and fervent, and traffic around the plaza solid. The plaza, east of the Carriedo LRT station, is also where fiery speeches were delivered by politicians and left-wing leaders during the early 1970s, protesting against Marcos and martial law. In 1972 scores of opposition figures were killed or wounded by a bomb here that was said to have been planted at the behest of Marcos to give him an excuse for further military crackdowns, although this was never proven.

Inside the church, hunched old women will, for a fee, tell your fortune, pray the rosary for you or light candles for lost loved ones. The brazen religious piety can be overwhelming. Even Imelda Marcos sometimes worships here, crawling down the central aisle on her knees as a sign of penitence and humility.

The area around the church is a good area for bargain-hunters. Several stores that sell **handicrafts** at local prices are squeezed under Quiapo Bridge, a place known to all Manila's bargain-hunters as Sa Ilalim ng Tulay (under the bridge). Outside the church itself, vendors sell anting-antings (amulets) and all manner of herbal remedies.

San Miguel and Sampoloc

San Miguel is an old residential area on the north bank of the Pasig, about 2km from Intramuros across Quezon Bridge. A bustling, claustrophobic area of town, it's only worth visiting to see **Malacañang Palace**, the place the president of the Philippines calls home.

A little further afield, 2km northeast of Binondo in **Sampoloc**, the **Santo Tomas Museum of Arts and Sciences** houses a vast private collection in the oldest university in Asia. Also in Sampoloc, the **Chinese Cemetery** is a sometimes ostentatious tribute to the power and influence of the Chinese community.

Malacañang Palace and Museum

While much of Malacañang Palace is off-limits to the public, you can visit the wing that houses the **Malacañang Museum** (Mon–Fri 9am–4pm; P50; ⓦwww. op.gov.ph/museum), covering Philippine presidential history. Visits are by appointment only, so you'll need to call the museum director (ⓣ02/736 4662) at least seven days ahead; you'll be told how to submit a request, which must be in writing with passport details for clearance by the Presidential Security Group. You can visit the former president's office, the cabinet room and the council of state room, which were used by every president until Marcos, and were restored in 2002. The palace is in J.P. Laurel Street; use the entrance at Gate Six.

Malacañang was once a stone house, purchased by Colonel Luis Miguel Formento in 1802 for P1100. In 1825, the Spanish government bought it and, in 1849, made it the summer residence of the governor general in the Philippines. The palace of the governor general in Intramuros was destroyed in the great earthquake of 1863, so he moved to Malacañang permanently. Rooms were added and renovations made, but on a number of occasions the building was damaged either by earthquake or typhoon. During the last major renovation in 1978, it underwent extensive interior and exterior changes, and was expanded to its present size – only a portion of the basement remains from the original structure.

The palace will forever be associated with the excesses of the **Marcoses**. When Cory Aquino became president she didn't want to associate herself with her profligate predecessors and refused to use Malacañang as a residence, keeping it only for official functions. She did however, allow the opening of a **museum** of Marcos memorabilia in an attempt to remind people of a dark period of history that she did not want repeated. The museum acquired its present focus at the behest of Fidel Ramos, although the Marcos connection survives in the Marcos Room, housing some of the late dictator's personal belongings. President Gloria Macapagal-Arroyo uses about two-thirds of the palace for official functions and duties.

Santo Tomas Museum of Arts and Sciences

The **Santo Tomas Museum of Arts and Sciences** (Tues–Fri 10am–4pm; P30; ☏02/786 1611), on the second floor of the main building of the University of Santo Tomas (UST), is an immense and fascinating private collection of historic documents, 180,000 volumes of rare books and displays on ethnology, natural history, archeology and arts. The collection includes a stuffed orangutan, a chair used by Pope John Paul II when he visited Manila and a macabre pair of two-headed calves. Staff are exceptionally approachable and will help you make sense of the displays, some of which are not well labelled or not labelled in English.

UST itself has an interesting history. It was founded in 1611, making it the oldest university in Asia, and is also known as the Catholic University of the Philippines, taking as its inspiration the teachings and philosophy of Thomas Aquinas. The medallion arch above the university entrance has a commemorative plaque that honours José Rizal (see p.95), national hero and UST alumnus.

The university is about twenty minutes' walk (or a short ride on any jeepney marked UST) from Don José LRT station, along a busy road called Lerma. From M.H. Del Pilar Street, any jeepney marked UST or España will get you to UST. The museum is the main building at the back of the sports field, close to Dapitan Street.

The Chinese Cemetery

Four kilometres north of Chinatown, a short walk from Abad Santos LRT station in Sampoloc, is the impressive **Chinese Cemetery** (use the South Gate entrance on Aurora Blvd; daily 7.30am–7pm; free), established by affluent Chinese merchants in the 1850s because the Spanish would not allow foreigners to be buried in Spanish cemeteries. Entire streets are laid out to honour the dead and to underline the status of their surviving relatives. The cemetery is still in use today, with the price of a burial lot as high as P300,000. Many of the tombs resemble houses, with fountains, balconies and, in at least one case, a small swimming pool. Many even have air-conditioning for the relatives who visit on All Saints' Day, when lavish feasts are laid on around the graves with empty chairs for the departed. It has become a sobering joke in the Philippines that this "accommodation" is among the best in the city. **Tours** of some of the more Baroque excesses are available courtesy of the guards, who double as guides to make a bit of money on the side – slip them P100 for their trouble.

Makati

Makati, 5km east of Manila Bay, was a vast expanse of malarial swampland until the Ayala family, one of the country's most influential business dynasties, started developing it at the turn of the last century. It is now Manila's business district and is chock-full of plush hotels, international restaurant chains, expensive condominiums and monolithic air-conditioned malls. The main triangle of Makati is bordered by Ayala Avenue, Paseo de Roxas and Makati Avenue, and is where most of the banks, insurance companies and multinational corporations are sited.

For sightseers, Makati is something of a wasteland, but for shoppers and diners it's nirvana. Opposite the *Makati Shangri-La*, the biggest mall is **Glorietta**, which has a central section and side halls numbered 1–4, and heaves with people seeking refuge from the traffic and heat. A short walk from Glorietta to the other side of Makati Avenue is **Greenbelt Park**, a landscaped garden with a pleasant, modern, white-domed church. Right next to the park is Makati's other main mall, **Greenbelt**, which, like Glorietta, is divided into various numbered halls.

The **Ayala Museum** (Tues–Fri 9am–6pm, Sat 9am–7pm; P350 adults/P250 children; ☎02/757 3589, ⍟www.ayalamuseum.org), in Greenbelt 4 on Makati Avenue, features dioramas illustrating Philippine history as well as rotating exhibitions by artists, photographers and sculptors and a collection of oils by Fernando Amorsolo, one of the country's most famous painters, known for his idyllic depictions of rural Filipino life.

The privately owned **Filipinas Heritage Library** on Makati Avenue, opposite the *Peninsula Hotel*, is an interesting little piece of history: it was Manila's first airport, and Paseo de Roxas, the road to the north, was built where the runway used to be. The library has a bookshop selling Philippine books and a quiet café with Internet access.

On the southeastern edge of Makati, on the east side of EDSA and 3km away from Glorietta mall, is the beautiful **American Cemetery and Memorial** on McKinley Road (daily 6.30am–4.30pm; free), containing 17,206 graves of American military dead of World War II. The headstones are aligned in eleven plots forming a generally circular pattern, set among a wide variety of tropical trees and shrubbery. There is also a chapel and two curved granite walkways whose walls contain mosaic maps depicting the battles fought in the Pacific, along with the names of the 36,000 American servicemen whose bodies were never recovered. From the Glorietta area you can walk to the cemetery in about twenty minutes, heading across EDSA near its junction with Ayala Avenue and along McKinley Road, passing the Santuario de San Antonio (the white church) and the Manila Polo Club on your right. The cemetery entrance is at the big roundabout about 1km past the polo club. A taxi from the centre of Makati will cost no more than P100.

Manila's skyline is changing again, this time on the southeastern edge of Makati in **Fort Bonifacio**, where a huge tract of land that was once an armed forces base (part of it still is) has been snapped up for redevelopment with promises that by the time "The Fort" is completed, it will be a gleaming city within a city, a collection of luxury apartments, shops, restaurants and leisure facilities to rival anything in Asia. Development is slow, but has begun with a number of new apartment blocks and a handful of restaurants and bars. The best

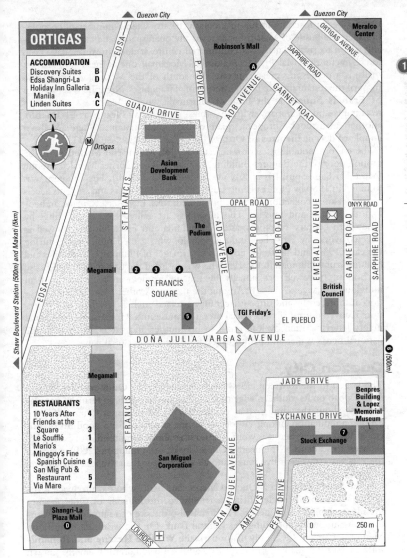

ORTIGAS

ACCOMMODATION

Discovery Suites	B
Edsa Shangri-La	D
Holiday Inn Galleria Manila	A
Linden Suites	C

N

Ⓜ Ortigas

Quezon City

Quezon City

Meralco Center

Robinson's Mall

ⒶＡ

ORTIGAS AVENUE

SAPPHIRE ROAD

EDSA

P. POVEDA

GUADIX DRIVE

ADB AVENUE

GARNET ROAD

ST FRANCIS

Asian Development Bank

The Podium

ADB AVENUE

OPAL ROAD

TOPAZ ROAD

RUBY ROAD

EMERALD AVENUE

ONYX ROAD

GARNET ROAD

SAPPHIRE ROAD

Ⓑ

Ⓐ ①

British Council

Shaw Boulevard Station (500m) and Makati (5km)

EDSA

Megamall

② ③ ④

ST FRANCIS SQUARE

⑤

TGI Friday's

EL PUEBLO

Ⓖ (500m)

DOÑA JULIA VARGAS AVENUE

Megamall

ST FRANCIS

JADE DRIVE

Benpres Building & Lopez Memorial Museum

EXCHANGE DRIVE

RESTAURANTS

10 Years After	4
Friends at the Square	3
Le Soufflé	1
Mario's	2
Minggoy's Fine Spanish Cuisine	6
San Mig Pub & Restaurant	5
Via Mare	7

San Miguel Corporation

SAN MIGUEL AVENUE

AMETHYST DRIVE

PEARL DRIVE

⑦

Stock Exchange

Shangri-La Plaza Mall

Ⓓ

LOURDES

Ⓒ

0   250 m

way to get there is to take a taxi from Makati (around P100). Getting back from a late night out in The Fort can be a problem because there are few taxis in the area, although that should change when the new "city" is complete.

Ortigas

Ortigas is a dense huddle of malls and offices, 5km north of Makati on EDSA, that can be reached by taking the MetroStar to Shaw Boulevard or Ortigas station. A taxi from the Malate area will cost about P150 and from Makati P120.

Ortigas began to come to life in the early 1980s, when a number of corporations left the bustle of Makati for its relatively open spaces, and can now justifiably claim to rival Makati as a commercial centre. It does, however, have even less character than Makati, if that's possible. Megamall, one of the region's largest malls, is a depressing great concrete slab south of the MetroStar station, and most of the restaurants are bland international franchises. Nightlife is centred on **St Francis Square** at the back of Megamall, where there are a number of restaurants and bars, many with live music from 9pm. Nearby is **El Pueblo**, another small mock European square of bars and restaurants. There are also a couple of decent **theatres** in Ortigas, for more on which see p.123.

There is one notable attraction here, the **Lopez Memorial Museum**, on the ground floor of the Benpres Building, Exchange Road corner Meralco Avenue (Mon–Fri 8am–5pm; P100; ⓦ www.lopezmuseum.org.ph). The museum was founded in 1960 by Don Eugenio Lopez to provide scholars and students access to his personal collection of rare Philippine books, manuscripts, maps, archeological artefacts and fine art. The museum's art galleries house paintings by nineteenth-century Filipino masters Juan Luna and Felix Hidalgo, as well as selected works by artist Fernando Amorsolo, who gained prominence during the early 1930s and 1940s for popularizing images of Philippine landscapes and beautiful rural Filipinas. In the 1950s he was awarded the title of National Artist, an honour bestowed occasionally by the government in recognition of an individual's service to the arts. Among the museum's other treasures is a collection of fourteenth- and fifteenth-century artefacts such as jewellery and silverware recovered from ancient burial sites. The museum's Rizaliana includes some ninety letters written by José Rizal to his mother and sisters, along with the national hero's wallet and paintbrushes, his flute and personal papers.

Quezon City

The largest of the fourteen cities that make up Manila, **Quezon City** sprawls from Cubao on its southern edge to Caloocan in the north. In terms of population, it's about the same size as Amsterdam or Manchester. Quezon City is gaining a reputation among visitors to Manila as a place for a good **night out** (see p.120), largely because word is spreading about the number of bars it has catering to students at the nearby University of the Philippines (UP). Many of the bars feature decent live music and all are cheaper than those in Makati and Malate.

At the heart of the area is Quezon Memorial Circle, whose centrepiece is the Quezon Memorial Circle Shrine, a tribute to the founder of Quezon City, President Manuel Luis Quezon. The area is also the site of a number of government organizations, including the Central Bank. On the west side of Quezon Memorial Circle is QC's only major park, the **Wildlife Rescue and Rehabilitation Center** (daily 7am–7pm; P12 adults, P6 children), formerly known (and still marked thus on many maps) as the Ninoy Aquino Parks and Wildlife Nature Center. The mini-zoo inside is home to numerous abandoned pets, many of which are rare species confiscated from owners who were keeping them illegally.

To get to Quezon from the south of the city (from Malate and Makati, for example) you can take the MetroStar Express and get off either at Kamuning station or Quezon Avenue station, a journey of about 25 minutes. Alternatively, hop on a **jeepney** in Taft Avenue bound for Fairview and get off at the Quezon City Welcome Rotunda, a towering structure that marks the western boundary of Quezon City. It stands near the United Doctors' Medical Center at the

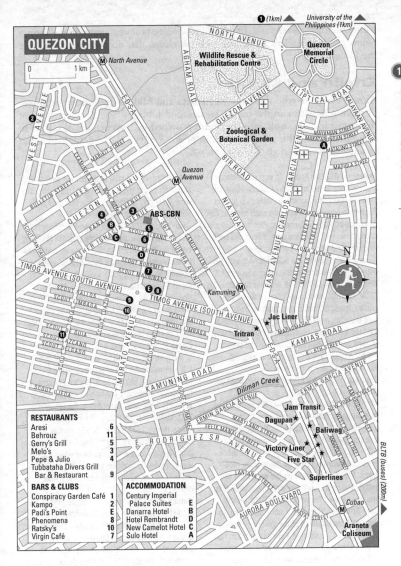

RESTAURANTS

Aresi	6
Behrouz	11
Gerry's Grill	5
Melo's	3
Pepe & Julio	4
Tubbataha Divers Grill Bar & Restaurant	9

BARS & CLUBS

Conspiracy Garden Café	1
Kampo	2
Padi's Point	E
Phenomena	8
Ratsky's	10
Virgin Café	7

ACCOMMODATION

Century Imperial Palace Suites	E
Danarra Hotel	B
Hotel Rembrandt	D
New Camelot Hotel	C
Sulo Hotel	A

junction of three busy roads: España, Quezon Avenue and E. Rodriguez Avenue. From here catch another jeepney bound for Timog.

Eating

Filipinos are fond of Western franchise **restaurants** of the kind you can see in every capital city – all of Manila's malls and business districts are full of familiar names such as *Starbucks* and *T.G.I. Friday's*. Most of the restaurants in the listings below are independent or belong to small chains that do not operate outside the Philippines.

Ermita and Malate

Almost everyone who dines out in **Ermita** and **Malate** does so either in one of the big hotels or in the trendy area around J. Nakpil Street, where most of the restaurants are small, intimate and not owned by big corporations. Bear in mind that J. Nakpil is always a work in progress – it's a fickle, faddish area, and restaurants come and go. See map on p.87.

Aristocrat 432 San Andres St, opposite Malate Church, close to the seafront. All plastic seats and linoleum floors, *Aristocrat* is an institution among Filipinos looking for comfort food such as *arroz con callo* (rice porridge with entrails; P65) and *dinuguan* (blood stew; P85). The less adventurous can settle for barbecued chicken or pork, noodles, sandwiches or *adobo*. The beef *machado* with rice (P286) is tasty and more than enough for one.

Bistro Remedios 1911 M. Adriatico St, Remedios Circle. Informal and homey little restaurant with pretty Filipiniana interior and charming staff. The food is exclusively Filipino, with cholesterol-filled fried pig's knuckles, beefy stews and hefty chunks of roast pork. There's also good fish and prawns, but not a great deal for vegetarians, although pineapple fried rice is on the menu.

Cabalen Robinson's Place, Level 2 Padre Faura Wing. Hugely popular chain of restaurants serving traditional dishes from the province of Pampanga, including *camaru* (rice-field crickets), *batute* (fried pigs' trotters), *kuhol* (escargots), *sinigang tiyan ng bangus* (milkfish belly) and desserts such as *tibok-tibok, tibok-mais* and *halayang ube*, all made from root crops. If you're daunted by the menu, try the buffet. There are six other branches, including one near Tower Records in Glorietta, Makati.

Café Adriatico 1790 M. Adriatico St, Malate. This chic but casual stalwart of the Malate nightlife scene opened a quarter of a century ago and was at the forefront of the area's revival. Light meals include salads, omelettes and fondues. Try the authentic *chocolate-eh*, a thick chocolatey drink served as an anytime "snack".

Café Breton 1810 M. Orosa St, Malate. As the name suggests it's French, but there's no traditional country cooking here – the speciality is crepes and the range includes a number of standards such as crepes with apple and some curiosities such as crepes with bacon. It also makes a pleasant place for a coffee and a snack.

Café Nakpil 644 J. Nakpil St, Malate. One of the great survivors of Nakpil Street, this unpretentious but still fashionable little bistro pulls in an eclectic crowd for pizzas, tasty curries and Thai dishes. The wine list is only average, so stick with cold San Miguel or one of the fresh juices.

Casa Armas 573 J. Nakpil St, Malate. Tapas bar and restaurant serving all-things Spanish including cochinillo, fiery shrimp gambas, chorizo and paella by the skillet – enough for three or four people – from P700.

Dean Street Café 612 Remedios St, Malate. Choose from thirty blends of coffee (P50–100) while using the off-track betting room to wager a few pesos on the nags at Santa Ana or San Lazaro. You can claim your winnings on site.

Dome *Pan Pacific Hotel*, Adriatico Square, Malate. In a city strangely short on a good cup of coffee, this international chain of urbane pseudo-French bistros perhaps has the best. The food is honest European, the service impressive and the cakes and tarts irresistible. Branches in the Greenbelt Mall, Makati and the Shangri-La Plaza, Ortigas.

Glass House 1771 M. Adriatico St, Malate. Right next to the *Malate Pensionne*, this European-style bistro is ideal for a light pasta meal while you watch the hectic world go by outside. Excellent shakes and a tempting range of home-made desserts.

Golden Sala 610 J. Nakpil St, Malate. One of the chicest restaurants in town, *Golden Sala* is a favourite haunt of celebs and socialites. The decor is sharp but relaxing and the service as good as you'll get in Manila. The signature dish is lamb shank with tomato (P740). For two people expect to pay around P2000.

Kamayan 532 Padre Faura corner A. Mabini St, Ermita. The word *kamayan* means "with your hands", which is how you eat here, without knife and fork. A traditional selection of unpretentious native dishes are dished up, including grilled fish, spicy crab, roast chicken and some good vegetables. The staff are dressed in elegant Filipino costumes and strolling minstrels work the tables doing requests. There's a branch in Glorietta mall, close to Tower Records.

Kashmir Merchants Center Building, Padre Faura St, Ermita. Curry, chicken tikka, a mouthwatering selection of breads and wonderfully cheesy ersatz Raj decor. Be warned, the *Kashmir* chefs can be liberal with the spices, so think twice when the waiters ask if you want it very hot. There's another branch at Fastejo Building, 816 Arnaiz Ave.

Komiks Café J. Nakpil St corner M. Orosa St, Malate. Fun, informal bistro that takes as its theme popular Tagalog "komiks" and their zany characters. The wall murals are terrific and the food not bad either. Specialities include native chicken, mango fried rice and tangy *adobo* with a hint of bayleaf.

Korean Ginseng Chicken Restaurant 1789 M. Adriatico St, Malate. One of a number of good Korean restaurants on this strip of M. Adriatico. Big, functional and with a large menu that includes some good dishes to share, such as fried beef, chicken or fish with piping hot rice and various side dishes including tangy pickled cabbage.

Seafood Market Restaurant J. Bocobo St, Malate ☎ 02/524 5761. Typical of the many seafood restaurants in the Malate area where the day's catch is laid out on ice and you pick from whatever the boat brought in. The choice typically includes giant prawns, lapu-lapu, lobster, fish lips and sea slug, all cooked as you watch by wok chefs in a glass-fronted kitchen. A huge meal for two with a few beers will cost around P800.

Sidebar Café 1771 M. Adriatico St, Malate. Agreeable little bar on the ground floor of the *Malate Pensionne*. What makes it so pleasant is that it has no themes or affectations, just good music, reasonably priced drinks and a menu whose most adventurous dish is Pinoy corned beef and cabbage, served in tamarind broth. The clientele is a happy mix of expats, travellers, young Filipinos and a few executive folk.

Zamboanga 1619 M. Adriatico St, Malate. Fresh seafood from the deep south, a trio of crooning guitarists and nightly cultural shows at 8pm. This is the restaurant that features on many travel agents' night-time city tours.

Zen Japanese Restaurant & Sake Bar Level 2, Robinson's Place. Unfussy and affordable Japanese restaurant with a big menu that includes sushi, tempura and inexpensive noodle dishes.

Intramuros

The old walled city of Intramuros doesn't have many restaurants, but those it does have are mostly in old colonial buildings and are significantly more atmospheric than anything beyond the walls. A number of newer, trendier places have been opening up on the eastern edge of Intramuros, in an area known as **Puerta Isabel II**. See map on p.93.

Aposento Bar & Grill Muralla St. One of a handful of fashionable bistros built inside the old eastern wall of Intramuros, just beyond *Starbucks. Aposento* is a popular hangout for students from San Juan de Letran college opposite and, later in the evening, a more urbane clientele of office workers and trendies takes over. Features a good menu of Filipino and Continental dishes such as pizza and pasta. Drinks are cheap.

Casa Manila Plaza San Luis. Elegant dining in a colonial setting, with woody interiors and rich Filipino food. Also known as *Barbra's*, this is a popular venue for lavish wedding receptions, usually on a Saturday afternoon when it might be closed to the public.

Ilustrado 744 Calle Real. Nothing compares to *Ilustrado* if you are looking for the ambience of colonial Manila. The floors are polished wood, the tables are set with starched linen, ceiling fans whirr quietly and the cuisine is rich and grand. Signature dishes include paella, Filipino beef stew, venison *adobo* and a three-course set dinner with steak (P1000) or fish (P800) as the main course.

Kuatro Kantos 744 Calle Real. This charming little bar and café in the same old building as *Ilustrado* opens for breakfast and stays open until 10pm – perfect for a good cup of coffee or a bite to eat while you're wandering around Intramuros. The hot *pan de sal* with corned beef or *carabao* cheese makes an excellent and very affordable snack, and their pesto is home-made and organic.

Binondo

Binondo has no fancy restaurants and no bistros or wine bars; people come here for cheap, nourishing Chinese food in one of the area's countless Chinese restaurants or hole-in-the-wall noodle bars. Inexpensive Chinese home-cooking is available at the food stalls known as the **esteros** at the western end of Ongpin at the foot of the North Bridge Arch, which offer fresh seafood and meat cooked any which way you like. Binondo also has a number of bakeries that are known in the Philippines for their *hopia*, a sweet cake-like snack with a soft pastry coating and thick yam paste in the middle. See map on p.102

Eng Bee Tin 628 Ongpin St. Filipinos often come to Binondo just to make a pilgrimage to this well-known bakery, which specializes in various kinds of sweet, sticky mooncake – and *hopia*. The bakers here invented *ube hopia*, made with sweet purple yam and now imitated throughout the country, and you can also buy *tikoy*, the sweet rice cake that is traditionally served during Chinese New Year.
Green Lake 778–780 Ongpin St. Large and popular Chinese restaurant spread over two storeys a few doors down from *Presidents*, with a very similar menu. Lunch or dinner for two will cost about P500.
Kim Hiong 1028 Ongpin St. Teahouse-style canteen with a range of very cheap dim sum, noodles and fried rice. You can eat a good lunch for less than P200. Two similar, popular and affordable

places close by on Ongpin are *Panciteria Mañosa* at no. 892 and *Four Season* at no. 786.
Ling Tiam's 616 Alonzo St. Busy and atmospheric dim sum and noodle parlour as authentic as anything you'll find on the backstreets of Shanghai. Choose from steaming hot noodles with black bean soup or Shanghai noodles with spicy pork. The shrimp dumplings are delicious and fresh, and there's also a reasonable vegetarian choice including spinach dumplings and fried rice.
Presidents 746–750 Ongpin St. Grand Chinese restaurant with an extensive and occasionally elaborate menu that includes bird's nest and shark's fin. More mundane and ecologically uncontentious dishes include excellent lemon chicken, spicy pork with bean curd and a good selection of fresh vegetables.

Makati

Most restaurants in Makati are either in **Glorietta mall** or the new, revamped Greenbelt. Many in Glorietta are international chains or functional places with plastic tables designed for office workers who need to eat quickly. Check the second floor of Glorietta for everything from sandwiches and pasta to Thai curries and Vietnamese soup. The **Greenbelt mall** has a great choice of more upmarket places that are still reasonably priced, while **Nicanor Garcia Street** is emerging as a fashionable area with a number of good independent restaurants.

About 1km west of Guadalupe MetroStar station, one of Manila's newer malls, **Rockwell** (also known as Power Plant) has a reputation for being a little upmarket. It's what Filipinos call a *sosyal* sort of place, somewhere you go for parading and people-watching. The basement is lined with fast-food outlets and cheap restaurants where you can eat and drink for a few hundred pesos; most of the more *sosyal* bars and restaurants are on the ground floor near the back entrance. On Friday night the road here is closed and tables are laid outside. See maps on p.89 and p.90.

Barrio Fiesta Makati Ave. There are various branches of this popular and colourful Filipino restaurant dotted around the metropolis, all serving indigenous food such as *adobo* and *lechon* with hefty portions of rice. Buffet lunch and dinner available.
Bianca's Café Vinotek 7431 Yakal St. A lovely, comfortable European café. The menu du jour (from P290) is excellent value: typically a salad starter followed by a pasta dish. Wine is P90 a glass and San Miguel P70. Owned by the same people as *Carpaccio* and located in the same building. Daily 8am–9pm.

Caffé Maestro 180 N. Garcia St, close to the junction with Kalayaan Ave. Pleasant, modern Italian restaurant managed by the same people who run *L'Opera*. Excellent salads, pastas and pizzas, with native touches in a few of the dishes, such as the use of lapu-lapu. Good choice of Valpollicelas and Chiantis from P90 a glass (P800 a bottle). Dinner for two will set you back around P2000, with wine.
Carpaccio 7431 Yakal St. Popular but never uncomfortably busy, this casual little restaurant tucked away down a side street behind Makati

Fire Station serves excellent regional Italian food and has a good, affordable wine list. The speciality is carpaccio – the beef carpaccio is delicious – but almost everything is good, including the home-made ice creams and sorbets. Expats love this place, and it's also got a loyal following among the Filipino office crowd.

Foodpark HSBC, Ayala Ave, opposite junction with Paseo de Roxas. Cheap food for Makati's legions of chattering office workers. *Foodpark* actually comprises dozens of small concessions lumped together under one roof, offering everything from dim sum and noodles to sushi, sandwiches, roast chicken and pizza. A good lunch need cost no more than P120.

Ihaw-Ihaw Kalde Kaldero at Kawa-Kawali Makati Ave corner J.P. Rizal St. Seafood and grill restaurant that's inexpensive and raucous but friendly, where the waiters and waitresses sing as they work. There's also a branch on the fourth floor of Megamall in Ortigas.

Il Ponticello 2/F Antel 2000 Building, 121 Valero St ⊕02/887 7168. A bit tricky to find, tucked away in the backstreets of Makati between rows of anonymous office blocks, but worth the effort. This agreeable Italian restaurant serves excellent pizzas – a refreshing change from the fast-food pizzas that Manila loves so much – and has a happy hour (5–8pm) when you get two San Miguels for P70. The best tables are by the window, but you'll have to book to get one of those. There's also a bar inside called *Azzuri*.

Le Soufflé Fort Bonifacio. A well-established Manila restaurant where the food is never flashy, but you can always rely on getting value for money. As the name suggests, the cuisine is mostly traditional French; the speciality, not surprisingly, is soufflé. Expect to pay about P2000 for a good meal for two, with wine. There's a branch in Ortigas (see p.116).

Nandau Restaurant 906 Arnaiz Ave. Simple and accessible Filipino cuisine, heavy on the meat and fish but with a good choice of vegetable dishes, and all at very reasonable prices. The grilled *pangga* (tuna jaw), flown from Davao every day, is delicious.

The New Bombay Canteen Buendia Shopping Plaza, Buendia Ave, close to the junction with the South Superhighway. Speak to Indian residents in Manila and most will tell you this functional little restaurant is peerless for authentic Indian food. The menu is extensive and includes snacks such as mixed pakora (P100) and samosas (P60), various curries and freshly prepared naan, roti and chapatti. Cheap, cheerful and exceptionally tasty. Also a branch in Dela Costa Street.

Old Swiss Inn 7912 Makati Ave, pavement level of the Olympia apartment complex. Traditional food, funky Alpine decor and waitresses in milkmaids' costumes – this place is as Swiss as cheese with a menu that even includes fondue.

Oody's Level 2, Greenbelt 3. Excellent choice for a quick, affordable light meal. The speciality here is noodles in all forms, including Thai, Japanese, Italian and Filipino. The rice meals are good value at less than P200; the bagoong rice is very fishy, but goes down well with a glass or two of fresh fruit juice.

Schwarzwalder The Atrium, Makati Ave, near the *Mandarin Oriental*. A favourite of Imelda Marcos, which feels like it has been around as long as she has. *Schwarzwalder*'s has endured because the food is simple, but consistently good. You won't go wrong here if you're looking for something reassuringly European. The menu includes wonderfully tender pig's knuckle, herby roast chicken and veal cutlets.

Sentro 1771 Level 2, Greenbelt 3. Well-run, straightforward Filipino restaurant that's packed with office workers at lunchtime and the pre-cinema crowd in the evenings. The affordable menu includes modern variations of classics such as *adobo, pancit* and *Bicol Express*.

Wasabi Bistro & Sake Bar Olympia Building, 7912 Makati Ave, not far from the junction with Ayala Ave. Minimalist, trendy Japanese restaurant with stone floors and a square bar where you can just have a drink if you don't want to eat. The clientele runs the gamut from office workers and politicians to diplomats and travelling Japanese executives. They do some good, fresh sushi such as California *maki* (P120 for two pieces). The excellent set lunch costs P250.

Around P. Burgos Street

Alba 38-B Polaris St. Cosy Spanish restaurant with faux adobe walls and a wandering guitarist who croons at your table. Dishes include paella, chorizo and *lengua* (tongue), but there's not much for vegetarians. Reasonable prices and an adequate wine list.

Danish Connection Kalayaan Avenue. This popular expat hangout serves up homey European/American cuisine, with a smattering of Asian; the burgers, grilled fish and pork steaks are all tasty and the portions immense. The decor is eccentrically Nordic, with a Viking boat suspended from the ceiling.

Handlebar 31 Polaris St. Hospitable biker bar owned by a group of Harley fanatics. It's primarily for drinkers (with lots of sport on the TVs) but the food also makes it worth a visit. The menu is nothing exotic, just solid, satisfying pizzas, burgers and pasta, or pies served with peas and mash.

Hossein's Persian Kebab 7857 LKV Building, Makati Ave. This glitzy take on a kebab house has frou-frou decor and prices to match. If you're not in the mood for a brain sandwich, you can choose from dozens of curry and kebab dishes. The food is very good, but it's become a little expensive in recent years.

North Park 1200 Makati Ave corner Kalayaan St. Basic, busy Chinese restaurant where you can eat cheaply to the sound of breaking crockery from the hectic kitchen. The food is nothing fancy, but it manages to be consistently tasty. There are sixteen choices of soup noodles ranging in price from P85 for noodles with Nanking beef to P143 with pork and wanton dumplings. Other choices include Yang Chow fried rice, congee, spare ribs, fried beancurd and Shanghai chicken, which is served with a tangy sauce. A good place to eat fresh food on a budget if you are staying in the P. Burgos area or rolling out of the nearby clubs and bars. Mon–Fri 11am–3am, Sat & Sun 24hr. Nearby is *Next Door Noodles*, which is part of the same company and has an almost identical menu.

Rockwell mall

Brazil Brazil G/F. In the middle of restaurant row close to *Seattle's Best Coffee*, this fashionable Latin café-cum-music bar does laidback lunches and dinners to the sound of piped samba and salsa, with live music in the evenings and tables outside for people-watchers. The food is a mix of Latin and Asian, with excellent tapas if you just fancy a snack and a drink.

Café Via Mare G/F. Smaller, trendier offspring of the *Via Mare* chain, specializing in bistro-style Filipino cuisine. Seafood is a speciality, as the name suggests, but there's much more on the menu, including toasted *pan de sal*, salad with Laguna white cheese and, for an afternoon snack with coffee, *bibingka* (cheese and coconut cake) with salted eggs. It's reasonably priced too; a good meal for two with drinks need cost no more than P600.

Cork Wine Cellar & Grill G/F. Wine bars are a fairly recent development in Manila, but are now sprouting everywhere. *Cork* charges from P80 up for a glass and P800 up for a bottle. It's open for lunch and dinner (pasta, steaks and seafood), but closes at 9pm when the clientele moves on to late-night haunts such as *Dish* (see p.119).

Ortigas

The malls at Ortigas are chock-full of small restaurants and fast-food outlets, while most of the major franchises and trendy theme restaurants are in St Francis Square at the back of Megamall. Robinson's Galleria, to the north of Megamall, has still more fast food outlets and small restaurants, all reasonably priced. Megamall itself features a strip of restaurants stretching for 200m. See map on p.109.

10 Years After St Francis Square. Fashionable, popular bar and restaurant with some top-notch live bands seven evenings a week and a busy happy hour of two-for-one drinks for workers from the many nearby offices. There's a simple menu of bar snacks and pizzas, but people don't really go for the food.

Friends at the Square St Francis Square. A restaurant and music bar that caters to a young crowd. The food is adequate, the music variable; the Wednesday evening acoustic jam session of laidback pop and rock is the best.

Le Soufflé 2/F Winsome Corporate Plaza, Ruby Rd. A branch of the popular French restaurant; see p.115.

Mario's St Francis Square. European-style restaurant that does a little bit of everything including steaks, seafood, pasta, pizzas and paella. Muted and relaxed, with a limited wine list.

Minggoy's Fine Spanish Cuisine 88 Dona Julia Vargas corner Meralco Ave. A minor

institution in Manila, popular for its paella (in three sizes, priced from P110 to P465), *adobo* and *lengua à la Minggoy's*.

San Mig Pub & Restaurant St Francis Square. Comfortable, comforting no-frills British-style pub with a range of Filipino food and cheap San Miguel. You can have a good meal and a few beers for P200.

Via Mare Penthouse, Philippine Stock Exchange Center, East Tower, Exchange Drive ☎ 02/631 7980. *Via Mare*, Imelda Marcos' favourite restaurant, is on the 33rd floor of one of Manila's tallest skyscrapers from where, on a clear day, you can see far into the hills of Antipolo and south to Laguna de Bay. A good place to relax and cool off after the rigours of a shopping expedition at nearby Megamall. If you want a seat with a view, make sure you book in advance. The most interesting appetizer is Balut Surprise, a duck embryo served with savoury sauce in puff pastry. Pastas start from P190; the set lunch is P220.

Quezon City

Quezon City is beginning to establish itself as an alternative to Makati and the Manila Bay area for restaurants and nightlife. Many elegant places have sprung up to cater for the growing corporate population, but there are also dozens of bars and cafés frequented by students from the nearby university. Most of the restaurants are in Tomas Morato Avenue, which runs north and south from the roundabout outside the *Century Imperial Palace Suites*. See map on p.111.

Aresi Tomas Morato Ave corner Scout Albano St. Contemporary European cuisine, cool interiors and a location opposite the ABS-CBN studios have combined to make *Aresi* (the name means "I like" in Greek) QC's restaurant of choice for celebs, their hangers-on and young couples on first dates. Prices are reasonable: you can have a decent dinner with a few drinks for around P400 per person.

Behrouz 63 Scout Tobias (Scout is abbreviated Sct on most maps). Another great late-night hole-in-the-wall snack place, run by a family of Iranians who cook authentic food, though alcohol isn't served. A single skewer of lamb kebab is P40, beef P50. Pitta bread is just P8, to dip in hummus or the aubergine-based moutabal (P30).

Gerry's Grill 24 Scout Albano St corner Tomas Morato Ave. Close to the ABS-CBN studios. Popular place, which is part of a chain, serving provincial Filipino dishes such as *pata* (pig's knuckle) and *sisig* (fried pig's ear and pig's face).

Melo's 58 Bohol Ave. A frilly restaurant with a white facade opposite the ABS-CBN studios, *Melo's* specializes in Australian and American steaks. Set lunches cost less than P400.

Pepe & Julio 121 Panay Ave. Laidback, open-air bamboo restaurant opposite the main entrance to the *Danarra Hotel*. Nothing exceptional about the menu, but the food is all authentic, fresh and well prepared, and includes six types of *sinigang* (tamarind soup), sizzling *bangus* belly and blue marlin.

Tubbataha Divers Grill Bar & Restaurant 295 Tomas Morato Ave. On the opposite side of the roundabout to the *Century Imperial Palace*. Popular and very casual native-style grill, with bamboo furniture, cheap San Miguel and barbecued meat served with large portions of rice.

Drinking and nightlife

Few visitors to Manila are disappointed by the buoyant, gregarious nature of its **bars** and **clubs**. This is a city that rarely sleeps and one that offers a full range of fun, from the offbeat watering holes and gay bars of Malate to the chic wine bars of arriviste areas such as Nicanor Garcia Street in Makati. Within Manila the debate rages about whether Malate is as trendy as it used to be and whether Makati might be making a comeback. Whatever the case, you won't find yourself short of options, from the grungy to the refined.

Manila also has a thriving **live music** scene, with dozens of bars where accomplished local bands play to packed houses almost every night. Venues with a serious emphasis on music are covered on p.121.

Ermita and Malate

Ermita and Malate went through something of a transformation in the early 1990s, when most of the girlie bars were closed down and new independent nightspots opened, catering to an audience that had grown tired of hanging out in Makati's malls. **Ermita** still has beer houses and a few pubs that are popular with male tourists, but the area around J. Nakpil Street and Remedios Circle in **Malate** has the densest concentration and greatest variety of bars and clubs. In Malate, whatever you want you can get: some bars have transvestite cabaret shows and some have ballroom-dancing nights, cashing in on a craze that has swept the Philippines. Don't make the mistake of arriving early because most places don't even warm up until after 10pm and are still thumping when the sun comes up, with crowds in summer spilling out onto the streets. Friday, as always, is the big night, with many places closed on Sunday.

Most places are inexpensive, depending on how chic they are. You can pay anything from P30 to P80 for a beer, while the cover charge for seeing a band is usually around P200, but can be as high as P400. This is often "consumable", which means it is deducted from your drinks bill when you pay. Most of the places listed below also serve food, ranging from *pica-pica* (finger food) for P70 to more substantial meals for around P200 per person.

Anthology 1786 M. Adriatico St, Malate. Live bands every night at this popular music bar. It's a young crowd and the acts are mostly pop, but with occasional folk and OPM.

Bedrock Bar & Grill Restaurant 1782 M. Adriatico St, Malate. Two live pop or mellow-rock bands play three sets every night until 4am and there's no entrance fee, which makes it popular with students. Stone-grilled food includes a hunk of premium Kobe beef for P850.

Bed J Nakpil corner Maria Orosa St. This new and brash – some say outrageous – addition to the Malate night scene is a gay club that also welcomes straights. Whatever you are, you'll need to be a hardcore partier to last the pace; *Bed* doesn't warm up until midnight and is still buzzing at dawn. The music is loud and the crowd is an entertaining mix of starlets, wannabes, expats and curious sightseers.

Café Havana 1903 M. Adriatico St, Malate. Uncomfortably busy on Friday and Saturday nights, but evidently the place to see and be seen.

The modus operandi is to get drunk and dance to live samba music, though the early evening features recorded sounds that can be intrusive. The cocktails are good, although for some reason the menu doesn't say what's in them, which means you have to go through the laborious process of asking. Not the place for a quiet chat. Also features the Ernest Hemingway cigar room.

Hobbit House 1801 A. Mabini St, Ermita. In the 1980s a young Manila entrepreneur decided to open a bar that would pay homage to his favourite book, *The Lord of the Rings*. He staffed it with twenty midgets and a legend was born. *Hobbit House* has somehow endured, still employing short people, with nightly appearances at 9pm by a variety of local bands, some good, some miserably bad. It has also become a notorious tourist trap, with busloads of visitors brought in every night to have their photographs taken alongside the diminutive staff. There's an "entertainment fee" of P100 per person.

In the Mood Dance Bar 1900 M. Adriatico St, Malate. Ballroom-dancing club where you can learn

Gay life in Manila

Young people in the Philippines, and Manila in particular, are generally open-minded about sexual inclination, with **gay life** very much out in the open and a large number of gay and gay-friendly bars, especially in the Malate area. Homosexuality is **legal**, but its complete acceptance is tempered slightly by the strong influence of the Catholic Church and more conservative attitudes among staunch Christians, both young and old. **Discrimination** isn't obvious, but it does exist with, for example, some colleges prohibiting the admission of gay applicants, though attempts are being made to outlaw such practices.

Yet the **gay scene** is vibrant and becoming more so, with several gay rights organizations, an annual gay parade in Malate, the Pink Film Festival in Manila every July and a number of massage parlours in Manila for gay men. Even bars and clubs that aren't obviously gay are unreservedly welcoming. Gay, straight, transvestite and transgender people mix easily and boisterously in the same nightclubs and bars. **Bars** come and go in Manila, but the best are not hard to find; one of the newest in Malate is *Bed* (see above), while in Makati there's *Club Government* (see opposite). A useful website for Manila gay listings is Utopia (Ⓦ www.utopia-asia.com). Other good web resources include Ang Ladlad (the National Organization of Filipino Lesbians, Gays, Bisexuals and Transgenders; Ⓦ www.geocities.com/angladlad) and Task Force Pride (Ⓦ www.pridemanila.cjb.net), whose site has a useful calendar of events.

the basics from a DI (dance instructor). You can choose whatever music you want from a range covering tango, cha-cha, rumba, salsa and swing. Menu specials include knockout pig's knuckles.

L.A. Café 1429 M.H. Del Pilar St, Ermita. Once the infamous *Rosie's Diner* pickup joint, this still has its share of single customers on the make, but is generally more wholesome than *Rosie's* was, despite its sepulchral interior. The waitresses are friendly, the San Miguel is on draught, and there are live bands upstairs at 9pm most evenings. The menu includes all the staples of global cuisine: pasta, steak, pizza, Mexican and Indian, with most main dishes costing P150–200. Every Friday there's an Indian curry buffet noon–3pm.

Library 1179 M Adriatico St, Remedios Circle. Live music, karaoke singalongs, bar food and cheap beer – *Library*'s simple formula for success sees it packed out most nights with a young crowd intent on a good time. Originally a gay bar, but friendly to everyone.

Sky Lounge *Manila Diamond Hotel*, Roxas Blvd corner Dr J Quintos St. The view across Manila Bay is memorable, and so is the *Sky Lounge*'s hypnotic fibre-optic ceiling, a representation of the galaxy with shooting stars. Romantic cover versions every night from various sultry dames. Get there for cocktails and grab a table by the window. Happy hour 5–9pm.

Suburbia 1718 M. Adriatico St. Favourite live venue of many of Manila's most popular showbands, including Freestyle, Side A and Mulatto, all of whom play a vapid brand of low-risk romantic pop and funk that gets local audiences extremely excited. The P400 cover charge is steep, but is consumable, which means you can drink about six bottles of San Miguel for no extra cost.

Tia Maria's 532 Remedios St. Branch of a popular Mexican restaurant chain that has become known less for its food, which is average, than for its cheap drinks (a pitcher of San Miguel costs P140) and live bands. The music starts at 9pm every night and goes on until the small hours, by when most of the audience have abandoned their seats and taken enthusiastically to the dance floor. The bands are a walking Filipino cliché: four-piece combos with two pretty girls sharing lead vocals on a standard selection of smoochy ballads and groovy pop.

Top of the Century *Century Park Hotel*, 599 P. Ocampo St. Convivial cocktail lounge with live easy-listening music every evening and panoramic views of the city and the bay. Daily 6pm–1am, happy hour until 9pm.

Makati

Makati has a reputation as a yuppie ghetto frequented by office workers spilling out of the nearby banks and corporate skyscrapers. Much of the nightlife is inside the malls, which does tend to make hanging out here a rather antiseptic experience. The best places, along Jupiter and Nicanor Garcia streets, for instance, are enormously popular with locals and expats. The Greenbelt mall has some fashionable bars and restaurants on the upper floors. See maps on p.89 and p.90.

Conway's *Makati Shangri-La Hotel*, Makati Ave. The most popular happy hour in Makati, with all-you-can-drink San Miguel for P180 (6–9pm) and live music (6pm–1am) from some excellent middle-of-the-road bands. The crowd is a happy and hard-drinking mix of young Filipino *corpies* (corporate types), expats and travelling executives staying at the hotel.

Club Government 7840 Makati Ave. Makati's biggest gay club has pumped-up acid jazz, disco and tribal music, plus guest DJs on most nights. P200 entrance (Mon–Sat) and two-for-one beers every Wednesday.

The Craic 3/F Max's Chicken Building, Jupiter St. Irish-style pub with memorabilia from the Emerald Isle on the walls and cold Guinness in cans. The menu offers a good selection of reasonably priced Irish home grub. Popular with expats.

Dish 3/F Rockwell mall. Trendy and hugely popular restaurant, bar and nightspot with soft red lighting, beautiful people and good live bands every night at 9pm. This is often the venue for sponsored theme parties where toothsome guests are photographed for the society pages of Manila's press. The food, to be frank, is mediocre, with just a few food stalls at the back of the main concert area where you can buy light meals and snacks.

Flute Plaza Royale Building, L.P. Leviste St. Faddish, minimalist wine bar with muted decor and an avid following of young people on the make who turn up obligingly every Thursday for the weekly *Sex and the City* night, when people watch the show and cocktails named after its characters are served. Look out for the sign next to Ralph's Liquor Store, close to Makati Sports Club, a good landmark for your taxi driver.

Ice Vodka Bar Level 3, Greenbelt 3, Makati Ave. Manila has a pathological obsession with beauty and glamour, prompting British novelist James Hamilton-

Paterson to write of its surfeit of "famous nonentities". If you're a famous nonentity yourself, come here on Wednesday night, when all models get unlimited vodkatinis and canapes for P395. How do you prove you're a model? Well in Manila, as long as you're tall, fair-skinned and are streetwise enough to know a little of the local gay patois, everyone will think you couldn't possibly be anything else.

Pravda 225 Nicanor Garcia St. One of Manila's newest and busiest wine bars, a saucy hangout with red and brown interiors intended to invoke old St Petersburg. The music is a mixture of house and Latin and the crowds just keep on coming, sometimes until the small hours. Behind the bar area is a restaurant called *Beluga*, again with a Russian theme, where you can indulge in caviar washed down with shots of ice-cold vodka.

V Glorietta 2, Ayala Center. Posh bistro and wine bar that for years has been packing in a flaky crowd of execs, expats, socialites, models and personalities. Look out for the kitsch blue doors at street level at the back end of Ayala Center, facing Arnaiz Ave.

Around P. Burgos Street

Heckle & Jeckle Villa Building, Polaris St. *Heckle & Jeckle* scooped everyone when it became the first bar in the Philippines to show live English Premier League football on Saturday and Sunday nights from 10pm. Live bands on Fridays and pool tournaments on Thursdays. Beer and local spirits are half-price 4–8pm.

Jools 5043–5045 P. Burgos St. A camp, flamboyant Burgos Street institution with cheesy but fun cabaret shows every night from 7pm until 4am. There are also excellent live bands every evening and downstairs there's an English pub, the *Woodman's Head*, with traditional ale and football on the TV.

Rogues P. Burgos St corner Makati Ave, next to *Pizza Hut*. Perhaps the least girlie girlie-bar on the strip, *Rogues* has live televised sport, three pool tables and regular promotions including an extended happy hour until 10pm and even free San Miguel for an hour on Wednesday evenings – a clever trick designed to get the punters so drunk they won't leave.

Quezon City

Quezon City's entertainment district is focused on Tomas Morato and Timog avenues, which intersect at the roundabout in front of *Century Imperial Palace*

The bars of P. Burgos Street

The quintessential Philippine **girlie bar** is a shopworn simulacrum of 1970s kitsch, with faux velvet seats, strings of flashing fairy lights, spinning disco balls and a stage at one end where listless dancers in bikinis go through uninspiring routines to some of the most dreadful pop music ever inflicted on humankind. As the music drones on, the waitresses become increasingly persistent and aggressive, asking time and again if you want another drink while half of your existing one remains. It's not unusual for drunken tourists to spend a few hundred dollars before they realize – through the fug of alcohol and hormones – what's going on.

Among tourists, the most popular girlie bars in Manila are those along **P. Burgos Street** in Makati. The young women employed here as GROs – guest relations officers – receive no salary, and are dependent on **"ladies' drinks"** for their pay. It's a simple scheme. If a customer sees a girl he likes he can buy her a minuscule glass of watery mango juice or iced tea for P300; she gets P80 and the bar takes the rest. In most of these bars, ten ladies' drinks buys the right to take the girl home. No one involved uses the word "prostitution", but it's the same thing. Most of the women are uneducated and arrive in Manila from distant, poor provinces in the hope of making it big in the city; their cut of the "bar fine" is too much to resist. Other services are discreetly rendered in the bars' darker corners – for a charge, of course.

It's a credit to many of the women that they remain cheerful and optimistic, although most have a hard-luck story to share given the chance (for obvious reasons this is discouraged by the management, who want to create an impression of carefree bacchanalia). Some find themselves stuck in these bars because they earn more than they would by working in a shop or as a secretary. Others are trying to cobble together enough cash to pay their way through school, or to provide food for their parents and siblings.

Suites hotel. By day the landscape is drab and suburban but when the lights come on at dusk it begins to jump. The area has a growing reputation for quality live music (see below), while for more mainstream nightlife there are plenty of chic bars and franchised hangouts at the southern end of Tomas Morato Avenue, near the junction with Don A. Roces Avenue. Fans of the original QC, tatty but full of campus character, complain it is being "Makati-ized" – turned into another sterile entertainment district with global coffee shops and bland international cuisine. See map on p.111.

Conspiracy Garden Cafe 59 Visayas Ave. This wonderfully ethnic little performance venue and café is a meeting place for artists, musicians, poets, songwriters and women's groups. *Conspiracy* was set up by the artists who perform there, among them luminaries of the independent Filipino music scene such as Joey Ayala, Cynthia Alexander and Noel Cabangon, who all perform regularly. Well worth the taxi ride out there, but check first to see who's on (T02/453 2170).

Padi's Point G/F *Century Imperial Palace Suites*, Tomas Morato Ave. Boisterous beer hall that serves very average Filipino food, although most guests are too drunk to care. Thursdays and Saturdays are disco nights. There's another branch at Citimall in Diliman, near the university, which has live bands.

Phenomena Timog Ave, next to *Century Imperial Palace Suites*. The unassuming entrance hides a concert venue of warehouse proportions, the setting for live performances and DJ raves of wildly differing quality, sometimes glitzy showbands, sometimes big names from MTV Asia and sometimes foam parties. Food and drink is cheap and the crowd young and boisterous. Entrance fee P300–500.

Entertainment

Manila is known for **live music**, with a huge variety of bands, from grungy rock combos in the beer halls of Quezon City to highly accomplished pop outfits playing in major hotels or venues such as the *Hard Rock Café* in Makati and the clubs of Malate. For the more traditional performing arts – **dance and theatre**, for example – there are daily performances at the Cultural Center of the Philippines and a handful of other venues. For **films** every mall seems to have half a dozen screens. The **Araneta Coliseum** in Cubao is the usual venue for large-scale events. Tickets for many of the more high-profile events can be booked through TicketNet (T02/911 5555, Wwww.ticketnet.com.ph) or Ticketworld (T02/891 5610).

Pop, rock and jazz venues

Quezon City in particular has a reputation for live music, especially from up-and-coming bands formed by students from the nearby University of the Philippines and offering an eclectic range of music – from pure Western pop to grunge, reggae and indigenous styles. Many of the venues in the area are dark, sweaty places that open late and don't close until the last guest leaves. Most serve food, usually snacks, although the culinary arts are not their forté. In Makati and Malate too, you're never far from a club with a live band, especially at weekends. Again, the music covers a range of genres.

70s Bistro 46 Anonas St, Quezon City. Legendary (in the Philippines) live-music venue playing host to some of the country's best-known bands as well as to impromptu jam sessions with big local names who happen to turn up. A great Manila experience and a cheap one too. Admission is rarely more than P100 and beers are P30. The only problem is it's a bit tricky to find: Anona St is off Aurora Blvd on the eastern side of EDSA, Quezon City.

Hard Rock Café Glorietta 3, Makati. Apart from serving the usual range of hamburgers, the estimable *Hard Rock*, close to Tower Records in the Glorietta mall, has become an established venue for some of Manila's more prominent recording artists. The crowd is young and enthusiastic. Entrance costs P300–400, depending on the stature of the performer.

Kampo 47 West Ave, Quezon City. One of the area's most enduring and insalubrious establishments, with a good selection of rock bands Mon–Sat at 9pm.

Kidd Creole Level 3, Greenbelt 3, Makati. It's the music that draws the crowds on Friday and Saturday nights – some of the most accomplished blues and jazz bands in Manila perform "outdoors" on a balcony overlooking the traffic jams on Makati Ave. These "Jazz on the Deck" concerts feature luminaries of the local scene such as the quintet Affinity, whose mellifluous brand of "*adobo* jazz" – smooth and creamy, like the dish – has secured them high-profile gigs at the *Blue Note* in New York. Flip-flops and vests are out, but pretty much anything else goes. The music starts at 9pm, but aficionados show their practised cool by never turning up before 10pm.

Mayric's Bar 1320 Macaraeg Building, España St, Sampoloc. A hole-in-the-wall affair, opposite the University of Santo Tomas and so attracting a studenty crowd, with concrete walls, plastic furniture and a reputation for appearances by some of Manila's most popular bands. Regular acts, many of whom you'll spot on MTV Asia, include Parokya ni Edgar, Wolfgang, Eraserheads, Mojofly, Barbie's Cradle and Razorback, all big names in the Philippines.

Monk's Dream 2/F Jupiter Place, 138 Jupiter St, Makati. Mellow lighting, affordable cocktails and, every night from 9pm, different jazz artists – not trad jazz, more the sultry lounge type. Named, in case you were wondering, after the Thelonius Monk composition.

Ratsky's 243 Tomas Morato Ave, Quezon City. On your right a short walk south along Tomas Morato from the *Century Imperial Palace Suites.* Perhaps the most famous live-music venue in QC, the club that gave a number of popular acts their break. There are live rock and alternative bands every night except Sunday from 9pm.

Virgin Café 308 Tomas Morato Extension, Quezon City. A short walk north of the *Century Imperial Palace Suites.* Trendy joint with upwardly mobile pretensions that stages regular concerts by middle-of-the-road jazz and fusion bands.

Theatre, dance and classical music

The Philippines has a rich **folk arts** heritage, but a scarcity of funds and committed audiences with money to spend on tickets means it's in danger of being forgotten. Folk dances such as *tinikling*, which sees participants hopping adeptly between heavy bamboo poles which are struck together at shin-height at increasing speed, are seen in cultural performances for tourists, but are only performed occasionally in theatres. The same goes for *kundiman*, a genre of music that reached its zenith at the beginning of the twentieth century, combining elements of tribal music with contemporary lovelorn lyrics to produce epic songs of love and loss.

In Manila there are only a handful of professional artistic companies, while in the provinces patronage of the performing arts is almost nonexistent, with very few theatre or dance companies and no notable venues. Talented Filipinos usually opt for areas of the arts where they can make decent, regular money: performing in cabarets on cruise ships, in lounge bands in Hong Kong hotels or joining the Manila showbiz circuit in the hope of a break in local movies.

Most performances at the following theatres are listed in the Manila English-language daily press, usually the *Philippine Daily Inquirer* and the *Philippine Star.* It's also worth checking listings websites such as ⓦ www.clickthecity.com.

Cultural Center of the Philippines Roxas Blvd, Ermita ☏ 02/832 1125 to 1139. Events here range from art exhibitions to Broadway musicals, pop concerts, classical concerts by the Philippine Philharmonic Orchestra, *tinikling* and *kundiman*. The CCP is also home to the Tanghalang Aurelio

Tolentino (CCP Little Theater), where smaller dramatic productions are staged and films shown; Ballet Philippines (ⓦ www.ballet.com.ph; ☏ 02/551 1003 or 0221 or 0114 for programmes and tickets); an art gallery; and a museum of musical instruments. The CCP's resident theatre group,

Tanghalang Pilipino, is dedicated to the production of original Filipino plays, both historical and contemporary, and occasionally tries its hand at Shakespeare in Tagalog. Nearby is the Folk Arts Theater, built for the Miss Universe Pageant in 1974 and now staging occasional rock concerts and drama.
Meralco Theater Meralco Ave, Ortigas. Stages everything from ballet by overseas companies to pantomimes with local celebs.

Paco Park and **Rizal Park**. Paco Park has free classical concerts at 6pm on Friday, performed under the stars in the historic cemetery; Rizal Park stages similar free concerts every Sunday at 6pm.
William J. Shaw Theater 5/F, Shangri-La Plaza, Ortigas ⊕ 02/633 4821 to 4824. Small venue mainly staging drama by local theatre groups, including Repertory Philippines.

Cinemas

Screenings at Manila cinemas generally start at around noon and continue until 9pm or 10pm. At some cinemas you can buy a ticket for a guaranteed seat (about P160), but at others you buy an unreserved ticket (P120) and then fight with everyone else for somewhere to sit. At cinemas without reserved seats films are often shown continuously and people are entitled to come and go as they please, which means it's not uncommon for people to watch the end of a film, then watch the beginning before leaving at the point they came in, causing a disturbance for everyone else. Thankfully, this system seems to be dying out in Manila, although it is still used in some of the older cinemas and in the provinces.

Plenty of malls house **mainstream cinemas**, including The Podium mall (on ADB Ave in Ortigas; ⊕ 02/633 8976), with guaranteed seats and late-night screenings on Fridays and Saturdays; Greenbelt 3 (⊕ 02/729 7777) and Rockwell (⊕ 02/898 1440). In the Malate area, try Robinson's Place Movie-world in M. Adriatico St (⊕ 02/536 7809). Tickets for Greenbelt and Glorietta cinemas can be reserved online at ⓦ www.sureseats.com for collection at the venue.

Besides a multi-screen complex, Makati's Glorietta mall (same number as for Greenbelt above) also houses the **Arts Film** cinema, which shows the kind of foreign-language films and alternative movies that would otherwise hardly get a look-in in a country hungry for Hollywood pizzazz. Another venue for arthouse and independent films is the **UP Film Center** (screenings from 3pm; ⊕ 02/926 3640) at Magsaysay Ave, to the northeast of Quezon Memorial Circle. However, it occasionally panders to popular tastes – and the need for revenue – with mainstream Hollywood titles, so don't make a special journey without calling first to see what's on. In Ortigas, the **Shangri-La Plaza** has two cinemas (⊕ 02/635 2079), which, apart from showing the usual Hollywood releases, also stage occasional European and Asian cinematic festivals.

Shopping

The combination of intense heat and dense traffic means many Manileños forsake the pleasures of the outdoors at weekends for the computer-controlled climate of their local **mall** – there can be few cities that have as many malls per head of population as this one. Philippine malls are American in feel, with new examples of sanitized monoliths being built every year: on land reclaimed from the sea, on vacant inner-city lots, anywhere there's room to sink the foundations. The developers rarely pay as much attention to the surrounding roads as

Sport in Manila

For a general overview of sport in the Philippines, see pp.49–51. In Manila you'll have quite a bit of choice if billiards, bowling or golf is your thing. The most high-profile **bowling alleys**, operated by AMF-Puyat, are located in cavernous buildings that also have **billiard halls**. In Malate you can try Bowling Inn, 1941 Taft Ave; in Makati, Coronado Lanes, Anson's Arcade, Pasay Road or Superbowl, Makati Cinema Square; in Ermita, Paeng's Midtown Bowl, Level 2, Robinson's Place. There are three **golf** courses in Manila where non-members can turn up and pay for a round. Fort Bonifacio Golf Club, in the army's Fort Bonifacio base south of Makati (℡02/826 9188), has some of the lowest green fees in the country. Nearby is the Villamor Air Base Golf Club (℡02/833 8630), home of the Philippine Masters. Club Intramuros east of Bonifacio Drive (℡02/527 6612 or 6613) has a compact eighteen-hole course that runs along the walls of the old city. A caddie here costs P300, club rental P500–700, while green fees for non-residents are P1200 between 5.30am and 3.15pm, P2000 from 3.30pm to 8.30pm.

Oddly enough in a country with so much heat and sunshine, public **swimming pools** are almost unheard of, and Manila has none. There are pools at private clubs in the suburbs and the bigger hotels, where you'll have to pay an expensive day rate. Some mid-range hotels have indoor pools, but they're usually small and not especially inviting. Most **gyms** cater to members only and rarely offer affordable day rates. One place to try is Fitness First, where P500 pays for a one-week "starter membership"; they have a branch in Ayala Avenue, Makati (℡02/813 0761).

Spectator sports

Basketball Games are played on Tuesdays (6.30pm), Thursdays (6.30pm) and Sundays (times vary) at the Araneta Coliseum in Cubao, the Cuneta Astrodome on Roxas Boulevard and the Philsports Complex (PSC) in Pasig to the northeast of Makati. Tickets in the cheap seats, the "bleachers", cost as little as P20, while a ringside seat will set you back P250. Tickets are available from Ticketnet and Ticketworld (see p.121).

Boxing Regular bouts are held in Manila on Sundays (details from the Philippine Amateur Boxing Federation, ℡02/838 8977), with hopefuls setting out to establish themselves in the capital before going on to the Olympics, where the Philippines has an exceptional record. The usual venue is the Joe Cantada Sports Center in Tanyag, Taguig, half an hour south of Makati by taxi.

Cockfighting Major venues in Manila include Libertad cockpit in Pasay City, where "derbies" start at 7pm, Araneta Coliseum on Roxas Boulevard, Mandaluyong Coliseum in Mandaluyong, 10min in a taxi from Makati, La Loma cockpit in Quezon City and Roligon Cockpit in Quirino Avenue, Paranaque.

Horse racing There are two venues for horse racing in Manila, the Santa Ana Racetrack in Santa Ana, Makati, and the San Lazaro Hippodrome (closest LRT stations for the latter are Tayuman or Blumentritt). Races take place on Wednesday, Thursday, Saturday and Sunday; the weekend races are held in the afternoon and the weekday races in the evening under floodlights. Admission is P5. For more details, contact the Manila Jockey Club (℡02/711 1251 to 1260, ⓦwww.manilajockey.com).

they do to their precious real estate. This means extra traffic, more tailbacks and headaches for residents.

At least you can buy, eat or drink almost anything in the malls, without raising a sweat. They're full of affordable restaurants and bars, supermarkets and brand-name stores. They're also noisy places, with concerts, promotions, events and small-scale shows, each competing for your attention with brash music played at maximum volume. For indigenous products such as religious art and tribal

Baclaran market

Immortalized in Filipino pop songs, and known to every Manileño who cares about their budget, **Baclaran market** in Pasay is a lugubrious street five minutes' walk south of Baclaran station. The little stalls under the LRT line here sell everything from fake designer watches and clothes (it's also known among Filipinos as the best place to pick up pirated CDs and DVDs) to household gadgets such as telephones and alarm clocks. The market is a big, noisy, pungent place, where food is very much part of the experience. Among the street snacks on offer are satay sticks, slices of *lechon* and hot chestnuts. To get to Baclaran market by public transport, you can take the LRT to Baclaran station and turn left along Dr Gabriel Street, or take a jeepney or bus along EDSA and get off close to the junction with Roxas Boulevard, from where you can walk. A taxi to Baclaran from Makati will cost about P100.

The market is open all week, but especially crowded every Wednesday, the so-called **Baclaran Day**, when devotees of Our Lady of Perpetual Help crowd into the Redemptorist church on Dr Gabriel Street (west of F.B. Harrison St and a 10min walk from the market) for the weekly *novena*. You might spot the occasional Manila celeb there: Cory Aquino's daughter, TV personality Kris, is a regular, as is the singer Pops Fernandez.

artefacts, you'll have to scout around a little. Ermita has the highest number of shops specializing in native goods. Most malls and shops are open daily from 10am until 8pm, later if there's a sale on.

Malls

Glorietta Makati. A maze of passageways spanning out from a central atrium, Glorietta has a large branch of Rustan's department store, and clothes and household goods on the other four floors. At the Makati Ave end of the complex is Landmark, a big, functional department store that sells inexpensive clothes and has a whole floor dedicated to children's goods. Most of the restaurants are near the atrium and there's a food court on the third floor, above Marks & Spencer.

Greenbelt Off Makati Ave, Makati. This whole area has undergone – and is still undergoing – extensive redevelopment. Greenbelt 3 and 4 on Makati Avenue are the newest additions, and as far as malls go, are among the most comfortable for a stroll and a spot of people watching. Most of the stores are well-known chains – Greenbelt 3 has the affordable stuff (including Nike, Adidas and Marks & Spencer) and Greenbelt 4 is full of expensive big names such as Ferragamo and DKNY. Music One on the first floor of Greenbelt 3 sells a good range of CDs, DVDs and VCDs. There are some excellent restaurants in Greenbelt 3 for all budgets, and coffee shops such as *Seattle's Best* and *Starbucks*.

Harrison Plaza A. Mabini St, Malate. Huge concrete mall with a gloomy interior and the usual range of fast-food restaurants, cafés and shops. The two big department stores inside, Rustan's and Shoemart, both have supermarkets.

Rockwell Rockwell Dr, about 1km west of Guadalupe MetroStar. From P. Burgos you can walk it in 15min. Also known as Power Plant Mall (it's built on the site of an obsolete power plant), it's home to Front Page, one of the city's best bookshops (see p.126), and a Rustan's supermarket, as well as some furniture shops selling imported teak items from Indonesia. Most of the mid-range brand names are also here, along with small shops selling fashion items for teenagers, a couple of good baby clothes shops, and electronics shops selling mobile phones and cameras.

Virra Mall Ortigas Ave, San Juan. Sweaty, labyrinthine mall north of Makati and notorious for its illegal bargains: fake designer goods as well as pirated software and DVDs. There's also an area full of stalls selling jewellery made with pearls from Mindanao; a good-quality bracelet or necklace made with cultured pearls will cost from P1000, depending on the style and the number of pearls used. There's also attractive costume jewellery on sale. Other sections of the mall offer cheap mobile telephones (some secondhand), household goods and home decor.

△ One of Manila's many shopping malls

Books, CDs and DVDs

The best general bookshop in Manila is **Powerbooks**, which has three branches around the city: at Glorietta (inside Tower Records) and Greenbelt 4 in Makati, and in Megamall (Building A) Ortigas. **Front Page** in Rockwell, Makati, also has an excellent selection of most genres. There are branches of **National Bookstore**, the country's major bookshop chain, in Ermita and Malate – at Harrison Plaza and Robinson's Galleria – but as ever their stock is limited to contemporary thrillers, literary classics and *New York Times* bestsellers, with much of what's on offer stocked specifically for students. The bookshop with the best literary section in town is **Solidaridad Bookshop**, 531 Padré Faura Street, Ermita. It's owned by the Filipino novelist F. Sionil José and, apart from stocking his own excellent novels, has a small selection of highbrow fiction.

For **CDs**, **DVDs** and **VCDs**, the best places are Music One in Greenbelt, Tower Records in Glorietta and Powerbooks in Megamall. None of these stocks a good range of Western music, but the OPM (Original Pilipino Music) section is comprehensive, covering everything from high-profile bands like Parokya ni Edgar to pop divas such as Sharon Cuneta and folk singers Grace Nono, Freddie Aguilar and Joey Ayala.

Handicrafts and tribal art

The first stop for tourists looking for indigenous gifts and **handicrafts** is usually **Balikbayan Handicrafts** (Ⓦ www.balikbayanhandicrafts.com). They sell a mind-boggling array of souvenirs, knick-knacks, home decorations, reproduction native-style carvings and jewellery, plus some larger items, such as tribal chairs, drums and musical instruments; staff can arrange to ship your purchases if requested. The biggest of their outlets is at 290–298 C. Palanca Street, Quiapo, with others on Pasay Road, Makati and A. Mabini Street, Ermita.

Next door to Balikbayan in Pasay Road is **Teosoro's**, another handicraft chain selling woven tablecloths, fabrics, *barongs* and reproduction tribal crafts such as *bulol* (see below). You can hunt down woodcarvings, *capiz*-shell items, *buri* bags and embroidery under **Quezon Bridge** in Quiapo.

For a range of bargain goods, from fabric and Christmas decorations to clothes, candles, bags and hair accessories, try fighting your way through the crowds at the immense **Divisoria market** in C.M. Recto Street, Binondo, open every day from 10am. The pretty lanterns (*parols*) made from *capiz* seashells that you see all over the country at Christmas cost P750 here, half what you would pay in a mall. Divisoria is very busy sometimes and while it's not notorious for pickpockets and snatchers, it's best to dress down and leave valuables at your hotel, just in case. You also stand a better chance of picking up a bargain if you don't look well-heeled. Finally, Venetian-style mirrors and photo frames are one of the Philippines' most eye-catching products and make excellent gifts. There's an excellent selection costing from P400 at **Jo-Liza Antique Shop**, a cavernous place at 664 J.A. Santos St, San Juan, ten minutes' taxi ride north of Makati.

Tribal art

There are tourist shops all over the place selling reproduction **tribal art**, especially **bulol** (sometimes spelt *bulul*) – depictions of rice gods, worshipped by northern tribespeople because they are said to keep evil spirits from the

Santos

A. Mabini Street in Malate has a number of shops selling crucifixes, candle-holders and wall carvings, though most of them specialize in **santos**, the carved wooden religious figures of saints and martyrs that decorated the Philippines' Catholic churches during the Spanish period. Many of the *santos* in the Philippines are known as *de gosne santos*, figures with joints that can be moved into various poses. They are usually bare wood, but at one time would have been dressed in fine silk garments and displayed as part of a shrine with votive candles. One of the most popular *santos* is, of course, Christ, usually represented in the form of the Santo Niño or on the Cross (Cristo Crucificado).

Santos have become collectors' items, with some relics of the Spanish era available, though most aren't especially ancient, and some items you'll come across are in fact reproductions. The best advice when purchasing is to be guided by price. A run-of-the-mill *santo* need cost no more than P3000, though exceptional items have been known to go for huge sums when sold on in the West.

home and bless farmers with a good harvest. Genuine *bulol* are made from *narra* wood and are dark and stained from the soot of tribal fires and from blood poured over them during sacrifices.

Balikbayan Handicrafts charges from P800 for a small, sitting *bulol* to P5000 for a more imposing one. Finding a genuine *bulol* poses a challenge, partly because any *bulol* that dates back further than the twentieth century is usually snapped up and sold to a collector overseas. You may strike it lucky in one of the small antique shops along A. Mabini Street in Ermita, or at **Casa Tesoro** in the same street. A collection of small shops under one roof, Casa Tesoro is a great place to browse through all sorts of tribal artefacts and Filipino bric-a-brac, where you can stumble across a bargain as long as you're prepared to root around and haggle. Some outlets sell little more than junk, while some stock a range of trendy tribalware such as baskets, wall hangings and masks. Opposite San Agustin Church in Intramuros is the **Silahis Center**, a complex of small art and tribal shops selling everything from *bulol* and oil paintings to native basketware and jewellery.

Listings

Airlines The main Philippine Airlines ticket office is at Philippine Airlines Center, Legaspi St, Makati, and there's another major office at the *Century Park Hotel*, P. Ocampo St, Malate. You can also buy PAL tickets at any travel agent, or by calling their 24hr reservations number ☎02/855 8888. Other airlines with offices in Manila include: Air Canada, 21/F Tower 2, The Enterprise Center, 6766 Ayala Ave, Makati ☎02/892 9215; Air France, 18/F Trident Tower A, 312 Gil Puyat Ave (Buendia) ☎02/887 4979; Air India, Gammon Center Building, Makati ☎02/815 1280 or 817 5865; Air Macau, 508 Plaza del Conde, Binondo ☎02/243 3111; Air New Zealand, The Enterpise Center, Tower II, Ayala Ave, Makati ☎02/884 8097; Air Philippines, 15/F Allied Bank Center, 6754 Ayala Ave, Makati ☎02/893 6086 or 114 Legaspi St, Makati ☎02/892 1459; American Airlines, G/F Olympia Condominium, Makati ☎02/810 3228 and 3229; Asian Spirit, LPL Towers, 112 Legaspi St, Makati ☎02/855 3333, 853 1496 or 853 1957; British Airways, Filipino Building, Dela Rosa corner Legaspi St, Makati ☎02/817 0361; Cathay Pacific, 22/F LKG Tower, 6801 Ayala Ave, Makati ☎02/757 0888 or 2/F Tetra Global Building, 1616 Dr Vasquez St corner Pedro Gil St, Ermita ☎02/525 9367 or 522 3646; Cebu Pacific, Express Ticket Office, Beside Gate 1, Terminal Building 1, Domestic Airport ☎02/636 4938, and 16/F Robinson's Equitable Tower, ADB Ave, Pasig City ☎02/702 0888; China Airlines, G/F, Golden Empire Tower, 1322 Roxas Blvd ☎02/523 8021 to 24; Emirates, 18/F Pacific Star Building, Makati Ave corner Buendia Ave, Makati

☎02/811 5278 to 5280; Continental Micronesia, G/F SGV Building, 6760 Ayala Ave, Makati, ☎02/551 3565 or 551 3566; Japan Airlines, 2/F 6788 Oledan Square, Ayala Ave, Makati ☎02/886 6868; KLM Royal Dutch Airlines, 8/F The Athenaeum Building, Leviste St, Makati ☎02/815 4790 to 92 or 832 1756; Korean Air, G/F LPL Plaza, 124 Leviste St, Makati ☎02/ 812 8721 to 812 8723; Lufthansa, 134 Legaspi St, Makati ☎02/810 4596; Malaysia Airlines, 25/F World Center Building, Buendia Ave, Makati ☎02/867 8767; Northwest, G/F La Paz Center, Salcedo St, Makati ☎02/810 4716 and G/F Gedisco Building, 1148 Roxas Blvd ☎02/521 1928 or 819 7341; Qantas, Filipino Merchants Building, Dela Rosa corner Legaspi St, Makati ☎02/812 0607; Qatar Airways, G/F The Colonnade Residences, 132A Legaspi St, Makati ☎02/812 1888; Royal Brunei Airlines, 5 Saville Building, Buendia Ave, Makati ☎02/896 3041 to 3048; Saudi Arabian Airlines, 345 Buendia Ave, Makati ☎02/896 3046 to 3051; Scandinavian Airline System, 8735 Paseo de Roxas, Makati ☎02/892 9991; Seair, 303 Lao' Center Building, Arnaiz Ave corner Makati Ave, Makati ☎02/849 0100 or 522 1662; Singapore Airlines, 138 Dela Costa St, Salcedo Village, Makati ☎02/810 4951 to 4959; Swiss, Zuellig Building, Makati ☎02/818 8351; Thai Airways, Country Space 1 Building, Buendia Ave, Makati ☎02/817 4044; Vietnam Airlines, c/o Imex Travel, G/F Colonnade Building, 132 Carlos Pelanca St, Makati ☎02/810 3406, 810 3653 or 893 2083.

Banks and exchange Most major bank branches have 24hr ATMs for Visa and Mastercard cash advances. The moneychangers of Ermita, Malate, P. Burgos Street (Makati) and in many malls offer better rates than the banks. Bank of the Philippine Islands, 1955 M. Adriatico St, Malate and Paseo de Roxas, Makati, close to the *Mandarin* hotel; Citibank, 8741 Paseo de Roxas, Makati ☎02/813 9101; Hong Kong & Shanghai Banking Corp, Ayala Ave, Makati ☎02/635 1000; Solidbank, 777 Paseo De Roxas, Makati ☎02/811 4769; Standard Chartered Bank, 6756 Ayala Ave, Makati ☎02/892 0961.

Camping equipment shops Adventure Shack, 494 Soldado St, Ermita ☎02/524 2816; Expedition Plus, 27 Buendia Shopping Plaza, Buendia Ave, Makati ☎02/894 4092; Habagat, Shop 124-A, G/F Megamall Hall A, Ortigas ☎02/637 5492, ⓦwww .habagat.com; Mike's Outdoor Shop, Park Square 1, Ayala Center, Makati ☎02/812 8382.

Car rental Avis ☎02/525 2206 in the Manila Bay area and ☎02/844 4844 in Makati; Budget, head office at the *Peninsula* hotel, Ayala Ave, Makati ☎02/818 7363; Dollar Rent-A-Car, offices at the airport and locations throughout Manila ☎02/893 3590 or 892 5708 for details; Hertz ☎02/897 5179; Nissan Rent-A-Car ☎02/894 4820 or 810 6845.

Couriers There are dozens of courier companies in the *Yellow Pages*. For the closest branch of DHL Worldwide Express in Manila call the customer services hotline ☎02/879 8888. The FedEx hotline is ☎02/854 5454; for UPS call ☎02/853 3333. Two local couriers who also do international deliveries are 2Go (☎02/898 7845) and LBC (☎02/854 4848).

Credit card agents American Express is at the ACE Building, Rada St corner Dela Rosa St, Makati ☎02/815 9311 to 9318; and at 1810 Mabini corner Remedios St, Malate ☎02/524 8681 to 8684. Thomas Cook, G/F Skyland Plaza, Buendia Ave (☎02/816 3701 to 3710), will change their own brand of travellers' cheques and arrange replacements if necessary.

Cultural centres Alliance Française de Manille, 209 Nicanor Garcia St, Makati (☎02/895 7441; ⓦwww.alliance.ph), runs French classes, a video club showing French films every Wed at 8pm and regular social evenings. The British Council, 10/F Taipan Place, Emerald Ave, Ortigas (☎02/914 1011 to 1014; ⓦwww.britishcouncil.org/philippines) hosts arts events, conferences and forums; the use of some of their library resources – newspapers and periodicals, for example – is free. The Goethe-Institut, Adamson Center, 4/F 121 Leviste St, Makati (☎02/840 5723; ⓦwww.goethe.de/manila) organizes cultural and academic events and has a small German-language library. Instituto Cervantes, 855 T.M. Kalaw St, Manila (☎02/526 1482 to 85;

ⓦwww.manila.cervantes.es), has a good Spanish library reflecting Spain's history in the Philippines. Instituto students can use the library for free, but others have to pay P500 a year. The institute organizes a number of arts events and Spanish-themed social gatherings.

Dive operators Aqua One, Aquaventure House, 7805 St Paul St ☎02/899 2831, ⓦwww .aquaventure.com; Dive Buddies, G/F Robelle Mansion, 877 J.P. Rizal St ☎02/899 7388, ⓦwww .divephil.com; Eureka Dive, Suite 306, 38 Rockwell Dr, Rockwell Center, Makati ☎02/890 8800 ⓦwww.eurekadive.com; Adventure Bound ⓦwww .adventurebound.com.ph; Unit LG2 Alfaro Place Condominium, Leviste St, Makati ☎02/840 5523; Ocean Colors, G/F Cancio Building, 1047 Metropolitan Ave ☎02/890 4142; Scuba World, 1181 Pablo Ocampo St ☎02/895 3551, ⓦwww.scubaworld .com.ph.

Embassies and consulates Australia, Dona Salustiana Building, 104 Paseo de Roxas, Makati ☎02/750 2850; Brunei, 11/F BPI Building, 104 Paseo de Roxas, Makati ☎02/816 2836; Canada, 9–11/F, Allied Bank Center, 6754 Ayala Ave, Makati ☎02/867 0001; Indonesia, Xanland Center, 152 Amorsolo St, Legaspi Village, Makati ☎02/892 5061; Ireland, 3/F 70 Jupiter St, Bel-Air 1, Makati ☎02/896 4668; Malaysia, 107 Tordesillas St, Salcedo Village, Makati ☎02/817 4581; Netherlands, 9/F King's Court Building, 2129 Pasong Tamo, Makati ☎02/812 5981; New Zealand, 23/F Far East Bank Center, Buendia Ave, Makati ☎02/891 5358; Singapore, 6/F ODC International Plaza, 219 Salcedo St, Legaspi Village, Makati ☎02/816 1764; Thailand, Royal Thai Embassy Building, 107 Rada St, Legaspi Village, Makati ☎02/815 4219; UK, 15–17/F LV Locsin Building, 6752 Ayala Ave corner Makati Ave, Makati ☎02/816 7116; US, 1201 Roxas Blvd ☎02/523 1001; Vietnam, 670 Pablo Ocampo St, Malate ☎02/524 0354.

Emergencies The main number for all emergency services in Metro Manila is ☎117. The Department of Tourism has two tourist assistance lines (☎02/524 1703 or 524 2384) and two tourist hotlines (☎02/524 1728 or 524 1660). You can call any of these numbers for the location of the closest police station, hospital and so on. Staff will also put you in touch with the tourist police.

Ferries The big ferry companies have ticket offices throughout Manila: Aleson Shipping Lines, Pier 2, North Harbor ☎02/712 0507; Negros Navigation, 849 Pasay Rd, Makati ☎02/818 4102 and Pier 2, North Harbor ☎02/245 5588, ⓦwww .negrosnavigation.ph; Sulpicio Lines, Pier 2, North Harbor ☎02/245 0616 to 0630, ⓦwww .sulpiciolines.com; WG&A, 1105 A. Francisco St corner Singalong St, Malate ☎02/528 7000,

By plane

International **flights** leave from Ninoy Aquino International Airport (☎02/877 1109): Philippine Airlines flights depart from the Centennial Terminal II, all others from the main terminal. This will change when the new terminal opens, so check with your airline. Philippine Airlines domestic flights use the Centennial Terminal II; other domestic flights go from the nearby Domestic Airport (☎02/832 3566). The domestic departure tax from Manila is P100 and you need identification to enter the terminal buildings. Addresses of airlines are given on p.128; for details of domestic flights from the capital, see "Travel details", p.144.

By ferry

Hundreds of ferries large and small leave Manila every day; the major routes are listed in "Travel details", p.145. Nearly all inter-island **ferry** departures sail from the North Harbor, though WG&A sailings use the new Eva Macapagal Super Terminal at South Harbor (Pier 15). All North Harbor piers have even numbers, all South Harbor piers odd numbers. For details of the major ferry operators, see p.129.

By bus

Buses from the Pasay terminals usually head south; those from Cubao usually go north. The bus operators include:

Heading South

Alps Transit Villegas St, near Intramuros on the western side of busy P. Burgos St. No phone. They operate a useful bus service that departs every thirty minutes from Villegas Street to the ferry terminal in Batangas City. The departure point is the Concepcion Street entrance to Intramuros, opposite City Hall.

BLTB All buses use a new, shared terminal behind the Araneta Coliseum in Cubao ☎02/913 1525. There are services south to Nasugbu, Calamba, Batangas City, Santa Cruz, Lucena, Naga and Legaspi, plus epic 28-hour journeys to towns in the Visayas and to Sorsogon in southern Luzon; northbound buses include regular departures to Dalahican (for Marinduque) and Batangas City.

Jac Liner Taft Ave, Pasay City ☎02/831 8977. Every thirty minutes to Lucena (via Alimos) and Lemery in Batangas.

JAM Transit Taft Ave, Pasay ☎02/831 0465; with a second terminal on the corner of EDSA Monte de Piedad Street in Cubao ☎02/414 9925. To various destinations in Batangas, Lucena and Laguna.

JB Bicol Express Line Aurora Bvd, Pasay City ☎02/833 2950. Hourly buses heading south through the Bicol region to Naga and Legaspi, usually stopping at Lucena on the way. The terminal is near the *Winston Lodge* hotel and next to the Five Star bus terminal.

Philtranco EDSA corner Apelo Cruz St, Pasay ☎02/833 5061, ⓦ www.philtranco .com.ph. Daily runs as far afield as Quezon, Bicol, Masbate, Leyte, Samar and even Davao.

ⓦ www.wgasuperferry.com, and at the Domestic Airport. Travel agents also sell ferry tickets. **Hospitals and clinics** Makati Medical Center, 2 Amorsolo St, Makati (☎02/815 9911) is the largest and one of the most modern hospitals in Manila. It has an emergency department and dozens of specialist clinics (the latter are usually open daily 10am–noon & 2–4pm). You can't make an appointment for the clinics – you just have to turn up and join the queue. An initial consultation costs around P400–P500 and if you need further tests they can usually be carried out on the same day if they're routine (such as blood tests). The HCS Medical Care Center, also in Makati at 3/F Equitable Bank Building, Buendia Ave (☎02/897 9111 to 9120), is a good place to go for basic care and prescriptions, but has no emergency facilities. A consultation costs P350. In the Manila Bay area, there's the Manila

Superlines EDSA, Cubao. Small bus company operating to Batangas and the Bicol region, including Daet and Legaspi.

Tritran EDSA corner East Ave, Pasay ⓣ02/831 4700. Buses every thirty minutes to Batangas City and Lucena, the latter via San Pablo.

Saulog Transit Anda St, just outside the northeastern wall of Intramuros, close to Magellanes Street ⓣ02/442 5391. Departures every 15 minutes to Cavite and Ternate.

Victory Liner Five terminals: Rizal Ave, Caloocan ⓣ02/361 1506 to 1510; EDSA, Pasay ⓣ02/833 5019; EDSA, Cubao ⓣ02/727 4534; EDSA, Quezon City ⓣ02/921 3296; and Espana St corner Galicia St, Sampoloc ⓣ02/741 1436; ⓦwww.victoryliner.com. All five serve destinations north of Manila, including Dau (for Clark), Alaminos, Dagupan, Olongapo, Zambales province, Baguio and Mariveles. The Quezon City terminal, in an area known as Kamias, is the place for buses north to the Cagayan valley (Santiago, Roxas, Tuguegaroa, Aparri, Ilagan, Tabuk and Tuao).

Heading North

Autobus Transport Systems Corner of Dimasalang and Laong Laan Sts, Sampoloc ⓣ02/735 8098. Overnight services to Banaue leaving at 10pm and regular departures for Tuguegarao, Vigan and Laoag. Jeepneys from Taft Avenue or A. Mabini Street heading for Blumentritt will pass the terminal.

Baliwag Transit 199 Rizal Ave Extension, Caloocan ⓣ02/364 0778 or 363 4331; and EDSA corner New York St, Quezon City ⓣ02/912 3343. Buses north to Bulacan province, Baliwag, San José and Tuguegarao.

Dagupan New York St, Quezon City ⓣ02/929 6123. Services to Baguio, Dagupan and Lingayen.

Dominion Bus Lines EDSA, Cubao ⓣ02/741 4146. Hourly departures for San Fernando in La Union, Vigan and Bangued (Abra province).

Farinas Transit Laong Laan St, Caloocan ⓣ02/731 4507. Hourly buses to Vigan and Laoag, with stops en route at Bagabag (change for Banaue), San Fernando in Pampanga, Tarlac, Dagupan and San Fernando (La Union).

Five Star Bus Lines Aurora Blvd, Pasay, near *Winston Lodge* hotel, next to the JB Bicol Express Line bus terminal; EDSA, Cubao; and Rizal Ave, Caloocan ⓣ02/833 4772 or 833 3009. Hourly buses north to Cabanatuan and Dagupan..

Philippine Rabbit 1240 EDSA, Quezon City ⓣ02/364 3477, with another terminal in Quipao on C.M. Recto St for points north. Popular for destinations in the north such as Angeles, Balanga, Baguio, Vigan, Laoag, San Fernando and Tarlac.

By train

There are two daily departures from Manila to Legaspi via Calamba and Naga. Tickets are available only at the train stations and there are no printed timetables. The only telephone number for the railways is the Philippine National Railways management centre (ⓣ02/287 3062).

Doctor's Hospital, 667 United Nations Ave (ⓣ02/524 3011) and the Medical Center Manila at 1122 General Luna St, Ermita (ⓣ02/523 8131).

Immigration For visa extensions, head to the Bureau of Immigration and Deportation, Magellanes Dr, Intramuros (Mon–Fri 8am–noon & 1–5pm; ⓣ02/527 3257 or 3280). It's best to get there early or you might have to hang around through their lunch break for your application to be processed.

Internet access Internet access is not hard to find anywhere in Metro Manila. Try *Global Café*, 3/F Pedro *Gil Wing*, Robinson's Place, Ermita ⓣ02/536 8023; the Filipinas Heritage Library, Makati Ave, Makati ⓣ02/892 1801; *MailStation*, 30-A Park Square 1, Glorietta, Makati ⓣ02/817 8134 or 3135. There are half a dozen Internet cafes in the P. Burgos area, including Durban Business Center (Durban St).

Left luggage At the time of writing there was no left-luggage service at the airport, the train station or any of the bus stations.

Massage Massage parlours are not as common here as they are in some Asian cities, but there are a few reputable ones. The Olympia Reflexology Center in Makati Ave (next to the *Wasabi* Japanese restaurant; ⊤02/817 9509), offers Swedish or shiatsu massage for P490, including use of the sauna and whirlpool bath. Most hotels can arrange for a masseuse to visit you in your room; expect to pay around P600 for an hour.

Pharmacies You're never far from a Mercury Drug outlet in Metro Manila – at the last count there were two hundred of them. In Ermita, there's one at 444 T.M. Kalaw St and another at the Robinson's Place Complex in M. Adriatico St. In Makati there's a big branch in Glorietta on the ground floor, near Tower Records.

Police Tourist Police, Room 112, Department of Tourism Building, Teodoro Valencia Circle, T.M. Kalaw St, Ermita ⊤02/524 1660 or 1728.

Post The Central Post Office at Liwasang Bonifacio, Intramuros, near MacArthur Bridge on the Pasig River, has a poste restante service. In Makati, there is a post office at the junction of Buendia and Ayala avenues, next to Makati fire station. Look out also for MailStation outlets in many malls where you can post letters, make telephone calls and often find email services.

Travel agents There are a number of reliable travel agents in the tourist belt of Ermita and Malate and more in Makati. Among the more established firms are: Baron Travel, Cityland 10, Tower 2, Makati ⊤02/817 4926; Bridges Travel & Tours, Unit 801 Liberty Center Building, 104 Dela Costa St, Makati ⊤02/750 3372 to 3375 and 117 Buendia Ave ⊤02/523 9705, ⊛www.bridgestravel.com; Broadway Travel, 416 United Nations Ave ⊤02/521 1608; Caravan Travel & Tours, 6758 Ayala Ave, Makati ⊤02/810 2411; Filipino Travel Center, G/F Ramona Apartment Building, 1555 M. Adriatico Street, Malate, ⊤02/528 4507 to 4509, ⊛www.filipinotravel.com.ph; Manila International Travel & Tours, G/F Ermita Center Building, 1350 Roxas Blvd ⊤02/521 1312; Magsaysay Travel & Tours, G/F Magsaysay Building, 520 T.M. Kalaw St, Ermita ⊤02/524 8410 or 521 9151; Rajah Travel, G/F Plywood Industries Building, A. Mabini St corner T.M. Kalaw St, Ermita ⊤02/ 523 8801 to 8807; Southeast Travel Corp, 451 Pedro Gil corner M.H. Del Pilar St, Ermita ⊤02/524 5676 to 5686; Thomas Cook, G/F Skyland Building Plaza, Malugay St, Makati ⊤02/816 3701.

Around Manila

With most tourists spending only a day or two in the capital before heading to the beaches of the south or the northern mountains, the provinces around Manila have failed to develop as serious tourist destinations, held back by a lack of visitors and poor infrastructure. That doesn't mean there's nothing to see, just that there are no world-class attractions and no reason to make special plans to visit Laguna, for instance, when you could be in Boracay or Palawan in about the same time. All the destinations covered here are within day-tripping range of the capital, though some places make reasonable overnight trips; attractions slightly further afield in Batangas and the southern part of Quezon province are covered in Chapter 2.

In Manila Bay, the island of **Corregidor** is the excursion of choice for many visitors who haven't time for more than one day-trip from Manila. Corregidor was the scene of fierce fighting during World War II, but isn't just a destination for those interested in great battles; there are some good jungle walks through the interior and two hotels where you can arrange fishing trips and rent boats to see the coastline. The island is a fragment of the province of **Cavite**, which borders the southwestern end of Manila beyond Parañaque. Most of Cavite has been swallowed up by industry and commuter housing, becoming another concrete and traffic-clogged suburb. It isn't worth a special trip unless you are seriously interested in its chief historical landmark, General Aguinaldo's House in the town of **Kawit**.

Also south of the capital, **Laguna** province, known for hot springs and mountain pools, was named after **Laguna de Bay**, the lake that forms its northern boundary, and is a major source of fragrant *sampaguita* flowers, orchids, coconuts, rice, sugar, citrus fruits and *lanzones*. The province is a favourite weekend escape for city-dwellers, and near the busy university town of **Los Baños** are dozens of **resorts** with hot spring baths, although the accommodation at these places varies wildly in quality and can be expensive. Laguna's best-known and most photographed destination – Francis Ford Coppola even made a film here – is **Pagsanjan Falls**, where you can take a wet and exciting canoe ride downriver across a series of rapids.

The province just to the north of Manila, **Bulacan**, is known for revolutionary heroes, poets and the quality of its sweets. This was the site of the nation's revolutionary republic and birthplace of Marcelo H. Del Pilar, patriot, revolutionary and editor of the incendiary underground newspaper *La Solidaridad*. The busy provincial capital, **Malolos**, is where the Revolutionary Congress was convened in 1898, while the town of **Obando** is scene of the province's best-known festival, the **Obando Fertility Rites**. **Biak-na-Bato National Park** in the northeast corner of Bulacan can be visited in a day from Manila and has some invigorating treks through the rocky foothills of the Sierra Madre mountains. **Bataan** province, the peninsula northwest of Manila, was the site of fierce fighting and atrocities during World War II, commemorated here by the **Shrine of Valor** atop Mount Samat. Reached most quickly by ferry from the capital, Bataan also has a dense interior of thick jungle and offers challenging treks and climbs in the **Bataan Natural Park**, while around the coastal town of **Mariveles** there are some wide, sandy beaches and a few resorts.

Cavite

Once a peaceful agricultural and fishing province, **Cavite** ("ka-vee-tay") is now an ill-planned jumble of busy market and industrial towns connected by bad roads that are invariably congested at peak times. For most Filipinos, Cavite will forever be associated with the revolution. In 1872, three Filipino priests – José Burgos, Mariano Gomez and Jacinto Zamora – were implicated in the Cavite Revolt, in which two hundred Filipinos rose up in arms against the Spanish forces in the garrisons. They were garrotted by the Spanish in what is now Rizal Park, where a memorial stands at the execution site (see p.96).

Corregidor

The tadpole-shaped island of **CORREGIDOR**, less than 5km long and 2.5km wide at its broadest point, is a poignant living museum to the horrors of war, where you can wander among the ruins of barracks and explore tunnels that were used as a hospital for wounded soldiers. The island was fought over bitterly by the Japanese and Americans during World War II, especially in 1942 when it was defended bravely by an ill-equipped US contingent under continual bombardment from Japanese guns on the nearby Bataan peninsula.

Corregidor is also where General Douglas MacArthur, seeing that the cause was hopeless, is alleged to have said, "I shall return." He actually made the pronouncement in Darwin, Australia, having escaped from Corregidor in a gunboat as the Japanese rolled across the narrow straight from Bataan. Public relations officers in Washington suggested dropping chewing gum across the Philippines with "I shall return" printed on the wrappers, in a bid to keep up morale under Japanese occupation. They also suggested that MacArthur revise the wording to "We shall return", so the rest of the army and the White House could bathe in his reflected glory. The chewing gum was never dropped and the speech was never revised, but MacArthur did return, three years later on March 2, 1945, when Corregidor was liberated.

△ Memorial, Corregidor Island

"Corregidor needs no epitaph from me," he said. "It has sounded its own story at the mouth of its guns." At the end of the war not a living thing stood on the island; it had been so utterly denuded by bombardment that it looked like a jagged end of incinerated bone, poking through the blue skin of the South China Sea.

Corregidor is a fascinating, haunting place. Make sure you visit the **Malinta tunnels**, a labyrinthine network of damp underground bunkers where MacArthur set up temporary headquarters and where vicious hand-to-hand combat took place. There are bullet holes everywhere, carbon burns from grenade explosions, bunk beds left behind from the makeshift hospital, and old Underwood typewriters whose keys are seized with rust, but which are otherwise exactly as they were when used by administrative staff to type MacArthur's paperwork. There is also a small **museum** containing weapons and uniforms that were left behind, a Japanese cemetery and a memorial to the thousands who died here. Little wonder Corregidor is said to be haunted.

Away from the reminders of one of the war's most horrific battles, Corregidor is unspoiled, quiet and a great break from the city. You can walk marked **trails** that meander through the hilly interior (look out for the monkeys and monitor lizards), rent a mountain bike to explore on your own, or circle the island on a banca and do some fishing. Try to visit during the week when it's quieter and you almost feel you've got the whole place to yourself; at weekends dozens of tour groups head out from Manila.

Practicalities

To regulate visitor numbers, Sun Cruises (G/F Magsaysay Building, 520 T.M. Kalaw St, Ermita or Cultural Center of the Philippines, Terminal A, CCP Complex, Roxas Blvd, Manila; ℡02/526 9626, 831 8140 or 834 6857, Ⓦwww.corregidorphilippines.com) has a monopoly on **transport to the island**. They run day- and overnight trips, departing from the Cultural Center of the Philippines pier at 8.00am and returning at 2.30pm. A day-trip with buffet lunch costs P1690 per person; overnight excursions start at P2500 per person sharing a twin or double room. All rates include transport and island tour, with an optional light-and-sound show in the tunnels for P150. The *Corregidor Inn* is the best place to stay, a creaky but atmospheric little place with polished wooden floors, thirty air-conditioned rooms and a large swimming pool. Alternatively, the *Corregidor Hostel* has two forty-bed dorms (P150 a night) sharing two bathrooms. The *Corregidor Inn* has a reasonable restaurant on a veranda overlooking the pool and with views of the sea. There's also a campsite (P50 per person) on South beach, a scenic spot on the south side of the island.

The Emilio Aguinaldo Shrine and Museum

The only attraction in mainland Cavite is the **Emilio Aguinaldo Shrine and Museum** (Tues–Sun 8am–5pm; free) in **KAWIT**, 23km south of Manila by road. The building, on the east side of the main street running through the centre of town, is the house where Aguinaldo, first President of the Republic, was born and raised, and where he is buried in a simple marble tomb in the back garden on the bank of the river. This is also where Philippine independence was proclaimed and the Philippine flag first raised by Aguinaldo on June 12, 1898, which is commemorated on this day every year with the president waving the flag from the balcony.

With its secret passages and hidden compartments, the house is testimony to the revolutionary fervour that surrounded Aguinaldo and his men. A number of the original chairs and cabinets have secret compartments that were used to conceal documents and weapons, while the kitchen has a secret passage that he could use to escape if the Spanish came calling. In the general's bedroom, one of the floorboards opens up to reveal a staircase that led to his private one-lane bowling alley under the house and an adjoining hidden swimming pool. Downstairs, the museum displays various Aguinaldo memorabilia including clothes, journals and his sword, while upstairs there is the general's bedroom, a grand hall, a dining room and a conference room. You can also see his desk – an elegant Art Deco piece with a carabao's head carved into the seat's backrest.

There isn't much else in Kawit, a grey industrial town blighted by traffic. You can get here on any southbound bus from Manila heading for Naic or Ternate. Baclaran LRT station is a good place to find jeepneys and FX taxis, which leave regularly for **Zapote**, where you can change for another vehicle for Kawit. From Makati you can catch an FX taxi to Zapote in the car park between Glorietta and Greenbelt malls on Makati Avenue. Buses operated by the Saulog and Saint Anthony companies leave every few minutes for destinations throughout Cavite from just outside the Intramuros walls, opposite Letran College.

Laguna

The largely agricultural province of **Laguna** – coconuts are a major crop – follows the south and southeastern coast of Laguna de Bay, its topography dominated by the massive hulk of **Mount Makiling**. On the province's western edge is the town of **Calamba**, birthplace of national hero José Rizal, and on its eastern edge the town of **Pagsanjan** and nearby **Pagsanjan Falls** and **Lake Caliraya**. The area around **Los Baños** has a number of resorts with bathing pools fed by **hot springs** on the slopes of Mount Makiling. The provincial capital, **San Pablo**, is part of a good area for hiking, while along the eastern shore of the huge Laguna de Bay you can buy hand-crafted souvenirs in the quaint woodcarving town of **Paete**.

Jac Liner, Tritran, JAM Transit and BLTB buses all operate at least hourly from the Pasay terminals to Calamba, Los Baños (and Mount Makiling), San Pablo and **Santa Cruz** (for Pagsanjan and Paete), and there are some Calamba services from the Taft Avenue end of Rizal Park. For towns on the far side of Laguna de Bay from Manila most buses marked for San Pablo or Santa Cruz pass through Calamba and Los Baños. The **train** line from Manila runs through Calamba and San Pablo. From Batangas City (see p.151), it's straightforward to get buses to all these destinations.

Calamba

The town of **CALAMBA** – once a rural backwater, now a choked and noisy extension of Manila – hugs the coast of the southern tip of Laguna de Bay at the foot of Mount Makiling, just 54km from the capital. There's nothing to see in the new part of Calamba, just the usual malls, fast-food outlets and hundreds of din-making tricycles. The old town, however, was built in Spanish colonial style, with a shady plaza in front of a town hall and a church, San Juan Bautista. A marker inside the church indicates that national hero and revolutionary **José Rizal** was baptized here by Fray Rufino Collantes on June 22, 1861, and that his godfather was Fray Pedro Casañas. Rizal's stature in the Philippines, a country notoriously short of heroes, is such that a number of religious cults have sprung up in his honour, most of them professing that Rizal is the Son of God and will one day return to lead his disciples to salvation. One such group has its headquarters near the church, on Lecheria Hill.

Opposite the church is the house where Rizal was born on June 19, 1861. Now a **museum** (Tues–Sun 8am–noon & 1–5pm; free), the building is a typical nineteenth-century Philippine *bahay na bato*, with lower walls of stone and upper walls of wood, plus *narra* wood floors and windows made from *capiz* shell. The house, which was restored in 1996 for the Centennial of the Philippine Revolution, has a small stable for horses and storage for carriages on the ground floor, while the upper floor is the living area. All the rooms feature period furniture and there are displays of Rizal's belongings, including the clothes he was christened in and a suit he wore as a young man. In the garden is a *bahay kubo* (wooden) playhouse, a replica of one where Rizal used to spend his days as a child.

The big concrete jar at the centre of the town plaza next to the Rizal house commemorates an apocryphal story about how the town got its name. It is said that a Spanish civil guardsman met a young woman carrying a jar of water and inquired as to the name of the place. In her confusion she replied "*kalan-banga*" ("it's a water jar"), and scurried away.

Laguna hot springs

The area of Laguna between Calamba Los Baños on the main road connecting both towns, trades heavily for its tourist custom on the health properties of its **hot springs**, which bubble from the lower slopes of Mount Makiling. There are dozens of resorts of varying quality that use the hot springs to fill swimming pools which become wallowing holes for visitors from Manila, especially at the weekend. Many of these resorts are big and cater to company outings, day-trippers and conferences, so don't expect Zen-like peace and quiet.

The biggest concentration of resorts – more than forty in all – starts around the fifty-kilometre marker south of Manila. To get there either take a local bus or jeepney from Calamba, or get a southbound bus in Manila for Los Baños, though check it actually passes the resorts.

The standard of **accommodation** at the resorts is generally disappointing – instead of pretty nipa huts, you find concrete air-conditioned boxes with tatty furniture and no views. At the 57-kilometre marker, on the right if you're arriving from Calamba, *Crystal Springs* (T02/895 9423; ⑤–⑦) has a variety of water rides (pools close at 5pm). The place feels a little down at heel, however, with a hot, grubby restaurant and faded, though spacious, rooms with double bed, plastic sofa and a deep bath that can be filled with hot-spring water. Next to *Crystal Springs* is *Makiling Highlands* (T049/545 9702 or 02/899 8488 in Manila; ⑥–⑧), which has villas and very large air-conditioned rooms, hot pools spread out over many hectares of ground, and – just in case you should start feeling too healthy – 24-hour room service from *Max's*, the fried chicken restaurant. One of the biggest resorts in the area is *Monte Vista Hot Springs & Conference Resort* (T049/545 1259; ⑤–⑦), on the right if you're heading south from Calamba. It has eighteen hot mineral pools, assorted giant slides and enough room for 1500 day-visitors. Rooms are air-conditioned and en suite.

UPLB

Just outside Los Baños is the **University of the Philippines Los Baños** (UPLB; Wwww.uplb.edu.ph), the forestry campus of the Manila-based university. The campus lies at the base of **Mount Makiling**, and there are some nice walking trails through the surrounding unspoilt rainforest. There are a number of attractions on the campus itself, including the International Rice Research Institute, which is home to the unexpectedly excellent **Riceworld Museum** (Mon–Fri 8am–noon & 1–5pm; Wwww.riceworld.org), showcasing the importance of the staple that feeds half the world's population. Apart from an overview of the developing world's food shortages, the museum has a number of small but intriguing displays, including one where visitors can inspect live paddy-field insects under a microscope, including damselflies, wolf spiders and aggressive fire ants. Another museum worth making time for is the **UPLB Museum of Natural History** (Mon–Sat 8am–5pm; P10), which has more than 200,000 biological specimens of Philippine plants, animals and micro-organisms.

Mount Makiling

The dormant volcano of **Mount Makiling** (1110m) is identifiable by its unusual shape, rather like a reclining woman. The mountain is named after Mariang Makiling (Mary of Makiling), a young woman whose spirit is said to protect the mountain. On quiet nights, tribespeople say, you can hear her playing the harp, although the music is rarely heard any more because Makiling is rumoured to be angry about the scant regard paid to the environment by the authorities.

There is a well-established and strenuous trail to the summit starting at UPLB, but climbing it alone is not recommended. Enquire at the university's administration building, on the left just inside the main gate, about hiring a **guide**, which will cost at least P1000 excluding provisions for the guide. You'll need to bring all your own gear, including tent, food and enough water for 48 hours. Most climbers camp below the summit for the night and then walk the remaining distance to the top early the following day to watch the sunrise.

San Pablo and around

Before the Spanish arrived, **SAN PABLO** was a prosperous hamlet called Sampalok near the town of Bay Laguna, where *sampalok* (tamarind) trees grew in abundance. It was originally inhabited by tribal groups and Muslims who migrated from Mindanao. These days, it is known as the City of Seven Lakes, lying as it does to the southwest of six lakes and a five-minute jeepney ride (P15) south of the largest of the lakes, **Lake Sampalok** which you can circumnavigate in a few hours. There are trails leading through lush jungle and farmland to all seven lakes, and the Lake Sampalok shore boasts floating restaurants serving native freshwater fish such as tilapia, bangus, carp and several species of shrimp. There are numerous jeepneys from Los Baños to San Pablo, but only a limited number from Pagsanjan (daily 5am–4pm; 2hr).

The **Underground Cemetery** (daily 8am–5pm; free) makes a pleasant enough side trip about thirty minutes east of San Pablo. It's an intriguing remnant of the Spanish colonial period, built by Spanish Franciscan missionaries in the sixteenth century to stop the spread of disease. The only portion that is actually underground is the crypt, which you can explore by crawling down a flight of stone steps inside the baroque Spanish chapel. In the nineteenth century the cemetery gained notoriety when the crypt became a hiding place for revolutionaries plotting against Spanish rule. The cemetery lies 2km south of **Nagcarlan**, from whose centre you can get a jeepney to the site.

The resorts

There are plenty of **resorts** in the area to choose from if you feel a day-trip here is too rushed. The best is *Villa Escudero Plantations & Resort* (T02/523 2944, Wwww.villaescudero.com; ❻–❽ full board), half an hour by road south of San Pablo near **Tiaong**. A working coconut plantation in a beautiful location surrounded by mountains, it has pretty cottages with verandas overlooking a lake, and the price includes all meals plus a tour of the plantation on a cart pulled by a *carabao*. Also inside the plantation, within walking distance of the cottages, is the **Escudero Private Museum**, with a trove of religious art, consisting of silver altars, gilded *carrozas* (ceremonial carriages), ivory-headed *santos*, Oriental ceramics, costumes, dioramas of Philippine wildlife and ethnography, rare coins and antique Philippine furniture. There's also a beautiful rose-pink baroque church that is a favourite venue for weddings, the bride usually arriving by horse-drawn carriage.

To the west of San Pablo on the road to Santo Tomas is the town of **Alaminos**, site of the *Hidden Valley Spring Resort* (T02/818 4034; ❻–❽), which sits amid rainforest in a volcanic crater 100m deep. There are air-conditioned cottages and seven natural spring pools at the resort, some deep enough for swimming. The entrance fee for day-trippers is P1200, which includes a welcome drink, buffet lunch, afternoon snacks and use of all the pools. Tricycle drivers in Alaminos will demand P100 for the honour of taking you to the gate, which is only 1500m or so away. To get to Alaminos itself, you can catch a local bus or jeepney from San Pablo or Los Baños. The film *Apocalypse Now* was partly filmed in this area, and director *Francis Ford Coppola* was so enamoured with the resort that he extended his visit for a few months after the final shooting date, prompting the owners to build a helipad for his personal use.

Pagsanjan and the Pagsanjan Falls

There's little to see in **PAGSANJAN**, but it's the logical place for budget accommodation if you plan to visit nearby **Pagsanjan Falls**, chosen by Francis Ford Coppola as the location for the final scenes in *Apocalypse Now*. Most tourists come not for the Hollywood nostalgia value, however, but to take one of the popular, if overpriced, boat trips down the fourteen **rapids** of the Bombongan River. The rapids are at their most thrilling in the wet season; during the dry season the ride is more sedate. You don't need to be especially daring to do the trip, though you will get wet, so bring a change of clothes.

Practicalities

The falls are 80km southeast of Manila. Many tour operators in the capital offer **day-trips** here, costing around US$55 per person for a minimum of two, including transport and lunch at a hotel in the area, though the rapids trip itself may not be included, so ask when booking. There are no buses between Manila and Pagsanjan, though you can easily get a bus to the nearby small town of **Santa Cruz**, on the southern shore of Laguna de Bay. Watch out for touts who will intercept you as you get off the bus and try to sign you up for one of their rapids trips, charging P200 more than at the falls themselves. Others will offer "special rides" to the falls, but it's straightforward to get one of the jeepneys that regularly make the easy ten-minute journey from the plaza in Santa Cruz to Pagsanjan or the falls, which are east of the town.

At the falls, the boatmen have also gained a reputation for being hard-nosed when the time comes to demand a tip. Prices are already rather steep for the thirty-minute, seven-kilometre ride, starting at P1000 for a single passenger. The official Department of Tourism rate is P580 per person, so you should refuse to pay more. It's best to get to the falls early before the hordes arrive and to avoid weekends if possible. The last rapids trip is usually a couple of hours before sundown, at around 4pm.

There is no shortage of **accommodation** in and around Pagsanjan. In the town itself, the *Pagsanjan Youth Hostel*, at 237 General Luna St, has singles and doubles with fan, plus dorms (℡049/645 2347; ❷–❸, dorm beds P150). Guesthouses include the simple, clean *Willy Flores Guesthouse*, 821 Garcia St (℡049/808 1730; ❷–❹), offering singles and doubles with fan and bath. *La Corona de Pagsanjan*, on the road from Pagsanjan to Cavinti (℡049/808 1753 or 808 1793; ❻), is the best accommodation in the area, but a little more expensive. It has en-suite air-conditioned doubles, triples and quads, a nice pool, a campsite at the rear where you can pitch a tent for P180 a night and includes breakfast in the room rate. *Pagsanjan Falls Lodge* in the barangay of Pinagsanjan (take a jeepney from General Luna St in Pagsanjan; ℡045/828 4051 or 02/632 7834; ❸–❹) has a good range of very ordinary but clean and quite spacious rooms including fan rooms, air-conditioned doubles and fifteen rooms for up to three people. The resort arranges rapids trips for P650 per person.

J.P. Rizal Street in Pagsanjan is the place to look for **restaurants**. Almost next to one another are three reasonably comfortable places serving mostly Filipino food. *83 Gallery Café* does everything from big breakfasts with rice to pizzas and grilled meat. *Lampsas Pagsanjan Kalikansan Grill* serves more tasty fare for carnivores, while *Pansita sa Plaza* is a workmanlike canteen with noodles, *adobo* and crispy pig's knuckle. There's also a popular Japanese restaurant at *Pagsanjan Falls Lodge*.

Lake Caliraya

The impressive man-made **Lake Caliraya**, 5km north of the town of **Cavinti** and easily reached by jeepney from Pagsanjan (P22), is 400m above sea level. Created in 1943 when a hydroelectric dam was built, the lake stands on top of a fertile volcanic plateau and boasts marvellous views of nearby Mount Banahaw (see p.161). Most visitors are weekend trippers from Manila taking advantage of the solitude. The lake and the lush jungle around it are still unspoilt, making it a good area for trekking, biking (bring your own bike as there is none to rent), fishing for largemouth black bass (gear can be rented at the resorts) or straightforward relaxation. On the lake itself you can rent jet-skis, water skis, kayaks and windsurfers.

Jeepneys from Pagsanjan go to Caliraya (P20), passing the accommodation en route. The most popular **place to stay** is the *Lagos Del Sol Resort* (℡02/526 8088 or 523 1835; **⑤-⑦**), set in immense tropical gardens where you can walk and jog, and offering water-skiing, windsurfing, tennis and a swimming pool. Accommodation here comprises spacious, comfortable native-style lakeside cottages for up to four, or a choice of rooms in the main building. The native-style restaurant is run down and the food isn't very good for the price, so people spending the weekend here tend to bring their own sandwiches and snacks.

Paete

In the woodcarving town of **PAETE** ("pa-e-te"), north of Pagsanjan on the road that hugs the east coast of Laguna de Bay, artisans produce woodcarvings, oil paintings, wooden clogs (*bakya*) and the gaily painted papier-mâché masks that are used in fiestas. Accomplished and elaborate, the woodcarvings have been sold around the world – in St Peter's Basilica in Rome there's a life-sized crucifix that was carved in Paete. All of the products are for sale, either in a number of small shops along the main road that runs through Paete or directly from the workshops. A small wooden statue of Christ or one of the saints (called *pu-on* locally) will cost around P1000 and a large one – and that can mean up to a metre or more in height – as much as P20,000. Some craftsmen also make **yo-yos**, said to have been invented in the Philippines as an ingenious if unlikely weapon, wielded by sitting in a tree and dropping the yo-yo onto the head of a passing victim (there's no conclusive evidence for this). The town's crumbling but atmospheric baroque **Santiago Apostol Parish Church** dates right back to 1646, but in common with many Philippine churches built by the Spaniards, it has been reduced to rubble by earthquakes on a number of occasions and rebuilt. The present structure (daily 7am–8pm; free) actually dates from the middle of the nineteenth century and has a beautiful sculpted altar finished in gold leaf. During the second week of January every year Paete marks its **salibanda festival**, a thanksgiving celebration that includes a parade on the lake and a rowdy procession along the main street, with participants and spectators splashing water over each other.

There is no **accommodation** in Paete, but you can visit it easily in a day from Pagsanjan. A couple of kilometres south of Paete on the main road look out for *Exotik*, which has snake and frog on the menu. If that's too much, there's crispy fried pork and tangy beef broth with vegetables. There's a souvenir shop where you can buy bottles of bubble-gum flavoured liquor.

From **Santa Cruz** (see p.139), it's easy to pick up a local bus or jeepney for the short trip north to Paete.

Bulacan

The province of **Bulacan** ("bu-la-CAN"), which begins 45km north of Manila, isn't a major tourist destination, though it does have a number of sights and events that have made it famous throughout the Philippines. You can reach most destinations in Bulacan, barring the **Biak-na-Bato National Park**, in less than an hour from Manila.

Bulacan's **history** is dominated by a battle with the British who, soon after capturing Manila in 1762, turned their attention to establishing a foothold in Bulacan. Filipino revolutionary Simon de Anda y Salazar had fled the capital for Bulacan, irritating his putative colonial masters by proclaiming himself Supreme Governor of the Philippines. The British promised a reward of P5000 for his capture, dead or alive; Anda countered with an edict awarding ten million pesos to anyone who could kill or capture a British officer. Then the British came in hot pursuit in a fleet with four hundred of their own soldiers and two thousand Chinese allies. In the ensuing Battle of Bulacan the British burned the province's churches, but in June 1763 they were forced back towards Manila in disarray by a marauding force of eight thousand Filipino and Spanish troops.

Bulacan is known for a number of major festivals, including the **Obando Fertility Rites**, which climax from May 17 to May 19 in the town of **Obando** on the southern edge of the province. Childless couples from all over the country come here to dance in the streets in the hope that they will be rewarded for their devotion with a baby. The festival – mentioned by José Rizal in his book *Noli Me Tangere* – also gives farmers the chance to pray for a good harvest and fishermen for a good catch. Single men and women also dance, on different days, in the hope of finding a partner. A **fluvial procession** is held every first Sunday of July in **Bocaue**, a short road trip north of Obando, and there's a **Carabao Festival** in **Pulilan**, not far northeast of Malolos, on May 14. The latter is an extraordinary sight, with *carabaos* groomed like pedigree dogs and made to kneel down in homage to San Isidro de Labrado, the patron saint of farmers.

Baliwag Transit buses from the terminals at Caloocan and Cubao leave every hour between 5am and 1pm for the provincial capital, **Malolos** (P90). Victory Liner and Philippine Rabbit buses also have hourly departures to Malolos, both from their terminals in Cubao. From Malolos you can get a jeepney to every town in the province, including Obando, Pulilan and Bocaue. Some buses pass through Obando and Bocaue on the way to Malolos, saving you a jeepney ride; check with the driver. There's no tourist **accommodation** in Obando, Pulilan or Bocaue and most festival-going tourists travel for the day from Manila. If you want to spend the night in the area there's limited accommodation near Malolos (see below). The festivals can also be reached easily in a day-trip from Clark (see p.421).

Malolos

Foremost among Bulacan's attractions is the impressive **Barasoain Church** in the provincial capital, **MALOLOS** (daily 6am–6pm; free). It was in this church that the Revolutionary Congress convened in 1898 and General Emilio Aguinaldo proclaimed the first Philippine Republic on 23 January 1899. Aguinaldo made his headquarters at the nearby Malolos Cathedral of the Immaculate Conception (daily 7am–8pm; free). Opposite the cathedral, the **Casa Real**, a nineteenth-century printing press used to print insurrectionist material, is now a municipal library and museum (Tues–Sat 10am–4pm; P20), with displays of priceless sixteenth-century Spanish religious artefacts and various incendiary pamphlets published by the revolutionaries.

The provincial **tourist office** is in the Capitol Building (Mon–Fri 9am–4pm; ☎044/791 0487). There's limited **accommodation** in Bulacan, most of it in Malolos. *DJ Paradise Resort*, a few kilometres south of Malolos along the

MacArthur Highway (℡044/791 5129; ❹–❽), is a sprawling water park with dorms, standard rooms, suites and cottages. It's got six swimming pools and a bowling centre, but it can be insufferably crowded and noisy at weekends.

Biak-na-Bato National Park

Biak-na-Bato, where revolutionary General Emilio Aguinaldo hid during the war against the Spanish, takes its name from its distinctive rocky environment – the name translates as "split boulders". The national park, encompassing the southern edge of the mighty Sierra Madre range, lies in the northeast corner of Bulacan and can be reached from Manila in a couple of hours. Biak-na-Bato has some excellent **hiking trails** (the highest point in the park, the 1009-metre Mount Silid, offers a relatively easy hike to the top) and hundreds of **caves**, although be wary of exploring them if you are an inexperienced caver and do not have a local guide. The most famous of the caves is La Mesa de Aguinaldo, where the general lived in hiding and received occasional guests. It was also here that he signed a peace treaty with the Spanish, known as the Pact of Biak-na-Bato.

Sadly, the park is fragile, and because of an increase in limestone quarrying environmentalists are concerned about its future. Blasting is said to be contaminating the water and causing underground streams to dry up.

From Manila, the best way to reach the park by public transport is to take a bus from outside the SM North City mall in Quezon City for **San Miguel** in Bulacan; ask the driver to let you off at the park entrance. It's also possible to negotiate a private FX van for the day – get to SM North City early and be prepared to pay up to P1500. If you're starting out from Olongapo or San Fernando, change in Malolos for a bus or jeepney to San Miguel. Entrance to the park costs P15, or P150 if you're camping overnight. You can buy water, soft drinks and snacks at sari-sari stores around the park entrance, but there are no campsites inside the park, so come prepared.

Bataan

With 85 percent of it covered in mountainous jungle, the **Bataan peninsula** is one of the most rugged places in the country and remains relatively undiscovered, apart from a number of beach resorts along the south coast around **Mariveles**. The province, forming the western side of Manila Bay, will always be associated by most Filipinos with one of the bloodiest episodes of World War II. After the outbreak of hostilities between the United States and Japan in 1941, Bataan became a strategic retreat for Filipino and American defenders. For four months, 65,000 Filipinos and 15,000 Americans held out here against the superior arms and equipment of the Japanese, in the hope of relief from the United States, until a revitalized Japanese army forced them to surrender on April 9, 1942. Filipino and American soldiers, weakened by months of deprivation, were forced to walk to detention camps in Tarlac province. About 10,000 men died along the way. A marker in Mariveles indicates the spot where the Death March began, while on the east coast, the Shrine of Valor on **Mount Samat** commemorates those who lost their lives. Also within the province is the pristine **Bataan Natural Park**, with some marvellous trekking possibilities.

El Greco Jet Ferries (℡02/831 9978, ⓦwww.elgrecomanila.com) runs three trips a day from Manila to the Mount Samat Ferry Terminal just south of the town of **Orion** on Bataan's east coast (7.30am, 10.30am and 5.15pm), departing from the Cultural Center of the Philippines; call first because departures have been erratic recently. Fares start at P195 one-way. From Orion, you can get a bus or jeepney to Mariveles, **Pilar** (for the Shrine of Valor) or the provincial capital **Balanga**, near the entrance to Bataan Natural Park. You can also do the whole journey by bus from Manila: many Philippine Rabbit buses leave the capital daily for Balanga and Mariveles. From Olongapo, Dau, Tarlac City and San Fernando, there are regular buses to Balanga.

Mount Samat and the Shrine of Valor

A paved path leads to the **Shrine of Valor** (Dambana ng Kagitingan; daily 8am–5pm; P50) at the summit of Mount Samat, a little way north of the coastal town of Pilar. The shrine has a chapel and a small museum of weapons captured from the Japanese, but the centrepiece is a ninety-metre **crucifix** (Mon & Tues 10–11am & 3–4pm, Wed–Fri 9–11am & 2–4pm, Sat & Sun 9–11am & 1–4pm) with a lift inside that takes you to a gallery at the top with views across the peninsula and, on a clear day, to Manila. On Bataan Day, April 9, Mount Samat is the focal point for remembrance, war veterans and their families arriving from all over the country and from overseas. You can visit the shrine in a day from Manila via Orion, then get a local bus or jeepney to Pilar, and cover the final 7km by jeepney or tricycle or on foot.

Bataan Natural Park

The **Bataan Natural Park**, an ancient and dense volcanic landscape in the northwest of the peninsula with the Mount Natib caldera (1253m) at its heart, offers some challenging trails and overnight treks. There's a steep trail to the summit of Mount Natib, and other trails exploring the park's lower regions, passing through a mixture of forest and farmland, and leading to beautiful waterfalls. It's estimated that a thousand households make their living within the park's boundaries, including some Aeta tribespeople, who are believed to be the oldest native inhabitants of the Philippines, settling in the islands more than 30,000 years ago. Many Aetas lived on the slopes of Mount Pinatubo, but were forced to move when it erupted in the 1990s, with some still living as refugees on the plains of Pampanga province. Flora and fauna include more than ten rare plant species, the Philippine macaque and the Luzon warty pig.

There are very few facilities for visitors, although guides can be hired at the park office (☎047/237 3550, ☏237 1938) at Bataan State College, on the eastern edge of the park in the barangay of Bangkal, **Abucay**. You can reach Abucay by bus or jeepney from any of the towns along Bataan's east coast, then take a tricycle to the office. Another place to enquire about trails and guides is the Bataan NGO Consortium (☎047/237 5238 or 0917/946 0104) in Palmera Subdivision, a residential district of **BALANGA**, 10km from the park's eastern boundary. In Balanga itself there's a small tourism office (Mon–Fri 8am–4pm; ☎047 237 4785) inside the provincial Capitol building in the main square, where staff can help with directions and accommodation.

The closest **accommodation** to the park is around Bagac or Morong, on Bataan's west coast, which can both be reached by bus from Balanga. The best resort in the area is the popular *Waterfront* (☎02/822 3070; ❼-❽, dorm beds P1050), on an impressive stretch of wide, sandy beach just south of Morong.

Mariveles and around

There are some picturesque wide **beaches** on Bataan's southwest coast between **Mariveles** and Bagac. Of a number of resorts used mostly by local travellers for weekend breaks, the best is *Montemar Beach Resort* (☎047/888 4719; ❺-❼) in Barrio Pasinay, Bagac. It's a large, well-established place on a five-hundred metre stretch of clean sandy beach, with watersports facilities and a swimming pool. The rooms have air-conditioning and a private balcony overlooking either the beach or the gardens. If you book in advance the resort will pick you up from the Orion ferry terminal, otherwise take a jeepney or bus from Orion (P70; 1hr). To the East of Mariveles there are a number of less impressive resorts along the southeast coast. Here, from Cabcaban Beach 20km east of Mariveles (30km south of Balanga) you can rent a banca to take you to Corregidor (see p.133). Note that these are unofficial bancas and once on Corregidor you won't be entitled to use any of the facilities included in the official Sun Cruises tours (see p.135). You will, however, be able to wander around and then hop a banca back to Bataan.

From Mariveles you can strike out for the summit of **Mount Mariveles**, a tricky overnight climb that starts with a twenty minutes' tricycle ride (P100 "special price") from Mariveles in the barangay of **Alasinan** (also known as Alasasin), where you register at the barangay hall and ask for a guide. Apart from food and water, you'll need a good tent or bivouac, a sleeping bag and a warm jacket – it can be surprisingly chilly when night falls.

Travel details

Trains

Tutuban PNR station to: Legaspi (2 daily; 10hr) via Calamba (2hr), San Pablo (3hr), Lucena (4hr), Naga (7hr) and Iriga City (8hr). Trains call at Buendia station 20min after leaving Tutuban.

Buses

Manila (Baclaran) to: Kawit (every 10min; 1hr); Zapote (every 15min; 45min).
Manila (Cubao or Pasay) to: Alaminos (hourly; 3–4hr); Angeles/Dau (12–15 daily; 2hr); Aparri (3–4 daily; 13hr); Baguio (12–15 daily; 6–8hr); Banaue (5–6 daily; 7–9hr); Bangued (4–5 daily; 8–10hr); Batangas City (18–20 daily; 3hr); Bolinao (3–4 daily; 6–7hr); Bulan (2–3 daily; 18–20hr); Cabanatuan (6–8 daily; 4hr); Calamba (1–12 daily; 2hr); Daet (6–8 daily; 7–8hr); Dagupan (8–10 daily; 6–7hr); Iba (3–4 daily; 6hr); Laoag (6–8 daily; 8–10hr); Legaspi (8–10 daily; 8–10hr); Lingayan (8–10 daily; 6–7hr); Los Baños (hourly; 3hr); Lucena (10–12 daily; 3hr); Malolos (hourly; 1hr); Mariveles (several daily; 4hr); Naga (6–8 daily; 6–8hr); Nasugbu (6–8 daily; 3hr); Olongapo (8–10 daily; 4–5hr); Pagsanjan (10–12 daily; 3hr); San Fernando (La Union; 4–6 daily; 6–8hr); San Fernando (Pampanga; 8–10 daily; 2–3hr); San Pablo (10–12 daily; 3hr); Santa Cruz (6–8 daily; 2–3hr); Sorsogon Town (2–3 daily; 24hr); Taal Town (10–12 daily; 2–3hr); Tagaytay (10–12 daily; 2–3hr); Tuguegarao (1–2 daily; 10–12hr); Vigan (6–8 daily; 8–10hr).

Manila (Intramuros) to: Kawit (every 30min; 1hr); Maragondon (every 30min; 2hr); Zapote (every 20min; 45min).
Balanga to: Dau (hourly; 2hr); Manila (hourly; 3–4hr); Olongapo (hourly; 1hr 30min); Orion (every 30min; 30min); San Fernando (Pampanga; several daily; 3–4hr); Tarlac City (several daily; 3hr).
Calamba to: Batangas City (several daily; 2hr); Manila (hourly; 1–2hr).
Los Baños to: Batangas City (several daily; 2hr); Manila (hourly; 3hr).
Malolos to: San Miguel (for Biak-na-Bato; several daily; 1hr).
Mariveles to: Dau (hourly; 3hr); Manila (several daily; 4hr); Olongapo (hourly; 2hr 30min); Orion (hourly; 1hr); San Fernando (Pampanga; hourly; 2hr 30min).
Orion to: Balanga (every 30min; 30min); Dau (hourly; 2hr); Mariveles (hourly; 1hr); Olongapo (hourly; 1hr 30min); San Fernando (Pampanga; hourly; 1hr 30min).
Santa Cruz to: Batangas City (several daily; 2–3hr); Manila (hourly; 3–4hr).

Jeepneys and FX taxis

Alaminos to: Calamba (several daily; 1hr); San Pablo (hourly; 45min).
Calamba to: Alaminos (several daily; 1hr); Los Baños (via hot-spring resorts; every 30min; 45min).
Los Baños to: Pagsanjan (6–8 daily; 1hr 30min); San Pablo (hourly; 1hr).
Lumban to: Pagsanjan (every 20min; 45min).

Manila (Makati) to: Zapote (every 15min; 1hr).
Manila (SM City mall) to: Biak-na-Bato (hourly; 2hr).
Malolos to: Bocaue (every 30min; 45min); Obando (every 30min; 1hr); Pulilan (every 20min; 45min); San Miguel (hourly; 2hr).
Pagsanjan to: Lake Caliraya (hourly; 45min); Paete (hourly; 1hr); Santa Cruz (every 15min; 30min).
San Miguel (near Biak-na-Bato) to: Cabanatuan (hourly; 2hr); Malolos (hourly; 2hr).
San Pablo to: Alaminos (hourly; 45min); Dolores (every 30min; 1hr 15min); Nagcarlan (hourly; 45min).
Santa Cruz to: Paete (every 15min; 1hr); Pagsanjan (every 15min; 30min).

Ferries

The services from Pier 15 in South Harbor belong to WG&A.
Manila CCP pier to: Corregidor (2 daily; 1hr); Orion (3 daily; 50min).
Manila North Harbor to: Bacolod (3–4 week; 19hr); Bohol (1–2 daily; 28–36hr); Butuan (1–2 weekly; 32hr); Cagayan de Oro (1–2 daily; 36hr); Catbalogan (4–5 weekly; 24hr); Cebu City (1–2 daily; 21hr); Coron Town (2–3 weekly; 14hr); Cotabato (2–3 weekly; 44hr); Davao (1–2 daily; 52hr); Dipolog (1–2 weekly; 38hr); Dumaguete (5–6 weekly; 22hr); Dumaguit (3–4 weekly; 17hr); Estancia (1 weekly; 20hr); General Santos (2 weekly; 43hr); Iligan (2–3 weekly; 34hr); Iloilo (1–2 daily; 18–25hr); Masbate (weekly; 7hr); Nasipit (2–3 weekly; 26–53hr); Ormoc (Tues & Fri at noon; 18hr); Ozamis (1–2 weekly; 32hr); Palompon (2 weekly; 18hr); Puerto Princesa (1–2 daily; 28hr); Romblon (2–3 weekly; 15hr); Roxas (1–2 daily; 16hr); San Carlos (1 weekly; 28hr); Surigao (2–3 weekly; 26–53hr); Tacloban (Tues & Fri at noon; 26 hr); Tagbilaran (3–4 weekly; 28hr); Zamboanga (1–2 weekly; 28hr).
Manila South Harbor (Pier 15) to: Bacolod (weekly; 17hr); Cebu City (5 weekly; 21hr); Coron Town (weekly; 11hr); Cotabato (weekly; 53hr); Davao (weekly; 50hr); General Santos (weekly; 43hr); Iligan (weekly; 31hr); Iloilo (weekly; 19hr); Puerto Princesa (2 weekly; 21hr); Zamboanga (2 weekly; 27hr).

Domestic flights

Philippine Airlines flights use Centennial Terminal II; other airlines use the Domestic Airport.
Manila to: Bacolod (up to 9 daily; 1hr 10min); Baguio (1–2 daily; 1hr 10min); Busuanga (daily; 1hr); Butuan (daily except Wed; 1hr 30min); Cagayan de Oro (8 daily; 1hr 25min); Calbayog (4 weekly; 1hr 30min); Catarman (5 weekly; 1hr 30min); Caticlan (5 daily; 1hr); Cauayan (daily; 1hr); Cebu City (up to 21 daily; 1hr 10min); Cotabato (1–2 daily; 1hr 40min); Davao (up to 10 daily; 1hr 40min); Dipolog (five weekly; 1hr 20min); Dumaguete (up to 3 daily; 1hr 10min); General Santos (2 daily; 1hr 40min); Iloilo (10 daily; 1hr); Kalibo (7–8 daily; 50min); Laoag (daily; 1hr); Legaspi (3–4 daily; 1hr 10min); Marinduque (5 weekly; 40min); Masbate (2 daily; 1hr 20min); Naga (2–3 daily; 1hr); Puerto Princesa (2–3 daily; 1hr 10min); Romblon (Tugdan; 2 weekly; 1hr); Roxas (Mindoro; 2 daily; 1hr); Roxas (Panay; 11 weekly; 55min); San Fernando (La Union; 4 weekly; 1hr); San José (Mindoro; 1–2 daily; 1hr); Tablas (5 weekly; 1 hr); Tacloban (6–7 daily; 1hr 10min); Tagbilaran (daily; 2hr); Tuguegarao (3 weekly; 1hr); Virac (2 daily; 1hr 20min); Zamboanga (4–5 daily; 1hr 30min).

2

Southern Luzon

CHAPTER 2 # Highlights

* **Anilao** A scenic stretch of coast with some choice resorts and the best scuba diving in Luzon. See p.154

* **Taal Volcano** Take a banca across the surrounding lake and scramble up to the crater at the top of one of the world's smallest volcanoes. See p.154

* **Pahiyas festival** Creativity runs riot as residents decorate their houses with fruit and veg, in one of the most colourful festivals in the Philippines' calendar. See p.160

* **Mount Banahaw** The ascent to the summit of the country's most mystical mountain is a strenuous climb through dense jungle and past crashing waterfalls. See p.161

* **Moriones festival** Every Easter the beautiful little island of Marinduque lays on a boisterous religious pageant celebrating the life of Longinus, the Roman soldier who pierced Christ's side at the Crucifixion. See p.164

* **Mayon Volcano** Even if you don't climb it, you shouldn't miss it. In fact it's hard to miss, its almost symmetrical cone standing imperiously above Legaspi. See p.182

* **Whale shark-watching in Donsol** Snorkel with the gentle giants of the sea. See p.188

* **Bulusan Volcano National Park** A lush wilderness area with an active volcano at its heart; raptors circle overhead and lizards are a common sight in the forest. See p.191

* **Puraran Beach, Catanduanes** A prime surfing beach it may be, but it's not only for surfers; the offshore coral reef is thick with marine life. See p.199

△ Taal Volcano

Southern Luzon

The area of Luzon immediately south of Manila encompasses some of the country's most popular tourist destinations – as well as a number of undeveloped provinces that few tourists take time to see. The province of **Batangas**, two hours south of Manila by road, contains the most popular tourist attractions and beaches around Manila and has a number of good resorts and hotels that get busy at weekends with trippers coming down from the capital. The two main destinations here are the area around **Taal Lake** and its **volcano**, and an area further south known as **Anilao**, where there's some excellent scuba diving.

A lengthy trip by road from the capital, the southern part of **Quezon province** hasn't anything rivalling either the beautiful beaches of the Visayas and Palawan or the interesting tribal communities of the far north and Mindanao. It's best known for the colourful annual **Pahiyas festival**, celebrated mostly in the town of **Lucban**, but also in many other towns and barangays. Quezon also offers access to the southern flank of **Mount Banahaw**, a revered dormant volcano that presents one of the toughest but most rewarding climbs in the country. The province is linked by ferry to the island of **Marinduque**, which is the place to sample barrio life in its purest form, untouched by mass tourism and with none of the unfettered development that has encroached on provinces closer to Manila. Marinduque also has some lovely, unspoiled coast and cheap resorts, and is known for its annual Easter festival, the Moriones, one of the biggest and most colourful in the country.

The region south of Quezon is technically called Region V, but is known to Filipinos as **Bicol** (or Bicolandia or South Luzon), a narrow finger of land whose southern tip is close to the Visayan island of Samar. Bicol is a raw and exotic part of the country, full of exciting opportunities to get off the beaten track and see the rural Philippines without the distraction of shopping malls and luxury resorts. Most visitors to the region head straight for the most alluring sight, **Mount Mayon**, an immense active volcano near Legaspi. Bicol also has a number of other wilderness areas offering some adventurous trekking and climbing, while further south, off the coast of **Donsol** in Sorsogon province is the best place in the country to spot **whale sharks**.

Batangas province is served by frequent buses from Manila and makes a feasible overnight destination or even a day-trip, though that would require a very early start to make it worthwhile. There are also regular, if not quite so frequent, buses through Quezon and Bicol, though if you're heading for Legaspi it's worth flying – this can save up to ten hours on the road journey.

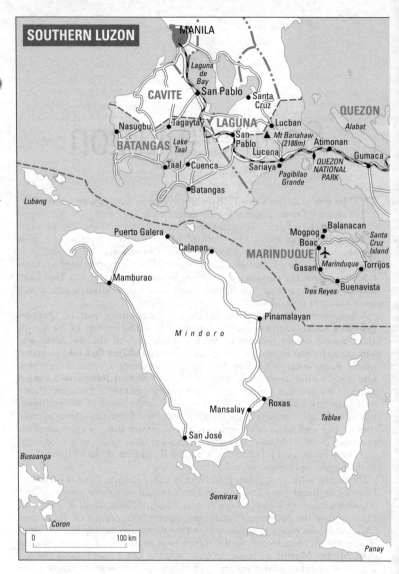

Batangas

Batangas province has some impressive natural attractions, most notably **Taal Lake** and the small, active **Taal Volcano** at its centre. Nearby **Taal Town** retains some of the period atmosphere of Spanish colonization, while on the

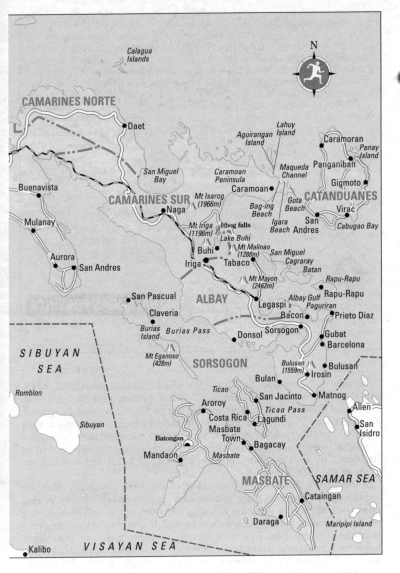

southeastern shore of Taal Lake is **Mount Maculot**, one of the best easy climbs in the Philippines. In the southwest there are also beach resorts at **Nasugbu** and **Anilao**, the latter offering terrific scuba diving.

There are signs that the provincial capital, **BATANGAS CITY**, is springing into life, with a new pier and talk of numerous industrial zones. Its only significance for most visitors is as a transit point on the journey to Puerto Galera on Mindoro (see p.209). BLTB buses to Batangas City leave from Pasay in Manila (P120), going first to the **ferry pier** (ferry tickets can

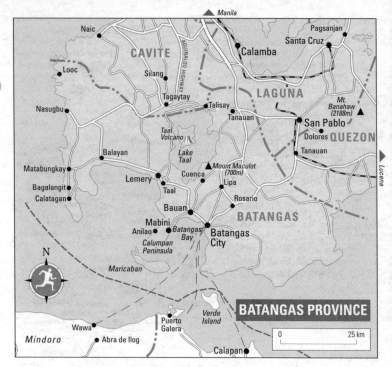

▲ *Manila*

Naic

Pagsanjan

Santa Cruz

CAVITE   Calamba

Looc

Silang

LAGUNA

Mt.
Banahaw
(2188m) ▲

Nasugbu

Tagaytay

Talisay

Tanauan

San Pablo

Dolores QUEZON

Taal
Volcano

Lake
Taal

Tanauan

Balayan

▲ Mount Maculot
(700m)

Matabungkay

Lemery   Cuenca

Lipa

Bagalangit

Taal

Calatagan

Rosario

Bauan

BATANGAS

Mabini   Batangas
Bay

Batangas
City

Anilao

Calumpan
Peninsula

N

Maricaban

BATANGAS PROVINCE

Wawa

Puerto
Galera

Verde
Island

0   25 km

Mindoro   ● Abra de Ilog

Calapan

Lucena ▶

AGUINALDO HIGHWAY

be bought in the terminal building; ferry schedules are on ☎043/723 8245) and then to the **bus terminal** in J.P. Rizal Avenue, near the cathedral. Numerous buses wait at the pier for the trip to Manila; try to take a direct bus marked for Pasay – some buses go through the barrios, making it a long journey – so either ask the driver what route he's taking or look out for the "Direcho" sign in the window. Among the ferry companies represented in Batangas City are Viva Shipping Lines (☎043/723 1422) and Montenegro Lines (☎043/723 8294).

Be careful on buses heading to and from the ferry terminal, which are sometimes the focus of petty thieves who target tourists, adroitly slitting open your bag with a sharp knife, taking a few belongings and then getting off the bus before you realize what's happened. If you get stuck overnight in Batangas you can take your pick from a number of poorly maintained flophouses, or try the rather better *Avenue Pension House* (☎043/725 3720; ❸) at 30 J.P. Rizal Avenue. There's also a *Days Hotel* (☎043/980 7321; ❻) in the Pallocan suburb on the northern outskirts of the city; the rooms are good, but the hotel is a twenty-minute drive from the city so you'll need to take a hotel taxi from here to the pier. If you're arriving by bus from the north, ask the driver to let you off on the main road near the hotel and get a tricycle the rest of the way; arriving at the pier, you'll need to head into the centre, then get a jeepney for Pallocan from J.P. Rizal Avenue.

Beach resorts

The closest beaches and scuba diving to Manila are in Batangas, mostly around **Nasugbu** on the west coast and the barangay of **Anilao** on Janao Bay, 20km west of Batangas City. Nasugbu is a slightly shorter journey, and boasts a handful of good, established beach resorts where accommodation is inexpensive and the atmosphere is relaxed. However, the diving here is nowhere near as good as it is at Anilao, where you can charter a banca to take you out to offshore islands such as Sombrero, Culebra and Bunny, offering good snorkelling and diving as well as many small, sandy coves on which to relax. The beach at Anilao itself is stony but clean, and for accommodation there are more than a dozen resorts stretched along the coast to the west.

Nasugbu and around

The coastline around **NASUGBU** is lined with resorts, mostly clearly signposted from the main road, grouped largely in three areas: to the north of Nasugbu on the white-sand beach to Fuego Point; around Nasugbu itself on Nasugbu Beach, which has darker sand and is more crowded; and about twenty minutes south of Nasugbu by road the town of **MATABUNGKAY** has a number of decent resorts. Heading to Nasugbu from Manila, there are hourly BLTB **buses** from their Pasay terminal, and regular Crow Bus Company services from the terminal at the junction of EDSA and Taft in Pasay, opposite the LRT station. The buses are usually marked for **Lian**, 25 minutes south of Nasugbu by road, but some actually continue south to Calatagan, passing through Matabungkay on their way. If you can't find a bus passing the resort you want, you'll have to take a tricycle or a jeepney (these run on set routes, so ask if one goes near your resort) from Nasugbu's town hall. There are jeepneys every few minutes between Nasugbu and Matabungkay. Accommodation prices at many of the establishments here increase by ten to twenty percent at weekends; the price codes below represent weekday rates.

Coral Beach Club On Matabungkay Beach south of Lian ☏ 0912/318 4868, ⓦ www.coralbeach.ph. A quiet, attractive place with restaurant, bar, pool tables, beachside pool and a/c rooms, all with cable TV and hot showers. ⑤–⑦

Lago de Oro Beach Club Overlooking the beach near Matabungkay ☏ 0917/504 3719 or 0926/710 4754, ⓦ www.lago-de-oro.com. Modern hacienda-style resort run by friendly Germans. There's good food in the European-style restaurant and a lagoon for water-skiing. ⑦

Matabungkay Beach Resort & Hotel Matabungkay ☏ 043/750 1459, ⓦ www .matabungkay.net. Clean if basic rooms with large balconies; many rooms are in a concrete barracks-style building 100m from the beach. There are two pleasant restaurants, a karaoke club and a swimming pool. The beach itself isn't great, with brown sand and water that's not especially clean or clear. ⑥–⑧

Maya-Maya Reef Resort Barangay Natipuan, north of Nasugbu ☏ 0918/903 9735 or 0918/909 7170, ⓦ www.mayamaya.com. This is a more upmarket resort than many in the area: there's a good choice of well-maintained a/c rooms, some big enough for four. That said, it's good value and reasonably priced, with excellent service and a menu featuring everything from Greek salad to chicken curry and Salisbury steak (P280). The new spa offers massage and beauty treatment from P950. ④–⑦

Punta Baluarte Resort In private grounds on a promontory 8km south of Balayan (about 20km south of Lian). ☏ 02/892 4202. Sprawling development with upmarket pretensions and a wide range of rooms, from a double with a sunrise view to your own native-style Bicol house for four. The beach is on the muddy side and therefore not suitable for swimming, though there are two swimming pools, one with salt water. The resort banca can take you further afield to better beaches and also to coral reefs for scuba diving and snorkelling. Buffet meals are served in the seashore restaurant. To get here by public transport from Nasugbu, take a jeepney southeast to Balayan (45min) and another heading west from Balayan along the only road. Ask to get off at the resort's gate, from where it's a 1km walk down a private lane to reception. ❹

Twins Beach Club ☎0912/322 8163, ⓦwww. twinsbc.de. Homely pension on the seafront 5km

south of Lian, offering en-suite doubles with tiled floors. Small beach, swimming pool and alfresco bar. Some of the best value accommodation in the area if you're content with the simple life. ❹

Anilao and around

ANILAO is less than 100km from Manila by road, but with the shortcomings of the road network it can take four hours to get there by car, longer by public transport. City folk make the trip for the weekends, when Anilao can get a little busy, but during the week it's much more peaceful and you can often negotiate a discount on your accommodation.

To reach Anilao by public transport, take a BLTB bus for Batangas City. You can ask to be let off in **Bauan**, a busy little coastal town, from where you can take a jeepney west to Mabini or the wharf at Anilao, then continue by tricycle along the coastal road to the resort of your choice. Alternatively, stay on the bus until you reach Batangas City and then catch one of the regular jeepneys to Anilao from outside *McDonald's* on P. Burgos Street. All the **accommodation** reviewed here is on the road beyond the wharf at Anilao, along the west coast of the Calumpan peninsula.

Anilao Seaport Center ☎043/807 4570 or 807 4574. Good range of double rooms opening onto the veranda, plus family rooms for five people. ❹

Aquaventure Reef Club ☎02/899 2831. Comfortable, unpretentious resort 3km along the coastal road beyond Anilao. Operated by Manila-based dive outfit Aqua One, it's primarily a scuba resort, though it also offers island-hopping and snorkelling trips in rented bancas. Double rooms come with fan and bath; buffet-style meals are served in a nice open restaurant overlooking the sea. ❸

Dive Solana ☎02/721 2089, ⓦwww .divesolana.com. Along the coastal road beyond the *Aquaventure Reef Club*, this is a charming and slightly bohemian little retreat owned by Filipina film-maker Marilou Diaz-Abaya. There are a/c and fan rooms, some right on the beach, with an ethnic touch, and the rate includes three buffet meals a day. It's always full at weekends because people keep going back, so book in advance. Prices rise ten percent at weekends. ❽

Eagle Point Resort Anilao ☎02/813 3553 or 02/750 6524, ⓦwww.eaglepoint.com.ph. Almost at the end of the Anilao coastal road, where it peters out into little more than a rutted, bumpy track, are these pleasant cottages with balconies that face the sea. Good diving with the resort's own dive guides, a large pool and a restaurant serving mostly Filipino food and boasting dreamy views out to sea. ❼

El Pinoy Dive Inn ☎02/726 8861. Close to the end of the dirt road, past *Eagle Point* and *Dive Solana*. Detached cottages and deluxe rooms with their own bath, or economy rooms with two to four beds and shared facilities. ❸

Planet Dive ☎02/410 6193, ⓦwww.planetdive.net. The last of the resorts along the Anilao strip, these native-style cottages are opposite the Twin Rocks dive site, where the bay is sheltered enough for good snorkelling. You can have candlelit dinners on the shore and there's a viewing deck from which to take in Anilao's wonderful sunsets. Accommodation ranges from the very basic to cottages for six, all of it clean and comfortable. ❸ ❻

Lake Taal and around

In part because of the cool climate – on some days it even gets foggy – **Lake Taal** and the surrounding area is a popular weekend retreat from the heat of the nearby capital. **Taal Volcano**, which stands right in the middle of the lake, is said to be the smallest active volcano in the world, and there are occasional rumblings that force the authorities to issue evacuation warnings to local inhabitants. If you're visiting for views of the lake and volcano, you can easily have a good look around on a day-trip from Manila, and you could just about climb the volcano too if you made an early start from the capital. However, it's worth spending the night down by the lakeshore, in the small town of **Talisay**, where there's affordable accommodation, and take the opportunity to climb the volcano the next day. This is a much better option than staying in the city of **Tagaytay**, which sits on the ridge above the lake.

The volcano last erupted in 1965 without causing major damage, but when it blew its top in 1754, thousands died and the town of **Taal** was destroyed; it was rebuilt in a new location on safer ground an hour by road from Tagaytay to the southwest of the lake. The town is an interesting side trip from the lake area, an atmospheric settlement with one of the finest old basilicas in the country.

Close to the town of **Cuenca**, on the southeastern side of Lake Taal, 50km east of Taal, **Mount Maculot** is relatively wild and less of a tourist attraction than Taal Volcano. Its summit is a modest 700m, making it a suitable day-climb for novices; if you've limited time available, this is your best opportunity to do some trekking in the Philippines.

Lake Taal

Beautiful **LAKE TAAL**, which sits in a caldera formed by huge eruptions between 500,000 and 100,000 years ago, is the country's third largest lake. The active **Taal Volcano**, which is responsible for the lake's sulphuric content, lies in the centre of the lake, on **Volcano Island**.

The departure point for trips across **Lake Taal** to the **volcano** is the small town of **Talisay** on the lake's northern shore; here you arrange to hire a banca and a guide. With an early start, you can climb to either the new crater or the old crater (both are active) and be back in Talisay in time for a good fish lunch at one of the many native-cuisine restaurants along the shore. There isn't much shade on the volcano, so don't go without sunblock, a good hat and plenty of water.

The compact but busy city of **Tagaytay**, 70km south of Manila on a 600-metre-high ridge overlooking the lake and volcano, has seen rash, unchecked development making it a hellish town, with congested roads and menacing

△ Lake Taal

shoals of tricycles. Thankfully, you don't have to go as far as Tagaytay itself to enjoy the volcano and the lake, which lie to the southeast of town.

Practicalities

From Manila, you can approach Talisay from two directions: from the west **via the Tagaytay Rotunda**, the big roundabout east of Tagaytay; or **via Tanauan**, northeast of the lake, which is the fastest route. BLTB buses from Pasay marked for Lemery stop at Tanauan, and from Tanauan's public market, there are jeepneys to Talisay along the bumpy lakeshore road, a thirty-minute ride. Several BLTB buses run daily from Pasay **to Tagaytay** on their way to the beaches at Nasugbu (see p.153); if you're on one of these buses and want to reach Talisay, get off the bus at the Tagaytay Rotunda, then continue by one of the jeepneys that shuttle back and forth all day between Tagaytay and Talisay, traversing the ridge en route. **From Batangas City**, some buses for Pasay in Manila pass through Tanauan, while others travel via Tagaytay; check the route with the driver.

Hiring a **banca** with a guide to take you out to the volcano will cost around P1000 if you arrange it independently in Talisay. If you're staying the night by the lake, your hotel can arrange this for you, with food and refreshments included, typically for P2000–3000.

Accommodation

The views from the ridge at Tagaytay overlooking the lake make it more expensive to stay here than in one of the barangays by the lake around Talisay, but most of the accommodation here is disappointing and you don't get the views you pay for. Down by the lake, it is quieter and more convenient if you intend to climb the volcano. Most of the lakeside resorts are between Talisay and Laurel, a few kilometres to the south.

Days Hotel Tagaytay On the main road through Tagaytay, just beyond the big roundabout ☏046/413 2400. The only hotel on the ridge really worth considering, this is a concrete box but it has neat and tidy singles and doubles, a swimming pool and terrific volcano views from the garden. Breakfast is included ❹–❼

Mountain Side Just beyond the barrio of Leynes on the lake's north shore, 8km west of Talisay ☏043/773 0138. Comfortable, cheap rooms with fans and bath. A boat to the volcano costs P800 including a guide. ❹

Rosalina's Place In the barangay of Banga, on the opposite side of the road to the lakeshore ☏043/773 0088. Some of the cheapest double rooms in the area, boats to the volcano for P700 and there's a P100 seafood buffet lunch daily. ❸

San Roque Beach Resort Less than 1km west of Talisay and close to the lakeshore ☏0918/290 8384. Accommodation here is mainly in nipa huts with room for two or more. ❹

🏃 **Sonya's Secret Garden** Barangay Buck Estate, Alfonso, Cavite ☏0917/532 9097, ⓦwww.sonyasgarden.com. Romantic cottage accommodation in a remarkable garden nurtured by the eponymous Sonya. Rooms are wonderful and the

rate includes a delicious breakfast, prepared with mostly home-grown, organic ingredients. If you're not staying the night, drop by for lunch or dinner. Daily set menus cost P500 (P250 for children) and include delights such as home-grown organic salad with mango, pasta with sun-dried tomatoes and anchovies, and banana fritters for dessert. It's very popular, so book ahead. Sonya's is on a private estate more than 10km beyond Tagaytay, so is tricky to reach without private transport: go past Splendido golf course and then look out for the signs on the right. From Tagaytay, you can take a tricycle, but you'll pay a special rate of around P200. ❻–❽

Taal Lake Yacht Club About 1km east of Talisay on the shore ☏02/811 3183 or 02/811 3283, ⓦwww.sailphi.org.ph. Popular and well-run sailing club with a pleasant, secure campsite with showers and toilets. Small yachts, kayaks and sailing boats are available for rent; you can also rent bancas to the volcano. It costs $2 to enter the site and $3 to pitch a tent for the night.

🏃 **Talisay Green Lake Resort** Next to Taal Lake Yacht Club. ☏043/773 0247 or 02/833 3860. Range of concrete rooms set in a large, private compound right on the lake shore. Quiet, friendly and comfortable, and with a perfect location. ❹–❺

Eating and drinking

The ridge above the volcano has dozens of **restaurants**, though it has also been rather overrun by big chains and fast-food joints. Two hundred metres east of the *Taal Vista Lodge Hotel*, on the main road that runs along the ridge to Tagaytay, is *Josephine's*, an institution among Filipinos, serving good home-style Filipino dishes such as *sinigang* with mounds of steamed rice. A little west of the *Taal Vista Lodge Hotel*, *Angelino's Pizza Parlor* cooks its pizzas in a wood-fired oven. Look out also for street vendors selling the local speciality, delicious **buko** (coconut) **pie**. The best place to buy it hot is a small stall known as *Collette's*; on the road heading towards Talisay, turn left at the Tagaytay Rotunda, and *Collette's* is 200m down on the left. Along the ridge, stalls also sell another speciality, piping hot *bulalo*, a rich beef bone-marrow soup for just P50 a bowl. Vegetarians will appreciate *Mushroom Burger*, a small roadside restaurant near the *Taal Vista Lodge Hotel* selling burgers made from fresh local mushrooms, which thrive in the cooler climate. Down by the **lakeshore** in and around Talisay, along Wencislao Road, there are good rustic eating places selling barbecued meat and fish.

Many Manileños make the journey here partly just to have lunch at *Gourmet Café* on the Aguinaldo Highway (5km north of the Tagaytay junction, on the left if you're heading south). Travelling on any bus for Tagaytay, you can ask the driver to let you get off close to the restaurant, and it's easy to pick up an onward bus after you've eaten. This is the biggest and best of a well-known chain of country-cottage-style restaurants with wooden interiors, pretty checked tablecloths and a range of organic dishes, the ingredients for which come from the restaurant's own farm nearby. There is also a small shop where you can buy organic products such as unrefined sugar, spicy vinegar, rice wine and salad dressings. Finally, try not to miss lunch or dinner at *Sonya's Secret Garden* (see above).

Taal

The name Taal is usually associated with the brooding volcano. Most visitors overlook the town of **TAAL**, which is a shame because it offers a blast from a glorious past, with faded Spanish colonial architecture and the magnificent **Basilica of St Martin de Tours** (daily 7am–8pm; free), said to be the biggest church in Southeast Asia. The original church on the site – five minutes' north of the town square – was also the first constructed in Southeast Asia, completed in 1575 but destroyed by the volcanic eruption in 1754. The present church, built in 1856 and inaugurated by Augustinian friars in 1865, has been made a national shrine by presidential decree. You can climb to the top of the bell tower for panoramic views over the ocean on one side and Lake Taal on the other.

The town's ancestral **houses** and Spanish-era buildings are being preserved by the Taal Heritage Foundation. Two of these houses, both on the street that runs downhill from the market, are especially noteworthy: the house of Gliceria Villavicencio (Tues–Sat 9am–noon and 1–4pm; P10), where the revolutionary Katipunan group (see p.498) met, and the house of Marcella Agoncillo (same times; P20), who sewed the first Philippine flag. Behind the Agoncillo house is a **Lourdes grotto** with water that is believed to have healing powers.

The **market** in Taal is a good place to look for local embroidery, including cotton sheets, pillowcases and tablemats. They're all made by hand in the town's small workshops and are much cheaper here than in Manila's department stores, as long as you're prepared to do some haggling. The area is also well known for the manufacture of *balisong*, knives which have a hidden blade that flicks out from the handle. The knives, once carried by revolutionaries against the Spanish, are now manufactured largely as souvenirs and sell at dozens of roadside stalls for P150–1000, the more expensive ones with carved or inlaid handles and bigger blades. The stalls also sell *bolos*, the vicious curved machetes used in the provinces for everything from splitting open a coconut to slaughtering a pig.

The DoT organizes **guided tours** of Taal, leaving Manila at 6am. A typical trip costs P550 per person and includes a native breakfast in Taal, a walking tour of the town, lunch, crafts demonstrations and afternoon *merienda*. For details call ⓣ0916/552 2074.

Some **buses** from Batangas City to Manila pass through Taal, dropping passengers on the main road a short walk from the market and town square. From Tagaytay you can either catch a local bus marked for Lemery – these travel via Taal – or take a jeepney. From Manila, a number of bus companies (BLTB, Jac Liner, Tritran and JAM Transit) ply the Manila–Lemery–Taal route (P118), stopping at the northern edge of town, not far from the plaza. If you want to **stay** overnight in Taal, try the beautiful and historic *Casa Punzalan* in the town square (❸), a traditional old house that has been converted into a simple but comfortable guesthouse and offers a real taste of provincial life in the Spanish-era. You can also contact the Taal Heritage Foundation (ⓣ043/421 1053 or 421 3034), which can put you in touch with homestays.

Mount Maculot

If you set out from Manila very early – as most local climbers do – you can climb **Mount Maculot** and still be back in the capital for dinner. One reason for Maculot's popularity is an area of sheer rock near the summit known as the **Rockies**, rising vertically up from the jungle and with a platform at the top affording unbroken views across Lake Taal to Taal Volcano. There's a steep but walkable path around the Rockies that takes you to the platform. Bear in mind, however, that because this is the closest climb to the capital, and the easiest (you don't need a guide), the trail can get congested at weekends.

From the foot to the area on the mountain's shoulder, where it's possible to camp, takes about two hours, and from the shoulder to the peak another hour. At weekends such is the influx of enthusiastic city folk that it can be hard to find space on the shoulder to pitch a tent; some climbers simply bring a sleeping bag, though it does get cool and windy on top.

To get to Mount Maculot from Manila, take one of the hourly JAM Transit buses from Pasay for **Cuenca** (2hr; P95). Cuenca can also be reached by public transport from towns on the south side of Laguna de Bay; coming from Batangas City, you change at Los Baños or San Pablo for another bus or jeepney. There's no direct transport from Talisay, but you can get a bus from Tagaytay to Cuenca. Once at Cuenca, take a tricycle or jeepney 5km north to **Siete**, where all climbers must register at the town hall. The trail to the summit starts behind from the little sari-sari shop known as the "mountaineer's store".

Quezon and Marinduque

Quezon (pronounced "kezz-on") **province** doesn't see many tourists. The south of the province serves mainly as a staging post on the road from Manila to the Bicol region, though it does have a nearby beach at **Sariaya** and two excellent climbs, **Mount Banahaw** and **Mount Cristobal**. On the south-eastern fringes of the province you can explore **Quezon National Park**, which has some fairly easy marked trails. If you happen to be here in mid-May, you can check out what is by far the biggest festival in the province, the **Pahiyas**, held in and around **Lucban**, not far from the very ordinary provincial capital, **Lucena**.

The peaceful heart-shaped island of **Marinduque**, 170km southeast of Manila in the Sibuyan Sea, is a quintessentially provincial place, with no renowned beaches (although some are good), no notable hotels and no nightlife. The island's charm as a destination lies precisely in its comparative lack of the sort of attractions that pull in today's worldly tourists. You can reach Marinduque by ferry from Lucena.

Lucena and around

LUCENA, a bustling trade entrepot with a revolutionary history and a popula-tion of almost 200,000, has few attractions. The tourism brochure for Quezon province lists only three sights worth seeing in Lucena, but even this is to stretch a point: the first is the Provincial Capitol Building, the second a metal statue of Manuel Quezon (the dapper second president of the Philippines) and the third Perez Park, which in reality is a ragged square of grass and concrete where teenage lovers gather after dark and pop music blasts from public speakers.

One attraction the brochure doesn't mention is the **Museo ng Quezon** (Mon–Fri 10am–4pm; free though a donation is expected), a small repository of the former president's personal belongings, including clothing and books. It's inside the Provincial Capitol Building at the eastern end of Quezon Avenue. There's also a fine, wide beach and a handful of resorts on the coast to the south of the town of **Sariaya**, 10km southwest of Lucena. Any jeepney from Lucena's Capitol Building marked for Bignay or Sariaya will get you there, though if the jeepney isn't going to the beach itself you'll be let off nearby in the barangay of **Marazapan**, in which case you can take a tricycle the rest of the way.

Practicalities

JAM Transit, Jac Liner and Tritran all have **buses** leaving for Lucena from Pasay in Manila (on Taft Avenue near the Gil Puyat LRT station). The fare is P140 and the trip takes about four hours. The **bus station** in Lucena, called Grand Central, is on the northern edge of the city on Diversion Road. Jeepneys take arriving passengers to Quezon Avenue, the main thoroughfare. Buses leave Grand Central every hour for the trip south through Bicol (to Daet, Naga and Legaspi) and also for the short hop to **Dalahican**, where you can catch a ferry to Marinduque (see p.162). Grand Central is also the place to find buses for Atimonan and Quezon National Park, and for Lucban. The run-down **train**

station is next to the Provincial Capitol Building. Trains do come and go to Manila, but the service is poor with one or two trips a day at the most, and also uncomfortable.

The **Quezon Tourism Association** has an office in the Provincial Capitol Building (☏042/373 5740) where you can pick up a list of hotels and resorts in the city and around. **Accommodation** in Lucena is limited: you can stay either at the modern *House of Halina* in Gomez Street (☏042/373 3681; ❹), which also has a restaurant, or the *Queen Margarette Hotel* in Diversion Road, five minutes' drive east of the city in the Domoit suburb (☏042/710 6218; ❸). The best **place to eat** in Lucena is *Tang's*, a dark, cavernous Chinese restaurant with whirring ceiling fans, right opposite Lucena Cathedral, the pretty whitewashed Spanish building midway along Quezon Avenue. The menu is extensive, with a good choice of vegetarian dishes, and the food is inexpensive: a meal for two with drinks will only cost P250–300.

Lucban

Quezon province's major tourist draw is the **Pahiyas festival**, held every year on May 15 in **LUCBAN**, at the foot of Mount Banahaw, 26km north of Lucena. Lucban is a quiet farming town whose only claim to fame, apart from the festival, is that Apolinario de la Cruz, a crusader for religious freedom, lived here in the early nineteenth century. The colonizing Spaniards refused the young Apolinario permission to enter their seminaries to study, so he founded a religious society of Filipinos and fought bigotry under the *nom de guerre* Hermano Pule. When he was executed for treason and sedition in 1841, the Spaniards hung his head on a pole outside his house. His hands and feet were displayed gruesomely at the four corners of Lucban.

The Pahiyas started life as a thanksgiving festival for a good harvest, with the usual prosaic offerings of fruit and veg. But when the church got too small to

△ Harvesting rice in Quezon

hold the produce, people started stacking food outside their houses. Later they used it to decorate their houses. These days, every May, the town is transformed from sleepy hollow into something from a fairy tale, the houses decorated in the most imaginative way with fruit, vegetables and brightly coloured *kiping* (rice paper), which is formed into enormous chandeliers that cascade like flames from the eves. There is good reason for this creativity: every year the winner of the best-decorated house wins a **cash prize**. And every year the winning household is blessed for twelve months by San Isidore, whose pious image dangles from the rear-view mirrors of a thousand smoke-belching public tricycles. The organizers regularly change the route the judges walk, so different households can participate.

The festival starts with a solemn Mass at dawn and goes on well into the night, with much drinking of liquor and dancing in the streets. There is a parade, a beauty contest, a marching band and a *carabao* parade, in which the enormous water buffalo, more used to rice fields and mudholes, are led through the streets in outrageous costumes. It's open-house for visitors during Pahiyas, and everyone is especially honoured to have foreigners at their table.

From Lucena there are local buses and jeepneys to Lucban. **From Manila**, you could either travel via Lucena or take a bus to San Pablo (see p.138) or Santa Cruz (see p.139) in Laguna province, where you can change for a local bus to Lucban. There is no accommodation in Lucban, and there are just a few **restaurants** around the plaza and the road leading south off it, mostly utilitarian canteens selling local specialities such as *longganisa* and *pancit habab*, a type of fried noodle with vegetables. During the fiesta, however, there's food everywhere, served from carts in the street and from temporary stalls outside the church and near the marketplace.

Mount Banahaw and Mount Cristobal

Northwest of Lucena, the town of **Dolores** is the starting point for treks up **Mount Banahaw** and **Mount Cristobal**, which lie either side of the town. There are JAM Transit buses to Dolores from Pasay in Manila and Lucena and local buses from Batangas City, San Pablo and Los Baños.

Considered sacred, 2188-metre Mount Banahaw has spawned a vast number of legends and superstitions: one says that every time a foreigner sets foot on the mountain it will rain. Every Easter thousands of pilgrims climb Mount Banahaw in the belief that bathing in its waterfalls will cure their ailments. This isn't a good time to visit – you're likely to find yourself in a queue to reach the top. Pilgrims include members of a number of sects, who dress in religious garb and claim the mountain imbues them with supernatural and psychic power. Others believe this is the New Jerusalem and that Christ set foot here. There are also those who say Banahaw's crater makes a perfect landing pad for UFOs and hence is the site of a number of alien abductions.

Aliens or not, Banahaw is a challenging but rewarding climb, its slopes thick with jungle and with panoramic views of the surrounding country from the crater rim. Treat this mountain seriously because although the trail looks wide and well trodden early on, it soon peters out into inhospitable rainforest – even experienced climbers allow three days to reach the summit and get back down and a crater descent should only be attempted by expert climbers. To get to the start of the trail from Dolores, take a jeepney or tricycle to the barangay of **Kinabuyahan**. You will need to hire a **guide** at the barangay hall and sign the logbook before proceeding. If you haven't time to reach the summit, you might prefer to trek to **Kristalino Falls** (Crystalline Falls) and back, which can be done in a day. One and a half hours further on is a second waterfall, whose surroundings make an ideal **campsite**.

Mount Cristobal

Mount Cristobal is known as the Devil's Mountain because of the evil spirits who are said to live there and exert strange powers over climbers. It takes up to six hours of serious trekking along an awkward trail to reach the summit, so the climb isn't recommended for beginners or unaccompanied climbers. You can ask about guides at the barangay hall in Dolores, opposite the PNB (Philippine National Bank) in the plaza. It's impossible to make it up the mountain and back again in a day, so you'll have to take a tent and spend the night either at the crater or – in the rainy season, when the crater becomes a lagoon – on the rim.

Quezon National Park

Quezon National Park, less than two hours east of Lucena by road near the town of **Atimonan**, is off the well-beaten trail, far from the picture-postcard beaches of the Visayas and too distant from Manila to make it a viable weekend trip. Though relatively small, just ten square kilometres, the park is so dense with flora and fauna that you have a good chance of seeing anything and everything from giant monitor lizards to monkeys, deer and wild pigs. This is also home to the *kalaw*, a bird known as the clock of the mountains because it cries out at around noon every day. A paved trail leads to the highest point, 366m above sea level, which has a viewing deck from where you can see both sides of the Bicol peninsula. The walk to the summit takes about two hours. There are also numerous **caves** in the park that can be explored by experienced climbers with guides and the right equipment. Enquire about **guides** at the Quezon Tourism Association in Lucena (see p.159) or at the Parks and Game Warden's office, which is just inside the park boundary. There's no accommodation or restaurants in the park, though you can **camp** overnight with a permit from the warden (P50).

The **entrance** to the park is on the Maharlika Highway, which runs from Lucena to Atimonan. The winding approach road to the park, known locally as *bituka ng manok* (chicken's intestine), is a challenge for buses. From Lucena's Grand Central station, you can get any bus heading east through Bicol (to Daet, for instance) or an Atimonan-bound bus, as all these vehicles pass the park entrance.

Marinduque

For all its geographical closeness to Manila, the island of **Marinduque** (pronounced "mar-in-DOO-kay") might as well be a world away. Most of the 200,000 residents lead a marginal life of subsistence coconut farming and fishing, many dreaming of a better life in the big city. To put it in sobering perspective, around 3.4 million *magniniyog* – small-time coconut farmers – in the Philippines are said to live on an annual income of P2000. When the Canadian-owned mining company Marcopper started operations here in 1968 many thought it was the dawn of a new era for the island; residents got jobs and saw their lifestyles improve. Sadly, the dream ended in disaster and recrimination (see box on p.169).

Marinduque is a marvellous island to tour at leisure, working your way slowly around the coastal road to the pretty beaches south of **Boac**, then across the island to **Torrijos** and **Poctoy White Beach**, where you can live cheaply in simple huts in the shadow of majestic **Mount Malinding**. There's some good island-hopping around Marinduque too, with beaches and coves to explore around the Tres Reyes Islands off the southwest coast and the Santa Cruz Islands off the northwest coast. For a feel of life on Marinduque, read James Hamilton-Paterson's *Playing With Water: Passion and Solitude on a Philippine Island* (see p.523).

Marinduque is also known for its **Moriones festival**, an animated Easter tradition featuring masked men dressed like Roman soldiers (see box on p.164).

Island practicalities

Marinduque has become harder to reach since Asian Spirit stopped flying there recently; check to see if these flights have resumed. The long journey to Marinduque from Manila by **bus and ferry** starts at one of the southbound bus terminals in Manila, where buses depart for the port of **Dalahican** on the outskirts of Lucena (3hr). Some of these buses may say they are going to Lucena, but most also pass through Dalahican; ask if you're in doubt. Ferries sail from here to **Balanacan** on the north coast of Marinduque (P140). Blue Magic Ferries (℡042/710 4168) runs two boats a day between Dalahican and Balanacan; Montenegro Shipping Lines (℡042/373 7084) has four trips daily (P140). Be prepared to wait in Dalahican because departure times do change, particularly in inclement weather. From Balanacan it's easy to get a jeepney south to Boac via Mogpog, and beyond to Gasan and Buenavista. There are also boats from **Pinamalayan** on Mindoro to Balanacan.

Transport on the island is limited to jeepneys, tricycles for shorter distances and small boats for island-hopping. It is possible to make the trip in two days, but four or five would be more comfortable. Be prepared for a lack of reliable information regarding destinations and methods of getting around. There are regular jeepneys between some communities, but if you miss the last one (the service usually stops around 4pm) you can easily find yourself stranded.

It is possible to circumnavigate the island by road, stopping off at small resorts along the way. A typical itinerary would see you moving **anti-clockwise** from **Boac**, the provincial capital, to **Gasan**, then to **Poctoy White Beach** (via **Buenavista**), then on to **Santa Cruz** and finally back to Boac. You can do the trip in the opposite direction, but the jeepneys are less regular. If you do travel around Marinduque, make sure you have ample water and food, just in case. Keep a good supply of small notes and coins for jeepney fares: the fare from one point to the next is in the P10–20 range and it's unlikely that anyone will be able to change anything bigger than a P100 note.

Take pesos to Marinduque because it can be difficult to change dollars, and there's absolutely no chance of changing any other currency or travellers' cheques. If you have to change dollars, try the Philippine National Bank, Allied Bank or Land Bank, all in Boac. There is a telegram station and a small **post office** in Boac, while the telephone company Piltel has a **phone office** near the plaza for long-distance calls. Mobile telephones work in some parts of Marinduque, but there is no Internet access.

Boac

BOAC ("bow-ak") is an orderly, compact town with neat streets and low-rise buildings laid out around a central plaza. On top of the hill on the town's north side, a ten-minute walk from the plaza, is an atmospheric old Spanish–Gothic **cathedral** (daily 6am–9pm; free). Built in 1666 in honour of the Blessed Virgin of Immediate Succour, the cathedral was also used in its early days as a refuge from pirate attacks. Most of the original main structure, including the red-brick

Moriones festival

The **Moriones festival** celebrates the life of Longinus, the Roman soldier who pierced Christ's side during the Crucifixion. Blood from the wound spattered Longinus' blind eye, which was immediately healed. Converted on the spot, he later attested to the Resurrection and, refusing to recant, was executed. The Marinduqueyo version is colourful and bizarre, involving fanciful masked figures dressed as centurions chasing Longinus around town and through nearby fields. Thrice he is caught and thrice he escapes; the fourth time he is captured and led to his public beheading. The legend itself is old, but this version isn't. The festival was introduced by a Jesuit in the nineteenth century, since when it has been given the inimitable Filipino treatment. You're just as likely to see participants dressed as Madonna, Miss Piggy and Batman running through town as you are Roman soldiers.

Several Moriones pageants are staged in Marinduque during **Holy Week**, with extra events added in recent years for the benefit of tourists. The major Moriones festival is in **Boac**, although other towns have their own, smaller versions, including Santa Cruz and Mogpog. This timetable is based on the Boac Moriones.

Palm Sunday Early morning procession through the streets followed by blessing of the palms at Boac cathedral.

Holy Monday to Black Saturday The Moriones participants, dressed in costumes and masks, begin to roam the streets.

Holy Wednesday & Good Friday A procession takes place at 5pm of religious icons in their *carrozas* (silver and tin-plated carriages).

Maundy Thursday The religious re-enactment of Christ's washing of the apostles' feet takes place at 4pm in Boac cathedral. The Sinaklo, or passion play, is re-enacted at 8pm on the banks of the Boac River on the west side of town. The drama lasts several hours.

Good Friday The Way of the Cross, commemorating Christ's last walk, commences from the Boac River, finishing at the Boac cemetery where "Christ" is placed upon the cross. This is not an actual crucifixion with real nails, although there are said to be some in Mogpog at around noon. Flagellants beat their backs hard enough to draw blood and when they have finished gather at the river to wash away their sins. At 5pm the Santo Entierro procession winds its way slowly from Boac cathedral, through the streets, and back to the cathedral, with all the saints on display.

Black Saturday The highlight of the Moriones festival, with parades throughout the day culminating in the beheading of Longinus in the evening, usually at around 10pm. It is repeated at 10am on Easter Sunday morning.

Easter Sunday The last day of the festival, the celebrations starting at 4am, with every town on the island acting out the Resurrection and the subsequent meeting between Mary and Christ. An angel (played by a child) is lowered from an arch and removes Mary's veil of mourning, and the choir sings hallelujah.

facade and the belfry, is well preserved and there's a small, pleasant garden outside. The vast interior needs funds for renovation and the vestry has become home to a colony of bats, but there's a sedate beauty and worn refinement about the place that gives a tangible sense of history. Look out above the main doors for a stone niche containing a statue of the Blessed Virgin, enshrined here in 1792. Devotees say it is the most miraculous statue in the country and tell of blind people who have regained their sight after praying fervently underneath it day and night. The quaint streets behind the cathedral are full of typical Filipino *bahay ng buto* (wooden houses), the windows boasting carved wooden shutters instead of glass, and the balconies exploding with bougainvillea and frangipani. Many of these houses were built in the nineteenth century and are now a photogenic, if faded, reminder of a style of architecture that is rapidly disappearing.

The only other tourist spot in town is the small **Marinduque Museum** on the plaza (Mon–Sat 8am–noon, 1–5pm; free). The museum's exhibits are limited, but the displays that chart Marinduque's history help you get a handle on the island's turbulent past. The plaza itself is a good central landmark, although Boac is so tiny it's hard to get lost. During the war against the Spanish colonizers the plaza was used as an execution site for revolutionaries. Today it is used for everything from political rallies and religious gatherings to high-school graduations and beauty contests.

△ Moriones festival, Marinduque

Accommodation and eating

The best **accommodation** in Boac is the new *Tahanan sa Isok* (℡042/332 1231; ❶ with fan, ❹ a/c), a white building in Canovas Street on the eastern edge of town, with en-suite rooms. The hotel also has a café, a lovely garden restaurant, and is about the only good place to get **tourist information**. In the shadow of the cathedral, the estimable *Boac Hotel* (℡042/332 2065, 332 1121 or 311 1096; ❷) has boxy singles and doubles with fan, toilet and shower. On the south side of town in an area known as Mercado is the splendidly named *Happy Bunny's Lodging House* (℡042/332 2040; ❶), where there are three double rooms with toilet and shower. Another option is to stay in Mogpog (see p.168) – it's easy enough to shuttle between there and Boac by jeepney – or in one of the resorts south of Boac.

The *Boac Hotel* has a coffee shop serving noodles and bread. The *BFC Restaurant* opposite the northern side of the market in Magsaysay Street is clean and quiet, with double beef *mami* (a type of noodle soup) for P30 and fried chicken for P40. There is no menu at *Tahanan sa Isok* in Canovas Street, but the hospitality-industry students who learn their trade here can rustle up something simple such as chicken *adobo* with steamed rice. A good dinner with a few beers will cost less than P150. The *Kusina sa Plaza* overlooking the plaza on Meralco Street is a typical Filipino eating place, with *pancit*, stews and some European-style pasta.

Boac to Buenavista

The west coast from Boac south to Gasan and a little beyond boasts a number of **resorts**. The beach here doesn't have white sand, but does offer fine views of the sunset and across the sea towards Mindoro in the distance. These resorts are often full for the Moriones festival, but at any other time you might find you are the only guest. During the low season (June–Dec) many put up the shutters. Continuing south from Gasan takes you to the sleepy town of **Buenavista**, where the road swings east across the hills to Torrijos and the beautiful beach at Poctoy. Jeepneys heading south along the coast road from Boac often terminate in Buenavista, so if you want to continue to Torrijos you'll have to wait here for an onward jeepney.

The beautiful **Tres Reyes Islands – Baltazar**, **Melchor** and **Gaspar** after the Biblical Three Kings, although the locals also refer to them as Polo, Manya and Pangikol – lie a few kilometres off this stretch of the coast. There is some good scuba diving here and, on the far side of Gaspar Island, a nice white beach with good coral for snorkelling. In 1981, a sunken galleon was found 40m under-water buried deep in sand between the waters of Gaspar and the mainland. The galleon yielded millions of pesos' worth of artefacts and treasures, mostly porcelain jars and plates, some of which are now on display at the National Museum in Manila. The only village is a small fishing community on the eastern tip of Gaspar Island, but there's no formal accommodation. Getting to any of the islands takes about thirty minutes from Marinduque. Many of the resorts can arrange a boat for you, or you can ask around among the fishermen in Buenavista.

The resorts

A&A Resort ℡042/382 3317. One of the first resorts south of Boac, *A&A* stands on an average stretch of beach and has a choice of a/c and fan rooms. The restaurant serves simple home-cooking and though service is often slow, it's also very friendly. ❷

Aussie-Pom Guest House About 4km from Boac ℡042/382 1148. Simple bamboo cottages on the beach, each big enough for two. The restaurant serves good grilled seafood, native dishes such as *adobo* and cold beer. ❶

The Blue Sea Resort 6km south of Boac

☎042/3832 1334. Fan or a/c rooms in concrete cottages on the beach. ❷

Club Marinduque A few kilometres south of Gasan near the barrio of Pingan ☎042/333 7116, 02/729 4486 or 02/834 1431, ⓦwww.clubmarinduque.com. The a/c rooms are spacious and there's a nice swimming pool. Finding it is no problem: take a southbound jeepney from Boac and ask the driver to let you off at the gated entrance. ❹–❺

🏃 **Katala Beach Resort & Restaurant** 3km south of Gasan, approximately 45min by jeepney from Boac ☎042/333 7117. This modern concrete place lacks the rustic charm of the resorts closer to Boac, but does have spick-and-span fan and a/c rooms with balconies at a very reasonable rate. The restaurant, on the water's edge, has a good range of food and drink. There's a boat you

can rent for day-trips (the resort is closer to the Tres Reyes Islands than other resorts) and the owners can also arrange scuba diving. ❸

Sea View Hotel Next to the *Blue Sea Resort*. ☎042/382 1239. Quiet place offering a handful of cottages with toilet and shower. There are occasional dances on Friday night where you can let your hair down with the locals. ❷

Sunset Garden Resort About 5min south of the airport and 2km north of Gasan in Pangi barrio ☎042/342 1004. Pleasant cottages on the beach. Run by a German and his Filipino wife, and set in a large garden. There's a restaurant and bar, and they offer scuba diving (from US$40 for two dives), boat rental and a tennis court. If you want three good meals a day, add P420. ❸

Buenavista

BUENAVISTA is described in the Marinduque local government tourist brochure as "buzzing with activity as air-conditioned tourist buses become familiar sights". Don't believe a word of it. Buenavista is a sleepy community where the arrival of even a solitary tourist is such a significant event that it soon results in the gathering of an inquisitive and excitable crowd. The town is built around a crossroads, with a jetty on one side and a number of sari-sari stores, and not much else, on the other.

The only **accommodation** in the area is at the *Susanna Hot Spring Resort*, 2km east out of Buenavista (☎042/332 1997; ❷), with very basic, somewhat tatty huts and a small thermal swimming pool. There is no food or drink, so make sure you bring your own; there are no restaurants in Buenavista itself, though you can buy instant noodles at the canteen near the crossroads or snacks from one of the stores. A tricycle ride to the resort from Buenavista costs from P20. If you're continuing east from the resort, make sure you arrange for the driver to collect you on the morning of your departure, so you can get back to Buenavista in time to get a comfortable seat on the jeepney.

Torrijos

The journey from Buenavista east to Torrijos is the best part of the round-island trip, the road winding precariously upwards through the foothills of Mount Malindig (1157m) before reaching a clutch of pretty little barrios where the people see few visitors and are extraordinarily friendly. The descent is equally exciting as the road snakes down to the southeast of the island. Jeepneys on this route are limited, however, and tend to leave early, so make sure you are in Buenavista by 8am at the latest.

In the barangay of Pulang Lupa, just before you reach Torrijos, look out for the **Battle of Pulang Lupa** marker, on the site of the bloody conflict between the Marinduque Revolutionary Forces and the Americans on July 31, 1900 (the first major battle won by Filipinos against Uncle Sam). However, as monuments go this has to be one of the most unspectacular ever erected, a squat stone slab that you risk missing if you blink. **Torrijos** itself is an orderly and friendly little town of painted wooden houses, but it has no beaches, accommodation or restaurants, though there are a number of sari-sari stores.

If you take a tricycle 2km to **Poctoy** you can stay at Poctoy White Beach, where there are rudimentary **huts** (❶) with no fan, no water and an outside toilet. You will have to collect your own water from the standpipe near the beach. Linda, the proprietor, can cook simple dishes and serves cold beer at her nearby house, and also has a small store where you can buy essentials. The beach is acceptable if not spectacular, but the views across the bay to Mount Malindig are.

To move on from Poctoy White Beach, take a tricycle back into Torrijos and board a jeepney at the crossroads for Santa Cruz. The jeepneys do pass Poctoy White Beach, but by the time they get there are so crowded that you won't get on, short of clinging perilously to the roof.

Santa Cruz and around

You can base yourself in the northeast at **SANTA CRUZ** for a day or two while you explore the area around it. The town is unmemorable, the only sights a whitewashed Spanish-era church and the dilapidated wooden convent next to it. The narrow streets in the town centre are choked with tricycles and jeepneys from dawn to dusk, so be prepared for noise if you stay here. From the town centre it's a bumpy thirty-minute tricycle ride to the **Bathala Caves**, but worth the pain. There are seven caves; four are accessible and one contains human bones believed to be the remains of World War II soldiers. You've a good chance of seeing pythons here, along with the thousands of bats that call the caves home. The caves are privately owned and you have to pay the caretaker P100 for a guided tour. There is a natural pool for cooling off after the rigours of the journey.

Rico's Lodging House (☎042/321 1085; ❶), opposite the town hall and the Philippine National Bank, is your only chance of a bed for the night, with very basic **rooms** with toilet and shower. The dingy coffee shop downstairs serves noodles, sandwiches and chicken.

There are no tourist facilities on Maniuaya, Mompong and Polo, collectively known as the **Santa Cruz Islands**, but there are a number of white sand beaches that are good for snorkelling. Access to the islands is by boat (around P300 one-way) from **Buyabod**, 10km southeast of Santa Cruz and accessible by tricycle or jeepney. Another interesting if rather depressing trip from Santa Cruz is to the ghostly site of the vast mine, now closed, that was responsible for one of the Philippines' most infamous environmental disasters (see box opposite). The journey takes about thirty minutes and costs around P50 there and back.

Mogpog

Attractive little **MOGPOG** is a hillside town a few kilometres north of Boac, which holds its own, smaller version of the Moriones festival during Holy Week. From here you can take a tricycle to **Tarug Caves**, actually one enormous cave with three chambers, set inside a 300-metre-tall limestone spire that is barely 3m wide at the top. Your reward for climbing to the top is a panoramic view of the Bondoc peninsula to the east and the Tablas Strait to the west. Another trip to consider is to **Paadjao Falls**, a series of gently cascading falls with a large pool at the bottom where you can swim.

The only **place to stay** is the pleasant colonial-style *Hilltop Hotel* (☎042/332 3074; ❸ ❹), a homestay belonging to the Garcia family. If you arrive at Balanacan you can hire a tricycle to take you to the *Hilltop* for P50. All the tricycle drivers know how to reach it – it's up a driveway on the right-hand side of the main road, less than 1km before you reach Mogpog from the north.

Marinduque mining disaster

It was in 1956 that Canadian prospectors found extensive deposits known as hydro-thermal sulphides in the northeast of Marinduque, outside Santa Cruz. These proved to contain mineable quantities of copper, and in 1968 open-pit mining began on the slopes of **Mount Tapian**, in the island's north-central zone. By then the Marcopper Mining Corporation had been formed, with the Philippine government owning sixty percent and Placer Dome Inc. of Vancouver owning the rest. A steady thirty thousand tonnes of ore were mined 365 days a year, operations going on day and night. The effects of the Marcopper operation were dramatic. Santa Cruz became a mini-boomtown, overtaking Boac in size as workers flooded in. A satellite township formed in the hills at Tapian, with a golf course, swimming pool and plush villas for foreign executives.

But on March 24, 1996, disaster struck. A huge jet of mine tailings burst into the headwaters of the Boac River from a little-known drainage tunnel that led to the bottom of a pit at Tapian. This pit had been used as a dump for years and held upward of 20 million cubic metres of slurry. The greyish mass surged downstream, killing the Boac River as it went and wiping out the livelihood of 1104 families. Techni-cians were not able to stop the leak until 2.5 million tons had escaped and most of the Boac River was dead. The disaster was reported worldwide and became a cause célèbre for environmentalists.

Placer Dome has since spent an estimated US$71 million cleaning up the Boac River, but its plan to dispose of the remaining waste in coral-rich Calancan Bay is still a source of debate on the island. The company no longer has shares in Marcopper, which is under new ownership who are looking for ways to rehabilitate the mine, a move Marinduqueños universally oppose. The government supports plans to reopen the mine, but local opposition has delayed any resumption of work. Tribal groups and NGOs have taken their case to the courts, arguing that according to the Constitution mining in the Philippines should not be open to foreign investment.

There are spacious double fan rooms and more expensive double air-con rooms. The communal balcony, with views over the hinterland, is perfect for relaxing with a cup of coffee or a cold drink. Try to call in advance to tell the owners of your arrival.

Bicol

Known throughout the Philippines as an area of great natural beauty, **Bicol** ("bee-col") comprises the mainland provinces of Camarines Norte, Camarines Sur, Albay and Sorsogon, and the island provinces of Catanduanes and Masbate. The local people call Bicol *magayon* (beautiful) and retell legends of a fertile land of brave people and the warrior-heroes Baltog and Handyong, who battled fierce monsters and powerful beings and made the region prosperous. This is also an area rich in **adventure tourism** possibilities, with surfing in Camarines Norte, volcano-climbing in Albay and whale-shark-watching in Sorsogon. Such is the variety of scenery and activity in Bicol that word is at last getting around, and the region is showing signs of becoming the destination it deserves to be. Another bonus is that Bicolano **cuisine** is some of the best in the country, characterized by the use of chillies (unusual in the Philippines) and coconut milk.

The downside to the region is that during the rainy season it is prone to typhoons, which tend to approach from the Pacific and make landfall in this area. Typhoon Durian, which slammed into the Philippines in late November 2006, killed over a thousand people when high winds and floods triggered devastating landslides in central Albay province.

The first province you reach if you head south from Manila is Camarines Norte, with its capital **Daet**. The National Highway meanders south from here to Camarines Sur through **Naga**, **Iriga** and **Legaspi**. The last of these is the jumping-off point for **Mount Mayon**, one of the nation's great icons, whose almost symmetrical cone broods over the city. It's one of three active volcanoes in the Bicol region, and, along with a number of inactive volcanoes, forms part of the **Bicol Volcanic Chain**, which also comprises Labo, Isarog, Iriga, Malinao and Bulusan. The coast to the east of Legaspi has some exceptional and very untouristy **beaches**, while islands such as **Cagaray** and **Rapu-Rapu** off the eastern Bicol coast are so far off the beaten track that they remain untouched by modern development and are home to no one except fisherfolk and farmers. The beautiful **Caramoan peninsula** has some of the best beaches in the country, with islands nearby you can island-hop to by banca and spend the night. The coast to the north of Naga, particularly around **San Miguel Bay**, also has some good beaches and very cheap accommodation; you can grab yourself a cottage on the shore for a few hundred pesos a week. Another natural wonder to make time for is **Lake Buhi** in Albay, close to the dormant volcanoes Mount Malimas and Mount Iriga, both of which can be climbed.

Continuing further south, you reach the coastal town of **Sorsogon**, a good place to base yourself for day-trips up and down the coast. The most popular of these is the fifty-kilometre ride west to the backwater of **Donsol**, which has seen an increase in tourism recently because of the number of plankton-eating whale sharks that congregate here.

The island provinces of **Catanduanes** and **Masbate** add more variety to Bicol's heady mix. Catanduanes, known as the "land of the howling winds" because of the typhoons that roar in from the Pacific, has long ribbons of sand colonized during the wet season by surfers. Masbate is the Philippines' wild east, where cattle are raised and the biggest tourist draw is the annual rodeo in May.

The only **airports** in Bicol served by regular flights from Manila are Virac in Catanduanes, Naga in Camarines Sur and Legaspi in Albay, all of which are served by Philippine Airlines, Air Philippines or Asian Spirit. Philtranco and BLTB have **buses** that run up and down the National Highway daily, taking you to most major jumping-off points in the area. BLTB even has services that run all the way to Sorsogon from Manila, but the journey is a long one: be prepared to sweat it out for the best part of twenty hours. Many choose to take a bus that leaves Manila in the evening and travels overnight when the roads are quieter, arriving in Daet very early the next day and in Legaspi around dawn. Philtranco has a service that goes all the way from Manila to Davao, using ferries where it has to. It runs through Daet, Naga and Legaspi and on to Matnog, where it boards the ferry for Samar. Some of the larger bus companies serving the region, notably Philtranco, have introduced first-class buses; fares are slightly higher, but there's more room, the a/c works and there's likely to be an onboard toilet. The **train** runs twice a day from Manila to Legaspi. There are **ferries**

The New People's Army

Dire warnings circulate in Manila about personal security in Bicol, a result of the area's reputation as a lair for guerrillas belonging to the **New People's Army** (NPA), an avowedly Maoist group formed in December 1969 with the aim of overthrowing the government through protracted guerrilla warfare. There's no doubt that the Bicol region, with its almost impenetrable rainforest and scattered rural barrios, is an area of occasional NPA activity. But it's worth remembering that the NPA itself is a weakened force, more concerned with extorting revolutionary taxes from farmers and engaging in urban terrorism against corrupt politicians and drug traffickers than making life difficult for tourists. This does not mean the threat doesn't exist, only that it's generally not great enough to change your travel plans.

The NPA – Bagong Hukbong ng Bayan in Tagalog – is the armed wing of the Communist Party of the Philippines (CPP), headed by the wily old campaigner José Maria Sison, who lives in exile in the Netherlands. Both factions reached their zenith in the 1970s when they were at the forefront of the campaign to remove Ferdinand Marcos from power. Since then things have not gone well for either the NPA or the CPP. The NPA is in disarray because of various internecine battles, never mind a lack of money and successful government operations against it during the 1990s. And in 2002 the CPP was designated a foreign terrorist organization by the US State Department, prompting the Dutch government to freeze its assets and stop payment of Sison's housing and health benefits. Sison is only being allowed to remain in the Netherlands because the Dutch government believes he will face the death penalty if extradited.

Because of these setbacks the strength of the NPA has dropped from an estimated 40,000 members during the 1970s to fewer than 8000 today. In recent times their activities have been largely limited to extortion, sabotage attacks on power plants or mobile phone installations, and occasional revenge killings against former guerillas who have deserted. Lives have been lost in these exchanges, and while rural civilians do become embroiled in the violence, accidentally or otherwise, the NPA has not specifically targeted tourists.

As for Bicol, it is still talked about as a stronghold, but given the diminished strength of the NPA and its lack of capital, that's probably too emotive a word. One thing that does seem certain is that enigmatic CPP spokesman Gregoria "Ka Roger" Rosales is hiding somewhere on the peninsula. When the military sent extra troops there in 2002 to look for him they drew a blank. He later called journalists on his mobile phone, urging the government to "catch me if you can".

across the Bernardino Strait between Samar in the Visayas and Matnog in Sorsogon province.

Daet and around

DAET, a commercial centre 200km southeast of Manila, is overrun with tricycles and there's little here to detain you, but it's a good place to bed down for the night before setting out to explore the rest of the province of Camarines Norte. The area around Daet is rich in natural attractions and has undeservedly been largely overlooked as a tourist destination. If it's unspoiled beaches you are after, the coastline east of Daet has more than its fair share, while to the south, there are desert islands to explore in San Miguel Bay.

The town's busy little central plaza is a popular meeting place in the evenings, with residents gathering to buy snacks from hawkers or do some roller-skating in the small rink. One block north is the 1950s Provincial Capitol building. In front of it is Kalayaan Park (Freedom Park) with a small boating lake and the tallest statue of **José Rizal** outside Manila. Erected in 1899, this was the first monument to Rizal in the country and set the trend for thousands of others in town and barrio plazas across the archipelago. The Daet monument was built after a decree from General Emilio Aguinaldo, then President of the Revolutionary Government, that December 30, the anniversary of Rizal's martyrdom, would henceforth be a national holiday in the "Free Philippines". Rizal never visited Daet or the province of Camarines Norte, but the people are proud of the passion with which they honour him. Every year on Rizal Day, residents of Daet stage a one-hour **street play** commencing at the Capitol building, and re-enacting the life and times of Rizal from childhood to execution. More modestly, in the third week of June, there's a festival celebrating one of the area's most important agricultural products, the pineapple.

Practicalities

Buses arriving in Daet stop on the edge of the city on the National Highway, from where it's less than 2km into town; plenty of tricycles ply the route. The only **tourist office** is on the ground floor of the Provincial Capitol building, where staff can give you directions, bus details or a few old brochures, but not much else. For transport to destinations in the vicinity, there's a station on Pimentel Avenue, near the Shell petrol station two blocks south of Kalayaan Park.

For **food**, there are hole-in-the-wall canteens all over town selling various dishes for as little as P20. Opposite the *Mines Hotel* on the third floor of Vinzons Arcade in Vinzons Avenue, which runs through the heart of town, is a big, bright Chinese place called the *Ho-fun Garden*, which serves huge portions of fried rice, fried chicken, pork in black-bean sauce and sweet-and-sour fish. There's another Chinese restaurant, *Golden Palace*, one block east in Zabala Street.

Accommodation

Accommodation in Daet is basic, with only a handful of hotels in the city itself, all offering a similar choice of functional rooms. The best thing to do is head straight to Vinzons Avenue, where there are a number of hotels within walking distance of each other.

Dolor Hotel Vinzons Ave ☎054/721 2167. Spacious a/c en-suite rooms with hot water. Some of the rooms are used as offices, so there's a great deal of coming and going during the day, which can be irksome. Also features a coffee shop, small restaurant and Internet access. ❸–❹

Mines Hotel Vinzons Ave ☎054/721 2566. Small, adequate fan or a/c rooms in a slightly shabby building on the edge of town. The best rooms are the a/c doubles, which have their own fairly clean bathrooms. Most of the single fan rooms have shared toilets and showers. ❹

Sampaguita Tourist Inn Vinzons Ave ☎054/511 2221. Of the two *Sampaguita Tourist Inns* in Daet (the other is in J. Pimentel Ave), this one has the better location and marginally nicer rooms. There's a dreary café in the lobby serving sandwiches and noodles. ❸

Wiltan Hotel Vinzons Ave ☎054 721/2525. Another mediocre but affordable hotel on the incredibly noisy Vinzons Avenue strip, the *Wiltan* looks like it has seen better days, although the rooms are clean and orderly. The suites are worth considering if you have a bit more to spend – they have much more space, cable TV and fridges. ❹

Around Daet

One of the most pleasant surprises around Daet is **Bagasbas Beach**, 4km northeast of Daet and accessible by jeepney and bus from the station on Pimentel Avenue. The waves crash in from the Pacific and are sometimes big enough for **surfing**. In fact, the whole area of coast east of Daet has become something of a beatnik surfers' hangout. If you're interested in surfing, the best man to see in Bagasbas is Alvin Obsuan, owner of *Alvinos' Pizza and Surf Camp* (no phone; ❶, dorm beds P100), a small guesthouse, at the back of the beach on a road known as the Boulevard, with dorm rooms and a couple of private rooms. It also has a pleasant restaurant serving good pizza, sandwiches and French fries. Behind *Alvinos'* is *Kusina ni Angel* (Angel's Kitchen), a lovely, down-to-earth little native restaurant specializing in catch of the day (swordfish, tuna, lapu-lapu and dorado) and fresh shakes.

San Miguel Bay

To the southeast of Daet lies **San Miguel Bay**, which has little in the way of tourist infrastructure, but does have a number of quiet beaches and islands worth exploring. The best beaches, around the northwestern edge of the bay, are as good as anything the Visayas have to offer, and they're often deserted because few tourists make the trip. You can hire a banca (around P500 for a half-day) in the little mainland town of **Mercedes**, 8km east of Daet, to explore the islands. Jeepneys to Mercedes run from Pimentel Avenue in Daet, and take about half an hour (P32). To get to Mercedes from Naga (see below), you'll first have to get a bus to Daet.

The only **place to stay** is *Apuao Grande Island Resort* (☎054/721 1545; ❸), with its rustic cottages for up to four people, clean swimming pool and white sand beach. At low tide you can wade through ankle-deep water to explore the neighbouring islets of Canton Island and Little Apuao Island. The resort's cottages, made of wood and nipa, have simple bamboo beds, clean white linen and private showers. You can also book through Swagman Travel, which has a number of branches in tourist areas nationwide (☎02/523 8541 in Manila).

Naga and Mount Isarog

Centrally located in the province of Camarines Sur, **Naga** is one of the country's oldest cities, established in 1578 by Spanish conquistador Pedro de Chavez. Although there's not a great deal to see, the city is a clean and friendly place with a dash of metropolitan style, and makes a good place to spend the night before striking out for the **Mount Isarog National Park**, which is hard to beat for an authentic wilderness experience, offering some exhilarating trekking and climbing along rough trails. At the park's centre stands Mount Isarog, a dormant volcano whose steep slopes are cut by narrow rivers, creeks and gorges.

Naga

NAGA is a reasonably compact town centred on a main square, **Plaza Martinez**, which is surrounded by fast-food restaurants, convenience stores and pharmacies. The main drag, **Elias Angeles Street**, runs north to south; to the east, along Panganiban Drive, is the Naga River.

The town's main tourist draw is the annual **Peñafrancia festival**, celebrated on the third Saturday of September. The festival is preceded by a *novena*, nine days of prayer, in honour of the Madonna. On the ninth day, an image of the

Domingo Abella

Domingo Abella, whose monument stands in Naga's town plaza, was one of numerous unsung heroes in the fight for an independent Philippines, free from Spanish rule and the tyranny of the friars. The son of a rich landowner and businessman, he was born in 1872 in Naga, then known as Nueva Caceres. When the Katipunan, a revolutionary organization, raised the call for insurrection, he attended secret meetings and was active in recruiting Negritos from Mount Isarog to join the fight. After his activities became known to the Spanish authorities, he was arrested on charges of rebellion and planning to assassinate Spaniards in Naga. Along with other Bicolanos he was taken to Manila in chains on board the steamer *Isarog*, locked up and tortured in Fort Santiago.

His cause was not helped by the envy he inspired among his accusers. Taller than the average Filipino, he was an accomplished fencer, horseback rider and martial artist, and was often seen in the company of Naga's most beautiful women. Needless to say, he was sentenced to death. On January 4, 1897, together with his father who had been charged with harbouring him, he was executed by firing squad on the spot where José Rizal had been shot five days earlier.

Madonna is taken downriver in a barge to its shrine. The colourful evening procession consists of numerous boats, lit by thousands of candles. Naga can get very busy for the festival, which is known throughout the country, so this is the one time of year when you should try to book a hotel room in advance.

Practicalities

Buses to Naga arrive at the **Central Terminal** across the river to the south of the town centre; you'll have to take a tricycle from here. Philippine Airlines has five flights a week from Manila to **Naga Airport** (also known as Pili Airport), 12km out of town to the east, along Panganiban Drive. It's a rough trip into town by tricycle (P100), but incoming flights are all met by willing drivers with private cars who will ferry you to your hotel. Make sure you agree a rate first – they'll ask for P300, but you should be able to bargain them down to P200. Philippine Airlines has an office at 2/F Galleria de San Francisco, Peñafrancia Ave (℡054/473 2277). There's a jeepney terminal on Elias Angeles Street, next to Peñafrancia College, for jeepneys and FX taxis to Calabanga, Pili, Tabaco and Daet.

The **Naga City Visitors Center** is in the DOLE Building, City Hall Complex, J. Miranda Ave (Mon–Fri 8–11am & noon–4pm; ℡054/811 3961), 1km east of the Naga River to the east of the city centre. Staff have general information on bus and ferry services, and can help you find accommodation or guides for Mount Isarog. They also arrange walking tours and trips to the **Caramoan peninsula** (see p.176).

Naga has a number of cheap **Internet cafés**: NagaNet is in Shopper's Mall at the junction of General Luna Street and Prieto Street, while Internet Naga is on the north side of Plaza Rizal above *Dunkin' Donuts*. There's a branch of Metrobank on Plaza Martinez, while Equitable PCI is on the southern edge of town at the junction of Carceres Street and Elias Angeles Street. The **post office** is next to the Naga City Visitors Center.

Accommodation

Naga has an adequate range of budget and mid-range **places to stay**. During the Peñafrancia festival many places, particularly the budget ones, are fully booked by devotees and tourists, so plan ahead.

Aristocrat Hotel General Luna St ℡ 054/473 8832. A few minutes' walk south of the centre, this is a low-rise brown concrete building where options range from ordinary fan singles to a/c family rooms. A TV will set you back an extra P100 a day. There's also a coffee shop. ②–④

Crown Hotel & Restaurant Famous Plaza, Elias Angeles St corner P. Burgos St ℡ 054/473 8305. Low-rise hotel right in the noisy centre of Naga. The cheapest room is a spartan a/c single with cable TV, hot water and a fridge. There's a small bar and a coffee shop. ③

Grand Imperial Plaza P. Burgos St, a 2min walk west of Plaza Martinez ℡ 054/473 6534, ℻ 473 9003. This is Naga's idea of a posh hotel and, despite some eccentricities (such as bright purple bedsheets), it's good value and has a decent location close to the city centre. Rooms are spacious and have a/c, plastic furniture and two double beds. ⑤

Hotel Mirabella Magsaysay Ave, a 5min walk northwest of the cathedral ℡ 054/473 9537 or ℡ 02/810 8773. Very comfortable and well-run hotel with carpeted a/c rooms that all have hot showers and cable TV. They also have a bistro, poolside grill and swimming pool. ④

Lucky Fortune Hotel & Restaurant 27 Abella St ℡ 054/472 0324. On the western edge of the city, just north of the market. A good, modern hotel away from the din of the city centre, but within walking distance of shops and restaurants. The a/c singles have hot water and cable TV, while the big executive twins are worth a bit extra for the additional space. ③

Mirabella-Liboton Hotel Liboton St ℡ 054/473 3862. Whitewashed, low-rise establishment on the western edge of the city with clean a/c rooms ranging from standard singles to family suites. Coffee shop, laundry and bar. ③

Sampaguita Tourist Inn Panganiban Dr ℡ 054/473 8896. Central location a stone's throw southeast of Plaza Martinez. Rooms are acceptable, but nothing special; it's worth paying for one with a/c and a private shower and toilet, because the shared facilities are far from wonderful. ②–④

New Crown Hotel Elias Angeles St corner P. Burgos St ℡ 054/473 9730. Clean, comfortable, modern hotel with small but well-kept a/c singles, doubles and suites, plus a café, snack bar and lounge bar with occasional live jazz. A 3hr "wash-up" costs P350, ideal if you need somewhere to relax before continuing your journey. ③

Villa Caceres Hotel & Restaurant Magsaysay Ave ℡ 054/473 6530 to 6533. Modern hotel with carpeted a/c rooms ranging from a decent single to a pricey Presidential Suite. Facilities run the gamut: Internet access, restaurant, café, nightclub and swimming pool. ⑥

Eating

As in most Philippine towns and cities, you don't have to look far for **fast food** in Naga. There's a branch of *Jollibee* on P. Burgos Street, a *McDonald's* on General Luna Street and a *Shakey's* on Elias Angeles Street. Perhaps the best place for a low-cost blowout is *Oyster Villa* (close to *Shakey's*), where the menu consists largely of grilled fish and other seafood served with rice. Next to the *Sampaguita Tourist Inn* on Panganiban Drive is the Chinese fast-food canteen, *Wok's*. P. Burgos Street also has a number of restaurants, including *Geewan*, which serves Filipino dishes and some fiery Bicol specialities including a veggie version of Bicol Express, Café *Frederico* (Chinese) and *Bigg's* (steak and pasta). *Café Candice* is a quiet little place on General Luna Street that offers various European and local light meals.

Mount Isarog National Park

One of the Philippines' richest and least trampled areas, **Mount Isarog National Park** covers forty square kilometres in the heart of Camarines Sur, about 40km east of Naga. At its centre stands **Mount Isarog** (1966m), the highest forested peak in southern Luzon and part of the Bicol volcanic chain that also includes Mayon. Like Mayon, Isarog is active, although its last recorded eruption was in 1641.

The park is relatively easy to reach, but once on the lower slopes of the mountain you feel as if you have stepped through a portal into the Jurassic age. The jungle is thick and steamy, and the **flora and fauna** are among the most varied in the archipelago. Long-tailed macaque monkeys and monitor lizards are a pretty common sight, while with a little luck you may also spot shrew rats, reticulated pythons and rare birds such as the bleeding-heart pigeon, red-breasted pitta and blue-nape fantail. Reaching the summit takes two days of strenuous climbing. At the top are two craters, the lower of the pair containing a number of fumaroles from which streams of sulphurous gas pour.

A number of paths on Isarog's lower slopes lead to **waterfalls** such as Mina-Ati, Nabuntulan and Tumaguiti, all of which are surrounded by thick rainforest and have deep, cool pools for swimming. The easiest waterfall to reach is beautiful Malabsay, a powerful ribbon of water that plunges into a deep pool surrounded by forest greenery. There are also some hot springs, but these are harder to find than the waterfalls, hidden in thick jungle.

Practicalities

You need a **permit** (P220) to climb Isarog, which you can get at the **ranger station** in **Panicuasan**, the barangay at the park's entrance, or at the Mount Isarog Protected Area Extension Office, 35 Panganiban Dr in Naga (☎054/472 8018). To head up, you will also need to secure the services of a local **guide** in Naga (around P1000 a day; ask at the Naga City Visitors Center or at the ranger station). A good place in Naga to glean additional information about the climb is the Oragon Sunrise Outdoor Shop, 16 Dimasalang Street (just north of Metrobank), where you can rent basic equipment. It's also a meeting place for the local Hagahag Mountaineering Club.

To get to the park, take a **jeepney** from Abella Street in Naga to Panicuasan, a journey of 16km, from where it's a five-kilometre walk along a well-marked trail to the ranger station, Malabsay Waterfall and the entrance to the park proper. There's only one trail to the summit open to the public, and it's not hard to miss because it starts at the ranger station. Allow at least three days to reach the summit and return.

There are no jeepneys from Panicuasan back to Naga after 4pm, so keep an eye on the time. If you get stuck you'll have to pay to rent one privately, usually costing around P1000.

Caramoan Peninsula

The wild and sometimes windswept Caramoan peninsula, 50km to the east of Naga, presents more adventurous visitors with the opportunity to explore a virtually unknown paradise with some rugged, scenic countryside and terrific beaches and islands off the peninsula's east coast, many with rocky cliffs and blue-water coves that rival anything in the Visayas and Palawan. **Gota Beach**, a few kilometres from Caramoan Town, reachable on foot or by tricycle, can be busy with locals at weekends, but during the week you're almost guaranteed to have it to yourself; it's a lovely, golden-sand cove with crystal clear water and, sometimes, crashing waves. You can hire a banca from Bikal Wharf just outside Caramoan Town (all the tricycle drivers know it) for the twenty-minute trip to wonderful **Lahuy Island**, also known as Treasure Island. Lahuy has a fine stretch of seemingly endless white beach on one side and some scenic coves on the other. There's no accommodation, but it's possible to camp out for the night on the beach, as long as you make sure the boat will be back for you the following day. You can rent tents from the Kadlagan Outdoor Shop in Caramoan Town. Nearby is **Aguirangan Island**, which has a beautiful coral reef for snorkelling. Other beaches well worth striking out for include **Bichara Beach**, which has deep, clear water and stunning limestone cliffs, and **Bag-ing Beach**, a scenic crescent of white sand on a lagoon-like deserted bay. Both are north of Gota Beach.

Practicalities

There's very little in the way of reliable transport or **accommodation**, so be prepared to go with the flow out here. The best way to explore the area is to base yourself in Caramoan Town, where there are a few small guesthouses, and use jeepneys, tricycles and bancas to get around. The *Rex Tourism Inn* (❶) in Real Street has six monastic and faded fan rooms, while *Roa Pension House* (❸) in Sirangan Street is a little more plush, with reasonably spacious air-conditioned singles and doubles.

Caramoan Town can be reached by bus and jeepney from Naga and Pili, passing along the edge of the Mount Isarog National park (see p.175) with unforgettable views of Mount Isarog. From Naga and Pili you can also take a bus or jeepney to the small port of Sabang, from where bancas run east along the coast to Guijalo. From here it's a short hop by tricycle to Caramoan Town.

Iriga and around

Sixty kilometres south of Naga, **IRIGA** is a bustling provincial town of 82,000 souls lying in the shadow of **Mount Iriga**. It's a logical place to base yourself not only to climb the mountain – a trek that takes you through some wild countryside inhabited by tribal people – but also if you intend to explore the area around **Lake Buhi**, sited in a stunning location between volcanic peaks.

Iriga has some interesting colonial architecture and a few sorry-looking plazas and parks, but nothing in the way of tourist sights. The best view of the city is from **Calviro Hill**, behind the *Ibalon Hotel*, where locals once thought a deadly *aswang* (witch) lived. During World War II the Japanese Imperial Army built a garrison there and tortured and executed countless Iriguñeos who opposed their rule. It is now a grotto to Our Lady of Lourdes and a pilgrimage site for Catholics.

The major event of the year is a thanksgiving festival called **Tinagba**, also known as the Feast of Our Lady of Lourdes, celebrated on February 11. The word *tinagba* is derived from the Bicol word *tagba*, meaning "to gather the harvest and offer it to God". The festival starts at dawn with a solemn procession through the streets and a thanksgiving Mass. In the afternoon there's a colourful mardi-gras parade along the main street and in the evening local pop groups perform in the plaza.

Practicalities

Iriga straddles the busy National Highway (also known here as the J.P. Rizal Highway). The **Philtranco bus station** is on the highway just north of the centre; almost all buses on the Manila–Legaspi route also make a quick and convenient stop in front of the City Hall and the market. Local buses stop next to the Philtranco bus station. The **train station** is in the city centre, on the National Highway close to the small coliseum where events such as basketball and cockfighting are held. There's no tourist office, though the **Mayor's Office** in City Hall can help find accommodation and guides for Mount Iriga.

The best place to **stay** is the hacienda-style *Ibalon Hotel* on San Francisco Street opposite Rizal Park, two minutes' walk from City Hall (☏054 299 2352; ❺). The rooms haven't been renovated in some time, but are nevertheless acceptable, if a little spartan. The hotel also has its own restaurant, coffee shop and small discotheque that rarely sees any punters. Over on San Roque Street, on the opposite side of Rizal Park from the *Ibalon*, the *Parkview Hotel* (☎054 299 2405; ❹) is a concrete box overlooking a busy road, so ask for a room at the back. It's bleak from the outside and a little grubby inside, although bathrooms are clean and the water is sometimes hot.

For **food**, *Iggy's* in San Francisco Street serves very cheap rice dishes with chicken or pork kebabs, while the coffee shop at the *Ibalon Hotel* has a largely Filipino menu along with sandwiches and pizza. In J.P. Rizal Street there's a branch of the local fast-food chain *Bigg's* where you can get burgers and pasta; a few doors along is *D'Nadal's Bakery & Restaurant*, for cakes, fresh sandwiches and rice dishes.

Lake Buhi and Mount Iriga

Beautiful, mystical **Lake Buhi** sits 100m above sea level in a valley between two ancient volcanoes, Mayon's "little sisters" Malinao and Iriga. A romantic legend surrounding the creation of the lake speaks of a peaceful village where the people were so content they became profligate and abandoned their religious duties. When an old man showed up begging for alms, he was turned away and hours later rains came, flooding the village and forcing the residents to flee in panic. It is said that on clear days, if you look deep into the lake, you can see those who were left behind still going about their business, attending to chores and weaving on looms. Spanish history books contain another account, that the word Buhi in the local dialect means "to escape from danger" and that people fled to the lake to escape a series of catastrophic volcanic eruptions in 1641.

Buhi

Mostly enclosed by mountains that rise to 300m in places, Lake Buhi is just 16km from Iriga. Jeepneys for the town of **BUHI**, the only realistic access point for the lake, leave from Alfelor Street in Iriga, immediately behind the cathedral, and take about an hour. On the south shore of the lake, the town is a surprisingly busy little place with a cinema, cockpit, two small discos and dozens of

Lake Buhi's small fry

It may be little, but the **sinarapan** (*Mistichthys luzonensis*), a type of goby that thrives in Lake Buhi, is said by locals to be tastier than anything else that swims. These tiny transparent fish, no larger than 12mm, are the smallest commercially harvested fish in the world, caught by the fishermen at Buhi using a time-honoured and ingenious method. The fishermen make a trap by planting a bamboo pole in the lake, palm leaves floating on the surface at the end that protrudes above water. During the day the fish find the palm leaves and rest on them, leaving the fishermen to return at dusk to gather them into a net.

The people who live around Buhi regard the *sinarapan* not as a delicacy but as a staple food, frying them in oil, or boiling them with *laing* (taro leaves). When more of the fish are caught than the local market demands, the surplus is salted or dried in cakes and exported to neighbouring towns. The diminutive fish's fame is spreading and the municipality now grants the right to catch them to the highest bidder for each sector of the lake. Stocks of *sinarapan* have dwindled, but you can still find them to eat in Buhi. The *Buhi Café* on the plaza mixes them with various greens, while around the plaza and the lakeshore street vendors sell them dried and salted in plastic bags. The taste is less fishy than anchovies or sardines, almost like potato crisps.

shack-like karaoke bars. Many of the population of 60,000 are fisherfolk; because of their relative isolation, the residents have developed their own dialect, **Buhinon**, for which academics at the University of the Philippines are trying to compile a dictionary. On May 25 every year Buhi celebrates its town **fiesta** with a catholic selection of activities ranging from a thanksgiving Mass to an arm-wrestling competition in the plaza and a basketball competition between local barangays.

Buhi is centred around a grey concrete plaza with a memorial to Buhinons who served in World War II. On one side of the plaza is a nineteenth-century Spanish church and on another the whitewashed town hall. Buhi's most dominant landmark, however, is Mount Iriga, which can be seen on the opposite shore of the lake from just about anywhere in town. There's no accommodation in Buhi and the only places to **eat** are street canteens or a couple of fast-food restaurants on the plaza: *Lake House*, which serves mostly rice and meat dishes, and *Buhi Café*, where fresh fish with rice costs only P50.

You can charter a **banca** at the lakeside market in Buhi and take a trip across the water (P500). If you've time, don't miss **Itbog Falls** in the barangay of Santa Cruz, 5km from Buhi and north of the lake; these wonderful twin falls come crashing through thick rainforest vegetation into deep pools that are perfect for swimming. Once you're across the lake, the boatman can guide you (this will cost around P200 extra) on the terrific one-hour trek to the falls through rice paddies and along rocky trails.

Mount Iriga

It takes two days to reach the summit of **Mount Iriga** (1196m), known to the locals as Mount Sumagang, or Mountain of the Rising Sun. An extinct volcano whose last recorded eruption was in 1611, Iriga is best reached through the barrio of **Cabatuan** on the far side of the lake from Buhi. Don't go it alone because it's highly likely you'll get lost, and the climb itself is tricky. A catastrophic landslide some time in the sixteenth century left a huge crater in the side of Iriga, a natural amphitheatre whose edges you have to negotiate to reach the top. This is rough, undeveloped country, so you'll need to be experienced in the wilderness and to take a **guide**: inquire about this at the town hall in Buhi, or one of the two tourist offices in Legaspi (see p.181), or ask around at the mayor's office in Iriga.

Mount Iriga is home to a number of small **Negrito tribes** who rarely see visitors and, while always welcoming, are rather shy. It's also a popular habitat for leeches; locals say the best way to prevent them sticking to you, apart from wearing long sleeves and securing your cuffs and ankles, is to rub your skin with soap beforehand.

Legaspi and around

The port city of **LEGASPI** (sometimes spelt Legazpi), is an unimpressive, tricycle-ridden metropolis with a congested and polluted main road (Peñaranda Street, also called the National Highway), very few restaurants and a poor selection of hotels. About four hours south of Naga and less than two hours north of Donsol by bus, Legaspi is, however, the best place to spend a night if you are going to climb **Mount Mayon**, whose almost perfect cone-shaped bulk rises from paddy fields to the north of the city. The countryside

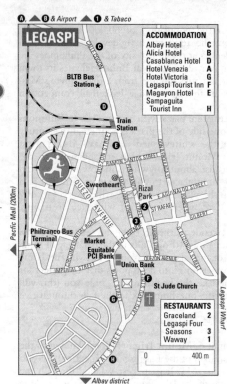

LEGASPI

ACCOMMODATION

Albay Hotel	C
Alicia Hotel	B
Casablanca Hotel	D
Hotel Venezia	A
Hotel Victoria	G
Legaspi Tourist Inn	F
Magayon Hotel	E
Sampaguita Tourist Inn	H

RESTAURANTS

Graceland	2
Legaspi Four Seasons	3
Waway	1

Pacific Mall (200m)

BLTB Bus Station ★

Train Station

Sweetheart

Rizal Park

Philtranco Bus Terminal ★

Market

Equitable PCI Bank

Union Bank

St Jude Church

Legaspi Wharf

0   400 m

▼ *Albay district*

and coast around Legaspi are marvellous and worth taking time to get to know, with some quiet beaches around the town of **Santo Domingo** to the north, one well-preserved Spanish Baroque church and the eerie remains of another church that was buried in the devastating eruption of Mayon in 1814.

In Legaspi itself there's really not much to see. At the rear of the City Hall compound there's a small **museum** in the Albay district (Mon–Fri 9am–5pm; free) that doesn't offer much to detain anyone except the most ardent historians and occasional high-school student. The miscellaneous exhibits include old coffee-grinders, World War II tin helmets and stuffed lizards. Museum staff are working valiantly to improve it, but have no budget and are dependent on donations. It is, believe it or not, the only functioning museum in the Bicol region.

Practicalities

Legaspi is in two distinct parts at either end of the National Highway. The old town, where you'll find the City Hall, is centred on Peñaranda Park and known as the **Albay** district. A couple of kilometres to the northeast is the new town, a muddle of small businesses, banks, cinemas and market stalls, and also where the hotels are located. It's a 25-minute walk between the two areas of Legaspi along a busy, polluted road lacking a decent pavement. The only sensible option is to add still further to the pollution by taking a tricycle or one of the many jeepneys that go back and forth.

The **BLTB bus station** is on Peñaranda Street next to *Casablanca Hotel*; the **Philtranco terminal** is a little west of the city centre, on Imperial Street. There's also a local bus station used by transport to and from destinations such as Sorsogon and Tabaco. Legaspi's **train station** is a rather attractive but ill-cared for stone building next to the *Casablanca Hotel*, a two-minute walk south of the BLTB bus station. The **airport** is only a couple of kilometres northwest of the new town. There are no taxis in Legaspi, but incoming flights are met by drivers with private cars who can take you the short distance to the city; a fair rate for this is P100 for one person and P150 for a small group. There are also tricycles at the airport (P20 to the city) and at the city's other transport terminals. Philippine Airlines, which has daily flights from Manila to Legaspi, has an office inside the airport (☏052/245

5024), open when flights are arriving or departing. Air Philippines flies to Legaspi from Manila every Tuesday, Thursday and Saturday, and Cebu Pacific flies daily every afternoon; both airlines have small offices at the airport. The **wharf** is at the eastern end of Quezon Avenue, ten minutes from Peñaranda Street by tricycle. It's not served by passenger ferries, although it's possible to negotiate with boatmen here for a banca to take you along the coast to Santo Domingo and even as far as the islands of San Miguel, Cagrary, Batan (see p.187) and Rapu-Rapu (see p.192). There are no **car rental** companies, but you can hire a car with driver by asking at your hotel or by negotiating with one of the drivers waiting for arriving planes at the airport.

Legaspi has two **tourist offices**, both in Albay. One, run by the city government, is on the ground floor of City Hall, through the main entrance and then through the first door on your right; the other is the Albay provincial tourist office, the pale brown building on Captain F. Aquende Drive close to City Hall. Inquire at either about arranging a guide for Mount Mayon. You can also ask to be put in touch with the Mayon Mountaineers Club, whose members can offer advice and find a guide. Another excellent source of information about activities around Legaspi is Bicol Adventures and Tours (☎052/480 2266), Quezon Avenue, in the same building as the *Legaspi Tourist Inn*. As well as offering advice, staff can arrange private tours, caving, trekking, scuba diving and island-hopping. This is also a good place to secure a reliable guide for climbing Mayon; the rate for two days is P2600.

The **post office** is on Lapu-Lapu Street at the junction with Quezon Avenue, and there are a number of **banks**, including Equitable PCI and Union Bank, near the market. The main **police station** is in Quezon Avenue at the junction with Mabini Street and the Philippine National Police command post is on the western side of Peñaranda Park. There are half-a-dozen small **Internet cafés** in the narrow road that runs behind City Hall, and also *Sweetheart Internet Café* in the new part of town at 122 Magallanes St, next to Jovid's Billiard Hall.

Accommodation

Most of the **accommodation** in Legaspi is along the main road so rooms at the front can be noisy.

Albay Hotel 88 Peñaranda St ☎02/893 5733. Modern hotel a little north of town beyond the BLTB bus station. All rooms are doubles with a/c and private facilities, but it's a little overpriced compared with other hotels in the city. There's a café in the lobby that serves breakfast, included in the rate. ④–⑤

Alicia Hotel F. Aquende Dr ☎052/481 0801. Good, clean a/c doubles in a quiet location very close to the airport. Being able to stay away from the mayhem of the main street makes up for the hassle of taking tricycles back and forth into the city. ④

Casablanca Hotel Peñaranda St ☎052/480 8334 to 8336. Popular, modern, mid-range hotel with enormous rooms. Standard rooms have two double beds so at a pinch they can sleep four. There's a restaurant called the *Orient Garden*, a cheesy karaoke bar called *Santuario* and a 24hr café in the lobby. Philtranco tickets can be reserved at the front desk. ④

Hotel Venezia Washington Dr ☎052/481 0877, ⓦ www.hotelvenezia.ws. Two minutes from the airport, this modern establishment is in a residential area and has 22 comfortable, clean a/c rooms with hot and cold water. There's a coffee shop and a small business centre with Internet access. ④–⑥

Hotel Victoria Rizal St ☎052/214 3176. Modern hotel near the market, so some of the rooms are noisy, though they are at least reasonably well-maintained and clean, with hot showers and cable TV. There's a patio garden on the roof and a small, quiet café in the lobby. ③

Legaspi Tourist Inn 3/F, V&O Building, Lapu-Lapu St ☎052/480 6147. Opposite the post office, this small and friendly place has well-kept fan rooms for a reasonable price. Not the height of luxury, but good value. ③

Magayon Hotel Peñaranda St ☎052/480 6147. The cheapest hotel in Legaspi, with cell-like singles and more spacious twins and doubles; bathrooms are a little grubby and the water's cold. There is, however, a spacious restaurant where the cook can whip up a cheap meal of eggs and rice for breakfast. **②**

Sampaguita Tourist Inn Rizal St
☎052/480 6255. One of Legaspi's newer

accommodation options, on a busy part of Rizal St at the Albay district end, but set back a little from the road behind a Petron petrol station. Good choice of boxy but comfortable a/c singles, doubles and triples, with clean en-suite bathrooms and a small coffee shop in the lobby area. Go for one of the quieter rooms at the back. **④**

Eating

It's remarkable that in Legaspi, capital of a province known for its inventive, spicy cuisine, there should be so few restaurants. The population seems to subsist almost entirely on **fast food**. In Pacific mall, the brown and green building in Imperial Street a short walk from the market, there are branches of *Jollibee*, *McDonald's* and *Chow King*. There's also a branch of *Graceland*, a local fast-food restaurant that serves dishes such as barbecued pork or chicken, and *adobo* with rice. Another *Graceland* can be found opposite Rizal Park and a third on the main road at the Albay end of the city.

The best **restaurant** in Legaspi is the *Legaspi Four Seasons* at 205 Magallanes St, up a concrete staircase, close to Rizal Park. It's a simple, clean **Chinese** place: portions are huge and freshly cooked, so choose a few different dishes and share them around. For native **Bicol cuisine** – including a tangy Bicol chicken and spicy regional dishes such as swordfish cooked in coconut milk with chillies and fish paste – try the *Waway* restaurant in Peñaranda Street, a ten-minute walk north beyond the *Albay Hotel*. There's a lively **market** at the southern end of Quezon Avenue, close to Pacific Mall market, where you can buy *ponkan* (small native oranges) and bananas.

Mount Mayon

The smooth cone of **Mount Mayon** (2421m) in Albay province makes it look benign from a distance, but don't be deceived. Mayon is a devil in disguise and has claimed the lives of a number of climbers in rock avalanches in recent years, as well as 77 people including American volcanologists during an eruption in 1993. The most active volcano in the country, it has erupted more than thirty times since 1616, the date of its first recorded eruption. In the second half of 2006, Mayon was again at a high level of unrest, seemingly on the brink of eruption, with sudden ash explosions and lava flows. An "extended danger zone" was in force, with everyone evacuated from an area 7km from the summit crater. Matters were made worse by Typhoon Durian in November 2006, which caused mudslides of volcanic ash and boulders on Mayon that killed hundreds. Most of the victims were buried alive when three communities at the base of the volano were swamped by mud. Clearly, climbing the volcano or even getting close to it under these conditions is impossible.

It's no wonder the locals spin fearful stories around Mayon. The most popular legend has it that the volcano was formed when a beautiful native princess eloped with a brave warrior. Her uncle, Magayon, was so possessive of his niece that he chased the young couple, who prayed to the gods for help. Suddenly a landslide buried the raging uncle alive, and he is said to be still inside the volcano, his anger sometimes bursting forth in the form of eruptions.

The presence of Mayon results in strange meteorological conditions in and around Legaspi, with the volcano and the surrounding area often blanketed in rain when the rest of the country is basking in unbroken sunshine. The only

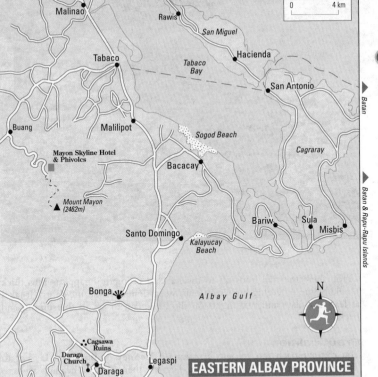

EASTERN ALBAY PROVINCE

window of opportunity for an ascent is **March to May**, and even then you'll have to be well prepared for cold nights at altitude and the possibility of showers. At any other time of year you could be hanging around for days waiting for a break in the weather. Furthermore, the slopes of Mayon are not as silky smooth as they look from a few miles away. It takes at least two days to reach the summit, working your way slowly through forest, grassland and deserts of boulders. Above 2000 metres there's the possibility of being affected by poisonous gases.

The usual approach is from the northwestern slope, which starts at 762m above sea level on a ledge where the Philippine Institute of Volcanology and Seismology (PHIVOLCS) research station and, next door, the ruins of the **Mayon Skyline Hotel** are located. The hotel is a damp, eerie monument to the grand ambitions and follies of the local politicians who decided to build it. Soon after it opened, it became apparent there was no way to secure a regular water supply, a fact you would expect to have been considered during the planning stages. The hotel subsequently closed, and has now been commandeered by poor farmers from Mayon's fertile lower slopes, some of whom sleep in what was once the ballroom. It's worth getting to the hotel even if you aren't climbing Mayon, just to see the **views** over the province of Albay.

△ Mount Mayon

From here the trail leads off to the left and promptly disappears into thick jungle before emerging higher up onto steep slopes of volcanic debris. It takes at least two days and two nights on the mountain to get to the summit and back.

Practicalities

You can approach the volcano by taking a **jeepney** or **bus** from Legaspi to **Tabaco** (see p.186), 26km north of Legaspi, then another heading west to **Buang**, where the narrow concrete road up to the *Mayon Skyline Hotel* is on the left just before you reach Buang itself, marked by a green signpost. The alternative approach is via **Daraga** (see opposite), though this may take longer as transport from Daraga to Buang is less frequent. It's just over 8km from the turnoff to the ruins, so if you don't fancy the walk, catch one of the tricycles that hang around at the turnoff. A quicker and more comfortable way to get there is to rent a vehicle in Legaspi. Whatever you do, don't go without a **guide**. Local authorities have made guides mandatory and setting out without one would be foolhardy in the extreme. You can arrange one at the tourist offices in Legaspi, or at Bicol Adventure & Tours (see p.169), and also check here whether conditions are suitable for climbing Mayon (volcanic unrest and the devastation caused by Typhoon Durian had made the mountain's slopes a no-go area at the end of 2006). Another good source of information is PHIVOLCS in Manila (☏02/426 1468, ⓦ www.phivolcs.dost.gov.ph). If you are able to climb Mayon, you'll have to bring all your food with you from Legaspi; there are sources of water on the volcano, but you'll need purifying tablets.

Cagsawa Ruins

Fifteen kilometres northwest of Legaspi beyond the town of **Daraga**, the **Cagsawa Ruins** (daily 7am–7pm; P5) are the remains of a Spanish church that was destroyed by the 1814 eruption of Mayon. More than a thousand people who took refuge here during the eruption were buried alive. In his colourful account *Erupcion de Volcan Mayon de Albay en 1814*, parish priest Francisco Argoneses tells of how he ordered his altar boy to ring the church bells warning people to flee. Most of those who remained were entombed in lava and still are – the Catholic Church has so far refused to have the ruins excavated.

To get to the ruins, take a jeepney from Legaspi to Daraga and then another for Camalig. Jeepneys don't stop automatically at the ruins, so tell the driver where you want to get off. The ruins are small and there's not much to explore, but they are picturesque, standing in gardens close to paddy fields with marvellous views across the plain to Mount Mayon. This is one of the best places from which to view Mayon, but it's also popular, so if you want peace and quiet take an early jeepney and get there before the crowds and the hawkers show up. Early morning is the best time to take photographs, before the day gets too hot and the cumulus rolls in to obscure Mayon's tip. There are a number of souvenir stalls and sari-sari stores right outside the ruins where you can buy drinks and snacks.

Bonga

The verdant paddy fields and farmlands around the tiny farming hamlet of **BONGA**, fifteen minutes by road north of Legaspi, offer some of the best vantage points for Mayon, well away from the touristy atmosphere of Cagsawa. Don't confuse Bonga with the barrio of the same name further north on the road to Tabaco. This Bonga is closer to Legaspi and you reach it by turning down a narrow concrete road on your left in Arimbay, 2km beyond Rawis (look out for the Shell petrol station on the right). By public transport, take a jeepney to Arimbay and then a tricycle. The road up to Bonga winds for a couple of kilometres through dazzling countryside with Mayon on your right. Not many travellers come this way so locals tend to be inquisitive, sometimes even a little wary about what you might be up to in the area. Take a few sweets for the children and don't be belligerent if you find yourself surrounded by puzzled locals; everyone is very friendly as long as you are too. There's nowhere to eat or even to buy a cold drink, so take whatever you need with you.

Daraga Church

Fifteen minutes northwest of Legaspi by jeepney, **Daraga Church** in the busy market town of **DARAGA** is an imposing and beautiful eighteenth-century Baroque church built by Franciscan missionaries from blocks of volcanic lava. The exterior, now stained by patches of moss, was decorated by skilled stonemasons with statuary, carvings, alcoves and niches. But although the facade is old, the interior has been nicely renovated and is still used for regular Catholic services.

The only problem is the location. In an effort to keep it safe from the wrath of Mayon, the church was built on top of a col with no access by road, leaving worshippers and tourists to negotiate a considerable ascent to get to it. To get there, take any jeepney from Legaspi marked for Daraga and then take a tricycle (P20) to the church, which is on the western edge of town.

Santo Domingo and Bacacay

About thirty minutes northeast of Legaspi along the coastal road is the small town of **Santo Domingo**, a tidy, friendly little barrio with an atmospheric old Spanish church, a brown stone structure on the north side of the narrow main street. From here you can either turn east along the coast or take the Tabaco road north to **Bacacay**. **Sogod Beach** near Bacacay, 45 minutes from Legaspi, is a pleasantly rustic beach of black lava sand known as the Mayon Riviera;

unfortunately there is nowhere to stay in the area. There are jeepneys from Legaspi's market to Santo Domingo and to Bacacay, where you can change for a tricycle to Sogod Beach.

East of Santo Domingo

The route east from Santo Domingo is a concrete road that winds its way up and down through some delightful, pristine countryside, with Tabaco Bay on the left and Albay Gulf on the right. Tabaco Bay, where locals moor their boats during typhoons, is so sheltered that when you first see it, it's easy to mistake it for an inland lake.

On the road east out of Santo Domingo there are a handful of average **resorts** on **Kalayucay Beach**, which is pretty but not spectacular, though the views across Albay Gulf are hypnotizing and it's a good place to relax. As you drive along the coastal road beyond Santo Domingo, the first resort on your right, on the shore, is *Ocean View Beach Resort* (❷–❸), followed by *Reyes Beach Resort* (❷), which has breezy and tidy fan doubles and a pleasant restaurant. Next is *Costa Palmera* (☎0919/587 3158; ❸–❹), in a concrete building set back a short walk from the beach. Clean and orderly, it boasts a seaside restaurant and its own generator in case of blackouts. Three kilometres further along the coast, at **Buhatan Beach**, are the remains of a seventeenth-century Spanish galleon five fathoms deep in clear water; scuba divers with their own equipment (or who can afford a tailor-made package from a Manila dive operator) can explore the wreck. The ship's relics are kept at the National Museum in Manila. It's also possible to hire a banca at the beaches along this coast to take you out to Cagraray island (see opposite). From Santo Domingo there are jeepneys along the coastal road to these resorts and beaches, but they don't follow any kind of timetable and leave only when they are full. Another option is to hire your own tricycle and driver in Santo Domingo.

Tabaco

The fourth largest town in the Bicol region, **TABACO**, 26km northeast of Legaspi via **Malilipot**, is a busy little port. Four of the Philippines' wilder **islands** – San Miguel, Cagraray, Batan and Rapu-Rapu – lie off the Pacific shore of Albay and can be reached by ferry from Tabaco, though Rapu-Rapu is easier to reach from Prieto Diaz in Sorsogon (see p.192). The main industry is the production of fibre, used to make ropes, sacks and handicrafts, from a plant known as *abaca*. Tabaco is not a tourist destination, but in some ways it's more interesting and atmospheric than Legaspi. The market is always frenetic and there's an old Spanish church opposite a small square, lit with fairy lights after dark.

You'll pass through Tabaco on the bus or jeepney if you're heading out from Legaspi to climb Mayon. All **local buses** arrive at the terminal on the main street, Ziga Avenue (next to the Caltex petrol station). This is where you change buses for the onward trip to Buang for Mayon Volcano. The **jeepney terminal** is behind the indoor market, opposite the church on the main street. **Philtranco buses** from Manila and Naga arrive at a terminal next to the market. The **port** is a ten-minute walk down the road next to the market. Besides ferries to Cagraray, San Miguel, Batan and Rapu-Rapu, there are services from here to Virac (P70–100) and San Andres (P40), both in Catanduanes.

The most modern and comfortable **accommodation** in Tabaco is at the *Casa Eugenia Hotel* on Ziga Avenue (☎052/830 0425, ℗830 1948; ❹), the green building on your right as you enter the city from the south. It's smart, clean and friendly, with a good café, air-conditioned rooms and cable TV.

Behind the Philippine National Police building on Bonifacio Street is the *Easter Apartelle* (℡052/830 0366, ❷ ❹), which has boxy air-conditioned and fan rooms which are just about all right for a night.

The best **restaurant** in Tabaco, although to be honest it doesn't enjoy much competition, is at the *Casa Eugenia*, serving sandwiches, burgers, fries and a number of rice dishes. Around the market there are dozens of little stalls selling barbecued kebabs. At the junction of Ziga Avenue and Cabile Avenue is *Food Garden*, a very simple al fresco native place offering barbecued chicken and grilled meat with rice.

Cagraray, San Miguel and Batan

The islands of Cagraray, San Miguel and Batan, bucolic and undeveloped, offer some great opportunities for more hardy travellers to get beneath the skin of the Philippines, in a dramatic and unspoilt part of the country. There are no hotels on any of these islands, so if you want to stay overnight you'll either need to camp or you'll have to ask locals if anyone can put you up in return for a token of your appreciation, which should be at least P100 a night. Hiring a banca to see the beaches and coves should cost no more than P500 for a full day.

The best island to visit, and the most accessible, is **Cagraray**, which has some wonderful white sand beaches in the barrios of **Sula** and **Misibis** on the southeast coast. It can be reached in two hours from Tabaco, the ferry (P55) taking you to the fishing community of **San Antonio** (also known as Sulong) on the northwest side of the island. However, ferries are sometimes cancelled as the eastern coast of Albay province is buffeted by strong onshore winds, especially during the typhoon season (May–Oct). A **bridge** has recently been built to Cagraray from the peninsula east of Santo Domingo, and this route is served by jeepneys from Tabaco and Legaspi.

San Miguel Island, to the north of Cagraray, and **Batan**, to the south, both have tiny populations of fishermen and farmers, and offer pristine waters for snorkelling and powdery beaches where you can sleep under the stars. The ferry to San Antonio continues to Batan (P40; 1hr), returning to Tabaco via Cagraray; for San Miguel, there are occasional bancas from San Antonio. To the south of Batan is **Rapu-Rapu** (see p.192), which is served by sporadic bancas from the port of Batan on the east side of Batan Island, and by ferries from Prieto Diaz in Sorsogon.

Donsol

The peaceful fishing community of **DONSOL** lies in the far northwest of Sorsogon province, almost equidistant between Legaspi and Sorsogon Town; you can get there by bus from either in less than two hours. The area around Donsol is best known for one of the greatest concentrations of **whale sharks** in the world, and your first stop in town should be the **Visitor Center** (daily 7am–4pm; ℡0927/233 0364), next to the Municipal Hall, where you can complete all the formalities of hiring a boat for a whale shark-watching trip. The number of sightings varies: during the peak months of December and January there's a good chance of seeing ten or fifteen whale sharks a day, but on some days you might strike out and see none.

Tourists are not allowed to board a boat without first being briefed by a **Butanding Interaction Officer** (BIO), who explains how to behave in the water near one of these huge creatures. The number of snorkellers around any

Whale sharks

Known locally by a number of names, including *butanding*, *balilan* and *kulwano*, the whale shark is a timid titan resembling a whale more than the shark it is. It can grow up to 20m in length, making it the largest fish in the seas. Unlike other sharks, these gentle giants are not carnivorous; they gather here every year around the time of the northeastern monsoon (Dec or Jan) to feed on the rich shrimp and plankton streams that flow from the Donsol River into the sea, sucking their food through their gills via an enormous vacuum of a mouth.

Whale sharks were rarely hunted in the Philippines until the 1990s, when demand for their meat from countries such as Taiwan and Japan escalated. Cooks have dubbed it the **tofu shark** because of the meat's resemblance to soybean curd. Its fins are also coveted as a soup extender. Tragically, this has led to its near extinction in the Visayas and further south in Mindanao. Though the government is trying to protect the whale sharks by fining fishermen who catch them, it's an uphill battle, largely because enforcement in a sparsely populated region like this is difficult. For poor fishermen, money talks, and a good whale shark can fetch enough to keep a rural family happy for months. In Donsol, however, attitudes seem to be changing, with locals beginning to realize that the whale sharks can be worth more alive than dead, attracting tourists and thus investment and jobs. Donsol fishermen claim they never hunt whale sharks and that those who do travel long distances from other parts of the Philippines in the hope of a quick profit.

one whale shark is limited to six; flash photography is not allowed, nor is scuba gear, and don't get anywhere near the animal's tail because it's powerful enough to do you some serious damage. Take plenty of protection against the sun and a good book. Once a whale shark has been sighted you'll need to get your mask, snorkel and flippers on and get in the water before it dives too deep to be seen.

Boats **cost** a hefty P2200 for up to six people, and there's also a registration fee of P300 for foreigners and P100 for Filipinos. Each boat has a crew of three, the captain, the BIO and the spotter, each of whom will expect a token of your appreciation (at least P100 to each person) at the end of a successful day (and even an unsuccessful one). All this makes it an expensive day out by Philippine standards, but take heart from the fact that your money is helping the conservation effort.

Practicalities

Buses, jeepneys and air-conditioned minibuses arrive in Donsol at the **market**. There are hundreds of tricycles buzzing around that will take you anywhere within the town for P20. The Visitor Center is a little out of town and the tricycle ride costs P30. Five hundred metres west of the market is a small **pier** where there are daily ferries to Claveria on Burias Island (see p.196).

In Donsol itself, you can **stay** at the *Santiago Lodging House* (T056/411 8311; ❷), close to the market. In the home of a pleasant woman who used to be a schoolteacher, this has cosy, impeccably clean rooms with fan and shared facilities. The owner will prepare simple meals for you, including packed lunches for the boat, if you notify her in advance. There are a number of modest **homestays** springing up in Donsol to cater for budget conscious whale-watchers. For information it's best to ask at the Visitor Center. There are two good resorts outside Donsol, both of which can arrange transport into town. *Amor Farm Beach Resort* (T056/411 1109; ❹) is a twenty-minute jeepney ride east of Donsol in **Dangcalan**, on the road to Sorsogon. It offers pretty bamboo and nipa cottages on the shore, with a native restaurant that serves fresh fish, *adobo* and anything else available in the nearby market. The cottages are simple but decent, with well-kept bathrooms. ☆*Woodland Farm Beach Resort* (☎056/411 3113; ❸) is another simple, quiet, pretty resort about 6km along the road to Sorsogon, with half-a-dozen double cottages on the shore and views across Ticao Island towards Masbate.

Around the market in Donsol there are dozens of canteens and fast-food **restaurants**, none exceptional. *Kim's Fastfood* does offer very cheap rice meals, usually consisting of rice and fish or meat barbecue. The Bicol fast-food chain *Graceland* also has a branch.

Sorsogon Town and around

In the southeast of the Bicol peninsula, about 60km from Legaspi, **Sorsogon Town**, capital of the province of that name, has little value as a tourist destination, but does make a good base for exploring Sorsogon province, a toe of land with a striking volcanic topography and some little-known beaches, lakes, hot springs and waterfalls. One of the nicest stretches of sand is **Rizal Beach**, in the barrio of **Gubat**, a twenty-minute jeepney ride east of Sorsogon Town, but there are many other pristine coves you can explore along the coast around **Bacon**, fifteen minutes north of Sorsogon Town by road, and Bulusan, south of Gubat. Northeast of Sorsogon Town is the little-visited, unspoilt island of **Rapu-Rapu** in the Albay Gulf. South of Sorsogon Town, **Mount Bulusan** is an active volcano which takes two days to climb, while on the southernmost tip of the Bicol peninsula is the busy little port town of **Matnog**. This is the end of the Philippine "mainland" and the beginning of the Visayas: a sign at the ferry terminal reads, "You are now leaving the island of Luzon."

Sorsogon Town has a number of **festivals**. The Kasanggayahan festival (Oct 24–27) celebrates the town's history with street parades, banca races and beauty pageants; the Pili festival (June 20–29) pays homage to one of the province's major sources of livelihood, the *pili* nut, which when roasted tastes a bit like an almond and can be used in chocolate, ice cream and biscuits.

Sorsogon Town

All buses terminating in Sorsogon – long-distance buses from Manila and local buses – arrive at a terminal at the end of Rizal Street in the southeast corner of town, close to the sea. There's also a busy jeepney terminal here for jeepneys to Bacon, Prieto Diaz and Gubat. Air-conditioned minibuses leave when they're full for Legaspi, and Matnog (for the ferry to Samar).

The fare for any tricycle trip within the town boundaries is P4, rising to P10 if you want to go further. Buses passing through Sorsogon drop off and pick up passengers at the northern edge of Rizal Street, about five minutes' walk from the town plaza. There are a number of **banks** (BPI, PNB and UCPB) and small **Internet cafés** on Rizal Street.

The best source of **tourist information** in town is the Sorsogon Tourism Council, located within the well-known **hotel**, *Fernando's Hotel*, in Pareja Street one block west of Rizal Park on Rizal Street. Staff can help arrange everything from mountain-biking and whale shark-watching to tours around the province, as well as help find guides and secure equipment for climbing Bulusan. The hotel itself (☎056/211 1357; ❸–❺) is a cosy, two-storey white building with a lovely little café that has wrought-iron furniture and polished terracotta floors.

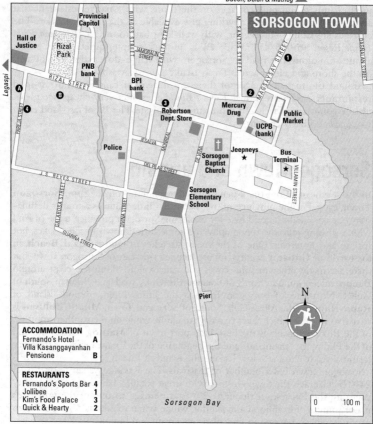

SORSOGON TOWN

Bacon, Bulan & Matnog ▲

Legaspi

Provincial
Capitol

Hall of
Justice

Rizal
Park

PNB
bank

RIZAL STREET

BURGOS STREET

JAMORALIN
STREET

PERALTA STREET

M. SANTOS STREET

MAGSAYSAY STREET

❶

DAGNALAN STREET

BPI
bank

❸
Robertson
Dept. Store

Mercury
Drug

❷

UCPB
(bank)

Public
Market

Police

JESALVA

MONREAL

DE LIMA

DEL PILAR STREET

Sorsogon
Baptist
Church

Jeepneys
★

Bus
Terminal
★

VILLAMIN STREET

J. S. REYES STREET

GALAROSA STREET

DIVINA STREET

Sorsogon
Elementary
School

GUARINA STREET

Pier

N

Sorsogon Bay

0   100 m

ACCOMMODATION
Fernando's Hotel   **A**
Villa Kasanggayanhan
Pensione   **B**

RESTAURANTS
Fernando's Sports Bar **4**
Jollibee   **1**
Kim's Food Palace   **3**
Quick & Hearty   **2**

All the rooms are air-conditioned and have clean bathrooms. The owner, David Duran, is a gracious host and a good source of local information. Opposite Rizal Park is *Villa Kasanggayanhan Pensione* in Rizal Street (☎056/211 1275; ❸), a low-rise mint-green building in a quiet compound with good air-conditioned, en-suite twin rooms (no singles). Staff here can arrange whale shark-watching tours.

Food in Sorsogon are mostly of the quick and cheap variety, with three branches of *Jollibee* and a couple of *Quick & Hearty* fast-food outlets. *Kim's Food Palace* in Rizal Street is a popular Chinese restaurant offering fried rice, sweet-and-sour chicken, and a great variety of noodle and rice dishes. *Fernando's Sports Bar*, next to *Fernando's Hotel*, has sandwiches, noodles, burgers, *adobo* and cold San Miguel.

Rizal Beach

In a nation of beaches, it's not going too far to say that **Rizal Beach**, a short tricycle ride beyond the barrio of **Gubat** on the eastern tip of Sorsogon province about 12km east of Sorsogon Town, is one of the best, stretching for

2km in a perfect crescent and sloping gently into calm, clear water. It's an idyllic spot, a rustic, uncorrupted corner of the world where you can idle away days in one of the beach's two simple and now rather careworn little resorts. The *Rizal Beach Resort Hotel* (℡056/311 1829; ❸) is not as grand as the name implies, with mediocre accommodation, in a converted schoolhouse with a choice of fan or air-conditioned rooms and a restaurant that serves fresh, locally caught fish. There's also a swimming pool. Next door is *Veramaris Resort* (℡056/311 1824; ❸), a four-storey, villa-style white building with small rooms on the top two floors. Make sure to get a room with a sea view, even if you pay a little extra.

Bacon and Paguriran

The small town of **BACON**, half an hour north of Sorsogon Town by jeepney, is a good place to hire a banca and explore some of the islands in the eastern half of Albay Gulf. The best of these is **Paguriran** about forty minutes by banca from Bacon. Paguriran is nothing more than a circle of jagged rock, much like the rim of a volcano, inside which is a seawater lagoon, a great place to swim and snorkel. Turtles were once a common sight here, but haven't been seen for a number of years. The local government plans to re-establish the island as a sanctuary, encouraging the turtles to return.

Only ten minutes by tricycle west of Bacon is the black sand **Libanon Beach**, where surf hammers dramatically against immense, black rocks that were spewed centuries ago by Mayon – the volcano is actually visible in the distance.

Barcelona and Bulusan Volcano National Park

Ten kilometres south of Gubat is the quiet and friendly little coastal town of **BARCELONA**, with a lighthouse overlooking the ocean and some evocative Spanish ruins on the shore. The church here dates from 1873 and if it's open it's worth climbing the belfry for the views out to sea. From Barcelona there are regular jeepneys north along the scenic coastal road back to Gubat and south to Bulusan, starting point for visits to the Bulusan Volcano National Park.

Mount Bulusan in **BULUSAN VOLCANO NATIONAL PARK** is one of three active volcanoes in the Bicol region. The area surrounding Bulusan was designated a national park in 1935 and, apart from a deep covering of lush rainforest, it also has a number of waterfalls, hot springs and caves, with a number of decent trails and a concrete path around Lake Bulusan, the most accessible of a number of lakes in the park at 600m above sea level. At Bulusan's peak (1559m) is a crater lake and, a short walk away through tricky terrain, the small Blackbird Lake.

The park is relatively easy to reach: a motorable road leads from the villages of **Bulusan** and **Irosin** right up to Lake Bulusan. From Sorsogon Town, you can take a jeepney to Irosin (45min; P18) and then another right up to the lake. Coming from Rizal Beach, Gubat or Matnog, take a jeepney down the scenic coast road through the towns of **Barcelona** and **Layog** to Bulusan, then another to the lake. If you want to reach the peak, get a lakebound jeepney from Irosin and get off in the village of **San Roque**, where you'll find the trailhead. Hikers will be refused access by rangers if an eruption warning is up; for **guides** and up-to-date details about the state of the volcano, inquire at the Sorsogon Tourism Council (see p.189).

Rapu-Rapu

Part of Albay province, **Rapu-Rapu** is a quiet agricultural island with a number of unspoilt beaches on its south coast and, on the east coast, some islets and lagoons you can explore by banca. The island's small *poblacion*, also called Rapu-Rapu, has a **town hall** where you can ask around for details of transport and accommodation; the islanders – whose ancestors came from nearby Catanduanes (see p.197) – are famed in the Philippines for their hospitality, so it's not difficult to find someone who will offer you a room.

To the amusement of the locals, tales are still told on the Bicol mainland about the number of **witches** (*aswang*) who live on Rapu-Rapu. The story seems to have originated in the nineteenth century, when islanders used to sail to Legaspi in small boats called *parao* that depended on the wind, not on oars. Because passengers often reached the mainland pretty quickly, worried townsfolk quickly concluded they had used supernatural powers to fly there.

Rapu-Rapu is tricky to reach, one of the reasons it has remained untouched by tourism. You have three options to get there – find a banca from the port of Batan on the eastern side of Batan island (see p.187), get a ferry from **Prieto Diaz**, one hour east of Sorsogon Town by jeepney, or charter a banca from Legaspi (see p.179).

Matnog

The only reason to visit **MATNOG** is to catch a boat to somewhere else. Buses here stop at the ferry terminal, where boats leave every hour between 5am and 3pm for **Allen** (see p.235) or between 6am and 11pm for **San Isidro** (see p.235) in northern Samar. Some buses go on the ferry to Allen and continue their journey south through Samar and, in some cases, through Mindanao to Davao. If your bus arrives too late for the last boat, you'll either have to spend the night on the bus or amble into town, where there's not much to see or do. The ferries are not especially comfortable and the onboard canteen offers only very basic local fare, so make sure you've got enough sustenance for the crossing, which takes two hours.

The only place worth spending the night in Matnog is *Matnog Grand Mansion* (no phone; ❸), simple lodgings with air-conditioned rooms and private bathrooms, but no hot water. It's in San José Street, five minutes' walk north from the ferry terminal.

Masbate

The province of **Masbate** ("Maz-bah-tee") lies in the centre of the Philippine archipelago, bounded to the north by the waters of the Ticao Pass, which separate it from Bicol, to the south by the Visayan Sea, to the west by the Sibuyan Sea and to the east by the Samar Sea. It comprises the **island of Masbate** with its small capital town of the same name, two secondary islands of **Burias** and **Ticao**, and fourteen small islands dotted around the beach-fringed coastline. None of the islands – Masbate included – is particularly easy to reach, which means that they get few tourists. To make the most of the area you'll have to be the type of traveller who doesn't get ruffled by the slow pace, or by the occasional night in basic accommodation. There are a number of exceptional beaches on Masbate, at **Bagacay** for instance, and immense caves in thick jungle such as **Kalanay** and **Batongan**. It's the infrastructure that's lacking. There are no dive shops or tour operators, so to visit the outlying islands you'll have to take small public bancas or hire your own. Make sure you have enough pesos to cover your stay in Masbate, as it's almost impossible to find a working ATM or a bank that will change dollars.

Masbateños, depending on which part of the province they live in, speak one of three distinct local **languages**, namely Cebuano, Ilonggo and Masbateño. If that's not confusing enough, the province is officially part of the Bicol region, but Masbateños hesitate to introduce themselves as Bicolanos because they can't speak the language. In disposition and culture they veer more towards the island people of the Visayas, yet Visayans have never fully welcomed them into their fold. Masbate has something of an identity crisis.

The province also has something of a reputation for violence, with an image throughout the Philippines as a lawless frontier province where swaggering politicians tote guns and private armies do battle for petty fiefdoms. Like many isolated areas of the archipelago, Masbate does seem a law unto itself, but its reputation for goonish violence is unfair, probably springing from its carefully cultivated tourist image as a Wild East rodeo outpost unsullied by the jejune sophistications of Manila. Life here is rustic and unaffected, and the people are gentle and friendly, making it an ideal place to experience the Philippines in the raw.

The Wild East moniker is apt for reasons other than lawlessness. Masbate ranks second only to the landlocked province of Bukidnon, Mindanao, in raising cattle, and there's an **annual rodeo** in Masbate Town in May, where cowpokes do battle for big prize money. Apart from the bulls and cows, there's not much else going on. Farming is the second most common form of livelihood, fishing the third. Gold and copper have been mined here for centuries, but any fortunes that have been made seem not to have gone into local pockets.

Masbate's **history**, about which little has been written, has been sketchily traced back to the tenth century, when the islands were populated only by indigenous Negritos. When Spanish captain Luis Enriquez de Guzman arrived on the shores of Masbate in 1569, he found tiny coastal settlements engaged in flourishing trade with China. In December 1600, Dutch commander Admiral Oliver van Noorth sought refuge at San Jacinto harbour on Ticao Island after his fleet lost to the Spanish armada at Manila. He was later engaged in a fierce clash with the notorious Chinese pirate Limahong. In 1864, Masbate was declared a separate province from Albay and, shortly before the declaration of Philippine independence, the town of Masbate was established as the provincial capital. Like much of the Philippines, Masbate suffered terribly under the Japanese occupation, which reduced it to an economic shambles. Food production ground to a halt, and locals succumbed to beri-beri or malaria. When Masbate was formally liberated on April 3, 1945, the population had fallen by forty percent and all trade had ceased.

Getting to Masbate island

Asian Spirit has five early morning **flights** a week to Masbate Town from Manila. Sulpicio Lines has two departures a week on Tuesdays (8pm) and Fridays (10pm) from Manila to Masbate Town. The trip takes 11 hours. Sulpicio also has sailings to Masbate from Cebu, Surigao, Ormoc and Masaain. Trans-Asia has two ferries a week from Cebu. Smaller ferries run to Masbate Town every morning from the port town of **Bulan** on the southwestern coast of Sorsogon.

Masbate Town

The provincial capital of **MASBATE TOWN** is pretty enough, nestling between the sea and the hills, but spoiled slightly by unstructured development and the nerve-jangling presence of the ubiquitous tricycle. The main thorough-fare, which runs behind the port area, is Quezon Street, and there's a busy **market** seven days a week in Zurbito Street. The only notable tourist attraction is the **Rodeo Masbateño**, a four-day orgy of bull-riding and steer-dogging which takes place every year in May (usually May 6–9). It's not only for cowboys and cowgirls: teams from universities, agricultural colleges and local government offices also take part. The prize money is big, as much as P300,000, while spectators have the chance to win one of the 25 cows that are raffled off each day. For more information, contact the Office of the Governors in Masbate Town (☎056/333 2176).

Practicalities

Masbate Town is only a five-minute ride from the **airport**. There are no taxis, so from the airport you'll have to take a jeepney or a tricycle. Asian Spirit has an office at the airport (☎056/333 3937). The **ferry pier**, close to the town centre and within walking distance of the hotels, has a ticket outlet for WG&A ferries (☎056/333 2373). **Buses**, **jeepneys** and **tricycles** for other destinations on the island leave from the main square, opposite the Provincial Capitol Building.

Most of the accommodation, together with places to eat, convenience **stores** and a PNB **bank**, are centrally located on Quezon Street, which heads north off the main square. If you want to make a long-distance call, you'll have to join the queue at the **BayanTel** office in Quezon Street. There's a police outpost, little more than a shack, beside the main pier. Cervante's on Quezon Street has **Internet** access.

As there are no taxis and not many buses, it's either tricycles or jeepneys for transport in and around Masbate. Jeepneys run to coastal destinations in both directions, as well as across the island to Mandaon.

Accommodation

Masbate is not known for its sights, so the chances are you'll be moving on pretty quickly along the coast to one of the beaches. Most places to stay are simple, friendly **boarding houses** and lodges.

Masbate Lodge Quezon St ☎056/333 2184. Spick-and-span little guesthouse with shining floors and fresh, clean linen on the beds. The rooms are nothing grand, but they are well maintained and those at the back of the lodge, away from the tricycles on Quezon St, are quiet. ❷
Rancher's Hotel Tara St ☎056/333 3931. Grey concrete building on a street parallel to Quezon St, with ordinary rooms that are a little careworn. There's also a budget canteen, selling *adobo* and noodle dishes for P40–50. ❸

St Anthony Hotel Quezon St ☎056/333 2180. A typically run-down provincial boarding house where folks hole up for one night on their way to or from Manila. Pleasant enough communal areas downstairs, but the rooms are small and musty. Choice of a/c or fan with private shower (no hot water). ❸
Sampaguita Tourist Inn Quezon St ☎056/333 4729. Dark, boxy a/c or fan rooms in a noisy location. Some of the twins and doubles are a reasonable size, but there's hardly room to swing a cat in the singles. ❸

Eating

Masbate Town has few restaurants that you would keep going back to. Most of what it does have are small *carinderias* where the day's choices are laid out in aluminium pots. On Quezon Street there are also a couple of bakeries where you can buy bread and pastries, and two convenience stores selling soft drinks, candy and instant noodles. *Ronnie's Restaurant* on Quezon Street has rice dishes and sandwiches for as little as P30, while the nearby *Lantau Restaurant* offers a large menu of Chinese basics such as fried rice and sweet and sour pork. For fresh fruit there's a **market** at the northern end of Quezon Street where, depending on the season, you'll find fresh coconuts, bananas and *ponkan* (small oranges).

Aroroy

The ramshackle little fishing village and gold-panning town of **AROROY** is 20km northwest of Masbate Town along the coast road, and easy to reach by jeepney. Aroroy has a white beach that is popular with locals but is not the kind of place you'd linger to sunbathe. Fishermen use it for making boats and mending nets, so much of the time it's a scenic open-air workshop – a good place for watching the quotidian rituals of provincial life. The village does have one eccentric attraction though, held every year in October. The **Aroroy Wacky Rodeo** tests participants' skill at handling that notoriously bad-tempered and uncontrollable beast, the crab. Crabs are a major livelihood source for the area and this day-long festival, after the usual parades and street dances, includes crab catching, crab tying, crab races and, of course, crab eating. The culmination is the crowning of a beauty queen, Miss Crab.

Bagacay Beach

The sand at **Bagacay Beach**, 14km south of Masbate town and 2km down a dirt road from the barangay of **Bagacay**, is not as blindingly white as some, but that's a minor quibble. Some 2km long, the beach, with palm trees at the edge and beautifully clear shallow water, is still an exceptionally pretty crescent bay that has lost none of its easygoing rural charm to development. The only **place to stay** is *Bituon Beach Resort* (℗056/333 2342; ❶–❸), a humble development of bamboo huts and more recent concrete rooms with a balcony. There's nothing sophisticated to eat, but the staff will rustle up a rice-based breakfast in the morning and some fish for lunch and dinner. As for entertainment, you can watch the sunrise and the sunset. That's the good news. The bad news is that you won't feel quite so alone at weekends, particularly on Sundays when half the population of Masbate Town seems to descend to eat, drink, be merry and make a great deal of noise. Try to time your visit for a weekday, when only local fishermen and their families are around.

There are tricycles and jeepneys to Bagacay from Masbate Town. The jeepneys stop on the main road, from where you can either walk to the beach or take a tricycle down the track.

Mandaon

The town of **MANDAON**, the fourth largest in the province of Masbate, is 64km west of Masbate Town on the opposite coast of the island. The trip by jeepney (P40) is a rugged one, taking you along a scenic but rough road that passes pastureland, paddy fields and a number of isolated barrios inhabited only by subsistence farmers and ragged children. Once you get to Mandaon there's not much to catch your eye in the town itself, but it's a good base for exploring two of the island's most noted natural wonders, **Kalanay Cave** on the northwest coast 40km from Mandaon, and **Batongan Cave**, 20km inland from Mandaon. Both make intriguing day-trips, but Batongan is the better, with

2

immense caverns and a large population of bats whose guano is collected and used as fertilizer. About 100m away is an underground river, said to have been discovered only a few years ago by agricultural students on a field trip. It's easy to get lost in these parts and if you fall and get injured you might not be found for days, so don't explore the caves or the river without a local guide. In Mandaon you can ask at the town hall; the mayor or his staff will appoint someone to take you. The going rate is about P500 a day, and the guide will expect you to buy food and drinks for him at sari-sari stores along the way.

Cataingan

The port town of **CATAINGAN**, 70km south of Masbate Town, sees very few travellers except islanders looking for a cheap ferry south to Cebu. Large bancas and the occasional ferry leave for the eight-hour trip at 6am and 7am. It's a potentially exciting but risky journey, the sometimes old and overcrowded vessels crossing an open sea that can be rough even in the dry season. There are plenty of dilapidated old local buses from Masbate to Cataingan and several jeepneys a day from 7am.

If you have to spend the night in Cataingan, the only option is *Jayvee's Lodge* (①) close to the wharf, with tiny, spartan singles and doubles, some with cold showers, though most rooms share a couple of showers on the second floor. The daily menu in the canteen on the ground floor might include squid *adobo* and rice and fried chicken. The wharf area is noisy, so expect to be woken up early by the din of cargo being moved and jeepneys revving their engines.

Ticao Island

The rarely visited island of **TICAO**, across the Masbate Passage from Masbate Town, can be reached in less than one hour on one of the big bancas (P40) that go back and forth from Masbate pier to either **Lagundi**, on Ticao's southwest coast, or **Costa Rica**, a little further north. You can also explore Ticao by chartering a banca in Masbate Town (P500–1000) or, from **Bulan** in Sorsogon province, you can catch a ferry across the Ticao Passage to the east coast fishing village of **San Jacinto**, from where you can get a jeepney to Lagundi.

Ticao is worth the trip: the island is beautifully rural and as you cross the Masbate Passage there's a decent chance of seeing pods of dolphins. Arriving in Lagundi or Costa Rica by public banca, you can hire another banca and ask the boatman to take you to **Catandayagan Falls**, about an hour along the coast. In a country known for its waterfalls, this is one of the most impressive, plunging more than 30m into a gin-clear pool at its base, ideal for swimming. The island's finest beach is **Talisay**, on the southeast coast, 25km south of **San Jacinto**. There's a rustic resort here where you can pay P100 for overnight accommodation in basic huts.

Burias Island

There is no accommodation for tourists on the remote island of **Burias**, a three-hour trip by ferry northeast of Masbate Town. This is a backwater even by provincial Philippine standards, most of it not electrified and populated only by subsistence fishermen, farmers and their *carabaos* (buffalo), and by American missionaries who have established a number of churches here. Burias holds some intriguing possibilities if you can get up early for the ferry, which leaves Masbate pier at 5am for the town of **Claveria** on Burias's southeast coast. You can also reach Claveria on the daily early-morning ferry from **Donsol** (see p.187) in Sorsogon province.

Burias's most prominent landmark is topographical: the dormant volcano **Mount Eganaso** (428m), which you'll see in the distance as you approach from the sea. From December to May keep your eyes peeled for **whale sharks**, which are often seen feeding in the Burias Passage. The island is too big to explore in a day, so aim to limit yourself to the area around Claveria, which has some pretty beaches known for their impressive rock formations. A little further north, the church at **San Pascual** is said to be the oldest in the Philippines. It was built in 1569 by Fray Alfonso Jimenez, one of the priests in Miguel Lopez de Legazpi's sixteenth-century expedition from Spain to the archipelago.

Catanduanes

The eastern island province of **Catanduanes** is another area of the Philippines ripe for exploration, a large, rugged, rural island with mile upon mile of majestic coastline. It hasn't felt the impact of tourism because getting there has been a problem until recently, and the island itself has little in the way of infrastructure. Resorts are rustic and in the hectic and disorderly little capital, **Virac**, accommodation is limited to a few dreary lodges.

This is no reason to stay away, however. There are now daily flights to Virac from Manila, and Catanduanes is gaining a reputation among travellers for the quality and beauty of its beaches, at **Magnesia** for example, while inland at **Lictin** there are some immense caves for exploration. Other sights include spectacular **waterfalls** at Maribina and San Miguel, both good areas for jungle trekking. On the island's wild **east coast** is **Puraran Beach,** a lovely crescent bay that has become a favourite with surfers – both foreign and local – because of the big waves that roll in from the Pacific. The **west coast** is even less developed, offering visitors with time and patience the opportunity to blaze a trail into areas few travellers see.

Catanduanes is also a rather wet island, lying as it does on the exposed eastern edge of the archipelago. The best **time to visit** is from March to June, when the chances of rainfall are slight and the wind is less wicked. Catanduanes lies smack in the middle of the "typhoon highway" and during the wet season can be hit half a dozen times by typhoons that often prove to be catastrophic, causing extensive damage to crops and homes and sometimes loss of life.

The quickest way to get to Catanduanes from Manila is

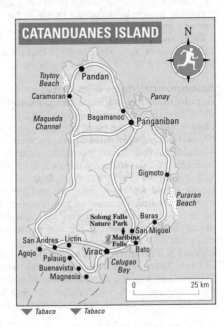

CATANDUANES ISLAND   N

Toytoy Beach
Pandan
Caramoran
Panay
Maqueda Channel
Bagamanoc
Panganiban
Gigmoto
Puraran Beach
Solong Falls Nature Park
Baras
San Miguel
San Andres Lictin
Maribina Falls
Agojo
Palauig Virac Bato
Buenavista
Calugao Bay
Magnesia
0   25 km

▼ Tabaco   ▼ Tabaco

to take the 6.15am Virac **flight** with Asian Spirit (Mon, Wed & Fri). A number of **ferries** run back and forth between Tabaco in Bicol (see p.186) and Virac or **San Andres**, on the southwest coast. It's a long (4hr) and potentially rough journey, so don't consider it if you're not a sea dog. The biggest ferry plying the route is the M/V *Eugenia*, which leaves Tabaco at 7am; otherwise the boats are usually small roll-on, roll-off ferries packed with passengers and cargo. Transport on the island itself is limited to old buses, jeepneys and tricycles.

Virac and around

VIRAC is an anonymous provincial town, busy with the mercantile activity of traders and the noise of jeepneys. There is one cinema, a small central plaza where the cathedral stands and a busy market, but nothing to detain the average visitor.

Virac's **airport** is 4km west of the town. When you arrive you'll have to take a tricycle into town or negotiate with one of the private vehicle owners (P100 is fair) who wait for arriving flights. Asian Spirit's Manila flight leaves at 8am; the airline has an office at Greypac Corporation (☎052/811 1056), San Juan Street, a two-minute walk from the northeastern side of the plaza. The combined **bus and jeepney terminal** is near the central market on Rizal Street, a short distance across the Santo Domingo River from the town centre. The **wharf** on the eastern edge of town, at the end of Geronimo Tabuzo Street, is where ferries arrive from Tabaco, along with dozens of other small craft bearing cargo from Manila and Cebu, or fish and produce from other areas of Catanduanes.

Hiring a car with a driver is a good way to see the island; ask around the drivers at the airport, visit the **tourist office** in the Provincial Capitol Building in Rizal Street (Mon–Fri 8am–4pm; ☎052/233 0989), a five-minute tricycle ride northeast from the plaza, or simply ask your accommodation to arrange it. For about P1000, for instance – good value if you can split the cost with others – you can get a ride to Puraran Beach without suffering the heat and discomfort of a jeepney.

There are two **banks** in Virac where you can change dollars: PNB is on the east side of the plaza and Equitable PCI on the west side. The **post office** is behind the PNB, and on Rizal Street there are a couple of **Internet cafés**.

Accommodation and eating

Accommodation in Virac is unremarkable. The newest and plushest hotel is the *Catanduanes Midtown Inn* (☎052/811 0527; ❸–❹), on Quezon Street one block northeast of the plaza, where rooms are air-conditioned and have cable TV and private white-tiled bathrooms with hot showers. The hotel **café** does a good Bicol Express and blue marlin is almost always the day's special. On San Pedro Street, a ten-minute walk north from the wharf along Rizal Street, is the new *Rakdell Inn* (☎052/811 0881; ❸–❺), which has large, modern rooms with balconies and a pleasant restaurant and bar on the roof deck. Another good option is a family room at the long-established *Marem Pension House* on Rizal Street (no phone; ❷). These rooms are reasonably spacious, well tended and have private bathrooms without hot water; the single rooms, while cheapest, are dingy and have shared facilities.

Virac's best **restaurants** are at the busy roundabout on the northeastern edge of town. There are a couple of local fast-food outlets here such as *Hogs* and *Peking Chow*, plus the friendly *Sandy Blossom's*, where most of the dishes are "rice toppings" meals, which means you get a hefty portion of rice topped with a choice of beef, sausage, barbecued pork or barbecued chicken.

Around Virac

There are some good, surfable **beaches** west of Virac in the villages of **Magnesia**, **Buenavista** and **Palauig**, although none is as pretty or as popular as Puraran, where on a clear day there are views across to Mount Mayon. While you're in the area it's well worth arranging a trip to the old observatory that stands derelict on a cliff above Buenavista overlooking Cabugao Bay. Take your camera, climb the old spiral staircase in the tower, and marvel at the views from the top. *Bosdak Beach Resort* at the beach in Magnesia has very simple cottages for rent (❶) and is busy at weekends with day-trippers from town.

Inland from Palauig there are some enormous limestone **caves** in the village of **Lictin**. To get there you'll have to find a guide in Lictin (P500 is a reasonable amount to pay); you can ask at the barangay hall or in any of the village stores. The best known is Luyong Cave, whose waters are said to have healing properties. Another spot that makes a good half-day trip from Virac is **Maribina Waterfalls** in the barrio of **Maribina**, fifteen minutes inland by jeepney. The fall plunges more than 10m and the pool at the base is crystal-clear and good for swimming.

Northeast of Virac near **San Miguel**, **Solong Falls Nature Park** is a wilderness area where you can trek along the banks of the Solong River and swim in numerous jungle pools. Jeepneys from Virac to San Miguel take thirty minutes and cost P10. On your way to San Miguel hop off the jeepney at **Bato** and take a look at **Batalay Church**, an atmospheric Baroque structure built in the sixteenth century following the arrival of Spanish Captain Juan de Salcedo, who had been hunting for pirates on the coast.

The east coast

The first decent beaches you reach as you head north along the **east coast** from Virac are around **Baras**, a small trading and fishing town where there's no accommodation and where the only visitors are surfers who come occasionally to spend the day. The beach isn't special, but it's worth stopping in Baras to climb the hill to the disused radar station. It's a thirty-minute scramble to the top, but when you get there you're rewarded with uninterrupted views of the coast.

However, for many visitors the only stop on the east coast is at beautiful **Puraran Beach**, with a "break" referred to as Majestic by surfers. Majestic is fickle though: good conditions can occur any time of year, as can bad ones, though it's generally thought that from August to October, when low-pressure areas lurking out in the Pacific help kick up a swell, is the best bet for good waves. Of course, these low-pressure areas can turn into tropical storms and typhoons that batter the coast, making surfing all but impossible except for experts and the very brave.

You don't have to be a surfer to enjoy a few days on a beach as stunning as this one. There are extensive **coral gardens** just offshore that make for wonderful snorkelling, and swimming is safe inside the line of the reef (once you get beyond the reef, where the rollers break, the currents are strong and unpredictable).

Puraran is still mercifully undeveloped and the handful of small resorts on the beach offer plain, perfectly adequate bamboo huts with concrete foundations and **restaurants** where staff will cook you the catch of the day with soup and rice. With beer at P20 a bottle and local rum even cheaper, there's not much else you need. At *Puting Baybay Resort* (☎0926/710 8711; ❶–❸) the rooms are simple, clean cottages with cold water only, and for an extra

P200 a day all your meals are included. *Elena's Majestic Resort*, one of the newer establishments (☎0919/558 1460; ❶–❸), is another simple place with six small cottages right on the sand, each with its own rickety terrace where you can relax with a cold drink at the end of a day's surfing.

The road north of Puraran reaches **Gigmoto**, then degenerates into a rough track. A number of jeepneys continue north through **Panganiban**, where there's an atmospheric old Spanish church and a town hall where, if you can't get any further and need a room, you can ask about homestays. The next stop to the north is **Bagamanoc**, a simple, pretty village with a clean beach. It's worth chartering a banca here (P750 a day) to take you out to **Panay Island**, where there are a number of fantastic, isolated beaches, though no accommodation. The only residents are farmers and fishermen, so bring provisions from Bagamanoc.

The west coast

The **west coast** of Catanduanes faces the Maqueda Channel with views across to Bicol and Mount Mayon. The landscape is brilliant green and blue, with paddy fields and jungle-clad mountains to the right and the sea to the left if you're heading north. However, most of the area is difficult to reach because the road that runs the length of the coast is rough and unpaved. It's a trip that has its rewards if you've the patience to sit in a slow-moving jeepney for hours as it bumps and grinds its way from pothole to pothole with passengers inside, on the back and sitting precariously in rows on the roof.

There's little formal accommodation along the way. The only major resort is in **Agojo**, 30km west of Virac along the coastal road, where *Paradise Resort* (☎0917/344 6677; ❷–❸) has whitewashed stone cottages for two in a neat garden leading on to a long, sandy beach. The price includes breakfast, and there's a big, clean swimming pool, but the real bonus is the view on a clear day of distant Mount Mayon. At **Toytoy Beach** in the far northern barrio of **Caramoran** the local government has built huts on the beach that can be rented for P200 a night.

Travel details

Trains

Iriga to: Legaspi (2 daily; 2hr); Manila (2 daily; 10hr); Naga (2 daily; 2hr).
Legaspi to: Iriga (2 daily; 2hr); Naga (2 daily; 3hr); Manila (2 daily; 8hr).
Lucena to Manila (2 daily; 4hr).
Naga to: Iriga (2 daily; 2hr); Legaspi (2 daily; 3hr); Manila (2 daily; 5hr).

Buses

Batangas City to: Lucena (8 daily; 4hr); Manila (every 30min; 3hr); Nasugbu (8 daily; 2hr); San Pablo (8 daily; 1hr 30min); Santa Cruz (6 daily; 3hr); Taal (several daily; 1hr 30min); Tagaytay (several daily; 1hr 30min); Tanauan (8 daily; 2hr).

Daet to: Calbayog (daily; 10hr); Davao (daily; 20hr); Legaspi (23 daily; 6hr); Matnog (3 daily; 8–9hr); Mercedes (23 daily; 30min); Naga (12 daily; 1hr); Sorsogon Town (6 daily; 7–8hr); Surigao (daily; 15hr).
Donsol to: Sorsogon Town (12 daily; 1hr).
Iriga to: Legaspi (23 daily; 3hr); Matnog (3 daily; 5–6hr); Sorsogon Town (6 daily; 4–5hr).
Legaspi to: Daraga (12 daily; 30min); Davao (daily; 18hr); Matnog (12 daily; 2–3hr); Sorsogon Town (24 daily; 1–2hr); Surigao (daily; 13hr); Tabaco (24 daily; 1hr).
Lucban to: Lucena (several daily; 2hr); San Pablo (several daily; 2hr); Santa Cruz (several daily; 3hr).
Lucena to: Atimonan (hourly; 1hr 30min); Daet (hourly; 3hr); Dalahican (for Marinduque ferries;

hourly; 1hr); Davao (daily; 23hr); Dolores (several daily; 1hr); Legaspi (hourly; 6hr); Manila (hourly; 4hr); Naga (hourly; 4hr); Surigao (daily; 18hr).

Masbate Town to: Cataingan (8–12 daily; 2–3hr).

Matnog to: Daet (hourly; 6hr); Davao (daily; 17hr); Iriga (hourly; 4hr); Legaspi (hourly; 2hr); Naga (hourly; 5hr); Sorsogon Town (hourly; 1hr); Surigao (daily; 12hr).

Naga to: Allen (3 daily; 11hr); Daet (12 daily; 1hr); Davao (daily; 20hr); Iriga (23 daily; 2hr); Legaspi (23 daily; 4hr); Matnog (3 daily; 6–7hr); San Isidro (3 daily; 12hr); Sorsogon Town (6 daily; 5–6hr); Surigao (daily; 15hr).

Nasugbu to: Batangas City (hourly; 2–3hr); Manila (hourly; 2hr 30min).

Sorsogon Town to: Donsol (12 daily; 1hr); Matnog (12 daily; 2hr).

Taal to: Batangas City (hourly; 1hr 30min); Lemery (hourly; 30min); Manila (hourly; 3hr).

Tabaco to: Buang (6 daily; 1hr).

Tagaytay to: Manila (every 30min; 2hr 30min).

Tanauan to: Batangas City (hourly; 2hr); Manila (every 30min; 2hr 30min).

Jeepneys and FX taxis

Batangas City to: Anilao (several daily; 2hr); Bauan (hourly; 1hr 30min).

Boac to: Balanacan (hourly; 45min); Buenavista (several daily; 1hr); Gasan (hourly; 45min); Mogpog (hourly; 30min); Santa Cruz (hourly; 1hr).

Daet to: Legaspi (1 daily; 1hr); Mercedes (4–5 daily; 30min–1hr).

Daraga to: Camalig (12 daily; 45min).

Iriga to: Buhi (4–6 daily; 1hr).

Legaspi to: Bacacay (6 daily; 2hr); Daraga (24 daily; 1hr); Santo Domingo (6 daily; 1hr); Tabaco (24 daily; 1hr).

Lucena to: Atimonan (several daily; 2–3hr); Lucban (hourly; 1hr 30min); Sariaya (hourly; 1hr 30min).

Masbate Town to: Aroroy (4–6 daily; 1hr); Bagacay (4–6 daily; 1hr); Cataingan (8 daily; 3hr); Mandaon (8 daily; 2–3hr).

Naga to: Panicuasan (for Isarog; 2–3 daily; 1hr).

Nasugbu to: Balayan (6–8 daily; 45min); Calatagan via Matabungkay (every 20min; 45min).

Sorsogon Town to: Bacon (6 daily; 30–45min); Donsol (6 daily; 1hr); Gubat (6 daily; 1hr); Irosin (6 daily; 1–2hr); Prieto Diaz (6 daily; 1hr).

Tabaco to: Buang (8–10 daily; 1hr).

Tagaytay to: Taal (several daily; 1hr); Talisay (every 30min; 40min).

Talisay to: Tagaytay (every 30min; 40min); Tanauan (every 15min; 30–45min).

Tanauan to: Tagaytay (every 15min; 30–45min); Talisay (every 15min; 30–45min).

Virac to: Agojo (6 daily; 2hr); Bagamanoc (2–3 daily; 6hr); Baras (6 daily; 1hr); Caramoran (2–3 daily; 6hr); Gigmoto (2–3 daily; 4hr); Lictin (6 daily; 1hr); Magnesia (8–10 daily; 1hr); Maribina (4 daily; 15–30min); Panganiban (2–3 daily; 5hr); Puraran (6 daily; 3hr); San Miguel (6–8 daily; 1hr).

Ferries and scheduled bancas

Balanacan to: Dalahican (2 daily; 3–5hr); Pinamalayan (Mindoro; 1–2 weekly; 5hr).

Batan to: Rapu-Rapu (several daily; 1hr).

Batangas City to: Puerto Galera (several daily; 2hr); Romblon (various destinations; 6 weekly; 8hr).

Bulan (Sorsogon) to: Masbate Town (daily; 3–4hr); San Jacinto (Ticao; several daily; 2hr).

Cataingan to: Cebu City (2 daily; 8hr).

Dalahican to: Balanacan (2 daily; 3–5hr).

Donsol to: Claveria (1–2 daily; 3hr).

Masbate Town to: Bulan (2–3 daily; 4hr); Burias (1 daily; 3hr); Calbayog (weekly; 4hr); Catanduanes (1 daily; 1hr 15min); Cebu (2–3 weekly; 7hr); Claveria (daily; 3hr); Manila (2-3 weekly; 11hr); Ticao (6–8 daily; 1hr).

Matnog to: Allen (hourly; 2hr).

Prieto Diaz (Sorsogon) to: Rapu-Rapu (1–2 daily; 3hr).

San Andres (Catanduanes) to: Tabaco City (2 daily; 4–6hr).

Tabaco City to: Batan (1–2 daily; 4hr); San Andres (Catanduanes; 2 daily; 4–6hr); San Antonio (1–2 daily; 2hr); Virac (2 daily; 4–5hr).

Virac to: Tabaco City (2 daily; 4–5hr).

Domestic flights

Legaspi to: Manila (1 daily; 1hr).

Masbate Town to: Manila (5 weekly; 1hr).

Naga to: Manila (5 weekly; 50min).

Virac to: Manila (3 weekly; 1hr 15min).

Mindoro

CHAPTER 3 # Highlights

✳**Tribal visits** Get an intriguing insight into a marginalized culture by meeting Mindoro's original inhabitants, the Mangyan. See p.206

✳**Puerto Galera** The area around this picturesque little coastal town has some terrific beaches, challenging treks and scuba diving for every level. See p.208

✳**Mount Halcon** Among the toughest and most rewarding climbs in the country, through dense rainforest and across montane streams. See p.221

✳**Mounts Iglit-Baco National Park** See the rare *tamaraw*, a type of water buffalo, as you trek through some of the most beautiful countryside on Mindoro. See p.224

✳**Sablayan Watershed Forest Reserve** Wilderness area offering reasonably easy day-treks around Lake Libao, whose shores are known for birdlife. See p.225

✳**North Pandan Island and Apo Reef** North Pandan is an island hideaway where you can join a trip to Apo Reef, which has superlative diving in one of the most pristine marine environments on Earth. See p.225

△ Sabang beach, near Puerto Gakera

Mindoro

T hough the seventh largest of the nation's 7107 islands, **Mindoro** remains undeveloped even by Philippine provincial standards, with barrios that have no electricity and a population of about 670,000, most of them Tagalog-speaking who exist on agriculture, tourism and the scraps they can make from trade with Luzon. Much of the island is wild and rugged, with some near-impenetrable hinterlands and an often desolate coastline of wide bays inhabited by fisher families. The northern coast is only 80km from the grime of Manila, but it's a different world, with unreliable telecommunications (although mobile phones now work in many areas), no taxis and most of the food coming straight from the sea or the fields.

Agriculture remains the island's foremost economic activity, with great tracts of fertile land along the coastal foothills given over to rice, corn, citrus fruits and rubber plants. Fishing can also be lucrative, at least for those who have enough to cover the cost of getting their catch to market or to a middleman in Manila. As with so much of the country, even this is a problem, with most cargo having to bump its way along unpaved island roads.

Divided lengthways into two provinces, **Mindoro Occidental** and **Mindoro Oriental**, the island deserves much more attention as a tourist destination than it's getting. Most visitors head this way only for the beaches, scuba diving and nightlife around the picturesque town of **Puerto Galera** on Mindoro's northern coast, a short ferry trip from Batangas. But there's much more to the island than this. Few people, Filipinos included, realize that Mindoro is home to several areas of outstanding natural beauty, all protected to some degree by local or international decree. In the north of the island, Puerto Galera itself is a marine reserve whose reefs are the habitat of some beautiful and extraordinary species. Nearby **Mount Malasimbo** is also protected, this time by UNESCO, because of the biodiversity of its thickly jungled slopes. To the east of Puerto Galera, near the port of **Calapan**, is **Mount Halcon**, at 2587m Mindoro's tallest peak and a difficult climb even for experienced mountaineers.

The south of the island is even less populated than the north, with few tourists making it as far as **Roxas** on the southeast coast or **San José**, on the southwest. The latter is a departure point for the **Mounts Iglit–Baco National Park**, good for trekking and home to the *tamaraw*, a dwarf buffalo endemic to Mindoro and in acute danger of extinction. On the west coast, the fishing town of **Sablayan** is the jumping-off point for a sight no scuba diver should miss, the **Apo Reef Marine Natural Park**, a vast reef complex about 30km off the coast, offering some of the best diving in the world. If you don't organize a trip there in Sablayan, you can do so in advance at a dive shop in Manila (see p.129) or Busuanga (see p.362). Sablayan is also a base for a visit to Mounts Iglit-Baco

The Mangyan

From many areas of Mindoro, including Puerto Galera and San José, you can organize a gentle trek into the foothills to visit communities of the **Mangyan** people, Mindoro's original inhabitants. It's estimated that there are around 100,000 Mangyan on the island (southern Luzon, too, has small groups of Mangyan), their way of life not much changed since they fought against the invading Spanish in the sixteenth century. With little role in the mainstream Philippine economy, they subsist through slash-and-burn farming, a practice the elders insist on retaining as part of their culture, despite the destruction it causes to forests. They also trap animals such as wild pig. Many who live in close contact with lowland Filipinos – around the coasts of Mindoro – sell cash crops such as bananas and ginger.

"Mangyan" is in fact the generic name given to eight indigenous groups, each with its own tribal name, language and customs. Mangyan tongues include Arayan, Alangan, Buhid, Hanunuo and Tadyawan. The **Iraya** live in the northern areas from Baco to Mamburao, inhabiting distinctive hexagonal wooden houses and producing handicrafts made from *nito*, a local vine. The **Alangan** live in a wide area around Mount Halcon and wear clothes made from long strips of woven *nito*. Belonging to an ethnic stock called proto-Malay, the **Batangan** or **Taobuid** inhabit the central highlands; they wear loincloths and leave their breasts uncovered. The **Hanunuo**, who consider themselves the "true" Mangyan, are found in the southern towns from Bongabong to San José in Occidental Mindoro and use an ancient indigenous script consisting of 48 characters, which they carve onto bamboo tubes. Their customs also include chanting words of wisdom called *inukoy* and folkloric poems called *ambahan*, accompanied by instruments made of wood and bows made with human hair.

Most Mangyan don't object to visitors, but aren't particularly welcoming. With the arrival of the Americans, the Mangyan were put to work on plantations and the resentment created by this still festers and perhaps accounts for some of their frostiness. The Mangyan are unlikely to invite outsiders into their homes, which consist of rudimentary wood-and-thatch houses on stilts. You can break the ice with a few treats such as cigarettes, sweets and matches, but if you want to take photographs, make sure you have their permission first. Cultural differences can result in awkward misunderstandings, and it's rare to find a Mangyan who understands English, so it's best to go with a guide who can act as an interpreter. Treks to Mangyan villages are possible in several parts of the island. For information on treks around Puerto Galera see box on pp.220–221; for Mounts Iglit-Baco National Park see p.224.

or the **Sablayan Watershed Forest Reserve**, a lowland forest with beautiful Lake Libao at its centre. The northwest of the island is little visited, though there are some unspoilt beaches around the town of **Mamburao**, the low-key capital of Mindoro Occidental.

Getting to Mindoro

There's a small **airport** at Calapan, northern Mindoro, although there were no scheduled flights to there at the time of writing (Seair has flown there from Manila in the past, so check to see if they have resumed). In the south, San José airport is served by daily flights from Manila with Asian Spirit and Cebu Pacific.

The main **ferry port** for departures to northern Mindoro is Batangas City (see p.151), from where there are many ferries to **Puerto Galera** including Super Diamond Lines' (℡0917/350 8121) M/V *Super 85* and Si-Kat's fast ferry which leaves at noon. Both charge P110 plus a P10 terminal fee. Viva Shipping Lines has ferries to the pier at Balatero, 3km west of Puerto Galera.

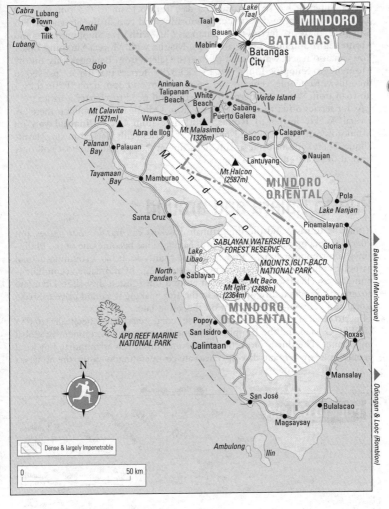

Labels on map:

Cabra, Lubang Town, Ambil, Lubang, Tilik, Gojo

Taal, Bauan, Mabini, Batangas City, BATANGAS, MINDORO

Aninuan & Talipanan Beach, White Beach, Verde Island, Sabang, Puerto Galera, Calapan

Mt Calavite (1521m), Wawa, Abra de Ilog, Mt Malasimbo (1326m), Baco

Palanan Bay, Palauan, Tayamaan Bay, Mamburao, Lantuyang, Mt Halcon (2587m), MINDORO ORIENTAL, Naujan, Pola, Lake Nanjan

Santa Cruz, Pinamalayan, Gloria

Lake Libao, SABLAYAN WATERSHED FOREST RESERVE, MOUNTS IGLIT-BACO NATIONAL PARK

North Pandan, Sablayan, Mt Iglit (2364m), Mt Baco (2488m), Bongabong

APO REEF MARINE NATIONAL PARK, Popoy, San Isidro, Calintaan, MINDORO OCCIDENTAL, Roxas

N, Mansalay

San José, Bulalacao, Magsaysay

Ambulong, Ilin

Dense & largely Impenetrable

0   50 km

Balanacan (Marinduque)

Odiongan & Looc (Romblon)

Si-Kat also operates a joint bus-and-ferry service from Manila (P790 per person return; ☎02/521 3344), leaving at 9am sharp from the *Citystate Tower Hotel* in Ermita (see p.86). Island Cruiser (☎02/523 8541, P790) offers a similar service leaving the *Swagman Hotel* in A. Flores Street, Ermita at 7.45am and the *Lotus Garden Hotel* in A. Mabini Street, Ermita at 8am.

Local bancas (P80) go back and forth from Batangas to **Sabang**, just east of Puerto Galera. Datinguinoo (☎0917/361 0772) has six departures a day to Sabang. M/V Brian Shipping has daily departures from Batangas to **White Beach**, west of Puerto Galera. Most of the bancas leave only in the mornings, so get to Batangas pier as early as you can.

Supercat ferries (🌐www.supercat.com.ph) and Viva Shipping Lines operate from Batangas City to **Calapan**, a route also plied by a number of slow ferries. Supercat has six departures a day, from 6.15am to 6.30pm and Viva has four departures a day, two early morning and two in the afternoon. For **San José**, there are ferries from Batangas City with Viva Shipping Lines and Montenegro Shipping Lines, and from Manila with Moreta Shipping Lines. You can also reach **Wawa**, west of Puerto Galera, from Batangas City on the Montenegro Shipping Lines' (☎043/723 8294) ferries that depart, packed to the gills with people, vehicles and cargo, at 8am and 3pm daily (P90); there's no road from Wawa to Puerto Galera so you'll need to charter a banca.

As for ferries other than from Luzon, from Odiongan in Romblon there are several weekly ferries to **Roxas**, with three from Looc. **Pinamalayan** on Mindoro's east coast is linked by irregular ferries with Balanacan on Marinduque. There's meant to be a daily departure at 6.30am, but the boat will only leave if there are enough passengers.

Puerto Galera and around

It may be touristy and the importunate hawkers can frazzle your nerves, but Puerto Galera on the northern coast of Mindoro has become one of the Philippines' most popular tourist attractions, and rightly so. It has a stunning natural harbour, countless coves and beaches, a good range of affordable accommodation and excellent scuba diving, with around thirty listed dive sites. There are dozens of accredited dive operators in the area, making it a good place to strike a deal and get yourself a discount on the going rate.

Puerto Galera's extensive and diverse coral reefs have been declared a UNESCO Man and the Biosphere Marine Reserve, an environment of global importance. The direct protection that comes from this is minimal, but local people, hotel owners and dive operators are co-operating to ensure the undersea

riches are not frittered away. There's plenty on offer in addition to diving, including excellent snorkelling, trekking into the mountains and beach-hopping by banca (see box pp.210–211), perhaps with a packed lunch so you can picnic in the deserted cove of your choice.

Puerto Galera is actually the name of a small town (*poblacion*), but is generally used to refer to the area between **Sabang**, 5km to the east, and White Beach, 8km to the west. Most visitors head straight for Sabang and the nearby beaches of **Small La Laguna** and **Big La Laguna**. Between them, these three locations offer the best choice of accommodation, diving, restaurants and nightlife. Sabang is the busiest beach, with a mind-boggling variety of accommodation dotted haphazardly along the shoreline and some above-average restaurants. It also has a couple of go-go bars, whereas Small La Laguna and Big La Laguna are rather more laidback and family-oriented, with accommodation to suit all budgets, a few beach bars and pleasant seafront restaurants. Also suited to families are a number of mid-range resorts which sprouted up near the village of **Palangan**, about halfway along the road from Puerto Galera to Sabang. Northeast of Palangan there's a small, isolated cove at **Sinandigan** with a handful of very peaceful resorts. In the other direction, to the west of Puerto Galera, the nearest beach is the picturesque **White Beach**, where accommodation is strictly of the bamboo-hut variety and restaurant menus are more limited than at Sabang. Beyond lie **Aninuan Beach** and **Talipanan Beach**, which have affordable, comfortable places to stay, though no nightlife or diving.

Many visitors come to Puerto Galera for the excellent **diving** (see box p.210), but there's plenty to do besides. There are many secluded beaches and coves around Puerto Galera and a number of **islands** close by that are worth exploring. The beaches west of Puerto Galera provide quick access to the foothills of **Mount Malasimbo** and make good bases for **trekking**.

Power failures are a regular occurrence in Puerto Galera, so it's worth asking resorts if they have a backup generator before committing yourself to staying. In and around Sabang most **restaurants** have European cuisine, with quite extensive menus at the larger resorts, but elsewhere in the Puerto Galera area eating is often a simple affair, usually revolving around whatever fish happens to have been brought ashore that day. Most areas have their own sari-sari stores, so you probably won't need to go into Puerto Galera to do your shopping.

The Town

Arriving at **PUERTO GALERA** by ferry from Batangas is a memorable experience, the boat slipping gently through aquamarine waters past a series of headlands fringed with haloes of sand and coconut trees. Brilliant white yachts lie at anchor in the innermost bay and in the background looms the brooding hulk of Mount Malasimbo, invariably crowned with a ring of cumulus cloud. The town itself is in a marvellous spot, overlooking Muelle Bay on one side and with green hills behind it, and you could sit for hours over a cool drink at the sleepy little cafés right on the waterfront on Muelle pier watching the bancas phut-phut back and forth. The town has various souvenir shops, general stores and a handful of modest places to stay, but despite its beautiful views and appealingly sleepy tropical ambience, there are no compelling reasons to base yourself here and most tourists move straight on to the beaches and dive resorts.

Practicalities

If you arrive by **fast ferry** from Batangas, you'll dock at **Muelle pier** in the town proper; the town centre is a short walk away up the hill. Larger, slower ferries use **Balatero pier** 3km to the west, and there are big bancas from

Diving and other activities around Puerto Galera

The beauty of scuba diving around Puerto Galera is the number and variety of **dive sites** that can be reached by boat in a matter of minutes. These offer something for everyone, from exhilarating dives in raging currents to gentle drifts along sheltered coral reefs. One of the standard dives is **Shark's Cave**, a drift dive along a reef that takes you past a cave where you might get a close-up of sleeping white tip sharks and, deeper down, leopard sharks. **Ernie's Cave**, named after a giant grouper who used to live there, is another reasonably easy dive, as is **Fish Bowl**, which takes you on a blue-water descent to the top of a reef where whitetip reef sharks, sweetlips and rainbow runners are common. **Sabang Point**, a half-hour banca ride from Sabang Beach, makes a good night dive, while **Monkey Wreck**, only five minutes from Sabang, is a local cargo boat that sank in fairly shallow water in 1993, and now plays host to large schools of batfish and snappers. Another good wreck for novices is the *St Christopher*, a retired diving boat that was deliberately sunk and is a refuge for the extraordinary frogfish, an ugly character with large fins and a flabby, drooping face.

More challenging dives include **Canyons**, which has a healthy reef split into three slab-like sections (hence the name) and some fierce currents that mean it's usually for advanced divers only. What makes it special is that it's the best place in the area to encounter large pelagics such as sharks and barracuda. Occasionally manta rays, eagle rays and hammerheads pass through. For a real thrill there's not much to beat the **Washing Machine**, a notorious dive near Verde Island, where currents are so strong and the topography so tricky that divers report being thrown around underwater and disoriented. It's definitely not for beginners.

There are dozens of **dive operators** in Sabang, Small La Laguna and Big La Laguna, though none west of Puerto Galera. They offer everything from the basic open-water certification course to wreck diving, night diving and specialist disciplines such as NITROX, using an oxygen/nitrogen gas blend that allows you to stay submerged longer. The established firms include: Action Divers (☏043/287 3320, ⓦwww.actiondivers.com), next to *Deep Blue Sea Inn* on Small La Laguna; Asia Divers (☏043/287 3205, ⓦwww.asiadivers.com) next door to *El Galleon*, Small La Laguna; and Frontier Scuba (☏0917/540 8410, ⓦwww.frontierscuba.com) near *Angelyn Beach Resort* in Sabang. Rates are around $27 for one dive with full equipment, or $22 if you bring your own wetsuit and buoyancy control device. The Open Water Course costs $300 inclusive of manuals, equipment and boat rental.

Batangas City to **Sabang** and increasingly to **White Beach**. **Jeepneys** from Calapan (there are no bus services to Puerto Galera) will drop you on the main road in town.

Boats arriving at Muelle pier are met by a welcoming committee of touts offering expensive "special rides" to Sabang or White Beach, but if you take the short walk to the end of the pier by the *Coco Point Hotel*, there's a **banca** departure area where you'll pay the standard fare to charter a boat – for up to six passengers, you'll pay around P440 to White Beach, P180 to Big La Laguna, P200 to Small La Laguna, and P480 to Aninuan or Talipanan; this is your best bet if you've plenty of luggage. You can instead hop on a **jeepney** (P18 to Sabang, P40 to White Beach), though they only leave when packed to the gills with people, baggage, produce and farm animals – on these routes it's not unusual for passengers to be hanging from the sides or sitting on the roof. Jeepneys to White Beach leave from close to the pier. For Sabang, from where you can walk to Small La Laguna and Big La Laguna, jeepneys leave from further away: walk up the hill, turn left at the blue bus stop and walk past the Puerto Galera Academy, then turn left again and continue up the hill for 100m. At Balatero pier, jeepneys meet arriving passengers to take them into town and

Some resorts charge less, but don't include equipment or boat rental. Advanced Open Water and Nitrox are both around $250.

Treks and day-trips

As for other activities in the area, local guides can lead you on a trek into the hills to visit Mangyan **tribal villages**, boatmen can take you on beach-hopping trips to secluded coves, and off the main road to Calapan are a number of caves and thundering waterfalls. The mother of all cascades here is the mighty **Tamaraw Falls**, thirty minutes by jeepney outside Puerto Galera and not far off the road to Calapan. Here cool mountain water plummets over a precipice and into a natural pool and manmade swimming pool. The falls have become a popular sight (hence the P10 entrance fee), so don't go at weekends, when they are overrun. One of the nicest day-treks is from White Beach into the foothills of **Mount Malasimbo**, where there are a number of tribal communities, as well as waterfalls with cold, clear pools big enough for swimming.

For a gentle walk, head to the old lighthouse at **Escarceo Point** by taking the dirt road out of Sabang up the hill to the east, then continuing through friendly barrios and across the clifftop to the lighthouse itself. The views are marvellous. A popular day-trip is to Python Cave and the **hot springs** about 3km out of town on the Calapan road. A narrow, unsigned trail leads up to the immense cave through thick vegetation and the piping hot springs are deep enough for a swim.

In Sabang you can arrange all the above trips, as well as kayak expeditions and overnight treks into the tribal hinterlands, at Jungle Trek Adventure Tours, opposite *Tropicana* on the main road or Tarzan Trek & Tours, behind the *Garden of Eden* resort on the northern half of the beach. In Puerto Galera itself Badladz Adventures (℡043/287 3184 or 0919/577 2823, Ⓦwww.badladz.com) near Muelle Pier in Puerto Galera town, offer scuba diving, paintball games, kayaking and trekking to Mindoro's native villages. Badladz also has accommodation (see p.212). If you're staying elsewhere, at White Beach for instance, simply ask around among the locals and find a guide (expect to pay about P500 for a trip leaving in the morning and returning after lunch) who's willing to take you. Another option for a day out is to **rent a motorbike** (P500 for half a day) in Sabang; you can do this at the agency on the main road close to the T-junction in Sabang, where they also have self-drive all-terrain vehicles for rent, taking two people including the driver.

other destinations in the area. There's no regular road transport to Aninuan and Talipanan beaches, so if you don't want to pay for your own private banca, you'll have to get a public jeepney to White Beach, then walk. It's also possible to hire a jeepney for a private trip to Aninuan and Talipanan when you arrive in Puerto Galera, but this will cost at least P400 and you'll have to be prepared to haggle.

There's a small **tourist office** at the end of Muelle pier (daily 8am–6pm; ℡043/281 4051), close to the Super Diamond Lines booking office and near *Coco Point Hotel*. They have a few brochures, details of accommodation and ferry schedules, but not much else. The **post office** is at the town hall (some resorts will post mail for a small fee). There are many **phone offices** in Puerto Galera where you can make calls to Manila for P12 a minute or overseas for P130 a minute; telephones are mostly cellular as there are few reliable landlines. **Internet** access is becoming more widely available, two of the best places being *Puerto Galera Online Internet*, on the main road in Sabang opposite the *Tropicana*, and *Rucke's* at Muelle Pier. The *Internet Café* in Sabang is just beyond the Big Apple resort walking south. Many of the more established resorts also have Internet

PUERTO GALERA TOWN

Muelle Bay

Bancas

Muelle Pier (i)

Si-Kat
Ferry Office ❶ ❷ ❸ Ⓐ
Ⓑ

Ⓒ

Margarita
Shopping
Center

★ Jeepnays to
White Beach

✝ Puerto Galera
Chruch

★ ★ Jeepnays
to Sabang

Puerto Galera
Medical Clinic

H. AXALAN STREET

P CONCEPCION STREET

E COBARRUBIAS SR STREET

R GARCIA STREET

E BRUCAL STREET

Balete
Beach

Varadevo
Bay

Ⓓ

N

RESTAURANTS
Hangout Bar & Restaurant **2**
La Galerie **3**
Pizza Pub & Restaurant **1**

ACCOMMODATION
Badlaz **C**
Bahay-Pilipino Pension House **D**
Coco Point **A**
Puerto Galera Resort Hotel **B**

Public Market

Hondura Beach

0   50 m

▼ Calapan

◄ White Beach

Sabang ►

access for guests.

The closest **ATMs** to Puerto Galera are a long jeepney ride away in Calapan, so it's advisable to bring whatever cash you'll need. Puerto Galera Rural Bank near the church changes cash but not travellers' cheques. The **police station** (☎043/281 4043) is inside the municipal compound a short walk from Muelle pier. The Puerto Galera Medical Clinic is in Axalan Street in town, a short walk up the hill from Muelle Pier, opposite the church. There are a number of other rudimentary **clinics** in the town; if in doubt you can always ask the dive operators, who know where the best doctors are. There are also a few small sari-sari-style pharmacies. As for **moving on** from Puerto Galera, there are jeepneys from the market to Calapan, and a clutch of ferries and bancas to Batangas City from Muelle and Balatero piers, and from Sabang.

Accommodation and eating

There are some simple, cheap places to **stay** along the pier, useful if you want to base yourself in town to catch an early ferry or jeepney. The best of these is *Coco Point* (☎043/442 0109; ❷), with a small café downstairs that serves snacks, shakes and instant coffee. The rooms are small and bare, each with a fan and its own tiny shower. Another good choice is *Badladz* (☎043/287 3184 or 0919/577 2823, ⓦwww.badladz.com; ❸), on the hill above Muelle pier, which has modest but very adequate and clean rooms, all with air-condi-

△ Puerto Galera

tioning and shady balconies with wonderful views across the bay.

Sitting incongruously above the laidback pension houses and budget rooms around the wharf, the *Puerto Galera Resort Hotel* (℡02/565 4241; ❹), is a sprawling concrete establishment with swimming pool, conference facilities and air-conditioned rooms with walls made from *sawali*, a native grass. Staff can help arrange all sorts of activities, including diving and golf. In the centre of the *poblacion* opposite Candava Supermarket and the *Dog & Duck* pub, the *Bahay-Pilipino Pension House* (℡043/422 0266; ❷) is a friendly place run by Bavarian Dr Fritz and his Filipina wife Jasmin. The rooms are small and well kept, with clean showers and fresh sheets. A common balcony overlooks the busy street, so you can buy yourself a cold San Miguel and sit and watch the world go by.

The best places for a simple **meal** in town are the little restaurants along the pier facing the sea, all serving light meals such as pizza, pancakes and toasted sandwiches. They include *La Galerie*, the *Pizza Pub & Restaurant* and the *Hangout Bar & Restaurant*, where the speciality is *halo-halo* (P40). The restaurant at the *Bahay-Pilipino Pension House* does simple but very satisfying German and Asian meals for as little as P100 a head, and the convivial *Badladz* restaurant, right at the water's edge on Muelle pier, serves Mexican, Asian and European dishes.

Sabang to Big La Laguna

The road leading into **Sabang** ends in a T-junction by the sea. The next beach to the west, **Small La Laguna**, is clean and scenic, if stony, and quieter than Sabang, but still with some friendly and popular bars on the shore. West of this and connected to Small La Laguna by a path over the headland, **Big La Laguna** is likewise much quieter than Sabang and popular with divers who aren't so keen on raucous nightlife.

At the **Tourist Information and Filipino Travel Center** office (daily 8am–6pm; ℡043/244 1228) on the main road opposite the *Tropicana Castle Dive Resort* in Sabang, staff can offer information as well as book local day-trips

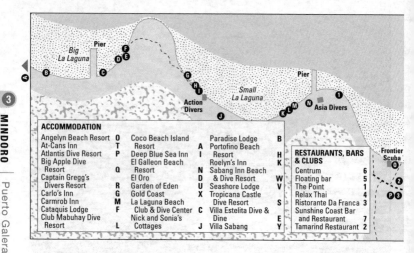

ACCOMMODATION

Angelyn Beach Resort	O	Coco Beach Island Resort	A	Paradise Lodge	B	
At-Cans Inn	T	Deep Blue Sea Inn	I	Portofino Beach Resort	H	
Atlantis Dive Resort	P	El Galleon Beach Resort	N	Roelyn's Inn	K	
Big Apple Dive Resort	Q	El Oro	D	Sabang Inn Beach & Dive Resort	W	
Captain Gregg's Divers Resort	R	Garden of Eden	U	Seashore Lodge	V	
Carlo's Inn	G	Gold Coast	X	Tropicana Castle Dive Resort	S	
Carmrob Inn	M	La Laguna Beach Club & Dive Center	C	Villa Estelita Dive & Dine	E	
Cataquis Lodge	F	Nick and Sonia's Cottages	J	Villa Sabang	Y	
Club Mabuhay Dive Resort	L					

RESTAURANTS, BARS & CLUBS

Centrum	6
Floating bar	5
The Point	1
Relax Thai	4
Ristorante Da Franca	3
Sunshine Coast Bar and Restaurant	7
Tamarind Restaurant	2

and plane and ferry tickets. Swagman Travel at the western end of Sabang beach offers currency exchange (they handle both cash and travellers' cheques), fax and phone facilities, organizes visa extensions and sells air tickets. Exchange (cash only) and telephone services are also available at *Centrum*, a club at the back of the beach and 50m west of the road from Puerto Galera. At the Metropolitan Doctors Medical Clinic, at the northern end of the beach in Sabang, a doctor specializing in hyperbaric medicine is on hand for diving-related complaints.

Sabang

The beach at **Sabang** is nothing special, and not particularly good for swimming, but this is a great place to stay if you want to be close to the bars, restaurants and dive shops. If you arrive here **by banca** from Batangas City, you'll be dropped a little way east of the main road. The accommodation west of the main road is in the thick of the action and slightly pricier than that to the east.

Accommodation

Angelyn Beach Resort ☎0912/306 5332 or 043/442 0038. Good location right on the beach and only a short walk from dive operators, bars and restaurants, with a choice of en-suite cottages with balconies and, in some cases, a/c. There's also a small open-air restaurant and a beauty parlour where you can get a haircut for P70 or a pedicure for P50. ❸–❹

At-Cans Inn ☎0917/463 8233. Good budget option at the quieter end of the beach, north from the main road. The rooms are plain but they do have big balconies right on the shore. ❹

Atlantis Dive Resort Near Swagman Travel at the far western edge of the beach ☎0917/562 0294 or 043/287 3066, ⟨w⟩www.atlantishotel.com. Luxurious a/c rooms in a whitewashed Mediterranean-style building overlooking the sea. All mod cons, scuba facilities, well-trained and knowledgeable staff and a good outdoor restaurant. ❽

Big Apple Dive Resort ☎043/287 3134 or 02/526 7592, ⟨w⟩www.dive-bigapple. com. Set back from the shore on the main footpath, this is one of Sabang's best-known resorts, with its own dive centre. There are fan cottages, a/c family cottages and a/c double cottages, all in a quiet garden surrounding a swimming pool. ❸–❼

Captain Gregg's Divers Resort Turn left at the end of the road in Sabang then it's a 5min walk along the beach ☎0917/540 4570. A popular, well-established resort catering mainly to divers, it offers acceptable rooms, decent food and useful advice from the resident divers in the dive shop, many of whom have lived in Sabang for years. ❸

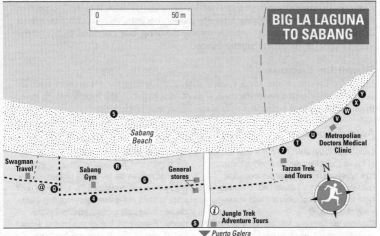

BIG LA LAGUNA TO SABANG

0   50 m

Sabang Beach

Metropolian Doctors Medical Clinic

Swagman Travel

Sabang Gym

General stores

Tarzan Trek and Tours

N

Jungle Trek Adventure Tours

Garden of Eden Turn right at the T-junction and the resort is a short walk along the beachfront. ☎0917/813 5392. There's a choice of nipa-style rooms with fan, a/c bungalows or lovely a/c suites with private patios. Bathrooms are all tiled, and the furniture is simple bamboo. All accommodation is set in a tropical garden planted with orchids, banana and papaya, and some of the rooms are on a hill with views towards Verde Island. ❹

Gold Coast Eastern end of the beach, no phone. Pleasant concrete rooms with shady balconies; for an extra charge you get your own small kitchen. ❸

Sabang Inn Beach & Dive Resort Eastern end of the beach ☎0912/311 4335, ⓦwww.sabang-inn.com. This small, friendly resort at the quieter part of the beach has new rooms with tiled floors, refrigerators and a/c or fan; many rooms also have pleasant balconies. There's a dive centre, small swimming pool, travel desk, pub and restaurant. ❹–❻

Seashore Lodge No phone. Almost at the far eastern end of the beach (a 5min walk from the main road), this is a pleasant, quiet, friendly resort

with large, airy bamboo huts on the beach, most with balconies, and a restaurant in the centre of a grass courtyard. ❸

Tropicana Castle Dive Resort Right on the main road ☎043/287 3075, ⓦwww .tropicanadivers.com. An extraordinary faux German schloss owned and operated by the Maierhofer family, *Tropicana* has medieval-themed rooms with all mod cons and four-poster beds that would make Lady Guinevere feel at home. There's a swimming pool, a small spa and gym, and a restaurant offering marinated grilled chicken, pepper steak and snapper fillet in herbs and white wine. Many guests are on all-in packages from Europe that include diving. ❻–❽

Villa Sabang ☎0917/562 0214. Modern, white-washed concrete rooms with a/c, reliable hot water and balconies. The large suites have a kitchen and mini-bar, and the location is great, along the beach to the east in a quiet area. Facilities include a swimming pool, billiards, a dive operation, bar and fast food. ❹

Eating, drinking and nightlife

For **eating**, if you want tropical charm right on the water, try the *Tamarind Restaurant*, with a menu of simple grills and salads that fluctuate in quality, but the view is wonderful. Opposite *Tamarind* is *Ristorante da Franco*, which serves excellent pasta and is popular with the après–scuba crowd. The *Relax Thai* restaurant is redolent of incense and does brisk business with its Thai curries (P150). For something very different, the *Sunshine Coast Bar and Restaurant* (turn right at the main junction and walk for 2min) has a Feeling Shitty Breakfast (P120) consisting of coffee, Coke, two cigarettes, cornflakes and fresh fruit.

Most of Sabang's **nightlife** centres around resort bars such as those at *Big Apple Dive Resort* or *Captain Gregg's Divers Resort*. Almost opposite *Relax Thai* is

215

Centrum, the only disco here that is no longer a go-go joint; it turned to putting on **live bands** from Manila after its owner became vice-mayor. For sunset drinks in your swimming costume, try the **floating bar** operated by Scandinavian Divers, on the main Sabang beach.

Small La Laguna

Small La Laguna is the ideal choice if you're looking for a range of friendly accommodation in a quiet location – most of it right on the beach – with good dive operators and a handful of informal bars and restaurants.

Accommodation

Carlo's Inn ☎0912/301 0717. In a quiet location at the far end of the beach, this laidback, friendly little family-run resort has various rooms and cottages built into the hillside. Good budget choice, close to the scuba operators and with wonderful views of the sea. ❸

Carmrob Inn No phone. Adequate fan or a/c double rooms in a white three-storey concrete house right on the shore. Make sure you take one of the rooms at the front, which have pleasant verandas. ❷

Club Mabuhay Dive Resort ☎043/ 287 3097, ⓦwww.mabuhay-dive-resort.com. A substantial resort set in expansive tropical gardens and finished to a high standard. All rooms are a/c and have balconies overlooking the central swimming pool. Their stylish *Mabuhay Beach Restaurant* is right on the shore and there's a silent 24hr generator should the power fail. ❻

Deep Blue Sea Inn No phone. On the west end of the beach, 30m from Action Divers. Very comfortable a/c apartments, cottages and doubles with bathrooms. The upstairs restaurant has fine views across the sea towards Verde Island. An excellent budget choice in a quiet location. ❹

El Galleon Beach Resort ☎02/834 2974. Professionally run tropical-style hotel with airy bamboo double rooms, many with balconies. Try to get one of the rooms on the upper level at the front, right on the beach. The pleasant seaside restaurant serves breakfast (P65–135) and a good range of lunch and dinner dishes including pasta, chicken, salads and seafood, produced by the resident French chef. There's also Internet access for P50 per half-hour. Next door is Asia Divers (see box on p.210) and on the hill above is the popular bar, *The Point*. ❹

Nick and Sonia's Cottages No phone. Simple nipa huts with a fridge, shower and their own cooking facilities; there's a choice of fan or a/c. ❸

Portofino Beach Resort ☎043/287 3227, ⓦwww.portofino.com.ph. A Mediterranean-style complex where accommodation ranges from a studio flat to a two-bedroom apartment overlooking the beach. Floors are of polished tile or wood throughout, and there's a lovely swimming pool with an alfresco bar and restaurant. ❻–❽

Roelyn's Inn Just past *El Galleon*, no phone. Simple place with a selection of concrete huts including some doubles with private showers. Set back from the beach, it has a small restaurant which stays open until 2am. ❸

Eating and drinking

Small La Laguna boasts the most popular **bar** in the area, *The Point*, which is next to *El Galleon Beach Resort*; it's open until midnight and offers a vast choice of cocktails. One of the most reliable **restaurants** here is the *Galley* at *El Galleon*, which occupies a beautiful spot on the beachfront and serves an excellent range of European and Filipino dishes, plus good home-baked bread. You could have breakfast, lunch and dinner here and still not feel like leaving, if only because of the view. *Carlo's Restaurant & Bar* at *Carlo's Inn* is a welcoming and relaxed place that's well worth the extra walk along the shore, and is especially noted for its grilled seafood, fresh off the boat not long before it reaches your table.

Big La Laguna

The sheltered cove of Big La Laguna has dive shops, a good choice of accommodation and a few convivial beach-style bars and restaurants at the resorts themselves.

Diving
in the Philippines

It's not surprising that many scuba divers say there is no better place in the world to take the plunge than the Philippines. This vast tropical archipelago of 7107 islands is at the heart of Southeast Asia's "coral triangle" that includes Indonesia and Malaysia and is the most biologically diverse underwater ecosystem on earth. The Philippines has 77 percent of the triangle's coral reefs – that's around 50,000 square miles – more than 300 coral species and 350 fish species. Extravagant coral gardens in the shallows are teeming with brilliantly coloured reef fishes, while at depth there are guaranteed opportunities to swim among the big pelagics. Affordable dive operators, where you can book lessons and rent equipment, are prolific, and what's more, the climate makes diving possible at any time of year, with surface water temperatures in the balmy 25–28°C range and visibility of up to 30m.

Clownfish

Unmissable marine life

The beauty of diving in the Philippines is that you don't have to dive deep to see some incredible marine life. Pottering about in warm coral waters at just a few metres, where sunlight is brightest, you'll come across a multitude of species. Among the commonest are the exotic and brightly coloured angelfish, damselfish and eye-catching humbugs, striped black-and-white like the sweet. In shallow coral gardens you'll see inquisitive clownfish defending their coral nests either singly or in pairs, perhaps with minuscule juveniles at their sides. Also unmissable are the frenetic shoals of dragonets and dottybacks, with their psychedelic colouring. Moray eels take shelter in crevices in the reef and it's not unusual to see one even in the shallows. Even rays and turtles can be seen at this depth, and the occasional baby reef shark looking for a snack.

Where the coral plunges away steeply into an inky darkness, the diving is equally as rewarding. Here, at depths of five or six metres, are bigger reef fishes, including bright green parrot fish and mesmerising batfish, who patrol the reef edge in family shoals. These slopes and fore reefs are also home to snappers, goatfish and wrasses, the largest of which – the Napoleon wrasse – can dwarf a person. Deeper still, but usually in the more isolated dive sites such as Tubbataha and Pescador, it's possible to see sharks, including white tip reef sharks and grey reef sharks, while if you're lucky an immense but gentle manta ray or whale shark might drift lazily past.

Two moray eels

Top five dive spots

Tubbataha Reef You'll need to book a liveaboard trip, but it's worth it, with guaranteed sightings of sharks, and a good chance of mantas and whale sharks. See p.353.
Busuanga The best wreck diving in the country, possibly in the world. See p.361.
Siargao Island Diving off the beaten track at many islets around Siargao. See p.386.
Puerto Galera Unrivalled all-round destination with something for everyone, from novices to old hands. See p.209.
Padre Burgos Out of the way in undeveloped southern Leyte and a prime spot for discovering new dive sites. See p.249.

Tawny nurse shark, Tubbataha Reef

Dangers of the depths

Few of the Philippines' ocean species present a significant threat to humans. There have only ever been a handful of shark attacks in the country and the last fatal attack was in 1960. You're more likely to suffer the inconvenience and short-term pain of a stinging rash from anemones or fire coral, but only if you brush against them. Being bitten by a moray eel or a beaky-mouthed trigger fish is rare and usually down to foolishness on the diver's part – both will bite if they feel threatened or cornered. Poisonous species include the spiny bottom-dwelling scorpion fish and the beautifully hypnotic lionfish (also called the flamefish), which hunts at night and has spines along its back that can deliver a nasty dose of venom. The lethal (and ugly) stonefish is remarkably well camouflaged as a gnarled rock and hard to spot, but fortunately rare. Shoals of jellyfish are common at certain times of year and needless to say you should watch from a safe distance. If you do get unlucky, a vinegar rinse can work wonders for a sting. Human urine is also said to be effective, but not everyone will want to put it to the test.

Most bites and stings are minor and can be avoided with common sense and care, but to be safe, make sure your dive operator, or the boat you're on, has a medical kit that includes antihistamine to block any allergic reaction, painkillers and cream containing hydrocortisone, which can help reduce swelling.

All aboard

Wreck diving, Coron Island, Palawan

If you're serious about your diving, booking a trip on a **liveaboard** can be a memorable experience, giving you the opportunity to get away from the more popular dive resorts and explore the wilderness. In turn, this means you'll have an almost guaranteed chance of some real thrills, including encounters with immense manta rays, whale sharks, dolphins, reef sharks and hammerheads. You'll be able to do as many as five dives a day, including deep, drift, wreck and night dives. And at the end of a hard day underwater you'll return to a good **dinner** prepared by the ship's cook. Everything is usually included in the rate – except the beer. For a list of liveaboards see p.47

Saving the reefs

Coral reefs are home to 25 percent of all marine life and form the nurseries for about a quarter of the oceans' fish. Sadly, they are increasingly under threat. Eighty percent of the Philippines' reef system is at risk of being lost as a result of coastal development, cyanide fishing, pollution, global warming and reckless tourism, including careless boating and diving, with people touching or collecting coral, stirring up sediment, and dropping anchors on reefs.

One illustration of the global-warming threat is a marked increase in the number of spiny, toxic coral-destroying crown-of-thorns starfish appearing around the archipelago, outbreaks of which often occur when ocean temperatures and nutrient levels increase.

Crown-of-thorns starfish

To make matters worse, some of the starfish's major predators, such as lumphead wrasse and giant triton, which usually keep the species in check, have declined in recent years as a result of overfishing, meaning that these voracious creatures can wipe out large areas of coral; an individual can consume up to six square metres of living reef per year.

For a list of what you can do to avoid endangering marine life while diving, see p.48.

Cataquis Lodge No phone. Very simple bamboo huts, clean and cheap and the location is exceptional, just paces from the sea. ❷

Coco Beach Island Resort Not strictly in Big La Laguna, but a little further along the coast to the west ☎02/521 5260, ⓦwww.cocobeach.com. Reachable only by private banca (they'll collect you in Batangas or at Muelle pier), this is secluded and idyllic, with airy rooms built of indigenous materials and a full range of activities on offer, including day-trips, diving and tennis. There's also a large outdoor swimming pool in the well-kept grounds. The Super Banana hut is particularly impressive, a small native house on the hill above the main resort area with a private veranda and enormous bed. Standard rooms are small, but can still fit four people. The only problem is that you'll have to depend on the resort's bancas to take you anywhere, even out for dinner at night. The resort does, however, have four restaurants of its own. ❺–❽

La Laguna Beach Club & Dive Center ☎043/287 3181 or 0973/855545, ⓦwww.llbc

.com.ph. Substantial resort with various palm-roofed rooms and cottages surrounding a beautiful swimming pool. All rooms have a/c, bathroom and hot water. On site are a reputable diving school, a first-class restaurant serving Asian and European fare and a relaxing upstairs bar with a large balcony for sunset-watching. ❻–❼

El Oro Roughly midway along the beach ☎0912/306 6642. Offers the usual range of basic nipa huts, with or without a veranda. The restaurant, open till 11pm, serves grilled fish, omelettes, salads and so forth, and has a pool table. ❸

Paradise Lodge No phone. Spacious fan doubles with shower and narrow balconies at the front. ❹

🏃 **Villa Estelita Dive & Dine** ☎0917/459 5485. Eleven simple, quiet rooms in a charming tropical garden, with an agreeable alfresco bar and restaurant on the sand. The owner, Speedy, is a good tour guide and can help arrange everything from diving to trekking. ❹

Palangan, Palangan Beach and Sinandigan Cove

There are some quiet and comfortable places to stay around the small barrio of **PALANGAN**, ten minutes by jeepney along the dirt road from Puerto Galera to Sabang. Some are on the ridge above the road, with marvellous views across Puerto's bays and islets and just a short walk from the beach. Not all of these resorts have dive centres, but they can all help arrange diving through operators at Sabang. Quiet **Sinandigan Cove**, also known as Coral Cove, is twenty minutes northeast of Palangan by jeepney.

Blue Crystal Beach Resort ☎0917/562 0129 or 043/287 3144, ⓦwww.bluecrystalbeachresort .com. Genteel place on the coast with concrete a/c rooms and a seaside restaurant with rattan furniture and daily specials ranging from seafood noodles to curry. There's also a secluded, private beach. ❹–❻

Coral Cove Resort ☎02/753 1129 or 845 0674, ⓦwww.coral-cove.com. This excellent little resort is the only place to stay in Sinandigan Cove and has large, comfortable, sea-facing fan rooms and cottages, a friendly little bar and a restaurant right on the seafront. There's also a dive operator here. ❻

Encenada Beach Resort West of *Blue Crystal* ☎0912/312 9761 or 02/524 0861, ⓦwww .encenada.com. There's a wide choice of accommodation here, set in a rambling hillside garden; some of the rooms are in an uninspiring motel-like

concrete building, but the individual cottages are better. Set meals cost $6 to $13 a head. ❹–❼

Franklyn Highland Beach Resort ☎0912/314 8133 or 02/522 3738, ⓦwww.franklynresort.com. Accommodation in thirteen attractive and spacious hillside cottages with lovely sea views. There's a pool and a restaurant that serves Filipino and European food. ❹–❼

🏃 **Kalaw Place** ☎043/422 0209 or 0917/532 2617, ⓦwww.kalawplace.com.ph. This is something special, a gracious and relaxed family-run resort on a promontory to the north of the road just before you reach Palangan. The rooms are beautifully furnished in native style and boast expansive bamboo balconies and unforgettable views. A *bahay kubo* (wooden house) for six people costs P2900 a night, while one for three that has its own kitchenette costs P1900. In the main house are elegant, simple doubles for P1500. The owners themselves prepare the food served in the restaurant, including vegetarian dishes. ④–⑥

Tanawin Bay Resort Next door to *Franklyn Highland* (to the east) ☎043/566 0117, ⊛www .tanawinbayresort.com. Beautiful resort in acres of hillside gardens with wonderful sea views and a

small, sandy private beach. The rooms are truly native and very atmospheric. Standards are teepee shaped with a double bed on the mezzanine level. Sunset rooms and family rooms are enormous, with polished tiled floors and private balconies. ⑥–⑧

White Beach

A once quiet crescent of sand, **White Beach** has in recent years been populated by many small resort hotels and cottage rooms. Unlike Sabang, this has no girlie bars and there are fewer scuba divers too, but it does have a few discos that can get a bit noisy. White Beach gets especially busy at peak times, notably New Year and Easter, when backpackers and students from Manila hold all-night rave parties on the sand. During holiday periods there are bouncy castles, jet skis, banana boats and crowds. No wonder tourists are now moving on to colonize beaches further along the coast such as Talipanan (see opposite).

There are no **banks** here, so make sure you bring cash; credit cards won't be accepted. There's also no Internet. M/V Brian Shipping has a small office on the beach where you can get **bancas** back to Batangas City.

Accommodation

When you arrive, touts will try to lead you to their own **accommodation**; for the cleanest rooms at the best price, take time to wander independently up and down the beach. Most of the accommodation here is simple, with dozens of places offering plain wooden cottages with cold showers.

Apartelle de Francesa ☎0916/737 3086, ⊛www.francescaresort.com. Twelve a/c rooms in a recently built resort with swimming pool, restaurant and small gym. This place isn't especially attractive and has no native ambience, but if you

really want something brand new, it's adequate. ⑤–⑦

Cherry's Inn ☎0917/788 8239. In a good spot at the northern end of the beach. Though the flimsy wooden cottages have become a little careworn

△ White Beach

over the years, they're still good value, with en-suite facilities and, in most cases, a veranda. ❸
Gray Wall Resort ☎043/287 3114, ⓦwww .graywallresort.com. Hacienda-style hotel that stands as concrete, air-conditioned symbol of just how quickly White Beach has developed. There's a choice of four types of room, a large swimming pool, a café and an oyster bar. You can also arrange scuba diving here. ❻–❼
Mylah's Nipa Hut & Restaurant No phone. Amiable place with a pleasant restaurant at the quieter eastern end of the beach. Accommodation is in standard wooden cottages big enough for two, and right on the sand. ❸

Summer Connection ☎0912/316 5910. Simple lodge and restaurant with nipa huts at the western edge of the beach, in a fine location right on the sand. It's friendly, laidback and humble, but comfortable enough, with reasonable private bathrooms. ❸
White Beach Lodge ☎0917/732 7674. At the west end of the beach near *Cherry's Inn*. Large wooden huts and cottages, some with balconies and all with their own bathrooms. ❸
White Beach Nipa Hut ☎0912/272 0774. Near *Cherry's Inn*. A slightly larger resort than most, with a choice of concrete cottages good for two, or fan rooms upstairs in the main building. ❹

Eating and drinking

Most of the resorts have their own simple **restaurants**, usually offering basic dishes such as grilled fish and *adobo*. About halfway along the beach, the *Sailor's Shack Bar & Restaurant* has spaghetti bolognese for P110 and vegetable curry for P100. *Simon's Place*, at the north end of the beach, is a homey café offering fish, grilled meat and rice dishes, while at the south end of the beach *Cococabana Snack Bar* has good breakfasts and fresh shakes, as well as lunch and dinner specials. *Peter's Restaurant & Bar* is a rustic place on the sand – just a few chairs and tables – with tasty curries and pasta dishes.

Aninuan and Talipanan beaches

With White Beach becoming increasingly busy, travellers looking for something more pristine are slowly moving further west along the coast. **Aninuan Beach** can be reached by banca from Muelle Pier or jeepney from White Beach; at low tide you can walk along the shore from White Beach. There are five **resorts** here, the best two being *Aninuan Beach Resort* and *Tamaraw Beach Resort and Cottages*. *Aninuan Beach Resort* is a marble-floored complex right on the sand (☎0912/287 1868; ❷–❺), with five double air-conditioned rooms and two small cottages with fan. Staff are helpful, and there's a relaxing open-air bar and a good restaurant. *Tamaraw Beach Resort and Cottages* (☎0912/304 8769, ⓦwww.tamarawbeachresort.com; ❸–❼) has an unbeatable location on the beach and pleasant rooms with balconies overlooking the sea, perfect for watching the sunset. The main building is an ugly motel-style box, so go for a separate cottage. They do good, reasonably priced food – grills and salads with rice, plus roast crab when available.

At **Talipanan**, a quiet stretch of sand a short hop beyond Aninuan, new resorts have also sprung up, but if you want something much more serene than White Beach, it's still the right choice. There's no nightlife or cosmopolitan restaurants, no karaoke – just you, the fishermen and the fireflies. The three **resorts** on Talipanan are rustic. *GM's Resort* (☎0917/732 3195; ❸) is a well-run place with various double rooms and a shaded outdoor eating area, and a surprisingly eclectic menu including fish, curry, noodles, sandwiches and Filipino favourites such as *adobo*. *Bamboo House* (☎0912/388 1283 or 02/872 0351; ❷) is also well managed and friendly, where the double and family rooms have fans, private bathrooms, bamboo furniture and clean linen. The restaurant serves fried fish or hotcakes – thick pancakes – for breakfast and grills for lunch and dinner. *Mengies Beach Resort* (☎0916/300 0068; ❷) is a modest but comfortable little hideaway right on the sand in the middle of the beach, with fan doubles and some family rooms for four.

The Last Surrender

Lubang Island, one of a number of undeveloped islands and islets off the northwest tip of Mindoro that rarely see any tourists, has a somewhat notorious recent history. In March 1974 it hit front pages around the world when a Japanese soldier, Second Lieutenant **Hiroo Onada**, finally decided to give himself up after hiding in the mountains of Lubang for thirty years. He emerged from the jungle with his rifle, five hundred rounds of ammunition and several hand-grenades, and said he had not surrendered earlier because he had not received orders to do so. It was only when his former commanders in the Imperial Army sent formal orders to him that he realized the war was over and Japan had been beaten. Onada became a celebrity and was feted by Ferdinand Marcos at Malacañang Palace before returning to Tokyo. Locals on Lubang feel differently about him. During his time on the island he is said to have stolen food, burned houses to the ground and, long after the war was over, continued to kill farmers who wandered near his lairs. When he returned to Lubang in 1996 to lay flowers at a memorial for local war dead, he was greeted with hostility.

The island's main port of entry is **Tilik** on the north coast, from where you can take a jeepney or a banca along the coast to beaches at Vigo, Mallig or Lubang Town, all nearby to the northwest. From Batangas there's a **ferry** every morning at 7am, returning at 2pm; departing from Puerto Galera, you'll have to negotiate a private boat. There's not tourist infrastructure on Lubang, so if you plan to stay overnight you'll have to camp or depend on the hospitality of locals for a roof over your head.

At both beaches you can charter a banca to do some beach-hopping, or ask your accommodation to help you arrange a trek to the lower slopes of **Mount Malasimbo** to visit waterfalls and Mangyan people. Across the road at the back of Talipanan Beach is a school for the children of Mangyan tribespeople (see box p.206). Teachers don't mind if you pay a quiet visit and donations of art materials or snacks are always appreciated.

Calapan and Mount Halcon

About 30km along an often unpaved road east of Puerto Galera, the compact, busy port city of **CALAPAN** is the capital of Mindoro Oriental. It's not a tourist destination, depending for most of its livelihood on trade, but it does have a small airport with a grass landing strip served by Seair from Manila and Cebu City, making it an emerging gateway to Mindoro's northern coast. It's also a base for a trek up **Mount Halcon**, the fourth highest mountain in the country and supposedly the toughest to climb.

Calapan

Calapan's **main street** is José P. Rizal Street, which is only 500m long and runs past Calapan Cathedral south to Juan Luna Street. If you arrive in Calapan by **fast ferry** from Batangas City, the city centre is a fifteen-minute ride away by tricycle. The **airport**, currently not served by any scheduled flights, although Seair has flown here in the past and may do so again, is on the northeastern fringes of the city, a three-kilometre tricycle ride from the city centre. If you're heading for Puerto Galera, many resorts will send transport to meet you if you book and pay in advance. Otherwise you can charter a banca at the pier (which will cost around P1500 for up to eight passengers) or take a jeepney to Puerto

Galera (P35) from the terminal at the market in Juan Luna Street. There are some terrific views during the second half of the jeepney ride as the road ascends into the hills above the palm-fringed coast. Note that many of these jeepneys don't stop at Sabang, for which you'll have to go all the way to Puerto Galera Town and then get a jeepney back. For destinations on the east coast, jeepneys and small buses head out from the market, while larger buses start from the ferry pier.

The **Supercat** ferry office in Calapan is at the pier (T043/288 3258), and you can buy tickets for all ferries at the pier or at the Aboitiz Shipping Office in the Tamaraw Center on J.P. Rizal Street. The main **tourist office** for Oriental Mindoro is in the provincial capitol building in J.P. Rizal Street (daily 9am–4pm; T043/288 5622). There are a number of **banks** on Juan Luna Street, including Metrobank, Equitable and BPI.

Accommodation options in Calapan don't set the pulse racing, but there are some budget hotels: *Riceland I Inn*, on J.P. Rizal Street (T043/288 4253; ❷), where the more expensive rooms are much bigger and in far better condition than the grubby singles; and, opposite, the *Hotel Ma-Yi* (T043/288 4437; ❸), which has air-conditioned doubles with bathrooms and cable TV. Much more preferable to staying in town, however, is to take a tricycle from Calapan pier fifteen minutes southeast of town to the *Parang Beach Resort* (T043/288 6120, Wwww.parangbeachresort.com; ❹–❺), which has a number of plain but comfortable and well-kept rooms in tin-roofed cottages right on the shore, with a beachside restaurant.

As for **eating** in Calapan itself, a walk along the traffic-clogged length of J.P. Rizal Street will take you past the usual Philippine fast-food outlets, including *Jollibee* (near the junction with José Laurel) and *Mister Donut*. There's good Chinese food at the *Hong Kong Restaurant* in M.H. Del Pilar Street, Santo Niño.

Mount Halcon

Rugged **Mount Halcon** rears up dramatically from the coastal plain of Mindoro Oriental, southwest of Calapan. At an altitude of 2587m, it's Mindoro's highest peak, distinguished by the dense tracts of rainforest that surround it, some of the most extensive forest on the island. To the Mangyans, Halcon is known as *lagpas-ulap*, which means "over the clouds".

Unusually for the Philippines, Halcon is not of volcanic origin, created instead by a massive geological uplifting millions of years ago. The lower slopes of Mount Halcon are about one hour from Calapan; chartering a jeepney at the market for the trip will cost around P1000. At the town of **Baco** you'll take a turnoff up an unsealed track to the Mangyan settlement of **Lantuyang**, where you pay a small fee – no more than P25 – to the barangay head. You can also approach the mountain from Puerto Galera, taking a jeepney for Calapan and getting off at the Baco turnoff.

Climbers who aim to reach the summit must conquer some wild terrain. From Lantuyang, it's a three-hour climb across fields before you first enter the forest. It's only after several more hours of walking that you reach the 1500-metre summit of **Mount Dulangan**, from there dropping steeply down to the **Dulangan River** and the start of the long, tough trek up Halcon's massive flank. On a ridge known as the **Knife's Edge**, near the summit, is a small shrine to a climber who died of exposure here in 1994, another reminder that even in a tropical country no climb of this nature should be treated with anything less than respect. It is customary to stop here, add a stone to the pile and say a short prayer.

The total climb – Dulangan and Halcon combined – is longer than that to the summit of Mount Everest from Base Camp; allow at least three days for the ascent and two for the descent. There are many obstacles, not the least of which is the sheer volume of rain that falls on Mount Halcon. There is no distinct dry season here and heavy rain is virtually a daily occurrence, resulting in an enormous fecundity of life – massive trees, dense layers of dripping moss, orchids, ferns and pitcher plants – but also making the environment treacherous and potentially miserable for climbers. Calm or even dried-up rivers and streams are soon transformed into raging torrents that can sweep away anything in their path. The crossing of the Dulangan River is especially hazardous and known as "The Gate of Strife". Then there's the diminutive *limatik*, a leech-like bloodsucker with a knack of finding its way through the most obscure gap in your clothing. Local climbers say you can fend it off by covering yourself with liniment.

Don't even think about climbing Mount Halcon on your own. The best place to begin making arrangements is the **Salong Paa Outdoor Shop** on Quezon Drive in Calapan (℡043/288 8161 or 0920/418 4938). The shop is a base for Halcon Mountaineers, a skilled and committed local group who will organize and guide the hike; expect to pay P3500 per person, including permit, guide fees and transport but excluding food and water. You'll be sleeping on the mountain for at least three nights, so if you need a tent and other equipment you can rent them at the shop. Halcon Mountaineers will also advise you on how much food and water to carry. Make sure you have good waterproof clothing and a waterproof cover for your backpack.

The east coast

Mindoro's east coast road from Calapan to the town of **ROXAS** is rough, dusty and rarely travelled by tourists. You might come here if you want to catch a boat to Marinduque from Pinamalayan or to Caticlan or Romblon from Roxas, but these journeys need some serious consideration because boats are often old and overloaded, crossing exposed ocean with heavy cargoes of grain, cement, diesel or farmyard animals.

The road south of Calapan runs past the immense **Naujan Lake** and skirts the eastern edge of the Naujan National Park before hitting the rather drab and uninspiring coastal towns of **Pinamalayan** and **Bongabong** and then Roxas itself, where there's a market, a busy high street, three average hotels and not much else. These east coast towns depend on trade and fish rather than tourism for their livelihood, and there are no pristine beaches, just long, hot stretches of grey sand. The coastal road continues from Roxas through **Mansalay** and on to **Bulalacao**, where it fizzles out into a rough track that few vehicles can negotiate – apart, that is, from the trusty jeepney. A couple of jeepneys try the journey west from Bulalacao every day, but it's a very rough and uncomfortable trip, with numerous stops to let people load and unload. Much more enjoyable is to take a banca from Bulalacao to **San José** (see opposite), a three-hour trip along the coast. The bancas don't operate to a timetable, but there's usually one that leaves Bulalacao at 6am. You can charter your own banca to San José at the wharf for about P1500 one-way.

Roxas practicalities

Buses and **jeepneys** run north and south from Roxas, leaving from near the market on Administration Street, and the **pier** is on the eastern edge of town. There's a one-man **tourism office** at the *Roxas Villa Hotel & Restaurant* (see opposite). There are three **hotels** on Administration Street, all facing the market and all noisy: inspect the rooms first and ask for one at the back. The *Santo Niño Hotel* (☎036/453 0056; ❷) is a rundown and creaky old place that has musty singles, plus some adequate larger rooms with three beds and private bathrooms. Right next door, the dusty, wooden *Hotel Dunnarose* (❶) has very cheap and tatty single fan rooms and a limited number of more acceptable doubles with fans and private bathrooms. Two doors down the street is the *Roxas Villa Hotel & Restaurant* (☎036/453 0017; ❷), which is newer and cleaner than its neighbours, offering spartan rooms, some significantly better than others, that at least have laundered linen and clean showers. The water supply in Roxas is a problem, as is power, so expect shortages and blackouts.

San José

On Mindoro's southwest coast, the intensely sun-bleached and noisy port town of **SAN JOSÉ** is a quintessential provincial Philippine metropolis, with traffic-dense streets lined with drug stores, cheap canteens and fast-food outlets. Travellers usually only see San José as they pass through on their way from the airport to Sablayan (see p.224) or the **Mounts Iglit–Baco National Park** (see p.224), for which **permits** can be obtained in San José. Though the Apo Reef is close by, there are no major dive operators in town and it's best to organize a trip there through the *Pandan Island Resort* offshore (see p.225).

Practicalities

San José is bounded on its northern edge by the **Pandururan River**, beyond which are the **pier** and the **airport**. The main thoroughfare, **Rizal Street**, runs across town starting from Cipriano Liboro Street in the west, and turns into the National Highway in the east, where it runs inland to Magsaysay. San José **airport** is a twenty-minute, P25 tricycle ride from town, or you could take one of the private cars that act as airport taxis, for which you'll pay P100. Air Philippines, which has daily flights from Manila to San José, has a ticket office at the airport (☎043/491 4157) and another in Burgos Street (☎043/491 4048), which runs north off Rizal Street. Asian Spirit (☎043/491 4151 or 491 4991) also has daily flights here from Manila.

If San José is your first port of call on Mindoro and you're en route to other destinations here, ask the tricycle driver at the airport or pier to take you straight to the main **bus terminal** at the junction of Rizal Street and Gaudiel Street, where you can catch one of the hourly buses heading north to Sablayan (P160).

For Mounts Iglit-Baco, you can apply for a permit (P125) and hire a guide at the Protected Area Office (Mon–Fri 8am–4pm; ☎043/491 4200) in the LIUCP Building on Airport Road. The park is a sixty-kilometre drive from San José: take a bus or jeepney along the coastal road to the barangay of **Popoy**, then a jeepney the rest of the way. If you want to reach Puerto Galera, you'll need to take a bus to Abra de Ilog, then a jeepney to Wawa on the north coast, and finally charter a banca the rest of the way.

Viva Shipping Lines (☎043/723 2986) operates two **ferries** that sail to Batangas City: M/V *Santa Maria* and M/V *Peñafrancia VIII*. Also serving Batangas is Montenegro Shipping Lines (☎043/723 8245). Moreta Shipping Lines has ferries to Manila (☎043/723 2839). All three firms have ticket offices at the pier.

There are a number of **banks** on Rizal Street, including BPI, a branch of Metrobank near the market in Sikatuna Street, one block south of the river, and a PNB on M.H. Del Pilar Street just south of Rizal Street. There are ATMs at BPI and Metrobank, but they're not reliable. Close to PNB are the **police station**, town hall and **post office**. Options are limited if you have to make a **phone** call: try the Globe Telecom Public Calling Office opposite Mercury Drug Store in Cipriano Liboro Street. In Liboro Street there are a handful of small **Internet cafés**, but connections are patchy.

Accommodation and eating

The best that can be said of **accommodation** in San José is that it's inexpensive. There's no reason to spend a night here, but if you do, the best place to head to is the *Sikatuna Town Hotel* (☏043/491 1274; ③), on Sikatuna Street next to the Globe Telecom Public Calling Office, which has air-conditioned rooms with cable TV and private showers. Close to the bus station, the *Jolo Hotel* on Cipriano Liboro Street (②) has rather depressing box-like air-conditioned singles and doubles. The *Sikatuna Beach Hotel* (☏043/491 2182; ②–③) on Airport Road is a reasonable budget option with ordinary but spacious rooms and a native-style restaurant overlooking the sea.

Most of the other **eating** places are fast food or *carinderias*; the best of these is *Dante's Eatery*, a short walk south of the *Jolo Hotel*. Opposite the town hall on M.H. Del Pilar Street, *Gold 98 Seafoods Restaurant* has very acceptable Chinese food such as sweet-and-sour pork, Shanghai fried rice and fresh *lumpia* – a Filipino version of the spring roll, served cold with sweet sauce (P50 for two).

Sablayan and around

Forty kilometres north of San José, the unhurried fishing town of **SABLAYAN** is the perfect jumping-off point for several nearby attractions. Inland, the **Mounts Iglit-Baco National Park** is being considered for UNESCO World Heritage Site status as it's the last refuge on Earth of the endangered **tamaraw**, or Mindoro dwarf buffalo. There's some terrific trekking in this area and it's a good place to get close to Mangyan tribes (see box p.206). Also inland, there are pleasant walks available in an area of rolling countryside around Lake Libao in the **Sablayan Watershed Forest Reserve**. Offshore, **North Pandan Island** has a wonderful tropical hideaway resort, and **Apo Reef** offers diving opportunities that are hard to beat anywhere.

The town, small enough to cover on foot in fifteen minutes, has a small plaza with a town hall and a stretch of beach lined by bancas. Buses north to Mamburao and south to San José use the **bus station** on the southern edge of town, on the National Highway. The **pier** is a five-minute walk south of the bus station. On the pier is the **Pandan Eco-Tourism Office** (daily 8am–5pm) where you can obtain a permit for Mounts Iglit-Baco (P125) and hire a guide for the park or the Sablayan Watershed Forest Reserve.

Accommodation in Sablayan is limited. The *Emely Hotel*, in a convenient location on the riverbank close to the market (②), has twenty plain rooms, all but four en suite. Along the National Highway close to the Municipal Plaza is *La Sofia Apartelle* (②), a small place where rooms are ordinary affairs with fans, and which has a restaurant, 24-hour water and a Globe telephone office.

Mounts Iglit-Baco National Park

The **Mounts Iglit-Baco National Park** is dominated by the twin peaks of **Mount Baco** (2488m) and **Mount Iglit** (2364m), which offer some challenging climbs; it can take up to two days to reach the peak of Mount Iglit, so these climbs are tough and not to be underestimated. Vegetation is so dense there have been no officially recorded ascents of Mount Baco. This is also a New People's Army (NPA) area and while there have been no notable events involving tourists, it's worth asking around for the latest information.

There are also a number of more leisurely treks through the foothills to areas where you are most likely to see the endangered **tamaraw** (*Bubalus mindorensis*), a dwarf bovine of which fewer than two hundred exist. The *tamaraw*, whose horns grow straight upwards in a distinctive "V" formation, has fallen victim to hunting, disease and deforestation, and to create more awareness of its plight there is talk of designating it the country's national animal. Apart from the *tamaraw*, the park is also prime habitat for the Philippine deer, wild pigs and other endemic species such as the Mindoro scops owl and the Mindoro imperial pigeon.

To visit the park, you'll first have to secure a **permit** and arrange a guide, either in San José (see p.223 for details) or Sablayan. Reaching the park by public transport from Sablayan means taking one of the regular buses or jeepneys south along the coastal road to the barangay of **Popoy**, then a jeepney up to the park itself. The road inland to the park is very rutted and bumpy in parts. Some hotels and resorts in both San José and Sablayan can help arrange trips, including visits to the "Gene Pool", a small laboratory where scientists are trying to breed the *tamaraw* in captivity. If you fancy staying overnight, ask the Protected Area Office in San José (☎043/491 4200) about the **rooms** it maintains inside the park, which are available for P100 per person per night.

Sablayan Watershed Forest Reserve

The **Sablayan Watershed Forest Reserve** is unusual among protected wilderness areas because it contains a **penal colony**, an open prison for low-risk inmates, surrounded by agricultural lands worked by the prisoners. The inmates are distinguishable from the guards only by the colour of their T-shirts and the fact that they are not armed. Nearby are a number of villages where staff and prisoners' families live; beyond the last of these villages is a motorable track that ends on the edge of thick forest, close to **Lake Libao**. This shallow, roughly circular lake is covered in lilies and alive with birds, including kingfishers, bitterns, egrets and purple herons. An undulating footpath around the lake makes for some wonderful walking, taking you through the edge of the forest and through glades from where there are views across the water; you'll see locals balanced precariously on small wooden bancas fishing for tilapia. If you're reasonably fit you can walk once round the lake in three hours, starting and finishing at the penal colony, though allow an hour to get between the colony and the main road.

To reach the penal colony you'll have to hire a vehicle and driver in Sablayan or take a bus along the coastal road and ask to be dropped at the turnoff for the colony, near the town of **Pianag**. There are buses and jeepneys from Pianag if you need one for the return trip.

North Pandan Island and Apo Reef

Idyllic **North Pandan Island**, ringed by a halo of fine white sand, coral reefs and coconut palms, lies 2km off the west coast of Mindoro. The island is the site of the well-run *Pandan Island Resort* (☎0919/305 7821, ⓦ www.pandan.com; ❷–❸), a back-to-nature private hideaway developed by a French adventurer who discovered it in 1986. In 1994 a sanctuary was established around the eastern half of the island so the **marine life** is exceptional; with a mask and snorkel you can see big grouper, all sorts of coral fishes, even the occasional turtle. On most days the resort's scuba-diving centre organizes day-trips to Apo Reef, one of the country's largest coral reefs, and longer overnight safaris both to Apo and to Busuanga off northern Palawan (see p.360) if there are enough passengers. Even if you don't dive, there's plenty to keep you occupied on and around the island itself, including kayaking, jungle treks, windsurfing and sailing.

It's easy to arrange a **boat** to Pandan (30min; P200 per person) from the Pandan Eco-Tourism office in Sablayan. There are four types of **accommodation** at the resort: five budget rooms, ten standard double bungalows, ten larger bungalows for four, and family houses for up to six. Family houses and bungalows all have private bathrooms, while the budget rooms, known as "The Bronx" to regulars, are perfectly adequate and share two bathrooms and two toilets. During the diving season (Nov–May) the island is so popular that all rooms are often taken, so it's important to book in advance. The resort **restaurant** dishes up excellent European and Filipino cuisine (try the tangy fish salad in vinegar) and the beach bar serves some unforgettable tropical cocktails. Breakfast is $3, lunch and dinner are $7 each (or $15 for all three).

Apo Reef Marine Natural Park

Lying about 30km off the west coast of Mindoro, **Apo Reef** stretches 26km from north to south and 20km east to west, making it a significant marine environment. There are two main atolls separated by deep channels and a number of shallow lagoons with beautiful white sandy bottoms. Only in three places does the coral rise above the sea's surface, creating the islands of Cayos de Bajo, Binangaan and Apo. The largest of these, **Apo**, is home to a ranger station and a lighthouse. The diving is really something special, with sightings of sharks (even hammerheads), barracuda, tuna and turtles fairly common. Most of the Philippines' 450 species of coral can be found here, from tiny bubble corals to huge gorgonian sea fans and brain corals, along with hundreds of species of smaller reef fishes such as angelfish, batfish, surgeonfish and jacks.

If you're not staying at the *Pandan Island Resort*, you can head to the reef on one of the **liveaboard** trips offered by many dive operators in Coron Town, Busuanga (see p.362) or Manila. Officially you need a permit to set foot on Apo Island, but the rangers will let you take a look around as long as you don't intend to set up camp.

The northwest

It's hard to believe that the quiet, relatively isolated west coast town of **MAMBURAO**, 80km north along the coastal road from Sablayan, is the capital of Mindoro Occidental. With a population of 30,000, Mamburao is significant only as a trading and fishing town, although the coastal road is undeniably scenic, with blue ocean on one side and jungled mountains on the other. North of town there are some alluring stretches of **beach** inhabited only by fishermen. The best of these is **Tayamaan Bay**, 4km north of Mamburao, where you can get a real rest and good, fresh food at the *Tayamaan Palm Beach Club* (☎043/711 1657; ●), well away from the din of tricycles and jeepneys. Cottages at the resort have twin or double beds, private bathrooms and verandas close to the sea. In Mamburao itself, you could stay at the *La Gensol Plaza Hotel* (☎043/711 1072; ❸), on the National Highway through town. The cheapest rooms are fan singles with tiny cold showers, though they have larger, more comfortable doubles, some with air-conditioning.

North of Mamburao the road forks. From here, jeepneys and some buses head northwest along the coast to Palauan, and northeast to **Abra de Ilog** near the north coast, where there's one small lodging house, *L&P Lodging House* (☎0918/528 2173; ❶), about 1km before you reach the pier. If you're coming in the other direction – arriving in Abra by ferry from Batangas – a tricycle to L&P from the Abra pier costs P20.

Palauan is the most northerly town on Mindoro and jumping-off point for treks through the foothills of **Mount Calavite** (1521m), which are criss-crossed by unsigned Mangyan trails. You can hire a guide at the town hall on the main road in Palauan. The journey from Mamburao to Abra de Ilog takes you past dazzling green paddy fields and farmland planted with corn. From here jeepneys continue to the coastal barrio of **Wawa**, a wooden fishing village with no accommodation or restaurants. The road ends here, though you can continue to Puerto Galera if you charter a banca (about 2hr; P1600). Montenegro Shipping Lines ferries leave a couple of times daily from Wawa for Batangas City.

Travel details

Buses

Abra de Ilog to: Mamburao (5–6 daily; 45min).
Bulalacao to: Pinamalayan (2 daily; 6hr); Roxas (3–4 daily; 1hr).
Calapan to: Bulalacao (4 daily; 6hr); Pinamalayan (8 daily; 2hr); Roxas (8 daily; 4hr).
Mamburao to: Abra de Ilog (5–6 daily; 45min); Sablayan (8–12 daily; 2hr).
Pinamalayan to: Bulalacao (2 daily; 6hr); Calapan (8 daily; 2hr); Roxas (several daily; 3hr).
Roxas to: Bulalacao (3–4 daily; 1hr 30min); Calapan (8 daily; 4hr); Pinamalayan (several daily; 3hr).
Sablayan to: Mamburao (8–12 daily; 2hr); San José (hourly; 3hr).
San José to: Sablayan (hourly; 3hr).

Jeepneys

Jeepneys operate between all towns and villages along the coast. Departures are more frequent between 6am and 9am and from 4pm to 6pm. Routes include:
Abra de Ilog to: Mamburao (5–6 daily; 1hr); Wawa (5–6 daily; 30min).
Bulalacao to: San José (2–3 daily; 3–4hr).
Calapan to: Pinamalayan (6 daily; 2hr); Puerto Galera (12–14 daily; 2hr).
Mamburao to: Abra de Ilog (5–6 daily; 1hr); Palauan (hourly; 1 hr); Sablayan (6–8 daily; 2–3hr); Wawa (several daily; 1hr 30min).

Pinamalayan to: Calapan (6 daily; 2hr).
Puerto Galera to: Baco (12–14 daily; 1hr 30min); Calapan (12–14 daily; 2hr).
Roxas to: Bulalacao (6–8 daily; 2hr); Pinamalayan (several daily; 3hr).
Sablayan to: Mamburao (6–8 daily; 2–3hr); San José (several daily; 3hr).
San José to: Sablayan (several daily; 3hr).
Wawa to: Abra de Ilog (5–6 daily; 30min).

Ferries and scheduled bancas

Balatero pier to: Batangas City (3 daily; 2hr).
Calapan to: Batangas City (7 daily; 1hr).
Pinamalayan to: Balanacan (Marinduque; daily; 5hr).
Puerto Galera to: Batangas City (several daily; 2hr).
Roxas to: Caticlan (for Boracay; 3 weekly; 8hr); Odiongan (3 weekly; 6hr).
Sabang to: Batangas City (several daily; 2hr).
San José to: Batangas City (1–2 daily; 10hr).
Tilik (Lubang) to: Batangas City (1 daily; 3hr).
Verde Island to: Batangas City (1 daily; 2hr).
Wawa to: Batangas City (2 daily; 2–3hr).

Domestic flights

San José to: Manila (14 weekly; 50min).

The Visayas

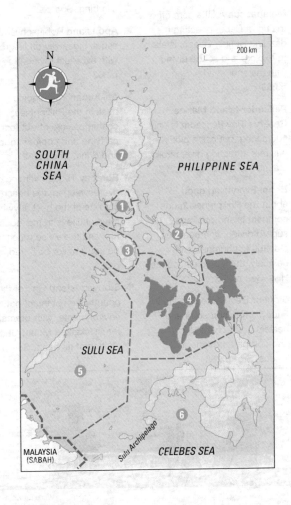

CHAPTER 4 # Highlights

* **Leyte Mountain Trail** Gruelling but memorable forty-kilometre walk through vast tracts of jungled wilderness. See p.247

* **Malapascua** A little gem off the tip of Cebu, boasting the dazzling Bounty Beach, islets to explore and scuba diving with thresher sharks. See p.269

* **Pescador Island Marine Reserve** Tiny Pescador is only 100m long, but has a glorious reef attracting divers from around the world. See p.273

* **Bohol** Everything good about the Philippines in one compact island package: superb diving, fine beaches, old Gothic churches and, uniquely, the iconic Chocolate Hills. See p.275

* **Siquijor** Best visited on Good Friday, when sorcerers and healers gather here to mix and compare potions and lotions. See p.285

* **Mount Kanlaon National Park** Active volcano at the centre of dense forest offering some extreme trekking and climbing. See p.297

* **Apo Island** Robinson Crusoe-esque hideaway off Negros, with excellent diving. See p.303

* **Ati-Atihan** The biggest bash in the Philippines: wild costumes, lots of outdoor partying and copious food and drink. See p.312

* **Boracay** Though verging on overdeveloped, the beach is still one of the best anywhere, the nightlife is tremendous fun, and there's so much to do you'll never be bored. See p.323

* **Sibuyan Island** One of the country's most intact natural environments, with dramatic forest-cloaked Mount Guiting Guiting at its heart. See p.338

△ White Beach, Boracay

The Visayas

The Visayas, a collection of islands large and small in the central Philippines, are considered to be the cradle of the country. It was here that Ferdinand Magellan laid a sovereign hand on the archipelago for Spain and began the process of colonization and Catholicization that shaped so much of the nation's history. The islands were also the scene of some of the bloodiest battles fought against the Japanese during World War II, and where General Douglas MacArthur waded ashore to liberate the country after his famous promise, "I shall return". Although there are almost too many islands to count in the Visaya group, the number certainly runs into the thousands. What is clear is that everywhere you turn there seems to be another patch of tropical sand or coral reef awaiting your attention, usually with a ferry or banca to take you there. There are nine major islands – **Cebu, Bohol, Guimaras, Samar, Leyte, Panay, Negros, Romblon** and **Siquijor** – but it's the hundreds of others in between that make this part of the archipelago so irresistible. A short journey can take you from air-conditioned ritziness to bucolic nirvana.

Despite recent efforts to turn **Cebu City** into a major international duty-free port, most of the islands remain lost in their own secluded little world. Vast areas of Bohol, Leyte, Panay, Samar and the sugar plantation island of Negros are relatively undiscovered, while beautiful Siquijor is said to be home to witches and faith healers. Romblon, still only accessible by boat, offers some of the country's most pristine wilderness areas, while sleepy Guimaras, known for the sweetness of its mangoes, has marvellous beaches that few tourists make the effort to see – although sadly some have been affected by an oil spill in 2006.

Of the smaller islands, some are famous for their beach life (nowhere else in the country will you find the same proliferation of bars and resorts as on Boracay, off the northern tip of Panay), some for their fiestas, some for sugar, and some for their folklore. No one can accuse the Visayas, and the Visayans who live here, of being a uniform lot. In some areas they speak Ilonggo or Waray Waray, in others Aklan; all three languages are closely related Malayo-Polynesian tongues, yet they have significant differences in vocabulary and phraseology. The diversity of languages is a symptom of the region's fractured topography, with many islands culturally and economically isolated from those around them, part of the Philippine archipelago in little more than name.

Getting around the Visayas is fairly easy, with increasingly efficient transport links. Boracay, Cebu, Panay, Bohol, Negros, Leyte and Samar are all accessible by air, with **flights** daily or every few days from Manila and, in some cases, Cebu City. Major **ferry** companies such as WG&A and Negros Navigation also ply routes between Manila and the Visayas. Within the Visayas, the ferry

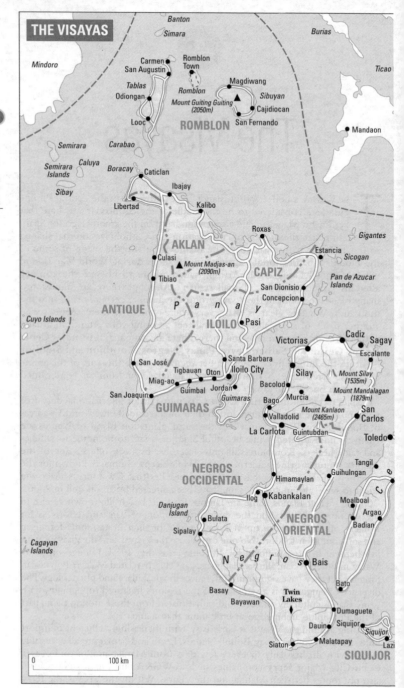

THE VISAYAS

Mindoro

Banton

Simara

Burias

Ticao

Carmen
San Augustin
Romblon Town
Magdiwang

Tablas
Odiongan
Romblon
Sibuyan
Cajidiocan
Mount Guiting Guiting (2050m)

Looc
San Fernando

Mandaon

ROMBLON

Semirara

Caluya

Carabao

Boracay — Caticlan

Semirara Islands

Gigantes

Sibay
Ibajay

Libertad
Kalibo

Roxas

Estancia
Sicogan

Cuyo Islands

Culasi — Mount Madjas-an (2090m)

AKLAN

CAPIZ

Pan de Azucar Islands

Tibiao

San Dionisio
Concepcion

ANTIQUE

P   a   n   a   y

ILOILO

Pasi

Victorias

Cadiz
Sagay
Escalante

San José
Santa Barbara

Tigbauan Oton

Miag-ao   Iloilo City

Silay

Mount Silay (1535m)

San Joaquin
Guimbal   Jordan

Bacolod
Murcia

Mount Mandalagan (1879m)

GUIMARAS

Guimaras

Bago

Valladolid

Mount Kanlaon (2465m)

San Carlos

La Carlota   Guintubdan

Toledo

NEGROS
OCCIDENTAL

Himamaylan

Guihulngan

Tangil

C   e

Danjugan Island

Bulata

Ilog Kabankalan

NEGROS
ORIENTAL

Moalboal

Argao
Badian

Sipalay

Cagayan Islands

N   e   g   r   o   s

Bais

Bato

Basay
Bayawan

Twin Lakes

Dumaguete

Siquijor
Siquijor

Dauin
Siaton Malatapay

Lazi

SIQUIJOR

0   100 km

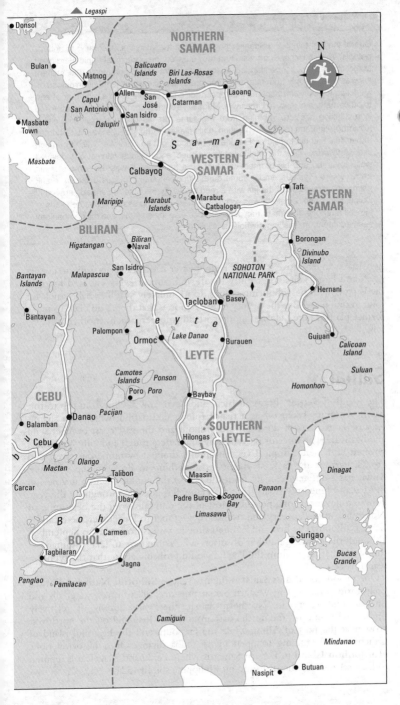

A history of hangovers

One of the first things the Spanish learned about the Visayans, according to anthropologist William Henry Scott, was that they enjoyed the occasional tipple. Ferdinand Magellan had no sooner landed in the settlement of Homonhon in the eastern Visayas when people from nearby Suluan presented him with a jarful of **arrack** spirit. Magellan drank it and became indisposed for days, unable to give orders or attend to other matters of ship. In Limasawa, Magellan's diarist **Pigafetta** became embroiled in a drinking session, imbibing from the same cup as the local chieftain, Rajah Kolambu. Pigafetta makes no mention in his diaries of the state he was in, but notes rather drily that his translator, Enrique de Malacca, got so drunk he "wasn't of much use". A few days later the drinking still continued, and the local harvest was delayed while Kolambu and his brother Awi slept off a hangover. It was the same story in Cebu, where Pigafetta, under some duress from another bibulous chieftain, drank palm wine straight from the jar with a reed straw. By the time the armada arrived in Quipit, Mindanao, Pigafetta was so wary of these drinking sessions that he excused himself after one draught of the local grog because the chieftain and his companions seemed intent on finishing a whole jar without eating.

network is so extensive it doesn't really matter if you can't get a flight. Ferries small and large, safe and patently unsafe, link almost every city and town in the Visayas with neighbouring islands, so it's unlikely you'll ever be stuck for long in one place. But the beauty of the region is that there's no need to make formal plans. There's always another island, another beach, another place to stay.

Samar

The island of **Samar**, between Bicol and Leyte and 320km from top to toe, has never quite taken off as a major tourist destination, which is a shame, because large parts of the coast are unspoilt and the east coast beaches wild and beautiful. The interior is even more dramatic, a rough and hilly wilderness covered with dense tropical vegetation and drained by numerous rivers and creeks. Perhaps the lack of visitors is something to do with the **weather**. Samar has a different climate from the rest of the country, with a dry period in May and June only. Apart from that, rainfall is possible throughout the year, although never for long periods. Most of the rain falls from the beginning of November until February and from early October to December there can be fierce typhoons. The best and sunniest time to visit is from May to September, although the growing number of surfers who come here to take advantage of the swells that rip in from the Pacific would probably argue that the typhoon season is best.

One reason not to miss Samar is the marvellous **Sohoton National Park**, a prehistoric wilderness in Western Samar province, full of caves, waterfalls and underground rivers. In Northern Samar, there are dozens of relatively untouched islands off the north coast around **San José** and off the northwest coast near the port of **Allen**, while the far south and the beautiful island of **Calicoan** are beginning to open up to scuba diving. On a historical note, **Homonhon Island** in Eastern Samar is where Ferdinand Magellan is reputed to have set foot for the first time on Philippine soil in 1521.

Getting to Samar

There are **airports** at Calbayog and Catarman, both served three times a week by Asian Spirit from Manila. **Ferries** from Matnog on the southernmost tip of Bicol make the one-hour trip to the Balwharteco Terminal in Allen, northwestern Samar, several times each morning. Tacloban on neighbouring Leyte is linked to Samar by regular **buses**, crossing the two-kilometre-long San Juanico Bridge, which spans the San Juanico Strait, and there's also a daily ferry from here to Guiuan in southeast Samar. F.J. Palacio Lines (☎032/255-5492 or 254-6629) sails four times a week at 7pm from Cebu City to Calbayog. The same company has a weekly service from Cebu City to Catbalogan, on Samar's west coast. From Manila, BLTB has a bus service that crosses on the Matnog–Allen ferry and runs down the coastal road to Calbayog, taking about twelve hours. The daily Philtranco bus service between Manila and Davao passes through Allen, Calbayog and Catbalogan.

Northern Samar

Arriving from Luzon by bus or ferry, your first taste of Samar is the small port town of **ALLEN**. From here there are dozens of buses and jeepneys a day that run east to Catarman and beyond, and south to Calbayog and Catbalogan, where you can catch an onward bus to the southern half of the island. Buses heading south and east from Allen all pick up passengers at the port itself where you can also catch a jeepney into town, 5km to the south.

There are limited **accommodation** options in Allen and the only reason you'd stay the night is if you couldn't move on. First choice has to be *Wayang Wayang Resort* (☎0918/338 8756; ❷–❸), a quiet, simple complex of double and treble cottages 5km south of town overlooking the sea. It's easy to get there from Allen by tricycle. In town, *Laureen's Lodging* (❶) is convenient for boats and buses, though the rooms are poky and get a lot of noise.

The Balicuatro Islands

The **Balicuatro Islands** off Samar's northwest coast include Ternate, San Vicente, Mahaba, Capul and Mongobongo, but the largest – and the only one with accommodation – is **Dalupiri**. From **San Isidro**, on the coast road south of Allen, there are bancas to Dalupiri (every 20min; 20min) and other islands in the group. The capital of Dalupiri, where bancas arrive, is **SAN ANTONIO**, a sleepy barrio with a post office, a small hospital and dozens of little bancas that can take you on day-trips to the other islands. You can stay 3km west of here at the eccentric *Flying Dog Resort* (❷), featuring eye-catching pyramid-style huts and an al fresco bamboo restaurant where simple food such as grilled fish and chicken is served. The huts are a little tatty, but the setting is marvellous, with a white sand beach and a coral reef offshore. This is a really tranquil "escape to nowhere" place, with electricity for only a few hours every evening and a clientele that seems mostly comprised of solo backpackers, hippies, gurus and poets. The other option on Dalipuri is the *Octopussy Bungalow Resort* (Ⓦwww. octopussy.ph; ❹) which has pretty concrete-and-thatch cottages in quiet gardens close to some marvellous beaches. There aren't many places to eat in the area, but the resort offers half board and full board for a little extra.

The rest of the islands, also largely unexplored by tourists, are mostly home to farmers and fishermen. **Capul**, for example, is a picturesque little island about one hour from San Isidro, with a majestic seventeenth-century fortified stone church built by the Spanish, and an almost derelict coastal road that takes you past some incredible coves and beaches. The people of Capul, known as the

Abak, speak a language called Abak-non that not even the people of mainland Samar understand.

The north coast

The ramshackle north coast port city of **CATARMAN** is served by Asian Spirit flights from Manila and – though it has never been a tourist destination – makes a good point of entry to Northern Samar if you want to save yourself a long bus or ferry journey. Tricycles and jeepneys wait at the **airport** to take arriving passengers the five kilometres into town. Asian Spirit has an office at Jacinto Street corner Magsaysay Street (☎055/500 9069). **Accommodation** in Catarman is unimpressive, most of it cheap and insalubrious. *Aileen's Lodging House* (☎053/354 1568; ❶) and *DCC* (☎053/354 1188; ❶), almost next door to each other on Bonifacio Street, have small rooms with fan and cold shower. The *Fortune Hotel* on Del Rosario Street (☎053/253 2114; ❷) is more appealing, with modern air-conditioned rooms and a quiet (there are few customers) coffee shop. The University of the eastern Philippines, 3km out of town and accessible by tricycle, has a number of cheap lodging houses aimed at students, plus some cheap **cafés** and **Internet cafés**. Otherwise, there's a good public market every day in town, with lots of fresh fruit. For a high-cholesterol quick meal try the fried chicken from one of the vendors who set up colourful stalls in the street. The only real tourist spot is walking distance from the university – a long and scenic stretch of fine, darkish sand for some reason known as **White Beach**.

From **San José** (all bus services stop here) thirty minutes east of Allen by road and 45 minutes west of Catarman, you can charter a banca (expect to pay at least P500 for a day-trip, and to have to provide food for the boatman) to explore the tantalizingly undeveloped cluster of islands called **Biri-Las Rosas**. Somewhere among this group of idyllic outcrops, many with fine beaches, you can find one to call your own for the day. Most are only inhabited by poor fisherfolk and infrastructure is nonexistent, so staying the night is difficult unless you're willing to rough it.

Western Samar

Sitting pretty with the Calbayog River on one side and the Samar Sea on the other, **CALBAYOG** on the west coast is less shambolic than many Philippine port towns. It has no good beaches or tourist sights nearby, but makes a pleasant enough place for a one-night stop on your way through Samar.

The **airport** is 8km out of town; a tricycle into the centre costs P100. At the **ferry port**, on reclaimed land 2km from town-ticket offices serve most of the ferry companies that operate from here, including Palacio Shipping Lines and Cebu Ferries. Most **buses** arrive at the Capoocan transport terminal north of the river, ten minutes by tricycle from the town centre. The Philtranco terminal is closer to town, south of the cathedral on the main drag, Senator Avelino Street, also known as the National Highway. Opposite the Legislative Hall one block inland from here is a park and a **post office**, and there's a daily **market** in Orquin Street, on the northern edge of town near the river. Asian Spirit's office is at the Riverview Cinema Building, at the junction of Senator Avelino and Gomez streets (☎055/209 1189 or 1364). There are a number of small **Internet cafés**, many on Magsaysay Street.

Calbayog is a compact place and most **accommodation** – the quality of which tends to increase the further you are from the centre – can be reached on foot from the pier. *Central Inn* on Navarro Street (☎055/209 1932; ❷), two blocks south of the market, is a plain, slightly careworn lodge. *Eduardo's Tourist*

Hotel (☎055/209 1558; ❶) on Pajarito Street close to the Legislative Hall, and the *San Joaquin Inn* (☎055/209 1386; ❶), in Nijaga Street on the northern edge of the market, both have ordinary fan singles and doubles. More airy and pleasant than the lodges in town, the *Riverside Inn* (☎055/209 1656; 1) beyond the market at the northern edge of town, has some rooms offering views across the river. Even better is the *Sea Side Drive Inn & Restaurant* south of town on the National Highway (take a tricycle from the pier; ☎055/209 1221; ❷), which has air-conditioned rooms with clean shower and a decent seafood restaurant that specializes in grilled fish, usually tuna.

Catbalogan

Provincial capital of Western Samar and a working port, **CATBALOGAN** is one of many towns on Samar that have fallen behind in the development stakes, hindered by the distance from Manila and a lack of passenger ferries and flights. You can, however, get buses here to **Taft** (P130) on the wild and raw east coast where great brown sweeps of beach are, very slowly, beginning to play host to Filipino and a handful of foreign surfers. Catbalogan does have one thing going for it though: peace and quiet, at least relative to most tricycle-ravaged Philippine towns. The far-sighted mayor has introduced a pedal-power only policy in the town centre, which means staying here for a night or two can be an attractive option. You might find it hard to resist the beautifully named *Rose Scent Pensionne House* (☎055/251 1899; ❷) on Curry Avenue, where the rooms are clean and functional, with powerful cold showers. It's hard to miss the *Rolet Hotel* (☎055/251 5512; ❷–❸), in Mabini Avenue because it's a rather brash shade of bright green. The rooms are fine though, with air-conditioning, cable TV and good bathrooms. The friendly proprietors, Odie and Lolit Letaba, can answer most travel-related questions for the area.

Marabut Islands

About an hour by road to the north of Catbalogan is Marabut, an excellent jumping off point for exploring the **Marabut Islands**, a wonderful and striking collection of toothy outcrops rising out of the sea only a few hundred metres offshore. In Marabut you can hire a banca and there are also one or two places in town where you can hire a kayak for the day. There's no **accommodation** on any of the islands, but in Marabut itself there's the wonderful **Marabut Marine Park Beach Resort** (☎053/520 0414; ❷), which has several simple but perfectly comfortable wooden cottages and a restaurant serving fresh seafood. A short jeepney ride east along the coast from Marabut is **Lawaan**, a rustic and friendly coastal community where you can stay at *Jasmine House* (☎0170/9630 543; ❹), a private holiday home set in peaceful gardens with a number of well-kept rooms and studio for rent.

Sohoton Natural Bridge National Park

Best known for a natural rock formation that forms a bridge across a gorge, the **Sohoton Natural Bridge National Park** includes some remarkable limestone caves and gorges and lowland rainforest where you can see, even around the park's picnic areas, monitor lizards, macaques and wild boar. Much of the area can be toured by boat, although to reach the natural bridge itself you'll have to get out and walk; and as there are few marked trails, you'll need to hire a **guide** (see p.283) to find your way around. The boat trip into the park is spectacular, heading up the Cadacan River's estuary which is lined by mangroves and nipa palms. As you approach the park the river begins to twist and is then funnelled into a gorge of limestone cliffs and caves. The most accessible of the park's many impressive caves is **Panhuughan I**, which has extensive stalactite and stalagmite formations in every passage and chamber, many that sparkle when the light from the guides' kerosene lamps falls on them. If you're lucky you might come across a number of specialized spiders and millipedes that live their lives here in total darkness. There have been many significant archeological finds in the caves, including burial jars, decorated human teeth and Chinese ceramics. During World War II Filipino guerrillas used the caves as hideouts in their campaign against the occupying Japanese forces.

Practicalities

The park is in the southern part of Samar, the only approach being through **Basey**, on Samar's southwest coast 10km from the barangay of Sohoton and the entrance to the park. The quickest way to get there is via **Tacloban** on Leyte, from where you can catch an early jeepney to Basey (1hr), then a tricycle to the Department of Environment and Natural Resources (℡055/276 1151) near Basey's plaza, where you pay the P150 entrance fee and can arrange a **guide** and a banca to take you to and from the park (P1100 for a half-day). You can also get information about visiting the park at the tourist office in Tacloban (see p.241). There's no **accommodation** in the park, but there are a couple of lodging houses in Basey. The best is *Distrajo's Place* (℡053/276 1191; ❷), which has singles and doubles with fan.

Eastern Samar

If you get as far as the untamed east coast of Samar it's worth taking a few more days to travel by jeepney between the surfing centre of **Borongan** and **Guiuan** in the southeast and south to beautiful, peaceful **Calicoan island** which has terrific beaches, caves and lagoons and seems ripe for tourism development. You can reach this part of the island by bus from Catbalogan, or on the daily Tacloban–Guiuan boat.

Borongan

The bus trip from Catbalogan across to the east coast is one of the great little road journeys in the Philippines, taking you up through the rugged, jungle-clad interior past isolated barrios and along terrifying cliff roads. The bus emerges from the wilderness at **Taft** after about four hours and turns south to **BORONGAN**, where you can find good surf most times of the year. If the surf's not up, you could always hire a banca at the wharf in Borongan and take a trip along the coast or out to the pretty island of **Divinubo**, which doesn't have any accommodation but is an idyllic day-trip destination for exploring and snorkelling; make sure you take something to eat and drink. A few **places to stay** have sprouted in Borongan to cater to surf dudes. The *Pirate's Cove Beach & Surf Resort* (℡055/261 2661; ❷) is easy to find right on Rawis Beach in the seaside barangay of **Bato**. It has solid double nipa cottages and bancas for rent; it also has a water park with slides which can get busy at weekends although mostly with day-trippers who don't stay overnight. *Borongan Pensionne* (℡055/261 2109; ❷) on the National Highway and *Domsowir Hotel* (℡055/261 2133; ❸) in Real Street, are both in town and not especially convenient for the beach. There is a small **tourist office** (Mon–Sat 8am–4pm; ℡055/330 1139) in the Provincial Capitol Building facing Borongan plaza.

Guiuan

By a strange twist of fate, **GUIUAN** was once one of the country's boom towns, a small economic miracle that began when it was chosen to take in six thousand Byelorussian refugees fleeing Communism in China. They came in waves from 1945 to 1951, and businesses prospered as local entrepreneurs sold them everything from food to clothes and lumber so they could build houses. A number of their descendants still live in the town.

At the heart of Guiuan, a tidy and friendly provincial town, is the strikingly white **Church of the Immaculate Conception** (daily 6am–9pm), whose construction was overseen by Augustinian friars who arrived during the second expedition to the Philippines from Spain. Completed in 1595 after twenty years of hard labour by the locals, the building is one of the most beautiful in the eastern Visayas and the only one in the region to be included in the recent conservation efforts of the Philippine Historical Commission. Designed to double as a fortress, the church once had a bulwark at each corner (only two remain) on which six pieces of artillery were once mounted. Inside the spacious interior an exuberant altar bears images of saints carved from ivory, as well as a ceiling painted by local artisans and based on the Sistine Chapel.

For great views of the east coast and the Pacific, head to the weather station at the top of **Tingtingon Hill**. You'll need to climb up from the former **US Air Force airbase** (you can get a tricycle there from the centre), where the remains of its immense runway are now grazing ground for chickens and hogs.

The best place to **stay** hereabouts is *Tanghay View Lodge* (❶) on the waterfront about 1km to the north of Guiuan, which has quiet, clean motel-style rooms and a **restaurant** that serves excellent cheap seafood. The owner, an avid photographer, is a great source of local information and advice.

Calicoan Island

From Guiuan it's a short hop by jeepney across a causeway to **Calicoan**, which has been getting a lot of attention in recent years as the country's most exciting new destination. It really is an extraordinarily beautiful and almost deserted area; don't be surprised to see the occasional monkey cross the road or find yourself sharing a beach with huge monitor lizards. There's plenty to do here, too, with walking trails, caves, lagoons, surfing, diving, kayaking and so on. To make the most of your time, take a guide.

Accommodation is thin on the ground, but on a beach known as ABCD, the island's prime surfing area, the upmarket *Calicoan Surf Camp* (☎0917/530 1828, ⓦwww.calicoansurfcamp.com; ❾) has just opened for business, with eight luxurious air-conditioned cottages overlooking the Pacific. On the northern tip of the island a ridge of Palawan-style limestone cliffs are attracting rock climbers, while south of here there's thick jungle perfect for trekking. Ask first in Guian about hiring a guide; even on a small island like this it's easy to get lost. The island's middle section has fantastic almost virginal beaches on either side. On the east coast is **Ngolos Beach**, which is very reminiscent of Boracay before tourism arrived, and on the west coast is **White Sand Beach** – eight kilometres of wild tropical beauty. There are ten other beaches dotted around the island; many of the small coves can only be reached on foot.

Homonhon Island

Two hours off the coast of Guiuan, or an hour by banca from the southern tip of Calicoan, lies **Homonhon Island**, where Magellan first set foot on Philippine soil on March 16, 1521. The island is a quiet backwater with a few good beaches and inland waterfalls, the same ones perhaps that attracted Magellan and his men to what Magellan's diarist called a "watering place of good signs". There's not much here that commemorates Magellan, just a faded old marker at the landing site and an annual **pageant** on or around March 17 that rè-enacts the landing. Magellan's expedition landed here with his servant Enrique from Melaka (in what's now Malaysia) as interpreter. Magellan extended a message of goodwill from the king of Spain and a feast was held and gifts were exchanged. On March 25, the crew sailed to Limasawa, where it is thought the first Mass in the Philippines was held on March 31, 1521.

You can get a public banca here from Guiuan, but the sea is fickle in this area so boats don't always run and if they do they might not be able to return right away. There's no formal **accommodation**, though as ever you can pay to be put up by local people.

Leyte

The east Visayan island of **Leyte** ("LAY-tay"), separated from Samar to the north by a mere slither of ocean, the San Juanico Strait, is another sizeable chunk of the Philippines that has a great deal to offer visitors but is often overlooked. You could spend a year on this island and still only scratch the surface: the coastline is immense, the interior rugged and there are lakes and mountains that are well off the tourist map, known only to farmers who have tilled their shores and foothills for generations.

In the sixteenth century, Magellan passed through Leyte on his way to Cebu, making a blood compact with the local chieftain as he did so. But to many Filipinos and war historians, Leyte will always be associated with **World War II**, when its jungled hinterlands became the base for a formidable force of guerrillas who fought a number of bloody encounters with the Japanese. It was because of this loyalty among the inhabitants that General Douglas MacArthur landed at Leyte on October 20, 1944, fulfilling the famous promise he had made to Filipinos, "I shall return." He brought with him the first President of the Commonwealth, Sergio Osmeña.

Around the provincial capital of **Tacloban**, the usual arrival point, there are a number of sights associated with the war, notably the Leyte Landing Memorial, marking the spot where General Douglas MacArthur waded ashore to liberate the archipelago. To the north of Tacloban is the beautiful island of **Biliran** and, a short banca ride away from Biliran, the islands of **Maripipi** and **Higatangan**, which both have terrific beaches, rock formations and caves. The town of **Ormoc** on the west coast is one of the starting points for the **Leyte Mountain Trail**, a spectacular and challenging trek through rugged tropical countryside. To the south of Ormoc the coastal road takes you through **Baybay** and **Maasin**, both big ferry ports, before reaching **Padre Burgos**, which is quickly gaining a reputation for scuba diving. Off the southern tip of Leyte is **Limasawa Island**, an isolated outcrop where some believe Magellan conducted the first Catholic Mass in the Philippines.

Getting to Leyte

Leyte's only major airport is at Tacloban, served by **flights** from Manila with Philippine Airlines and Cebu Pacific. Good **ferry** connections link the ports of Palompon, Ormoc, Baybay and Maasin, all on Leyte's west coast, with Manila and a number of other ports in Luzon, Cebu, Bohol and Mindanao. There are also sailings between Samar and Tacloban, and between Cebu City and Naval on the island of Biliran, as well as from Baybay and Maasin to Surigao. For access to Leyte's southwest coast and the developing tourism area around Padre Burgos, there are regular ferry connections from Cebu City to Maasin.

Buses to Leyte operate from Manila (a long haul through Bicol and Samar) and from Mindanao; there are also regular daily services to Tacloban from Biliran Island off Leyte's north coast, and from Samar via either the San Juanico Bridge or the car ferry from Basey.

Tacloban and around

On the northeast coast, **TACLOBAN** is associated by most Filipinos with that tireless collector of shoes, Imelda Marcos, who was born a little south of here in the small coastal town of Tolosa to a humble family called Romualdez. The airport has been renamed Daniel Z. Romualdez Airport, and numerous streets and buildings bear the same name. In her youth, Imelda was a local beauty queen, and referred to herself in later life as "the rose of Tacloban".

Tacloban is a busy, dirty city, with most activity centered around the port and the market. There are few tourist attractions, though if you are here for a day or two you'll find the city has everything you need: some good accommodation, numerous ticket outlets for onward journeys, and banks and restaurants huddled in the compact centre to the south of Magsaysay Boulevard, which runs along the shore with views of southwest Samar. The city's major fiesta is the **Tacloban Festival** in the last week of June, kicking off with the Subiran Regatta, a boat race held at the eastern entrance of the San Juanico Strait. Tacloban is also a good starting point for the **Sohoton National Park** in neighbouring Samar (see p.237).

Arrival, transport and information

Tacloban city centre occupies a thumb of land bounded by Cancabato Bay on the east side and Panalaron Bay on the west. There are three main streets running across the city, **Magsaysay Boulevard**, **J. Romualdez Street** and **Avenida Veteranos**; another major thoroughfare, **Rizal Avenue**, runs roughly southwards off J. Romualdez Street. Major city landmarks include **Plaza Libertad** in the north close to the port area, **Madonna Park** in the east and the **Mangonbangon River**, which marks the city's southern perimeter. **Roxas Park** on the city's western edge is surrounded by malls, a big market and fast-food restaurants.

A jeepney into the city from the **airport**, which is south of the city along Real Street, costs P20, a taxi around P80. **Philippine Airlines** has a ticket office at the airport (℡053/325 7832 or 321 2212); **Cebu Pacific**'s office is in Senator Enage Street (℡053/325 7747) near the Central Bank. **Buses** from all points arrive at a terminal in Quezon Boulevard on the northwestern edge of the city, an easy walk from Roxas Park. The city's main **jeepney terminal**, for jeepneys north and south along the coast, is next to the bus terminal.

As for **ferries**, the WG&A ticket office is in Trece Martirez Street southwest of Plaza Libertad. You can buy tickets for Supercat fast ferries, which run from Leyte's west coast to Cebu, at the Supercat office in Santo Niño Street opposite *Welcome Home Pension*. Other ferry ticket offices are in the **port** off Bonifacio Street beyond the post office, easy to reach by tricycle from anywhere in the city.

Staff at the **tourist office**, off Magsaysay Boulevard (Mon–Sat 9am–4pm; ℡053/321 2048 or 4333), are organized and helpful, and can provide advice on

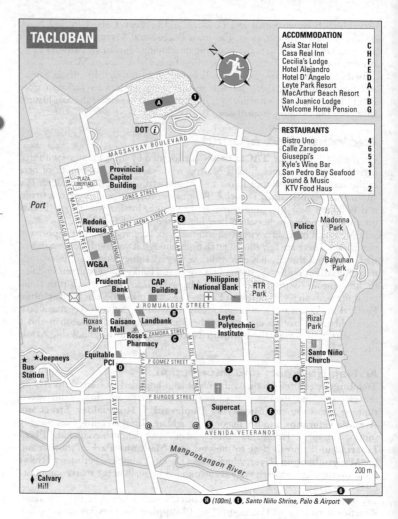

TACLOBAN

ACCOMMODATION
Asia Star Hotel	C
Casa Real Inn	H
Cecilia's Lodge	F
Hotel Alejandro	E
Hotel D' Angelo	D
Leyte Park Resort	A
MacArthur Beach Resort	I
San Juanico Lodge	B
Welcome Home Pension	G

RESTAURANTS
Bistro Uno	4
Calle Zaragosa	6
Giuseppi's	5
Kyle's Wine Bar	3
San Pedro Bay Seafood	1
Sound & Music KTV Food Haus	2

Ⓗ (100m), ❶, Santo Niño Shrine, Palo & Airport ▼

the Leyte Mountain Trail (see box on p.247). Their *Do-it-Yourself Tour of Tacloban & Environs* brochure outlines a number of interesting sights in and around Tacloban that you can cover, at a brisk pace, in one day on foot. The route starts at the tourist office and takes in the city centre before heading north towards the San Juanico Bridge (also known as the Marcos Bridge), which was presented as a gift and testimonial of love by Ferdinand Marcos to Imelda.

There's a **post office** near the harbour on Bonifacio Street, while the *Net Surf Café* at 170 Avenida Veteranos is one of dozens of small **Internet** places. Other good areas for Internet cafés are Gaisano mall near Roxas Park and Zamora Street around Leyte Polytechnic Institute; both have lots of small cybercafés, many with broadband. Most **banks** in Tacloban have ATMs and give cash advances against credit cards. Equitable Bank is on Rizal Avenue and Prudential Bank, Landbank and Philippine National Bank are on J. Romualdez Street. The grandly monikered Dona Remedios T. Romualdez Memorial Hospital and Puericulture Centre (named after Imelda's mum) is on J. Romualdez Street. Local **police** headquarters are located on the Paterno Extension near the RTR Park.

Accommodation

There's a good range of comfortable accommodation in Tacloban, ranging from simple budget accommodation that's adequate for a night or two, to affordable mid-range hotels where you can find better rooms than many budget places for not much more money. There are also a couple of plush hotels to consider, one of them a little way out of town at Palo but easy to reach by jeepney.

Asia Star Hotel Zamora St ☎ 053/321 4942. Quiet doubles with fan or a/c and all with private shower. Some rooms have cable TV and a fridge. Unattractive from the outside, but the rooms are fine, the staff friendly and the location central. ❸

Casa Real Inn Real St ☎ 053/321 2523. South of the city centre opposite the People's Center & Library. It's a short walk or tricycle ride back into town, but the extra peace and quiet compensate. Rooms are small and bare, but perfectly adequate and well maintained, with fan and shower. ❶

Cecilia's Lodge 178 Paterno St ☎ 053/321 2815. This modest but comfortable little pension house is the one many backpacker's head to. It offers simple, clean singles, doubles and family rooms, most with a private shower and toilet. Staff are friendly and helpful, and there's a decent café overlooking a courtyard. ❶

Hotel Alejandro P. Paterno St ☎ 053/321 7033. Attractive and well-managed hotel in a 1930s building two blocks from Santo Niño Park. Rooms are plain but spacious and feature a/c and shower (although the water pressure is poor and not always very hot). There's also a good restaurant and coffee shop. ❸

Hotel D' Angelo Rizal Ave ☎ 053/325 5342. Well-located and clean mid-sized establishment with simple, modern rooms with tiled floors and good

bathrooms. The rooms on the upper floors have pleasant views across the city and of the sea. ❸

Leyte Park Resort Magsaysay Ave ☎ 053/325 6000. This sprawling five-star resort-style development sits on top of a hill at the northeastern edge of Tacloban overlooking the San Juanico Strait and San Pedro Bay. Offers lush gardens, grand rooms with modern amenities, a swimming pool and regular live entertainment. ❽

MacArthur Beach Resort Palo, 5km south of Tacloban ☎ 053/323 3015. In a terrific location close to the Leyte Landing Memorial (see p.240), this government-run establishment has rooms decorated with native materials, immense landscaped grounds, plus restaurants and a swimming pool. ❻

San Juanico Lodge J. Romualdez St ☎ 053/321 9981. Very basic and careworn, but clean and adequate enough for a night, and centrally located. The rooms are small and dark, with nothing to see from the windows except concrete walls, but they have a/c and private bathrooms. ❶

Welcome Home Pension South end of Santo Niño St opposite the Caltex petrol station ☎ 053/321 2739. Mid-sized new establishment with a glittering lobby and modern rooms, with either fan or a/c, and cable TV. ❷

The City and around

One of your earliest stops on any tour of Tacloban must be to gawp at the **Santo Niño Shrine & Heritage Center**, a fifteen-minute walk south from the junction of Real Street and Avenida Veteranos, on the west side of the road opposite a Petron petrol station (Mon–Sat 8.30–11.30am & 1–5pm; P200). A grand folly of a house that Imelda Marcos ordered built but never slept in, it was sequestered by the government after the Marcos regime was overthrown. It's now another monument to Imelda's excesses, housing a dazzling collection of gifts and treasures that she acquired on her many overseas shopping expeditions. The building has a beautiful, delicate facade with clover-shaped fountains in front of the faded but still striking entrance. Inside there is evidence aplenty that nothing was too opulent or tasteless for La Imelda. Her personal chapel has sparkling diamond chandeliers, gold-framed mirrors and an expensive replica of the miraculous Santo Niño de Leyte (the original resides in the Santo Niño

△ Leyte Landing Memorial

Church opposite Santo Niño Park in Real Street). There are guides who can give you a tour, many of whom seem to be Marcos loyalists – jokes about the Iron Butterfly and her late husband are not appreciated.

It's worth the sweat of taking a walk to the top of **Calvary Hill**, on the western edge of Tacloban along Avenida Veteranos. This is a place of pilgrimage during Holy Week (before Easter) and the ascent is marked by the fourteen Stations of the Cross, with a five-metre statue of the Sacred Heart of Jesus at the summit. A good time to start the climb is late afternoon so you reach the top in time to watch the sun set. The views across Tacloban and San Pedro Bay are especially pretty after dark when the lights come on.

One of Tacloban's most remarkable legacies of World War II is the extraordi-narily flamboyant **CAP Building** on J. Romualdez Avenue. Formerly known as Price Mansion, this became General Douglas MacArthur's HQ after he landed in Leyte to set in motion the liberation of the Philippines; memorabilia of his stay are on display here in the MacArthur Room (Mon–Fri 9am–5.30pm, Sat 8.30am–noon; P25). A five-minute walk north, in Senator Enage Street, is another war curiosity, **Redoña House** (no admission), the residence of President Sergio Osmeña and his staff during the liberation.

Palo

About 5km south of Tacloban is the small town of **PALO**, known for its associations with General Douglas MacArthur and the liberation of the Philip-pines towards the end of World War II. It was at Palo's **Red Beach**, about 1km from the town centre, that MacArthur waded ashore on October 20, 1944, fulfilling his famous vow to return. The spot is marked by the dramatic **Leyte Landing Memorial**, an oversized sculpture of the general and his associates, among them Sergio Osmeña, walking purposefully through the shallows to the beach. Just outside Palo, on **Hill 522**, there's an old Spanish church that was turned into a hospital during the war, and the remnants of a number of Japanese foxholes and bunkers. It's worth chartering a tricycle for the day when you reach Palo to take you from sight to sight.

Eating, drinking and nightlife

The best place to try Tacloban's seafood is at *San Pedro Bay Seafood*, a large, popular restaurant that's part of the *Leyte Park Resort* complex, with beautiful views out to sea. It's not the cheapest place in town; P300 or so per person pays for a good meal from a menu that includes fresh tuna steaks, blue marlin, lobster, giant crabs and clams. *Giuseppi's* is a long-standing Italian favourite in the Anover Building on Veteranos Avenue, opposite the Divine Word Hospital, while the newer *Bistro Uno* at 41 Juan Luna St has sandwiches, burgers and traditional Filipino dishes such as *pancit* and *adobo*. The local delicacy *binagul*, a hot sticky concoction made of coconut and nuts, can be bought freshly made every morning from hawkers. In the evening, *Kyle's Wine Bar* on P. Gomez St has live music and serves a menu of pasta, salads and Philippine favourites. If karaoke is your thing, head straight for the *Sound & Music KTV Food Haus* at the northern end of M.H. Del Pilar St. For cheap drinks, decent food and wireless Internet head for *Calle Zaragosa* at 39 Independencia Street, a down-to-earth but enjoyable bistro and music venue that evolved from a 24-hour convenience store. There are live bands most nights and when there's not a live band music comes from the owner's collection of 10,000 CDs.

Biliran, Maripipi and Higatangan

The beautiful and largely undiscovered island of **Biliran** lies off the north coast of Leyte to the west of Tacloban, separated from mainland Leyte by the Biliran Strait, only a few kilometres wide, and connected by a bridge. Biliran's proximity to Leyte makes it appear that the two are part of the same province, but in fact Biliran was granted autonomous status in 1992, allowing it to detach itself from the distant bureaucracy in Tacloban and deal with Manila directly on matters of politics and budgets.

Biliran is the Philippines in microcosm, with a lengthy coastline of coves and beaches, a jungled, mountainous interior with some wonderful waterfalls and even its own small version of Banaue's rice terraces. Among the many natural wonders are three thundering waterfalls, all with deep, clear pools that are perfect for swimming: **Kasabanga Falls** is in the barangay of **Balaquid** on the south coast; **Casiawan Falls** a little further along the coast near **Casiawan** village; and **Tinago Waterfall** near Cabibihan in the island's southeast. There are **rice terraces** at Iyusan in the island's western interior, close to another splendid waterfall, **Bagongbong**.

Two of the best beaches on Biliran are on opposite sides of the island, but even on a day-trip you'll have time to see them both. On the east coast near Culaba is the beautifully deserted **Looc White Beach**, while the **Shifting Sand Bar**, 45 minutes by banca from the west coast capital of **NAVAL**, is a curving spit of sand surrounded by shallow water ideal for swimming, though note that there's no shade.

If you get to Biliran make sure you allow enough time to take a banca to some of the surrounding islands. **Maripipi** is a picturesque place of friendly people dominated by a stunning nine-hundred-metre volcano, while Higatangan Rocks on **Higatangan Island**, one hour west of Naval by banca, should also be on your itinerary. The beach here is beautiful and the rocks have been curved into extraordinary formations by time and tide. Ask your guide (see below) to take you to Cavintan Cave, said in local legend to extend all the way to Masbate and to contain deadly legions of venomous snakes – neither story appears true.

Practicalities

There are **buses** to Naval from Tacloban airport and from Ormoc. A direct **ferry**, the M/V *San Juan*, operated by San Juan Shipping Lines, sails from Cebu City to Naval. Sulpicio Lines also has sailings three times a week between Cebu City and Naval. There's a small provincial **tourist council** (☎053/500 9627; Mon–Fri 8am–4pm) in the capitol building in Naval, where staff can fill you in with latest details of transport and accommodation. To explore the more remote areas of the islands and to find the waterfalls, it's best to employ the services of a **local guide** which you can enquire about at the council. Staff at Naval accommodation may also be able to help in securing a guide, along with boat owners and tricycle drivers at the jetty. The going rate is at least P500 a day, plus food and drink. From Naval there is public transport (jeepneys) north to Kawayan and south to Caibiran, but no further in either direction. Jeepneys only leave when they are full (very full) and the road is bumpy and dusty (wet in the rainy season), so even a short trip can take time.

There are a number of simple **lodgings** in Naval. *Brigida Inn* (❶) in Castin Street close to the pier has seventeen rooms, some with air-conditioning, and provides snacks and meals on request. Nearby in the same street is *V&C Lodge* (❶), which has twelve fan rooms and one air-conditioned room. *LM Lodge* (❶) in Vicentillo Street has small rooms with fan and shared facilities. A few doors down is the friendly *Rosevic Pension* (❶), run by the helpful Vicente Felecia, which has rooms with fan, plus a small kitchen where staff can cook for you.

Ormoc

The small and relatively neat town of **ORMOC** on Leyte's west coast faces Ormoc Bay at the mouth of the Isla Verde River. A clean, attractive place, Ormoc has been largely rebuilt after floods in 1992 caused untold damage and resulted in the loss of eight thousand lives. It now has a lovely bayside park and drive from where the sunsets are marvellous, though there's nothing to see in town. Ormoc is also a possible starting point for the gruelling **Leyte Mountain Trail** (see box opposite).

Practicalities

There are Supercat ferries three times a day between Cebu City and Ormoc (P635, 2hr 35min), while Cebu Ferries operates twice weekly on Fridays and Wednesdays. In Ormoc, there's a **ticket office** (☎053/255 3511) for both services at the pier and another in Bonifacio Street (☎053/561 0154). Sulpicio Lines is the only operator sailing between Ormoc and Manila, with a weekly service that stops in Masbate en route. It also has sailings to Cebu City. The main **bus terminal** and **jeepney terminal** are next to each other on Ebony Street, near the pier. No airlines fly to Ormoc, but **Philippine Airlines** does have an office (☎053/225 2081) in the shopping mall on Lopez Jaena Street.

It's difficult to cash travellers' cheques or find an ATM that works in Ormoc. There's a branch of the Equitable PCI Bank at the junction of Rizal and Burgos streets, and a Philippine National Bank on Bonifacio Street, close to *Pongos Hotel*. **Western Union** has an office in the PPL Building. For **Internet access** there are a number of cybercafés in Gaisano department store in Real Street and

Don't tackle the beautiful but gruelling **Leyte Mountain Trail**, which winds from **Lake Danao** (also known as Lake Imelda) in western Leyte to **Burauen** in the east, without a guide. It's a forty-kilometre trek that can take up to eight days through rugged terrain. There are very few places along the way to buy anything, so you'll need to have supplies of food and water for yourselves and for the guide, whose fee will be in the region of P2000, excluding the cost of provisions. It's also worth having your own tent, though you may come across simple huts for overnight accommodation.

The trek snakes through some luscious countryside and across high plateaus, with panoramic views of Leyte's east and west coasts. If you're taking the trail from west to east, the first good area to camp is Lake Danao itself, a tranquil body of water of unknown depth lying 800m above sea level in a jungled bowl, and said to be home to a giant eel. At about the halfway stage you'll reach the trail's highest point on top of the Amandiwing mountain range, before descending again to Lake Mahagnao and the nearby **falls of Guinaniban**, where pristine mountain rainwater plunges into a deep pool that's perfect for swimming. There's a rudimentary rest hut (free) at the lake that can accommodate thirty people. At the eastern end of the trail you crisscross agricultural plantations and then ford the Marabong River, which runs about 10km west of Burauen. At Burauen you're around 80km south of Tacloban.

If you're starting at the Ormoc end of the trail, your best bet for assistance is the mayor's office in City Hall or the trail warden's office in the barangay of **Ga-as**, thirty minutes by jeepney from Ormoc. In Tacloban you can enquire at the tourist office (see p.241).

the Centurm Building in Aviles Street, opposite St Peter's Church. In Navarro Street is Net Bytz. Ormoc's **police** station is a little north out of town on Liia Avenue. There's a **hospital**, Ormoc Doctors' Laboratory, on Lopez Jaena Street near *Zenaida's Tourist Inn*.

Accommodation and eating

The best city accommodation is undoubtedly the *Ormoc Villa Hotel* (℡053/255 5006, Ⓦwww.ormocvillahotel.com; ❻–❼) in Obrero Street, the next block east from the Ormoc City Superdome. This is an attractive and upscale place with forty smart air-conditioned rooms, coffee shop, restaurant, swimming pool and spa. Even better, take a tricycle fifteen minutes eastwards out of the city to *Sabin Beach Resort* (℡053/255 8922; ❻–❼), which has luxurious cottages overlooking the sea, a swimming pool and an excellent restaurant. Budget options back in the city include *Don Felipe Hotel* (℡053/255 2460; ❶) and *Pongos Hotel* (℡053/255 2540; ❶), both in Bonifacio Street, and centrally located only a short walk from the bus, jeepney and ferry terminals. *Don Felipe* has plain singles and doubles, many of which face the noisy street. *Pongos* is a little further along from the ferry terminal and has a better choice of rooms. East off Bonifacio Street along Lopez Jaena Street is the *Zenaida's Tourist Inn* (℡053/255 2517; ❶), a friendly establishment where the rooms don't quite live up to the welcome. Singles have a fan and their own cold shower, while many doubles have air-conditioning and hot water.

Eating in Ormoc is limited, but one of the best restaurants is the native-style *Milagrina's* at the northern end of Real Street, where the Filipino food is wonderfully authentic and the *halo-halo* a popular speciality. *Chito's Chow* opposite the Ormoc Superdome, a short distance east of the pier along

Larrazabal Street, is a fast-food place with Chinese and Filipino dishes. Close to the *Jollibee* fast-food restaurant in Aviles Street are a few **bars**: *Bistro RJ* and *Asteroid Bar* are almost next to each other and offer mediocre food, loud music and inexpensive cold beer.

The southwest coast

Two hours south of Ormoc by road is the frenetic port of **BAYBAY**, which has some useful connections by small ferry to Cebu, Iloilo and Manila, as well as Ormoc. Baybay is a functional town with a very busy wharf area and a main street lined with *carinderias*, convenience stores, pawnshops and a few banks. The best place to stay is the *Uptown Plaza Hotel* in Magsaysay Avenue (℡053/335 2412; ❸), which has some rooms with air-conditioning and private bathroom, with occasional hot water.

About halfway between Baybay and Maasin, **HILONGOS** is a clean, easygoing town with fast ferry connections to Cebu City (P390). From the bus and jeepney terminal on the main road opposite the pier, numerous vehicles head south to Padre Burgos, or north to Baybay and Ormoc. There are a number of canteens huddled around a simple pier, but nowhere to stay. A little south of Hilongos, the port town of **Bato** has daily Kingswell Shipping Lines (℡032/255 7572 in Cebu) ferries to and from Cebu City. This is another useful jump-off point for Padre Burgos.

Maasin

At the mouth of the Maasin River in southern Leyte, **MAASIN** is a nondescript sort of place but an important port for hemp and copra; river valleys in the vicinity produce cotton, pepper, tobacco, rice, Indian corn and fruit. The town is well served by ferries from Cebu City and makes a good starting point if you're heading for the far south of Leyte, an area that is opening up for scuba diving and whale shark-watching. You can get up-to-date information on these activities from the Provincial Planning Development Office in Maasin's Provincial Capitol Building (℡053/570 9017).

Cokaliong and Trans-Asia Shipping Lines both run **ferries** between Cebu City and Maasin (P365). The boats are sometimes full, so make sure you book in advance; both these firms have offices at the pier itself. WG&A doesn't sail to Maasin, though it has a ticket office in Engage Building, Tomas Upos Street (℡053/381 3757), which runs along the seafront from the pier to the centre. There are also ferry connections with Surigao on Mindanao, though the ferries only sail if they are full. If you're arriving **by air** in Tacloban you can catch an air-conditioned L-300 van here from the airport (4hr; P150). Alternatively, take a jeepney from the airport to the bus terminal, where you can catch a bus for Maasin, although numerous unscheduled stops make this an unpredictable and frustrating trip.

Most travellers only pass through Maasin on the way to Padre Burgos, but if you do want to **stay**, take a tricycle for the short trip to *Maasin Country Lodge* (℡053/570 8858; ❸), which is a little inland on the banks of the Canturing River and has comfortable air-conditioned rooms that are spacious and well-maintained, some with a TV.

In town there are a number of basic, cheap places around the pier, including *Ampil Pensionne* (℡053/381 2628; ❶) in Tomas Upos Street, *National Pensionne House* in Kangleon Street (℡053/570 8424; ❶) and *Southern Comforts Pensionne* (℡053/381 2552; ❶) in Demetrio Street, right in the noisy centre of town.

Padre Burgos and Limasawa Island

The area around **PADRE BURGOS** on Leyte's southern tip is making a name for itself as an exciting scuba-diving destination, with more than twenty sites which have been documented by local divers. Whales, dolphins, manta rays and several species of shark can be seen in **Sogod Bay** immediately to the east.

The closest major port to Padre Burgos is **Maasin**, which is served by ferries from Cebu City. From Maasin there are jeepneys running south the rest of the way. *Peter's Dive Resort* in Padre Burgos (℡053/573 0015 or 0919/585 3891, Ⓦwww.whaleofadive.com; ❷–❺) has affordable **accommodation** in single rooms or cottages for two and breathtaking views of Sogod Bay. The main building's lower terrace also has a games room, where you can enjoy a round or two of pool and darts (free) and there's an excellent little restaurant where the owners serve home-cooked food. The resort provides a pickup service from Maasin and Hilongos. *Southern Leyte Divers* in San Roque, Macrohon (℡0918/589 2180, Ⓦwww.leyte-divers.com; ❷), fifteen minutes northwest of Padre Burgos by jeepney, is a small German-owned lodge with charming native-style cottages in an idyllic beachside location. The restaurant serves German food, fish dishes and curry; the owners can, of course, arrange diving trips. *Sogod Bay Scuba Resort* (℡0927/481 9885, Ⓦwww.sogodbayscubaresort.com; ❹) has lovely Spanish-style concrete rooms on the beach (twenty minutes to the north of Padre Burgos by jeepney), diving facilities and Internet. The restaurant has some appetizing fare, including beef and beer meat pies; steamed fish in banana leaves; curry laksa and the "world famous" Dopey Burger. The owners can help you arrange everything from diving and trekking to motorbike hire and caving trips.

Limasawa Island

Covering only six square kilometres, **LIMASAWA**, a sometimes choppy one-hour banca trip from Padre Burgos, is a simple island of six thousand farmers and fishermen and has electricity for a maximum of five hours a day, usually in the evening. It was on this island that, on top of a prominent hill, Magellan is said to have conducted the first Catholic Mass in the Philippines (though some revisionist historians claim the first Mass was most likely to have been said in Butuan, Mindanao). You can walk up concrete steps to a monument at the top of the hill, from where there are commanding views over the whole island. Limasawa also has some marvellous beaches and coves for snorkelling.

Bancas leave Padre Burgos two or three times early in the morning for the barangay of Magallanes on Limasawa. If you miss the boat back you shouldn't have much trouble finding a home to stay in for the night, though do the polite thing and enquire first with the mayor.

Cebu

Right in the heart of the Visayas, nearly 600km south of Manila, the island of **Cebu** is the ninth largest in the Philippines and site of the second largest city, **Cebu City**, an important transport hub with ferry and air connections to the rest of the Philippines. Cebu is a long, narrow island – 300km from top to bottom and only 40km wide at its thickest point – with a mountainous and rugged spine. All the towns and cities are located in the narrow strip of verdant lowland around its coast. Most tourists spend little time in the towns, heading

A quick guide to Cebuano

Filipino (Tagalog) might be the official language and English the medium of instruction, but **Cebuano**, the native language of Cebu, is the most widely spoken vernacular in the archipelago, not only used in Cebu but also by most of the central and southern Philippines. Cebuano and Filipino have elements in common, but also have significant differences of construction and phraseology. It's quite possible for a native Manileño to bump into a native Cebuano and not be able to understand much he or she says. The complex web of languages and dialects that spans the Philippines is one of the reasons for its political and social fragmentation.

Cebuano is evolving as it assimilates slang and colloquialisms from other Visayan dialects, as well as from Filipino and English. Confused? You will be. Most Cebuano conversations veer apparently at random between all three languages, leaving even Filipino visitors unable to grasp the meaning.

Some Cebuano basics

Good morning	*Maayong buntag*	Cheap	*Barat*
Good afternoon	*Maayong hapon*	Who?	*Kinsa?*
How are you?	*Kumusta?*	What?	*Unsa?*
Goodbye	*Ari na ko*	Why?	*Ngano?*
I'm fine	*Maayo man*	Near/Far	*Duol/Layo*
How much is this?	*Tag-pila ni?*	Idiot!	*Amaw!*
Expensive	*Mahal*	Go away	*Layas!*

off as soon as possible to the beaches and islands of the north or south. The closest beaches to Cebu City are on **Mactan Island** just to the southeast, although they are by no means the best. Head north instead to the marvellous island of **Malapascua**, where the sand is as fine as Boracay's, or to tranquil **Bantayan** off the northwest coast. The isolated **Camotes Islands** are a day's journey northeast from Cebu City, but well worth the trouble to reach, being truly picturesque and ideal for exploring at leisure. To the south of Cebu City, you can take a bus along the coast through the old Spanish town of **Carcar** and across the island to the diving haven of **Moalboal** and its nearby beaches.

Getting to Cebu is simple. There are dozens of **flights** daily from Manila and less frequent flights from a number of other key destinations, including Davao, Iloilo, Caticlan, Puerto Princesa and Siargao. The island is served by **ferries** from most key ports, including Manila, Iloilo, Davao and Tagbilaran. Cebu's position in the middle of the country makes it an excellent place to journey onwards by ferry, with sailings to Luzon, Mindanao and elsewhere in the Visayas.

Cebu City

Like many Philippine cities, **CEBU CITY**, nicknamed the "Queen City of the South", has become something of an urban nightmare, with jeepneys taking over the inadequate road network and pedestrians relegated to second-best. There's history and architecture in there somewhere, but you have to look hard for it among the clutter, the exhaust fumes and the nondescript concrete malls. Cebu City has always seemed less chaotic than Manila, but in recent years the impression is that it's catching up. Traffic has increased and the roads are often gridlocked.

The few attractions in the city itself mostly have some association with Magellan's arrival in 1521 and the city's status as the birthplace of Catholicism in the

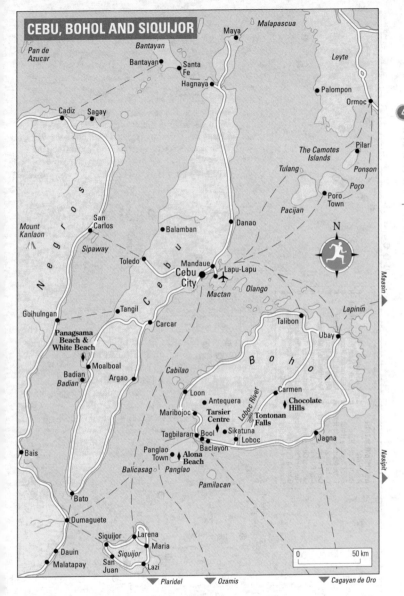

CEBU, BOHOL AND SIQUIJOR

Pan de Azucar

Bantayan

Bantayan

Santa Fe

Hagnaya

Maya

Malapascua

Leyte

Palompon

Ormoc

Cadiz

Sagay

Pilar

The Camotes Islands

Ponson

Tulang

Poro

Pacijan

Poro Town

San Carlos

Balamban

Danao

Mount Kanlaon

Sipaway

Toledo

Mandaue

Lapu-Lapu

Negros

Cebu

Cebu City

Mactan

Olango

Guihulngan

Tangil

Carcar

Talibon

Ubay

Lapinin

Panagsama Beach & White Beach

Moalboal

Badian

Badian

Argao

Cabilao

Bohol

Loon

Antequera

Carmen

Chocolate Hills

Maribojoc

Tarsier Centre

Tontonan Falls

Tagbilaran

Bool

Sikatuna

Loboc River

Lobuc

Jagna

Bais

Panglao Town

Alona Beach

Baclayon

Balicasag

Panglao

Pamilacan

Bato

Dumaguete

Siquijor

Larena

Maria

Dauin

Siquijor

San Juan

Lazi

Malatapay

Maasin

Nasipit

N

0   50 km

Plaridel   Ozamis   Cagayan de Oro

4

THE VISAYAS | Cebu

Philippines. The main tourist event here is the mardi-gras-style **Sinulog festival** in January (see box on p.260).

Orientation

Cebu City is a jumble of streets that in true Philippine urban tradition appears to have no particular heart. Some say the centre is the port area and the earthy,

251

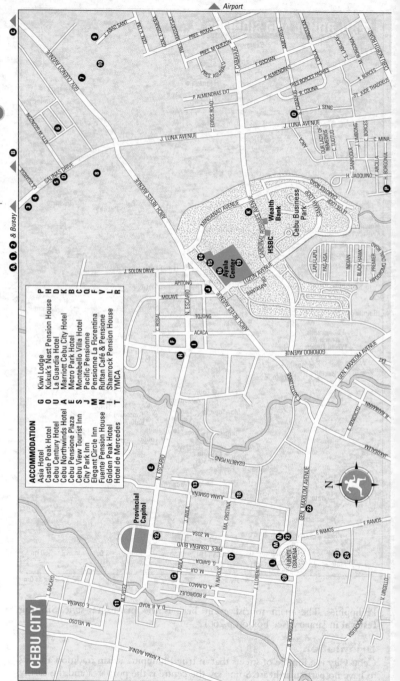

CEBU CITY

THE VISAYAS | Cebu

4

252

▲ Airport

ACCOMMODATION

Asia Hotel	G	Kiwi Lodge	P
Castle Peak Hotel	O	Kukuk's Nest Pension House	H
Cebu Century Hotel	U	La Guardia Hotel	K
Cebu Northwinds Hotel	A	Marriott Cebu City Hotel	D
Cebu Pensione Plaza	E	Metro Park Hotel	B
Cebu View Tourist Inn	S	Montebello Villa Hotel	C
City Park Inn	J	Pacific Pensionne	Q
Elegant Circle Inn	M	Pensionne La Florentina	F
Fuente Pension House	N	Ruftan Café & Pensione	V
Golden Peak Hotel	I	Shamrock Pension House	L
Hotel de Mercedes	T	YMCA	R

Provincial Capitol

Wealth Bank

Cebu Business Park

HSBC

Ayala Center

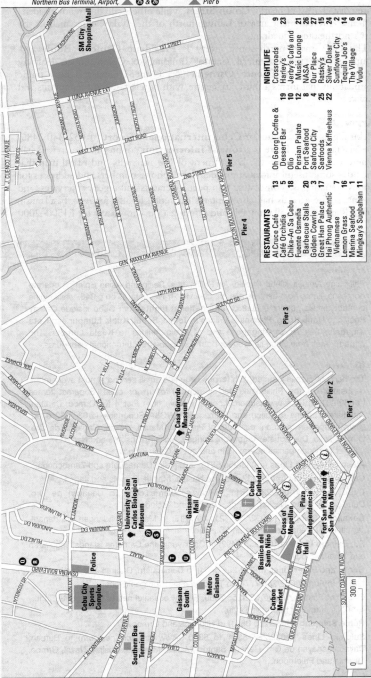

THE VISAYAS | Cebu

4

RESTAURANTS	
Al Cruce Café	13
Café Orchidia	5
Chika-An Sa Cebu	18
Fuente Osmeña	
Barbecue Stalls	20
Golden Cowrie	3
Great Han Palace	17
Hai Phong Authentic	
Vietnamese	7
Lemon Grass	16
Marina Seafood	1
Mingkay's Sugbahan	11
Oh Georg! Coffee &	
Dessert Bar	19
Olio	10
Persian Palate	12
Port Seafood	8
Seafood City	4
Seafoods	25
Vienna Kaffeehaus	22

NIGHTLIFE	
Crossroads	9
Harley's	23
Jerby's Café and	
Music Lounge	21
NASA	26
Our Place	27
Ratsky's	15
Silver Dollar	24
Sunflower City	2
Tequila Joe's	14
The Village	6
Vudu	9

careworn charms of nearby **Colon Street**, while others cite the trendy residential and entertainment area of **Lahug**, north of the Ayala Center mall in the city's northeastern quadrant.

The city's main north–south artery is **President Osmeña Boulevard**, running from the Provincial Capitol Building to Colon Street. Halfway between the two is **Fuente Osmeña** (aka Osmeña Circle), a busy traffic roundabout that forms a third city centre, with hotels, fast-food restaurants and hawkers.

Arrival

Cebu flights land at **Mactan Cebu International Airport** (℡032/340 2486) on Mactan Island. There is a **tourist information** counter in the arrivals hall where you can pick up the Department of Tourism's city and island map that includes some useful information such as telephone numbers and addresses for hotels, restaurants, consulates, transport operators, emergency services and hospitals. The arrivals hall also contains car-rental booths for Avis, FastTransit, Friends and e-Cars, all reputable and offering a car with driver for P1500–2000

Moving on from Cebu City

By plane

Philippine Airlines, Cebu Pacific, Air Philippines, Seair and Asian Spirit all operate domestic flights from here; routes are given in "Travel details" on p.340, while airline contact details appear on p.263. **International flights** from Cebu include Cathay Pacific to **Hong Kong**, Philippine Airlines to **Tokyo**, **Seoul, Kuala Lumpur** and **Kota Kinabalu**, Silk Air to **Singapore** and Malaysia Airlines to **Kuala Lumpur**. The departure tax from Cebu is P100 for both domestic and international departures.

By ferry

The harbour area is jammed with **ferries** large and small serving almost every major destination in the Philippines and a number of minor ones. Supercat ferries (℡032/231 9194, ⓦwww.supercat.com.ph) leave from Pier 4 for Ormoc, Dapitan, Tagbilaran, Larena (Siquijor) and Dumaguete. WG&A Superferry (℡032/232 0490, ⓦwww.superferry.com.ph) pulls out of Pier 6 to Manila, Davao, Cagayan de Oro, Ormoc, Iloilo, Dumaguete, Tagblaran, Surigao, Maasin, Masbate and Nasipit.

Other ferry companies operating in and out of Cebu include:

Aleson Shipping Lines (℡032/255 5673) to Dipolig, Dumaguete and Zamboanga.

Carlos A Gothong (℡032/232 9998) to Nasipit, Manila, Ozamis and Jagna.

Cebu Ferries (℡032/233 2611, ⓦwww.cebuferries.com) to Cagayan de Oro, Dumaguete, Iligan, Nasipit, Ormoc, Ozamis and Tacloban.

Cokaliong Shipping (℡032/232 7211 to 7218) to Maasin, Sindangan (Mindanao), Tagbilaran, Larena, Polompon and Surigao.

F.J. Palacio Lines (℡032/255 5492) to Calbayong, the Camotes islands, Tagbilaran and Larena (Siquijor).

Georg and Peter Lines (℡032/254 5404) to Dumaguete, Dapitan and Zamboanga;

Lite Shipping (℡032/253 7776) to Tagbilaran and Tubigon (Bohol).

Oceanjet Fast Ferries (℡032/255 7560, ⓦwww.oceanjet.net) to Dumaguete, Tagbilaran, Dapitan and Hilongos (Leyte).

Roble Shipping (℡032/255 3871) to Hilongos and Ormoc.

Sulpicio Lines (℡032/232 5361 to 5380, ⓦwww.sulpiciolines.com) to Butuan, Davao, Cagayan de Oro, General Santos, Manila, Masbate, Nasipit, Naval, Ormoc, Ozamis and Palompon.

per day. Most arriving flights are greeted by a handful of touts offering to take you straight from the airport by car to Malapascua or Moalboal. This is a convenient way of getting to these places and can save you the expense of a night in a city hotel. Make sure you agree a price first – and don't get in the car if the driver has companions.

Airport **taxis** charge about P180 to take you to Cebu City, 8km away across the suspension bridge that links Mactan to the main island of Cebu. The taxi booths are in the arrivals terminal, where you must buy a ticket and pay up front. You can also cross the road to the departures area and pick up a metered taxi, which will charge marginally less for the ride into the city.

The arrival point for ferries is one of six large piers in the **harbour** area beyond Fort San Pedro. Pier 1 is closest to Fort San Pedro, a matter of fifteen minutes on foot, and Pier 6 furthest away. Jeepneys and buses line up along the nearby Sergio Osmeña Boulevard for the short journey into the city. It's usually no problem flagging down a taxi in this area.

There are two bus terminals in Cebu. The **Northern bus terminal** on the coastal road, just east of the city, is used by buses and jeepneys to and from

Super Shuttle Ferry (☏032/345 5581 to 5583) to Ormoc, Camiguin, and Hagnaya and Santa Fe (Bantayan Islands).

Trans-Asia Shipping Lines (☏032/254 6491) to Cagayan de Oro, Ozamis, Iloilo, Masbate and Tagbilaran.

Weesam Express (☏032/231 7737, ⓦwww.weesamexpress.com) fast ferries to Dumaguete and Bohol, and from Toledo on Cebu's west coast to San Carlos in Negros.

For a list of domestic routes, see p.341. Note that Aleson Shipping Lines at 117 R. Palma Street (☏032/255 5673) has a ferry that sails every Monday at 10am for Sandakan in **Malaysia**, via Dumaguete, Dipolog and Zamboanga, taking 55 hours in total. For Negros, buses from Cebu to Moalboal run through **Tangil** on the west coast, where there's a daily ferry to Guihulngan; there are also Negros ferries from Toledo (see p.267) and Bato (see p.272).

A good place to get up-to-date ferry information is from the shipping pages of local newspapers. There's also a shipping schedules channel on the local Sky Cable TV network, available in some hotels.

By bus and taxi

Buses, many of them old and overloaded, run to the **southern** half of Cebu every thirty minutes or when they are full – and that means really full – from Cebu City's Southern bus terminal. These vehicles serve the full length of the east coast through Carcar to the port of Bato (P70), where you can hop on a boat to Negros. Buses for Moalboal and Badian also leave from this station, many of them continuing the length of the southwest coast to Bato. The typical fare to Moalboal is P80. Buses heading north to Hagnaya (for Bantayan Island) and Maya (for Malapascua) leave from the Northern bus terminal.

You may prefer to charter a **car with driver** to get around the island; many tourists simply flag down a taxi and negotiate a flat rate with the driver, usually P1000–1500 for the day or a one-way trip to, say, Moalboal or Maya. Many of the bigger hotels have their own cars with drivers, but you'll pay significantly more to hire one of these.

destinations north of the city. The **Southern bus terminal**, for buses and jeepneys to and from points south, is in Bacalso Avenue, west of President Osmeña Boulevard.

Information

The main **tourist office** is the Department of Tourism's Cebu regional office (Mon–Sat 8am–6pm; ☏032/254 2811, 254 6007 or 253 2047) in the LDM Building at the corner of Lapu-Lapu and Legaspi streets, near Fort San Pedro. At the fort itself is another tourist office (Mon–Sat 9am–4pm) with some basic maps and accommodation leaflets. For more urgent assistance, Cebu City also has a 24-hour tourist assistance hotline (Taskforce Turista; ☏032/254 4023 or 254 0080 after 5pm).

The only detailed **city map** is the **Cebu City Street Map** (P150), with a scale of 1:160,000; it's available from bookshops, as is E-Z Map's pocket map of both the island and the city, also available at many hotels in Cebu City. You can pick up a reasonable city and island map for free at the airport's tourist information counter. The tourist offices in Lapu-Lapu Street and Fort San Pedro have a small selection of maps, although the quality isn't great. There are a number of English-language local **newspapers**, including the *Cebu Daily News* (Ⓦwww.cebudailynews.com.ph), *The Freeman* and the *Sun Star Cebu* (Ⓦwww.sunstar.com.ph), all of which contain listings of local events and restaurant reviews.

City transport

Cebu City is reasonably compact with just a few buses operating within the city limits. There are, however, plenty of **taxis** in the city and it's not hard to find a driver who's willing to use the meter. The tariff is P2 per kilometre plus a flagfall of P25; a typical cross-city trip costs P50 outside rush hour.

There's a new breed of **jeepney** on the streets of Cebu – slick Isuzu vans often painted in outrageous colours with benches fitted in the back and windows cut in the sides. They ply dozens of cross-city routes in competition with the usual smoke-belching jalopies. From Colon Street, jeepneys old and new run almost everywhere: east to the piers and the SM City mall, north to Fuente Osmeña, northeast to Ayala Center and south to Carbon Market. There are also jeepneys along N. Escario Street, north of Ayala Center, heading east to Mandaue and west and southwest to the Provincial Capitol Building, Fuente Osmeña and the Colon Street area.

Accommodation

Some of the cheapest accommodation in Cebu City is in the old **Colon Street** area, though note that the streets in this neighbourhood can be a little scary at night, with roaming pimps and a number of shabby massage parlours and go-go bars. Hotels around **Fuente Osmeña** and **Lahug** are better, with the latter closer to the big malls and many of the city's more fashionable restaurants.

Around Colon Street

Cebu Century Hotel Colon St corner Pelaez St ☏032/255 1341 to 1347. Faded, airless rooms in a hotel that has seen better days, but is redeemed by its low prices. There's a range of singles, doubles and family rooms, all a/c; doubles and family rooms also have cable TV. ❹

Cebu View Tourist Inn 200 Sanciangko St ☏032/254 8333. Impressive new hotel, comfort-

able and secure, offering a variety of a/c rooms (though no singles) in a quiet road, with a little café downstairs. ❸

Hotel de Mercedes 7 Pelaez St ☏032/253 1105 to 1110. Solid concrete box of a hotel with a variety of room sizes. The recently renovated ones cost a little more than their unrenovated counterparts, but they're worth it: you get a fancier bathroom and a TV. ❹

Ruftan Café & Pensione 61 Legaspi St, near the Basilica del Santo Niño ☏ 032/256 2613. The rooms are as you'd expect for the price – small and dark, with prison beds and none-too-pleasant bathrooms – but staff and other guests are a great source of information. There's Internet access and a red-tiled café downstairs where you can get sandwiches for P30. A short stay (up to 5hr) is P100 and a "wash-up" P40. ●

Around Fuente Osmeña and the Capitol Building

Asia Hotel 11 J. Avila St ☏ 032/255 8536. In a good location north of Fuente Osmeña, a 10min walk from the Cebu Doctors' Hospital, this neat, medium-sized boutique hotel has an airy white-tiled lobby and small, well-appointed rooms, each with that travel essential, a high-tech Japanese toilet. The restaurant is open 24hr and there's a rooftop bar. ●

Cebu Pensione Plaza N. Escario St ☏ 032/254 6300. Large deluxe rooms, with more than enough room for two. Top-of-the-range suites also available. ●

Elegant Circle Inn Fuente Osmeña ☏ 032/254 1601. Modern glass edifice with a/c rooms and a coffee shop. ●

Fuente Pension House 0175 Don Julio Llorente St ☏ 032/253 4133 or 6789. Well-run place behind Fuente Osmeña in a quiet road offering ordinary but clean and comfortable doubles and trebles. There's also a restaurant and an Internet café. ●

Pacific Pensionne 313-A President Osmeña Blvd ☏ 032/261 1792. Next to the *Firehouse* go-go bar down a small side street off the boulevard, this is a welcoming, quiet little hotel with a bright café in the lobby and a range of rooms from very afford-able singles to four-bed family options. You'll get a discount if you take one of their fans and promise not to use the a/c. Staff are charming and can help with everything from tour arrangements to ticket reconfirmation. ●

Shamrock Pension House Fuente Osmeña ☏ 032/255 2999. Budget a/c accommodation in the hubbub of Fuente Osmeña, so close to the BBQ stalls that you can smell grilled meat from the lobby. Rooms range from standard and deluxe doubles to studios for two. ●

YMCA 61 President Osmeña Blvd ☏ 032/253 0691 or 4057. Good central location and a great range of affordable rooms from singles with a private bath to triples and women-only dorm beds. Set back from the busy road and quiet, with a small swimming pool (P25), billiards and a passable cafeteria. Dorm beds P150. ●

Ayala Center, Lahug and beyond

Castle Peak Hotel F. Cabahug corner President Quezon streets, Mabolo ☏ 032/ 233 1811, ⓦ www.castlepeakhotel.net. Clean and very affordable hotel in a quiet area a short walk from Ayala Center. Rooms are spacious and the bathrooms are well-maintained. Handily, there's a taxi rank right next to the hotel. Internet facilities are available and there's a decent restaurant. ●

Cebu Northwinds Hotel Salinas Dr (the continua-tion of J. Luna Ave) ☏ 032/233 0311 to 0313. Close to Lahug's bars and restaurants, this is a modern hotel with the usual mod cons, a coffee shop, restaurant and bar. You get a ten percent discount if you pay cash. ●

City Park Inn Archbishop Reyes Ave ☏ 032/232 7311. Modern hotel in a good spot opposite the Ayala Center mall, and convenient for taxis and jeepneys. Rooms are a/c and en suite. ●

Golden Peak Hotel Gorordo Ave ☏ 032/ 233 9770, ⓦ www.goldenpeakhotel.com. Good-value, mid-range hotel with efficient staff and tremendous views if you ask for a room on one of the higher floors. Decent buffet breakfast included in the price. Walking distance from Ayala Center. ●–●

Kukuk's Nest Pension House 157 Gorordo Ave ☏ 032/412 2026. This legendary, rather down-at-heel hangout for artists and beatniks is a ten-minute walk northwest of Ayala Center along the horribly busy Gorordo Avenue. Rooms, some with a/c, bathroom and cable TV, are kitted out with wooden antiques, and there's a garden restaurant on site where you can eat and drink to the sound of thundering traffic. ●

La Guardia Hotel Salinas Dr ☏ 032/232 3789. Spotless, peaceful, tile-floored sanctuary with seven types of room to choose from. Cheapest are the economy rooms, with three single beds. All rooms have a/c, cable TV, refrigerator, shower and hot water. ●

Kiwi Lodge 106 Tud Tud St, Mabolo ☏ 032/ 232 9550, ⓦ www.kiwilodge.org. Small and well-run family hotel in a great location in a residential area south of Ayala Centre and the Cebu Business Park. Range of comfortable a/c rooms at reasonable prices, with a restaurant that serves hearty western cuisine and a bar where the usually expat clientele can offer all sorts of travel advice. ●

Marriott Cebu City Hotel Cardinal Rosales Ave, Cebu Business Park ☏ 032/232 6100; ⓦ www.mariott.com. More than three hundred rooms, plus restaurants, a coffee shop, cocktail lounge and health club, in a twelve-storey building located in a pleasant green residential area close to Ayala Center. Plenty of taxis on the doorstep. ●

Metro Park Hotel St Lawrence St ☎032/233
0130. Simple, unfussy place with a range of rooms
in a good location behind the *La Guardia*. Besides
doubles, they have spacious two-bedroomed
"apartments", good for four. ❹

Montebello Villa Hotel In the suburb of Banilad
☎032/231 3681 to 3689, ⓦwww.montebellovilla-
hotel.com. Rambling, atmospheric establishment
which, despite noisy a/c and dodgy plumbing,
remains a great choice because of its quiet
isolation, neat gardens and clean swimming pools,

one for children and the other for adults. The only
disadvantage to staying here is that you'll have to
get a taxi to visit other parts of the city. Residents
of the Philippines get discounts. ❻

Pensionne La Florentina 18 Acacia St ☎032/231
3118. Friendly, family establishment in an old
building set back from Gorordo Avenue, so it's
reasonably quiet. The coffee shop offers simple
native dishes and the shops and restaurants of
Ayala are a short walk away. ❸

The City

The old part of Cebu City, known to bureaucrats as **Central Proper**, is a
seething cobweb of sunless streets between Carbon Market and Colon Street,
the latter said to be the oldest mercantile thoroughfare in the Philippines. You
can explore the area on foot, picking your way carefully past barrow boys selling
pungent limes, hawkers peddling fake mobile phone accessories and, at night,
pimps whispering their proposals from dark doorways. A vibrant, humming,
occasionally malodorous area of poorly maintained pavements and thick diesel
fumes, it's not a mainstream tourist sight but worth some time for its spirit and
vigour. About ten minutes' walk south of Colon Street, **Carbon Market** is an
area of covered stalls where the range of goods on offer, edible and otherwise,
will leave you reeling. Carbon is alive from well before dawn and doesn't slow
down until after dark. This is where produce is brought from the rest of Cebu
Island every morning – shining fat tuna, crabs, lobsters, coconuts, guavas,
avocados and mangoes. Cebu City has its fair share of malls, offering shops, fast
food, restaurants, Internet cafés and travel agents. The two biggest are **Ayala
Center** in the north of the city and **SM City** on J. Luna Avenue in the east on
the way to Mandaue City.

The Cross of Magellan

Cebu City's spiritual heart is an unassuming circular crypt in the middle of busy
Magallanes Street – the spelling, confusingly, is correct – that houses the **Cross
of Magellan** (daily 9am–7pm; free). The first of the conquering Spaniards to
set foot in the Philippines, Magellan began a colonial and religious rule that
would last four hundred turbulent years. The crypt's ceiling is beautifully
painted with a scene depicting his landing in Cebu in 1521 and the planting of
the original cross on the shore. It was with this cross that Magellan is said to
have baptized the Cebuana Queen Juana and four hundred of her followers. The
cross which stands here today, however, is a modern, hollow reproduction said
to contain fragments of the famous conquistador's original.

Basilica del Santo Niño and Cebu Cathedral

Next to the Cross of Magellan on President Osmeña Boulevard is the **Basilica
del Santo Niño**, built between 1735 and 1737, where vendors sell plastic
religious icons and amulets offering cures for everything from poverty to infer-
tility. Inside is probably the most famous religious icon in the Philippines, a
statue of the Santo Niño. It's said to have been presented to Queen Juana of
Cebu by Magellan after her baptism, considered the first in Asia, in 1521.
Another tale has it that 44 years later, after laying siege to a pagan village, one
of conquistador Miguel Lopez de Legazpi's foot soldiers found a wooden box
that had survived the bombardment inside a burning hut. Inside this box was

△ Carbon Market, Cebu City

the Santo Niño, lying next to a number of native idols. If you want to see the statue, let alone touch it, you'll have to join a queue of devotees that often stretches through the church doors and outside. A short walk from the basilica is **Cebu Cathedral**, a sixteenth-century baroque structure that's crumbling on the outside, though its interior has been restored.

Fort San Pedro and San Pedro Museum

When he arrived in 1565, conquistador Miguel Lopez de Legazpi set about building **Fort San Pedro** (daily 9am–6pm; P15) to guard against marauding Moros from the south. It was here, on December 24, 1898, that three centuries of Spanish rule in Cebu came to an end when their flag was lowered and they withdrew in a convoy of boats bound for Zamboanga, their waystation for the voyage to Spain. The fort, near the port area at the end of Sergio Osmeña Boulevard, has been used down the centuries as a garrison, prison and zoo, but today is little more than a series of walls and ramparts with gardens in between.

Sinulog

The big, boisterous **Sinulog festival**, which culminates on the third Sunday of January with a wild street parade and an outdoor concert at Fuente Osmeña, is held in honour of Cebu's patron saint, the Santo Niño. It's almost as popular as Kalibo's Ati-Atihan (see box on p.312), and hotels in Cebu are usually full during this period.

Sinulog is actually the name given to a **dance** performed in honour of the Santo Niño. Comprised of two steps forward and one step backward to the sound of drums, this swaying movement is said to resemble the current (*sulog*) of a river and evolved from tribal elders' rhythmic movements while praying at the image of the Santo Niño's original sanctuary, a waterfront chapel. Until the 1970s Sinulog was purely religious in nature, with the dance performed almost exclusively by old women in front of the Santo Niño in the Basilica del Santo Niño. In 1980 it took to the streets and thereafter assumed the status of an exuberant cultural show for locals and visitors alike. It's a memorable, deafening spectacle, with hundreds of intricately dressed Cebuanos dancing through the streets to the beat of noisy drums.

One of the most popular places from which to view the parade is President Osmeña Boulevard, but many of the prime positions are taken by dignitaries and a scrum of tourists, so get there early. If you want to escape the crowds, grab a spot on one of the smaller roads, such as N. Escario Street, where security is less zealous and you can slip underneath the velvet ropes and join the dancers. For information about Sinulog and details of the exact route, which varies every year as the festival grows, call the Sinulog Foundation on ☏ 032/253 3700 or visit ⓦ www.sinulog.ph.

A small **museum** (Mon–Sat 9am–5pm; free) inside the fort contains remnants of old galleons and their cargoes. If it happens to be closed you can always slip one of the security guards P100 for a private tour.

At weekends, especially on Sundays, the park opposite, Plaza Independencia, seethes with townies playing ghetto-blasters and families enjoying picnics.

Casa Gorordo Museum

Built in the middle of the nineteenth century by wealthy merchant Alejandro Reynes, the marvellous **Casa Gorordo**, 35 Lopez Jaena St (off the eastern end of Colon St; Mon–Sat 9am–noon & 2–6pm; P15), is one of the few structures of its time in Cebu that survived World War II. Owned by a succession of luminaries, including the first Filipino Bishop of Cebu, Juan Isidro de Gorordo, it was acquired in 1980 from the bishop's heirs and opened as a museum three years later.

From the outside, the house is a striking example of late Spanish-era architecture and native building techniques, with lower walls of Mactan coral cemented using tree sap, and upper-storey living quarters built entirely from Philippine hardwood held together with wooden pegs. The interior offers an intriguing glimpse into the way Cebu's rich Filipinos once lived, elegantly furnished with original pieces from America and the Old World – a Viennese dining set, a German piano, American linen and Catholic icons from Spain and Mexico. In the ground-floor library are photographs of Cebu during the American regime. Other curious exhibits include native gadgets used for grinding chocolate and a handheld cannon for launching fireworks.

University of San Carlos Biological Museum

Held in the Engineering Building of the USC Technological Center on Del Rosario Street, a short walk east of President Osmeña Boulevard, the collection of the **University of San Carlos Biological Museum** (Mon–Fri 8am–noon

& 1–5pm; Sat 8am–noon; free) is said to be one of the most impressive in Asia. It was begun in 1952 by Enrique Schoenig, a German priest and entomologist who started the tradition, continuing today, of annual USC field trips to Mindoro, Mindanao and the Visayas to gather specimens from as many different parts of the Philippines as possible. The museum has an enviable collection of creepy-crawlies and some morbidly interesting stuffed mammals such as a six-legged **carabao**.

Busay
The road that winds northwards out of Cebu City eventually finds its way to **Busay,** the high mountain ridge that rises immediately behind the city. There's a wide concrete lookout area known to locals as **Tops**, where you pay a P100 entrance fee, grab yourself a stick of barbecued chicken from one of the vendors, and sit and watch the sunset. Tops is popular at dusk, so don't expect romantic solitude, but the view is great and the air cooler and cleaner than in the concrete jungle below. A taxi ride there and back will cost in the region of P600, including a wait while you admire the view. Some jeepneys from SM City and Ayala Centre are marked for Busay, but they usually don't go all the way, leaving you with a hot uphill walk of almost one kilometre.

Jumalon Museum and Butterfly Sanctuary
On the western edge of the city, the **Jumalon Museum and Butterfly Sanctuary** (by appointment only; ☎032/681 6884, ⓦ www.jnjumalon.org; free, though donations invited), 20-D Macopa Street, is lepidopteran heaven, with rooms full of dead specimens in glass cases and a large garden at the back with an aviary of live ones. This is the country's oldest collection of butterflies and includes not just everyday species such as monarchs and viceroys but also specimens of malformed and freak butterflies such as albinos, melanics, dwarfs and Siamese twins. The museum is in **Basak**, a largely residential suburb about twenty minutes from the centre by taxi (P60). Alternatively, you can take any jeepney heading along the Cebu South Road to Friendship Village or Basak, get off at the Holy Cross Parish Church and look out for Macopa Street near Basak Elementary School.

Eating
There are an increasing number of independent **restaurants** in Cebu City, with a good blend of Filipino and foreign cuisine, plus some pleasant coffee shops and excellent seafood restaurants. All the big malls have food courts – in the Ayala Center there's one on the top floor. Malls also have numerous small restaurants dotted around, usually on the lower floors, where you'll find everything from quick Asian snacks to pasta and sushi. Coffee shops have become popular in Cebu; there are many in the malls.

Fuente Osmeña and around
Al Cruce Café J. Avila St corner Ma Cristina Extension, behind the *Cebu Vacation Hotel*. Friendly little family-run Spanish café. Try their *habas con jamon* (broad beans with ham), *chuleta de cerdo* (pork cutlet), potato omelette or spicy chicken wings. There's good home-made *lemonada* too.
Chika-An Sa Cebu Century Plaza Commercial Complex, Juan Osmeña St. A Cebu institution that serves popular rustic fare such as chicken, pork barbecue, *lechon kawali* (crispy pork), sizzling *bangus* (milkfish) and *bulalo* (beef bone stew). Close to Fuente Osmeña and probably your first stop for affordable native Cebuano cuisine.
Fuente Osmeña Barbecue Stalls Fuente Osmeña. Cheap and tasty, but only for carnivores. The cooking starts with a vengeance at dusk and the choice ranges from whole chickens cooked over coals to sticks of pork and street food delicacies such as chicken's feet and intestines.

Great Han Palace 18 President Osmeña Blvd. Perhaps the best of a number of authentic Chinese restaurants on Osmeña Blvd, *Great Han Palace* has a huge menu that includes a number of vegetarian options such as vegetable fried rice and fresh broccoli with tofu and black beans. The chilli dishes are delicious and there's a good choice of noodles.

Mingkay's Sugbahan Velez St. A couple of blocks west of the Capitol Building opposite China Bank, this modest native-style restaurant celebrates the Cebuanos' love of all manner of barbecued meat, served with spicy dips made of vinegar and soy and served with piping hot fragrant rice. Typical of the many BBQ places in the city. Not for vegetarians.

Persian Palate Restaurant President Osmeña Blvd corner Escario St, close to the Capitol building ☎032/253 6745. Very spicy Singaporean, Malaysian, Indian and Middle Eastern dishes, including a good range of vegetarian curries such as vegetable biryani served with tomato rice.

Vienna Kaffeehaus Mango Square mall, General Maxilom Ave. Founded more than 20 years ago by an expat Austrian who saw the need for good coffee in the Philippines, the *Kaffeehaus* is a little corner of imperial Europe in the tropics. There are eleven types of coffee including Viennese iced coffee and excellent espresso, which is still hard to find in the country. The lunch and dinner menu is also Austrian, with wholesome goulash and dumplings, schnitzel and sausage and a delicious home-made sauerkraut.

Lahug and beyond

Café Orchidia Nivel Hills, Lahug. Intimate and comfortable European-style restaurant specializing in Italian pasta dishes, but also offering excellent steaks and salads. At the northern end of Salinas Dr beyond the Cosmopolitan Chapel.

Golden Cowrie Salinas Dr, Lahug ☎032 233 4670. The interior is Philippine Zen with white walls and bamboo furniture; the food is chic traditional. Lots of seafood dishes such as tuna jaw and grilled lapu-lapu. The Bicol Express-style vegetables are very spicy. Busy, especially at weekends.

Hai Phong Authentic Vietnamese Restaurant Crossroad mall, Banilad. Unpretentious place with plastic tables offering promptly served and appetizing Vietnamese dishes such as beef noodle soup, spring rolls and spicy curries, all prepared with fragrant herbs. Right next door is a Thai equivalent, *Krua Thai*.

Lemon Grass Restaurant Ayala Center. On the northern side of the mall facing Archbishop Reyes Ave, this fashionable new restaurant is arguably the best place to sample Thai food in Cebu. The dishes are as close to authentic as they can be, with lots of well-herbed and spicy coconut curries. The soups have been smoothed down for local tastes, but if you like them hot the chef can oblige. The salads are a treat, made with slices of fresh mango and coconut shavings.

Marina Seafood Restaurant Nivel Hills, Lahug ☎032/233 9454. Laidback native-style alfresco restaurant on a hill above the city (a taxi from the centre will cost P100). Two people can feast on tuna belly, grilled marlin and shrimps with chilli and coconut for about P200 a head.

Olio Crossroads mall, Banilad. High-end "fusion" restaurant specializing in seafood and steaks, with a tempting but expensive (by local standards) wine list. The 750-gram Cowboy Steak is a carnivorous treat. A good meal here will set you back around P1000 per person.

Oh Georg! Coffee & Dessert Bar Level 1, Ayala Center. In a mall chock-full of fast-food restaurants and coffee shops, this one deserves special mention. The Batangas coffee is rich and strong and the menu full of real home-made dishes such as bean and vegetable soup, Greek salad and a Mexican salad that's big enough to share.

Port Seafood Restaurant *Waterfront Hotel*, Lahug ☎032/231 7441. An upmarket hotel reinvention of the quintessential Filipino seafood restaurant. The food is undeniably good, especially the baked oysters and fried lapu-lapu.

Seafood City Restaurant Salinas Dr, Lahug. Big, brightly lit and hugely popular seafood restaurant where you choose what you want from the displays and ask for it to be cooked any way you choose. The king prawns are enormous and delicious with chilli and garlic. Other choices include grouper, tuna jaw and tangy fish soup.

Seafoods Restaurant Hernan Cortes St, Mandaue. Immensely popular seafood restaurant – all the taxi drivers know it – on the road to the airport. Tuna jaw, flown in daily from Davao, is a speciality.

Drinking, nightlife and entertainment

Cebu, like its big brother Manila, is a city that never – or rarely – sleeps. You don't have to walk far in the centre to pass a pub, a karaoke lounge or a music bar. The colourful and friendly *Jerby's Café and Music Lounge* is one of many popular **nightspots** on Fuente Osmeña. Just south of Fuenta Osmeña, on President Osmeña Boulevard, late-night joint *Harley's* has a P150 cover charge which includes one drink and the chance to listen to Filipina pop singers putting Madonna and Mariah Carey to shame. Close to *Harley's* (look out for *McDonald's* next door) you'll find the *Silver Dollar*, something of a Cebu institution, a dark and boozy go-go bar where hustlers monopolize the pool table and cockroaches make occasional guest appearances on the sticky counter top. To enter, look for the small doorway set back from the pavement, surrounded by blue neon lights. *Our Place* in Pelaez Street, right on the junction with Sanciangko Street, is another Cebu stalwart, straight from the pages of Graham Greene. A small upstairs bar is cooled by inefficient ceiling fans, where expat men swill San Miguel into the early hours and complain about the hardships of life in the tropics. The air is warm and full of motes, the toilets are dank and the menu includes dishes with mashed potato and gravy.

One of the latest additions to Cebu's club scene is *Crossroads*, a development of various clubs and bistros in Archbishop Reyes Avenue, 100m east of the turnoff into Salinas Drive – the dance-bar *Vudu* among the most popular places here. On the opposite side of the road right on the junction with Salinas Drive is *The Village*, another fashionable complex of bars, restaurants and clubs. Further north along Salinas Drive is *Sunflower City*, a hyper-trendy entertainment complex where you can enjoy a cocktail at the bar, east-meets-west cuisine in the minimalist restaurant, and then move on to the nightclub for DJ music and live bands. There are also private karaoke rooms. Admission is P100 from Sunday to Monday and P150 on Friday and Saturday. There's a very similar place, *NASA*, on Fortuna Street in Mandaue City.

At Ayala Center two very popular nightspots – *Tequila Joe's* and *Ratsky's* – both have lively young crowds and live music from some excellent youthful bands. These establishments are almost next door to each other, on the north side of the mall facing Archbishop Reyes Avenue.

Listings

Airlines All these firms have offices at the airport, and you can book tickets in Cebu City at any travel agent: Air Philippines ☏ 032/417 2320 to 2322; Asian Spirit ☏ 032/341 2555; Cathay Pacific ☏ 032/254 0821; Cebu Pacific ☏ 032/340 3254; Malaysia Airlines ☏ 032/340 2977; Philippine Airlines ☏ 032/340 0422 or 0181; Seair ☏ 032/341 4879; Singapore Airlines/Silk Air ☏ 032/232 6211.

Banks and exchange There is no shortage of places to change currency, particularly along the main drag of President Osmeña Blvd and in all shopping malls. There are branches of Citibank in President Osmeña Blvd (just north of Fuente Osmeña) and in Cebu Business Park close to Ayala Center. In President Osmeña Blvd there's also Metrobank, Banko Central and HSBC. Near the massive SM City mall in J. Luna Ave Extension are RCPB and Equitable PCI Bank.

Bookshops National Book Store has branches in SM City mall, Ayala Center and close to Fuente Osmeña. The choice of literature isn't vast, but you will find various paperback best-sellers and classics such as Dickens.

Car rental Avis, Archbishop Reyes Ave ☏ 032/340 2486; Dollar, 36 President Osmeña Blvd ☏ 032/254 7425; Hertz, 34 Cebu Capitol Commercial Complex, N. Escario St ☏ 032/254 5004; Thrifty, *Waterfront Hotel*, Lahug ☏ 032/340 2486. Many firms also have outlets at the airport.

Consulates A number of countries have consular offices in Cebu, among them the UK, at Villa Terrace, Greenhills Rd, Mandaue City (☏ 032/346 0525) and the US, G/F Waterfront Cebu City Hotel Building, Salinas Drive (☏ 032/231 1261), though these are open only part-time and don't offer a full consular service.

Couriers Courier companies can be found in most of the city's malls; the Ayala Center contains offices for DHL, Fedex, UPS and TNT.

Dive operators Useful for packages to Moalboal or Malapascua, or a diving trip to nearby Mactan Island, are the following PADI-certified companies: Aquaventure Dive Shop 2/F *Myra's Pension*, 8 Escario St ☏ 032/234 1630; Scotty's Dive Center, *Shangri-La's Mactan Island Resort*, Mactan Island ☏ 032/231 5060; Scuba World, Maria Cristina Ave ☏ 032/231 6009.

Emergencies Apart from the usual emergency numbers (see Basics p.61), you can call Task Force Turista (☏ 032/254 1136), a 24hr tourist-assistance hotline.

Ferry tickets There are ticket outlets throughout the city, in malls, at Aboitiz Express offices (convenient locations include: Level 2, Ayala Center ℡ 032/281 0896; New Vision Theater, Colon St ℡ 032/253 0239; Level 3, Robinson's Place, Fuente Osmeña ℡ 032/254 0488; Lower G/F, SM City mall ℡ 032/232 0764) and at many travel agents (see below); many hotels can book ferry tickets as well.

Hospitals Among the best-equipped are Cebu Doctors' Hospital, President Osmeña Blvd (℡ 032/253 7511); Cebu Community Hospital, also on President Osmeña Blvd (℡ 032/588 1998); Chong Hua Hospital, J. Llorente St, just north of Fuente Osmeña (℡ 032/254 1461); and Cebu Velez General Hospital, F. Ramos St (℡ 032/253 1871), close to Swagman Travel.

Immigration The Cebu Immigration District Office is in P. Burgos St, Mandaue (℡ 032/253 4339 or 345 6443), a busy suburb 30min away by taxi. You can extend a 21-day visa to 59 days in less than a couple of hours.

Internet access Malls are a good place to look for small cybercafés; in Ayala Center there are a number on Level 4 above *Oh Georg! Coffee & Dessert Bar* and in SM City there are plenty on the top floor. Elsewhere, try *Ruftan Internet Café & Pensione* on Legaspi St, close to the port area, or *Sanciangko Cybercafe* on Sanciangko St outside the University of Cebu. *Café Intelleto* on Mango mall (General Maxilom) Ave next to *Vienna Kaffee-haus* has broadband connections and a paperback book lending library.

Pharmacies There are large pharmacies in all malls and you'll also find 24hr pharmacies that are often little more than holes in the wall, but carry a good stock of essentials. There's a big branch of Mercury drugstore at Fuente Osmeña.

Police The main Cebu City Police Office is south of Fuenta Osmeña (℡ 032/231 5802 or 253 5636), close to Cebu State College. There's a small police outpost known as Police Station 3 at Fort San Pedro, close to the post office and another, Precinct 4, a short walk north of SM City in J. Luna Ave Extension. Other emergency numbers include ℡ 166 for the mobile patrol and ℡ 032/254 8635 for the police station at Carbon Market.

Post The post office on Quezon Blvd close to the port area (at the back of Fort San Pedro) offers a poste restante service.

Shopping Away from the malls there's not much in the way of tourist souvenirs. Rustan's department store on General Maxilom Ave has a small section dedicated to souvenirs such as woven placemats and model jeepneys. Island Souvenirs, which has branches in SM City and Ayala Center, sells a good range of colourful T-shirts, caps and shorts. For *pasalubong* many visitors pick up candies and biscuits at one of the half-dozen souvenir stalls inside the airport departure lounge, where you can also buy hand-made guitars and ukuleles. There are also guitar shops in Borremeo St, a 10min walk south of Colon St, and on Mactan Island (see p.265).

Travel agents Adventure International Tours, 4/F Ayala Center ℡ 032/232 2968; Cattleya Travel & Tours, 126 Archbishop Reyes Ave ℡ 032/232 2055; Cebu Holiday Tours & Travel, 28 A. Morales St ℡ 032/231 5391; CNA Travel Express, Marvel Building, 1905 M.J. Cuenco Ave ℡ 032/232 2792; Interphil Travelers Service Center, 462 Gorordo Ave ℡ 032/231 4975; Marsman Travel & Tours, 4/F JRDC Building, President Osmeña Blvd; Rajah Travel, Upper G/F, SM City mall ℡ 032/231 2461; Swagman, F. Ramos St, near Fuente Osmeña ℡ 032/254 1365.

Mactan Island and Cordova Island

The closest beaches to Cebu City are on **Mactan Island**, linked to the main island of Cebu by the Mandaue–Mactan Bridge and the New Mandaue–Mactan Bridge. Off the southern coast of Mactan and linked by two short bridges is **Cordova Island**, an undeveloped slab of land with a couple of secluded, upmarket resorts on the beach. While the beaches on these islands don't compare with those in Malapascua, for instance, they are easier to reach. You can scuba dive along the Mactan coast and there are plenty of other watersports on offer at the many resorts here. The small capital of **LAPU-LAPU** has a heaving central market, a mall, a post office and some small hotels, but not much for tourists.

Magellan's Marker and Lapu-Lapu's Monument, both memorials to the battle that ensued when Magellan landed here in 1521, are in the north of the island on the main road that goes to the *Shangri-La's Mactan Island Resort*. Neither is really worth a special trip. There are a few sorry-looking souvenir stalls here, but not much else and the trip from the city can be a hassle; it takes two or three

The death of Magellan

Everything seemed to be going very nicely for Portuguese explorer **Ferdinand Magellan** when, as part of what would become the first circumnavigation of the globe, he made landfall in Samar early in 1521 and claimed the pagan Philippines for his adopted country, Spain, and the true religion, Catholicism. He stocked up on spices and sailed on, landing in Cebu. It was here that he befriended a native king, Raja Humabon and, flush with his conquest of the isles, promised to help him subdue an unruly vassal, Lapu-Lapu, who was simmering with anger over a long-running land dispute between himself and the king. His mind fogged by vanity, Magellan miscalculated badly. He believed he could knock some sense into these savage recalcitrants, seeing them off with superior Spanish weapons if it came to a fight. Early on the morning of April 27, 1521, he landed at Mactan and tried to coerce the intractable Lapu-Lapu into accepting Christianity. Lapu-Lapu wanted no such thing and when Magellan continued to hector him angrily ordered an attack. Most of Magellan's men fled quickly to their ships. Magellan, resplendent in polished body armour, backed away towards safety, but was felled by a spear aimed carefully at his unprotected foot, allowing Lapu-Lapu's men to move in for the kill. Seventeen months later, on September 8, 1522, the last remaining ship in Magellan's original fleet sailed into Seville with eighteen survivors on board. After three years and the loss of four ships and 219 lives, the first circumnavigation of the globe was complete.

sweaty jeepney rides through Mandaue City and then across the bridge to Lapu-Lapu City, or a P200 taxi ride each way.

For many tourists the obligatory souvenir purchase is a hand-made **guitar** from one of Mactan's diminishing number of small guitar factories, of which a couple remain on the Basak–Marigondon road. You can also buy guitars at the souvenir stalls around Magellan's Marker and Lapu-Lapu's Monument. The guitars are not so well constructed that you'd want to stake a musical career on one, but some of the smaller ukuleles and mandolins, starting from P1000, make novel gifts. A full-sized steel-stringed acoustic with shell inlay can be picked up for P2000–3000.

The rest of Mactan Island, notably the east coast, stands as a monument largely to bad taste. Most of its coastline has been colonized by leviathan air-conditioned resorts where the guests pay hundreds of dollars a night for the privilege of drinking cocktails on a man-made beach.

Practicalities

Mactan is a P14 jeepney ride from Cebu City's SM City mall in J. Luna Avenue Extension, close to the *Sheraton Cebu Hotel*. From the airport to anywhere on Mactan is a short traffic-free journey that costs no more than P150 by taxi. Getting to Cordova takes a little longer and will cost up to P200.

Lapu-Lapu is on the island's northern shore, close to the Mandaue–Mactan Bridge and the oil depots that service visiting container ships. Jeepneys stop near the small market square in Lapu-Lapu, where you can catch another jeepney onwards towards the beaches of Mactan's east coast. The **police station** (☏032/341 1311) is on B.M. Dimataga Street facing Upon Channel, the thin stretch of water that separates Mactan from the Cebu mainland, and there's a Philippine National Bank on Quezon National Highway. There are two **hospitals** on Mactan, the Lapu-Lapu General Hospital off the Basak–Marigondon road near the airport and the Mactan District Hospital on the Look–Basak Road.

Accommodation and eating

The northern town of **Lapu-Lapu** has a handful of functional, affordable hotels with air-conditioning and restaurants. On Mactan's eastern shore there are about twenty **beachfront resorts**, ranging from overpriced hotels to affordable native-style establishments. The beach here is not especially attractive and in some cases has been expensively groomed and landscaped to make it look like a tropical beach should – with the predictable result that it looks fake. This is jet-ski and umbrella cocktail country, and seems about as authentically Filipino as pie and chips. Most of the "upmarket" resorts are in fenced, private enclaves, so **eating** means taking expensive resort transport into Cebu City, or staying in for middling, overpriced food. The clientele at these places is a mix of rich Filipinos, package tourists from Hong Kong and South Koreans in Hello Kitty swimwear. If you're travelling independently room rates will be high if you simply show without a reservation. You'll save some money if you book in advance either with a travel agent or online. Some resorts offer scuba diving, but the coral here has long gone and you're better off heading for Malapascua or Moalboal.

Lapu-Lapu

BSM Hotel Marigondon Rd, Lapu-Lapu City ℗032/340 8314. Japanese-owned and well-run boutique hotel with single, double, treble and VIP rooms, all with a/c and large bathrooms. The main road outside is noisy, so ask for a quieter room at the back. ❹

Hotel Cesario Quezon Highway, Lapu-Lapu City ℗032/340 7480. Modern mid-range hotel with 33 a/c rooms and a buffet breakfast included in the rate. Helpful staff can handle travel reservations. ❹

Mactan Bridgeside Hotel Allan St, Lapu-Lapu City ℗032/340 1704. Uninspiring concrete box of a hotel, but with adequate enough mid-range double rooms, each with bathroom and hot water. Breakfast is included in the rate. ❹

East coast

Club Kontiki Maribago ℗032/340 9934. By far the best bet on Mactan's east coast if you're looking for somewhere with genuine charm and without the unnecessary frills and fuss of the five-stars. *Kontiki* is mainly geared to divers, with good simple rooms in a pretty building on the shore, which is rocky but has flat areas for sunbathing. The "house reef" is one of the best in the area. ❺

Cordova Reef Village Resort Cordova ℗032/340 6788. Luxury resort charging luxury prices. Villas

are secluded and spacious, with mod cons such as cable TV and piping hot high-pressure showers. The swimming pool is beautiful, overlooking the sea. ❻

Hilton Cebu Resort & Spa Punta Engaño ℗032/492 7777. The pink twin towers of the Hilton are the latest addition to the island's coastal skyline. The rooms at this upmarket beach resort – popular with honeymooning Japanese and Korean couples – are modern and comfortable, with some pleasing design touches and spacious marble bathrooms. Staff are clearly well-trained and efficient and there's a restaurant, coffee shop, beach bar and lovely swimming pool. ❽

Costabella Beach Resort Buyong ℗032/232 4811. Expansive tropical-style resort with palm trees, swimming pool and a/c rooms on the shore. Friendly, less showy and a little cheaper than many other Mactan resorts, there's the usual range of activities, including jet-skiing and scuba diving. ❺

Shangri-La's Mactan Island Resort Punta Engaño ℗032/231 0288, ⊛www.shangri-la.com. Grand name for a grand concrete edifice with more than five hundred rooms, eight restaurants and bars and, if the traffic is getting you down, a helicopter to meet you at the airport. Plenty of recreation, some of which you pay extra for, including scubadiving, windsurfing and banana-boat rides. ❾

Olango Island

Five kilometres east of Mactan Island, **Olango Island** supports the largest concentration of **migratory birds** in the country. About 77 species, including egrets, sandpipers, terns and black-bellied plovers, use the island as a rest stop on their annual migration from breeding grounds in Siberia, northern China and Japan to Australia and New Zealand. Olango is a major refuelling station, the birds feeding on the rich supply of insects and worms to replenish their fat reserves for the next leg of their journey, which may involve up to 15,000km of nonstop flight. Declared a **wildlife reserve** in 1998, the island is also home to about 16,000 resident native birds which live mostly in the northern half; the southern half of the island is made up of a wide, shallow bay and expanses of mudflats and mangrove. The reserve is at its best during peak migration months: September to November for the southward migration and February to April northbound.

Most resorts on Mactan will organize a day-trip here, though you could visit independently: there are hourly bancas (P40) to **Santa Rosa** on Olango Island from the wharf near the *Hilton* on Mactan Island or you can hire your own banca from the area around the *Tambuli Beach Resort* for around P1500 for the trip to the island and back. From the small Santa Rosa wharf it's only a short tricycle ride to the sanctuary. If you want a knowledgeable **guide**, make arrangements with the Coastal Resource Management Project of the Department of Environment and Natural Resources (☎032/232 1821 or 1822) located in the Capitol Building in Osmeña Boulevard in Cebu City, which runs an Olango Birds and Seascape tour.

The only **place to stay** is the *Nalusuan Island Resort & Marine Sanctuary* (☎032/425 8980 or ☎02/922 3199; ❼), a wonderfully informal place on an islet rising out of Olango's western coastal reef. Besides double rooms, the resort has duplex cottages on stilts in the water. All cottages and rooms have a shower, ceiling fan, TV and 24-hour electricity. The open-air restaurant specializes in seafood caught on the doorstep and there are nightly campfire cookouts where you can barbecue food as you like it. The resort can collect you in Mactan if requested in advance.

There are a number of other islets in the area, all with pretty good reefs, making it a good base for snorkelling and scuba diving. **Sulpa** is known for the quality of its giant clams, while **Gilutongan** has a more dubious claim to fame – it is sometimes said to have been the birthplace of dynamite fishing. The authorities, to give them credit, have teamed up with locals to put a stop to this destructive practice. The battle isn't over, but the problem is diminishing and reefs are recovering.

Toledo and Balamban

On the west coast of Cebu, less than two hours from Cebu City by road, **TOLEDO** has two piers, one built by a conglomerate that used to mine copper in the surrounding hills and the other by the local government. Ferries leave the municipal pier for **San Carlos** in Negros (see p.298) four times a day at 7am, 9am, 10am and 12.15pm (P40). Buses leave Cebu City's Southern Bus Terminal for Toledo from 5am daily (P35).

There's not much else in Toledo. It's a pleasant enough place, with an old church and plaza, but much of it is industrial and there are no noteworthy beaches. **Accommodation** is almost nonexistent, with one rudimentary place to stay, *Aleu's Lodge* (☎032/322 5672; ❷), on Polyapoy Street on the southern edge of town. If you're heading from Cebu City to Negros, catch an early bus to Toledo to make sure you don't miss the last ferry.

Twenty minutes out of Toledo is the town of **BALAMBAN**, around which you can explore a clutch of deserted black sand **beaches**. The German-owned *Sailor's Cabin* (☎032/465 2816; ❶) is located in the quiet residential area of Abucayan (look out for the big white and blue entrance). Accommodation here comprises three types of apartment, with cable TV and private bathroom. The menu at the restaurant includes German sausage, smoked ham with sauerkraut and Hungarian goulash. The proprietor can organize trips to some undiscovered areas of the rural west coast.

Bantayan Island

Bantayan Island, just off the northwest coast of Cebu, is quiet and bucolic, flat and arable, without the moody mountains of mainland Cebu. It's a great place to explore, though divers will be disappointed with the lack of coral left along the shore. Most of the island's resorts and beaches are around the attractive little town of **SANTA FE** on the southeast coast, which is where ferries from mainland Cebu arrive.

Along the west coast, the port town of **BANTAYAN** has no accommodation but it's worth a quick visit; there's an elegant Spanish-style plaza on the south side of which stands the **SS Peter and Paul Church**. The building has a bloody history: the original structure was torched by marauding Moros in 1640, and eight hundred local folk were taken captive and sold as slaves to rich Muslim chieftains in Mindanao. Every Easter Bantayan holds solemn processions of decorated religious *carozzas* (carriages), each containing a life-sized statue representing the Passion and death of Jesus Christ. The carriages are passed on through the generations; an apocryphal story tells of the scion of a local patriarch who, when told he could inherit either the family *carozza* or six hectares of land, chose the *carozza*. Thousands of locals and tourists turn out to join in the processions, many setting up camp on the beaches because resorts are full.

Practicalities

To reach Bantayan from Cebu City you can take a bus from the Northern bus terminal to the port town of **Hagnaya** (P75). The bus will take you to Hagnaya's pier, where you pay a P5 pier fee and P65 for the one-hour ferry crossing to Santa Fe; there are four departures a day, two in the morning and two in the afternoon. The overnight option is to take Palacio Shipping's rusty old **Don Martin** ferry (P175–275 depending on the type of accommodation), which leaves Pier 1 in Cebu City on Tuesday, Thursday and Saturday at 9pm, arriving in Santa Fe at 6am; it returns from Santa Fe at 9pm on Wednesday, Fridays and Sundays. From further afield, there are big bancas to Bantayan from Bacolod or Cadiz on Negros, and from Iloilo on Panay, departures depending on the tide.

The only **local transport** is the trusty tricycle, known on Bantayan as a *tricikad*. It's fun to hire a motorbike or moped and tour the island yourself by the coastal road, though inspect the bike thoroughly beforehand: some of the rental outlets will try to charge you for scratches that were already there. Get the renter to sign an agreement that details all existing damage, however insignificant.

Accommodation and eating

If you intend to **stay** in Santa Fe, you can get a tricycle from the pier to your accommodation, though some resorts can send a representative to collect you at the pier.

Kota Beach Resort A short ride west of Santa Fe by tricycle. ☏032/438 9042. Basic fan rooms and cottages with fan and bath. It's expensive for what you get, but the restaurant has excellent seafood and views. ❹

Ogtong Cave About 15min west of the Santa Fe pier by tricycle. Owned by the same family as the *Santa Fe Beach Club* (same phone numbers), and set in pleasant gardens with a swimming pool fed by water from a spring. Accommodation is in well-maintained a/c cottages with balconies and, in most cases, sea views. A short walk takes you down to the beach, where you can arrange fishing expeditions with the locals and bring your catch back to the *Ogtong* chef to be cooked. **⑤**

Santa Fe Beach Club On the beach in Santa Fe close to the pier where the ferries dock ☎032/438 0031 or 0917/360 8722, ⓦsfbci.bantayan.net.

Breezy and spacious non-a/c beach cottages, sleeping up to three. Avoid the rooms in the main building, which are airless and have poor views. **⑤**

St Bernard's Resort North of *Santa Fe Beach Club* on Alice Beach, and 5min by tricycle from the pier. ☎0917/963 6162. Quaint little circular cottages on the beach for two to four people. There's a small restaurant where you can get a good meal for P100–150. **❷**

Malapascua Island

Eight kilometres off the northern tip of Cebu, the island of **Malapascua** has been touted as the next Boracay, largely because of **Bounty Beach**, a blindingly white stretch of sand on the island's south coast where a dozen simple resorts have sprung up offering a good choice of accommodation. The beauty of Malapascua is that while it's every bit as scenic as Boracay (and, at 2.5km long and 1km wide, even smaller), it has none of the cosmopolitan development, with no big hotels, no fashionable nightclubs and only a handful of beach-style bars frequented largely by divers. For the time being, it remains an island unto itself, where most of the tourists are glad to take life without the frills, away from nightclubs and karaoke. It's worth taking a stroll in the cool of the late afternoon to the lighthouse tower on Malapascua's northwest coast: the tremendous views from the top across the Visayan Sea towards Masbate and Bantayan are particularly memorable.

Another advantage Malapascua has over Boracay is that the **diving** is much better, with a number of extreme dive sites that will get the adrenaline pumping more than your average gentle drift along a shallow reef. Anyone staying a few days is almost guaranteed a sighting of manta rays and thresher sharks, while two hours from Bounty Beach is the **wreck** of the passenger ferry **Dona Marilyn**, which went down in a 1984 typhoon and is now home to scorpion fish, flamefish and stingrays. **Gato Island**, 8km north of Malapascua, is a marine sanctuary and a breeding place for black-and-white-banded sea snakes, which are potentially deadly but do not attack divers. Other islets off the coast of Malapascua, all excellent places for exploring, snorkelling or diving, include **Dakit Dakit** off the south coast and **Lapus Lapus** off the north coast. Overnight trips can be arranged to the tiny volcanic island of **Maripipi** (see p.245), where reef sharks and dolphins are common.

Whether you're diving or not, don't miss the opportunity for a day-trip to **Calangaman**, a beautiful, remote islet that consists of no more than a strip of sand just a few metres wide with a few trees at one end. Another gem in the area – two hours to the northeast by banca – is the Robinson Crusoe-esque **Carnassa Island**, where you land at a picturesque bay fringed by palm trees.

Practicalities

You can reach Malapascua from Bantayan, Cebu City or San Isidro on Leyte. A number of public bancas ply the route **from Bantayan**, but departures are infrequent and depend on custom, tides and weather; only undertake this trip if the weather is set fair, as it's a four-hour journey in open seas. **From Cebu City**, take one of the hourly (4am–4pm) Rough Riders or Cebu Autobuses bus (P65) from the Northern bus terminal to **Maya** (also called Maya-Bagay). For a taxi to take you from Cebu City to Maya, expect to pay around P1500. It's best to set off early to avoid traffic and the heat. There are ferries to Malapascua from Maya (P50), or you could charter a banca for P350–500, but don't expect to have it exclusively to yourself – locals will take advantage of your generosity to avail themselves of a free ride. **From Leyte**, there is a daily boat at 7am from San Isidro to Maya (P70), returning at 10am.

Accommodation

There are about a dozen **resorts** on Bounty Beach and a number of others dotted on various beaches and coves around the island; all are available to independent travellers and apart from during the busiest holidays (Christmas, New Year and Easter) you shouldn't have any problem turning up and finding a room somewhere. Bounty Beach is the most developed area and where the divers tend to congregate.

Bounty Beach

Blue Water Beach Resort Middle of the beach ☏0927/490 9011, ⓦwww.malapascuabeachresort.com. Hard to miss, *Blue Water* is a pretty sight, with an elaborately thatched main building, a restaurant overlooking the sea and a patio at the front that's ideal for watching life go by on the beach. There's a new Italian restaurant and a lovely little chillout bar on the beach – perfect for sundowners. The rooms are plain but tastefully furnished with white linen and mosquito nets on the beds, and all with private facilities. ❸

Cocobana Beach Resort Next to *Blue Water Beach Resort* ☏032/437 1007 or 0919/305 0583. One of the first resorts on Malapascua, *Cocobana* has double bungalows, all with fan and private bathroom, in three categories – beach cottage, garden cottage and budget garden cottage. There's an excellent restaurant and a beach bar that's great for sunset-watching. ❸

Malapascua Exotic Island Dive & Beach Resort Far eastern end of Bounty Beach ☏0918/774 0484, ⓦwww.malapascua.net. This is one of the most popular places to stay, especially for divers, with pleasant, clean cottages, a small restaurant and 24-hour electricity, something of a luxury in these parts. ❸

Mike & Diose's Close to *Malapascua Exotic Island Dive & Beach Resort* ☏032/254 2510. A couple of very simple beach cottages in an excellent location at the east end of Bounty Beach. No frills, but everything's clean and you've got your own small terrace in a colourful garden. ❷

Sunsplash Beach Resort & Restaurant On the beach a short walk east of *Cocobana Beach Resort* ☏032/254 3520. One of the largest resorts on the island, with concrete tiled rooms built around a sandy courtyard facing the beach. It's very motel-like, but the rooms are big and clean, and there's a restaurant serving European and Asian cuisine. ❹

Around the island

Logon Beach Resort Logon, Daanbantayan ☏0918/913 7278. Ten minutes to the west of Bounty Beach by tricycle, this place has quaint little double cottages with fan, mosquito nets and dusk-to-dawn electricity, on a slight rise above a 200-metre-long private beach. Outside, the cottages have a small porch with table, chairs and sofa – a marvellous place to relax and admire the views. ❷

Los Bamboos Beach Resort Lapus-Lapus, Daanbantayan ☏032/ 253 2937, ⓦwww.los-bamboos.com. On the northwest tip of the island and excellent value if you're looking for something away from the dive-talk of Bounty Beach. Simple fan-cooled cottages with beautiful views and home-cooked food in the simple bamboo restaurant on offer. ❷

Mangrove Oriental Resort Logon, Daanbantayan ☏0916/218 5534, ⓦwww.mangroveoriental.com. About 3km northwards along the west coast from Bounty Beach (you can take a tricycle for about P50) this is a wonderfully romantic and secluded exotic hideaway with eight tastefully decorated cottages, all nestled around a secluded cove where the snorkelling is superb and the sunsets even better. Try the Kasbah, which is perched on top of the hill and furnished with inlayed furniture from Mindanao. It has a spacious private balcony and cool terracotta interior. The budget cottages right on the sand are the cheapest accommodations available; they have brightly painted exteriors and simple but comfortable furnishings. ❷–❽

The Camotes Islands

Northeast of Cebu City and nearly three hours from the Cebu mainland by boat, the three friendly, peaceful **Camotes Islands** are largely untouched by tourism, making them an excellent place to experience real Visayan barrio life. The Supercat fast ferry **Ocean Spray** departs for **Poro** island twice daily from Cebu City. Poro is also linked by public bancas with Cebu City and Danao on Cebu and with Ormoc on Leyte. From Poro, you can get to **Pacijan** island (connected with Poro at low tide by a thin strip of land and at high tide by a potholed road) either by chartering a banca or by motorbike (the only form of public road transport here). The easternmost (and smallest) Camotes island, **Ponson**, can only be reached by small banca from Poro.

On the coast of Poro there are beaches where you can hire a shed or camp on the sands for the night. The best beaches and the best places for snorkelling and diving are mostly around **Tulang**, a picturesque islet lapped by turquoise waters off the northern coast of Pacijan. At the caverns at **Bukilat** on Poro, you can pay P2 to swim in a series of small underground caves. The trip from Poro Town to the caverns and back costs about P50 per person by motorbike.

Southern Cebu

The journey along the southeast coast of Cebu takes you through green and pleasant scenery, with the sea on one side and rice paddies leading up to a mountainous ridge on the other. Nearly all southbound **buses** from Cebu City pass through **Carcar**, about one-third of the way along the southeast coastal road. From here they either continue south to **Argao** and **Bato** (from where you can head to Tampi on Negros), or head inland and wind their way along a mountain pass that eventually drops down to the western seaboard and **Moalboal**. It's Moalboal that is the most popular tourist destination in the southern half of the island, with plenty of accommodation, some lively bars and excellent scuba diving. From here you can explore the neighbouring small towns and beaches, the best of the latter being **White Beach**. Along the coast around the little town of **Badian** there's more good diving and a popular waterfall to visit.

Carcar

If you're on one of the buses heading south from Cebu City, you'll know when you've arrived in **CARCAR**, because the vehicle will immediately be surrounded by screaming hawkers peddling food at you through the windows. Few tourists get off the bus here and there's no accommodation, the town depending for its livelihood mostly on coconuts, shoe-making and black-smithing. But behind the dusty bustle there's an intriguing place waiting to be noticed, with some hidden backstreets where you can wander past some of the finest old houses in the country. These *balay na tisa* (houses of tile) are an Oriental variant of Spanish-American colonial architecture of the Caribbean, and feature enormous sliding windows that allow the air to circulate.

There are six such houses in Carcar, dating from around 1850, of which the best is the **Sarmiento house** in Santa Catalina Street. To reach the street, where most of Carcar's prominent families of the nineteenth century lived, head 50m south from the bus station and turn right at the busy junction. The house once belonged to Don Ramon Sarmiento, a *haciendero* who had large landholdings in Carcar and the surrounding barangays. Now lovingly restored, the building is not officially open to the public but the caretaker might allow you to take a look around. The ground floor is made of cut stone corals, the first floor of timber, with a piked roof and two striking attic dormer windows for ventilation, typical of *ilustrado* (affluent people's) homes of the time. Inside, the walls are panelled and there's a grand dining room with an embossed metal ceiling. Another of Carcar's architectural curiosities is 200m down the same street, **Saint Catherine's Church**, an inspired cupcake of a building built in 1876 in Byzantine style. The aisle is lined with statues of the twelve apostles, all painted white except Judas, who is painted black.

Argao

Another colonial-era outpost, now a noisy modern coastal town, **ARGAO** is about halfway along Cebu's southeast coast. If you're leaving Cebu via the port of Bato but don't want to do the journey in one go, Argao is a convenient place to stay the night, with a couple of decent lodgings nearby. There are also irregular bancas to Loon on Bohol from here.

The town centre has a busy marketplace, a crumbling Spanish baroque church, small park, municipal hall and post office, and a worthy little museum. The **Museo de la Paroquia del San Miguel** (Mon–Sat 9am–5pm; free), in a room next to the church, was the brainchild of Argao-born Supreme Court Chief Justice Hilario Davide, a key figure in Joseph Estrada's downfall. It houses a number of precious antiques including a gold Santo Niño, ivory icons, old altars and seventy sets of liturgical vestments used by early friars.

Accommodation and eating

There are no restaurants or bars in Argao itself, just a few local beerhouses with plastic tables and tin pots of food on the counter. As for **accommodation**, *Bamboo Paradise* (☎032/367 7271 or 485 8684; ❷), on the beach five minutes south by tricycle from the town centre, has four double rooms and one apartment, all air-conditioned, and a restaurant. Run by two retired Germans, it's set in lovely gardens with plenty of shaded areas, comfy chairs and sun loungers, perfect for relaxing with a cold drink and a good book. The beach is okay for swimming, collecting shells, or just hanging around and watching rural life. Ten minutes south of Argao by road, in the barangay of **Suba**, *Luisa's Place* (☎032/367 7281; ❶) consists of half a dozen rickety wooden cottages with a nipa restaurant serving pancakes, omelettes and fried fish for breakfast, and catch of the day, adobo and fried chicken for lunch and dinner. The setting is green and tranquil, even if the grey sand beach isn't great for swimming.

Bato

On Cebu's southern tip, **BATO** is a typical provincial port town. Life here is centred around the small concrete wharf where fishermen unload the day's catch. Without lodges, hotels or places to eat apart from *carinderias*, Bato is at least a friendly place from which to exit Cebu. Big bancas depart the wharf for **Tampi**, near Dumaguete on Negros's southern coast, hourly between 5am and 5pm (1hr; P35), with occasional larger boats (45min; P40) making the crossing. There are regular buses to Bato from Cebu City as well as from Moalboal. Many of the resorts in Moalboal can arrange for a private car to take you here for about P1500.

Moalboal

Three hours by road and 89km from Cebu City, on the southwestern flank of Cebu Island, lies the once drowsy coastal village of **MOALBOAL**, now a boozy hangout for travellers and scuba divers (see box opposite). The little town of Moalboal proper is on the road that follows the coast; what tourists and divers

Diving at Moalboal

It's hardly surprising that most of the activity in Moalboal is centred around **diving**: the sea is crystal clear and, while many reefs along the mainland coast were damaged by a typhoon more than a decade ago, **Pescador Island**, thirty minutes by banca from Moalboal, remains one of the best dive sites in the country, surrounded by a terrific reef that teems with marine life. Barely 100m long, the island is the pinnacle of a submarine mountain reaching just 6m above sea level and ending in a flat surface, making it look from a distance like a floating coin. Underwater though, it's a different story. Vertical walls plunge to 50m and contain a huge number of ledges, overhangs and crevices. The most impressive of the underwater formations is the Cathedral, a funnel of rock that is open at the top end and can be penetrated by divers. Pelagic fish are sometimes seen in the area, including reef sharks and hammerheads, while at lesser depths on the reef there are Moorish idols, sweetlips, fire gobies and batfish.

There are at least ten other dive sites around Moalboal, including the gentle Balay Reef, Ronda Bay Marine Park, Airplane Wreck and Sunken Island. Arranging diving trips is easy, with a dozen operators at Panagsama Beach, including Seaquest (☏032/346 9629), Ocean Safari (☏032/474 0010), Blue Abyss Dive Shop (☏032/474 0031) and Visayas Divers (☏032/474 0018).

refer to as Moalboal is **Panagsama Beach**, a P25 tricycle ride from the point on the main road where buses drop passengers.

Sun-worshippers looking for a Boracay-style sandy beach will be disappointed – there isn't one. The shoreline is a little rocky in places and not generally suitable for recreational swimming. Moalboal makes up for this in other ways, with a great range of cheap accommodation, a marvellous view of the sunset over distant Negros, and some good discounts on diving and rooms if you hang around long enough. Besides diving, many dive shops offer **activities** such as kayaking, mountain-bike rental and snorkelling. For P1200 you can have a day of horse riding along the shore or on pleasant jungle trails. A good place to plan such adventures is Planet Action Adventure in the middle of Panagsama Beach, close to *Roxy Cafe*.

A number of **bus** companies run regular services here from Cebu City's Southern bus terminal, but make sure the driver knows where you want to get off, as most buses continue beyond Moalboal. Buses operated by ABC and by Albines display Bato as their destination. You'll be dropped off on the main road, from where a tricycle will take you down the dusty track to Panagsama Beach, where all the resorts are. Kings Star runs two daily air-conditioned buses from the Southern bus terminal every day at 1pm and 3pm; these buses cost a little more than ordinary non air-conditioned buses, but are more comfortable. A quicker option than the public buses is the air-conditioned Fly-the-Bus shuttle service from Cebu City (3 weekly; P350 one-way); pickup points are Pier 4 (8.15am), Swagman Travel (who operate the service – see p.264 for contact details; 8.45am) and *Kukuk's Nest* (see p.257; 9am). The return trip leaves *Savedra-Great White Dive Centre* in Moalboal at 1pm.

Accommodation

There's a wide range of accommodation in Moalboal, most of it huddled in the same area along the beach.

Emma's Store & Restaurant At the southern end of the beach, just past Visayas Divers. Single and double wooden cottages, nothing fancy, but clean and quiet, with friendly staff and a small restaurant where a good barbecue chicken lunch can be had for P120. ❷

Eve's Kiosk Northern end of the beach. Plain doubles and there's no restaurant, but it doesn't matter because there are plenty of eating places nearby. ❷

Hannah's Restaurant & Lodge At the southern end of the beach ☎032/474 0091. Rooms are spacious and well maintained, with a private bathroom. There's an informal restaurant on the shore. ❸

Love's Lodge Right at the southern end of the beach along a dirt track ☎0915/817 8175, Ⓦwww.seaexplorersscuba.com. The owner, Elvie, does most of the cooking aided by her husband, known to everyone as Tata ("old man"). Fourteen of the twenty rooms are a/c, and all have hot water and a shower. There's a convivial restaurant and bar overlooking the ocean; the views are fantastic. ❸

Pacita's Roughly in the middle of the beach ☎0918/770 9982. Twenty-five double cottages, each with its own veranda and most with private bathroom, although the shower is little more than an old pipe sticking out of the wall. All cottages stand in a garden of colourful bougainvillea. ❷

Paradise Restaurant & Cottages Northern end of the beach. Doubles with fan located close to *Pedong's*. The rate includes a choice of American or Filipino breakfast. ❸

Pedong's Place Northern end of the beach. Simple resort with modest little double huts and private cold showers, perfectly adequate for a good night's rest after a day's diving. ❷

Quo Vadis Beach Resort Next to Visayas Divers ☎0918/770 8682, Ⓦwww.moalboal.com. Eight deluxe rooms and fourteen solid cottages in a beachside tropical garden. The little outdoor bar, *La Payag*, is a great place to sit and watch the sunset. There's also a restaurant, *Arista*, offering Filipino and German cuisine. ❸

Savedra Centre of the beach ☎032/474 0014, Ⓦwww.savedra.com. Simple, clean beach resort whose nine a/c rooms (doubles and twins) are right on the beach with fantastic ocean views from their spacious balconies – perfect for sunset-watching at the end of a satisfying day's diving. Rooms are tidy and comfortable, with bamboo beds and tiled floors. There's a good dive centre a few steps away, operated by the resort owners. ❸

Sumisid Lodge Near Seaquest Divers ☎0917/770 7986, Ⓦwww.seaquestdivecenter.net. Two-storey building constructed entirely from native materials. The a/c twin rooms with cold shower are downstairs; upstairs, rooms have fan and share two bathrooms. ❸

Sunshine Pension House 50m inland from the sea beside Blue Abyss Dive Shop ☎032/474 0049. Set in a lovely garden with its own swimming pool and friendly staff. The rooms come with fan and private bathroom. ❹

Eating, drinking and nightlife

There are as many **places to eat** in Moalboal as there are places to stay, and there's also some convivial nightlife, usually in beach bars serving cold San Miguels for a bargain P25 or less. *Roxy Cafe & Restaurant*, a short walk inland from the centre of the beach, has probably the biggest menu in town, offering squid stuffed with vegetables, prawn tempura, twelve types of pizza and various pasta dishes. It's an all-purpose hangout, with billiards, sport on cable TV and even a couple of rooms – don't stay here if you relish peace and quiet, because there's live rock music from the local combo a couple of times a week. The British-owned *Royal Bulldog*, a few steps from *Savedra*, is decked in British flags and offers a good choice of spicy Indian and Thai curries. The preparation takes a while, but the food is worth waiting for. *Last Filling Station*, on the main path along the shore, is another Moalboal favourite, with pitta-bread sandwiches, Thai curries and pizza. Right on the shore in the middle of the beach you'll find two relaxed places with views, food and drink: the *Sunset View Restaurant* and the *Visaya Restaurant*. *Chief Mau Station Bar & Disco*, a short walk back from the shore behind Seaquest Dive Centre, is for serious drinkers and dancers, while *Tabu Piano Bar* at the northern end of the beach is more laidback, with a great-value happy hour and occasional live entertainment.

Around Moalboal

Travellers tend to stay put in Moalboal because it's got everything they need, but there are some wonderful islands and beaches a little further afield that are gaining a reputation in their own right. In an area known as Basdaku, 8km northwest of Moalboal on the Saavedra peninsula, **White Beach** is one of Cebu's lesser-known gems, an idyllic stretch of fine sugary sand. A tricycle here from Moalboal costs around P100. The best place to stay is *Ravenala Beach Bungalows* (℡0917/640 1920; Ⓦwww.ravenala-resort.com; ❸), which is the only resort here and is right on the beach; it's a homey, romantic little hideaway with nine separate, spacious cottages, each designed and furnished differently, but in native style. There's a small swimming pool and a restaurant and the location couldn't be better, with views of Pescador in the distance.

On the coast road, twenty minutes south of Moalboal by bus or jeepney, the unimpressive fishing town of **Badian** is little more than a huddle on the shore surrounding a pungent market. This is where you can catch a private banca to **Badian Island**, site of the well-manicured grounds of the *Badian Island Resort & Spa* (℡032/475 1103, Ⓦwww.badianhotel.com; ❾), where luxurious cottages sit on a green hillside above a private ribbon of fine white sand. The swimming pool is beautifully clean and gin-clear; at the spa you can get a sixty-minute Island Paradise Massage for $50 or a Badian Deluxe Four-Hand Massage for $75. Round-trip transfers from Cebu City or the airport cost $50 per person.

Staff at *Badian* can arrange just about anything for you, from an excursion in a glass-bottomed boat to tennis, scuba diving and a trip to **Kawasan Waterfalls**. The last of these offers a pleasant day-trip into a rural area, where people still live in flimsy nipa houses and cook over open fires. The falls themselves are only accessible by foot, the last half-hour being a pleasant uphill walk through isolated barrios along the banks of a river; you can reach the start of the path by tricycle from near Badian's market.

Bohol

It's hard to picture it today, but the quiet island of **Bohol** (see the map on p.251), a two-hour hop south of Cebu by fast ferry, has a notoriously bloody past. The only reminder of the unpleasantness is a memorial stone in the barrio of **Bool**, denoting the spot where Rajah Sikatuna and Miguel Lopez de Legazpi concluded an early round of hostilities in 1565 by signing a compact in blood. Even before Legazpi arrived and brought Catholicism with him from Spain, members of the indigenous Bool tribe were using the island's coves and inlets to hide from vicious Muslim marauders who swept north through the Visayan islands from their bases in Mindanao. These days, however, apart from some mercantile activity in **Tagbilaran**, the island is an attractive, dozy sort of place where life in the barrios and hinterlands is pastoral and quiet. The only sign of frenzied activity is on the beautiful beaches of **Panglao Island**, where scuba divers gather in incongruous neon wetsuits. Everywhere else, Bohol is on Filipino time and runs at a strictly Filipino pace. Even the *carabao* chew slowly. For most visitors the only reason to leave Panglao's beaches is to see the island's iconic attraction, the **Chocolate Hills**, about thirty minutes inland from Tagbilaran by road. However, Bohol is also a historical attraction, site of a number of the most wonderful old **Spanish churches** in the country, many of them built with coral.

An interesting time to visit Bohol is during May, which is **fiesta month**, with island-wide celebrations including barrio festivals, beauty pageants, street dancing and solemn religious processions.

All bus journeys **around the island** start at the Dao Integrated bus terminal in E. Butalid Street, ten minutes outside Tagbilaran by jeepney or tricycle. Buses leave here every thirty minutes or hourly for all destinations along the coast from Baclayon and Loon to east coast towns such as Ubay (2hr). They also travel the cross-island road via Carmen, passing close to the Chocolate Hills. Jeepneys likewise leave from Dao, making trips clockwise and anti-clockwise around the coast, but they stop often and become uncomfortably overloaded, so are best used only for short trips. Chartering a taxi in Tagbilaran to take you from one sight to another costs around P500 per day.

Tagbilaran

There are a few small hotels and lodges in **TAGBILARAN**, the hectic port capital of Bohol, but with the feverish hum of tricycles and so many sights nearby, it's unlikely you'll actually want to stay here. And indeed, there's no real reason to do so. From Tagbilaran you can be on Panglao Island in less than twenty minutes and even the Chocolate Hills, hidden in the hinterlands, are less than an hour away by road.

As for sights, there are a number in the vicinity, but few in Tagbilaran itself. **Tagbilaran Cathedral** opposite the plaza in Sarmiento Street is a nineteenth-century hulk standing on the site of an original that was destroyed by fire in 1789. The **Bohol Museum** (Mon–Fri 10am–4.30pm; P10) in Carlos P. Garcia Avenue is in the former home of Carlos Garcia (fourth President of the Philippine Republic), and contains various presidential memorabilia and a collection of shells. The **Tagbilaran City Fiesta** takes place on May 1.

Practicalities

Tagbilaran's main drag is **Carlos P. Garcia Avenue**, also known as CPG Avenue, where you'll find a dense line of canteens, convenience stores and some banks. The **airport** lies less than 2km outside the city; tricycles from the airport into town cost P50, but a number of private "taxis" greet every flight so negotiating for a car to take you straight to Panglao Island is no problem. Philippine Airlines has two flights a day from Manila to Tagbilaran; it has three ticket outlets on Bohol: at the airport (☎038/411 2232), at the **Metro Centre Hotel** in Carlos P. Garcia Avenue (☎038/411 3552) and nearby at 38 Carlos P. Garcia Ave (☎038/411 3102).

The **ferry pier** in Tagbilaran is off Gallares Street, a ten-minute tricycle or jeepney ride from the city centre. A number of private cars wait to meet passengers arriving on ferries. As for ferries to Tagbilaran **from Manila**, WG&A's *Our Lady of Sacred Heart* sails every Monday and *Our Lady of Medjugorje* every Friday. The trip takes about 31 hours via Cebu and fares range from P1600 for a dorm bed to P4800 for a two-person stateroom. There are ferry-ticket outlets for WG&A at the Dao Integrated bus terminal in E. Butalid Street (☎038/411 5182), on Carlos P. Garcia Avenue (☎038/411 4906) and at the pier (☎038/235 4510). Negros Navigation's *St Peter the Apostle* sails every Friday at 11am from Manila to Tagbilaran via Cebu, arriving on Saturday at 1pm. The Negros Navigation ticket office is in Bigal Building, Carlos P. Garcia Avenue (☎038/411 5717). Sulpicio Lines operates between Tagbilaran, Dipolog and Iligan, while Cebu Ferries sails from Jagna, to the east of Tagbilaran, to Cagayan de Oro.

From **Cebu City**, Supercat has three fast ferry trips a day to Tagbilaran (P300). Supercat tickets are sold in Tagbilaran through Aboitiz Express outlets: there's one at the pier (☎038/235 4008) and others in San José Street, Carlos P. Garcia

Wisdom on wheels

Tagbilaran's two thousand licensed tricycles make the same shrill din and belch and the same toxic fumes as tricycles everywhere else in the Philippines, but at least they have some pensive **reading matter** to make you feel good about the pollution you're helping cause. In 1988 the city fathers passed a resolution forcing drivers to turn their machines into sermons on wheels, with quotations from the Bible and the Koran displayed prominently in passenger sidecars. To get the initiative going, the mayor gave free plywood panels with pre-printed texts to 150 tricycle drivers. Since then, the drivers have chosen their own messages, with mixed results. Nothing wrong with "Better to be poor and fear the Lord than rich and be in trouble" or "There is no pillow as soft as a clear conscience". But mangled English has produced some tricycle wisdom that has a surreal ring to it, such as "Ask and you shall received" or "One who walks with Christ is a walking summon". Some drivers have gone for laughs ("Lead me not into temptation, I can find it myself") and others for deeply felt political doctrine ("You can find the world's shortest sermon on a thousand traffic signs: Keep right"). However, nothing beats careering through the chaotic streets of Tagbilaran, heart in mouth and white knuckles gripping the seat, on a tricycle that carries the message: "Prepare to meet thy God".

Avenue, Starlite Avenue and Gallares Street. Smaller operators such as Trans Asia and Cokaliong also have daily, slower services between Cebu City and Tagbilaran.

From Dumaguete there are two Supercats a day, both via Cebu. **From Dapitan** in Mindanao there's a Supercat departure at 2pm (P700). There's also a useful Supercat trip daily at 5.15pm between Tagbilaran and Larena on Siquijor, via Dumaguete (P420). Weesam Express has five daily trips from Cebu City to Tagbilaran, one stopping on the way at Dumaguete.

There's a new **tourist information and assistance centre** (Mon–Sat 9am–5pm; ☎038/235 5497) in Grup Street, opposite the market a short walk north of Plaza Rizal. ATMs can be found at a number of **banks** in Tagbilaran; Philippine National Bank is on the junction of Carlos P. Garcia Avenue and J.A. Clarin Street and PCI Bank at the southern end of Carlos P. Garcia Avenue. There's a Metrobank on Carlos P. Garcia Avenue. The **police station** is near City Hall, behind St Joseph's Cathedral; the **post office** is also near here, at the end of the City Hall car park. To get **online**, try *D&G's Cybercafe* in Noli Me Tangere Street next to the PLDT International Telephone Office. Alternatively, there are Internet cafés on almost every corner in Tagbilaran, particularly on M.H. Del Pilar Street a little north of Agora Market, where you'll find *Internet Cathedral*.

Accommodation and eating

There's not much notable **accommodation** in the city. The best hotel is the *Metrocentre Hotel & Convention Centre* (☎038/411 2599, ⓦwww.metrocentre-hotel.com; ➏), a short walk north of the Caltex petrol station on Carlos P. Garcia Avenue. The marbled lobby has a coffee shop, there's a gym and a nice pool on the top floor, and the rooms themselves are tasteful and comfortable, all with cable TV and fridge. The hotel also has reliable Internet access that's only slightly more expensive than the Internet cafés, without the queues. *Nisa Traveller's Inn* (☎038/411 3731; ➊) on Carlos P. Garcia Avenue is the best budget place in town featuring good doubles with fan and clean bathroom, as well as more expensive air-conditioned rooms. Out of town, not far from the pier, the homely *Hotel La Roca* (☎038/411 3796; ➌) in Graham Avenue has a choice of rooms ranging from standard doubles to penthouse.

Metrocentre's *Asiatika Bar & Grill* is one of the better *restaurants* in Tagbilaran, with a good choice of grilled fish and meat. For something a bit more rustic, try *Jovings Seafood* and *MR Seafood Restaurant* on Gallares Street. Both have immense menus that include grilled tuna, marlin and lapu-lapu, chilli crab, king prawns and clams. All dishes are served with a hefty mound of steaming hot rice; two people can fill up here for less than P500.

Chocolate Hills

The surreal **Chocolate Hills** are known throughout the Philippines as one of the country's great tourist attractions. Some geologists believe that these unique forty-metre mounds – there are said to be 1268 of them if you care to count – were formed from deposits of coral and limestone sculpted by centuries of erosion. Most locals, however, will tell you that the hills are the calcified tears of a giant, whose heart was broken by the death of a mortal lover. Some prefer the idea that they were left behind by a giant *carabao* with distressed bowels.

What you think of the hills will depend largely on what time you choose to visit. During the glare of day the light casts harsh shadows and the hills lose their definition. But at dawn or dusk, when the sunrise and sunset cast an emollient light, they look splendid. During the dry season (Dec–May is best) the scrub vegetation that covers the hills is roasted brown, and with a short stretch of the imagination, they really do resemble endless rows of chocolate drops.

One way to see the hills is on one of the day-trips which most hotels or resorts on Bohol offer; expect to pay about P1500. Along the way you'll be taken to attractions east of Tagbilaran, such as the Baclayon Church, the Blood Compact Site, Loboc River and the Tarsier Visitor Centre. The hills are usually the last stop. Otherwise you could take one of the buses to **Carmen** which leave hourly from the Dao terminal in Tagbilaran. It's a dusty and bumpy ride, often with every inch of bus space taken by locals returning from Tagbilaran market with produce and livestock. From Carmen it's a pleasant four-kilometre walk south up to the hills and then up the 213 steps to the concrete lookout area. You can also hop on a motorbike from Carmen: there are always plenty of young bucks who'll take you up the final stretch for around P50. Another option – a thoroughly enjoyable one if you know what you're doing – is to rent your own **motorbike** from one of the resorts on Panglao Island (see p.282).

North of Tagbilaran

The scenic road north from Tagbilaran takes you through the pretty coastal town of **MARIBOJOC**, 14km from Tagbilaran and not hard to reach by bus or jeepney. The town is the site of the old Spanish **Punta Cruz watchtower**, one of a number of old watchtowers of note on Bohol. Once a lookout for marauding pirates, Punta Cruz is now a viewing deck from where you can gaze across to Cebu and Siquijor.

Loon, Cabilao and Antequera

Another 8km along the coastal road from Maribojoc is **LOON**, which has at its centre the imposing and atmospheric Loon Church. Built in 1803 by Recollect Friars, it's the largest church in Bohol and has a maw-like interior with three immense naves. On the outside it's equally impressive, with twin bell towers at the front and Corinthian architectural flourishes on its columns and pilasters. Loon can be reached easily via Maribojoc by bus or jeepney from the Dao terminal.

From the pier in Loon you can take a banca (15min; P15) to the tiny island of **Cabilao**, eight kilometres square, where there are a handful of modest but very comfortable resorts aimed largely at divers. *Cabilao Beach Club* (t 0917/454 5897, Ⓦwww.cabilao.com; ②) has simple, clean wooden cottages in green surroundings right on the beach near the village of Cambaquiz on the island's northeast coast. The place is well run by a Swiss–German management team and the staff are helpful. *Polaris Dive Centre* on the main beach on the island's northwest coast (☎0918/903 7187; ①), offers a choice of cottages ranging from simple wooden treehouses to more substantial air-conditioned doubles. These resorts can arrange trips to local dive sites such as the **Wall at Cambaquiz**, where there are turtles and baby sharks, and **Shark View Point**, where one of the attractions – apart from sharks – is pygmy seahorses.

A number of resorts offer half-day trips for around P2000 per person to the town of **ANTEQUERA**, north of Tagbilaran (you can get here independently by bus or jeepney from the Dao terminal). The attraction for tourists here is the lively **market**, twice a week on Thursdays and Saturdays. Craftsmen and traders from around the island congregate to sell locally made handicrafts such as baskets, hats and various home decor items such as linen tablecloths, mirrors and attractive bowls made from stone or coconut shells. Prices are significantly cheaper than in the cities and it's a fun place to haggle and pick up a few inexpensive souvenirs.

Tarsier Visitors Centre

The **Tarsier Visitors Centre** (Tues–Sat 8am–4pm; ☎0912/516 3375 or 0919/874 1120; P20) is a bumpy ten-kilometre drive northeast from Tagbilaran on dirt lanes lined with village huts. The journey is half the fun, and the centre, which is operated by the Tagbilaran-based Philippine Tarsier Foundation, dedicated to protecting what is left of the native tarsier population, is well worth a visit. Often mistakenly referred to as the world's smallest monkey, the **tarsier** – all 11cm of it – is in fact not an anthropoid but a prosimian, more closely related to lemurs, lorises and bushbabies, with oversized humanlike hands and tiny ears. A bashful little furball whose once expansive turf is slowly being razed by logging and development, the saucer-eyed beastlets are now listed as one of the Philippines' officially endangered species. The tarsiers need all the help they can get if they're going to survive: they're not the smartest of creatures (each of their eyes is bigger than their brain). They do, however, have durability on their side, having been around for about 45 million years, making them one of the longest-surviving land species on the planet.

The centre's captive-breeding programme has been a success, and the tarsiers, left alone and unhunted in their jungle reserve, have swelled to number some one thousand. There's a forested corner of the centre that's open to visitors (daily 9am–4pm; P25), but it's only a small fraction of Bohol's breeding grounds. Knowledgeable **guides** at the centre keep close tabs on their tiny charges and can usually lead visitors to their favourite haunts, though spotting the tarsiers nestled among the thick foliage is difficult, especially during the daylight hours when the nocturnal creatures rarely move. But when they are awake they study visitors with wide-eyed curiosity, sometimes swivelling their heads a disconcerting 180 degrees to get a better look.

There are two ways to reach the Tarsier Centre. You can take public transport (bus, taxi or jeepney) from Tagbilaran to **Corella** or **Sikatuna** and then a tricycle the rest of the way. The other option is to take a bus or jeepney to **Loboc** (see p.281), 10km east of Tagbilaran, then hike 5km along the well-marked **tarsier trail**, which isn't difficult and takes you through some gentle

△ A tarsier

countryside of paddy fields and coconut groves. You can, of course, do the trail from the other end, starting at the centre and walking to Loboc, from where there are plenty of buses and jeepneys back to Tagbilaran.

East of Tagbilaran

Heading east from Tagbilaran takes you first to the coastal fishing town of **BOOL**, 5km away. Said to be the oldest settlement on the island, it's also the site of an attractive bronze sculpture on the seafront that denotes the spot where local chieftain Rajah Sikatuna and Miguel Lopez de Legazpi concluded an early round of Philippine-Spanish hostilities in 1565 by signing a compact in blood. Every year for one week in July, Boholanos gather in Bool for the **Sandugo** (One Blood) **festival** which, apart from the usual beauty pageants and roast pigs, includes a passionate re-enactment of the blood ceremony.

About 2km east of Bool, **BACLAYON** is the site of Baclayon Church, the oldest stone church in the Philippines. Much of the existing facade was added by the Augustinian Recollects in the nineteenth century, but the rest dates back to 1595 and was declared a national historical landmark in 1995 by the National Historical Institute. The church's convent has been transformed into an intriguing **ecclesiastical museum** (Mon–Sat 9am–4pm; P10) that houses a number of priceless religious icons, artefacts and vestments. One of the most impressive collections is of Spanish colonial **santos** (statues of saints), including the Nuestra Señora de los Dolores, which has miracles attributed to it. The museum also contains librettos of sacred music printed in Latin on animal skins.

Loboc and around

Another twenty minutes by road east of Baclayon, **LOBOC** hasn't much to see except the grand old **San Pedro Church**, built by missionaries in the eighteenth century. If you head inland from Loboc towards **Sevilla**, you follow a bumpy road along the banks of the Loboc River through a valley planted with rice and lush with bamboo. About 5km along the road are the **Tontonan Falls**, where water thunders over a low cliff into a bubbling pool that has some quiet corners for swimming. River trips are becoming popular and you can rent a banca at the jetty in Loboc to take you to the falls, a pretty journey past idyllic barrios and green paddies. The further up you get, the more dense the vegetation becomes and before long you find yourself gliding through a primordial pea-green landscape of twisted roots, towering palms and thick mangroves.

There is a **resort** in the area, the *Nuts Huts Retreat* (℡038/525 9162; ❸), that makes an excellent base for exploring the river and Bohol's untouristy interior. The resort presides over sweeping views of the surrounding hills and is run by two charming Belgians, Rita and Chris, who seem to know what every traveller wants: great cooking, well-chosen music and the option to do nothing at all in several different locations – a shady terrace, a library or a herb-infused sauna. The outdoor restaurant is magic, perched on a hill with views down the valley across a dense green canopy of rainforest. If you manage to summon up the energy you can go rafting, trekking or mountain-biking. To get to *Nuts Huts,* take a jeepney that runs through Loboc to Carmen and get off 1km past Loboc at the Sarimanok Boat Company, where you can charter a banca (P500) for the ten-minute trip to the resort.

Jagna

While **JAGNA**, a busy and clean little town about 60km east of Tagbilaran, is a pleasant enough place, with people every bit as friendly as everyone on Bohol, all it really offers the traveller is an alternative port for getting away from Bohol. Mindanao-bound boats operated by Cebu Ferries leave for Cagayan de Oro at noon every Sunday and for Nasipit (near Butuan) at midnight on Sunday. There's an Aboitiz ticket office at Jagna pier where you can buy tickets for these ferries, plus services operated by WG&A and Supercat. The only **place to stay** is *Garden Café* (❶), which has simple en-suite rooms and serves Filipino food; it's close to the church in the town centre.

Panglao Island

A short road bridge from Tagbilaran and another from Bool connect the Bohol mainland to the island of **PANGLAO**, a tropical diving paradise with some lovely sand beaches and a friendly little capital with an old Spanish church. Most of the resorts and most of the diving action are focused on the 800m of **Alona Beach** on Panglao's sandy southwest coast, but there are also two good beaches on the north coast, **Duljo Beach** and **Momo Beach**. The best quiet, undeveloped stretches of white sand on the east coast are **Bikini Beach**, **San Isidro Beach** and **Libaong Beach**. Nowhere near as busy as Alona Beach, with only a few small resorts, this is an ideal place to relax if you really want to get away from it all.

The **reef** at the western end of Panglao, a few minutes by banca from Alona Beach, is in good condition, with healthy corals, a multitude of reef fish and perpendicular underwater cliffs that drop to a depth of 50m. This is where most of the island's dive sites are, though you can go further afield to Doljo Point and Cervira Shoal, or use Alona Beach as a base for diving at Cabilao, Balicasag (see p.284) or Pamilacan (see p.284). Some of the bigger dive operators on Alona Beach organize overnight safaris as far as Masaplod, Dauin and Apo in Negros; try Sea Explorers at the *Alona Tropical* (☏038/502 9024 or 9031) or Seaquest Divers (☏038/502 9038).

Practicalities

It's not hard to find a **taxi** at the airport or pier in Tagbilaran to whisk you across the bridge and out to Panglao. If you negotiate a little you won't pay more than P250. JG Express **buses** to Alona on Panglao leave every hour or when they are full from the Dao terminal, but if you don't want to hang around you could always take a tricycle (P100). You can **rent a motorbike** at a resort for around P500 per half-day – excellent for heading back to the Bohol mainland and up to the Chocolate Hills or along the Bohol coast.

For **ferry tickets**, there's an Aboitiz booking office at the *Alona Kew White Beach Resort* where you can make reservations for Supercat, Cebu Ferries and WG&A. There are a few moneychangers on Alona Beach, but it's best to bring enough cash in dollars or pesos. The only place on Alona Beach changing travellers' cheques is the small **tourist office** (daily 8am–8pm) near the beach next to the *Alona Kew White Beach Resort*. Staff here can arrange trips and have a free map of Bohol and Panglao to hand out. In the same building you'll find a **travel agent**, Sunshine Travel & Tours, where you can arrange accommodation, transport, tours and visa extensions. There's another travel agent, Panglao Island Travel & Tours, on the main road next to the **tourist assistance centre**, where you can get general tourism advice, report lost and stolen property or ask to see the police.

Accommodation

An excellent choice of unpretentious, comfortable budget beach accommodation can be found on Panglao Island, mostly on **Alona Beach**, as well as a number of smarter, more expensive resorts. The beach is a few hundred metres long and all the resorts are within walking distance of one another. **Bolod Beach**, a short walk to the east, is as beautiful as Alona and is home to just a couple of resorts where prices are higher. There's also some stylish accommodation in the resorts along the northern coast.

Alona Beach

Alona Kew White Beach Resort At the eastern end of the beach ☏038/502 9042, ⓦwww .alonakew.com. Comfortable and well-managed native-style resort standing in lush grounds, with a stylish restaurant and enormous suites and cottages with a/c and shower. The standard rooms are also comfortable and very affordable, with some right on the beach. Staff are knowledgeable and can arrange scuba diving, Loboc River safaris and day-trips to the Chocolate Hills. ❹

Alonaland A short walk inland on Ester Lim Street ☏038/502 9007, ⓦwww.alonaland.ch. *Alonaland* has a big choice of accommodation, ranging from budget single nipa cottages to family rooms with their own small kitchen. ❷–❻

Alona Palm Beach Resort & Restaurant Western end of the beach ☏038/502 9141, ⓦwww.alonapalmbeach.com. One of the most

luxurious resorts here, with stylish double cottages set back from the beach around a big, beautiful swimming pool. There's even separate dormitory accommodation for your nanny and chauffeur. ❾

Alona Tropical Eastern end of the beach ☏038/502 9024 or 9031. Large resort with a choice of a/c rooms and beachfront cottages with fan, all built from native materials such as nipa and bamboo. The outdoor restaurant is pleasant and there's a large swimming pool. Staff can arrange diving and excursions. ❸

Bohol Divers Lodge & Restaurant On the western half of the beach close to *Philippine Islands Divers*. ☏038/411 4983. Simple and convivial French-run place with 42 native-style double rooms and cottages with fan or a/c, some right on the beach. There's a good restaurant and bar. ❸

Flower Garden Resort Eastern end of the beach, close to *Alona Kew* ☏ 038/502 9012, ⓦ www.flowergarden-resort.com. Efficiently managed by a resident Swiss couple, this wonderful little family resort has pretty chalet-style houses and spacious bungalows, all set in tropical gardens a short stroll inland from the beach. Not luxurious, but comfortable, quiet, clean, friendly and excellent value. For longer stays you can negotiate a monthly rate. ❹

Isis Bungalows Middle of the beach ☏ 038/502 9292, ⓦ www.isisbungalows.com. Eyecatching modern resort with eight spanking new white-washed a/c bungalows with large terraces and idyllic ocean views. Neatly manicured gardens lead straight to the beach and there's a large restaurant, also with terrific views. ❺

Tierra Azul Alona Beach House Western end of the beach ☏ 038/502 9065. Peaceful, family-run resort, five minutes from the bars and restaurants. The ordinary but comfortable mid-range concrete and bamboo rooms are spacious, and either fan-cooled or with a/c. ❸

Peter's House Eastern end of the beach ☏ 038/502 9056. Simple and cosy nipa rooms close to Genesis Divers. An excellent budget option. ❹

Swiss Bamboo House Western half of the beach ☏ 038/502 9070 or 0918/600 0245. Seven cottages built in native style, with simple bamboo beds and balconies looking out onto pleasant gardens. The beach is a stone's throw away and the resort has its own diving school. Manager Manny Slovic, a fount of local knowledge, has been in the Philippines for decades and is a patient diving instructor. ❷

Around the island

Alumbung Resort Near the barangay of Danao, 15min north of Alona Beach by tricycle ☏ 038/502 5528, ⓦ www.alumbungbohol.com. Wonderfully atmospheric accommodation in two rice-barn cottages built exclusively from native materials. The A-frame cottages, based on a traditional design and spacious enough for four, have an upper floor for sleeping and a downstairs area that's perfect for lounging around or cooking in the kitchenette. The sea is five minutes away, although there's no sandy beach here. You can wander eastwards along the road to Alona Beach (25 minutes) or hop on a banca (5 minutes). Staff can prepare meals from a limited menu on request. Weekly rate for a cottage is an affordable P9000. ❹

Ananyana Beach Resort Duljo Beach ☏ 038/502 8101, ⓦ www.ananyana.com. Stylish, intimate resort on Duljo Beach with eight fashionably decorated double rooms and two family suites of two storeys. Breathtaking sea views from your private balcony and less than fifty metres to a beautiful stretch of white sand beach that's nowhere near as busy as Alona Beach, add to the allure. Tasty Asian food in the restaurant and the native-style beach bar is perfect for a drink at sunset. ❻

Bohol Beach Club Bolod Beach ☏ 038/411 5222, ⓦ www.tambuli.com/Bohol.htm. Spacious cottages with big verandas right on beautiful Bolod Beach a short distance to the north of Alona Beach. A range of five-star facilities and services. ❼

Dumaluan Beach resort Bolod Beach ☏ 038/502 9081. Next to *Bohol Beach Club* and offering a similar range of upmarket rooms on the beach. Large swimming pool and restaurant with dreamy sea views. ❼

Panglao Island Nature Resort Near Dauis, on the island's north coast ☏ 038/411 2599, ⓦ www .panglaoisland.com. Upmarket resort that can be reached by taxi from Tagbilaran in 20min. Spacious villas are either on the beach or in a quiet garden, all with large *lanai* (veranda). A good restaurant, a large swimming pool, gym and massage are also available. ❽

Eating and drinking

Most of the resorts on Panglao, especially those on Alona Beach, have their own **restaurants** open to non-guests. One of the best is at *Alona Kew White Beach Resort*, where the reasonably priced grilled tuna and blue marlin are as fresh as they come. Right on the shore in front of *Alona Kew White Beach Resort* is *Tawara Seaside*, a wonderfully simple little outdoor place mostly serving fresh fish. During the day you grab a table under the shade of palm trees and at night the dining area is candle-lit. The vast menu at the popular *Kamalig Bar & Restaurant* includes pasta, seafood and burgers; it's a short walk down the path leading inland from Alona Beach. Next door is *Beach Rock Café*, a friendly beach bar with occasional live music, pool tables and friendly staff. *Safety Stop Bar* is little more than a bamboo hut facing Alona Beach, but it has a pleasant atmosphere at night, with cheap beer, a billiard table, good music and barbecued food.

Balicasag Island

Southwest of Panglao, the almost perfectly circular divers' paradise of **BALICASAG**, barely 600m in diameter, is flat and featureless, covered with coconut palms and scrub. It's what goes on underwater that makes it such a gem: the island is fringed by an incandescent halo of coral, the reef ending abruptly in massive underwater walls that drop sharply into the depths and teem with life. If you think the island, where the only noise at night is the beating of fireflies' wings, might be too quiet for you, it's worth noting that all dive operators on Alona Beach arrange day-trips.

Despite its isolation from Bohol, Balicasag is home to about sixty families who, inevitably, make their meagre living from fishing. The island has in fact been inhabited since 1870, when a watchtower was built to guard against attacks from Mindanao. The only **place to stay** is *Balicasag Dive Resort* (T02/812 1984; ❸), which has ten duplex cottages and a restaurant.

Pamilacan Island

Around 22km east of Balicasag, the tiny island of **PAMILACAN** makes another superb day-trip for scuba divers from Alona Beach. There are a number of beaches around its circular coast and, on the island itself, a crumbling Spanish fort.

The island's name is derived from the word *pilak*, which is a large hook used by the islanders to capture manta rays, whale sharks and bryde's whales, all of which breed in the area and can be seen from January to April. If you take a stroll among the fishermen's houses you'll notice many of them are decorated with the jaws and bones of marine mammals. These creatures are now protected, but their hunting isn't eradicated, merely less common. The method used to catch the enormous whale sharks is ingenious, cruel and exerting. Equipped only with a hook attached to a one-hundred-metre rope, a "hooker" jumps on the whale shark's back and hooks the animal, allowing the boatmen, often after hours of exhausting effort on behalf of both man and beast, to bring the whale shark close to the banca. Once close enough, the animal is paralyzed by a deep cut through its spinal cord, securely tied through holes bored in its jaw, and dragged back to land. The whole process often takes as long as ten hours.

Ubay and around

On the opposite side of Bohol to Tagbilaran, about two hours away by bus, **UBAY** is an agricultural town with a municipal hall and a pier. Its most notable feature is a livestock farm on the outskirts where research is conducted into the breeding, physiology and nutrition of cattle and small ruminants. For the tourist this is about as far from the well-trodden path you can get, even in the Philippines. The offshore island of **Lapinin** is totally undeveloped, but offers some good diving, some of it extreme in subterranean caves. You can rent a banca for the day at the small pier in Ubay; it will cost about P500. There are no dive operators in the area, so if you want to do some underwater exploring, you'll have to arrange to bring all your gear. Dive operators at Alona Beach can help. There's no accommodation in Ubay and for food there are just a few simple canteens around the pier. It's a good idea to bring your own food and drink.

A number of **ferries** depart from Ubay, including a daily trip to Maasin on Leyte (P180), another to Cebu (P200) and a weekly ferry to Manila (P480), although it's more for cargo and passenger berths are limited. Further along the north coast, in **Talibon**, you can catch one of VG Lines' daily ships to Cebu (P75).

Siquijor

Siquijor, a laidback island where life is simple and tourists are made very welcome, lies slightly apart from the rest of the Visayas off the southern tip of Cebu (see the map on p.251) and about 22km east of Negros. Very little is known about Siquijor and its inhabitants before the arrival of the Spanish in the sixteenth century. The Spanish sailors nicknamed it the Isla del Fuego ("Island of Fire") because of the eerie luminescence generated by swarms of fireflies nestled among the foliage of *molave* trees. This sense of mystery still persists today, with many Filipinos believing Siquijor to be a centre of **witchcraft and black magic**. It's a view that's enforced by the annual staging of the Conference of Sorcerers and Healers in the mountain village of San Antonio every Easter.

Shamans aside, Siquijor is peaceful, picturesque and bursting with attractions. The **beaches** alone make it worth a visit, with a number of lovely little resorts dotting the coastline where you can rent a cottage on the sand for a few hundred pesos a night. The most popular beaches are **Sandugan**, half an hour by jeepney north of the port of **Larena**, and **Paliton** on the west coast. The island's relatively small size makes it a joy to tour by public transport, rented vehicle or even on foot. Good **scuba diving** can be found on the coast and a number of resorts have certified dive operators who will take you on half-day or day-trips to places such as Sandugan Point and Tambisan Point, both known for their coral and abundant marine life. At Paliton Beach there are three submarine caves where you can see sleeping reef sharks and at Salag-Doong Beach on the eastern side of the island divers have occasionally reported seeing manta rays and shoals of barracuda. In the interior there are some good treks and climbs, including up **Mount Bandila-an**, which at 557m is accessible to anyone reasonably fit.

Arrival and island transport

Siquijor is not accessible by plane, but there is an excellent fast **ferry** connection with Supercat, which has one trip daily from Cebu City to Larena (P465), via Tagbilaran on Bohol and Dumaguete on Negros. Other options include a Palacio Shipping ferry that sails to Larena from Tagbilaran in Bohol. There's also a wharf in Siquijor Town (the island capital) where local bancas from Dumaguete dock; the trip can be very rough and wet. Irregular ferries, most of them rusty old tubs, from Plaridel in Mindanao arrive in Lazi, a small port town on Siquijor's southeast coast.

Black magic, white magic

"There's black magic and there's white magic," says Siquijor's governor. "What we do here is white magic." Every Good Friday herbalists from around Siquijor and from the rest of the Visayas and Mindanao gather in **San Antonio**, in Siquijor's pea-green hinterlands, to mix and compare medicinal potions made from tree bark, roots, herbs, dirt and insects. The culmination of this annual Conference of Sorcerers and Healers – now rebranded the **Folk Healing Festival** because it sounds less menacing – is the mixing of a mother-of-all-potions in a large cauldron filled with coconut oil. As the potion is stirred, participants gather in a circle and mumble incantations said to imbue the mixture with extraordinary healing powers. The herbal preparation takes place on Good Friday because Christ is dead and there is no God, opening a window of opportunity for entities and forces not of this realm to roam the Earth. It's evidently a strong brew, with wide-ranging powers that include provoking a good harvest, securing a spouse or getting rid of that troublesome zit.

You can circumnavigate Siquijor by tricycle or jeepney along the 72-kilometre **coast road** which is paved all the way – a rare delight in the Philippines – so renting a motorcycle or mountain bike from one of the resorts is a good option for getting around. To take you along the coast by sea, bancas can be chartered in Larena, Siquijor Town and Lazi. As an example, the trip from Larena to Siquijor Town costs P150 and takes about 45 minutes.

Larena and Sandugan

The bustling port of **LARENA** will probably be your first taste of Siquijor, as most ferries arrive here. It's only a short walk from the pier to the town centre, which has a town hall, plaza, church and post office, but not much else. There's a Supercat ticket office on the pier, though the main ticket office is on the main road (☎035/484 1144), the National Highway.

There's no reason to stay in Larena, and the only options if you do want to stay are *Luisa & Son's Lodge* (❶) and *Mykel's Garden Pension House* (❶), both near the pier and both a little run-down. You can get online at Siquijor Internet on Rizal Street, right opposite the Allied Bank, although the computers are usually monopolized by schoolboys playing Donkey Kong and Tomb Raider.

Sandugan

Six kilometres northeast of Larena is the village of **SANDUGAN**, where there's a big beach and a number of hospitable resorts, one with professional scuba-diving facilities (see below). To reach the beach, take a tricycle or jeepney from Larena to Sandugan and then negotiate the rutted path that leads to the shore. All the tricycle drivers know it, so you won't get lost.

Kiwi Dive Resort is at the eastern end of the beach (turn right at the end of the path; ☎0921/643 0031, ⓦwww.kiwidiveresort.com; ❷) and has cottages for two on a low hill overlooking a private cove, all with private bathrooms and hot water. Home-baked bread, omelettes, nourishing meat and potato stews, curry, fish, spaghetti and sandwiches are some of the tasty dishes available at the restaurant. There's also a small vegetarian menu. One of the owners is a dive instructor and can organize trips to good nearby dive sites. *Islanders Paradise Beach Resort* (☎0919/446 9982; ⓦwww.islandersparadisebeach.com; ❷), also to the right as you hit the beach, has lovely little beachfront cottages with fan and private shower. In the opposite direction is the largest resort on the beach, *Casa de la Playa* (☎035/484 1170, ⓦwww.siquijorcasa.com; ❹), whose owners Terry and Emily have established a New Age tropical spa that offers yoga sessions, food made with organic vegetables from the resort's own garden, and even massages from a local shaman. Accommodation is in a range of lovingly built huts; some are set back from the shore in a pretty garden bursting with frangipani and white *sampaguita* blossom, while others are on the beach and have sea views.

Siquijor Town and Paliton Beach

SIQUIJOR TOWN, twenty minutes southwest of Larena by jeepney, is a laid-back, likeable enough place without anything to keep you there for long. There is an atmospheric eighteenth-century church on the seafront, the Church of St Francis of Assisi, which was built in 1783 partly from coral and with a bell tower you can climb for views across the town and out to sea.

The provincial **tourist office**, in the New Capitol Building facing the plaza (Mon–Fri 9am–3pm; ☎035/344 2088), hasn't much in the way of maps and brochures, but can help arrange transport and guides. The main drag, **Rizal Street,** is chock-a-block with ludicrously cheap canteens and bakeries selling fresh *pan de sal*. There's an Internet café – called *Internet Café* – on Legaspi Street, opposite church. Supercat has an office on the National Highway, the main road through town.

There's nowhere worth **staying** in town itself, though 1km to the northeast is *Calalinan Beach Garden Mini Hotel and Restaurant* (℡0912/515 0370; ❷), a Dutch-owned place with a restaurant serving better food than anywhere in town. The menu includes curry, spaghetti and fresh salads.

Paliton Beach

Twenty minutes west of Siquijor you come to **PALITON BEACH**, 1km down a bumpy track from the main road (take the turnoff at the church in Paliton), but well worth the pain inflicted on your buttocks (and on your head – every time the tricycle hits a pothole, you hit the roof). A west-facing cove of sugary white sand, Paliton is sheltered from big waves by the promontory of **Tambisan Point**, and has views of tropical sunsets you'll never forget.

There's no accommodation here except a few **huts** where you can take refuge from the sun during the day and unfurl your sleeping bag for P20 a night. Half a dozen fishing families have made their homes in wooden shacks in the coconut grove at the back of the beach, and may be able to cook up fish for you. In return it's worth having a bottle of local rum to share among the adults and some cola for the kids. It's a magical experience sitting around a fire with the locals at night and waking before dawn to help them launch their bancas and cast their nets. People are reserved but courteous, and enjoy showing clumsy foreigners how to catch fish.

San Juan

On the south coast, **SAN JUAN** has an unusual focal point: the sulphurous San **Juan de Capilay Lake** (P5) where locals gather, especially at weekends, to wallow in the eggy water, said to have miraculous healing qualities. For more energetic activity, try the scenic but strenuous trek from San Juan along a jungled trail to San Antonio.

For **accommodation** in the San Juan area, the cottages at the *Coco Grove Beach Resort* (℡035/481 5006 or 0918/740 3707; ❷) are spacious, in good condition and stand in landscaped gardens around a swimming pool and restaurant. The resort is situated in a beautiful spot overlooking the sandy beach and blue sea at **Tubod**, a short trip east of San Juan. Standard air-conditioned doubles have a balcony and private cold shower. For hot water you'll pay about P100 extra per night. The resort's dive shop can arrange trips around Siquijor and further afield to Apo Island near Dumaguete (see box on p.303). Less than two kilometres east of San Juan on a small sandy beach lapped by glass-clear water is *Royal Cliff Resort* (℡035/481 5038; ❸) which has spacious, cool rooms with ceiling fan, private toilet and bath. All rooms are overlooking the sea with a beautiful flower garden around.

Another option in this area is the well-established *Coral Cay Resort* (℡035/481 5024 or 0919/269 1269, ⓦwww.coralcayresort.com; ❸) on the beach at **Solangon**, 3km to the west of San Juan. The resort is owned by an expat and his Filipina wife who know the island like the back of their hand, and who can arrange jeepney tours, trekking, scuba diving, mountain bikes and anything else you care to ask for. Accommodation ranges from clean, simple rooms with fan and cold shower to spacious air-conditioned cottages with a small living area and separate bedroom. The restaurant menu is surprisingly urbane for such an isolated place, featuring *coq au vin* and Australian Chardonnay. There's another excellent resort along this pretty stretch of coast, the *Charisma Resort* (☎035/481 5033, ⓦwww.charisma-resort.com; ④) with its spic-and-span white motel-style rooms arranged around a swimming pool and right on the beach. The restaurant serves excellent Spanish cuisine.

The east coast

Siquijor's picturesque east coast is a rural littoral of sun-bleached barrios and hidden coves, some of the most secluded around **Kagusua Beach**, reached through **Minalonan** and then the sleepy little fishing village of **Kagusua**. There's a sealed road from the village to the edge of a low cliff, where steps take you down to the sand and a series of immaculate little sandy inlets. To proceed north from Kagusua you'll have to backtrack to the coastal road at Minalonan, where you can catch a jeepney through **Maria** and on to **Salag-Doong**, another untouristed beach with no accommodation or restaurants, just a sari-sari store selling basics such as water, soft drinks and instant noodles. For Salag-Doong Beach, look out for the signposted turning about 6km north of Maria. You can walk it in about twenty minutes from the main road.

Heading to Minalonan from the west you'll pass through **Lazi**, with its delightful nineteenth-century church built of coral and stone and right opposite it, the oldest convent in the Philippines, a low-rise wooden building now sagging with age but still beautiful. There's a Supercat office here in Cortes Residence, an office building on the main road 200m west of the church.

Mount Bandila-an

At the centre of Siquijor, **Mount Bandila-an** lies in an area still recovering from damage inflicted during World War II, when acres of forest were razed by retreating Japanese troops in a final, desperate effort to flush out local guerrillas. The inevitable deforestation has been blamed for floods and the silting of rivers, but now the entire area is part of the Siquijor Reforestation Project and while rehabilitation is not yet complete, wildlife such as the leopard cat and long-tailed macaque survives.

Mount Bandila-an can be climbed in a day; you can enquire about **guides** at the tourist office in Siquijor Town, although many resorts can also offer advice and arrange for a local to show you the way. Access is via either the village of **Cantabon**, which can be reached by tricycle or jeepney from Larena on the north coast, or **Cangmonag** on the south. On the way to the peak you'll pass the **Stations of the Cross**, where a solemn religious procession re-enacting the Passion of Christ is held every Easter, and there are a number of springs and caves. Ask the guide to point out the old **balete tree** at the side of the trail, a tree known to locals because of its age and immense size. In the way of Philippine myths and legends, this impressive old tree is said to be home to spirits, imps and guardians of the forest, so you'll need to ask their permission to pass. The polite thing to say is *tabi tabi lang-po*, which means "excuse me, please step aside."

Negros

The island of **NEGROS**, fourth largest in the country and home to 3.5 million people, covers 13,000 square kilometres – about the size of New Jersey – and

I chop your feet, I drink your blood. What am I?
Sugar cane

Visayan riddle

Land reform – or the lack of it – has been at the root of simmering discontent on Negros that began in the 1970s under Ferdinand Marcos and continues to this day. The case for land reform is stark. Seventy percent of the island's population is impoverished; half of it makes a living off the land but eighty percent are landless. All of the sugar-producing land is held by two percent of the people and half the arable land by five percent. Of course if you happen to own the land people want reformed, things look different. Negros's gentry assume reform means their land will be taken and handed over to ignorant peasants. They see the land as a way of life, while the Church, the New People's Army (NPA; see p.171) and various peasant organizations see it as a source of food. The NPA has been screaming about land reform for years, intimidating *haciendas* and seizing land. The *haciendas* have responded with private armies and acts of repression, turning Negros into a battleground for the struggle between rich and poor, in which the rich have all the guns. What the government wants is some middle ground, but it's as elusive as a mirage in the desert.

In the 1970s and 1980s this struggle was played out against the background of Ferdinand Marcos's thieving dictatorship. Between 1974 and 1978 Marcos monopolized sugar trading, placing it in the hands of crony **Roberto Benedicto** who was, after the dictator himself, probably the greatest kleptomaniac in Philippine history. A native Negrense, Benedicto owned or controlled 106 sugar farms, 85 corporations, 17 radio stations, 16 television stations, a Manila casino, a *Holiday Inn* and a major piece of the national oil company. Known as the Sugar Czar, he effectively controlled the supply chain, allowing him to steal tens of millions of dollars from his neighbours on Negros by paying them a third or fourth the price he received when he resold their sugar. For good measure Marcos gave him control of the bank that was the planters' principal lending agency.

In 1974, as prices of sugar on the world market rose steadily with no end in sight, Benedicto began hoarding, speculating that the price would continue to rise. Sugar reached a peak of 67 cents a pound and then began to plummet, hitting four cents in 1984. Benedicto responded by paying planters less for their sugar than it cost to grow. The planters took their land out of cultivation and as a result, production in 1985 was half that of ten years earlier. Thousands were thrown out of work and hunger and malnutrition set in on a massive scale. Benedicto got out of the sugar business and was promptly appointed Philippine ambassador to Japan.

In 1981 the **Pope** visited Negros and thrust the island into the international limelight. Imelda Marcos told an audience of more than half a million in Bacolod, "Negros is not an island of fear, but an island of love." The Pope's message was different: "Injustice reigns," he said. The oligarchs and Imelda squirmed. His Holiness used the words "justice" and "injustice" seventeen times in his speech, casting his lot with the labourers and appearing to endorse land reform, the idea the *haciendas* most despised.

Five years later Marcos was overthrown, and **Cory Aquino** gave the impression during her election campaign that she was willing to give up her own family's hacienda north of Manila in the name of nationwide land reform. But once elected she began to equivocate and produced a watered-down land bill which she dumped in the lap of a newly elected Congress dominated by landed oligarchs. "She might as well have appointed a crack addict to run her drug treatment programme," said an opposition senator. As for Benedicto, under a deal struck with Aquino's Presidential Commission on Good Government, established to recover the ill-gotten wealth of Marcos and his cronies, he was allowed to keep $15 million of the fortune he amassed. He lived quietly in Negros until his death in 2000.

lies at the heart of the Visayas, between Panay to the west and Cebu to the east. Shaped like a boot, it's split diagonally into the northwestern province of Negros Occidental and the southeastern province of Negros Oriental. The demarcation came when early missionaries decided the central mountain range was too formidable to cross, even in the name of God, and is still felt today. Impenetrable rainforest and a lack of roads so completely separated the eastern and western plains for centuries that the two populations continue to speak mutually incomprehensible languages. It's an island many tourists miss out and as a result is largely unspoilt, with miles of wild, untouched coastline and a dramatic western plain that's a vast silver-green expanse of sugar-cane plantations stretching from the Gulf of Panay across gentle foothills and on to volcanic mountains. It is because of these plantations that Negros is known as "Sugarlandia", its rich lowlands growing two-thirds of the nation's sugar cane. Needless to say, sugar processing is a major industry, as is the production of paper made from cane fibre. Rice, coconuts, bananas and corn are also grown, though only around the coast.

Much of Negros's interior is jungled and uncultivated, rising to a giddy 2465m at the peak of **Mount Kanlaon**, the highest mountain in the Visayas. Like much of the Philippines, Negros is a volcanic island and has six volcanoes, four on the Negros mainland (Kanlaon being one) and two on offshore islands, making up the Negros Volcanic Belt. For the intrepid this means there's some extreme trekking and climbing on Negros, from Mount Kanlaon itself to **Mount Silay** in the north and the **Northern Negros Forest Reserve,** an antediluvian landscape of peaks, waterfalls and fumaroles. From **Bacolod**, the capital of Negros Occidental, you can follow the coastal road clockwise to **Silay**, a beautifully preserved sugar town with grand antique homes and old sugar locomotives. Much of the north coast is given over to the port towns through which sugar is shipped to Manila, but at the southern end of the island around **Dumaguete** there are great beaches and scuba diving, with a range of excellent budget accommodation. The **southwest coast** – the heel of the boot – is one of Negros's great secrets, with **beaches** that compare to Boracay's (such as Sugar Beach near Sipalay) and unforgettable tropical sunsets. Much of this coast is charmingly rural and undeveloped, with *carabao* in the fields and chocolate-coloured roads winding lazily into the farming barrios of the foothills.

Among Negros's earliest inhabitants were dark-skinned natives belonging to the Negrito ethnic group – hence the name Negros, imposed by the Spanish when they set foot here in April 1565. After appointing bureaucrats to run the island, Miguel Lopez de Legazpi placed it under the jurisdiction of its first Spanish governor. Religious orders wasted no time in moving in to evangelize the natives, ripe for conversion to the true faith. The Augustinians were here first, then the Recollects, the Jesuits, the Dominicans, the Seculars and, again, the Recollects, returning in the 1800s. The latter half of the eighteenth century was a period of rapid economic expansion for Negros, with its sugar industry flourishing and Visayan ports such as Cebu and Iloilo open for the first time to foreign ships. In the last century the rapacious growth of the sugar industry and its increasing politicization were to have disastrous consequences that are still being felt today (see box p.289).

Getting to Negros

The main **airports** on Negros are Bacolod, with daily flights from Manila and Cebu City, and Dumaguete, served by flights from Manila. The biggest and busiest **ports** on Negros are Bacolod and Dumaguete, both connected by regular ferries with Manila, Cebu City, Tagbilaran on Bohol and Dapitan and

Iligan on Mindanao; Bacolod also has ferry connections with Iloilo on Panay and Cagayan de Oro and Ozamis on Mindanao. Many other coastal towns on the island, including Cadiz, San Carlos and Guihulngan, have smaller ferries going back and forth to Iloilo, Cebu, Guimaras and Siquijor, as well as to other destinations on Negros itself. There are regular ferries on the useful crossing from the southerly tip of Cebu to the east coast of Negros. These ferries sail between Bato (Cebu) and Tampi (north of Dumaguete); and Lilo-an (Cebu) and Sibulan, also north of Dumaguete.

Bacolod

On the northern coast of Negros, the city of **BACOLOD** is a heaving provincial metropolis centred around City Plaza and San Sebastian Cathedral. Its tourist attractions aren't significant enough to make you linger for more than a day or two, but it's a major transit point for Negros and a good place to head for if you want to see some of the nearby towns, such as Silay and Victorias. Some visitors choose to stay a little outside the city in Singcang, a quiet area of new homes and hotels close to the airport.

About 300m north of the centre, the 1930s Provincial Capitol Building is one of the few architectural highlights. Next door is the excellent **Negros Museum** (Mon–Sat 9am–6pm; P20), which details five thousand years of island history. Housed in an elegant Neoclassical building dating from the 1930s, the museum is dominated by the **Iron Dinosaur** steam engine, which used to haul sugar cane in nearby Silay. Over the road is an open area that has been turned into the **Biodiversity Conservation Center** (Mon–Fri 9am–noon & 1–4pm; P10), a rescue centre where conservationists care for endangered animals endemic to Negros, including leopard cats and Visayan spotted deer.

During the third week of October everybody who is anybody attends the flamboyant **Masskara festival**, a mardi-gras jamboree of street dancing and beauty pageants (the event's name is derived from the local word for the colourful masks worn by participants).

Practicalities

The **city centre**, chaotic and choked with traffic, is best defined as the area around the City Plaza at the northern end of Araneta Street, where jeepneys and tricycles congregate. Bacolod's main thoroughfare is **Lacson Street**, a long, busy north–south drag that is lined with shops, fast-food restaurants, banks and some reasonably priced hotels. It is crossed by a number of busy secondary streets, including Burgos Street and Rizal Street, both teeming with convenience stores and fast-food restaurants.

The **airport** is 5km south of the centre on Araneta Street. Turn left outside the airport to pick up a jeepney going to the city (P20). Philippine Airlines, which operates four flights a day from Manila, has an office at the airport (☏034/434 7878). Cebu Pacific, also has an office at the airport (☏034/707 3933 to 3935) and another in Victoria Arcade, Rizal Street (☏034/434 2020 to 2023), and fly here from both Manila and Cebu City. Air Philippines has a daily afternoon flight from Cebu to Bacolod and a daily early morning flight from Manila. Its main Bacolod ticket office is at the airport (☏034/433 9211).

Ticket offices for major ferry companies operating out of Bacolod are at **Palanca port**, on reclaimed land 500m west of the plaza. This is the arrival and departure point for most major ferries, including Supercat, Superferry and Weesam Express, which between them connect Bacolod with Manila, Cebu City, Dumaguete, Iloilo and Mindanao. Negros Navigation uses the old

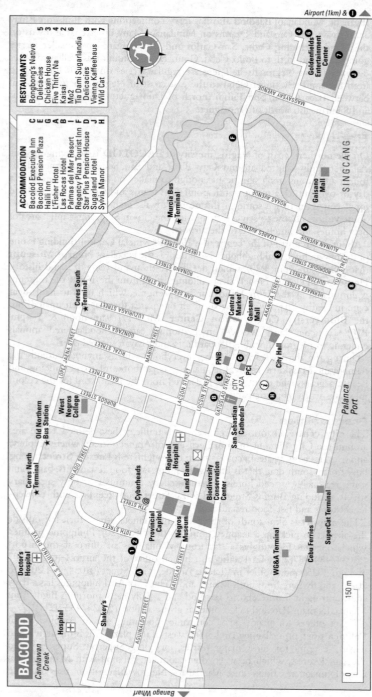

BACOLOD

Canalawan Creek

Doctor's Hospital

Hospital

Shakey's

AGUINALDO STREET

10TH STREET

7TH STREET

HILADO STREET

B.S. AQUINO DRIVE

Provincial Capitol

Negros Museum

Cyberheads @

Regional Hospital

Land Bank

Biodiversity Conservation Center

West Negros College

BURGOS STREET

GATUSLAO STREET

SAN JUAN STREET

Old Northern Bus Station

★ Ceres North Terminal

LOPEZ JAENA STREET

GONZAGA STREET

LUZURIAGA STREET

★ Ceres South Terminal

RIZAL STREET

MABINI STREET

GALO STREET

LACSON STREET

LOCSIN STREET

GATUSLAO STREET

San Sebastian Cathedral

CITY PLAZA

PNB

PCI

City Hall

Central Market

Gaisano Mall

SAN SEBASTIAN STREET

RONANO STREET

LIBERTAD STREET

Murcia Bus Terminal ★

LIZARES AVENUE

ROXAS AVENUE

ARANETA STREET

ALUNAN AVENUE

QUEZON STREET

RODRIGUEZ STREET

HERNAEZ STREET

OLD STREET

MAGSAYSAY AVENUE

Gaisano Mall

SINGCANG

Goldenfields Entertainment Center

Airport (1km) & ❶

Palanca Port

WG&A Terminal

Cebu Ferries

SuperCat Terminal

Banago Wharf ▲

0 — 150 m

ACCOMMODATION

Bacolod Executive Inn	C
Bacolod Pension Plaza	E
Haili Inn	G
L'Fisher Hotel	A
Las Rocas Hotel	B
Palmas del Mar Resort	I
Regency Plaza Tourist Inn	F
Star Plus Pension House	D
Sugarland Hotel	J
Sylvia Manor	H

RESTAURANTS

Bongbong's Native Delicacies	5
Chicken House	3
Five Thirty Na	4
Kaisai	2
Mo2	6
Tia Dami Sugarlandia Delicacies	8
Vienna Kaffeehaus	1
Wild Cat	7

Banago wharf 8km north of Bacolod and has its ticket office there (although there are dozens of outlets in the city itself). From Banago Wharf you'll have to take a tricycle or jeepney into the city, but from the new wharf it's possible to walk (or take a short tricycle ride for P10).

There are two **bus terminals** of the Ceres Liner bus company, next to each other on Lopez Jaena Street on the eastern edge of the city. One, the Ceres North terminal, is for buses heading north along the coastal road to Silay and Cadiz. Some of these buses continue from Cadiz to San Carlos and on to Dumaguete 313km away (8hr; P150). There's also a Ceres service from here that travels clockwise around Negros from Bacolod to San Carlos, where it boards a ferry for Toledo on the western coast of Cebu and continues on to Cebu City. Buses heading south along the coast road leave from the Ceres South terminal. The old **northern bus station** on Lopez Jaena Street is used by Royal Express Transport and by express air-conditioned buses leaving for Dumaguete (P120), heading south and across the island; most other buses hug the coast. From the **Murcia bus terminal** off Libertad Street near the market you can catch slow, non-air-conditioned buses to Silay and Victorias. Jeepneys and FX taxis use the City Plaza.

The **tourist office** (Mon–Sat 8.30am–5.30pm; ☎034/433 2515 or 435 1001) is in the administrative building of the provincial government complex in City Plaza, San Juan Street. Many little **cybercafés** can be found on Hilado Street around the West Negros College northeast of the centre, and also in hotels and at the city's two Gaisano malls, one near the central market in Gatuslao Street and the other in Singcang. The trendy *Cyberheads Café* is one of a number around the junction of Lacson and 7th Street. The **post office** is on Gatuslao Street, near the junction with Burgos Street. Most of Bacolod's **banks**, including PCI and PNB, are near the City Plaza in Araneta and Gonzaga Streets; Landbank is north of here next to the post office. **Police** headquarters are located on Magsaysay Avenue in Singcang, and there's a good **hospital**, the Bacolod Doctors' Hospital, on B.S. Aquino Drive northeast of the centre.

Accommodation

You've got two choices for accommodation in Bacolod: either head for the city centre and find a room in one of the many ordinary budget hotels, or stay in **Singcang**, a quiet area close to the airport where there are a number of mid-range business hotels that offer a higher standard of accommodation at affordable prices. From Singcang to the city it's only a few minutes by tricycle or fifteen minutes on foot along Araneta Street.

City centre

Bacolod Executive Inn 52 San Sebastian St ☎034/433 7401 or 433 7404, ⊛www.bcdexecutiveinn.com. Good-value and well-run mid-range hotel with single "tourist" rooms, deluxe doubles and suites. The coffee shop serves snacks and light meals. ❸

Bacolod Pension Plaza Cuadra St, opposite City Plaza ☎034/433 4547. Not to be confused with the *Bacolod Pension*, this place is bigger and more central, with rooms ranging from singles with fan to a/c family rooms that sleep up to five. At the front desk you can book air and ferry tickets. ❸

Halili Inn Locsin St ☎034/81548. Close to *Las Rocas* (see below) and as cheap, with small singles and doubles that share a bathroom, but are not so threadbare as to be uncomfortable. Not a bad choice for one night, although the location can make it noisy; ask to look at the quieter rooms at the back. ❶

Las Rocas Hotel Gatuslao St ☎034/433 0933. Dark, small rooms with no views, but they're among the cheapest in Bacolod and at least it is right in the middle of the action, opposite City Plaza and the cathedral, a stone's throw from shops and restaurants. ❶

L'Fisher Hotel Lacson St ☎034/433 3731. One of Bacolod's best mid-range hotels, this glass-fronted establishment on the main drag has well-kept a/c doubles that have clean bathrooms, cable TV and a fridge. There's a 24hr poolside café that offers buffet lunches and dinners. ❹

Star Plus Pension House Lacson St corner Rosario St ☎034/433 2948. Small singles and doubles with a/c and nice showers. The restaurant is a bit dowdy and serves *carinderia*-style fare. ❶

Sylvia Manor St Juan St ☎034/434 9801, ⓦwww.sylviamanor.com. New boutique hotel in a central location one block south of the main city plaza. Wide range of comfortable a/c rooms and suites, all tastefully decorated and with cable TV and, in some cases, a kitchenette. There's a laid-back café-bar in the lobby. ❹

Singcang

Bacolod Convention Plaza Hotel Magsaysay Ave ☎034/434 4551. Reasonably modern establishment close to the airport, with impressive modern rooms

and a large swimming pool. The hotel's large Chinese restaurant is popular with business types. ❺

Palmas del Mar Resort J.R. Torres Ave ☎034/435 3527. Family resort in a residential area close to the sea. There's a good range of accommodation, including regular a/c rooms, one family room and three cottages. The swimming pool is Olympic-size and the restaurant serves local specialities and European dishes. Pleasantly quiet during the week, when you might have the pool to yourself, but weekends can get busy. ❹

Regency Plaza Tourist Inn Lacson St ☎034/433 1458. Unfussy accommodation in a/c rooms with hot showers. The choice of rooms ranges from bright singles to family rooms big enough for five, all with fridge and cable TV. ❷

Sugarland Hotel Araneta St ☎034/435 2690, ⓦwww.sugarland.com. Reasonably affordable modern hotel with a/c rooms. There are two quaint and convivial restaurants with terracotta tiled floors and antique-style furniture. Recreational facilities include tennis, a swimming pool and a nearby golf course. ❹

Eating, drinking and nightlife

The **restaurant** scene in Bacolod is far from urbane, with choice largely limited to the usual fast-food outlets, and a number of average international restaurants in hotels. One of the better independent restaurants is the Austrian-owned *Vienna Kaffeehaus* on Lacson Street, where a good Teutonic breakfast, lunch or dinner will cost P120–200 a head. Next door is an affordable little Japanese restaurant, *Kaisai*, which does noodles, tempura and some excellent sushi. On Araneta Street, *Chicken House* is known beyond Bacolod for the quality of its fried and barbecued chicken, sold in enormous quantities in a range of styles and sauces. It's fun to eat here in the evenings when it's packed out with locals and the atmosphere is lively, and it's cheap too: a big meal with a couple of drinks costs less than P200. A short walk south on Araneta is *Bongbong's Native Delicacies*, where you can grab a cup of Negros coffee and nibble on sweet treats such as *piyaya* (a hardened pancake with sugar melted inside) and *bay ibayi* (sugar and coconut served in a coconut shell). There's a similar place not far away, *Tia Dami Sugarlandia Delicacies*, on Yulo Street.

For **drinks**, food and billiards, there are a few popular places clustered around the Goldenfields Entertainment Center in Singcang, including *Mo2*, *Wild Cat* and *Five Thirty Na* (the name is a play on the way Filipinos state the time).

Silay

The elegant city of **SILAY**, about 20km north of Bacolod, is an atmospheric relic of a grander age, when Negros was rich from its cultivation of sugar cane and its affluent residents, keen to emulate the sophistications of Europe, turned it into an aspirational enclave of art and education; in the late eighteenth century it was talked about as the "Paris of Negros", with performers from Europe arriving by steamship to take part in operettas and *zarzuelas*. This passion for music and the arts gave Silay – and the Philippines – its first international star, **Conchita Gaston**, a mezzo-soprano who performed in major opera houses in Europe in the postwar years. Ms Gaston was reportedly the first Filipina to cut a record in America and is still talked about fondly by locals. Silay's reputation as a hotbed of intellectual activity was enhanced in November 1898, when townspeople attacked the Spanish garrison and overthrew their colonial masters in a bloodless revolution, raising the Philippine flag in a victory ceremony at the public plaza.

Japanese forces occupied the city in World War II, after which the sugar industry declined and Silay lost its lustre – many of its European residents departing for home. Today, Silay's major tourist draw is its **ancestral homes**, most of them built between 1880 and 1930 and some of the best open to the public.

The major annual festival here, the **Kansilay**, lasts one week and ends every November 13 with a re-enactment of a folk tale showing the bravery of a beautiful princess who offered her life for justice and freedom.

The City

Two ancestral houses have been turned into lifestyle museums that give a glimpse of what life was like for the sugar barons. The **Balay Negrense Museum** on Cinco de Noviembre Street, five minutes' walk west of the plaza (Tues–Sat 10am–6pm; P25), was once the home of Don Victor Gaston, eldest son of Yves Germaine Leopold Gaston, a Frenchman who settled in Silay during the latter part of the nineteenth century. Yves Gaston had worked as a technician on a sugar farm in Batangas and is credited with the development of the sugar industry in northern Negros. It is probably safe to say that it was Gaston and his descendants who imbued Silay with its unmistakable French flavour, giving rise to the "Paris of Negros" tag. After World War II the house was left deserted and by 1980 was a sad ruin, known only by locals for the ghosts that were said to roam its corridors. In the latter part of the 1980s restoration work started, courtesy of the Negros Foundation, and the house is now a glorious monument to Silay's golden age, its carved ceilings painstakingly restored and rooms of polished mahogany furnished with antiques donated by locals.

The **Don Bernardino-Ysabel Jalandoni House Museum** is at the northernmost end of Rizal Street (Mon–Sat 9.30am–6pm; P25), which runs north–south directly to the east of the plaza. Built in 1908 with hardwood from as far off as Mindoro, it's hard to miss because it's pink (affectionately referred to by locals as the Pink House). Within are displays of antique law books and Japanese occupation currency, and in the garden is a huge metal vat that was used to make muscovado sugar.

A short walk from Balay Negrense, the **Manuel and Hilda Hofileña ancestral house** (open by appointment; enquire at the tourist office) is notable for housing works by contemporary Filipino painters and by masters such as Juan Luna and Amorsolo. It's also worth taking time to visit the **Church of San Diego**, on the north side of the public plaza. Built in 1925, it is a dramatic sight, with a great illuminated crucifix on top of the dome that is so bright at night it was once used by ships as a navigational aid. Behind the church are the ruins of the original sixteenth-century Spanish church, now converted into a grotto and prayer garden.

Silay is also known for **pottery** and in the barangay of **Guinhalaran** (about ten minutes by tricycle or jeepney from town) on the National Highway you can visit the potters and buy quality jars and vases at bargain prices.

Practicalities

Buses and jeepneys arriving in Silay stop in Rizal Street on the eastern side of the plaza, from where it's a short walk or tricycle ride to accommodation. The Silay **tourist office** (Mon–Fri 9am–4pm; ☏034/495 5145) in Plaridel Street, opposite the **police station**, has some helpful staff with information about Silay's attractions. The office can arrange informal guided tours of some ancestral houses that aren't usually open to the public. For long-distance calls there's a **PLDT office** in Rizal Street; the *Silay Internet Cafe* is next door.

The only **accommodation** in Silay is the atmospheric former ancestral home *Baldevia Pension House* on busy Rizal Street (☏034/495 0272; ❷), close to its junction with Burgos Street (head 200m north from the Church of San Diego and it's the big white building on your left). *Baldevia* is low on modern amenities, but high on faded old-world charm. The hotel has its own bistro-style **café**, but don't miss the opportunity to try some of the freshly baked pastries, pies and breads from *El Ideal Bakery & Refreshment* – locals swear it was once featured in a BBC cookery documentary – sited close to the plaza. Established in 1920, it does a range of specialities that include coconut pie, cassava cake, meringue and *halo-halo*. Silay is also full of *manuglibod*, or sweet-sellers, who carry their home-made goods in baskets on their heads. Milksweets – made with *carabao* milk – are delicious and cost P1 for two.

Northern Negros Forest Reserve

The mountainous **Northern Negros Forest Reserve** lies approximately 20km east of Bacolod and, while access is difficult, offers some fantastic jungle treks for the persistent and athletic. The reserve's importance to the biodiversity of the Phillipines cannot be overestimated. Protected since 1935, it contains more than half of Negros's old-growth forest and so has become a vital reservoir of flora and fauna, much of it – like the Visayan deer and Visayan warty pig – endemic to Negros, and some of it highly endangered. There are two areas of the reserve accessible to visitors: the slopes of **Mount Mandalagan** directly to the east of Bacolod, and an area known as **Patag** on the slopes of **Mount Silay**, northeast of the city.

To get to the slopes of Mandalagan mountains you must travel to **Campestuehan** (accessible from Bacolod and Silay), where a motorable track ends close to an abandoned school now used as headquarters for the Negros Forest and Ecological Foundation, whose staff and rangers can act as guides. From here it's possible to hike along a number of undulating trails and head deep into the interior, where a narrow valley known as **Dinagang Dahat** contains an active fumarole that pours out sulphurous smoke and steam. Close by is an attractive lake that usually dries up during the dry season, making a convenient camping site. If you want to climb Mount Mandalagan, whose highest point is **Marapara Peak** (2056m), allow at least two days in total to reach the summit and return. You should hire a guide from the Negros Forest and Ecological Foundation.

To reach Patag, take a jeepney from Silay or Bacolod (P15) to the Mount Silay Registration Office, close to the World War II-era former Japanese hospital, which has been partly modernized and is now used to accommodate park rangers. You can hire guides here (P250 a day), who can lead you through dense jungle to three thundering waterfalls, all within an hour's trek. You can go further, even to the summit of Mount Silay, but this is a strenuous climb for which you'll need the right equipment. Tents can be rented through the Department of Environment and Natural Resources opposite the Provincial Capitol Building in Bacolod (☏034/434 7769), but you'll have to obtain other gear elsewhere. If necessary, you can stay a night in the hospital building – there are no beds, but you can roll out a mattress on the floor and, for P10, get a lantern to read by.

Mount Kanlaon National Park

At 2435m **Mount Kanlaon**, two hours south from Bacolod by jeepney, is the tallest peak in the central Philippines and offers a potentially dangerous challenge. It is still one of the thirteen most active volcanoes in the country and there's the possibility of serious, violent eruptions. Climbers have died scaling it, so don't underestimate its fury.

Around the rim of the crater there is no flat area, just a circular knife-edge that overhangs a gaping and apparently bottomless chasm. The dense surrounding forest contains all manner of wonderful fauna, including pythons, monitor lizards, tube-nosed bats and the *dahoy pulay*, a poisonous green tree snake. Locals say this magnificent mountain and its slopes are home to many spirits. As well has having spiritual connections, the mountain is of historical note: it was on these slopes that President Manuel Quezon hid from invading Japanese forces during World War II.

The park has 40km of trails so day treks are possible in the foothills, although even for these you'll need permits (P300) and a guide. You can get both at one of two locations in the park area: the village hall in **Guintubdan** on the western edge of Kanlaon or in the information centre at *Guintubdan Nature Camp* a country holiday resort seven-kilometres east of Guintubdan itself in the barangay of *Ara-al*. The best way to get here is by jeepney in three stages: from Bacolod to Murcia, from Murcia to La Carlota, then eastwards to either *Guintubdan* or *Guintubdan Nature Camp*.

From *Guintubdan* or *Guintubdan Nature Camp* there are dozens of challenging day treks that take you through jungled foothills, past hot springs and deep waterfalls. There are also several routes up the volcano, most involving three tough days of walking and two nights of camping.

Guintubdan Nature Camp (**①**) is an ideal place to rest up before and after trekking. It's set in manicured grounds surrounded by verdant jungle and water-falls. There are simple twin and triple rooms with shared cold showers, or you could camp if you've got a tent – there are none for rent.

If you access Kanlaon by a route other than the two mentioned above, you must first register and buy a permit at the Department of Environment and Natural Resources in Bacolod (see p.291).

△ Foothills of Mount Kanloan

The north and northeast coast

North of Silay along the rugged coast, the first significant settlement is **VICTORIAS**, where the **Victorias Milling Company**, the largest integrated mill and sugar refinery in Asia, is open to the public (daily 9am–4pm; P25). The mill, a ten-minute tricycle ride east from Victorias plaza, has some fine examples of the old locomotives that were used for hauling sugar cane from the fields, including American Baldwins and German Henschells. Inside the mill compound stands one of the country's religious curiosities, the **Church of St Joseph the Worker**, built between 1948 and 1950. The church is home to a controversial modern mural called **The Angry Christ**, which depicts a square-jawed Jesus sitting in front of the hands of God, straddling a serpent-spewing skull. Other murals depict Mary and Joseph as Filipinos in native attire, the first such representation in liturgical art. There's a small public relations office (Mon–Fri 8am–5pm) just inside the mill gates where you can ask if any staff are available to show you around. It's an informal arrangement so there's no guarantee you'll even get in, but if you do the usual price of a tour is P15 per person.

Cadiz

A rough-and-ready port and fishing town 30km east of Victorias and 50km north of San Carlos, **CADIZ** is where much of Negros's sugar is stacked on cargo boats for shipment to Manila and beyond. For tourists it's little more than a possible exit point for Roxas on Panay (see p.321) and for Bantayan (see p.268). Cadiz's uninspiring **hotel** options include the *Cadiz Hotel* (❸) on the city plaza, with air-conditioned rooms and a tennis court; *RL Apartelle* (❶) near the Ceres bus depot on the main road; and – opposite – the *EC Pension Plaza* (❶).

Sagay

SAGAY is a hectic industrial and fishing city 15km east along the coast from Cadiz, at the mouth of the Bulanon River. The city is the jumping-off point for one of the Philippines' least-visited natural wonders, the beautiful **Sagay Marine Reserve**. This scenic little huddle of islets and atolls about 5km off the coast was declared a reserve in 1980 when Sagay's enlightened city mayor finally decided he'd had enough of the destruction caused by illegal fishing methods. He enlisted the help of the Silliman University Marine Laboratory in Dumaguete and established a sanctuary around Carbin Reef, one of the area's two major reef systems. The sanctuary, which you can visit for a day (free admission) on a half-hour banca ride from Sagay wharf, was later expanded to include a number of smaller reefs and the nearby Molocaboc Islands. There are some marvellous beaches, slender strips of sugary sand surrounded by gin-clear water, and the reefs are a picture of health; with a mask and snorkel you can see giant clams, pufferfish, immense brain corals and the occasional inquisitive batfish.

There's one other thing to do in Sagay: head for the city plaza and take a look at the **Legendary Siete**, or Train Number Seven, an iron dinosaur that once hauled lumber for the Insular Lumber Company and now stands in the middle of the plaza, restored and sparkling in all her 75-tonne liveried glory.

San Carlos

SAN CARLOS on the northeast coast is the closest major urban centre to the Negros Occidental/Oriental border, from where the road continues south to Dumaguete, about three hours away, via Bais (more commonly visited from

Dumaguete; see p.303), where there are opportunities for whale- and dolphin-spotting. Regular ferries run every day from San Carlos to Toledo (see p.267) on the west coast of Cebu.

Short on charm and tourist attractions, San Carlos does nevertheless have a **tourist office** (Mon–Fri 8am–4pm; ☎034/312 5112) in the municipal building on the city plaza. Here you can ask about ferry schedules and trips to **Sipaway Island** (also known as Refugio Island), 3.5km offshore, where there's a white sand beach, clear water and a couple of government-owned swimming pools.

Dumaguete

DUMAGUETE ("dum-a-get-eh"), known in the Philippines as the City of Gentle People, is capital of Negros Oriental and lies on the southeast coast of Negros, within sight of the southerly tip of Cebu Island. The city is becoming more of a mainstream tourist destination these days and it's easy to understand why: it has exquisite architecture, a laid-back university town ambience, and a lovely concrete path along the **seafront promenade** shaded by acacia trees and coconut palms,. The seafront is lined with cafes, restaurants, bars and hotels, and is especially lively at dusk with the after-work crowd and then again towards midnight, when the serious nightlife begins. Dumaguete is also close to some of the country's best scuba diving and has opportunities for whale- and dolphin-watching, while the coast to the south boasts good beaches and some restful little native resorts.

Arrival and information

The small **airport** is a few kilometres north of the city centre on the far bank of the Bona River. Tricycles make the trip to the city for about P50; there are also jeepneys waiting for city-bound passengers outside the airport perimeter fence, or you can haggle with one of the private car drivers who greet incoming flights. Air Philippines has two, sometimes three, daily flights to Dumaguete from Manila, as does Philippine Airlines. The **ferry pier** is near the northern end of Rizal Boulevard, within easy walking distance of the centre. WG&A sails to Manila, Tagbilaran and Cagayan de Oro; Negros Navigation serves Manila and Tagbilaran; and Supercat has two daily sailings to Cebu City via Tagbilaran and one to Larena on Siquijor. There are ticket offices for all three of these operators close to the pier on Flores Avenue. From Siquijor local **bancas** arrive several times a week at Silliman Beach, 1km north of Dumaguete along Flores Avenue and easy to reach by tricycle or jeepney.

Ceres Liner **buses** arrive and depart at the Ceres terminal in Governor Perdices Street, on the southern side of the Banica River. A jeepney into the city costs P10, but if you haven't got much luggage you can walk it almost as fast. For bus departures to the north of the island, it's worth making sure you get on an express bus, shaving a few painful hours from journey times. There's a **tourist office** (Mon–Sat 8.30am–6pm; ☎035/225 0549) in the City Hall complex on Colon Street, near Quezon Park. There's also a provincial tourist office (☎035/225 1825) behind the provincial Capitol Building.

Accommodation

There's plenty of inexpensive accommodation in the city centre or within walking distance of it. If you haven't booked anything in advance, take a tricycle from the airport or pier to the junction of Hibbard Avenue and San Juan Street where there are half a dozen lodges and small hotels. Another option is to base yourself in Dauin (see p.303) and see Dumaguete on a day-trip – there are

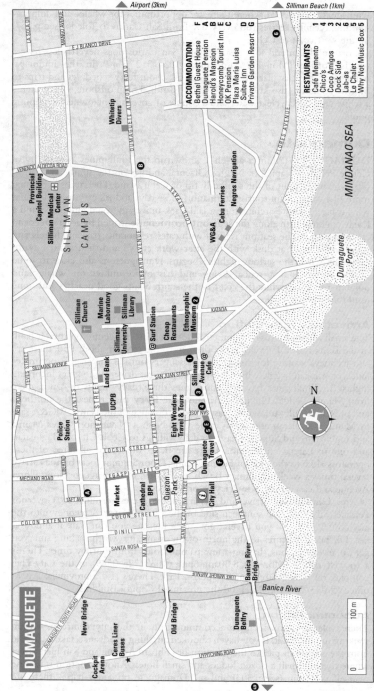

DUMAGUETE

▲ Airport (3km)   ▲ Silliman Beach (1km)

ACCOMMODATION
Bethel Guest House   F
Dumaguete Pension   A
Harold's Mansion   B
Honeycomb Tourist Inn   E
OK Pension   C
Plaza Maria Luisa   D
Suites Inn
Private Garden Resort   G

RESTAURANTS
Café Memento   1
Chico's   4
Coco Amigos   3
Dock Side   2
Lab-as   6
Le Chalet   5
Why Not Music Box   5

MINDANAO SEA

Dumaguete Port

N

0   100 m

plenty of jeepneys and buses going back and forth between the two most hours of the day and night.

Bethel Guest House Rizal Blvd ☎035/225 2009. In an excellent location on the seafront, this is a modern four-storey building with clean studio rooms and doubles, some with a sea view (for which you'll pay extra). Rooms at the front are big and bright, with picture windows. Efficient and friendly staff, and a reasonable restaurant. ❹

Dumaguete Pension Taft Ave ☎035/225 4631. Long-established, friendly place on the west side of the market, with small, ordinary rooms and a coffee shop. Fan doubles present a good budget option and you can pay a little extra for a private shower. ❶

Harold's Mansion 205 Hibbard Ave, a short walk north from Silliman University ☎035/225 8000. Functional, bright (pink) and friendly mid-range hotel with simple rooms. The lobby café does simple fare, coffee and milk shakes. ❸

Honeycomb Tourist Inn Rizal Blvd ☎035/225 1180. Though rooms are small, everything, including the bathrooms, is clean and tidy. On the seafront next to *Music Box,* the *Honeycomb* also has a bar and small café. ❸

OK Pension Santa Rosa St ☎035/225 5925. On the southern edge of town between Quezon Park and the river. There's a wide range of fan, a/c, deluxe and "super" rooms, few of which seem to have windows. Ask to see a selection before choosing a room. ❷

Plaza Maria Luisa Suites Inn Legaspi St ☎035 422 7382 or 422 7984, ⓦ www.fil. net/plazamar. Attractive little family-run hostel with hacienda-style architecture, bright, tiled interiors and twenty clean a/c rooms. There's a swimming pool on the roof and a little café called *Tico's* with views over the park opposite. ❹

Private Garden Resort National Highway, Dumaguete City ☎035 225 0658, ⓦ www.privategardenresort .com. Popular and laid-back resort on the main beach three kilometres south of the city. Rooms are plain, but clean and comfortable, with affordably priced fan-cooled economy and budget rooms, rising to more spacious a/c deluxe and superiors. The convivial restaurant is surrounded by plants and chock-full of bamboo furniture. There's scuba diving, motorbike rental and mountain bikes. ❶–❸

The City

Dumaguete isn't a city of major sights, just a pleasant place to relax for a day or two. Dominated by the respected **Silliman University**, the oldest Protestant university in the Philippines, the city has a casual campus feel that's lacking in many of the country's other bustling ports. Much of Silliman's reputation has been built on the work of its **marine laboratory**, which provides technical assistance throughout Negros for pollution monitoring, mangrove reforestation and maricul- ture, and spearheads efforts to end illegal fishing. Laboratory staff and students are happy to talk to visitors and give guided tours of the various projects and collec- tions, including one of whale bones, but you must make an appointment (☎035/422 8880). The university also has an **ethnographic museum** (Mon–Fri 9am–4pm; free) housing an extensive collection of artefacts and archeological finds, including Sung and Ming porcelain dating back 2000 years and relics from minority tribes in the Philippines. The museum is in the Assembly Hall, built in 1903 with leftover construction materials from a New York theatre (go through the university gate on Hibbard Avenue and past the fountain to the building).

A walk south along Rizal Boulevard and across the Banica River bridge brings you to the old Dumaguete Belfry **bell tower** on the seafront. The thick stone structure was built in 1811 for a neighbouring church (now gone) and was used to warn townsfolk against piratical raids; if you climb to the top there are marvellous views across the sea, especially at sunrise and sunset. From here it's a short walk past the Ceres Liner bus terminal to the **Dumaguete Cockpit Arena**, where fights are held regularly at weekends, usually on Sundays after church, and sometimes on weekday evenings.

Eating, drinking and nightlife

Dumaguete's premier expat hangout is *Why Not Music Box* on Rizal Boulevard, a good place to gather travel intelligence over a few drinks at the friendly bar. European and Asian fare are included on the menu and Internet access and air-conditioned transport to nearby beach resorts are also on offer. After 10.30pm Silliman students wander in and the place transmogrifies into a disco. *Music Box* also has a Swiss restaurant, *Le Chalet*, attached, serving specialities such as pig's knuckle and schnitzel. Nearby in Rizal Boulevard, *Chico's*, a fashionable little bistro and delicatessen, opens at 6am to serve breakfast and is still open at 2am doing cocktails and snacks. A short walk north, *Dock Side* is a grill bar that does lots of barbecue dishes and inexpensive San Miguels. If you continue north out of town on Flores Avenue, past the *Coastal Inn* and the ice plant, you'll reach a cluster of small bars and restaurants overlooking the promenade. At the *Lab-as* seafood restaurant here you can feast on on grilled squid and sour swordfish soup for a few hundred pesos a head. For really inexpensive fare, all you have to do is wander along Silliman Avenue between the university in the west and Rizal Boulevard in the east. At the junction of Silliman and Rizal is *Café Memento*, a pleasant place to sit over a coffee or shake and watch the world go by on the promenade. On Rizal Boulevard itself, *Coco Amigos* does delicious mango splits (P75).

Listings

Airlines Philippine Airlines is at the airport (☎035/419 6020) and at the *Honeycomb Tourist Inn* in Rizal Blvd (☎035/225 1181). Cebu Pacific has offices at the airport (☎035/225 8758 to 8760) and at Rama Services, 479 Governor Perdices St (☎035/225 6850), in the city centre. The Air Philippines office is at the airport.

Banks There are a number of banks with ATMs, including BPI on Governor Perdices St opposite Quezon Park and UCPB (United Coconut Planters Bank) and Landbank, both on the western edge of the city centre in Real St.

Car rental A good place to rent a car is R&R Rent-a-Van at 97 L. Rovira Rd in Bantayan (☎035/225 2285), a residential area north of town close to the airport. You can also inquire at any travel agent (see below).

Ferries Ticket offices for WG&A and Negros Navigation are conveniently located on Flores Ave near *Coastal Inn*, opposite the pier. There are two Aboitiz Supercat ticket outlets in Dumaguete, one at the pier (☎035/225 5811) and the other in Ma Cristina St (☎035/225 1540).

Hospitals The Silliman Medical Centre is in Venencio Aloecoa Rd opposite the university's athletics stadium; the Provincial Hospital is a little further north still, on Dumaguete North Rd.

Immigration The office for visa extensions is in the Lu Dega Building, 38 Dr V. Locsin St (☎035/225 4401).

Internet access As you'd expect of a university town, there's no shortage of places to check your email and surf. The cafés around the junction of Hibbard and Silliman avenues are a good bet; try *Surf Station Internet Café* on Katada corner Hibbard Ave or *Silliman Avenue Café* and *Scooby's* on Silliman Ave. The most "upmarket" Internet café in town is *Cyberbox Business Centre* at *Why Not Music Box* on Rizal Avenue, where you can enjoy an (alcoholic) drink or fresh fruit shake while online.

Post The post office on Santa Catalina St offers poste restante.

Police The main police station is at the west end of Locsin St near the Central Bank.

Travel agent There are a number of good travel agents on Rizal Blvd close to the *Honeycomb Tourist Inn:* Dumaguete Travel (☎035/225 6212), Eight Wonders Travel and Tours (☎035/225 5968), Paradise Travel (☎035/422 9820) and Why Not Travel (☎035/225 9028), Orientwind Travel and Tours is at LAB-AS Compound, E.J. Blanco St (☎035/255 3536). All these are authorized ticket agents for airlines and ferries.

Around Dumaguete

From Dumaguete you can arrange a trip inland to the **Twin Lakes** of Balinsasayao and Danao. The walk from the town of San José up to the lakes is demanding, but takes you through terrific jungle and some tribal settlements. For dolphin- and whale-watching head to **Bais**, while for affordable resort

Diving off southern Negros

The small, volcanic **Apo Island**, 7km off the south coast of Negros, has become a prime destination for divers, most of whom head out for the day from Dumaguete or Dauin. Site of one of the Philippines' first and most successful marine reserves, Apo has a series of reefs teeming with marine life, from the smallest nudibranch to the largest deepwater fish. The sanctuary area is on the island's southeast coast, while much of the flat land to the north is occupied by the only village, home to four hundred fisherfolk and farmers. Non-divers needn't be bored; Apo has some fantastic snorkelling and it's a great little island to explore on foot.

Most tourists visiting Apo take an organized trip from Dumaguete or Bais, though you can travel independently on one of the regular bancas from Silliman Beach in Dumaguete and from Malatapay (see p.299). The trip takes about 45 minutes and the usual fare is P50. There are only two simple places to **stay** on the island, neither with telephones, air-conditioning, TV or hot showers: *Kan-Upi Cove Beach Resort* (❶) has double cottages on the beach, and *Liberty's Resort* (❶) boasts singles, doubles and a diving school.

Among other dive sites, **Calong-Calong Point** off the southern tip of Negros is known not for big pelagics, but for its dazzling number of smaller reef fish. Nearby is **Tacot**, a tricky deep dive where sharks are common. From the coastal towns to the south of Dumaguete you can take a banca to Siquijor (see p.285), where sites such as **Sandugan Point** and **San Juan** go as deep as 65m, and where you can expect to see tuna, barracuda and sharks plus, from March to August, manta rays. You can arrange trips to these sites through the dive operators in Dauin (see below) or, in Dumaguete, at Whitetip Divers, just north of the Looc Bypass on Dumaguete Airport Road in the Bantayan suburb (☎035/225 2381 or 422 7770).

accommodation near Dumaguete the best place is **Dauin**, where you can also arrange scuba diving. **Malatapay Market** and **Tambobo Beach** make pleasant day-trips.

Bais and Twin Lakes

The town of **BAIS**, about 40km to the north of Dumaguete, is a good place to arrange day-trips to see dolphins and whales in Bais Bay as they migrate through the Tanon Strait separating Negros from Cebu; March to September is the most promising time of year. The best accommodation here is at *La Planta Hotel* in Mabini Street (☎035/752 0307; ❺), a quaint and cosy place in a white-washed old building that used to be the city's power plant.

A walk to the **Twin Lakes**, Balinsasayao and Danao, makes an excellent but strenuous day-trip; most hotels in Dumaguete and many of the resorts in Bais will help find a guide and arrange transport to the start of the trek. The lakes lie nestled in a jungled crater a fifteen-kilometre hike west from the main coastal road. The little town of **San José**, nearly midway between Dumaguete and Bais, is where you actually start heading inland for the lakes, taking you past a couple of waterfalls where you can swim and through settlements of the indigenous Bukidnon people who inhabit the area.

Dauin

South of Dumaguete is beach-resort country, with a good range of clean and affordable accommodation close to the sea, often with dive schools attached. **DAUIN** is a popular port of call twenty minutes' journey from Dumaguete. The unspoiled beach has a dramatic backdrop of palm trees and ruined watchtowers built in the nineteenth century as protection against raiding Moro pirates from the south. Buses and jeepneys leave Dumaguete for Dauin from either the Ceres terminal or the area around the market.

The *Atlantis Beach Resort* (☎035/424 0578, ⓦwww.atlantishotel.com; ❾) has air-conditioned singles and doubles with TV, mini-bar and private bathroom but no beach view, for which you'll have to pay for one of the slightly larger Seaview Suites. *Atlantis* is primarily a dive resort, though it offers non-divers a large pool, loungers on the sand and day-trips to Dumaguete, Bais (for dolphin- and whale-watching) and Apo Island. The *El Dorado Beach Resort* (☎035/425 2274, ⓦwww.eldoradobeachresort.com; ❹, dorm beds P150) is a charming rustic hideaway that's well geared up to cater for scuba trips to Apo and Siquijor. Besides a good range of accommodation, from dorms to family cottages with all mod cons, there's a swimming pool and a native-style restaurant with thatched roof. The menu includes soups, salads, pasta, steak, Asian specialities and vegetarian dishes.

Malatapay Market and Tambobo Beach

About fifteen minutes southwest of Dauin by road – twenty kilometres from Dumaguete – one of the most unusual markets in the Philippines is held every Wednesday in the seaside barrio of **MALATAPAY**. Buyers and sellers at Malatapay market, also known as Zamboanguita market, still use the traditional native barter system, with farmers from the surrounding villages and Bukidnon tribespeople from the interior meeting with fishermen and housewives to swap everything for anything – livestock, fish, exotic fruit, strange vegetables and household items. Most of the resorts in Dauin arrange trips to the market, but you'll have to be up bright and early: the bartering begins at first light and is usually over well before noon.

If you want to make a day of it, combine a trip to the market with a visit to **Tambobo Beach**, a little further along the coast near **Siaton**. Tambobo is a beautiful palm-fringed crescent of glistening sand, a great place to spend a lazy afternoon swimming and snorkelling. Again, you can organize trips at most of the resorts, or you can hop on any jeepney from Dumaguete or Dauin going south along the coast. Ask to get off at Siaton, where you can either walk or take a tricycle to the beach itself.

If you're looking for somewhere friendly and quiet to stay in the Malatapay area, look no further than *Hans & Nenita's Malatapay Beach Resort* (❷), a small place with four charming duplex cottages right on the delightfully unspoiled Malatapay Beach, with views to Apo Island in the distance and in-your-face sunsets. The fresh food in the bamboo restaurant is excellent and the owners will arrange trips not only to the market but also to nearby hot springs, water-falls and reefs.

Sipalay and around

About 100km northwest of Siaton, **SIPALAY** is a surprisingly big town for such a rural location, surrounded by a scattering of islands and, on the mainland itself, some wild and wonderful beaches, especially to the north of the city, with some good native-style **accommodation**.

Sipalay's historical focal point is the plaza and the church, but these days most activity centres around its pier and the main road, where there are numerous canteens, bakeries and a couple of convenience stores. The mayor's office in the plaza has a municipal **tourist office** where you can enquire about transport and accommodation. **Buses** stop at the Ceres terminal on the National Highway, a short walk north of the pier. The best **dining** in town – such as it is – is at the *carinderias* around the pier.

Around Sipalay

Campomanes Bay, also known as Maricalum Bay, is a natural harbour that's said to be deep enough to hide a submarine. Shaped like a horseshoe and 2km wide, it's backed by steep cliffs and accessible by tricycle from Sipalay and then on foot. It's a fantastic day-trip with some good snorkelling and scuba diving (the latter can be arranged through Artistic Diving in nearby Punta Ballo or by resorts in Dauin – see p.304), though there's no accommodation here.

There are also two excellent beaches in the area. The long and lovely **Sugar Beach**, reachable from Sipalay by tricycle, has a backdrop of coconut groves and mountains and faces due west, with wonderful sunsets. *Sulu Sunset Beach Resort* here (T0919/716 7182, W www.sulusunset.com; ❷) only has eight simple fan-cooled thatched cottages, but what a location: you step from the little wooden veranda right onto a crescent of almost deserted white sand that slopes gently into the sea. The busiest Sugar Beach gets is when local children get out of school and gather there to play in the relative cool of the late afternoon. Another clean, quiet and beautiful beach is **Punta Ballo**, fifteen minutes from Sipalay by tricycle. You can stay here at the *Artistic Diving Beach Resort* (T0918/930 5703, W www.artisticdiving.com; ❶), which has beachfront accommodation in fan or air-conditioned rooms and can arrange scuba diving and banca rides. To get to Punta Ballo from Sipalay you can go pillion on a local motorbike for P100. Ask at the bus station or at *Pat's Restaurant* near the bus station.

Danjugan Island and Bulata

Lying 3km off the southwest coast of Negros and accessible through the small town of **Bulata** a little north of Sipalay, **Danjugan** (pronounced "Danhoogan") **Island** is a little gem. It's fringed completely by vibrant coral reefs and so well forested that it's home to such rarities as the white-bellied sea eagle and the barebacked fruit bat. The sea eagles nest every year in a tall tree that overlooks Typhoon Beach on the island's east coast, while many of the island's beaches are nesting grounds for green and hawksbill turtles. Danjugan isn't the only island to explore here: there are a number of small islets, including Manta Island and Manta Rock, and three offshore reefs that are home to about 270 species of fish. The best way to investigate the area is to charter a banca for the day in Bulata.

In 1995 the then newly formed Philippine Reef and Rainforest Foundation Incorporated (PRRFI), a non-governmental organization based in Bacolod, bought the island, since when they have been implementing a largely successful conservation policy designed to restore Danjugan's environment and improve the livelihoods of the local fishermen. Dozens of volunteers were brought to map the reefs and engage in community work to earn the trust of the fishermen. Already the project is starting to bear fruit, with the fishermen themselves declaring a number of sanctuaries where fishing is banned outright, and a buffer zone where only fishing with landlines is allowed.

There is no accommodation on Danjugan and it would be nice to think it will stay that way. There is, however, a great **place to stay** in Bulata, which can arrange day-trips to Danjugan: the *Punta Bulata White Beach Resort* (T034/433 5160, W www.puntabulata.com; ❺), on a lovely white sand beach to the west of the town centre, has a fantastic range of comfortable huts, family cabins for six, rooms and tents, all air-conditioned. There's also a pleasant bar and a hillside native-style restaurant with ocean views.

Ilog

The road north from Bulata, plied by Ceres Liner, Royal Express and Victorias Transit buses, winds gently along the coast through huge tracts of farmland given over to sugar and rice. Around 100km north of Bulata is **ILOG**, which in 1632 under the Spanish became the first capital of Negros. The only accommodation option in the area is up in the hills at *Balicaocao Highland Resort* (③), a 45-minute bus or jeepney ride south of the southeast of Ilog. The resort has a number of concrete huts in immense, manicured gardens, with a big swimming pool and pathways through the hills for walking and jogging. It's pleasantly cool up here, even in the height of summer, and on a clear night you can see across the Panay Gulf to Guimaras.

Guimaras

Between the islands of Panay and Negros is the small island province of **GUIMARAS**, known in the Philippines for the sweetness and juiciness of its mangoes. Separated from the Panay mainland by the narrowest slither of ocean, Guimaras is a gentle island of few hassles, where the people (about 110,000 of them, living mainly in five small towns) depend largely on agriculture for their livelihood and treat tourists with a mixture of kindness and curiosity. You get the feeling that while tourism has begun to get its claws into Guimaras, it still can't quite hold on. In the hinterlands and most of the barangays, life continues to revolve around the harvesting of citrus fruit, coconuts and rice. Other industries are equally rural, including fishing, charcoal production, basket making and mat weaving. The island holds yet more evidence of the country's polarizing range of languages and dialects; most inhabitants speak Hiligaynon, of the Austronesian language family, but residents of some areas around the towns of Jordan and Nueva Valencia speak a variant of this known as Kinaray-a.

After the spill

Guimaras was badly affected by an oil spill from a tanker, *Solar 1*, which sank off the northern coast of the island in August 2006. Clean-up operations were under way at the time of writing and resort owners were saying beaches were fine for swimming. But as is often the case in the Philippines, resources for the clean-up were proving hard to come by, with volunteers resorting to using their bare hands to move sludge. The Philippine Coast Guard estimated that more than 500,000 litres leaked from the sunken vessel, resulting in a slick that polluted beaches on the east coast of the island facing the Guimaras Strait. The slick also affected vast areas of seaweed farms and mangrove, and threatened the livelihoods of an estimated 6,000 families who depend on the sea for food. Greenpeace said the vessel was leaking an estimated one tonne of oil every ten days and called it "a ticking time bomb that continues to imperil human lives and ecosystems". Remaining bunker fuel still needed to be siphoned out of the tanker to avoid further spills, but that work was not expected to begin until early 2007. A government report in November 2006 concluded 46 percent of the province's population of 150,000 was directly affected by the spill, especially residents of coastline villages engaged in fishing, banca operations, salt-making and agriculture. It said more than half, or 52 of the 98 barangays in the province, were directly affected by the oil spill. The worse-hit area was the west coast around Nueva Valencia. Owners of resorts on the east coast say they were not affected.

△ Villager harvesting coconuts in Guimaras

For all its provincial simplicity – perhaps because of it – Guimaras is much more than a day-trip destination. There are some good, affordable **resorts**, exceptional **beaches** – especially around **Nueva Valencia** on the southwest coast – and dozens of enticing **islands**, including **Taklong Island** in the south, which has been designated a marine reserve. Sadly, this whole area was affected by the 2006 oil spill (see box opposite) although authorities say it is now fine again for swimming. The undulating **interior** and its numerous trails have also made the island a popular destination for mountain bikers. There's even a smattering of history, with defiant old Spanish churches and the country's only Trappist monastery. During the Filipino-American War, the US Army maintained a military reservation, known as Camp Jossman, in **Buenavista**, as headquarters of the American forces in Panay. During this period, General Douglas MacArthur, then a first lieutenant, built the wharf at Buenavista, which is still being used today by ferries.

△ Farmer and water buffalo, Guimaras

Practicalities

Finding bancas **from Iloilo City** on Panay to the west-coast towns of **Jordan** (where they arrive just outside town at Hoskyn Port) or the pier near **Buenavista** is never a problem. Some resorts can send a banca to collect you at Iloilo, which usually adds about P1000 to your accommodation bill. **From Valladolid** south of Bacolod on Negros, there's a daily ferry to **Cabalagnan** on Guimaras's south coast.

Local **transport** comprises the usual three suspects: tricycle, jeepney and banca. If you want to charter a banca for the day to take you along the coast or hopping around some of the offshore islands, P500 is the usual price. For **tourist information**, there's an office at Hoskyn Port (daily 8am–4pm; ℡053/503 0328). The Philippine National Police station is in the barangay of Alaguisoc in Jordan. Medical care is better than you might expect, with a provincial hospital in San Miguel, Jordan, and others at Buenavista and Nueva Valencia. Making a telephone call from Guimaras is usually more effort than it's worth. If your resort doesn't have a phone, you could try the public phone office in the island's small capital, **San Miguel**.

Accommodation

Guimaras is a small enough island that it doesn't really matter where you base yourself. You can make day-trips around the island by public transport or, if available, a vehicle rented from your resort. Even if you choose the solitude of a resort on one of the smaller islands nearby, it's easy to hop on a banca back to Guimaras itself if you want to explore.

Baras Beach Resort On a sheltered inlet on the island's west coast ℡0917/241 1422, ⊛baras .willig-web.com. A pretty little hideaway with double cottages on stilts. Equipped with fan, they overlook the bay and are just a few steps away from the white sand beach. The food, almost all of it grown or caught by the staff, is good; there's not much of an à la carte menu, but there are ample buffet lunches and dinners for around P200, and a shot of local rum is P20. Provisions have to be brought in by boat, and staff say they need to know in advance if you intend to have plenty of alcohol.

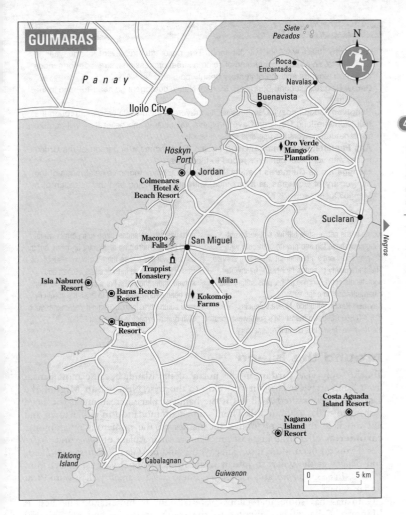

To get there either call ahead to arrange a pickup or take a banca (about P200) from Puyo wharf in Nueva Valencia. ④

Costa Aguada Island Resort Around 20min off the east coast of Guimaras by boat, on the island of Inampulugan ☏02/890 5333, ⓦwww.costa.com .ph. Swish complex with spacious duplex as well as detached bamboo cottages, each with bathroom, telephone and balcony, plus a swimming pool, a beachside bamboo restaurant, a poolside bar, riding stables and tennis courts. ⑧

Isla Naburot Resort On an island called Naburot off the west coast of Guimaras ☏034/321 1650. Beautiful and romantic, *Isla Naburot* has eleven

private cottages that were built partly from flotsam and jetsam, with driftwood for window frames and shells for walls. There's no electricity and no entertainment; after dark you'll have to read by paraffin lamp and eat by candlelight. All the food is caught or grown locally and prepared over primitive charcoal stoves. Activities include fishing, swimming, island-hopping, snorkelling, and scuba diving. ⑧

Nagarao Island Resort Nagarao Island off the southeast coast of Guimaras ☏0920/324 9086, ⓦwww.nagarao.com. Accessible only by banca, so either call ahead for pick-up (P2300 per boat) or charter your own in Iloilo or Jordan. All sixteen

Guimaras fiestas

Kinaradtu (third weekend of January). The major cultural event of the year in Buenavista, an eclectic confection of solemn street processions, street performances based on legends and the obligatory beauty pageant.

Paraw Regatta (second Sunday of March). Native outriggers go head-to-head in the Iloilo Strait.

Pangalap (Good Friday). Devotees recite prayers in Latin while crawling through the half-kilometre-long Catilaran Cave in Nueva Valencia, in the belief they will acquire supernatural powers for use against evil spirits.

Ang Pagtaltal sa Guimaras (Good Friday). Re-enactment in Jordan of the Crucifixion, with volunteer penitents roped to the cross.

Manggahan sa Guimaras festival (May 22–24). Commemorative celebration of the anniversary of Guimaras as a province, with street dancing and the selection of a Mango Queen.

rooms in the native-style hillside or beachfront bungalows have fan and private bathroom with shower, and there's a restaurant with room service. There are plenty of sports facilities – freshwater pool, tennis court, jogging paths, plus sailing and other activities on offer. ❷

Raymen Resort Alubihod, Nueva Valencia. ☎0920/336 9296. On the island's southwest coast, the *Raymen Resort* has clean if rudimentary

cottages with verandas, close to a perfect white sand beach. There's no restaurant or menu, but the owners will make sure there's always a supply of fresh fish, prepared in their small kitchen and served under the stars. For a simple few days on the beach, *Raymen* is hard to beat. It's 40min by road south from Jordan, 30min if you charter your own banca (expect to pay about P300). ❶

Around the island

Tourists only visit **Jordan**, in the north of the island, because most bancas from Iloilo arrive at Hoskyn Port 2km to the west. Nearby **San Miguel**, the capital, is rarely visited at all but is the handiest place hereabouts if you need cash or to make a phone call. There's no accommodation in either town and not much in the way of food – the names on the numerous no-nonsense **carinderias** offer little hope of much more than a plate of *adobo* and rice – but if you do need some sustenance, you could try *Gladys' Refreshment House* and *Sailor's*, at the wharf in Jordan while in San Miguel you can select from *Victor's*, *Edna's*, *Vangie's* and *Gonzaga's*. There's also a small police outpost at Jordan wharf.

Guimaras has some marvellous waterfalls in its hinterland. The best is **Macopo Falls**, fifteen minutes to the south of Jordan and ten minutes northwest of San Miguel by tricycle, where you can pay P5 to swim in a beautifully chilly mountain pool formed by water gushing through a rocky gorge from high above. For some really off-the-beaten-track accommodation try the little native **huts** here (❶). At night all you'll hear is the sound of water, geckos and some very sonorous frogs. There's nowhere to buy food or drink, so bring your own if you think you'll end up staying the night, plus a small consideration for the caretaker who'll help you cook it over a real log fire. The huts have no showers, but with the waterfall nearby you don't need any.

Another place well worth a visit is **Our Lady of the Philippines Trappist Monastery**, which lies on the main road southwest from San Miguel and twenty minutes by jeepney from Macopo Falls; you can do the falls and the monastery in a day. Founded in 1972 by Americans, it's the only Trappist monastery in the Philippines. The monks seem to do very nicely, with orchards that grow assorted tropical fruit and an interesting souvenir shop where cashews, peanuts and mangoes are sold under the Trappist Monastic Products brand name. A jar of mango jam costs P45 while a one-litre bottle of mango juice is P50.

Another good day trip is exploring the **beautiful islands** and islets in the south of Guimaras; all you need to do is rent a banca. Off the southeast coast there's Sereray island and Nao-wai island, both with tiny sandy coves where you can picnic and swim. Off the southwest coast is Taklong Island, a marine reserve whose mangroves and beds of sea grass are breeding grounds for hundreds of marine species. However, Taklong was badly affected by the oil spill (see box p.306).

Navalas and the north

The barangay of **NAVALAS** on the island's northern coast has two interesting sights, one religious, the other an imperious temple to Mammon. The seventeenth-century **Navalas Church**, an atmospherically decrepit relic of the Spanish regime, is a good starting point for exploring this coast. A short walk away on a promontory overlooking Iloilo Strait stands a villa known as **Roca Encantada** (Enchanted Rock) or, more sneeringly, Lopezville, vacation house of the wealthy Lopez clan who hail from Iloilo. Opposite the Lopezville promontory is a picturesque group of coral islets called **Siete Pecados** (Isles of the Seven Sins) that can be reached in thirty minutes from Navalas or the neighbouring north coast barangays of Bacjao and San Miguel (not to be confused with the island's capital). The largest of the islets has an impressive house perched on top, but the others are bare. There are no beaches but it's worth the trip for the snorkelling.

The mango plantations

You could hardly leave Guimaras without a visit to one of the **mango plantations**. All have just the right elevation and exposure to the elements to ensure the timely maturation of the tree blossoms into succulent fruit. Guimaras's soil also has a balanced combination of sand, clay and loam, making it ideal for planting; one island anecdote says all you need do is scatter seeds on Guimaras ground and they will grow. But probably the most important factor is the island's micro-climate: unlike its neighbours, Guimaras has consistent tropical weather with equal wet and dry seasons that come and go like clockwork.

The most visitor-friendly plantation on the island is **Kokomojo Farms** near **Millan** (℡033/337 7620 or 02/759 2302, ⑩www.kokomojomangos. com), roughly in the centre of Guimaras, where the owners will show you around personally if you call ahead. If your interest in mangoes runs deep, you can also visit the **National Mango Research and Development Centre** (℡033/237 0912) just west of San Miguel on the road to Lawi. Staff will show you around and there's information on mango varieties, research and mango cultivation.

Panay

The substantial, vaguely triangular island of **Panay** has been largely bypassed by tourism, perhaps because everyone seems to get sucked towards **Boracay** off its northern tip instead. There's room enough on Panay, though, for plenty of discovery and adventure: the island has a huge coastline and a mountainous, jungled interior that has yet to be fully mapped.

Among the Visayan people, a pious Spanish friar wrote in the sixteenth century, "it is not quite proper to drink alone or to appear drunk in public". Drinking in those days was always done in small groups or in "gatherings where men as well as women sat on opposite sides of the room". The good friar would have been dismayed then if he had witnessed **Ati-Atihan** (ⓦwww.ati-atihan.net), a quasi-religious mardi gras held every January in **Kalibo**, where much of the fervour is fuelled by a liberating mix of locally brewed grog.

The culmination of the two-week event is a procession through the streets on the third Sunday of January, a sustained three-day, three-night frenzy of carousing and dancing, often with strangers. The locals have an unwritten rule that there are no wallflowers at Ati-Atihan and no choreographed steps that isolate participants from spectators. If the best you can muster is a drunken conga line, that's fine. Transvestites bring out their best frocks and schoolgirls with hats made of coconuts join aborigines, national heroes, priests and spacemen in a fancy-dress parade that makes your average costume party look like afternoon tea at the rectory in comparison. Throw in the unending beat of massed drums and the average Filipino's predisposition for a good party, and the result is a flamboyant alfresco rave that claims to be the biggest and most prolonged in the country. The Ati-Atihan mantra *Hala Bira, Puera Pasma* translates as "Keep on going, no tiring."

The festival's **origins** can be traced to 1210, when refugees from Borneo smeared their faces with soot in affectionate imitation of the Filipino natives. The Borneans, comprising ten ruling families and their followers, had fled north to escape the tyranny of an enemy and found themselves on Panay Island. Panay's Negrito natives, known as Atis, were quick to capitalize on the refugees' arrival, selling them land in exchange for a gold hat and a basin. In addition, the Ati chief's wife wanted an ankle-length necklace, for which the natives gave a bushel of live crabs, a long-tusked boar, and a full-antlered white deer. It wasn't the most lucrative real-estate deal ever concluded, but both parties were satisfied and held a feast that same night to celebrate. The Atis slaughtered livestock and the Borneans blackened their faces.

The Ati-Atihan's religious element is in honour of the **Santo Niño** (see p.258), the concept of which was introduced to Panay by opportunist Spanish friars, who spread the word among islanders that the baby Jesus had appeared to help drive off a pirate attack. It was a cynical move calculated to hasten the propagation of Catholicism throughout the Philippines, and it worked. It gave rise to the ritual of *patapak* in local churches, during which revellers can be seen with the image of the Holy Child on their shoulders shouting, "Viva el Senor Santo Niño!" (Long live the Holy Child).

The Ati-Atihan has become so popular that similar festivals have cropped up all over the Visayas. Elsewhere in Aklan province, Ati-Atihan is celebrated in the towns of Makato, Altavas and Ibajay, all of which claim to be the birthplace of the Ati-Atihan, as do countless other small towns throughout Panay. Antique province has its Binirayan and Handugan festivals, while Panay's capital, Iloilo, has a more lavish and choreographed version called **Dinagyang**. Bacolod on Negros too holds an annual Ati-Atihan, while every January Cebu City has the **Sinulog** (see box on p.260). Historians generally agree, however, that the Kalibo Ati-Atihan is the real thing.

Panay comprises four provinces, **Antique** ("ant-ee-kay") on the west coast, **Aklan** in the north, **Capiz** in the northeast and **Iloilo** ("ee-lo-ee-lo") running along the east coast to the capital of province, **Iloilo City** in the south. The province that interests most tourists is Aklan, whose capital **Kalibo** is the site of the big and brash **Ati-Atihan festival**, held in the second week of January (see box above). This doesn't mean you should give the rest of Panay the brushoff. The northeast coast from **Concepcion** to **Batad** offers access by banca to a number of unspoilt islands, the largest of which is **Sicogon**, eleven square kilometres fringed by white sandy beaches and home to monkeys, wild pigs and eagles. On the other side of Panay, Antique is a raw, bucolic province of pictur-esque beaches and scrubby mountains. This is the gentle, rural side of the island, with little in the way of tourist infrastructure but plenty of natural splendour.

Getting to Panay

There are four major **airports** on Panay, all served by daily flights from Manila. Panay's main airport is in Iloilo on the south coast. On the north coast there are airports at Roxas, Kalibo and Caticlan, the latter two used mainly by visitors on their way to Boracay. Philippine Airlines and Cebu Pacific have a number of flights from Cebu to Iloilo, Roxas and Kalibo, while Air Philippines has a daily flight from Cebu to Iloilo. Seair and Asian Spirit both operate the Cebu–Caticlan route, an enjoyable 55-minute hop that takes you low along the north coast of Panay with terrific views on a clear day.

Passenger **ferries** operated by WG&A and Negros Navigation leave from Manila and Cebu to Iloilo and to Dumaguit, just outside Kalibo. Numerous smaller ferries sail from Manila, Cebu, Masbate, Bacolod and other Visayan ports to Caticlan and Culasi (the port at Roxas). Among connections from Romblon, there are bancas to Roxas from Santa Fe on Tablas Island and San Fernando on Sibuyan Island. You can also take a banca from Romblon to Carabao Island, north of Boracay, and from there to Boracay itself.

Iloilo City and around

ILOILO CITY is a useful transit point for Guimaras Island (see p.306) and has good ferry connections to many other Visayan islands, but there's nothing to keep you here for more than a day or two. The city's handful of sights include a couple of reasonably interesting heritage-style museums. If you're visiting in January, the **Dinagyang** festival, loosely based on Kalibo's Ati-Atihan, adds some extra frenzy to the city during the fourth weekend. Three kilometres out of town, the old areas of **Molo** and **Jaro** both make pleasant half-day trips. The former has a church made of coral and in the latter an impressive Spanish-era cathedral. In Jaro you can also wander among the old colonial homes of sugar barons and mooch through a number of dusty old antique shops, where prices are lower than in Manila.

There are at least two churches in the vicinity of the city, besides the ones in Molo and Jaro, that you shouldn't miss: **Miag-ao Church** (see p.319) and **Santa Barbara Church**. The latter, 16km to the north of town in Santa Barbara, is a Neoclassical red-brick and coral church where General Delgado convened the junta that raised the first cry of revolution against Spain. The neighbouring convent, built around a small rectangular garden, has a gallery that's reminiscent of medieval England and thick brick columns that are vaguely Roman in style. To get to Santa Barbara, take any bus or jeepney from Iloilo heading inland through **Pavia**; the trip takes about forty minutes.

Arrival and orientation

Iloilo's Mandurriao **airport** is about 7km northwest of the city. A taxi from the airport to the city centre costs about P120. A cheaper option is to take one of the jeepneys marked Iloilo–Mandurriao that run between the city and the airport. The **wharf area** used by ferries is on the eastern edge of the city, a fifteen-minute walk or short jeepney/tricycle ride from General Luna Street.

Ortiz wharf, used by ferries from Jordan on Guimaras, is at the southern end of Ortiz Street near the market. The **Ceres bus terminal** on Rizal Street in

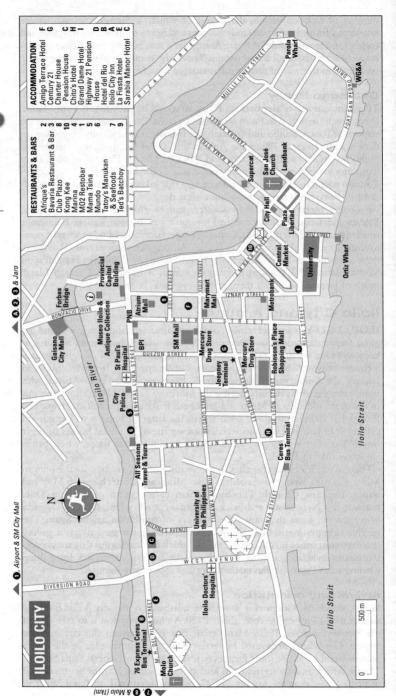

ILOILO CITY

RESTAURANTS & BARS

Afrique's	2
Bavaria Restaurant & Bar	3
Club Plazo	8
Kong Kee	10
Marina	4
MO2 Restobar	1
Mama Tsina	5
Mundo	6
Tatoy's Manukan	
& Seafoods	7
Ted's Batchoy	9

ACCOMMODATION

Amigo Terrace Hotel	F
Century 21	G
Charter House	C
Pension House	I
Chito's Hotel	H
Grand Dame Hotel	D
Highway 21 Pension	
House	B
Hotel del Rio	A
Iloilo City Inn	E
La Fiesta Hotel	C
Sarabia Manor Hotel	

Iloilo Strait

Iloilo River

0   500 m

N

① Airport & SM City Mall   **Ⓐ ② ③ & Jaro**

Ⓑ ⑦ & Molo (1km)

the south of the centre is the arrival point for buses from the north coast. Buses from points west of the city, including Antique and Libertad, arrive at the **76 Express Ceres terminal** on M.H. Del Pilar Street in Molo, close to the *Hotel del Rio*. From here it's a ten-minute tricycle ride into the centre.

Iloilo has little to distinguish it from any other urban area in the country, with most of its central streets a claustrophobic jungle of fast-food restaurants, malls and overhead telephone cables. The city centre occupies a thin strip of land on the southern bank of the Iloilo River, with views across to Guimaras. General Luna Street, running from west to east along the riverbank, is where you'll find most of the shops and banks.

Information and transport

The city's **tourist office** (Mon–Sat 9.30am–5.30pm; ℡033/337 5411 or 8874) is in the grounds of the Capitol Building on Bonifacio Drive one block north of J.M. Basa Street next to the Museo Iloilo. There are very few taxis in Iloilo, but you can cover much of the city centre on foot or take a tricycle or jeepney. There's a **jeepney terminal** on Ledesma Street where you can catch a ride to Molo, Jaro and along the coast in either direction.

Accommodation

Finding reasonably priced accommodation in Iloilo City isn't a problem, with much of it right in the city centre close to shops and transport.

Amigo Terrace Hotel Iznart St corner Delgado St ℡033/335 0908. Upmarket, marbled, a/c sanctuary in the heart of the city, with its own bistro, restaurant, disco and outdoor swimming pool. Standard doubles have all mod cons, including cable TV and refrigerator. ❺

Century 21 Quezon St ℡033/335 8821. Mid-sized glass-fronted building offering basic, affordable rooms with a/c and cable TV. Singles are among the cheapest in town for this sort of quality. Family rooms for four are good value at P1400. ❷

Charter House Pension House General Luna St ℡033/508 1853. Arguably the best budget option in town, the *Charter House* is in the same quiet complex as the *Serabia Manor Hotel*. Rooms are showing signs of age, but they're very big and as an added bonus you can use the hotel's swimming pool. ❸

Chito's Hotel 180 Jalandoni St corner de Leon St ℡033/337 6415. Very pleasant accommodation in a/c en-suite rooms with cable TV. The outdoor *Lobby Café*, surrounded by greenery and overlooking a small swimming pool, is a civilized place to eat. ❸

Grand Dame Hotel Rizal St ℡033/508 8881, ⓦwww.granddame.net. One of the city's more upmarket establishments and a good bet if you're looking for a night or two of real comfort. Rooms are spacious and have all mod cons. There's a relaxed lobby coffee shop and a decent restaurant. ❻

Highway 21 Pension House General Luna St ℡033/335 1839 or 1840. Excellent budget choice close to the *Serabia Manor Hotel* with recently refurbished rooms and staff who are on the ball. Good location with lots of restaurants on the doorstep. ❸

Hotel del Rio M.H. Del Pilar St, Molo ℡033/335 1171, ⓦwww.hoteldelrio.net. Comfortable modern hotel with views of the river from some rooms. Standard doubles have a/c, cable TV and hot water. ❹

Iloilo City Inn 113 Seminario St, Jaro ℡033/320 6290 or 329 0078, ⓦwww .nagarao.com. Large comfy a/c rooms and a pleasant restaurant, *Bavaria*, where you can get home-made German bread and wheat beer. Owned and operated by a German and his Filipina wife, who are both friendly, efficient and a good source of local knowledge. The roof deck has views of the nearby cathedral. ❷

La Fiesta Hotel M.H. Del Pilar St, Molo ℡033/338 0044. In a good location, 3km from the airport and less than 2km from the various piers, this newish hotel has spic-and-span a/c rooms, car rental and Internet access. ❺

Sarabia Manor Hotel General Luna St ℡033/336 0908, ⓦwww.smxhotel.com.ph. You can't miss it – the biggest and most upmarket hotel in this neck of the woods, with hundreds of comfortable rooms, a swimming pool, casino and a disco. ❽

The City

The old residential and commercial buildings that do exist in Iloilo City date back to Spanish and American colonial periods; they are mostly in J.M. Basa Street, which runs from Ledesma Street to the port area. In the southeastern quadrant of the city is **Plaza Libertad**, where the first flag of the Philippine Republic was raised in triumph after Spain surrendered Iloilo City on December 25, 1898. There's little to remind you of the history though – the square today is a concrete affair with fast-food restaurants and busy roads on all sides.

The only notable museum is the **Museo Iloilo and Antique Collection** on Bonifacio Drive (Mon–Sat 9am–5pm; P10). An engaging and clearly presented repository of Iloilo's cultural heritage, it has a diverse range of exhibits including fossils, shells and rocks indicating the age of Panay Island, ornamental teeth, jewellery excavated from pre-Spanish burial sites, pottery from China and Siam, coffins, war relics and some modern art.

Molo

On the western edge of the city, the district of **Molo** makes for an interesting wander; it can be reached on foot from the city centre in twenty minutes (half that by tricycle or jeepney). In the sixteenth and seventeenth centuries Molo was Iloilo's Parian, a Chinese quarter like that near Intramuros in Manila, where immigrants from the Middle Kingdom established their trades and began to integrate into Philippine life by marriage.

One of Molo's major historical landmarks is **Molo Church** (St Anne's), a splendid nineteenth-century Gothic Renaissance church made of coral, with rows of female saints lining both sides of the aisle. It's not hard to reach on foot from Iloilo's centre – head out along Tanza Street and you'll be there in twenty minutes. Next door is the renowned **Asilo de Molo**, an orphanage (visits possible daily 10am–noon & 1–4pm; donation expected) where vestments are made, hand-embroidered by orphan girls under the tutelage of nuns. The orphans also make hand-embroidered **barongs** (shirts) from **piña**, pineapple fibre. Molo holds its own **fiesta** on every July 26 in honour of its patron, Saint Anne.

Jaro

Another historical enclave worth exploring is **Jaro**, 3km north across the Forbes Bridge from the centre. You can get there on any jeepney marked Jaro or Tiko. Jaro's **plaza** is an inspiring little piece of old Asia, dominated by a dignified but crumbling old belfry that was partially destroyed by an earthquake in 1984. Opposite is the **Jaro Metropolitan Cathedral**, seat of the Catholic diocese in the Philippines, with its ivory-white stone facade, crooked bell tower of red brick and steps either side of the main doors leading up to a platform and the Shrine to the Divine Infant and Nuestra Señora de la Candelaria.

To the south of Jaro's plaza, Luna Street and Burgos Street are the site of a number of colonial houses that belonged to sugar barons. The best of these homes is **Nelly Garden**, which stands back from Luna Street down a pictur-esque driveway lined with eucalyptus. This grandiose mansion, with murals on the walls and a U-shaped dining room with a fountain in the middle, can only be visited by arrangement with the Iloilo tourist office (P800 per person).

Jaro is a good place to browse **souvenir shops**, two of the best being Lourdes Dellota's on East Lopez Street (☏033/337 4095) off Luna Street, and Letecia Jesena's at 59 Commission Civil St (☏033/337 2681), one block south of Lourdes Dellota's. Both sell religious artefacts such as **santos**, and jewellery.

Eating and drinking

Iloilo City is one of the best places in the country to try seafood prepared the Filipino way. It's also known for a number of unique regional delicacies, including **pancit Molo soup**, a garlicky noodle soup containing pork dumplings, which is named after the Molo area of the city and is sold at numerous street stalls. **Batchoy**, an artery-hardening combination of liver, pork and beef with thin noodles, is also widely available. Goold old San Miguel beer is the drink of choice in most of the city's bars and restaurants, although a number of more fashionable bistro-style places are springing up where you'll find cocktails and a modest wine list.

Afrique's Right behind the cathedral in Jaro. Atmospheric European restaurant in a lovely old colonial house. Patios and open spaces have been converted into charming dining areas so you can either eat outside or inside in a/c comfort. The menu is largely Italian with specialities such as pasta with chorizo and saffron.

Bavaria Restaurant & Bar 113 Seminario St, Jaro. Reliable European food at the *Nagarao City Inn*, including pork knuckle, schnitzel and roast chicken for P120.

Club Plazo M.H. del Pilar St, Molo. Hugely popular club for Iloilo's young night crowd. There's some sort of themed party here every night of the week, with guest DJs from around the Philippines, fashion shows and various drinks promotions.

Kong Kee J.M. Basa St. Venerable institution in the heart of the city. The interior is faded, but

people don't come here for the décor. The food is simple but delicious Chinese fare including dim sum and crispy fried chicken.

Marina Diversion Road, north of the river. The menu here includes lobster, *lapu-lapu*, all sorts of grilled meat and fish, and some non-Visayan Filipino specials such as *kare-kare* (oxtail) and Bicol Express. Two can eat and have a few drinks for around P500, with live music thrown in on Friday and Saturday nights.

MO2 Restobar Out towards the airport in Benigno Aquino Drive, Mandurriao. This new nightlife area has a number of good restaurants including *MO2 Restobar*, a lively native place that does excellent seafood; try the vinegary *kinilaw*, which is made with blue marlin or swordfish.

Mama Tsina General Luna St. This Iloilo fast-food chain, established by a woman who used to sell

Moving on from Iloilo City

Buses connect Iloilo City to other towns on Panay. The Ceres Liner (☎033/321 2491) bus terminal in Rizal Street is the departure point for the long journey to Caticlan (for Boracay), Kalibo, Roxas and Estancia (P130). The usual route (and the quickest) for the Iloilo–Caticlan bus trip is inland on the main road that runs through Passi and Dap before hitting the north coast at Kalibo. Ceres also runs three early morning trips (3am, 4am, 5am) to Manila, with the bus boarding a ferry at two points en route. The trip takes about 17 hours and fares are from P1,050. From the 76 Express Ceres terminal, buses run clockwise along the coastal road to San José, capital of Antique, and on to Libertad in the north.

Iloilo is a busy port with good **ferry** connections. From their dock on Fort San Pedro Road, WG&A Superferry operates sailings to Manila, Cagayan de Oro, Davao, General Santos City, Iligan and Ozamis, while Negros Navigation connects Iloilo with Manila, Bacolod, Cagayan de Oro, Zamboanga, General Santos, Ozamis and Iligan. From the river near the post office there are daily Supercat fast ferries to Bacolod on Negros. For **Guimaras**, there are big public bancas leaving Ortiz wharf every thirty minutes for the short crossing to Jordan, starting at 5am, and regular bancas to Buenavista throughout the day from Parola wharf off Muelle Loney Street. Fel-Am Transport Ferry Service is the major operator of larger ferries to Guimaras. Their M/V *Filipe,* for example, leaves Ortiz wharf daily at 9am and 2pm for Hoskyn Port near Jordan. At both of the wharfs you can try haggling for your own boat to take you anywhere on Guimaras; expect to pay at least P300. Finally, there are **flights** to Cebu City, Davao and Manila. For details of airline and ferry company offices, see p.38.

snacks from a street stall, serves standard Chinese dishes and is cheap and popular. No frills décor with lots of plastic.

Mundo General Luna St. One of a new generation of urbane bistro-style restaurants and bars that have sprung up in Iloilo. *Mundo* caters very much to a young crowd, but specializes in very traditional, no-nonsense Ilonggo fare with European classics such as pasta and wood-baked pizza thrown in. The native appetizers such as spicy chorizo, sardines and anchovies are delicious with

a glass or two of San Miguel.

Tatoy's Manukan & Seafoods Villa Beach in Arevalo, ten minutes west of the city by taxi, beyond Molo. This is a favourite with locals for fresh oysters and other seafood, and should be your first stop if you are looking for something with an authentic Visayan flavour.

Ted's Batchoy Solis Street, near the river. Try this down-to-earth canteen-style restaurant for an authentic helping of *batchoy*.

Listings

Airlines Air Philippines (℡033/320 8048), Cebu Pacific (℡033/320 6889) and Philippine Airlines (℡033/320 3030 or 3131) all have small ticket offices at the airport. Air tickets can also be obtained at any of the eight Aboitiz outlets in the city, including one at SM City on Iloilo Diversion Rd and at Marymart mall at the junction of Delgado and Valeria streets.

Banks There are a number of banks with ATMs. PNB and BPI both have branches on General Luna St near the junction with Iznart St. Equitable PCI has three branches: Iznart St, Ledesma St and Quezon St.

Ferries The main WG&A office is on Fort San Pedro Dr (℡033/337 7151), and there are others at the Atrium in General Luna St and Gaisano mall in Luna St, just north of the river across Forbes Bridge. Negros Navigation is also at Fort San Pedro (℡033/336 2396), in the Atrium and Gaisano City mall, and in SM City, out near the airport. Supercat's ticket office is at their terminal on the river (℡033/336 1316).

Hospital St Paul's Hospital is at the eastern end of General Luna St (℡033/337 2741) close to the junction with Bonifacio Dr. Iloilo Doctors' Hospital is a 5min drive to the west of the city centre in Timawa Ave (℡033/337 7702).

Immigration The Bureau of Immigration is at the Old Customs House on Aduana St.

Internet access Malls are the best place to check your email and surf. Try the cybercafés in the Gaisano City mall, the Atrium mall on General Luna St or *Robinson's Place* on Quezon St. On the top floor of the humungous SM City mall, to the north of the city proper on Diversion Rd, are a number of computer shops and Internet cafés. There's also a smaller SM Mall in the city centre on Quezon St. Many hotels have small business centres with Internet access.

Pharmacies There are pharmacies in every mall. Outside SM mall in the centre is a large Mercury branch and there's another next to the Interface Computer Center in Ledesma St.

Post Iloilo's main post office is in Muelle Loney St, close to the junction with Guanco St, opposite the pier where boats leave for Jordan on Guimaras.

Police The main city police department is in General Luna St (℡033/337 5511).

Travel agents Gaisano City mall is a good place to look for travel agents and also for ticket outlets selling airline and ferry tickets. All Seasons Travel & Tours at Sarabia Manor Building, 101 General Luna St (℡033/335 1021), offers ticketing, city tours, adventure tours and vehicle rental.

The south coast

Heading southwest from Iloilo City along the coastal road – the only road – takes you through the towns of **Oton**, **Tigbauan**, **Guimbal**, **Miag-ao** and **San Joaquin**. At San Joaquin the road turns northwards and into the province of Antique. Much of this southwest coast is flat, sparse and undeveloped, with next to no accommodation for tourists. What does strike you is how completely it came under the influence of the friars. For students of the Spanish era this coast is one of the most atmospheric and revealing in the country, with some sort of relic at almost every turn. Every town has an old Spanish church, including the Baroque Tigbauan Church in Tigbauan (22km from Iloilo City) and Guimbal Roman Catholic Church in Guimbal (35km from Iloilo City), which stands close to a number of ruined seventeenth-century watchtowers erected by the Spanish to help guard against Moro raiders from the south. Pride of place, however, goes to **Miag-ao Church** (also known as the Church of Santo Tomas de Villanueva), built by the Augustinians between 1786 and 1797 as a fortress against Moro invasions. Declared a national landmark and a UNESCO World Heritage site, the church is built of a local yellow-orange sandstone in Baroque-Romanesque style, a unique example of Filipino rococo. All transport from Iloilo City bound for San Joaquin passes through Miag-ao (a 45min journey).

There are two options if you want to **stay** in the area. The *Shamrock Beach Resort* (℡0912/520 0501; ❶) in the barangay of **Nanga**, a few minutes west of Guimbal, has motel-style concrete rooms on the shore (though the beach isn't great) with a restaurant serving grilled chicken and seafood, and a small music bar that's open, and making a lot of noise, until 2am. At the eastern edge of Miag-ao, *Sea Breeze Beach Resort* (℡0912/769 0916; ❶) has cottages with fan or air-conditioning. Note that this coast isn't really made for swimming and the black sand beach at *Sea Breeze* is not especially picturesque.

The west coast

Most of the west coast of Panay, made up largely of the province of **Antique**, is untouched by tourism and has next to nothing in the way of infrastructure or accommodation. This is one of the poorest areas of the Philippines, with a solitary coastal road connecting a series of isolated villages and towns where the main source of livelihood is subsistence farming and fishing. It's an attractive coastline, untamed, unrefined and with a savage backdrop of jungled mountains which separate the province from the rest of Panay, and which are only just beginning to be explored and climbed. The residents of Antique have had barely any exposure to tourists and few have ventured far beyond their communities, which means questions about transport and geography are inevitably met with a smile and an equivocal reply. Antique represents the Visayas at its most untouched, with a number of long beaches, none of which offers anywhere to stay beyond the simplest shed. The journey along the province's coast, from **San José** in the south to **Libertad** in the north, takes you through some quintessential Southeast Asian countryside – green rice paddies, stands of banana trees and palms. It also provides an excellent opportunity to experience a simple provincial life that goes on today much as it has done for most of the last century, shielded from the rest of the Philippines by mountains on one side and sea on the other. In some areas you still meet *babaylans*, native priestesses who claim to divine the future, heal the sick and conjure spells of protection.

San José

SAN JOSÉ, sometimes known by its grander name of San José de Buenavista, is a busy little port town whose major claim to fame – apart from being capital of Antique – seems to be that its cathedral has the tallest bell tower in Panay. There are no tourist sights here, just a chaotic wharf, a cracked plaza and a main street, the National Highway, lined with pawnshops, canteens and rice dealers. The town's annual **Binirayan Festival**, held from April 30 to May 2, commemorates the landing in the middle of the thirteenth century of ten Malay chieftains who established the first Malayan settlement in the Philippines.

76 Express Ceres and Ceres Liner have **bus stations** in Isabel Street, 1km west of the centre. The **pier** is easy to find on the western edge of the town off the main road. The Negros Navigation ticket office is on Carretas Street, which leads east from the market; Asuncion Shipping Lines is on Libertad Street

opposite the pier, MBRS is on T. Fornier Street and Moreta Shipping Lines in CB Arcade, Preciado Street. There are ferries from here to Manila, Bacolod and occasionally Cebu, as well as to the Cuyo Islands in Palawan.

Accommodation in San José is limited and strictly functional. The *Susanna Guest House* in T. Fornier Street (❶) has small rooms with cold showers.

Tibiao

About halfway along Panay's west coast, the town of **TIBIAO** is at the head of the Tibiao River and in the shadow of Panay's highest peak, Mount Madjas-as (2090m). Tibiao is trying to sell itself as a base for white-water **rafting** and **trekking**; for information, call Tribal Adventures (☎02/821 6706), a small family-run firm that runs adventure tours to Tibiao from its base at *Sandcastles Resort* on White Beach in Boracay. Tribal Adventures has a small lodge called *Kayak Inn* in the foothills outside Tibiao from where you can join kayaking trips, climbing expeditions and outings to nearby waterfalls. North of here the coast road continues to Libertad and Caticlan (see p.326).

The east coast

Panay's **east coast** – from Iloilo City north to **Estancia**, a route served by Ceres Liner buses – is an undeveloped area of wilderness and sun-drenched barrios rarely seen by tourists. There are a number of reasons why travel along this coast is challenging. First, there's hardly anywhere to stay, and secondly, reliable information and services are hard to come by. There are some wonderfully pristine islands off the coast, many of them unfamiliar even to locals, and the potential for exploration is remarkable, but you'll need time on your hands, patience and a willingness to spend nights camped in the wilderness or on beaches.

Both of the fishing towns of **CONCEPCION** and **SAN DIONISIO** make good jumping-off points for the many islands and islets off the northeast coast of Panay, the biggest of which is **Pan de Azucar** (Sugar Loaf) **Island**, which can be reached in about 45 minutes. Few of the Iloilo–Estancia buses pass through Concepcion and Dionisio, but you can hop off in nearby **Sara** and take a jeepney or tricycle. Concepcion is probably the better base of the two because you can stay at the *SBS Iyang Beach Resort* (❶) on the seafront, where the owners can help you arrange a banca for island-hopping. Mount Manaphag on Pan de Azucar is a remarkable sight as you approach from the sea: it's not high (about 1000m) but its sides are steep, giving the impression of a blunted triangle. The mountain can be climbed from the friendly barangay of **Ponting** on the island's east coast, though it's a real wilderness trek, for experienced climbers only.

The unassuming seaside town of **ESTANCIA** offers more opportunities to explore beautiful islands off the coast, among them **Sicogon**, which has wide, sandy beaches, and **Gigantes** (Giant) where a rock formation does look undeniably like the inert profile of a man. In Estancia you can stay at *Terry & Em Lodge* (❶) on Cement Street, but there's no accommodation on any of the islands apart from homestays with friendly locals.

The north coast

The section of Panay's north coast from **Roxas** in the east to **Caticlan** in the west (transport gateway to Boracay; see p.326) is mostly industrial and has no notable beaches. Its biggest – in fact its only – attraction is the town of **Kalibo**, a rather drab place that every year transforms itself into the country's party capital by staging the **Ati-Atihan** festival.

Roxas

It's about 25km from Estancia to **ROXAS**, capital of Capiz province, which has a reputation among Filipinos as being a hotbed of witches and shamans. Roxas is a hot, hectic urban sprawl that probably won't form part of your Philippines itinerary unless you decide to use it as a gateway to Panay's unexplored northeast corner and the islands around Estancia.

The **airport**, ten minutes north of the city by jeepney or tricycle in Arnaldo Boulevard, is served from Manila by Philippine Airlines and Cebu Pacific. Philippine Airlines' ticket office is at the airport (☏036/621 0618), while Cebu Pacific has two offices, one at the airport (☏036/621 0663) and the other in Legaspi Ilawood Street (☏036/621 0307).

Ferries from Manila, including WG&A's *Our Lady of Lipa*, dock at the **Calusi pier**, a short distance to the west of the city. The main ticket office for WG&A is in Jugo Building, Rizal Street (☏036/621 5567), although there's also one at the pier and another at Hughes Street corner Arnolda Boulevard (☏036/621 0231). Other companies sailing here from Manila include Moreta Shipping Lines (at Calusi Pier; ☏036/621 0238) and Negros Navigation (their office is at the 1km marker, Roxas Ave; ☏036/621 1473 or 3822).

Jeepneys and buses for Kalibo and Estancia use the Alba terminus south of the Panay River, reachable by tricycle (P6). This is also a good place to pick up FX vans to Kalibo. The **Ceres Liner bus station** for buses to and from Iloilo via the interior is next to the Caltex petrol station on the National Highway.

The best **accommodation** in Roxas is the central *Roxas President's Inn* at the junction of Rizal Avenue and Lopez Jaena Street (☏036/621 0208; ❷). Rooms are spacious, en suite and well looked after, and the rate usually includes breakfast. *Halaran Plaza Hotel* in Rizal Street (☏036/621 0649; ❶), opposite the city hall, has a choice of comfortable fan and air-conditioned rooms, plus a popular ground-floor Chinese restaurant.

Kalibo

KALIBO, the capital of Aklan province, lies on the well-trodden path to Boracay and for most visitors is simply the place they get off the plane and onto the bus. It's an uninteresting town, full of tricycles and fast food outlets, but every second week of January it hosts what is probably the biggest street party in the country, the **Ati-Atihan** (see box on p.312), an exuberant festival that celebrates the original inhabitants of the area and the later arrival of Catholicism.

Arrival and information

Kalibo has sprawled beyond its original compact boundaries in recent years, but most of the essential places – banks, shops and accommodation – are within walking distance of one another. The major thoroughfare is **Roxas Avenue**, which runs into town from the **airport** in the southeast, with most streets leading off it to the southwest. The ten-minute tricycle ride into town from the airport, a distance of about six kilometres, costs around P100 for a "special ride".

The **Ceres bus terminal** used by Iloilo services is 1km south of the town centre on C. Laserna Street; Caticlan buses use a terminal on Roxas Avenue. **Ferries** arrive in **Dumaguit**, a fifteen-minute jeepney ride outside Kalibo.

WG&A has three ferries a week from Manila, Negros Navigation has twice weekly sailings from Manila and one departure a week (Wednesday) from Cebu City.

There are a number of **banks with ATMs**, including BPI and PNB, on Martyr's Street, which runs along the southern edge of the main green space,

Pastrana Park, close to Kalibo Cathedral. BPI also has a branch in Roxas Avenue, near Metrobank. The **post office** is in the Provincial Capitol Building in Mabini Street, off Roxas Avenue. There are many small **Internet cafés**, including *Webquest* on Roxas Avenue, although the best place to surf is at one of the many clean, comfortable outlets on Level-2 of Gaisano mall, at the southern end of Roxas Avenue. For **telephone calls** there's a PLDT office in Burgos Street a short walk east of the market, but there are also many so-called call centres in Gaisano mall. The Kalibo provincial **hospital,** an immense, modern, rose-pink building, is on Mabini Street.

Accommodation

Good accommodation can be hard to find during the Ati-Atihan, when rates increase by up to a hundred percent, so if you're visiting during the festival, make sure you've booked a room (and, if you want to fly in, your plane ticket) in advance.

Apartelle Marietta Roxas Ave ☎036/262 3353. Friendly place offering rooms with fan, balcony and shower. ❶

Beachcomber Inn 467 N. Roldan St ☎036/262 4846. Well-furnished, airy, a/c rooms in a good location on the eastern edge of Kalibo, within walking distance of Gaisano mall and other shops. Staff are efficient and helpful, and can arrange plane and ferry tickets. There's a relaxed ground-floor restaurant where you can set yourself up for the day with a good Filipino breakfast (P110). ❺

Garcia Legaspi Mansion Roxas Ave ☎036/262 5588. Good mid-range option with comfortable, spacious a/c rooms, cable TV and lots of hot water.

The only disappointment is the "restaurant", which usually has only chicken or noodles. But there are plenty of other places to eat nearby. ❸

Gervy's Gourmet & Lodge One block to the east of *Glowmoon* in Pastrana St ☎036/262 4190. Quiet rooms with fan, but only a few with their own bathroom. ❶

Glowmoon Hotel & Restaurant S. Martelino St ☎036/262 2373. Close to Pastrana Park, with seven small fan rooms and seven slightly bigger a/c rooms. Only the latter have their own shower. There's also a reasonable restaurant with a range of Filipino and continental dishes. ❷

The Town

Kalibo is home to one of Panay's best museums, the **Museo It Akean** in San Martelino Street at the junction with Burgos Street (Tues–Sat 10am–5pm; P10). Though modest, it's the only museum to document the cultural heritage of the Aklañons (Aklan people), and contains exhibits of the area's old **piña** textiles, pottery, religious relics, literature and Spanish-era artefacts, many on loan from affluent local families. Among the most interesting exhibits are rare costumes that were worn by Aklan tribespeople during festivals. The ground floor is where you'll find the permanent displays, while the first floor is reserved for temporary exhibitions by local artists. In July 1980 a powerful earthquake destroyed the original museum and it wasn't until the end of 2002 that it opened again after years of fund-raising. The rehabilitated museum retains some of the original structure which, since its construction by the Spanish in 1882, has also been used as a school, a courtroom and a garrison.

Eating

There's no gourmet dining in Kalibo, so the choice is largely between fast food at malls such as Gaisano mall or tasty street food such as the roast chicken that's sold from mobile stalls every evening.

Peking House Restaurant, on Luis Barrios Street, is a popular place for inexpensive Chinese food – noodles, fish in black bean sauce and immense portions of fried rice. The *Wilhelm Tell Deli & Restaurant* on Roxas Avenue has European steaks and pastas from P120. It also has a good selection of German

Moving on from Kalibo

For **Caticlan** (the jumping-off point for Boracay; see p.326), buses (2hr 30min; P100), jeepneys (4hr) and FX vans leave hourly from the Roxas Avenue terminal. From the airport, a more convenient way to make the trip is to take one of the FX taxis or L300 vans which meet incoming flights (2hr; P150 for the trip to Caticlan wharf). Every flight landing at Kalibo is also met by drivers with private vehicles; you can usually find someone with a Toyota van to take you to Caticlan for around P1500, divided among as many as nine passengers. If you're arriving in Kalibo by ferry, you can get a bus or jeepney from Dumaguit to Caticlan. From the Ceres Liner bus terminal there are buses east to Roxas, south to Iloilo and along the west coast road south through Antique to San José. Gunding Lines in Roxas Avenue has hourly buses to Caticlan, but they're mostly old bangers without air-con and the trip can take four hours.

From Dumaguit, there are Negros Navigation **ferries** on Wednesday to Cebu City and twice a week to Manila, one going via Roxas on Mindoro. The Negros Navigation office is in C. Laserna Street (☎036/262 4943), south of the market. WG&A's M/V *Our Lady of Lipa* sails to Manila on Tuesday, Thursday and Sunday at 3.30pm; tickets can be obtained from the WG&A office in Archbishop Reyes Street at the junction with Acevedo Street (☎036/268 4391). Moreta Shipping (☎036/262 3003) at the northern end of Roxas Avenue, opposite Metrobank, has one boat a week to Manila. MBRS Lines, also on Roxas Avenue, near the junction with Ramos Street (☎036/268 6850), operates a boat to Cajidiocan on Sibuyan Island and on to Romblon Town. All these ferry operators also have ticket outlets at the pier in Dumaguit. For tickets there's also a convenient Aboitiz outlet right in the centre of Kalibo at the junction of Burgos Street and Luis Barrios Street.

There are several **flights** to Manila daily. Philippine Airlines (☎036/262 3260), Air Philippines (☎036/262 4444) and Cebu Pacific (☎036/262 5406) all have ticket offices at the airport; Cebu Pacific also has an office in Legaspi Street, behind Kalibo Cathedral and there's an Air Philippines office on Roxas Avenue.

sausages and the owner, who's also the chef, makes *rösti* and mashed potatoes fresh every day. *Kamay Kainin*, about halfway along Archbishop Reyes Street (which runs along the north side of Pastrana Park), is a charming little Filipino place with rice lanterns hanging from the ceiling. Portions are freshly cooked and generous; they include tangy *sinigang* and *kinlaw*. Beside *Kamay Kainin* is *Kurts*, a functional canteen-style restaurant that specializes in tasty, piping-hot *mami* noodle soup.

Boracay

BORACAY, off the northeastern tip of Panay about 350km south of Manila, is not the dozy tropical backwater it used to be. That's the bad news. The good news is that Boracay is still an exceptional destination. It may be only 7km long and 1km wide at its narrowest point, but it's a big tropical island in a small package, with thirty beaches and coves, and sunsets that are worth the journey on their own. The most famous of the beaches is **White Beach** on the island's western shore, 4km of the kind of powder-white sand that you thought only existed in Martini advertisements. The word Boracay is said to have come from the local word *borac*, meaning cotton, a reference to the sand's colour and texture.

One of the most popular activities in Boracay is simply doing nothing. Another is sitting on the beach at dusk watching the sun drift towards the horizon, or having an outdoor massage from one of the roaming beach masseuses. You can also go horse riding, rent mountain bikes, motorcycles or kayaks, or scuba dive with one of the many dive operators. There are 24 official **dive sites** around the island (see box on p.331), and because of the calm waters near the shore outside the rainy season it's a good place to learn to dive.

The influx of tourists has made Boracay the most cosmopolitan patch of sand in the world. A walk along the beach takes you past restaurants serving a United Nations of cuisine, including Filipino, Greek, Indian (cooked by a Bengali master chef), Caribbean, French, Thai, German, English and more. The beach is also dotted with interesting little bars and bistros, some of them no more than a few chairs and tables on the beach, others raucous places that turn into discos as the night wears on and stay open until dawn.

On the downside, there is hardly a patch of beachfront that has not been appropriated for some sort of tourism-related development. The laidback Boracay of the 1970s and 1980s, with its rickety barbecue stalls and bamboo

△ White Beach, Boracay

Moving on from Boracay

For Manila, there's a choice of MBRS Lines' M/V *Virgin Mary* (sailing from Caticlan Wed & Sun at noon) or M/V *Mary the Queen* (Fri at noon), or HSF Lines' M/V *Florinda* (Wed & Sat at 4pm). *Mary the Queen* sometimes stops at Odiongan, Romblon Town and Cadjidiocan. WG&A has a ticket office (☎043/288 3012) at *Oro Beach Resort* near Allied Bank, close to Boat Station 3. The Boracay Tourist Center also sells ferry tickets. Another way to fit Romblon into your island-hopping schedule is to take the banca that goes from Boat Station 2 daily at 7am to Santa Fe on the southern tip of Tablas Island (P220) and on to Looc. There are also bancas from Caticlan to San Fernando on Sibuyan and from Boat Station 1 to Carabao Island.

Boracay could hardly be better served by flights, with numerous daily flights to Manila and Cebu City from Caticlan. For details of airline offices and other ticket outlets, see p.333.

Kalibo aside, it's a long haul from Caticlan to almost anywhere on Panay **by road**. The mammoth trip from Iloilo takes at least seven hours, while from Roxas it's six hours. Tickets can be bought on board the buses themselves.

beach huts, has been almost totally usurped by a modern strip of hotels, jet-skis, inflatable banana boats and all-night raves. Where you could once only get catch of the day and a grog of rum, you can now sit in air-conditioned luxury eating Chateaubriand and smoking Cuban cigars. Some areas of the beach are restful, but others suffer badly from radios blasting out music. The authorities, who have now realised that unchecked development could end up being a turn-off, are threatening to demolish establishments that have been built without permission, but this being the Philippines any action of this sort is likely to take years to be given the go-ahead, never mind enforced. Also of concern is the pollution from the tricycles which roar up and down the main road at all hours. Many resort owners are aware, however, of how fragile Boracay is and organize beach clean-ups and recycling seminars. You can do your bit by taking all your plastic bags and batteries with you when you leave.

Stray dogs can be a nuisance, as can the vendors who stream along the beach in packs selling everything from massages to boat trips, fake watches, sunglasses and model Spanish galleons. If you do decide to show the colour of your money, make sure you check the going rate for all these products and services in advance. It's easy to blame the vendors for ripping off visitors, but not always fair. With the minimum daily wage in the Philippines at no more than P350, tourism has resulted in temptations that are hard to resist.

The two distinct **climatic seasons** in the Philippines have a marked effect on day-to-day life in Boracay. Because of the island's north–south orientation, White Beach takes the brunt of onshore winds during the southwest monsoon, the wet season, so don't expect to find White Beach looking its well-barbered best at that time. The waves can be big, washing up old coconuts, seaweed and dead branches. Many beachfront resorts and restaurants are forced to erect unsightly tarpaulins to keep out the wind and sand; some even give up the fight against the elements completely and close for a few months, usually during July and August, the wettest months. At this time of year boats from Caticlan are forced to dock on the south side of the island, leaving you with a bumpy tricycle ride on a potholed and puddle road to White Beach. The onshore wind makes for some thrilling windsurfing and kiteboarding, but all other activities move to calmer waters on the island's east side.

There are two gateways to Boracay: **Caticlan** and **Kalibo** (from where you can get transport to Caticlan; see box on p.323). During peak season Seair flies to Caticlan six times daily from Manila and nine times a week from Cebu City. Asian Spirit has up to ten flights daily during peak season to Caticlan from Manila and one daily from Cebu City. Philippine Airlines and Air Philippines both fly frequently from Manila and Cebu City to Kalibo, with Cebu Pacific also flying from Cebu City. One-way fares from Manila start from P2350.

MBRS Lines operates two **passenger ferries** from Manila: the M/V *Virgin Mary* leaves Manila at 5pm on Monday and Friday and arrives in Caticlan early the following morning; the M/V *Mary the Queen* leaves Manila at 5pm on Wednesday. On both ships a deluxe ticket (a bunk in an a/c dormitory) costs P950 while a "cabin" ticket, entitling you to one bunk in a four-bunk cabin, costs P1350. On the M/V *Virgin Mary* a few two-person suites are available (❽), each with a queen-sized bed and a bathroom shared with the suite next door. Both ships have cafeterias, karaoke and a late-night disco. The M/V **Florinda** belonging to HSF Lines sails here from Manila North Harbour's Pier 6 on Mondays and Thursdays at 6pm. There are three classes of ticket: economy (P750), deluxe (P825) and cabin (one bunk in a six-bunk cabin, P1290).

Some **buses** drop you on the main road through Caticlan, about 1km from the pier and airport, although many continue to the pier itself. There are always tricycles waiting to take you the rest of the way.

From Caticlan to Boracay

Caticlan airstrip is a five-minute tricycle ride (P20 per person) from the **ferry terminal**, where you buy tickets for the twenty-minute banca journey to White Beach (P19.50 during the day and P30 at night, plus a P50 environmental fee and P2 boat terminal fee). If you're flying in and have booked to stay at a resort, you'll be met at the airstrip by their representative. The public bancas to Boracay mostly go to Boat Station 2, right in the middle of White Beach. Some stop first at Boat Station 3, with a few calling at Boat Station 1; ask the boatman if you need to know the route. In the rainy season they go to Tambisaan, a beach on the island's south side. There's a new ferry terminal being built near here. Once it's complete all bancas will arrive here, whatever the season.

Information and transport

The Department of Tourism has a small **tourist office** in D'Mall, on the right hand side as you enter, opposite *Gasthof*. Just south of it, also on the beach, the **Boracay Tourist Center** (daily 9am–10pm; ☎036/288 3704) is by far the most useful place on the island for getting general information and making reservations for onward travel. You can buy maps here and there's a useful noticeboard advertising new boat services, adventure tours, activities, nightlife and accommodation. There's also a branch of the **Filipino Travel Centre** (Ⓦwww.filipinotravel.com.ph) here, perhaps the best travel agent on the island and a good source of general information about accommodation and transport, including international flights. Another good source of information is the website of the Boracay Foundation (Ⓦwww.boracayisland.org), a government-funded environmental and social task force that works with businesses and individuals on Boracay to formulate policies for the island. The site is updated regularly with listings, accommodation news and events.

Tricycle fares should be no more than P20 per person for a trip along the length of the island's main road, but make sure you agree a fare before you climb

RESTAURANTS, BARS & CLUBS

Bazura	14
Beachcomber	5
Blue Berry Restaurant	16
Bom Bom Bar	11
Boracay Steakhouse	7
Charlh's Bar	21
CNN Café	19
English Bakery and Tea Rooms	2, 9 & 23
Floremar Pizzeria de Mario	H
Gasthof	17
Hey Jude's	15
La Capinnina Italian Restaurant, Café & Wine Bar	25
Lemon i Cafe	16
Manjana	12
Moondogs Shooters Bar	6
Prana	4
Red Coconut Bar & Restaurant	10
Red Pirates Pub	3
Restaurante Banza	22
Summer Place	18
Tesebel's	1
True Food Restaurant	13
Wave	20
The Wreck Bar	24
Zuzuni	8

ACCOMMODATION

Angol Point Beach Resort	G
Balinghai	A
Boracay Beach Chalets	S
Boracay Beach Houses	I
Boracay Scuba Diving School	W
Boracay Tropics	V
Calypso Villa	U
Casa Pilar	bb
Chalet Y	C
Dave's Straw Hat Inn	ee
Fat Jimmy's	P
Fiesta Cottages	M
Fridays Boracay	D
Green Yard Beach Resort & Seasport Center	Q
Jemlee's	Y
Jony's Beach Resort	L
Le Soleil de Boracay	R
Little Corner of Italy Resort & Restaurant	H
Lorenzo Main	Z
Lorenzo South	J
Lorenzo Villas	K
Mabini's Place	F
Mango-Ray	O
Michelle's Bungalows	dd
Mona Lisa White Sand	aa
Nami	B
Nigi Nigi Nu Noos 'e' Nu Nu Noos	T
Saigon Resort	cc
Seabird Resort Bar & Restaurant	N
Tirol and Tirol Beach Resort	X
Trafalgar Garden & Lodge	ff
Waling-Waling	E

Banyugan Beach
Puka Beach
Bat Cave
Punta-Bunga Beach
Punta Bunga
MAIN ROAD
Yapak
Punta-Ina
Hagdan
Ilig-Iligan
Balinghai Beach
A
Shell Museum
Ilig-Iligan Beach
Diniwid Beach
B
Diniwid
Fairways & Bluewater (Hotel & Golf Club)
Lapuz-Lapuz Beach
Horse Riding Stables
C
D
E
Lapuz-Lapuz

See inset map for detail
Balabag
Bolabog
N
Bolabog Beach
White Beach
i
i
Boracay Rock

Willy's Rock
0   200 m
Balabag
5   6
L
Boat Station 1
Boracay Safari Divers
7
Land Bank
Fisheye Divers
M
8
N
Boracay Medical Clinic
11
12   13
Aquarius Diving
Lapu-Lapu Diving Center
Dive Gurus
14
D'Mall
Victory Divers
15
16
17 18
P
Allied Bank
19
S
L   PT&T
20
i   DOT
21

2
Ambulon
F
SULU SEA
G
3   H
Angol
J
4
Mandala Spa
SIBUYAN SEA
Tulubhan
MAIN ROAD
Malabunot
Tambisaan

22   U   23   V
Boracay Tourist Center
Police   Allied Bank
i
Boracay Scuba Diving School
W   24
Calypso Diving
Boracay Imperial Beach Resort
X
Z   Y   Talipapa Market

Manoc-Manoc
K
New Ferry terminal
Crocodile Island
Cagban Beach
aa
bb
Manoc-Manoc Beach
cc   dd
Tabon Strait
ee
25   Immigration Office
Allied Bank
ff

BORACAY

0   1 km

Boats to Boracay
Panay
Caticlan Airport

on board. Some drivers have a habit of adding "extras" at the end of the journey.

Accommodation

There are about two hundred **resorts** on Boracay, from the monastic to the luxurious, which means that except at peak times (Christmas and Easter, when prices rise sharply) you should be able to find a place to stay simply by taking a stroll down White Beach from south to north. Prices have risen sharply in recent years and Boracay is no longer the bargain basement destination it used to be, with the best rooms in even some of the mid-range resorts going for a couple of hundred US dollars a night. Standards vary wildly, with some budget resorts offering better value than some of the five-stars, which can seem overpriced for what you get. It's always worth negotiating for a discount, especially if you plan to stay a while. The prices used in our price codes in the reviews below are for most of peak season excluding Christmas and Easter, when they rise by as much as fifty percent.

Most of the **budget** accommodation is in the areas of Boat Stations 2 and 3. The "exclusive", quiet end of the beach, beyond Boat Station 1, is a little fancier and correspondingly more expensive. Few visitors stay on the eastern side of the island where there is a very limited choice of accommodation and from where White Beach is a half-hour walk or banca ride away.

Boat Station 1 and points north

Chalet Y Northern end of the beach a few steps from Boat Station 1 ☏ 036/288 5808, ⓦ www .chalety.com. Modern, serviced beachfront duplex home for four people, making it ideal for families if you don't want the restrictions of a hotel. Chalet Y is tastefully decorated, comfortable, in a perfect location – and at more than P14,000 a night for the whole house, expensive. ❾

Fiesta Cottages Northern end of the beach near Boat Station 1 and Fisheye Divers ☏ 036/288 2818. An unbeatable location with peace and quiet at night in simple nipa and bamboo rooms, but only a 10min walk from other resorts, bars and nightlife. ❹

Fridays Boracay Almost the last resort on White Beach, right at the northern end beyond Boat Station 1 ☏ 036/288 6200 or 02/892 9283 or 02/810 1027, ⓦ www.fridaysboracay.com. Rates of US$120 a night upwards for native cottage-style rooms, in a splendidly peaceful location with five-star service – right down to your own pair of hand-made Manila hemp slippers. The beach bar is ideal for an aperitif before you dine under the stars. The food is pricey by local standards, but if money is no object you can wash it down with a bottle of vintage Louis Roederer champagne for P14,000 before retiring to your balcony with a Filipino-made Fighting Cock Flyboy cigar (P350). ❾

Jony's Beach Resort On the road behind the northern end of the beach, about 100m south of

Cocomangas Shooters Bar ☏ 036/ 288 6119, ⓦ www.jonysboracay.com. Rightly popular family-style resort with comfortable a/c rooms close to the beach. Some rooms are built around a garden a matter of metres inland on the other side of the road. Some are on the beach itself, so if you want one of these it's best to book ahead. A lovely restaurant serves big breakfasts and some tasty Mexican dishes. ❼

Seabird Resort Bar & Restaurant Set back from the beach a short walk north of D'Mall ☏ 036/288 3047. A range of rooms, the cheapest of which is a pleasantly simple double with fan and shower. Good coffee, pancakes, breakfasts and fish in the restaurant. ❸

Waling-Waling Northern end of the beach beyond Willy's Rock ☏ 036/288 5555 to 5560, ⓦ www .waling.com. One of a new generation of modish, upmarket resorts, *Waling-Waling* has native-chic rooms, including a premier suite with a bamboo four-poster and tribal tapestries on the walls, for $240 a night. At night torches are lit along the resort beach and you can dine alfresco, sitting on cushions around low tables in trendy little bamboo shelters. ❾

Boat Station 2

Boracay Beach Chalets 50m north of the Tourist Center, roughly in the middle of the beach ☏ 036/288 3993. Standard rooms good for one or two people, and family rooms for five, though the "rooms" are actually big, pleasant cottages standing in a quiet, tropical garden. Perks include

The **music** of the Philippines

Music is everywhere in the Philippines. Street musicians strum locally produced, cheap guitars in the shade; rock and pop from around the world blast from pumped-up speakers in jeepneys; chanteuses sing ballads in hotel piano bars; and in the clubs, pubs and cocktail lounges of every city there are bands playing every night. Top quality bands too. Filipinos can mimic just about any big name or style, but during the last couple of decades have also established themselves as an original musical force in their own right.

Traditional tribal

Among the ethnic and tribal groups of Mindanao and the Sulu archipelago there's a sophisticated musical genre called **kulintang**, in which the main instruments are bossed gongs similar to those used in Indonesia. *Kulintang* is commonly performed by small ensembles playing instruments that include the *kulintang* itself (a series of small gongs for the melody), the **agung** (large gongs for the lower tones) and the **gandingan** (four large vertical gongs used as a secondary melodic instrument). *Kulintang* music serves as a means of **entertainment** and a demonstration of **hospitality**; it's used at weddings, festivals, coronations, to entertain visiting dignitaries and to honour those heading off on or coming back from a pilgrimage. It is also used to accompany healing ceremonies and, up to the beginning of the twentieth century, was a form of communication, using goatskin drums to beat messages across the valleys.

The Manila Sound

The "Manila Sound" was the sound of the **seventies** in the Philippines. Against a backdrop of student riots and martial law, some audiences found comfort with bell bottom-wearing bands, like the Hotdogs and the Boyfriends, who set romantic **novelty lyrics** to catchy **melodic hooks**. Some sneered at the frivolity of it all, but the Manila Sound was as big as disco. Today the Manila Sound is effectively extinct and hardly any survives on CD, but it gave rise to a number of **major stars** who evolved and are still going strong. The most well-known is indefatigable diva **Sharon Cuneta,** who is known throughout the country by the modest moniker "The Megastar". She first appeared in the Philippine pop charts at the age of 12 singing the disco tune "Mr. D.J" and has since released thirty-eight albums including one of duets with other apparently ageless Filipina singers such as Pops Fernandez and Sunshine Cruz.

Sharon Cuneta in concert

The folkies

Far removed from the jaunty happy-pop of the Manila Sound, folk singer **Freddie Aguilar** became popular in the eighties under ironic circumstances involving Imelda Marcos (see p.516) and inspired a generation of artists whose music turned into a **social force**. One of the most well-known groups of that new generation was **Apo Hiking Society**, a foursome from Ateneo University whose anthem "Handog ng Pilipino sa Mundo" ("A New And Better Way") has been covered by fifteen Filipino artists. Its lyrics are carved on the wall of Manila's Our Lady of Edsa Shrine, traditionally a focal point of **protests** and **revolutions**.

Guitar making is prolific throughout the Philippines

Tribal-pop

In the nineties – largely as a reaction to the decline of the protest movement and the creeping Americanization of Filipino music – a roots movement emerged that took the **traditional rhythms** and chants of tribal music such as *kulintang* and merged them with **contemporary instruments** and **production techniques**. One of the chief exponents of so-called **tribal-pop** was **Grace Nono**. She never quite cracked the big time, but cleared the path for others, including **Pinikpikan**, the most successful tribal-pop band in the country today.

The mainstream

Any consideration of mainstream popular music in the Philippines won't get off the ground without reference to the irreverent **Eraserheads**. After more than a decade at the top they disbanded in 2003, but remain the most popular Filipino band ever. Many current popular groups have been inspired by their infectious blend of irony and irresistibly melodic pop, including **Rivermaya**, still producing platinum-selling albums at a rate of knots, and **Parokya ni Edgar**, one of the few bands that have come close to equaling the Eraserheads; their 1996 debut album, "Khangkhungkherrnitz", features a tribute to the nation's favourite food: instant noodles.

Manila's top live venues

Suburbia, Malate. See p.119.
Hobbit House, Malate. See p.118.
Conway's, Shangri-la Makati. See p.119.
Kidd Creole, Makati. See p.122.
Mayric's Bar, Sampoloc. See p.122.
Ratsky's, Quezon City. See p.122.
70s Bistro, Quezon City. See p.121.

Parokya ni Edgar accept an award

For more on Philippine music see Contexts, p.515.

cable TV, fridge, free coffee or tea and free mineral water. ⑤

Boracay Tropics About 150 metres inland along the path beside the tourist centre and police station. ⑦ 036/288 4034, ⑩ www.boracaytropics .com. Not on the beach, but it's only a short walk away and the rooms are of a high standard, built around a large garden with a swimming pool. Premier suites are luxurious and pricey, but there are also standard rooms with a garden view and fantastic, trendy little "dorms" for six people at $120 – great value of you're splitting the cost. ⑤

Calypso Villa Down a footpath at the back of the Tourist Center, on the left ⑦ 036/288 3206. This place is worth the effort to find if you're looking for good-value, comfortable accommodation close to the beach but away from the noise of the bars and clubs. In a new, whitewashed house standing in peaceful gardens, the downstairs rooms have French windows that open onto a patio area, while the upstairs rooms have large balconies. Simple, charming and immaculately clean. ⑦

Fat Jimmy's 100m inland, next to D'Mall ⑦ 036/288 3748. One of a number of excellent budget resorts along a path next to D'Mall. Relaxed, quiet and friendly, *Fat Jimmy's* has 16 simple but charming fan-cooled or a/c rooms, five of which have their own small patio garden. Family rooms sleep four with a bunkbed for the kids and rates include a choice of Filipino or American breakfast. All-round good value. ⑤

Green Yard Beach Resort & Seasport Center Halfway down the beach at the rear of Calypso Diving ⑦ 036/288 3748. Good-value huts with fan and shower. As the name suggests, watersports can be arranged. ⑤

Le Soleil de Boracay A few minutes' walk inland, about halfway along White Beach ⑦ 036/288 6209 to 6212, ⑩ www.lesoleil.com.ph. In its own quiet gardens, this cheesy Mediterranean-style hotel has a range of rooms and suites, including apartments from P3500. There's also a restaurant, health spa and business centre. ⑨

Mango-Ray On the beach 50m north of Boat Station 2 ⑦ 036/288 3301, ⑩ www.mangoray.com. Four large a/c furnished rooms for two (each more like a small apartment) with shower, fridge, TV, telephone and spacious porch. If you plan to hang around for a while, they're worth considering at P40,000 a month. Floors are tiled, the whitewashed walls are decorated with tasteful Filipino art and the surrounding gardens are lush and peaceful. Breakfast included. ⑥

Nigi Nigi Nu Noos 'e' Nu Nu Noos A 5min walk north of the Boracay Tourist Center ⑦ 036/288

3101. Longstanding and popular resident of White Beach, close to the PT&T telephone office. The Indonesian-style cottages have thatched pagoda roofs and shady verandas. ⑤

Boat Station 3 and points south

Angol Point Beach Resort At the south end of the beach ⑦ 036/288 3107 or 032/522 0012. It's a little more pricey than many resorts of its ilk because the conservationist owner, Francis, has built only one cottage where most developers would have put three or four – which means you get expansive rooms, huge verandas and the benefit of acres of space in the peaceful coconut grove where the resort stands. It's a short walk from bars and restaurants and very quiet. Good choice for families. ⑥

Boracay Beach Houses Southern end of the beach ⑦ 036/288 3315. Daniel and Esther Vogel have built three self-catering beachfront houses which they rent out by the floor, a peaceful and homely alternative for those who don't want to stay in a resort. Each floor sleeps up to four. The ground floor has direct access to the beach and a small kitchenette for cooking. The top floor has no kitchenette, but it does have a large seaview veranda. The rate includes daily breakfast and the services of a maid. ⑨

Boracay Scuba Diving School Between Boat Stations 2 and 3 ⑦ 036/288 3327. Plain but comfortable rooms in a great location. There's Internet access, and not surprisingly, a full range of diving courses. ⑤

Casa Pilar About 100m south of Boracay Tourist Center ⑦ 036/ 288 3073. In a concrete motel-style building in an orchid garden right on the beach. There's a range of bright, airy rooms, some with a/c; other facilities include a restaurant and bar and Internet access. ⑤

🏃 **Dave's Straw Hat Inn** Down the path next to *Angol Point Beach Resort.* ⑦ 036/288 5465, ⑩ www.davesstrawhatinn.com. The kind of simple but well-run establishment that Boracay badly needs more of. *Dave's* is a charming, homey little resort with comfortable cottages and good food; the kind of place where you instantly feel right at home and aren't paying through the nose for it. Fan-cooled rooms for two are one of the best deals on the island, while even deluxe doubles have extra roll-out beds so a family of four can fit in at no extra charge. ④

Jemlee's Behind Boat Station 3 ⑦ 036/288 6327. One of a number of small resorts along the footpath at the rear of White Beach. Affordable and thus popular with Filipino students, *Jemlee's* has a mixed bag of cottages, some in better repair than others, all in a reasonably quiet garden in a good location. ❷

Little Corner of Italy Resort & Restaurant At the southern end of the beach ☎036/288 5078. Besides dorm beds, there are a/c doubles and group rooms for twelve. Slightly faded but very friendly, and the Italian owner, Mario, cooks some mean pasta. Dorm beds P100, ❶

Lorenzo South Southern end of the beach ☎032 928 0719, ⊛www.lorenzo-resorts-boracay.4t.com. One of three *Lorenzo* establishments on Boracay, this one is a bit of a landmark because it's the last resort you reach if you walk south along White Beach. The others are *Lorenzo Main*, halfway along White Beach, and *Lorenzo Villas* at Manoc Manoc. All three resorts have big, comfortable a/c rooms, restaurants, cable TV and aqua sports. ❽

Mabini's Place Southern end of the beach. ☎036/288 3238. Mabini's consists of half a dozen very plain, cheap cottages, one of which is right on the sand and offers probably the most affordable sea view on the island. There's no restaurant and only cold water to shower with, but for this price and in this location, do you really care? ❶

Mona Lisa White Sand 200m south of Boracay Tourist Center ☎036/288 3012. A/c cottages with pretty *capiz* (seashell) windows and shady balconies, or slightly cheaper cottages with fan; all boast bamboo furniture, white linen and nice private showers. The garden is beautiful, with orchids and frangipani, and the place generally has an air of being cared for and well run. ❻

Saigon Resort Next to Western Union and the WG&A office near Talipapa market ☎036/288 3203. *Saigon* is so ordinary that it's easy to miss. The half-dozen cottages are, however, clean and

sturdy, and have balconies where you can swing in the complimentary hammock. Friendly staff, reasonable rates and right on the beach. An excellent budget option. ❸

Tirol and Tirol Beach Resort 5min walk along the beach to the north of Boracay Tourist Center ☎036/288 3165, ⊛www.tirolandtirol.com. Large bamboo cottages in a leafy garden. Standard rooms don't have a/c but are big and breezy enough not to need it. An unpretentious, well-run little resort in a good location. ❽

Balinghai and Diniwid beaches

Balinghai Balinghai Beach ☎036 288 3646. If you are looking for desert-island solitude and don't mind being a few minutes' tricycle ride from the buzz of White Beach, *Balinghai* fits the bill. On a small, secluded cove surrounded by cliffs on the northern part of Boracay, it's set into a steep slope with lots of steps, and boasts a handful of private bungalows and houses built from local materials, with consideration for the environment. One house has a tree in the kitchen and another is carved from the rockface, with a balcony facing the sunset. There is a small restaurant where you can get three good meals a day. ❺

Nami Nestled on the cliffside 20m above Diniwid Beach, the next cove along from White Beach ☎032/818 6237, ⊛www.namiboracay.com. Spacious villas with a 180-degree ocean view, jacuzzi, butler service and DVD player (with pirated DVDs available from reception). *Nami* bills itself as a very upmarket establishment, but in reality the service doesn't make the mark and the villas are showing wear and tear. ❾

The island

Most visitors fall in love with **White Beach**, but don't miss **Puka Beach** on the north coast, which is famous for shiny white seashells called *puka*. The best way to get there is to hire a banca on White Beach for half a day (P500) per group. To the north of White Beach sits the little village of **Diniwid** with its two-hundred-metre beach, accessible from White Beach on a path carved out of the cliffs. At the end of a steep path over the next hill is the tiny **Balinghai Beach**, enclosed by walls of rock.

On the northeast side of the island **Ilig-Iligan Beach** has coves and caves, as well as jungle full of fruit bats. From the beach here a path leads a short way up the hill through the scrub to **Bat Cave**, which you can climb into and explore. It's fantastic to be here at dusk when the bats leave the cave in immense flocks.

The Boracay Tourist Center can help arrange **activities**. A banana-boat ride (on which you get towed behind a speedboat on an inflatable banana) is P150 each for a minimum of four people. There's also water-skiing (P750 for 15min), jet-skiing (P1000 for 30min), ocean kayaking (P500 per half-day), parasailing (P2500 including 15min actual flying time). Speedboat rental costs P2500 per

Diving around Boracay

Boracay's diving isn't as varied or extreme as diving in Palawan or Puerto Galera, but there's still enough to keep everyone happy. The dive sites around the island, all easily accessible by banca, include gentle drift dives, coral gardens and some deeper dives with a good chance of encounters with sharks. At **Crocodile Island,** fifteen minutes southeast of Boracay, there's a shallow reef that drops off to 25m and a number of small canyons where sea snakes gather. **Big and Small Laurel** are neighbouring islets with some of the best soft coral in the Visayas and shoals of snappers, sweetlips, eels, sea snakes, morays, puffers and boxfish. Probably the star attraction for divers here is **Yapak**, where you freefall into the big blue, eventually finding at 30m the top of a marine wall where there are batfish, wahoo, tuna, barracuda and cruising grey reef sharks. On Boracay's northern shore are the **Bat Caves**, where a swim through one of the caves brings you out into an immense cavern inhabited by thousands of fruit bats. The smell is unforgettable. **Lapu Wall** is a day-trip from Boracay to the northern coast of Panay, but the diving is some of the most challenging in the area, with overhangs and caverns. Another good day-trip is north to Carabao Island (see p.339), in the province of Romblon, where there are splendid reefs, some peaceful, powdery beaches and one resort if you want to stay overnight.

There are dozens of licensed **dive operators** (see p.333) along White Beach. A Discover Scuba introductory session with a dive master costs $35 if you do it off the beach or $65 if you are taken by banca to Coral Garden or Friday's Rock. The full PADI Open Water Course (3–4 days) costs around $325.

hour. There's been a boom in **kiteboarding** on Boracay, with boarders gathering on White Beach during the off-season to catch the onshore winds and take advantage of the challenging waves and lack of water-traffic during the rainy months. In the peak season there's more sedate boarding to be had on the eastern side of the island, although even here waves can get big. There are a number of kiteboarding schools offering lessons, including rental of all the equipment. Two hours of "discover kiteboarding" costs around $50 and the International Kiteboarding Organisation (IKO) beginners' course takes 12 hours over three or four days and costs around $275. There's information on boarding in Boracay at ⓦ www.kiteboardingboracay.com.

Mountain bikes can be rented at a couple of stalls along the beach path for P300 per half-day. An enjoyable, not too rigorous option is to take the main road at the rear of White Beach north, heading through the quaint little barangay of **Yapak** to Puka Beach. For **horse riding** try Boracay Horse Riding Stables (ⓣ036/288 3311), on the opposite side of the road to *Chalet Y* north of Boat Station One. Gentle one-hour rides start at P550 per person, with discounts for groups.

Eating

Restaurants come and go in Boracay, but you can eat and drink your way up and down White Beach almost 24 hours a day. Some of the best food is prepared alfresco by the local vendors, who set up barbecues on the beach at sundown to cook everything from fresh lapu-lapu and squid to the tasty local bananas, which are sprinkled with muscovado sugar. There are many affordable places in D'Mall, where you'll find everything from Swiss and Italian to Chinese and Caribbean.

Blue Berry Restaurant At the rear of D'Mall towards the road. One of many small restaurants in D'Mall offering cheap food. *Blue Berry* is among the best, with home-made pancakes and rice dishes and, as the name suggest, irresistible pies. There's nothing fancy about this place; just pull up a stool and point to what you want.

Boracay Steakhouse A few steps from Boat Station 1. Excellent steak and salad restaurant that also offers vegetarian dishes such as potato pie and cheese pasta. The dining area is on the first storey with pleasant views.

Charlh's Bar Right on the beach about 100m north of the Boracay Tourist Center. A modest and relaxing place with cheap drinks of all descriptions. Simple menu of chicken and fish dishes available, along with live acoustic music on the beach from sunset.

CNN Café A short walk north of Boracay Tourist Center. Oddly named restaurant in a fine beachside location, with tables on an open terrace giving views of the sea. Swiss owner and chef Pascal dishes up wholesome European fare such as rosti potato with bacon and onion, spaghetti Bolognese, and cheese omelettes.

English Bakery and Tea Rooms There are three branches of this establishment; the main branch is a short walk south of the Boracay Tourist Center. As the name suggests, the fresh bread is excellent, as are the breakfasts and shakes. Fish and chips costs P170 and a glass of yoghurt is P50.

Floremar Pizzeria de Mario Inside the *Little Corner of Italy Resort*, at the southern end of White Beach. Thin-crust pizza, pasta and risotto, all cooked by the Italian owner.

Gasthof Right at the beachside entrance to D'Mall. A friendly German-run place with daily seafood specials and a delicatessen where you can buy cheese and cold cuts.

La Capinnina Italian Restaurant, Café & Wine Bar South of Boat Station 3 right next door to the Boracay Tourist Center. Home-style Italian food cooked by a resident Italian. Delicious pasta and thin-crust pizza, plus a good choice of daily specials and delightful desserts.

Lemon i Cafe In D'Mall. Terrific little European-owned café which is an oasis of calm in the middle of the shops and fast-food outlets. *Lemon i* serves a variety of breakfast dishes and light meals, as well as tasty sandwiches and healthy main courses. The Thai lemon chicken is a treat, while for breakfast there's a delicious eggs Benedict. In the evening, check the specials board for daily main courses such as grilled mahi-mahi fish on warm potato salad with a spicy dressing of capers and chilli.

Manjana Northern end of the beach between Boat Stations 1 and 2. Cute little beachfront hut offering delicious Mexican food and some good drinks. A fine place to chill out in the shade with a good book, a frozen mango daiquiri and a plate of nachos or spicy potato cakes.

Prana Inside Mandala Spa, at the southern end of the main road. Classy vegetarian restaurant at the upmarket Mandala Spa (W www.mandalaspa.com). The menu, created by a Swedish chef especially for the restaurant, includes interesting starters such as wasabi salad, main courses like penne pasta with roasted vegetables and pan-fried tofu with asparagus, pechay, sprouts, cucumbers, crushed peanuts and peanut sauce.

Red Coconut Bar & Restaurant A short walk north of D'Mall. Stylish beachfront restaurant at the *Red Coconut Beach Resort*. Tables are on the sand under palm trees and the menu includes grilled seafood, barbecues, pizza and French crepes.

True Food Restaurant Next door to *Mango-Ray*, a short walk north of Boat Station 2. Simple place where you sit on cushions around a low table on the bamboo floor and choose from the day's range of tasty curries (some vegetarian).

Tesebel's Puka Beach. This long-standing restaurant is nothing fancy to look at, but people go back for the delicious fresh seafood, which includes garlic prawns with buttered honey and tangy *sinigang* with catch of the day. Head here for a lazy lunch if you're in the Puka Beach area.

Zuzuni Boat Station 2. Trendy bistro-style Greek restaurant where you can enjoy your meal indoors or at a candlelit table on the beach. The menu includes fried cheese (saganaki), chicken souvlaki and lamb gyros. Service is efficient and the ambience intimate and peaceful.

Drinking and nightlife

Nightlife in Boracay starts with drinks at sunset and continues all night. Hardcore ravers don't even warm up until midnight, with many dancing and drinking until sunrise.

Bazura One hundred metres north of Boat Station 2. Lively and long-established disco with an outdoor dance floor, cheap drinks and a thumping sound system. Rarely gets going much before midnight.

Beachcomber At the far north of White Beach.

Simple bamboo bar on the sand, ideal for a few casual drinks before you move on to something more lively.

Bom Bom Bar Right on the beach a few metres north of D'Mall. Another atmospheric little chilled-out beach hut, with cushions on the sand where you can stretch out while listening to local musicians come together for jam sessions on native instruments.

Charlh's Bar On the beach halfway between Boat Stations 1 and 2. An agreeable place to start the evening, listening to guitarists play live under the stars from 6pm. Drinks are cheap: happy-hour gin and 7-Up (tonic is hard to come by) costs P30.

Hey Jude's At the entrance to D'Mall. Popular glass-fronted bistro where you can eat pizza and guzzle a margarita while watching beautiful people stroll past inches away on the beach. After dinner there are hip DJs and a op-arty crowd of Manila's beautiful people, tourists and expats.

Moondogs Shooters Bar On the road at the back of the *Cocomangas Beach Resort* at the northern end of White Beach. (In)famous for drinking games involving potent cocktails. Raucous until the wee hours.

Red Pirates Pub South end of White Beach beyond Boat Station 3. Bare feet and sarongs are the order of the evening at this chilled out little beach club far from the madding crowd. The music ranges from reggae to chill-out to tribal, ethnic and acoustic sounds. Occasionally you can enjoy a live jamming session with bongo drums, rain sticks and various other native instruments. The owner, Captain Joey, has a sailing boat and offers sunset cruises, adventure tours and snorkelling trips around the island.

Summer Place A few steps south of D'Mall. U-shaped bamboo bar facing the beach, with a dance floor and music until the sun comes up, or until the last customer leaves.

Wave *Boracay Regency Beach Resort*, near Boat Station 2. A subterranean a/c cavern (apparently the only underground disco in the Philippines) with live bands, DJs and karaoke rooms.

The Wreck Bar Calypso Diving Center, just south of the Boracay Tourist Center. Casual native-style bar where divers gather for après-scuba tall stories. Friendly atmosphere, live sport on cable TV and good food; the eclectic menu includes seafood Provencale, Hawaiian chicken, Swiss steaks and *adobo*.

Listings

Airlines Inside the Boracay Tourist Center is a branch of Filipino Travel Center where you can book tickets for Philippine Airlines, Air Philippines, Seair, Asian Spirit, Cebu Pacific and WG&A. The following airlines have ticket offices in the locality: Asian Spirit, at the southern end of White Beach near Boat Station 3 (☏036/288 3465); Philippine Airlines, on the beach path just south of Boat Station 3 at *Marzon Beach Resort* Seair, at D'Mall on White Beach (☏036/288 3704 to 3705) as well as at Dickson Travel in Caticlan (☏036/260 3131), right outside the airport; Seair, in D'Mall (☏036/288 5502).

Banks and exchange There are four banks on Boracay: Land Bank near Boat Station 1, Allied Bank along the main road behind White Beach, Metrobank at the back of D'Mall (near the elementary school) and a branch of BPI (Bank of the Philippine Islands) in D'Mall, a few minutes' walk north of the Boracay Tourist Center. All change travellers' cheques and BPI has an ATM. The best place to change travellers' cheques – with the least bureaucracy – is the Boracay Tourist Center.

Dive operators There are dozens of diver operators on Boracay, so you won't have to walk far to find one. These firms are all on White Beach: Aquarius Diving ☏036/288 3132; Aqualife ☏036/288 3276, ⓦwww.aqualife-divers.com; Boracay Safari Divers ☏036/288 3260; Boracay

Scuba Diving School ☏036/288 3327; Calypso Diving Resort ☏036/288 3206, ⓦwww.calypso. ph; Dive Gurus ☏036/288 5486, ⓦwww. divegurus.com; Fisheye Divers ☏036/288 6090, ⓦwww.fisheyedivers.com; Lapu-Lapu Diving Centre ☏036/288 3302, ⓦwww.lapulapu.com; Safari Divers ☏036/288 3260; Victory Divers ☏036/288 3209, ⓦwww.victorydivers.com.

Hospitals and clinics The main hospital is the Don Ciriaco Senares Tirol Senior Memorial Hospital (☏036/288 3041) off Main Rd by the *Aloja Delicatessen*. There are also a number of clinics: the Metropolitan Doctors Medical Clinic is on Main Rd (☏036/288 6357), by the market. It can provide first aid or deal with emergencies and will send a doctor to your hotel. The Boracay Medical Clinic is at the northern end of Main Rd (☏036/288 3141). and can be reached along the path next to Land Bank.

Immigration There's a small office at D'Mall (right-hand side near *Gasthof*) and another at the *Camilla Beach Resort* near Boat Station 3 where you can get visa extensions (☏036/288 5267; Mon–Sat 8am–noon & 1–5pm). Many resorts arrange visa extensions, as does the Filipino Travel Center on White Beach.

Internet access Getting online in Boracay is a little more expensive than in many parts of the country; reckon on anything between P60 and

P150 an hour. The Internet café at the Boracay Tourist Center is convenient and has fast connections. Other options are the Boracay Business Center, behind the *Swiss Bistro* near Boat Station 3; Netcom on the main road inland near Boat Station 1; the business centre at *Nigi Nigi's;* and the Computer Center at the *Boracay Imperial Beach Resort*. Station 168 is in a good location right at the beachside entrance to D'Mall.

Laundry The place you're staying will probably arrange laundry for you, but if not there are three launderettes on the island: Laundry Wascherei a little south of Boat Station 3, Lavandera Ko next to *Cocomangas*, and Speedwash laundry on the main road insland from Boat Station 3.

Post The post office in Balabag, the small community halfway along White Beach, is open Mon–Fri 9am–5pm. The Boracay Tourist Center on White Beach has poste restante costing P5 per letter.

Pharmacies There are pharmacies selling most necessities in D'Mall, Boracay Tourist Center and Talipapa market.

Phones Most resorts will let you make telephone calls, but the rates can be high. Cheaper options include the Boracay Tourist Center, the PT&T office just north of *Nigi Nigi's* on the inland side of the beach path, and RCPI Bayantal near Allied Bank at Boat Station 3.

Police The Philippine National Police have a new station a short walk inland between Boat Stations 2 and 3, immediately behind the Boracay Tourist Center. If you have lost something you can ask the friendly staff at the local radio station, YESFM 91.1, to broadcast an appeal for help. They claim to have a good record of finding lost property, from wallets and passports to labrador puppies. The station office (☎036/288 6107) is on Main Rd close to Boat Station 1.

Shopping Essentials are not hard to come by on Boracay. There's a minimart selling mineral water, toiletries and Agfa film at the Boracay Tourist Center, while at Talipapa market there are dozens of hole-in-the-wall stalls for beach basics such as shorts, sandals, sunblock and drinks. This is also a good place to invest in a sarong, ideal for using as a beach mat, for covering your head when the sun gets too hot, or even for wearing. D'Mall, a few minutes' walk north of the Boracay Tourist Center, is a booming conglomeration of stalls selling beachwear, souvenirs, T-shirts and home decor.

Western Union There's a branch of Western Union close to the entrance to Talipapa market.

Romblon

Off the northern coast of Panay, between Mindoro and Bicol, the province of **Romblon** consists of three main islands – Tablas, Romblon and Sibuyan. The province also includes a dozen or more smaller islands such as Alad Island and, to the north, Banton Island and Simara Island. Romblon is well known in the Philippines for its marble – and little else. The locals seem to like it that way: they fish, harvest copra and maintain their quiet little corner of the archipelago in something close to mint condition.

The province is largely overlooked by visitors because, to put it simply, there's not much here. There are few resorts and no shops, and don't expect European-style restaurants and nightlife anywhere on these islands. The most sophisticated Romblon gets is the occasional wooden shack with a karaoke machine. There are, however, some beautiful and rarely visited **beaches** and coral reefs, making Romblon an excellent off-the-beaten-track destination for scuba diving, snorkelling or just exploring and getting a sense of provincial life in the archipelago.

Romblon Town itself is a pretty place, with Spanish forts, a cathedral built in 1726 and breathtaking views across the Romblon Strait from Sabang lighthouse. On **Sibuyan** you can explore **Mount Guiting Guiting Natural Park** and climb the mountain itself, an extinct volcano. To the south of Tablas Island is beautiful little **Carabao Island** (usually visited via Boracay) where there's some terrific diving and a lovely resort.

Getting to Romblon

There's a small airport at Tugdan on Tablas, which at the time of writing was served by twice-weekly flights (Tuesday and Saturday) at 11:15am from Manila by Interisland Airlines (☎02/852 010 to 8013, ⓦwww.interislandairlines. com). The only **ferries** from Manila are MBRS Lines' (☎02/921 6716 in Manila, 042/243 5886 in Romblon) M/V *Mary the Queen* and M/V *Virgin Mary*. Three times a week one of these vessels sails a route from Manila to Odiongan (Tablas Island), then on to Caticlan and finally to Lipata (Antique province, Panay) and back the way it came. Once a week the M/V *Mary the Queen* sails from Manila to Romblon Town, and on to Cajidiocan (Sibuyan) and Dumaguit, near Kalibo, before returning the same way. The trip from Manila to Odiongan takes about 10 hours (from P450). There are also regular big bancas from Caticlan to Santa Fe and Looc on Tablas Island. From **Batangas City** there are regular ferries – operated by Viva Shipping Lines, Montenegro Lines and Shipshape Ferry Inc – variously to Odiongan, San Agustin on Tablas, Romblon Town, and Magdiwang, San Fernando and Cajidiocan, all on Sibuyan. Shipshape's (☎02/723 7615 in Manila) M/V *Princess Camille*, for example, sails the following route three times a week: Batangas–San Agustin (Tablas island)–Romblon Town–Magdiwang (Sibuyan).

From Dalahican near Lucena there are ferries three times a week to Romblon Town.

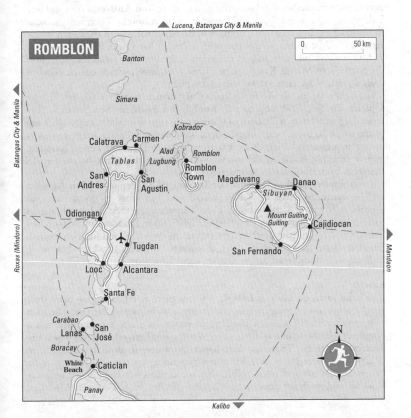

As for services **from Panay**, MBRS Lines has sailings from Dumaguit, Caticlan and Lipata in Antique province. From Roxas there are bancas to Santa Fe and San Fernando. There are also daily bancas from Caticlan to Carabao Island and from Dumaguit (near Kalibo) to Cajidiocan. Finally, **from Mindoro**, there's a ferry three times a week from Roxas to Odiongan, while Cajidiocan on Sibuyan's east coast is linked by banca with Mandaon on **Masbate**.

Tablas Island

Tablas, the largest of the Romblon group, is a narrow island with a sealed coastal road running around the coast. Chartering a jeepney for a tour around the island is worth considering. The usual day-trip winds past some pretty barrios up to **Carmen** on the island's northern tip, to San Agustin with its baroque church and back down through Tugdan. The road that cuts across the island from Concepcion to Odiongan is a real thrill, winding along a ridge with, on a clear day, views as far as Sibuyan in the east and Boracay in the south.

If you arrive by air, it's typical to head first to **Odiongan**, a pleasant little town with a few simple places to stay. The best place for a short stay is *Odiongan Plaza Lodge* (☎042/567 5760; ❷) which is in a central location opposite the town hall on the plaza and has acceptable, well-kept air-conditioned rooms with tiled floors and hot water showers. There's also a small **Internet café** right next door, although connections here are slow and not always reliable. From Odiongan it's easy to explore the beautiful northwest coast up to **San Andres**, a neat and tidy little place with paved roads and low-rise wooden houses. There's no accommodation here, but there are a number of houses at the rear of the beach where residents will be willing to put you up. San Andres has a beautiful sweeping bay of fine sand on one side and on the other dazzling paddy fields that stretch to the foothills of Mount Kang-Ayong (Table Mountain), which can be climbed with a guide – ask at the town hall in the plaza.

The next town north of San Andres is **Calatrava**, from where you can charter a banca for the short hop to the **Enchanted Hidden Sea**, an incredibly beautiful forty-metre wide pool of water barely 10m from the sea through a gap in the rocks. To most local folks the pool is an enchanted place, home to supernatural beings and elementals such as elves, fairies and gnomes. The surrounding area is certainly home to the monkey-eating eagle, the white-breasted eagle, monkeys, butterflies, sharks and turtles.

If you want to head to Romblon or Sibuyan, take a jeepney to **San Agustin** on the northeast coast of Tablas, where you can cross by local banca to Romblon Town or San Fernando. There's an adequate little lodging house in San Agustin, the *August-Inn* (☎0919/592 2495; ❶) in the town plaza, with air-conditioned rooms (the doubles have private showers too) and food on request. Another roption, right next door, is *Kamella Lodge* (❶), which has small, ordinary air-conditioned rooms that are okay for a short stay.

Looc

The main town on Tablas is **LOOC**, a scenic place huddled among palm trees against a curtain of jungle hills, and facing a wide natural harbour. There's a tourist office in the Capitol Building in the town plaza, a post office and a couple of telephone offices. Looc's pier is at the southern edge of town near the *Morales Lodging Inn*. There are daily bancas from here to Boracay and Caticlan (P120). One boat leaves at 7.30am, but depending on demand there may be others at 9.30am and noon. Note that some boats are too big to moor at Boracay, and so head directly to Caticlan. Ferries leave Looc on Mondays,

Thursdays and Saturdays for Roxas on Mindoro. For up-to-date information about ferries there's a useful **tourist office** (Mon–Fri, 8am–noon and 2–4pm) in Looc on the main square. Near here, also on the square, you'll find the Brain *Storm Internet Café*.

It's worth hiring a banca to explore the pretty bay and coves around Looc. Looc's main tourist attraction is **Looc Bay Marine Refuge and Sanctuary**, an area of the bay guarded 24 hours a day to allow corals damaged by dynamite fishing to regenerate. The guards, all volunteers, are stationed on a bamboo platform and are happy to welcome tourists aboard and let them snorkel in the area. Donations in the form of soft drinks, instant coffee and snacks are always appreciated.

Accommodation and eating

If you're spending a night in Looc while waiting for a ferry, head for the *Marduke Hotel* (☎042/509 4078; ❶), on Grimares Street near the town plaza. The eight rooms all have air-conditioning and private bathrooms, and there's a simple restaurant which manages to offer brewed coffee. The *Morales Lodging Inn* (❶) at the pier is a little run-down but reasonably comfortable. The owner is friendly and something of an oracle on ferry schedules. If you want to stay away from the noise of the town centre, the best option is *Roda I and II Beach Resort* (❷) 3km south in the barangay of **Kamandag**. Easily reached from Looc by tricycle, *Roda's* is right on a pleasant beach and has a choice of family cottages and air-conditioned twin or double rooms.

The best place to *eat* in Looc is the *Pacific Garden Restaurant*, a Chinese place serving noodle soup, piping hot fried rice and deliciously peppery *adobo* that comes with a lump of freshly steamed rice. For fresh fruit, there's a good daily market near the plaza.

Romblon Island

Romblon Island has been extensively quarried for decades to get at the beautiful Romblon marble used for the furniture and floors of the rich and famous in Manila. It's a picturesque island, with a pretty harbourside capital, an interior buzzing with wildlife and a coastal road, partly cemented, that you can whip around in half a day, past some enticing beaches with a number of simple resorts. The problem any traveller faces is getting there. The only way in is by ferry, a factor that has kept the island isolated and idyllic.

Romblon Town

One of the most attractive towns in the Philippines, low-rise **ROMBLON TOWN**, the provincial capital, sits on a sweeping deep port with red-roofed houses lining the water's edge and thickly jungled hills behind. Happily dozing in the balm of a more sedentary age, the town feels a few centuries behind the rest of the Philippines. In the mornings all you can hear is cockerels and in the afternoons almost everything stops for a siesta, stirring again at 3pm when the worst of the heat has gone from the sun and children can play along the shore.

The town has a few sights, all reachable on foot. Slap in the middle overlooking the quaint little Spanish plaza is **St Joseph's Cathedral**, a richly atmospheric seventeenth-century church where almost everyone in town turns out for Mass on Sunday at 8am and on weekdays in the early evening. On the seafront are the remains of **Fort San Andres** and **Fort San Pedro**, reminders of the risk Romblon Town once faced from pirates.

There's a helpful **tourist office** (Mon–Fri 8am–noon & 1–4pm; ☎042/507 2202 to 2204) in the Provincial Capitol Building, a short tricycle ride from the pier. There are car ferries to Batangas City (P380), and bancas to Dalahican near Lucena. For Sibuyan, bancas run daily to Magdiwang, Cajidiocan and San Fernando.

Accommodation and eating

The main **hotel** in town is the *Romblon Plaza* (☎042/507 2269 or 2277; ❶), one block away from the pier and, with four storeys, the tallest building in Romblon. There are six types of room, from en-suite doubles with fan to air-conditioned superior suites, also with private bathroom. The hotel has its own very pleasant rooftop restaurant with daily specials, including some delicious fresh seafood. *Jak's Restaurant & Bar* on the plaza has some surprisingly good Western favourites including spaghetti, plus curry and grilled fish.

Around Romblon Town

There are good beaches with very simple hut accommodation at **Lonos**, 3km south from Romblon. One of the best is **Bonbon Beach**, about 500m long and with a gently sloping ocean floor that makes it safe for swimming. Also here is **Tiamban Beach**, a short stretch of white sand flanked by palm trees and wooden shacks.

A number of **resorts** have sprung up along this stretch of coast. The first one you reach if you head south from town is *Tiamban Beach Resort* (☎02/723 6710; ❸), a well-run place with native-style cottages right on the beach, many with shady verandas and sunset views. There's a good restaurant and activities such as island-hopping, mountain-biking and diving. Next door are the bamboo cottages of the less grand but equally friendly *Palm Garden Beach Resort* (❷), which has a restaurant in a shady garden. Seven kilometres further south is *Ginablan*, where you'll find *Marble Beach Resort* (❷), which has bamboo cottages with shady verandas right on a pretty beach. A few minutes south of Ginablan in the barangay of **San Pedro** is *San Pedro Beach Resort* (☎0920/905 5780; ❶), a charming, relaxing hideaway with cottages nestled along a hillside overlooking sandy Talipasak Beach. There's home cooking in the restaurant and staff can arrange island-hopping and trekking.

There are a number of little-visited islands off the coast of Romblon Island, including **Alad**, **Lugbung** and **Kobrador**, with fine beaches. There's no formal accommodation though, and they're served by public bancas only twice a week; if you miss the banca back to town, you'll have to ask for a lift from fishermen.

Sibuyan Island

Dominated by the ragged saw-like bulk of Mount Guiting Guiting, the isolated **SIBUYAN ISLAND** is the easternmost of the Romblon group and has everything an adventure traveller could dream of: a sparkling coastline, a thickly forested interior and a couple of daunting mountain peaks. This magnificent emerald isle, covering 450 square kilometres, has one of the most intact natural environments in the entire country, a fact that was recognized in 1996 when a large part of Sibuyan was declared a reserve. Sibuyan's isolation has given it five unique species of mammals, 131 species of bird and more fish species than anyone has yet been able to record. The island's shoreline boasts extensive mangroves giving way to seagrass and seaweed beds in shallow waters, replaced in deeper waters by a halo of coral that rings the entire island. Sibuyan's 47,000 residents, mostly subsistence farmers and hunters who rely on the forest and the ocean to supplement their meagre incomes, rarely see tourists but know every cove, trail and cave on the island and are happy to act as guides. Most of them live in three towns, **San Fernando**, **Cajidiocan** and **Magdiwang**.

Mount Guiting Guiting alone is an unforgettable sight, rising directly from the coastal plain to a height of 2050m. The trail to the summit starts from the Mount Guiting Guiting Natural Park headquarters, a short tricycle ride to the east of Magdiwang where most ferries dock. The trail starts gently enough, winding through pleasant lowlands, but soon becomes very steep. You'll need four or five days to get to the summit and back. Next to Guiting Guiting is **Mayo's Peak** (1530m), a secondary summit that, like its neighbour, is cloaked in mossy forests, ferns and rare orchids. The trek to the top is more straightforward, requiring only 24 hours. If you plan on doing any serious trekking or climbing, you'll have to bring all your equipment with you.

Practicalities

Bancas leave Romblon Town every day for Magdiwang, Cajidiocan and San Fernando. There are also boats to Sibuyan from Panay and Masbate (see p.313). Ask around and you'll be pointed in the direction of one of the island's **homestays**. In Magdiwang, the Feliciano family has a pretty wooden house close to the pier with clean rooms and a shared cold shower; P100 a night is the usual rate, plus a little extra if you want Mrs Feliciano to cook. In San Fernando, *Vicky's Place* on M.H. Del Pilar Street is a family home featuring some bright, airy upstairs guest rooms, with a shared bathroom. Any tricycle driver at the pier can take you there.

Carabao Island

Less than one hour south of Santa Fe on Tablas Island by banca, beautiful little **CARABAO ISLAND** is also easy to reach from Boracay (see box on p.325). All the Boracay dive operators and resorts run trips to the island, or you can rent your own banca for around P1000 for the round-trip. Some resorts on Boracay have speedboats for rent that can do the trip in 45 minutes, about 30 minutes quicker than the quickest bancas.

Only 6km wide from the capital of **San José** on the east coast to **Lanas** on the west, Carabao Island is an idyllic place where fishing is the main industry and tourism has only just begun to have an impact. Divers arrive on day-trips to explore the surrounding reefs; there are a dozen well-known dive sites around the island, but there are no dive operators here so you'll have to bring all your gear.

It's a shame few visitors linger for long on Carabao, because the island is surrounded by beautiful white sand beaches and is small enough to amble from east coast to west coast and back in a day, walking through coconut groves and paddy fields. It's easy to hire a motorbike in San José to get around; an enjoyable ride takes you to Tagaytay Point, the highest point on the island from where there are magnificent views across to Boracay and beyond.

Bancas **arrive** at Carabao Island at **Port Said**, a couple of minutes walk from the island's best beach, **Inobahan Beach**, a one-kilometre stretch of powdery white sand. Here you can **stay** at the friendly and comfortable *Republic of Inobahan Beach Resort* (❶), which has four thatched cottages spacious enough for three. It also has a small restaurant – intriguingly named the *Sir Polyon Lounge* – serving breakfast, soup, hamburgers and grilled meat and fish. A matter of metres away is the *Ging Grill and Restaurant*, where the food is straightforward and cheap, including hot dog sandwiches, noodles and burgers for a bargain basement P20. Another accommodation option is to ask at Port Said for *Vista Violeta* (℡0919/890 9999), which is near the jetty and is actually the mayor's house. For P750 a night he can give you a room for four people, with small shower and toilet.

Travel details

Buses

Samar

Allen to: Calbayog (18 daily; 3hr); Catarman (18 daily; 2hr); Catbalogan (18 daily; 4hr); Davao (daily; 15hr); San José (8–10 daily; 1hr); Surigao (daily; 10hr); Tacloban (4 daily; 7hr).
Borongan to: Calbayog (2 daily; 8hr); Catbalogan (4 daily; 6hr); Guiuan (2 daily; 5hr).
Calbayog to: Borongan (6 daily; 6hr); Basey (8 daily; 6hr); Catbalogan (12 daily; 3hr); Davao (daily; 14hr); Manila (1–2 daily; 17hr); Surigao (daily; 9hr); Tacloban (4 daily; 6hr).
Catarman to: Calbayog (18 daily; 3hr); San José (8–10 daily; 1hr).
Catbalogan to: Basey (8 daily; 4hr); Borongan (4 daily; 6hr); Davao (daily; 12hr); Manila (1–2 daily; 16hr); Surigao (daily; 7hr); Tacloban (18 daily; 4hr).

Leyte

Baybay to: Davao (daily; 12–14hr); Hilongos (12 daily; 3hr); Maasin (12 daily; 4hr); Manila (daily; 14hr); Ormoc (12 daily; 3hr); Tacloban (12 daily; 5hr).
Biliran to: Ormoc (12 daily; 4hr); Tacloban (8 daily; 4hr).
Hilongos to: Baybay (12 daily; 3hr); Maasin (8 daily; 3hr); Sogod (8 daily; 4hr); Tacloban (8 daily; 7hr).
Maasin to: Baybay (12 daily; 4hr); Davao (daily; 10–12hr); Hilongos (8 daily; 3hr); Manila (daily; 16hr); Padre Burgos (8 daily; 2hr); Sogod (4 daily; 4hr); Tacloban (4 daily; 7hr).
Ormoc to: Baybay (12 daily; 3hr); Hilongos (12 daily; 5hr); Maasin (12 daily; 7hr); Naval (several daily; 4hr); Palompon (hourly; 2hr); Tacloban (12 daily; 4hr).
Padre Burgos to: Maasin (8 daily; 2hr); Sogod (8 daily; 3hr); Tacloban (4 daily; 8hr).
Sogod to: Hilongos (8 daily; 4hr); Maasin (4 daily; 4hr); Padre Burgos (8 daily; 3hr); Tacloban (4 daily; 5hr).
Tacloban to: Basey (8–10 daily; 2hr); Baybay (12 daily; 5hr); Biliran (8 daily; 4hr); Calbayog (12 daily;

4hr); Davao (1–2 daily; 12–14hr); Hilongos (8 daily; 7hr); Maasin (4 daily; 7hr); Manila (1–2 daily; 20hr); Ormoc (12 daily; 4hr); Padre Burgos (4 daily; 8hr); Sogod (4 daily; 5hr).

Cebu

Cebu City to: Argao (12 daily; 3hr); Badian (12 daily; 5hr); Bato (12 daily; 6hr); Carcar (12 daily; 2hr); Mactan (24 daily; 45min); Maya (12 daily; 4hr); Moalboal (12 daily; 4hr); Toledo (12 daily; 2hr).

Bohol

Tagbilaran to: Antequera (8 daily; 1hr); Baclayon (12 daily; 45min); Bool (12 daily; 45min); Carmen (12 daily; 2hr); Jagna (12 daily; 2hr); Loboc (12 daily; 1hr); Loon (12 daily; 1hr); Maribojoc (12 daily; 30min); Talibon (8 daily; 4hr); Ubay (8 daily; 4hr 30min).

Negros

Bacolod to: Cadiz (14 daily; 2hr); Dumaguete (4 daily; 6–8hr); Sagay (12 daily; 2hr 30min); San Carlos (8 daily; 4hr); Silay (20 daily; 1hr); Sipalay (4–6 daily; 5hr); Talisay (20 daily; 45min).
Dumaguete to: Bacolod (4 daily; 5–8hr); Bais (18 daily; 1hr); Cadiz (hourly; 4hr); Sipalay (6 daily; 3hr).

Panay

Caticlan to: Iloilo (several daily; 8hr); Kalibo (18 daily; 2hr 30min); Libertad (several daily; 9hr); Roxas (12 daily; 4hr).
Iloilo to: Caticlan (2 daily; 8hr); Estancia (several daily; 6hr); Kalibo (2 daily; 7hr); Roxas (2 daily; 6hr); San José (8 daily; 4hr).
Kalibo to: Caticlan (18 daily; 2hr 30min); Iloilo (several daily; 6hr); Roxas (hourly; 3hr); San José (1–2 daily; 9hr).
Roxas to: Caticlan (12 daily; 4hr); Iloilo (6–8 daily; 6hr); Kalibo (12 daily; 2 hr).
San José to: Caticlan (2 daily; 6hr); Iloilo (several daily; 4hr); Libertad (2 daily; 8hr).

Jeepneys

Samar

Allen to: Calbayog (18 daily; 3hr); Catarman (18 daily; 2hr); Catbalogan (18 daily; 3–5hr); San José (8–10 daily; 1hr); Tacloban (4 daily; 7hr).
Borongan to: Guiuan (2–4 daily; 5–6hr).
Calbayog to: Catbalogan (12 daily; 3hr); Borongan (6 daily; 6hr); Basey (8 daily; 6hr); Tacloban (4 daily; 6hr).
Catarman to: Rawis (24 daily; 2hr); Calbayog (18 daily; 3hr); San José (8–10 daily; 1hr).
Catbalogan to: Borongan (4 daily; 6hr); Basey (8 daily; 4hr); Taft (1–2 daily; 5hr).

Leyte

Baybay to: Hilongos (6 daily; 3–4hr); Ormoc (10 daily; 4hr).
Hilongos to: Maasin (10 daily; 3hr).
Maasin to: Hilongos (10 daily; 3hr); Padre Burgos (8 daily; 2hr).
Ormoc to: Baybay (10 daily; 4hr).
Padre Burgos to: Sogod (10 daily; 2hr 30min).
Tacloban to: Basey (12 daily; 1hr); Maasin (1–2 daily; 8hr).

Cebu

Jeepneys operate between all towns and villages along the coast. Useful routes in the city and its environs include:
Cebu City (Colon St) to: Ayala Center (every 15min; 20min); Lapu-Lapu (every 10–15min; 1hr); Mandaue (every 10–15min; 45min); SM City (every 15min; 30min).

Bohol

Jeepneys operate between all towns and villages along the coast. Routes include:
Tagbilaran to: Antequera (12 daily; 1hr); Baclayon (20 daily; 45min); Bool (20 daily; 45min); Carmen (8 daily; 2hr 30min); Jagna (10 daily; 3hr); Loboc (8 daily; 1hr); Loon (18 daily; 1hr 30min); Maribojoc (18 daily; 45min); Panglao Island (24 daily; 1hr); Talibon (2 daily; 5hr); Ubay (2 daily; 4hr 30min).

Siquijor

Jeepneys connect all points along the coastal road. Routes include:
Larena to: Cantabon (8 daily; 1hr); San Juan (8 daily; 2hr); Sandugan (12 daily; 45min); Siquijor Town (20 daily; 1hr).
Siquijor Town to: Cantabon (6 daily; 1hr); Paliton (12 daily; 1hr); Sandugan (6 daily; 1hr 30min); San Juan (12 daily; 1hr).

Negros

Jeepneys operate between all towns and villages along the coast. Routes include:
Bacolod to: Cadiz (20 daily; 3hr); Murcia (10 daily; 1hr); Sagay (12 daily; 4hr 30min); Silay (20 daily; 1hr 30min); Talisay (20 daily; 1hr).
Dumaguete to: Bais City (24 daily; 2hr); Dauin (24 daily; 1hr 30min); Malatapay (18 daily; 1hr 30min).

Guimaras

Jordan to: Buenavista (12 daily; 45min); Navalas (12 daily; 1hr); Nueva Valencia (12 daily; 1hr 30min).

Panay

Caticlan to: Kalibo (12 daily; 3hr); Roxas (6 daily; 4hr).
Iloilo to: Guimbal (12 daily; 1hr); Miag-ao (12 daily; 1hr 30min).
Kalibo to: Caticlan (12 daily; 3hr).

Romblon

On Romblon Island, regular jeepneys run around the coastal road to and from Romblon Town. On Tablas a jeepney every hour serves all towns and on Sibuyan jeepneys circle the island.

Ferries and scheduled bancas

Samar

Allen to: Matnog (4 daily; 2–3hr).
Guiuan to: Tacloban (daily; 4–6hr).

Leyte

Baybay to: Cebu City (3 weekly; 6hr); Iloilo (weekly; 14hr); Manila (1 weekly; 9hr); Ormoc (several weekly; 4–5hr); Palompon (daily; 5hr).
Biliran to: Cebu City (3 weekly; 6hr).
Hilongos to: Cebu City (1 daily; 2hr).
Liloan to: Surigao (2 weekly; 4hr).
Maasin to: Cebu City (6 weekly; 5hr); Surigao (2 weekly; 6hr); Ubay (several weekly; 4hr).
Naval to: Cebu City (3 weekly; 5hr).
Ormoc to: Baybay (several weekly; 5hr); Cebu City (5 weekly; 5hr); Poro Town (several weekly; 4–6hr).
San Isidro to: Maya (daily; 2hr).
Tacloban to: Basey (several daily; 1hr); Guiuan (daily; 5hr).

Cebu

Argao to: Loon (Bohol; 1–2 daily; 2hr).
Bato to: Tampi (at least 12 daily; 45min–1hr).
Cebu City to: Bantayan (3 weekly; 9hr); Cagayan de Oro (3 weekly; 8hr); Dapitan (3 weekly; 8hr);

Davao (daily; 18hr); Dumaguete (4 daily; 4–6hr); Dumaguit (daily; 14hr); Hilongos (1 daily; 2hr); Iloilo (2 daily; 8hr); Larena (daily; 4hr 15min); Maasin (daily; 5hr); Manila (1–2 daily; 21hr); Masbate (3 weekly; 8hr); Nasipit (3 weekly; 9hr); Naval (3 weekly; 5hr); Ormoc (5 weekly; 5hr); Poro (2 daily; 2hr 30min); Roxas (Panay; 2 weekly; 12hr); Sandakan (Malaysia; weekly; 55hr); Surigao (3 weekly; 7hr); Tagbilaran (3 daily; 1hr 30min); Talibon (5 daily; 3hr); Zamboanga (3 weekly; 12hr).
Danao to: Poro (2–3 daily; 3hr).
Hagnaya to: Bantayan (4 daily; 1hr).
Maya to: Malapascua (8–10 daily; 30min).
Poro Town to: Cebu City (2 daily; 2hr 30min); Danao (2–3 daily; 3hr); Ormoc (several weekly; 4–6hr).
Tangil to: Guihulngan (Negros; daily; 2–4hr).
Toledo to: San Carlos (4 daily; 2–4hr).

Bohol

Jagna to: Cagayan de Oro (weekly; 6hr); Nasipit (weekly; 6hr).
Tagbilaran to: Cagayan de Oro (3 weekly; 6hr); Cebu City (3 daily; 1hr 30min); Dapitan (1 daily; 4hr); Dumaguete (2 daily; 1hr 30min); Larena (1 daily; 2hr 15min); Ozamis (3 weekly; 6hr); Ubay (daily; 2hr).
Talibon to: Cebu City (5 daily; 3hr).
Ubay to: Cebu City (daily; 5hr); Maasin (daily; 3hr); Manila (weekly; 26hr).

Siquijor

Larena to: Cebu City (daily; 4hr 15min); Dumaguete (4 daily; 1hr 15min); Tagbilaran (3 daily; 2hr).
Lazi to: Plaridel (1–2 weekly; 8hr).
Siquijor Town to: Dumaguete (daily; 4hr).

Negros

Bacolod to: Cagayan de Oro (weekly; 12hr); Iligan (weekly; 13hr); Iloilo (4 daily; 1hr); Manila (7 weekly; 17hr); Ozamis (weekly; 10hr); Roxas (Panay; several weekly; 8hr); San José (Panay; 1–2 weekly; 8hr).
Cadiz to: Bantayan (daily; 4hr); Roxas (Panay; daily; 6hr).
Dumaguete to: Cagayan de Oro (several weekly; 6hr 30min); Cebu City (2 daily; 3hr); Dipolog (3 weekly; 6hr); Larena (1 daily; 30min); Manila (4 weekly; 22–25hr); Tagbilaran (2 daily; 1hr 30min); Siquijor Town (daily; 4hr).
Guihulngan to: Tangil (Cebu; daily; 3hr).
San Carlos to: Toledo (4 daily; 4hr).
Valladolid to: Cabalagnan (Guimaras; daily; 45min).

Guimaras

Cabalagnan to: Valladolid (Negros; daily; 45min).
Jordan to: Iloilo (24 daily; 1hr).

Panay

Boracay to: Caticlan (every 10–15min; 20min); Carabao Island (daily; 1hr 30min); Looc (Romblon; daily; 3–4hr); Santa Fe (Romblon; daily; 2–3hr).
Caticlan to: Carabao Island (daily; 2hr); Manila (several weekly; 12hr); Odiongan (Tablas; weekly; 3hr); Roxas (Mindoro; 3 weekly; 8hr); San Fernando (Sibuyan; 3 weekly; 4–6hr); Santa Fe (Romblon; daily; 2hr 20min).
Dumaguit (for Kalibo) to: Cajidiocan (2–3 weekly; 6hr); Cebu City (weekly; 14hr); Manila (several weekly; 17–24hr); Romblon Town (2–3 weekly; 8hr); Roxas (Mindoro; weekly; 7hr).
Iloilo to: Bacolod (4 daily; 1hr); Cebu City (2 daily; 8hr); Davao (weekly; 34hr); General Santos (weekly; 24hr); Jordan (Guimaras; 24 daily; 1hr); Ozamis (weekly; 14hr); Zamboanga (weekly; 28hr).
Roxas to: Bacolod (daily; 6hr); Cebu City (2 weekly; 12hr); Manila (3 weekly; 7hr); Masbate (3 weekly; 8hr); San Fernando (Sibuyan; 2 weekly; 9hr).
San José to: Bacolod (2 weekly; 6hr); Cuyo Town (weekly; 8hr); Manila (weekly; 20hr).

Romblon

Cajidiocan to: Dumaguit (2–3 weekly; 6hr); Mandaon (3 weekly; 6hr).
Looc to: Boracay (daily; 3hr); Roxas (Mindoro; 3 weekly; 4–5hr); Santa Fe (daily; 1hr).
Magdiwang to: Lucena (2 weekly; 14hr); Romblon Town (daily; 3hr).
Odiongan to: Batangas City (4 weekly; 8hr); Caticlan (3 weekly; 4hr); Looc (several daily; 1hr); Manila (3 weekly; 10hr); Roxas (Mindoro; several weekly; 4–6hr).
Romblon Town to: Batangas City (4 weekly; 7hr); Dalahican (3 weekly; 8–10hr); Manila (3 weekly; 10hr); San Agustin (several daily; 1–2hr).
San Fernando to: Caticlan (3 weekly; 4–6hr); Roxas (Panay; 2 weekly; 9hr).
Santa Fe to: Boracay (daily; 3–4hr); Carabao Island (several daily; 2hr); Looc (daily; 1–2hr).

Domestic flights

Bacolod to: Cebu City (daily; 35 min); Manila (several daily; 1hr 20min).
Calbayog to: Manila (3 weekly; 1hr 15min).
Catarman to: Manila (3 weekly; 1hr 15min).
Caticlan to: Cebu City (daily; 1hr); Manila (several daily; 1hr).
Cebu City to: Bacolod (daily; 35min); Bantayan (2 weekly; 30min); Cagayan de Oro (3 weekly; 1hr);

Camiguin (2 weekly; 35min); Caticlan (daily; 1hr);
Cotabato (3 weekly; 1hr 15min); Davao (several
daily; 50min); General Santos (daily; 1hr 15min);
Iloilo (daily; 40 min); Legaspi (2 weekly; 45min);
Manila (16 daily; 1hr 10min); Siargao (2 weekly;
50min); Tandag (weekly; 1hr); Zamboanga (4
weekly; 55min).

Dumaguete to: Manila (2–3 daily; 50min).
Iloilo to: Cebu City (daily; 40min); Davao (daily; 2hr
5min); Manila (8 daily; 1hr 15min).
Kalibo to: Manila (5 daily; 55min).
Roxas to: Manila (11 weekly; 55min).
Tablas to: Manila (2 weekly; 1hr).
Tacloban to: Manila (several daily; 1hr 10min).
Tagbilaran to: Manila (1–2 daily; 1hr 15min).

Palawan

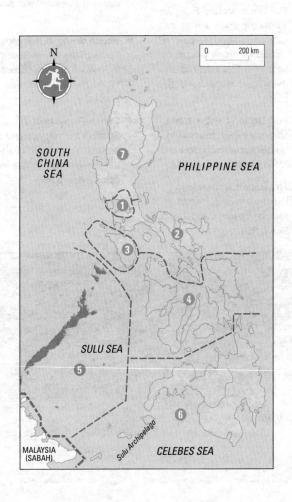

CHAPTER 5 Highlights

❋ **Tubbataha Reef Marine Park**
Take a liveaboard boat out to
dive among sharks and manta
rays. See p.353

❋ **The Underground River** Take
a boat trip under limestone
cliffs and through sepulchral
chambers, along a subterranean river that's said to be
the longest in the world. See
p.354

❋ **Port Barton** Laidback and
convivial beach town with
simple accommodation and
rustic nightlife. See p.354

❋ **The Bacuit archipelago**
Explore majestic limestone
islands, beaches and lagoons.
See p.359

❋ **Cayangan Lake** Arrive by
banca at a hidden blue
lagoon, from where you
scramble uphill to this
dazzling volcanic lake. See
p.360

❋ **Scuba diving in Busuanga**
Some of the wildest diving
in Asia, on sunken Japanese
World War II wrecks. See
p.361

❋ **Culion** Gentle people,
Spanish architecture and a
fascinating museum charting
the island's history as a leper
colony. See p.365

△ Rice field, Palawan

Palawan

f you believe the travel agent clichés, Palawan is the Philippines' last frontier, an unexplored and unexploited province of wondrous scenery and idyllic tropical beauty. For once it's practically true. Tourism has yet to penetrate much of this long, sword-shaped island to the southwest of Luzon, and travellers who make it here will find a marvellous Jurassic landscape of coves, beaches, lagoons and razor-sharp limestone cliffs that rise from crystal-clear water. Palawan province encompasses 1780 islands and islets, most of which have irregular coastlines that make excellent harbours. Many of the islands are surrounded by a coral shelf that acts as an enormous feeding ground and nursery for marine life. It is sometimes said that Palawan's **Tubbataha Reef** is so ecologically important that if it dies the Philippines will also die. Hyperbole perhaps, but it contains an element of truth: the reef is among the richest fishing grounds in Asia and its health is crucial to the health of the nation's marine environment and food supply.

Palawan's **history** can be traced back 47,000 years, as confirmed by the discovery of caveman remains in Quezon in the southwest of Palawan. Anthropologists believe the early inhabitants came from Borneo across a land bridge that connected the two. There are several stories regarding the origin of the name Palawan; some contend that it was derived from the Chinese words *pa lao yu* meaning "Land of the Beautiful Harbours", though popular belief has it that Palawan is a corruption of the Spanish word *paraguas* (umbrella), the main island being shaped like a closed umbrella.

The capital of Palawan, **Puerto Princesa**, is nothing special, but makes a good starting point for exploring the province. From here you can visit the islands of **Honda Bay** and the immense flooded cave systems that make up **St Paul's Underground River**. A few hours' travel from Puerto, **Northern Palawan** is a dazzling mix of superb dive sites, vertiginous cliffs and idyllic tropical islands and beaches. Here you'll find the pretty beach resort town of **Port Barton**, the old fortress town of **Taytay** and the incredibly beautiful islands and lagoons of **El Nido** and the **Bacuit archipelago**. Many areas are still relatively untouched by tourism, such as the friendly little fishing village of **San Vicente** and nearby **Long Beach**, one of the finest stretches of sand anywhere, yet rarely visited by tourists.

Many visitors to Palawan miss Puerto Princesa completely and head straight from Manila to the **Calamian group** of islands, scattered off the northern tip of the main island of Palawan. The biggest of these islands is **Busuanga**, which has a deserved reputation for some of the best **scuba diving** in Asia, mostly on sunken World War II wrecks. Even if you're not a diver, there's plenty to do here, including island-hopping, trekking and kayaking. The little town of **Coron** on

Busuanga has good, affordable accommodation and is the jumping-off point for trips to other islands in the area such as mesmerizing **Coron Island**, with its hidden lagoons and volcanic lake and, to the south, the former leper colony of **Culion**.

Undeveloped **Southern Palawan** contains some of the least visited areas in the whole country. **Brooke's Point**, a trading and fishing outpost, is the access point for trekking nearby at **Mount Matalingajan**. Further afield, a ferry ride or flight northeast from Puerto Princesa, the isolated **Cuyo Islands** feature volcanic islets to explore by banca.

Getting to Palawan by air is fairly simple. The main gateway is Puerto Princesa, served by daily flights with Philippine Airlines, Air Philippines and Seair. Seair and Asian Spirit fly to Busuanga in northern Palawan as well, with Seair also serving El Nido, nearby Rodriguez Airport at **Sandoval** via Busuanga and the Cuyo islands. Seair has flights from Busuanga to Clark (San Fernando) and Busuanga to Caticlan (Boracay), although these are seasonal so check before you travel. WG&A and Sulpicio Lines **ferries** sail from Manila to Coron and Puerto Princesa, while Negros Navigation operates from Manila to Puerto

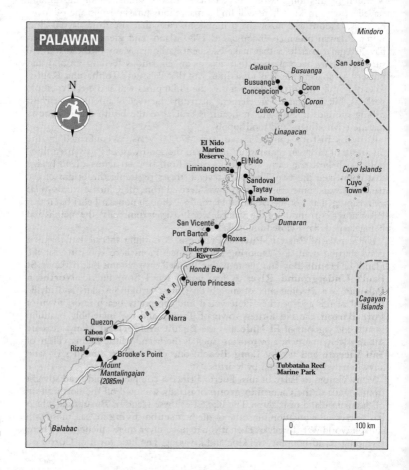

Princesa and between Bacolod and Puerto Princesa, via Iloilo. Cuyo is served by **ferries** from Iloilo and from Manila via San José on Panay, the latter route sailed by MBRS Lines' M/V *Romblon Bay*.

As for **getting around Palawan**, there are very few comfortable air-conditioned buses; many vehicles are battered old affairs with hard seats and may stop very often en route to let passengers off and on, in which case they're hardly quicker than jeepneys. It's best to **bring cash** to cover your stay in Palawan: outside Puerto Princesa credit cards are rarely accepted except by some of the more established resorts, banks are few and ATMs almost nonexistent.

Puerto Princesa and around

The provincial capital **PUERTO PRINCESA** is the only major urban sprawl in Palawan, with 120,000 residents. Puerto Princesa has been touted in the media as one of the country's cleanest and greenest cities, but the reality is different. The main drag, three-kilometre-long Rizal Avenue, is a deafening jumble of tricycles spewing noxious fumes. There are a few sights around Puerto Princesa, but hardly any in the city itself, which is why most visitors treat it as a one-night stop on the way to or from Palawan's beaches and islands.

Puerto Princesa's **Palawan Museum**, in Mendoza Park on Rizal Avenue (Mon, Tues, Thurs & Fri 8:30am–noon & 2–5pm; P20), offers an overview of the history, art and culture of Palawan, but is only worth the effort if you're really at a loose end. Most of the exhibits are fossils and old tools. The **Immaculate Concepcion Cathedral** at the west end of Rizal Avenue is a pretty angular structure with sharp turrets and spires, but it's not historically significant and the interior is ordinary. There are two major **fiestas** in Puerto Princesa: the Tabuan festival on March 4 and the City Fiesta on December 8.

Practicalities

Rizal Avenue runs from the **airport** at the eastern edge of the city to the **ferry port** at the west. If you want to stay in the airport area, you can easily reach the accommodation on foot from the terminal. Buses and jeepneys arrive on Malvar Street.

There are no taxis in Puerto Princesa, but it's not difficult finding a tricycle. The standard fare per person within the city – including the airport and port – is P6 per person, while hiring a tricycle privately for the ride will cost P50.

The **tourist office** (Mon–Sat 9am–5pm; ☎048/433 2968) is in the Provincial Capitol Building on Rizal Avenue, 1km west of the airport at the busy junction with the National Highway, and has maps of the city for P50, but they're not as useful as the *E-Z Map* of Puerto Princesa and Palawan, which many of the city's hotels sell. There's also a small tourist office at the airport itself (☎048/433 2983), with photographs and details of accommodation pinned on the wall. Swagman Travel in Rizal Avenue, opposite the WG&A office, is a good place to find information and make reservations.

The **post office** is on Burgos Street at its junction with Rizal Avenue. There are a growing number of **Internet** cafés in town including 2610 Computer Center in Rizal Avenue, a ten-minute walk west of Mendoza Park, and Moscom Internet in Roxas Street, opposite the Iglesia ni Cristo church. Many hotels and small resorts also have Internet access. There are plenty of **banks**, with PNB at the western end of Rizal Avenue, just beyond Mendoza Park, and PCI at the junction of Rizal Avenue and Lacao Street, a short walk west of the National

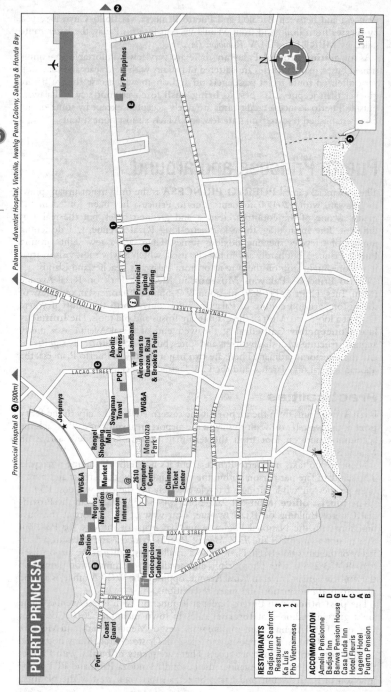

PUERTO PRINCESA

Provincial Hospital & Ⓐ (500m) ◀

Palawan Adventist Hospital, Vietville, Iwahig Penal Colony, Sabang & Honda Bay ▲

② ▲

ABREA ROAD

Air Philippines

N

100 m

0

③

Ⓔ

RIZAL AVENUE

MANALO STREET

ABAD SANTOS EXTENSION

RIZAL AVENUE

NATIONAL HIGHWAY

Ⓘ

ⓓ

Ⓕ

MANALO EXTENSION

Provincial Capitol Building

ℹ

FERNANDEZ STREET

ABAD SANTOS STREET

Aboitiz Express

Landbank

LACAO STREET

Ⓒ

PCI

Aircon vans to Quezon, Rizal & Brooke's Point

Swagman Travel

WG&A

Jeepneys

★

Rengel Shopping Mall

Mendoza Park

MANALO STREET

ABAD SANTOS STREET

WG&A

Market

2610 Computer Center

Chimes Ticket Center

MANALO STREET

MABINI STREET

BONIFACIO STREET

Negros Navigation

@

Moscom Internet

@

BURGOS STREET

Bus Station

Ⓑ

PNB

ROXAS STREET

Immaculate Concepcion Cathedral

✝

Ⓖ

SANDOVAL STREET

CONCEPCION

MALVAR STREET

Coast Guard

Port

RESTAURANTS

Badjao Inn Seafront
Restaurant   3
Ka Lui's   1
Pho Vietnamese   2

ACCOMMODATION

Amelia Pensionne   E
Badjao Inn   D
Banwa Pension House   G
Casa Linda Inn   F
Hotel Fleuris   C
Legend Hotel   A
Puerto Pension   B

Highway junction. Landbank is at the eastern end of Rizal Avenue opposite the *Chow King* fast-food restaurant, and on Rizal Avenue there are also branches of BPI and Allied Bank. There are two good **hospitals**, the Palawan Adventist Hospital on the National Highway, 4km north of the city centre, and the Provincial Hospital, 1km north of the city centre on Malvar Street.

Accommodation

There are more than fifty places to stay dotted around Puerto Princesa. The best of them are at the quieter, greener airport end of Rizal Avenue, although there are also a few reasonable options at the port end of the city.

Amelia Pensionne 420 Rizal Ave ☏048/433 7029. Within walking distance of the airport and offering a good range of en-suite rooms, from basic a/c doubles to larger deluxe doubles with cable TV. ❸

Badjao Inn 350 Rizal Ave ☏048/433 2761, ⓦwww.badjaoinn.com. An unattractive brick structure facing the road and close to the airport, but behind the facade there's a lovely garden and a good choice of spacious rooms overlooking the greenery. The efficient travel desk can book transport for you. Dorm beds $6, ❸

Banwa Pension House Liwanag St ☏048/434 8963, ⓦwww.banwa.com. Casual and friendly backpackers' guesthouse with simple native-style rooms with bamboo beds and private showers. The café serves breakfast, lunch and dinner, including some tasty vegetarian choices. Liwanag Street is at the southern end of town: walk south down Roxas Street past the Pilot Elementary School and it's on your right. Dorm beds P170, ❶

Casa Linda Inn Behind *Badjao Inn*, down a narrow road off Rizal Ave ☏048/433 2606.

Simple, friendly and convenient, with the bonus of good European and Asian food in the breezy café. The rooms are large and arranged around a spacious courtyard garden. All rooms are native-style, with wooden floors and walls made of dried grass, and the place is always clean and orderly – you even have to take your shoes off before you enter. ❶

Hotel Fleuris Lacao St ☏048/434 4338, ⓦwww.fleuris.com. Modest, well-maintained modern establishment, where all rooms have a/c, private bathrooms and cable TV. The rate includes a decent breakfast in the small poolside restaurant. ❼

Legend Hotel Northeastern end of Malvar St, not far from the centre ☏048/433 9076. Upmarket option with spacious a/c rooms and big, tiled bathrooms. The rate includes a buffet breakfast. ❽

Puerto Pension 35 Malvar St, close to the ferry port ☏048/433 2969 or 4149. Cool, clean and quiet, with native ambience and an alfresco top-floor restaurant that has views across the bay. Fan or a/c rooms, all with private bathrooms. ❷

Eating and drinking

There are two exceptionally good **restaurants** in Puerto Princesa. *Ka Lui's*, in Rizal Avenue almost opposite the *Badjao Inn*, is a pretty bamboo restaurant where you take your shoes off before you step inside. The daily set meals are built around either seafood or meat, and most come with a good salad and a small portion of fresh, raw seaweed. There's also an à la carte menu featuring items such as sweet-and-sour *mameng* (wrasse), spicy squid and grilled prawns. The *Badjao Inn Seafront Restaurant* is a classy but informal native-style restaurant on the shore south of the centre, reached on foot from Abueg Road, at the end of Bonifacio Street across a dainty bamboo bridge through a patch of mangroves. It's a little more expensive than *Ka Lui's*; expect to pay about P500 a head for fresh, wonderfully tasty grilled seafood. The main dining area, fashioned entirely from bamboo, is open-air and has terrific views of the sea. If you're here in the evening, getting transport back to the centre can be tricky, so you might want to pay a tricycle driver P100 to get you here and wait around for the return trip.

The area has a community of Vietnamese refugees, and a few 24-hour Vietnamese **noodle shops**, known locally as *chaolaongan*, operate near the market. If you'd prefer to eat at a restaurant, try the *Pho Vietnamese* on Rizal Avenue, a five-minute tricycle ride beyond the airport, for good soups,

Puerto Princesa is linked by **ferry** with Manila, Bacolod, Coron Town, Cuyo and Iloilo. There are a number of ticket outlets in Puerto Princesa for WG&A and Negros Navigation, but none for Sulpicio Lines, although you can buy a ticket for any ferry operator at the port just before departure. One of the most convenient WG&A outlets is the Aboitiz office at 371 Rizal Ave (☎048/433 4875), close to the junction with Lacao Street. There's another in Malvar Street on the north side of the market and one more, called Chimes Ticket Center (☎0918/739 0877), in Burgos Street, south of Rizal Avenue near the market. The Negros Navigation office (☎048/434 4735) is on the second floor of the Kentroy Building, Malvar Street, on the north side of the market.

Air tickets can be booked at travel agents and through many hotels. Philippine Airlines (☎048/433 4565), Air Philippines (☎048/433 7003) and Seair (☎048/434 5272) have offices at the airport, which generally open only when there are arrivals and departures. There's also an Air Philippines office at 420 Rizal Ave.

Moving on by **bus** and **jeepney** to all major destinations in Palawan is easy, with all manner of vehicles departing daily from the chaotic market area in Malvar Street. From here you can head north to Sabang, Port Barton, Roxas, Taytay and El Nido, and south to Quezon and, less frequently, Brooke's Point. There are also a/c FX taxis and various vans serving destinations in the north from the market, and heading south to Quezon and Brooke's Point from the junction of Rizal Avenue and Lacao Street. Your accommodation in Puerto Princesa may also have its own van heading north; they cost a little more, but are quicker and more comfortable than buses or jeepneys.

vegetarian dishes and seafood. A huge bowl of beef or chicken noodles is just P75. **Nightlife** is limited to a few bars at *Ka Lui's*, *Casa Linda Inn* and *Badjao Inn*.

Around Puerto Princesa

There are a few minor attractions around Puerto Princesa that you can easily visit in a day or less, with the **Underground River** slightly further afield (see p.354). Tricycle drivers might try to talk you into taking a personalized tour of some of these places, charging around P500 for half a day; it's not a bad deal for two or three people sharing.

Iwahig Penal Colony
In **Iwahig**, 23km to the northwest of Puerto Princesa, the **Iwahig Penal Colony** is one of the standard day-trips from Puerto Princesa. Jeepneys leave Malvar Street every day at 9.30am (P35) for the colony, which is also known as the Prison Without Bars (daily 8am–7pm; free). Prisoners live at Iwahig as if in an ordinary village, cultivating rice and root crops and fishing. Tourists are welcome to wander around and buy handicrafts made by the inmates, who are identifiable by their prison T-shirts and ID badges. Some long-term residents – those deemed least likely to make a run for it – are allowed to stay with their families in small nipa huts on site. Prison officials say the rate of repeat offending among those released from Iwahig is significantly lower than among those incarcerated in the country's traditional jails.

Vietville
Fifteen kilometres north of Puerto Princesa in the barangay of Santa Lourdes is **Vietville**, a military-owned seaside camp housing around three hundred

refugees who fled the Communist takeover of Vietnam. When UN funding for Vietville ended, the refugees feared they would have to go home, but the Catholic Church's Center for Assistance to Displaced Persons stepped in to pay for electricity and water; the refugees take care of their own food and pay for their children's schooling. There's not actually a great deal to see at Vietville – just people quietly going about their daily business – but there is the guarantee of a delicious meal at the authentic Vietnamese **restaurant**. Don't worry if your Vietnamese isn't up to scratch: all dishes are numbered and accompanied by a photograph.

Honda Bay

Picturesque **Honda Bay**, 10km north of Puerto Princesa, contains seven islands, among them Snake Island, with a good reef for snorkelling, and Starfish Island, which has a rustic restaurant where, on a good day, the seafood is as fresh as it comes, though at other times you might need your own tinned provisions as they often run out of supplies. Look out for Bat Island: in the late afternoon scores of bats leave here on their nocturnal hunting trips.

Any jeepney or bus going north from Puerto Princesa will take you to Honda Bay. You'll need to get off at the wharf in **Santa Lourdes** (reaching the wharf may involve a tricycle ride from where the bus or jeepney drops you), sign in at the little tourist office and book a banca. The boat will cost anything from P200 to P500 depending on which island you plan to visit and for how long. Some islands ask visitors to pay a fee (P20). **Accommodation** in Honda Bay is limited. On Starfish Island, the *Starfish Sandbar Resort* has rustic huts that sleep four (P500–800), but remember to bring your own tinned food because the

Tubbataha Reef Marine Park

Located in the middle of the Central Sulu Sea, 181km southeast of Puerto Princesa, **Tubbataha Reef Marine Park** has become a magnet for scuba divers, who reach it on liveaboard boats – most departing from Puerto Princesa between March and June.

The reef – actually a grouping of dozens of small reefs and coral islands – is one of the finest in the world, with sightings of sharks, manta rays and turtles a daily occurrence, as well as huge shoals of other marine life and a dazzling array of smaller reef fish.

But the visits of around two thousand divers annually, and the trade in shells and handicrafts fashioned from reef materials that has grown up around this, have taken their toll. Fishermen rely on major reefs such as this for their livelihood and as nurseries that regenerate stocks, but overfishing continues, much of it carried out illegally by large Chinese trawlers. Though the authorities regularly arrest Chinese fishermen and impound their vessels, the offenders are usually released after a token period of detention, for fear of jeopardizing diplomatic relations. Repeated anchoring on the fragile coral and dynamite fishing have both added to the damage at Tubbataha, but the authorities have had some success in limiting these activities. Scientists monitoring the reef say that in recent years there has been a slight recovery in marine life, though Tubbataha remains an extremely fragile environment.

Independent travel to Tubbataha is impossible, but dive operators in Manila, Puerto Princesa and Coron Town can arrange **packages** for around US$1200 for a one-week trip, including domestic flights, food and unlimited diving. A typical liveaboard schedule entails sailing overnight from Puerto Princesa to Tubbataha, followed by a number of days of diving at locations such as Jessie Beazley Reef, Black Rock and Bird Island. For details of liveaboards, some of which visit the reef, see p.47.

small restaurant often runs out. *Dos Palmas Arreceffi Island Resort* (Ⓦwww
.dospalmas.com.ph; ❽) is an upmarket place on a private island with chic
accommodation in huts either on stilts above the ocean or set around a lush
garden, and with restaurants, bars, water sports and a spa.

Northern Palawan

The part of Palawan north of Puerto Princesa is the area tourists come to see.
It's got everything: a subterranean river, jungled mountains, pristine beaches,
tropical island hideaways and hundreds of islets, lagoons and coves that you can
explore at your leisure by banca. **Port Barton** is the ideal place to break a
journey through this half of the island, relaxing for a few days and perhaps doing
a spot of exploring or diving. Nearby is **San Vicente**, a quiet fishing town
where the people are amiable and there are some sweeping beaches, including
one that must be the longest in the country. Another relaxing coastal town
where you can stop off for a day or two is **Taytay**, with its old Spanish fort.
From here it's not far to **El Nido** and the **Bacuit archipelago**, some of the
best island-hopping territory on the planet. Further north still is the terrific
Calamian group of islands, which offers some exceptional diving. And for
some real frontier travel, try the **Cuyo Islands**, in the northern Sulu Sea
approximately halfway between Panay and Palawan.

The Underground River

The **Underground River** (or to give it its proper name, **St Paul's Subterranean National Park**) is the sight most visitors to Palawan want to see. The
longest underground river in the world, it meanders for more than 8km
beneath the surface, passing a bewildering array of stalactites, stalagmites,
caverns, chambers and pools, the formations made eerier on your ride through
by the shadows cast by the boatman's paraffin lamp (trips daily 7am–5pm).

The jumping-off point for the river is Sabang, more than two hours north of
Puerto Princesa by road. Many northbound buses and jeepneys from Puerto
Princesa pass through **Sabang** or chartering a jeepney from Puerto Princesa
costs about P1000 one-way. From Port Barton there are daily bancas to Sabang
at 7am and 1pm, returning at 10am and 4pm (P120). At the Visitors' Assistance
Center in Sabang, close to the pier, you pay P150 per person to enter the cave,
plus another P400–500 for four passengers in the boat. It's twenty minutes by
boat from here to the Underground River, and the trip through the cave takes
about an hour. While you're at the visitors' centre, look out for the famous
resident **monitor lizards** (*bayawak*) that are tame enough to take food from
your hand.

Sabang has **beaches** to either side where there are a few simple places to
spend the night. The best of these is the quiet, idyllic *Mary's Beach Resort* (❷), a
ten-minute walk north of the pier along Sabang Beach, with no-frills cottages
right on the sand.

Port Barton

On the northwest coast of Palawan, roughly halfway between Puerto Princesa
and El Nido and around four hours from either by road, **PORT BARTON** is
an agreeable place on pretty, crescent-shaped Pagdanan Bay with fantastic sunset
views, and now something of a travellers' ghetto. There are fourteen white sand

islands in the bay, many of which are the target of diving trips organized by the resorts here. It costs about P800 to rent a banca for a day of island-hopping. Make sure you take snorkelling equipment with you, which can be rented for P150 a day.

Buses and jeepneys from Puerto Princesa arrive on Rizal Street, very close to the beach and the town centre. Bancas from destinations along the coast including Sabang, Taytay, El Nido and San Vicente arrive right on the southern end of the beach close to town.

The best-value accommodation is *Swissippini Lodge and Resort* (℡048/433 2540, ⓦwww.portbartonswissippini.com; ❷), right on the beach a short walk from Rizal Street. The resort has big A-frame cottages, all with balconies and private bathrooms, and also offers Internet access and air-conditioned vans to El Nido and Puerto Princesa. Close by, *Princesa Michaella's* (❷) offers basic, fan-cooled huts on the beach. There are two good resorts at the far (northern) end of the beach, reached either by walking along the sand or to the very end of Rizal Street beyond the junction with Roxas Street. *Greenview Resort* (℡0921/326 0565; ❷) and *El Dorado Sunset Resort* (❸) are both clean and quiet, with fan cottages on the shore, all with private bathrooms and verandas. Some of *Greenview's* cottages have a small kitchen, so you can prepare simple meals. Most of the eating in Port Barton is at the resorts themselves; *Swissippini* has a good restaurant offering Filipino and European food for P200 or less per person.

San Vicente

About 15km north along a rough coastal road from Port Barton is the sleepy fishing village of San Vicente, which has a market and a pier where bancas can be chartered. You can take a bus, jeepney or banca here from Port Barton, or a bus from Puerto Princesa via Roxas on Palawan's east coast. The road from Roxas cuts westwards across the island, through quiet barrios and then up a narrow rough road through dense rainforest before reaching the west side of Palawan. It's a long trip – at least four hours – but very scenic.

San Vicente isn't a tourist destination in itself, but around it there are some marvellous beaches including Long Beach, an undeveloped fourteen-kilometre stretch of sand south of town that ranks as one of the most extraordinary beaches in the country – you can see both ends only on a brilliantly clear day. A few kilometres north of the village, a quiet and charming resort right on a dazzling white crescent of sand, *Caparii Dive Camp* (℡0916/824 1252; ❻) is an idyllic, laidback sort of place, with few visitors except those who know it and return regularly. Accommodation is in solid wooden huts with air-conditioning and old Spanish-style four-poster beds with mosquito nets. The open-air beach-front restaurant offers a choice of meals; everything is fresh and the beer is ice cold.

To get to the *Caparii* or Long Beach you'll need to use the only form of local public transport, riding pillion on a motorcycle; you can get a ride from San Vicente's market, near the pier. The trip from San Vicente to Long Beach will cost around P50. At the resort you can ask staff to find motorbike transport for you if you want to get around.

Taytay and around

On the east coast of Palawan, about 140km north of Port Barton by road and 50km south of El Nido, the quaint and friendly town of TAYTAY ("tie-tie") was once capital of Palawan. The town is stretched out along a pleasant bay and offers great views across Taytay Bay from the smallish, squat **stone fort** built by the Spanish in 1622, a sign of its important trading history. Also well worth a look is the atmospheric old Spanish **Church of Santa Monica**, built in the seventeenth century with immense blocks fashioned from coral.

Taytay is a jumping-off point for a number of offshore **islands**, which you can reach by chartering a banca for the day from the little wharf. Make sure you take a mask and snorkel because the waters in these parts are gin-clear, with lots of coral and marine life. Among the islands, Elephant Island and Castle Island are known for the quality of their edible birds' nests (*nido*; see below). Elephant Island has an immense cave full of water, with a natural skylight in the roof that makes it a wonderful place to swim. There's a fine reef near Dinot Rocks Island where sea turtles make regular appearances, while Abalone Island, as the name implies, is a good source of the expensive seafood delicacy.

Lake Danao, the only lake in mainland Palawan, is another good side trip from Taytay. A twenty-minute jeepney ride from town takes you right to the lakeshore in the barangay of Danao, where there are kayaks and a few windsurfing boards for rent.

It's easy enough to reach Taytay. The small **airstrip** at Sandoval on the northern edge of the bay is served by Seair flights from Manila, and there are plenty of tricycles to take arriving passengers to Taytay. **Jeepneys and buses** from Puerto Princesa are limited, but there are three morning buses from Port Barton which arrive at the market in Taytay. **Bancas** from El Nido and Coron Town arrive either at Taytay itself or at the Embarcadero pier to the west, from where you can get a tricycle the remaining 8km to Taytay.

Accommodation in Taytay itself is limited to a handful of simple lodgings. *Pem's Pension House and Restaurant* (❶), on Taytay Bay near the fort, has single rooms with a shared bathroom, plus smallish cottages with private bathrooms and a choice of fan or air-conditioning. They serve simple but tasty food here, with breakfast for P80 and grilled-fish dishes with rice for lunch and dinner from P100. The other budget option is *Casa Rosa Cottages & Restaurant* (❶), a pleasant little resort on a low hill behind the town hall. Their double cottages are good value, with views of the ocean, while the restaurant has delicious home-cooked spaghetti, pizza, fish and grilled chicken. Out on the islands in Taytay Bay, the swish *Club Noah Isabelle* (☎02/844 6688, ⓦwww.clubnoah .com.ph; ❸) on Apulit Island offers accommodation in luxury cottages built on stilts over the water; you can actually see baby sharks from your balcony. The resort has various bars and restaurants, including a lovely little bar high on a rocky cliff at the back of the beach, reached up 109 steps. Another upmarket option is beautiful *Flower Island Resort* (☎02/893 6455 in Manila, ⓦwww .flowerislandresort.com; ❻) on Flower Island. It has seven romantic and attractively furnished huts scattered along the shore, a restaurants and lots of opportunity for sports such as kayaking, snorkelling and diving. *Club Noah* and *Flower Island* both include the cost of transfers from the airport and back in their rates.

El Nido and the Bacuit archipelago

The small coastal town of **EL NIDO** in the far northwest of Palawan is departure point for trips to the many islands of the **Bacuit archipelago**. This is limestone island country, with spectacular rock formations rising from the iridescent sea everywhere you look. These iconic karst cliffs with their fearsomely jagged rocky outcrops are believed to have been formed sixty million years ago, emerging from the sea as a result of India colliding with mainland Asia. As soon as the cliffs emerged, weathering and erosion started working on them to form deep crevices, caves, underground rivers and sinkholes.

El Nido's cliffs are home to the **swiftlet**, or *balinsasayaw*, which produces the rare **nido**, the edible birds' nests that gave the town its name. The nests consist of strands of the birds' own gummy saliva, which hardens when exposed to air. One kilogramme of *nido*, the main ingredient in the Chinese bird's nest soup, fetches up to P150,000. Access to the nests is only allowed during government-specified periods, to ensure that the swiftlets have reached maturity, but in an isolated region such as this the law is hard to enforce, and there's little doubt illegal gathering of the nests continues.

The archipelago itself has now been declared a **marine reserve**, the main purpose being to safeguard marine resources, especially the turtles which nest on many beaches and the fish which support the local people. The area's striking beauty has not gone unnoticed by developers, who have established a number of **exclusive resorts** on some of the islands. If US$200 a night for a taste of paradise is too much for you, stay in rustic El Nido itself – where electricity almost always cuts off at midnight – and island-hop by day.

El Nido

EL NIDO is a compact, relaxed town of narrow streets hemmed against the shore by the sheer Marble Cliffs at the back; you can walk from one end of town to the other in a matter of minutes. Don't miss the one-hour climb to the top of the Marble Cliffs; it's a strenuous haul, but the views are magnificent. The town's main beach has fantastic views, but the **beach** itself is only average and not especially attractive for swimming because of the number of bancas coming and going. Sunset Lover's beach is much better and only a short walk along the coastal path heading north.

Buses and jeepneys arrive at the northern end of Calle Hama Street, a stone's throw from the beach. From the **airport**, served by Seair, it's a twenty-minute

△ El Nido

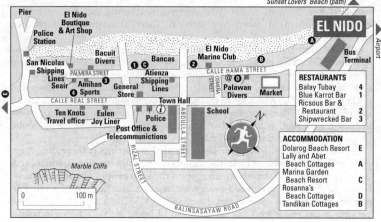

tricycle ride into town (P180 per tricycle). The **pier** is at the southern end of the beach, a short walk from accommodation.

The **tourist office** on Calle Real Street (daily 8am–6pm), near the town hall one block inland from the beach, is one of the best in the country, with useful hand-drawn maps of the area, a list of accommodation and information on trips and activities. Another good place to get up-to-date local information is the El Nido Boutique & Art Shop in Palmera Street. You can **change money** at many of the resorts and also at the general store on Calle Real Street, opposite the **police station**, which is next to the town hall; there's another police station at the end of the pier. There are a number of reliable **dive operators** including Amihan Sports, at the southern end of town in Palmera Street, and El Nido Marine Club (℡0916/668 2748), which is hard to miss right in the middle of the beach.

Accommodation

It's easy to walk from the bus and jeepney arrival point to all the town's accommodation, of which there's no shortage, most of it budget.

Dolarog Beach Resort ℡0919/321 9986, ⓦwww.dolarog.com. Peaceful beachside accommodation in the quiet and rather isolated little barangay of Corong-Corong, south of El Nido. The five thatched cottages stand in a grassy coconut grove on a private beach. The resort is well run, serves excellent meals and is easy enough to reach from town by tricycle (P100) or banca (about P200 for the boat). You can also make arrangements for resort staff to meet you at the airport. ⑥

Lally and Abet Beach Cottages ℡0920/905 6822, ⓦwww.lallyandabet .com. Long-established and well-run resort at the northern end of town right on the shore (off Calle Hama Street). More than thirty fan or a/c rooms and cottages, many with terrific views across the bay and with balconies where you can sit and

watch the world go by. They're also neatly furnished, with tiled floors, immaculate bathrooms and king-sized bamboo beds. There's a good restaurant where the bulk of the menu is fresh seafood. ⑦

Marina Garden Beach Resort ℡0916/562 2404. Small rooms and cottages, some with balconies and private bathrooms. Rooms are a little tired and the walls are thin, but the location is perfect, right in the middle of the beach. ②

Rosanna's Beach Cottages ℡0929/605 4631. A choice of four spacious doubles in a large building on the beach, and two cottages in a neighbouring small garden. The eponymous Rosanna and her husband are friendly and helpful hosts. ②

Tandikan Cottages ℡0927/562 6350. Rustic resort in a fine location with sea and mountain views. The cottages are simple, but the service is friendly; you'll wake in the morning to find a flask of hot water on your balcony for coffee. The bad news? The owner raises fighting cocks and they make one heck of a noise. ❶

Eating and drinking

Dining and nightlife in El Nido are very relaxed affairs, with a handful of laidback **beach bars** offering simple food and cold beer. *Blue Karrot Bar* on the beach is a convivial watering hole with a simple menu including burgers, pizza and grilled seafood. A little south of here, *Shipwrecked Bar* does cocktails and cold beer, plus pasta and more pizza and grilled seafood. Also on the beach, *Ricsous Bar & Restaurant* is a laidback travellers' haunt with a variety of Asian and European food and good music on the stereo. For live music, try the intriguing new *Balay Tubay* on Calle Real Street, which has regular jam sessions on native instruments, as well as well-prepared Filipino food.

The Bacuit archipelago

Finding a banca to take you **island-hopping** around the Bacuit archipelago for the day is no problem, either just around at the pier, or most accommodation in El Nido will arrange one for you, usually charging P300 per person or P800–1500 per boat for a whole-day tour, including a packed lunch. If you simply want to stay put on a beach for a few hours and do some snorkelling, you can charter a boat for P300 to take you to Commando Beach, Lapus-Lapus Beach or Paradise Beach, all with dazzling white sand and good coral. Masks and fins can be rented for P150.

There are more than forty islands in the area, so you've got a lot to go at, though a typical itinerary would include Miniloc, Snake and Pangalusian islands. **Miniloc Island**, 45 minutes from town, boasts one of El Nido's greatest treasures, **Big Lagoon**, surrounded by towering limestone cliffs which look like a cathedral rising from the water. The lagoon is spectacular at any time, but even more so during a full moon, when light pours in from the top, illuminating the water. Nearby **Small Lagoon** is only accessible through a small gap in the rocks by kayak or by swimming through. **Snake Island** has a serpentine sandbar

---

Moving on from El Nido

Bancas from El Nido are infrequent, but you can charter your own boat, usually for a maximum of six passengers, for P3800 to Port Barton and P6000 to Sabang. From **Liminangcong**, one hour south of El Nido by banca, there's a cargo boat twice a week to Coron Town and then Manila. Another maritime option is M/V *Asuncion IV*, which leaves El Nido every Sunday for Manila (P700 including food). You can buy tickets at the El Nido Boutique & Art Shop. *Eulen Joy Liner*, whose little office – no more than a desk in a hut – is on Calle Real Street, has ferries from El Nido to Puerto Princesa (P250), Roxas (P150) and Taytay (P80).

There's no public road transport north of El Nido. Southbound, there's a daily **bus** and **jeepney**, both leaving El Nido at 9am, to Taytay and on to Puerto Princesa; the bus (P380) is faster and more comfortable. During the rainy season, however, the road south is often washed out, in which event you'll have to charter a banca (P1800–2200) as far as Taytay, where you can catch a bus or jeepney for Puerto Princesa.

Seair flies regularly from El Nido to Manila via Puerto Princesa; they have an office next to the El Nido Boutique & Art Shop, or you can contact them on ☏0918/506 6123. Ask at the Ten Knots Travel Office on Calle Real Street about flights to Manila on Island Transvoyager (🌐 www.islandtransvoyager.com). This small charter operator serves *El Nido Miniloc Island* and *El Nido Lagen Island* resorts, and sometimes has spare seats up for grabs.

lapped by crystal-clear waters, making it a great spot for sunbathing and a dip, while **Pangalusian Island** with its long, palm-fringed, white sand beach is perfect for swimming and snorkelling. A good place to spot turtles and manta rays is **Tres Marias**, northwest of Miniloc.

Accommodation

Owned by the same company, *El Nido Miniloc Island* and *El Nido Lagen Island* (T02/894 5644, Wwww.elnidoresorts.com; ●) are both located on private islands with superb beaches and diving, and offer similarly stylish tropical accommodation in fan-cooled or air-conditioned cottages. Both also have package rates including meals and watersports such as kayaking and scuba diving, and if you're intending to be active during your stay these deals can represent better value than just paying for a room. On Malapacao Island, about thirty minutes south of El Nido by banca, there are another two resorts. Stridently and eccentrically New Age, the *Malapacao Island Retreat and Healing Spa Paradise* (T0917/896 3406, Wwww.malapacao.com; ●) offers a bewildering range of packages that include not just accommodation, meals and transfers from El Nido, but also detox therapy, yoga, colon therapy and goodness knows what else. There are discounts for women's groups and long-stayers. Alcohol is not allowed, nor are children under 6, while children under 12 are not encouraged. On the other side of Malapacao, *Marina del Nido* (T02/831 0597; ●) has spacious beach cottages for up to six, and good set meals from P200 per person.

The Calamian Islands

A great area for island-hopping, kayaking, diving and trekking, the **Calamian Islands** off the northern edge of mainland Palawan number a few hundred, the largest being **Busuanga**. Just to the southeast are the precipitous limestone cliffs of undeveloped **Coron Island**. It's only when you get close to them in a banca that they reveal dozens of perfect little coves, hidden in the folds of the mountains. Tribes still live in the interior, where, a short, steep climb takes you to the island's volcanic **Cayangan Lake**, not only a lovely place to swim but also one of the area's favourite dive sites. You could spend a lifetime around Coron Island and still not get to see every hot spring, hidden lake or pristine cove. South of Busuanga is the large island of **Culion**, home to a former leper colony and a fascinating museum, which is open to visitors. Off the northern tip of Busuanga, **Calauit** is where President Marcos sat under a tree (still standing) in August 1976 to sign Executive Order 1578, creating a bizarre **wildlife sanctuary** on the island that would be home to hundreds of African animals and dozens of rare Philippine species.

Most visitors arrive at the small **airport** on the northern side of Busuanga island, or by ferry at **Coron Town**, the main settlement on the island. There's a wide range of budget **accommodation** in Coron Town, and more expensive resorts scattered around the islands. The waters around the Calamians are a feeding ground for the endangered **dugong** (see box p.364) and some resorts can arrange snorkelling trips with the chance of seeing one of these gentle creatures.

Coron Town

Busuanga's main town is the rickety little fishing community of **CORON TOWN**, on the south coast. There's no beach here, but the presence of several Japanese World War II wrecks (see box opposite) in the bays nearby has

Volcanic **Cayangan Lake**, reached by climbing (with your tank and weights on your back) up a steep flights of steps into the interior of Coron Island, offers some of the most unusual diving in the country. On the surface the water is the usual temperature, but deep down it heats up so much that you can drift along on hot thermals.

However, it's the World War II **Japanese shipwrecks** in the Coron area that most divers come for. There are eleven wrecks in all, sunk by US aircraft on September 24, 1944. The best of these is the **Irako**, still almost intact and home to turtles and enormous groupers, who hang in mid-water and eyeball you as you float past. A swim through the engine room reveals a network of pipes and valves inhabited by moray eels and lionfish, which look like liquid flame and have spines that deliver a hefty dose of poison. Other wrecks include:

Akitsushima A big ship lying on her side with a crane once used for hoisting the seaplane. Between Culion and Busuanga islands, near Manglet Island, the wreck attracts huge schools of giant batfish and barracuda.

Kogyo Maru Japanese freighter lying on her starboard side in 34m of water. In the large cargo holds you can see loaded construction materials, a cement mixer and a small bulldozer, while there are anti-aircraft weapons on deck.

Morazan Maru Japanese freighter sitting upright at 28m. Large shoals of banana fish, giant batfish and pufferfish the size of footballs can be seen, especially around the mast, bow and stern. It's easy to get into the cargo holds, making this a good wreck dive for beginners.

Olympia Maru A beautiful dive, with big groupers, sweetlips, turtles and sea snakes around; you can swim through the cargo rooms and the engine room.

Taiei Maru Japanese tanker covered with beautiful corals and a large variety of marine life. The deck is relatively shallow at between 10m and 16m deep, and is well suited to wreck-dive beginners.

⑤

PALAWAN | Northern Palawan

inspired many scuba divers to make a pilgrimage to the area. To find your own patch of sand you can charter a banca and head off to the island of your choice.

Seair and Asian Spirit both have regular **flights** to Busuanga. The little **YKR Airport**, no more than a grass strip with a small terminal building and a few sari-sari stores, is half an hour north of Coron by jeepney (P100). There's always a jeepney waiting to meet incoming flights. For the return trip, a jeepney leaves from the respective airline office (both on Real Street; Seair ☎0920/909 8639; Asian Spirit ☎0921/691 4574) in Coron Town about two hours before every departing flight.

It's possible to make arrangements in advance with resorts to send a private air-conditioned van to meet you at the airport, although at P1000 this is a little expensive. For visitors staying at the more expensive island resorts such as Club Paradise (see p.365) private transport will be included.

WG&A and Sulpicio Lines ferries from Manila arrive at the **pier** east of Coron Town, from where it's a short tricycle ride into town. The WG&A ticket office (☎0919/540 1695) is opposite the Seair office in Real Street. Other operators serving Coron Town include San Nicolas Shipping, which has three trips weekly from Manila to Coron (Tues, Thurs & Sat; ☎0918/216 1764); and Atienza Shipping Lines (☎0927/406 6036), which operates a Liminancong–El Nido–Coron–Manila route twice a week. Big bancas from Culion and occasionally El Nido arrive at the smaller pier in Coron Town itself, close to the market.

△ Busuanga Island

The centre of Coron Town is around this smaller pier (where bancas can be chartered) and the nearby market. There are a dozen or so **dive operators** in town: Dive Right is near *L&M Pe Lodge*; Discovery Divers is a short walk out of town towards the airport; and *Sea Dive Resort* (opposite) has a well-equipped dive operation and is popular with beginners and advanced divers. West of the market are more dive shops and, at the next junction, Swagman Travel, next to which is a Western Union office and adjacent to that, Pascual Video, which has **Internet access**. At Globe Telecom & Internet Cafe, a short walk east of town along Don Pedro Street, you can make phone calls and access the Internet. There are a couple of small banks in town, including Landbank, a fifteen-minute walk to the east beyond *Darayonan Lodge*, which doesn't have an ATM but does change US dollars.

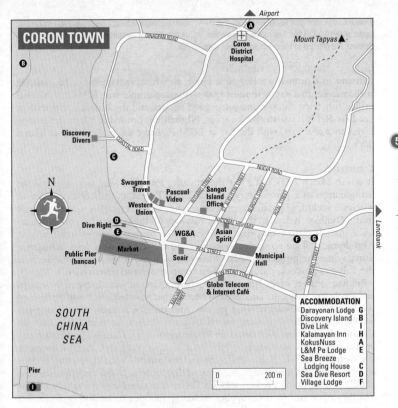

Accommodation

Most places to stay are around the pier and can be noisy as the locals perform some terrible karaoke at night and the cockerels start their chorus before dawn.

Darayonan Lodge A 5min walk east of the centre ☎02/821 0637 or 823 2752. This rambling bamboo house has well-kept rooms nicely furnished in native style, some with private facilities. They also have an alfresco restaurant serving breakfast, lunch and dinner. **2**

Kalamayan Inn In the town centre a little east of the market and pier ☎02/633 4701. En-suite, a/c rooms downstairs and standard rooms upstairs with fan or a/c and shared bathrooms. Choose a room away from the road if you can. Rates include breakfast. **2**

KokusNuss ☎0919/448 7879, ⓦwww .kokosnuss.info. A 10min tricycle ride from Coron, and the first accommodation you come to if you approach from the airport, this has decent double bungalows with private bathrooms built around a pleasant garden. **3**

L&M Pe Lodge ☎0918/514 5254. Built on a pier close to the market, with simple, small rooms and a popular bar and restaurant where divers gather in the evening to swap stories. **2**

Sea Breeze Lodging House No phone. Three small, basic nipa huts in a relatively quiet area, down a narrow track leading off the main road to the west of the market. Each hut has two double beds and private shower and toilet. **1**

Sea Dive Resort ☎0918/400 0448, ⓦwww.seadiveresort.com. Popular divers' resort offering a variety of simple but comfortable fan rooms, a/c rooms and dorm beds, built around a pier a few minutes west of the town centre. There's a decent restaurant and bar and Internet access, and the dive facilities are first-rate. **1**

Village Lodge Next door to *Darayonan*, east of the centre T0919/222 1161. The rooms here are the cleanest and quietest in town, and some have their own bathroom. An extra bed costs P100. Breakfast in the pleasant restaurant is included in the rate. ❶

Eating, drinking and nightlife

Cuisine in Coron Town largely amounts to whatever happens to be available at the market that day with most resorts offering simple fare. *L&M Pe Lodge* has grilled fish, fried chicken and some good curries, and the laidback restaurant at *Sea Dive Resort* is worth checking out. **Nightlife** is limited to tall stories among divers in a few bars, with the bar at *L&M Pe Lodge* a popular hangout after a day's diving.

Calauit

It was in March 1977, just a few months after President Marcos authorized the inauguration of a game reserve on **CALAUIT**, that animals of eight African species – including giraffes, zebras, elands, impalas and gazelles – were shipped from Mombasa, Kenya, to this part of Palawan. All the original 104 animals have since died, but their offspring have multiplied to number over five hundred. Also doing well are more than one thousand native Calamian deer (there were thirty when the project started). Other rare indigenous species present include the Palawan peacock, mouse deer, bearcats, pythons and porcupines.

But like so many of the late dictator's schemes, Calauit was hampered by scandal and cronyism. Rumours circulated in Manila that Marcos's son Bong Bong used the island as a private hunting reserve. And there was discontent among the island's aborigines, who were forced to leave Calauit for non-arable land on Culion Island, where they could no longer grow crops. Calauit's problems today are twofold: a lack of funding and the Balik-Calauit (Back to Calauit) movement, the members of which are settling in various parts of what they claim is their ancestral land and threatening the work of the wardens. In the circumstances, the island's staff are doing a remarkable job. Their salaries start at only P6000 a month, and they often run short of supplies, including food for themselves.

Most resorts in the area will arrange banca trips to **Calauit** for around P1000 per person. To reach Calauit on your own, your best bet is to charter a banca

Mermaids in danger

Culion is surrounded by thirteen islets, whose shallow bays serve as a breeding ground for the **dugong**. Mistaken for mermaids by ancient seafarers, dugongs are sometimes called sea cows, because they graze on a kind of sea grass that was once found extensively around the Calamian Islands. Dredging, development and pollution have resulted in the decline of sea-grass fields and a consequent fall in the number of dugongs here – there are fewer than a hundred left in the Philippines. It's the same sad story around the world: in Australia numbers have halved to around 1700 in the past twenty years.

Dugongs are extraordinary, gentle animals – five hundred kilos of muscle and blubber, with paddle-like flippers, a powerful spade of a tail and a vaguely human face with long whiskers and a morose lip. Being **mammals**, they breathe air through lungs and give birth to live young. Apart from its declining food source the dugong has another problem: females give birth to a single calf only every three to seven years, hardly a rate of procreation to keep numbers up. Even in Busuanga your chances of finding yourself face-to-face with a dugong are slim; your best hope is to tour to their feeding grounds, where you can snorkel among the sea grass and hope for a sighting. The best tours are arranged by *Club Paradise* ($20; 3hr; see opposite).

for the day (expect to pay around P1000) in **Salvacion**, on Busuanga's southwest coast. Admission to the island costs P100 for Filipinos, P300 for tourists, the fee going into central government coffers. The bancas take you to within walking distance of the warden's office and administration building, where you can arrange a motorized **tour** around the island (2hr; P500 for a group of six), getting you close to many of the animals. You can ask one of the wardens to take you on a walking tour, for which there isn't a fixed rate, though it should cost roughly the same as the motorized trip. The landscape in the reserve bears comparison to the African savanna, with low scrub and few hills, but that's where the resemblance ends: many of the animals, used to living close to humans, are tame enough to take food from your hand.

Culion

About two hours south of Coron Town by banca, **CULION** makes for a fascinating day or overnight trip. The approach to the pretty little capital, **Culion Town**, is dominated by a large Catholic church built on the site of an old Spanish fort. There are tremendous views from up here, north to Coron Town and east across a deep natural harbour, where Spanish ships once anchored.

The island was once the world's largest **leper colony**, begun with six hundred patients who were forcibly rounded up throughout the archipelago in 1908. Given the concern about leprosy at the time, this was considered neither cruel nor unusual, simply a way of bringing the sick together in one place so a cure could be found and transmission limited. An early twentieth-century travelogue described Coron as "suitable to the comfort of those who must die slow deaths within its boundaries". By 1922 more than four thousand patients were being administered a new treatment based on *chaulmoogra* oil, extracted from hydnocarpus trees. There are still a handful of people with leprosy left here, but with the disease no longer the problem it once was, the sanatorium has become a general hospital that serves all the islands in the area. A recently renovated **museum** in the hospital compound (Mon–Sat 10am–5pm; P25) details the history of the colony and contains medical relics and photographs from the turn of the last century, when American doctors employed by the colonial government in Manila searched desperately for a cure for leprosy. The museum is one of the most intriguing in the Philippines, with a vast archive of original photographs and patient records that you can browse. The rooms where doctors worked have been maintained as they were and contain equipment the doctors actually used, much of it looking like instruments of torture.

Culion can only be reached by banca from Coron Town (P110); the M/V *Santa Barbara* leaves at 11.30am daily from either the large pier where the ferries dock or the smaller pier outside the *Bayside Divers Lodge*. On Fridays the boat returns to Coron Town at 4.30pm, giving you only three hours or so in Culion – just enough for the main sights. Every other day it remains overnight in Culion so you'll have to stay unless you can find a local willing to offer a private return trip (about P800). Culion's only **hotel** is the *New Luncheonette Lodge* right on the water's edge (❶), with spartan doubles and a restaurant.

Resorts elsewhere in the Calamians

Around Busuanga there are a number of pricey resorts, most of them on their own private island or beach. There's no regular transport to most of these places, so you'll generally need to book in advance and arrange to be met at the airport.

Club Paradise Dimakya Island, off the northern coast of Busuanga ☎ 02/838 4956 to 4960, | ⓦ www.clubparadisepalawan.com. Slick, German-owned place with cosy a/c cottages a stone's throw from the sea, various watersports and diving. The rate includes the cost of collecting you at the airport. Full board ❾

🏃 **Coral Bay Marine Reserve** Popototan Island, at the western edge of the group ☎02/371 9928 or 372 6031, ⓦwww.coralbay .com.ph. Comfy, rustic accommodation in fan-cooled wooden huts on an island about 1hr from Coron Town by banca. This is a peaceful place to chill out, and you can trek around the island or snorkel just offshore on a beautiful reef teeming with tropical fish. Owned by the same people as *Dive Link*, so you can arrange a "twin resort" package. Full board. There are also a number of private homes on the island that can be rented when the owners are not staying there. ❼

Discovery Resort Decanituan Island, a 10min banca ride from Coron Town ☎0920/901 2414, ⓦwww.ddivers.com. Popular dive-oriented resort with a 24hr shuttle service back and forth to Coron Town. The bungalows all have private bathrooms and terraces with fine views of the bay. Staff are friendly and reasonably efficient, and there's a good restaurant. The beach here is nothing special, but horse riding and kayaking are available. ❻

Dive Link Uson Island, just a few minutes west of Coron Town ☎02/371 9928 or 372 6031, ⓦwww .divelink.com.ph. Twin, double and family cottages with fans and private bathrooms. There's only a small patch of brown beach amid the mangroves, but there's compensation in the terrific views from the cottages, and there's a large pool. Full board ❼

Maricaban Bay Marina Resort In a beautiful bay on Busuanga's north coast ☎02/838 4956 to 4960. Chic native-style resort set on a 500m beach. The double cottages are all spacious, comfortable and have big verandas facing the beach; facilities include a pool, diving, restaurant and floating bar. Staff can arrange various trips around the islands. ❾

🏃 **Sangat Island Reserve** Sangat Island, 30min from Coron Town ☎0919/299 5469, ⓦwww.sangat.com.ph. On a beautiful island with a giddy interior of cliffs and jungle, and a shore of coves and coral reefs. Accommodation is in pretty beach cottages. Full board. There's also a Sangat Island reservation office in Coron Town. ❾

The Cuyo Islands

The 45 tiny members of the **Cuyo Islands** are a world unto themselves. Effectively in the middle of nowhere, seventeen hours from Puerto Princesa by ferry, even the main island, **Cuyo**, has no resorts. The islands might see more tourists now that Seair has two flights a week from Puerto Princesa to the little landing strip on Cuyo. There's plenty to do in these parts, but you must be willing to put up with an almost complete lack of tourist infrastructure and the vagaries of the weather – Cuyo is in the path of some serious winds that can disrupt plans for island-hopping.

The best base is **CUYO TOWN** on the western side of Cuyo, a pleasant fishing village with an estimable old Spanish fort and church and a pier where ferries arrive and you can charter a banca. A typical day's island-hopping will cost P600 and include visits to uninhabited **Pandan Island**, a strikingly beautiful place with black volcanic rocks and a ribbon of sand, **Selad Island**, which has a fine beach and good snorkelling, and **Bisucay Island**, where there's also snorkelling. Cuyo Island itself is crisscrossed by paths leading through coconut and cashew groves, making it a good place to explore on foot. From Cuyo Town, for instance, you can walk 8km to **Quejano Beach** on the north side of the island, where a resort has been under construction for a number of years. Another good walk is to the summit of little **Mount Aguado**, from where there are panoramic views of the whole island. You can reach the trail in ten minutes by tricycle from Cuyo Town.

From Cuyo's **airstrip** it's a P15 tricycle ride into Cuyo Town. The **pier** is at the end of Sandoval Street, just 100m from the centre. The only **accommodation** in town is 200m inland from the pier: the *Paloma Lodge* (❶) in Sandoval Street has six rooms, each with a bunk bed and fan, and sharing a small toilet and cold shower. You can **eat** at the nearby *Sandoval Canteen*, where staff can rustle up scrambled eggs for breakfast, grilled fish and the local speciality, jackfruit and bean soup. Another favourite local dish as *lato*, a type of seaweed that looks like miniature bunches of grapes and is eaten raw. The **Seair office** is actually in the canteen.

Southern Palawan

A journey through southern Palawan represents one of the last great travel challenges in the Philippines. Much of the area is sparsely populated, with limited accommodation and nothing in the way of dependable transport, communications or electricity. The major attraction is **Tabon Caves**, a little south of the town of **Quezon**. Many caves in this immense network are still unexplored, and the site is one of the country's most significant archeologically. On the east coast, around **Brooke's Point**, travelling becomes a little tricky as there are hardly any buses and few jeepneys, but if you do make it here you'll find unspoilt countryside, quiet barrios and deserted, palm-fringed beaches backed by craggy mountains.

Tabon Caves

A number of hotels and travel agents in Puerto Princesa organize day-trips to the **Tabon Caves** for about US$40 per person. Alternatively, you can catch a bus to **Quezon**, a fishing village consisting mainly of wooden houses on stilts, around 100km from Puerto Princesa. At Quezon's wharf, bancas can be chartered for P500 for the thirty-minute ride to the caves and back.

There are actually more than 200 caves in the area, but only 29 have been fully explored and of those only three are open to the public (daily 9am–4pm; P15). The main entrance to the caves, measuring 18m high and 16m wide, overlooks a beautiful bay studded by islands with white sand beaches. It was inside these caves during the 1960s that archeologists discovered a fragment of the skull of "Tabon Man", dated to 47,000 years ago, making it the oldest known human relic from the archipelago. Crude tools dating back some 22,000 years have been unearthed in the caves, along with fossils and a large quantity of Chinese pottery dating back to the fifth century BC. Most of these items have been transferred to the National Museum in Manila for preservation, though some artefacts are on display in the caves. It's interesting to wander through the damp caverns and tunnels; researchers are still working here and are happy to show visitors the latest finds.

The best **place to stay** close to the caves is the *Tabon Village Resort* (❶) in the village of **Tabon**, which has simple cottage-style accommodation with fan and private bathrooms, plus a good restaurant. The resort stands on a small beach with ocean views, though the water here is muddy and not really suitable for swimming. You can, however, arrange a banca at the resort and go island-hopping: a short trip takes you to Mariquit Island, Sidanso Island or Marangas Island, all with beaches and good snorkelling, but no accommodation.

Brooke's Point

Deep in the southern half of Palawan, 192km from Puerto Princesa, the town of **BROOKE'S POINT** is flanked by the sea on one side and formidable mountains on the other. A limited number of buses leave the market in Puerto Princesa early every day for Brooke's Point, and there are usually one or two jeepneys a day going this far from Puerto Princesa. An alternative route is to catch a jeepney or bus to **Narra**, about three hours south of Puerto Princesa, then another the rest of the way.

The town was named after the eccentric nineteenth-century British adventurer James Brooke, who was driven by insatiable wanderlust to leave England for Borneo, where he helped the local chieftain suppress a revolt and was awarded the title of Rajah of Sarawak. From Borneo he travelled north to Palawan, landing at what is now Brooke's Point and building an imposing watchtower there, the remains of which stand next to a newer lighthouse. Brooke's Point has another claim to fame as the spot where, in 1934, a local free diver found the largest pearl in the world, the Pearl of Allah, measuring 23cm across. The chief of Palawan took possession of it until 1939, when a man named Wilburn Dowell Cobb saved the life of the chief's son and received the pearl in gratitude. Cobb's heirs sold it in 1980 to a Beverly Hills jeweller for $200,000; it's said to have been subsequently valued at $40 million.

There's not much to do in town, though if you're looking for adventure you can hire a guide at the town hall to climb nearby **Mount Mantalingajan**, at 2085m the highest peak in Palawan. This is a tough climb that can take up to four days, so make sure you come well prepared; there's no equipment for hire locally. Accommodation in Brooke's Point is functional. *Silayan Lodge* (➊) and *Villa Senior* (➊) are both on the plaza opposite the town hall and offer similar rooms with prison-type beds and a small, shared shower and toilet.

Travel details

Buses

El Nido to: Puerto Princesa (daily; 7hr); Taytay (daily; 2hr).

Puerto Princesa to: Brooke's Point (1–2 daily; 5hr); El Nido (1 daily; 5–6hr); Irawan (hourly; 45min); Iwahig Penal Colony (hourly; 45min); Narra (several daily; 2hr 45min); Port Barton (several daily; 3hr); Quezon (several daily; 3hr 30min); Roxas (several daily; 2hr 30min); Sabang (hourly; 2hr); San Vicente (1–2 daily; 4–5hr); Santa Lourdes (for Honda Bay; hourly; 1hr); Taytay (1–2 daily; 5hr); Vietville (hourly; 30min).

Narra to: Brooke's Point (several daily; 3hr); Puerto Princesa (several daily; 2hr 45min); Quezon (several daily; 2hr).

Port Barton to: Puerto Princesa (several daily; 3hr); San Vicente (daily; 1hr); Taytay (3 daily; 3–4hr).

San Vicente to: Port Barton (daily; 1hr).

Taytay to: El Nido (1–2 daily; 2hr); Port Barton (3 daily; 3–4hr); Puerto Princesa (1–2 daily; 5hr); Roxas (several daily; 3hr).

Jeepneys and FX taxis

El Nido to: Puerto Princesa (daily; 7hr); Taytay (daily; 2hr).

Narra to: Brooke's Point (several daily; 3hr); Quezon (several daily; 2hr 30min).

Port Barton to: Puerto Princesa (several daily; 3hr); San Vicente (2–3 daily; 2hr); Taytay (1–2 daily; 4hr).

Puerto Princesa to: Brooke's Point (1–2 daily; 6hr); El Nido (1 daily; 7hr); Iwahig Penal Colony (hourly; 1hr); Narra (2–4 daily; 3hr); Port Barton (several daily; 3hr); Quezon (several daily; 4hr); Roxas (several daily; 3hr); Sabang (hourly; 2hr 30min); San Vicente (1–2 daily; 4–5hr); Santa Lourdes (for Honda Bay; hourly; 1hr 15min); Taytay (several daily; 5hr); Vietville (hourly; 45min).

Taytay to: El Nido (1–2 daily; 3hr); Lake Danao (several daily; 20min); Puerto Princesa (several daily; 5hr); Roxas (2–3 daily; 3hr).

Ferries and scheduled bancas

Coron Town to: Culion Town (daily; 2hr); Liminingcong (2 weekly; 6hr); Manila (2 weekly; 10hr); Puerto Princesa (2 weekly; 6hr); Taytay (2–3 weekly; 5hr).

Cuyo to: Iloilo (2 weekly; 13hr); Manila (weekly; 22hr); Puerto Princesa (2 weekly; 17hr); San José (Panay; weekly; 8hr).

El Nido to: Liminingcong (2–3 daily; 1hr); Manila (weekly; 16hr); Port Barton (1 daily; 5hr); Taytay (1–2 daily; 2hr).

Liminingcong to: Coron Town (2 weekly; 6hr); Manila (weekly; 17hr).

Port Barton to: El Nido (1 daily; 5hr); Sabang (2 daily; 2–3hr); San Vicente (2–3 daily; 2hr); Taytay (1–2 daily; 4hr).

Puerto Princesa to: Bacolod (weekly; 15hr); Coron Town (2 weekly; 6hr); Cuyo (2 weekly; 17hr); Iloilo

(weekly; 12hr); Manila (2 weekly; 16hr).
Sabang to: Port Barton (2 daily; 2–3hr).
Taytay to: Coron Town (2–3 weekly; 5hr); El Nido (1–2 daily; 2hr).

Domestic flights

Busuanga to: El Nido (3 weekly; 30min); Manila (1–2 daily; 1hr); Puerto Princesa (3 weekly; 35min); Sandoval (daily; 30min)

Cuyo to: Puerto Princesa (2 weekly; 1hr).
El Nido to: Busuanga (3 weekly; 30min); Manila (3 weekly; 1hr 30min); Puerto Princesa (3 weekly; 45min).
Puerto Princesa to: Busuanga (3 weekly; 35min); Cuyo (2 weekly; 1hr); El Nido (3 weekly; 45min); Manila (2 daily; 1hr 30min).
Sandoval to: Busuanga (daily; 30min); Manila (daily; 1hr 30min–2hr).

PALAWAN | Travel details

6

Mindanao

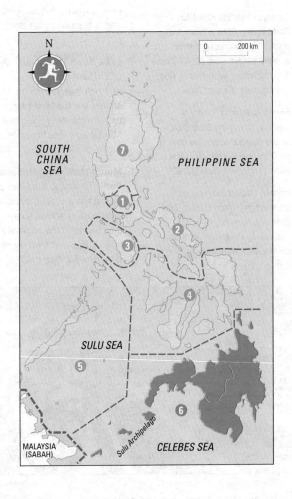

CHAPTER 6

Highlights

* **Lanzones festival**, **Camiguin** Time your visit to this dazzling little island for October, when the colourful Lanzones festival is held. See p.384

* **Agusan Marsh Wildlife Sanctuary** Take a boat trip back in time through this watery wilderness area inhabited by tribes who live in floating houses. See p.389

* **Siargao Island** Tranquil resorts, powdery beaches, secret lagoons, scuba diving, surfing and some laidback island nightlife. See p.390

* **Samal Island** Hop across on the ferry from Davao and spend a few days exploring sandy beaches, enticing coves and affordable resorts. See p.399

* **Mount Apo** The challenging trek to the summit of the highest mountain in the country takes you through thick jungle, past thundering waterfalls, geysers, sulphur pillars and a steaming blue lake. See p.401

* **Lake Sebu** This beautifully placid lake and the town of T'boli that stands on its shores are the best places to experience life among one of Mindanao's most hospitable tribes, the T'boli. See p.403

* **Mount Malindang National Park** The trail to the heart of the park is a classic tropical trek, leading across steep grasslands to the edge of a huge gorge and then up into dense forest. See p.407

△ Siargao Island

6

Mindanao

indanao, the massive island at the foot of the Philippine archipelago, is in many ways the cultural heart of the country, a place where indigenous tribes still farm their ancient homelands and Christians live alongside Muslims who first settled here in the fourteenth century. Mindanao is also a troubled island, with various indigenous Islamic or Moro groups agitating, sometimes violently, for autonomy (see box pp.378–379). Some parts of the island are considered unsafe for tourists, but this doesn't mean you should delete Mindanao from your itinerary. Large areas are peaceful, friendly and beautiful, with a range of activities, scenery and sights that can compete with anything the rest of the country offers.

Northern Mindanao remains largely bucolic and undeveloped, and includes terrific destinations such as **Siargao Island**, the volcanic island of **Camiguin**, reached via the city of **Cagayan de Oro**, and the vast floating world of the **Agusan Marsh Wildlife Sanctuary**. Also worth exploring are: the city of **Dapitan**, where national hero José Rizal was sent into exile; **Mount Malindang National Park**, a little-known area of dense rainforest near Ozamis; and the Muslim city of **Marawi**, which stands on the northern shore of serene **Lake Lanao**.

In recent years economic development has reached **Davao** in the south, the island's de facto capital. The city has changed from something of a backwater into a gentrified metropolis that can claim to have as much going for it as Manila or Cebu City. The malls and the nightlife are there, but what makes Davao a little different is that it still retains an almost pastoral ambience, flanked by ocean and islands on one side and rolling countryside on the other. It has few genuine sights, but is a relaxed place you can explore on foot for a day or two before heading to the beaches of **Samal Island** or facing bigger challenges, such as climbing nearby **Mount Apo**. West of the frenetic city of **General Santos**, around the shores of **Lake Sebu**, the friendly and gentle **T'boli** people still live in traditional wooden houses and wear hand-woven tribal garments and adornments.

The region to the west of Davao, beyond General Santos, is considered unsafe for travellers, with periodic violence particularly in and around **Cotabato**, the provincial capital of **Maguindanao** and the neighbouring provinces of Sultan Kudarat, South Cotabato and North Cotabato. The journey by road through these areas is a tough one, taking you to backward rural areas that are the petty fiefdoms of politicians. In the far southwest, **Zamboanga City** has also known violence, but not to the extent that it should be avoided. The city is the gateway to the **Sulu archipelago**, a dramatically beautiful chain of small islands that extends south to within sight of Sabah; travel is potentially dangerous here because of separatist violence.

The Mindanao problem

Both politically and in terms of security Mindanao is the most unstable part of the country, and it has been a nagging thorn in the side of successive governments. The situation is fluid and confusing, with a number of factions and splinter groups calling for varying degrees of autonomy from Manila. Mindanao's Muslims (or Moros) are seeking self-determination from the majority Christian Filipinos, while the indigenous Lumad peoples assert rights to their traditional lands.

The **Moro National Liberation Front** (MNLF) started a war for independence in the 1970s. Another group agitating for change is the **Moro Islamic Liberation Front** (MILF), which is at the forefront of the Islamic autonomy movement in the Bangsa Moro homeland. (Bangsa Moro is a generic term for ethnolinguistic tribes who live mostly in the Mindanao provinces of Maguindanao, Lanao del Sur and Sulu.) In 1987, the MNLF signed an agreement relinquishing its goal of independence for Muslim regions and accepting the government's offer of autonomy. As a result, the **Autonomous Region in Muslim Mindanao**, or ARMM, was created in 1990, covering the provinces of Basilan, Lanao del Sur, Maguindanao, Sulu and Tawi-Tawi, plus Marawi City.

Divisions along generational lines have emerged among Mindanao's Muslims, with many young Muslims asserting that old hierarchical structures are unnecessary in a modern Islamic society. But among themselves, these young reformers are divided between moderates, working within the system for their political goals, and militants, engaging in guerrilla-style warfare. The MILF, meanwhile, refused to accept the 1987 accord and initiated a brief offensive that ended in a series of uneasy truces, broken many times.

The formation of the ARMM didn't please everybody, and one disaffected group of fighters left the MNLF, accusing it of selling out to Manila, and formed **Abu Sayyaf**, whose centre of operations is largely Basilan Island, off Mindanao's south coast. Abu Sayyaf, whose name means "Bearer of the Sword", is said to have ties to a number of

Getting to Mindanao is easy, with regular **flights** from Manila and Cebu to a number of airports. Philippine Airlines flies from Manila to Davao, Cagayan de Oro, Butuan, General Santos, Cotabato and Zamboanga City. Air Philippines flies from Manila to Cagayan de Oro, Davao, General Santos and Zamboanga City, and from Cebu to Davao and General Santos. From Manila, Cebu Pacific serves Cagayan de Oro, Cotabato, Davao, Dipolog, General Santos and Zamboanga City. Seair flies from Cebu to Camiguin and Cotabato; it also flies from Zamboanga City to Cotabato, Jolo and Tawi-Tawi. By **ferry**, you can take the long trip from Manila (at least 18hr). There are also ferry links from Mindanao's many ports to destinations around the Visayas.

Northern Mindanao

North Mindanao, from the city of **Cagayan de Oro** in the west to Siargao Island in the east, is the area most tourists are interested in. It contains some of the area's great destinations, with a variety of small islands and activities, and accommodation for every budget. Cagayan de Oro isn't much in itself, but it makes a good starting point for trips to **Camiguin**, a stunning little volcanic

Islamic fundamentalist organizations around the world, including Osama bin Laden's al-Qaeda and Ramzi Yousef, who was convicted of organizing the 1993 bombing of the World Trade Center in New York. The group finances its operations mainly through robbery, piracy and ransom kidnappings, and may also receive funding from al-Qaeda. They are believed to have been responsible for the bombing of the WG&A *Superferry 14* in February 2004, which sank off the coast of Manila with the loss of 116 lives, making it the world's deadliest terrorist attack at sea. A television set filled with explosives had been placed on board.

Security forces in the Philippines have met with some success in their battle against Abu Sayyaf. In 2002 the group's high-profile commander Abu Sabaya, who was behind a number of notorious kidnappings and killings, was killed while trying to evade army soldiers and in 2006 the group's leader, Khadaffy Abubakar Janjalani, was killed in an encounter with government troops. Abu Sayyaf's profile has diminished somewhat in recent years, but it should not be considered a spent force. In 2006 it attempted to bomb the Association of Southeast Asian Nations political summit in Cebu, but the plot was foiled, and in early 2007 there were several bombings on the same day in General Santos City, Kidapawan City and Cotabato City, killing seven people and injuring at least 27 others. Public transport is a common target for attacks and kidnapping remains a threat.

As this book went to press, the British Foreign and Commonwealth Office was advising against all travel to Mindanao because of the possibility of terrorist activity. In fact, few visitors report even the slightest problem, but clearly the threat is there and visitors need to be aware of it. If you do travel in the area, keep a low profile, be alert to any suspicious packages and to people behaving suspiciously, avoid public transport as much as possible and never flaunt your (relative) wealth.

For specific security and safety information about Mindanao see p.61.

island off Mindanao's northern coast, and inland through the bucolic province of Bukidnon. Further east is the city of Butuan and, to the south, the beautiful wilderness area of the **Agusan Marsh Wildlife Sanctuary**, inhabited by the Manobo tribe. One of northern Mindanao's finest destinations is off the north-eastern coast, the many dazzling islands and beaches around **Siargao**.

Cagayan de Oro

CAGAYAN DE ORO on the north coast of Mindanao is the departure point of many travellers for trips to the dazzling little island of Camiguin. Cagayan itself is generally unimpressive, a noisy mish-mash of busy streets and fast-food restaurants, hardly enough to tempt you to stay longer than a day or night before moving on to greener pastures.

The city sits on the eastern bank of the wide Cagayan River and stretches from MacArthur Park in the north, near the Provincial Capitol Building, to circular Gaston Park in the south. In between it's mostly traffic and broken pavements, making the 45-minute walk between the two parks only for the brave. There's another park, a narrow strip of open space called Friendship Park, running east–west between Neri Street and Abejuela Street, a good area for convenience stores and fast food. You'll find few memorable sights, apart from the eighteenth-century **San Augustine Cathedral**, a pretty, off-white stone edifice just south of Gaston Park, with a gold-plated altar and immense stained-glass windows. The **Xavier Museo de Oro** (Tues–Sun 9am–5pm; P20

MINDANAO

N

0   100 km

Cebu, Iloilo & Manila

Manila

Manila & Cebu City

Manila

Siargao

Tandag

Bunawan

Agusan Marsh
Wildlife Sanctuary

Surigao

Nasipit

Butuan

Mambajao

Benoni

Camiguin
Island

Balingoan

Cagayan de Oro

Malaybalay

Maramag

Marawi

Iligan

Lake Lanao

Initao

Plaridel

Dapitan

Dipolog

Mount Malindang
(2404m)

Ozamis

Tagbilaran

Bohol

Siquijor

Negros

Dumaguete

M i n d a n a o

Mount Apo
(2954m)

Davao

Samal

Talicud

Gulf of
Davao

General Santos

Koronadal

Kidapawan

Lake
Buluan

T'boli

Lake
Sebu

Sarangani
Bay

Cotabato

Zamboanga
City

Basilan

S u l u   A r c h i p e l a g o

Jolo

Jolo

Tawi-Tawi

Bongao

Sandakan (Malaysia)

minimum donation) at Xavier University on Corrales Avenue gives an interesting overview of local culture stretching back thousands of years; there are evocative dioramas of the Spanish period, when gold was discovered in the Cagayan River (hence the "Oro" in Cagayan's name).

If you pass through the city's eastern suburbs (on the road to Balingoan, for instance), you'll notice the sweet smell of pineapples, the source of much of Cagayan's income. There are enormous **plantations** inland, mostly owned by Del Monte, and the fruit are brought to the suburbs for canning.

Practicalities

Lumbia **airport** sits 10km south of the city – a taxi ride into Cagayan will set you back at least P100. **Ferries** arrive at Macabalan wharf, 5km north of the centre, with regular jeepneys back and forth; a taxi from here into the city costs about P100. All buses arrive at the **integrated bus terminal** on the north-eastern outskirts next to Agora market, from where it's an easy tricycle or jeepney ride into town.

The regional **tourist office** (Mon–Sat 8am–noon & 1–5pm; ☎088/22 727 275) is on A. Velez Street, a short walk north of the city centre close to the library, and has maps, details of guided tours and lists of accommodation in the city and around, including Camiguin (see p.383). There's also a tourism information centre in a more convenient location, close to the *Grand City Hotel* on R.N. Abejuela Street. The **post office** is on T. Chavez Street, and one of the best places for **Internet** access is *Cyberpoint Café* on R.N. Abejuela Street (2/F R&M Building), close to a big branch of the Mercury pharmacy. There are few **banks** in Cagayan de Oro, so make sure you've got enough cash – Landbank is on the south side of MacArthur Park and Bangko Central on the north side. PCMC Hospital sits on the north side of Gaston Park and the police station on the south side.

Moving on from Cagayan de Oro

Philippine Airlines and Cebu Pacific have daily **flights** from Cagayan de Oro to Manila and Cebu City, while Air Philippines serves Manila. There are two Philippine Airlines ticket offices in Cagayan de Oro: one at the airport (☎088/858 8864) and another at 21 Tirso Neri St (☎088/851 2295), right in the centre of town close to *McDonald's*. Air Philippines has offices at the airport (☎088/858 8888) and in the Santiago Building (☎088/857 1124), on Gaerlan Street close to Gaston Park. Cebu Pacific (☎088/858 8856) is at the airport.

By **ferry**, WG&A and Negros Navigation both sail from Cagayan de Oro to Bacolod, Iloilo and Manila. The main WG&A ticket office is at the pier, but a number of more convenient outlets are located in town, including an Aboitiz One office in SM City mall. The Negros Navigation ticket office (☎088/856 9197) is in the Atco Building on Punta Street. There are also regular ferries operated by smaller companies from Macabalan wharf to Dumaguete (Negros) and Jagna (Bohol).

Buses heading east and west along the coast and south through Bukidnon all leave from the integrated bus station. There are dozens of routes covering all major destinations, with long-distance trips as far as Butuan, Davao, Iligan and Dapitan. Major bus operators include Ceres Liner and Bachelor. If you're heading to the bus terminal from the city you can take a taxi for around P50 or a jeepney marked for Agora.

To get to **Camiguin** from Cagayan de Oro, take one of the hourly buses from the integrated bus station to Balingoan and then a ferry from Balingoan to **Benoni** on Camiguin's southeast coast. Ferries run hourly throughout the day (6am–5pm); total travelling time is around four hours.

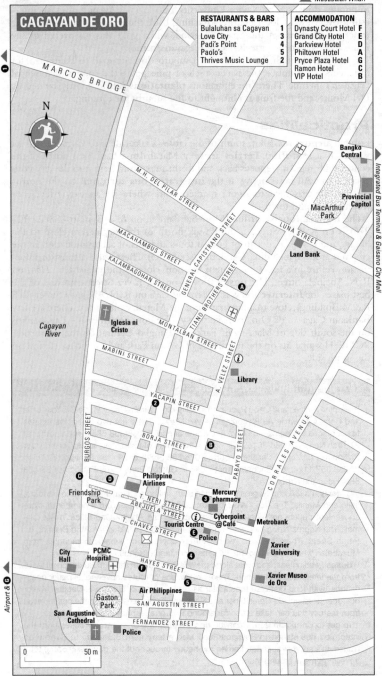

CAGAYAN DE ORO

Macabalan Wharf

RESTAURANTS & BARS
Bulaluhan sa Cagayan   1
Love City   3
Padi's Point   4
Paolo's   5
Thrives Music Lounge   2

ACCOMMODATION
Dynasty Court Hotel   F
Grand City Hotel   E
Parkview Hotel   D
Philtown Hotel   A
Pryce Plaza Hotel   G
Ramon Hotel   C
VIP Hotel   B

MARCOS BRIDGE

N

Integrated Bus Terminal & Gaisano City Mall

Cagayan River

M. H. DEL PILAR STREET

Bangko Central

Provincial Capitol

MacArthur Park

LUNA STREET

Land Bank

MACAHAMBUS STREET

GENERAL CAPISTRANO STREET

KALAMBAGOHAN STREET

TIANO BROTHERS STREET

A

Iglesia ni Cristo

MONTALBAN STREET

A. VELEZ STREET

MABINI STREET

Library

YACAPIN STREET
2

BORJA STREET
B

BURGOS STREET

PABAYO STREET

CORRALES AVENUE

C D

Philippine Airlines

Mercury pharmacy
3

Friendship Park

T. NERI STREET

ABEJUELA STREET

Cyberpoint @ Café

Tourist Centre

Metrobank

T. CHAVEZ STREET

E Police

City Hall

PCMC Hospital

Xavier University

HAYES STREET
F

4

Xavier Museo de Oro

Gaston Park

5

Air Philippines

SAN AGUSTIN STREET

San Augustine Cathedral

FERNANDEZ STREET

Police

Airport & G

0   50 m

Accommodation

The area between T. Neri Street and Gaston Park is the location of most of the town's budget **accommodation**. Some of it is of poor quality, with dank, dark rooms, so do look at your room before committing yourself. Cagayan also has some good mid-range hotels.

Dynasty Court Hotel Hayes St ☎088/857 1250. Affordable mid-range option in a good location right in the city centre; it's a grand, white-washed building and hard to miss. All rooms have a/c and private bathroom, and are neat and well kept. The rate includes breakfast. ❺

Grand City Hotel A. Velez St ☎088/857 1990. Acceptable mid-range establishment. Rooms are a little worn, but they're very clean and all have a/c and spacious bathrooms. ❺

Parkview Hotel T. Neri St. Long-established budget lodge overlooking Friendship Park. All rooms are a/c, and while very spartan and ordinary they are comfortable enough and clean. ❷

Philtown Hotel A. Velez St ☎088/857 1822. Squat, concrete block of a place – not at all appealing from the outside – three blocks south of MacArthur Park. Inside, the rooms are plain but clean, with a/c, bathrooms and cable TV. There's a Chinese restaurant downstairs offering a range of rather ordinary standards such as fried rice and noodles. ❹

Pryce Plaza Hotel National Highway, Carmen Hill ☎088/858 4536, ⓦwww.pryceplaza.ph. Cagayan's swankiest hotel, with five-star rooms and service, set in pleasant grounds on a hill to the west of the city, across the river. The location isn't ideal, but if you're looking for somewhere close to the airport for a night, and you've got the budget, it's better than anything else on offer. ❾

Ramon Hotel Burgos St ☎0822/727 608. If you get a room at the back with views of the river, *Ramon* is hard to beat. It's modern, clean, afford-able and, despite being on the river, only a 10min walk from the city centre. ❸

VIP Hotel A. Velez St ☎0822/726 080. Unattrac-tive from the outside, but a good-value budget option, with spick-and-span rooms, all with a/c and bathrooms, and with a 24hr coffee shop. ❸

Eating and drinking

Cagayan de Oro is a university city, which means there are a good number of affordable **restaurants** and watering holes. One of the liveliest places for food and drink is *Padi's Point* at the southern end of A.Velez Street: it's open until late and fills up with students after 9pm. A short walk south, *Paolo's* is a convivial candlelight bistro that serves an incredible range of pasta, pizza and Asian dishes. The most authentic Filipino restaurant is *Bulaluhan sa Cagayan*, across the river, which specializes in grilled seafood served with a steaming hot portion of rice: try the garlic rice or rice with *bagoong* for a change. *Love City* on Cruz Tael Street is the city's major **disco**, with half-price drinks between 9pm and 11pm. At *Thrives Music Lounge* on Capistrano Street good live bands play every night from 8pm; it's a popular place and gets packed out with students.

Camiguin

Sitting in the Mindanao Sea about 20km off the north coast of mainland Mindanao, the pint-sized island of **Camiguin** ("cam-ee-*gin*") is one of the country's most appealing tourist spots, offering ivory beaches, iridescent lagoons and undulating scenery. There's no shortage of adventure here either, with reasonable scuba diving and some tremendous trekking and climbing in the rugged interior, especially on volcanic **Mount Hibok-Hibok**. Camiguin also features six other volcanoes, a multitude of hot springs, a submerged cemetery for divers to explore near the coastal town of **Bonbon**, a spring that gushes natural soda water, and 35 resorts, most in the northern half of the island but some on the southwest coast near **Catarman**. Another major tourist draw is

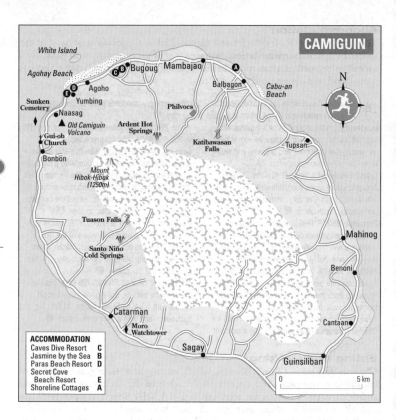

White Island

Agohay Beach

Bugoug   Mambajao

Balbagon

Cabu-an
Beach

Sunken
Cemetery   Agoho
Yumbing

Naasag

Philvocs

Old Camiguin
Volcano

Ardent Hot
Springs

Katibawasan
Falls

Gui-ob
Church

Bonbon

Tupsan

Mount
Hibok-Hibok
(1250m)

Tuason Falls

Mahinog

Santo Niño
Cold Springs

Benoni

Catarman

Moro
Watchtower

Cantaan

Sagay

Guinsiliban

ACCOMMODATION
Caves Dive Resort   C
Jasmine by the Sea   B
Paras Beach Resort   D
Secret Cove
  Beach Resort   E
Shoreline Cottages   A

0   5 km

the annual **Lanzones festival**, held in the fourth week of October. Revellers dressed only in lanzones leaves stomp and dance in the streets as a tribute to the humble fruit, one of the island's major sources of income. The festival is one of the liveliest and most welcoming in the country, and this on an island already renowned for the friendliness of its people. It's also a peaceful, almost spiritual island, where residents are proud of their faith. Old Spanish documents indicate that Ferdinand Magellan and Miguel Lopez de Legazpi passed this way in 1521 and 1565 respectively, but it wasn't until 1598, when the first Spanish settlement was established here, that the natives – mostly from nearby Surigao – converted to Catholicism.

The beauty of Camiguin is that it doesn't really matter where you stay because you can visit all the sights easily from anywhere. The **coastal road** is almost 70km long, making it feasible to circle the island in a day. If you don't want to depend on public transport, consider hiring your own private jeepney or tricycle for the trip. Many resorts also offer motorcycle rental.

Ferries from Balingoan, about 80km northeast of Cagayan de Oro, arrive at **Benoni** on Camiguin's southeast coast: the Camiguin Authorized Ticket Agent (℡08822/387 4000) in the Negros Navigation Office in Benoni will help you arrange tours, make long-distance telephone calls and book ferry tickets. From here, several jeepneys run every day to **Mambajao**, the bustling little capital on the north coast. If you know where you're going to be staying you can take a tricycle straight to your resort; in many cases the resort will send a vehicle to meet you.

The other way to get to Camiguin is on the twice-weekly Seair **flight** from Cebu City, which lands at the airstrip a few kilometres to the west of Mambajao, from where it's an easy tricycle ride into town or to your resort. The Philippine Rural Reconstruction Movement in Manila (℡02/372 3931, ⓦwww.prrm .org) runs **homestay tours** to Camiguin: guests stay with locals in old wooden houses and tour the island with their own guide and driver. One of the best **adventure sports** outfits on the island is Johnny's Dive 'n' Fun (℡088/387 9588, ⓦwww.johnnysdive.com), who can arrange scuba diving, trekking, motorbike tours, mountain biking, parasailing and fishing. It has outlets at three resorts around Mambajao: *Secret Cove Beach Resort*, *Caves Dive Resort* and *Paras Beach Resort*. Camiguin Action (℡088/387 1266, ⓦwww.camiguinaction.com) at Agohay, near Mambajao, is another reputable outfit, offering scuba diving, island tours and trekking, including on Mount Hibok-Hibok.

Mambajao and around

There's no reason to hang around in **MAMBAJAO**, the island's capital, other than to sort out the practicalities of your stay. The **tourist office** (Mon–Sat 8.30am–5pm; ℡08822/871 014) in the Capitol Compound has information about accommodation and climbing Hibok-Hibok. There are several **banks** in town and you can change travellers' cheques at most of them, although service is slow and rates are low. As always, it's best to make sure you have enough cash, either in pesos or dollars.

There are pleasant stretches of sandy beach either side of Mambajao. **Cabu-An Beach** to the east, near the barangay of Balbagon, is marginally the closest and has some nice coral close to the shore, as well as half a dozen decent resorts. **Agohay Beach**, 7km west of Mambajao, is wider and sandier than Cabu-An, with many resorts and is an ideal place to base yourself for all sorts of activities, including scuba diving, banca-hopping and walks into the island's interior. You can trek inland along a marked trail to **Katibawasan Falls**, a clear stream plunging over a rocky cliff into a deep pool that makes for a heavenly swim after the walk: getting to the falls on foot takes about two hours, or you can hire a tricycle. Most resorts at Agohay Beach will help you find a **guide** – the trail may be marked, but you can still get lost.

At **PHILVOCS** (Mon–Fri 9am–4pm), an easy trip inland from Mambajao by tricycle, vulcanologists who monitor Mount Hibok-Hibok will be only too happy to give you a few personal insights into their work, as well as showing spectacular photographs of past eruptions. Three kilometres inland from the barangay of Tagdo, **Ardent Hot Springs** (daily 9am–10pm; P20) can be reached in about an hour on foot from Mambajao or Agohay Beach. Hot means very hot: the water in these pools, which lie in a verdant valley surrounded by jungle, is warmed by the volcanic interior of Mount Hibok-Hibok and reaches 40°C. The best time to visit is from the late afternoon, when the sun is less fierce, or consider an after-dark visit, when you can sit in one of the pools with a cold drink and gaze at the stars. There's a good little restaurant, a coffee shop and accommodation in a number of simple cottages.

The only active volcano on Camiguin, **Mount Hibok-Hibok** had its last major eruption in 1951, with tremors and landslides that killed 500 people. At a relatively modest 1250m it can be climbed in a day, but the strenuous trail crosses some very steep slopes and treacherous rocks and shouldn't be attempted alone. Many resorts have lists of local **guides** who can be hired for around

△ White Island with Camiguin Island and Mount Hibok-Hibok in the background

P1500; the usual approach is through the barangay of Esperanza to the south of Mambajao. Along the way you'll see steam vents and hot pools, while at the top there's a crater lake. Views from the summit are unforgettable, with the coast of Mindanao to the south and the islands of the Visayas to the north.

About half-way between Mambajao and Bonbon off the island's northwest coast is one of Camiguin's most popular attractions, **White Island**, a dazzling serpentine ribbon of sand only visible at low tide and easily reached in a short banca hop from nearby resorts. It's less of an island and more of an extended sandbar. The views and the water are lovely, but there's no shade, so make sure you take a wide-brimmed hat and lots of sunblock.

Accommodation and eating

Most of the best beach **accommodation** in Camiguin is west of Mambajao on the beaches between the small towns of **Bug-ong** and **Naasag**. The resorts in this area are well prepared for foreign tourists and have lots of information about diving and trekking; resorts near the town of Agoho, a little west of Bug-ong, are popular because of their good access to White Island. To the east of Mambajao around the village of **Balgabon** you'll find more simple resorts, although the beach here isn't as good as Agoho, Yumbing and Naasag.

Eating on Camiguin is mostly limited to your resort or one of a few nipa-style restaurants dotting the beaches. In Mumbajao itself there are some local eateries clustered around the Capitol Compound, including the *Pachada Café* and *Parola* by the sea. On the beach at Agoho, the *Paradise Bar and Restaurant* is popular, with delicious fish and curry dishes and tremendous sunset views.

Caves Dive Resort Bug-ong, a short walk west of *Jasmine* ☏088/387 0077, ⓦ www.cavesdiveresort.com. Situated right on the beach, *Caves* has a range of cottages and smaller rooms in the main building. It is well set up for diving and adventures sports, and has a homey restaurant and bar. ❸

Jasmine by the Sea Bug-ong ☏088/387 9015. One of the closest resorts to Mambajao, *Jasmine* is excellent value, with spacious fan cottages on the shore and a restaurant that serves some organic dishes. ❷

Paras Beach Resort 4km beyond Bug-ong in

Yumbing ⓣ 088/387 9008 or 9081. This was a private beach house belonging to the Paras family until they decided to add eighteen a/c rooms and open it to the public. It's in a spectacular position on the shore, and the staff are efficient organizers of tours. ❻

 Secret Cove Beach Resort Yumbing ⓣ 088/ 387 9084, ⓦ www.secretcove-

camiguin.net. The Canadian–Filipino owned resort has four spacious and clean a/c rooms and three fan rooms, restaurant, bar and Internet access. ❸

Shoreline Cottages Balgabon, east of Mambajao ⓣ 088/387 9033. Typical of the accommodation on this stretch of beach, they have ordinary single, twin and double huts with cold showers. ❶

Bonbon and around

The small fishing town of **BONBON** on Camiguin's west coast has an attractive little plaza and a pretty, whitewashed church; it also lies a few kilometres south of the slopes of the **Old Camiguin Volcano**, which you can climb easily in an hour. The path to the summit, from where the views are stunning, is marked by lifesize alabaster statues representing the Stations of the Cross, beginning with Christ being sentenced and ending with his shrouded body being lowered into the sepulchre.

A little south of the old volcano you'll see the striking sight of an enormous white cross floating on a pontoon in the bay, its image reflected in the blue waters. This marks the site of the **Sunken Cemetery**, which slipped into the sea during a volcanic eruption in 1871. You can dive and snorkel in the cemetery and observe the reef fishes that mass around the decaying tombs. The same eruption destroyed the seventeenth-century Spanish **Gui-ob Church** on the northern fringes of modern Bonbon; its brooding ruins still stand, with a memorial altar inside.

Catarman and around

There are some quiet stretches of sandy beach near the ramshackle little town of **CATARMAN**, on the island's southwest coast, 24km south of Mambajao, but there's no accommodation in the area. Six kilometres north of Catarman are the **Tuasan Falls** and nearby **Santo Niño Cold Springs**, which can both be reached either on foot from the coastal road or by tricycle along a rather rough track. Both have deep pools that are good for swimming and the surroundings are pleasant, with rich vegetation and a few simple huts (P100 a day) where you can change and take a nap. On the southern coast near Guinsiliban, fifteen minutes east by jeepney from Catarman, is a 300-year-old **Moro Watchtower**: climb to the top for panoramic views of the Mindanao Sea across to mainland Mindanao.

Butuan and the Agusan Marsh Wildlife Sanctuary

The bustling capital of Agusan del Norte province, **BUTUAN** is not on the tourist trail, but it is served by flights from Manila and is a good place to head for if you're planning to visit the nearby **Agusan Marsh Wildlife Sanctuary**.

This major port is said by historians to be the site of the first coastal trading settlement in the Philippines; in 1976 a carefully crafted and ornate ocean-going outrigger (*balanghai*) was unearthed on the banks of the Agusan River and carbon-dated to AD 320. The boat is now in the small Butuan branch of the

National Museum (daily 9am–4pm; P12), 3km west of the city centre towards the airport in the suburb of Libertad, along with the remains of a number of other ancient boats and various archeological and ethnological treasures such as ceramics and coffins. There's **another branch** of the National Museum (daily 9am–4pm; P15) a kilometre north of the city centre in the City Hall compound, this one set in shady gardens and home to a small but intriguing collection including cooking implements and jewellery that prove Butuan's pre-Hispanic existence. The museum has two galleries: the Archaeological Hall which exhibits specimens of stone crafts, metal objects, pots, gold and burial coffins; and the Ethnological Hall, which focuses on the culture of the Manobo, Mamanua, Higaonon and lowland Butuanons. In the city centre, facing Rizal Park, is **St Joseph's Cathedral** (daily 6am–8pm; free), an austere old Spanish building which contains controversial documents, said to be pages from Magellan's diarist Pigafetta, that may indicate that Butuan was where Magellan first set foot in the islands. The cathedral also has the only ecclesiastical museum in Mindanao, the **Diocesan Ecclesiastical Museum** (it isn't always open, but you can get the key from the parish office next to the cathedral; free) in St Joseph's Convent at the cathedral. The museum showcases a collection of religious and liturgical arts ranging from all kinds of church vestments to chalices and relics of saints. Many of the artefacts belonged to sixteenth-century Spanish missionaries.

Butuan practicalities

There's a small **tourist information** office in City Hall. At the centre of Butuan is Rizal Park, on the park's south side the **police station** and on its west side St Joseph's Cathedral. You'll find a BPI on Montilla Boulevard, ten minutes' walk west of Rizal Park. The **airport**, served by Philippine Airlines and Cebu Pacific flights, is west of the city; both airlines have offices at the airport and Philippine Airlines has another in Villanueva Street (T085/341 5156). WG&A, Negros Navigation and Cebu Ferries all have **ferry** services here; they dock at the port town of Nasipit, 11km west of Butuan, from where it's a thirty-minute jeepney ride into town. **Buses** from Cagayan de Oro, Surigao and Davao arrive on the western outskirts of Butuan in Montilla Street; there are plenty of tricycles to take you the rest of the way.

The best place to **stay** in Butuan is the mid-range *Almont Hotel* (T085/342 5263; ❹), in Rizal Park, which has spacious and airy rooms, all with air-conditioning, private bathrooms and frills such as cable TV. Rooms at the front have pleasant city views and the coffee shop with tinkling indoor waterfalls offers light meals and pastries. *Emerald Villa Hotel* (T085/225 2141; ❹) is well located in Villanueva Street and has large air-conditioned rooms with spacious bathrooms and a good restaurant in the lobby where a big breakfast costs less than P100. For a real budget option, look no further than the *Hensonly Plaza Inn* (T085/342 5866; ❶), on San Francisco Street, where rooms are a little rough around the edges, but clean and quiet. The choice ranges from fan singles and doubles with shared bathroom to air-conditioned doubles with private bathrooms.

Dozens of fast-food **restaurants** line Burgos Street, a block north of Rizal Park, including *Jollibee*, *MacDonald's* and *Shakey's Pizza*, while the Otis Department Store on Aquino Street houses an average food court with stalls offering noodles and fried chicken. For something more formal try the restaurant in the *Balanghai Hotel*, a few minutes by tricycle west of the city on Doongan.

Agusan Marsh Wildlife Sanctuary

About 70km south of Butuan on the road to Davao, the **Agusan Marsh Wildlife Sanctuary** lies at the confluence of several of the Agusan River's tributaries and is the largest freshwater marsh in the Philippines. Whichever direction you're coming from, to reach the sanctuary you need to get off the bus in the town of **Bunawan** and then take a jeepney west to the **Protected Area Office**; this part of the trip takes about thirty minutes. From the office you can hire a boat for the three-hour ride along the river to the marsh area itself – be prepared for a full day out and take lots of water and sunblock.

The sanctuary consists of a great maze of interconnecting rivers, channels and lakes, with dramatic areas of **swamp forest** consisting largely of sago trees and inhabited by parrots, purple herons and serpent eagles. Think twice before taking a refreshing dip: in 1991 a comprehensive survey of the environment revealed it was home to a good number of saltwater and Philippine **crocodiles**. A day **tour** costs P600 plus a tip and some refreshments for the guide. Despite its isolation, the marsh is inhabited by about 2600 people, mainly the Manobo, an animist group that live across much of eastern Mindanao. Their houses are floating wooden structures with thatched roofs and rest on a platform lashed to enormous logs. Whole communities exist like this, their houses tethered to one another in one place, but moveable at any time.

Surigao, Siargao and Dinagat

The frenetic capital of the province of Surigao del Norte, **SURIGAO** provides nothing more for tourists than a place to pass through to reach the picture-postcard island of **Siargao** or the bigger, less touristy **Dinagat** island. There's not a lot to see or do in Surigao, although if you're waiting for an onward ferry you might be forced to spend the night – there are a number of average hotels.

Surigao sits on a thick promontory with the sea on one side and the Surigao River on the other, and has a neat plaza with an old church. It's a compact place and easy to negotiate on foot: the main street, Rizal Street, runs from north to south and is crossed by a number of secondary streets including Amat Street and Narciso Street.

A few good **beaches** west of the city are worth exploring if you're at a loose end, but are probably not worth a special trip. The best is **Mabua Beach**, a kilometre-long sweep of smooth stones 20km by bus or jeepney to the west. There are basic cottages to rent, but they're only designed for shade during the day, not for overnight stays. The sunsets here are something special, but don't go at weekends when everyone else has the same idea.

Surigao practicalities

In the City Hall, at the southern end of Rizal Street near the grandstand, you'll find a helpful **tourism assistance centre** where you can get information about accommodation and ferries to Siargao and Dinagat islands. Buses arrive at the terminal 4km west of the city on the National Highway. WG&A, Cebu Ferries, Cokialong Shipping Lines and Sulpicio Lines all serve Surigao, arriving at the wharf at the southern edge of Navarro Street; you can walk or take a tricycle from here to the city centre. **Ferries** to Siargao and Dinagat islands leave from

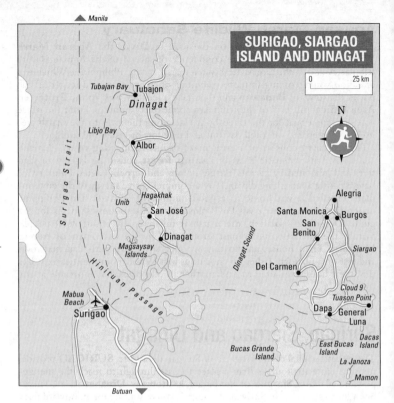

the pier off P. Reyes Street, close to the Cokialong Shipping Lines office. At the western end of Borromeo Street there's a branch of Equitable PCI, and you'll find **Internet** at *Surigao Internet Café*, next to the tourism assistance centre.

The best **accommodation** is the government-run *Garden Pavilion* (☎086/826 7779; ❹), a resort-style development of concrete cottages in the grounds of the Provincial Capitol Building in a quiet area on the southern outskirts of town, a fifteen-minute tricycle ride from the city centre. Closer to the ferry piers is the *Metro Pension Plaza* (☎086/232 4257; ❼), a modern building offering a range of comfortable air-conditioned rooms and various restaurants and bars. A couple of blocks to the east, half-way along Borromeo Street a block inland from the sea, the *Leomondee Hotel* (☎086/826 0634; ❸) is the best mid-range option. Rooms are ordinary but all have air-conditioning and good bathrooms, and there's a restaurant and Internet café.

There's no shortage of fast food in Surigao, but for something more substantial there are two **restaurants** near the ferry piers: *4As Fast Food* and *Adrian's STK By The Sea*, both offering straightforward rice dishes with meat and fish, as well as noodles and limited vegetables.

Siargao Island

Off the northeastern tip of Mindanao lies the teardrop-shaped island of **Siargao**, a largely undeveloped backwater with Boracay-type beaches and dramatic coves and lagoons. Siargao has got everything, with a typically tropical coastal landscape of palm trees and dazzling seas, and a verdant hinterland of rustic little barrios and coconut groves. Some of the first tourists here were **surfers**, who discovered a break at Tuason Point that was so good they called it Cloud 9, and though it's still off the tourist trail, word-of-mouth is bringing an increasing number of surfers from around the world.

Kayaking is a great way to explore the area, paddling through mangrove swamps or into hidden coral bays. You can also hire a banca to do some serious **island-hopping**, or rent a motorcycle for the day and tootle up the dusty coastal road to Alegria and Burgos at the island's northernmost tip, visiting beaches that few tourists see.

There are some modest but comfortable seaside resorts around the island's friendly little capital of **GENERAL LUNA**, known as GL. You can base yourself here to tour Siargao itself and also grab a boat and head out to Dacas Island, East Bucas Island and Bucas Grande Island, all with superb snorkelling in palm-fringed coves. Bucas Grande is especially striking, with mushroom-shaped limestone rocks, green with foliage, sprouting from its shimmering waters. There's a cove here that leads to a stunning lagoon – if you can hold your breath for long enough, you can swim through a short tunnel into a hidden cave where there are bats, strange fishes, stalactites, rock oysters, corals, cycads and wild orchids. You can organize this **trip** at any resort or simply by asking around to rent a banca for half a day. It will cost around P500 per person, but is well worth it.

Another good day-trip from Siargao is to the **Twin Islands**, La Janoza and Mamon, said to be the easternmost islands in the archipelago. There's a powdery white sand beach and a quaint fishing village on La Janoza and between the two islands is a pellucid lagoon that's wonderful for swimming and snorkelling.

For **surfers**, the main area is Tuason Point, less than 2km north of GL. Waves here include Cloud 9, Jacking Horse, Tuason Left and Cemetery. You can rent equipment from the resorts and lessons cost about P300 an hour. The annual **surfing cup,** held every year in late September or early October, has risen in profile over the past few years and attracts competitors from Australia, the US and Europe, as well as the Philippines. The winner picks up a useful 200,000 pesos.

Practicalities

Getting to Siargao has become much easier recently with regular Asian Spirit flights from Manila to Surigao, from where there are Aska Queen, Fortune Jet and Tropical Queen fast ferries twice a day (5am and noon; P120) which arrive on the southwest coast at **Dapa**; there are also plenty of slower and cheaper ferries making the crossing daily. Some ferries sail to Del Carmen, further up Siargao's west coast, but for tourists heading for the beaches, Dapa is best. It's very easy to hop on a tricycle or jeepney from Dapa to General Luna; from Del Carmen it can take a couple of hours on a bumpy road. In the town hall in General Luna there's a **tourist office** – although information from the many resort and bar owners is more reliable and up to date – and a public telephone office. There are no banks and credit cards aren't accepted, so bring **cash**. **Internet** facilities are becoming easier to find. Two resorts at Cloud 9, *Patrick's on the Beach* and Ocean *101*, have broadband, charging P1 a minute, with a minimum of P25.

On the main road in GL you can get cheap beer and Filipino **food** and watch the world go by at *Maridyl's* or *Lalay's*. Both are fairly primitive *carinderias*, but the food is good and the service very friendly. Next door to *Lalay's* is *Ruth's*, where the chicken and pork barbecue is said to be the best in Mindanao. For a really good-quality feed – prawns, fish steaks, banana leaves, curry, spaghetti, fish soup and salad, plus excellent breakfasts such as the Surfer's Superfry – head for the *Pub*, down by the sea in GL itself: go down the main street to the school, turn left, right at the end of this road and straight on to the shore.

Accommodation

Accommodation in Siargao covers the whole range, from modest lodges aimed at backpackers and low-budget surfers, to upmarket tropical resorts where you can be pampered. Most accommodation is a short distance from GL.

Cherinicole Beach Resort ☎0928/609 8963 or 032/420 7815 in Cebu City, ✆www.cherinicoleresort.com. A short tricycle ride from GL or a 15-minute walk. Mid-range, well-run place with 17 spacious and substantial wooden a/c cottages on the beach or in a pleasant garden. Family cottages with two double beds are good value. There's a swimming pool, café and beach bar. ❸

Drop In Resort Cloud 9. Five simple double cottages in a fine location on the beach. Each has a private bathroom with the luxury of a hot shower and there's a restaurant where specialities include chop suey and fried chicken. ❷

Ocean 101 Cloud 9. ☎0910/848 0893, ✆www.ocean101cloud9.com. Popular with surfers and offering spartan but spick and span beachside accommodation ranging from small singles at the back of the resort to a/c doubles with enough space for an extra bed. All rooms have well-maintained private bathrooms. There's also a cosy restaurant and bar. ❶

Pansukian Tropical Resort ☎032/234 1282 or 0918/903 9055, ✆www.pansukian.com. You can't

get any swankier than this on Siargao. Accommodation is of two types: the Tropical Pagoda and the Garden Cottage. Excellent location south of GL, attentive service and good food. ❾

Patrick's on the Beach Resort ☎0920/402 4356, ✆www.patricksonthebeach.com. Simple but comfortable local-style beach hut accommodation, with spacious beachfront cottages, garden cottages and a number of economy cottages that were being built at the time of writing. Helpful staff can arrange everything from boats, air tickets and babysitting to laundry, massage and manicure. Walking distance from GL. ❸

Sagana Resort Cloud 9 ☎0919/809 5769, ✆www.cloud9surf.com. The newest resort at Cloud 9, *Sagana* has six cottages – two a/c and four with fan – in a landscaped garden with coconut trees and large, leafy plants. Cottages are beautifully made following a Laotian motif. The restaurant is one of the island's best, with daily seafood such as tuna, marlin, and Spanish mackerel, as well as mud crabs and prawns from local fish farms. ❺

Dinagat Island

Wild and undeveloped Dinagat island, about 60km from tip to toe, is an adventure paradise-in-waiting, with only handfuls of travellers having made it this far. It's a shame, because Dinagat is only a short banca hop from Surigao and its rugged coastline has some wonderful **islets** and beautiful white sand **beaches** backed by sheer cliffs that are attracting an increasing number of **rock climbers**. The main problem with any kind of extended stay on the island is the lack of **accommodation**: there are some basic beach huts on the southwest coast around the town of Dinagat, but not much else. The best way to get an overview of what Dinagat has to offer is to hire a banca when you get to the island; you can do this for about P400 for half a day in Tubajon or Albor, where ferries arrive from Surigao. On the west coast islet of **Unib** you'll find unspoiled Bitaug beach and several immense, largely unexplored caves. The waters of this area are fringed by good coral and deep sea walls, so the scuba diving potential is obvious. There's no equipment for rent so whatever you need you'll have to bring, including snorkelling gear. In the same area, the uninhabited islet of **Hagakhak** is another beauty, with spectacular above-water and underwater rock formations. At a group of islets called **Magsaysay**, again off Dinagat's west coast, there are several beaches with pure white sand.

At least getting to Dinagat is straightforward. There's a daily **ferry** (P120) from Surigao to Tubajon on the northwest coast at noon. The trip takes four hours and the ferry does not return until 6am the following day, so you'll have to be prepared to spend the night on the island. Another ferry sails daily at noon from Surigao to Albor (also known as Libjo) on the west coast, returning early the following morning.

Southern Mindanao

The major city in southern Mindanao and the arrival point for many visitors is **Davao**, a friendly, low-key metropolis with a range of accommodation from where you can explore nearby attractions such as the pretty islands of **Samal** and **Talicud**, just off the coast, both with resorts, beaches, scuba diving and snorkelling. It's also an easy trip from Davao to the **Philippine Eagle Foundation**, where dedicated staff are striving to keep the majestic bird from extinction. The foundation is in the foothills of **Mount Apo**, the tallest mountain in the Philippines – bear in mind that access to this wonderful natural environment is restricted, and you need to get permission in advance. From Davao it's possible to travel south by road to the region's other metropolis, workaday **General Santos**, the starting point for inland travel through the tribal provinces of southern Mindanao and to the city of Cotabato, de facto capital of the Autonomous Region in Muslim Mindanao.

Davao and around

DAVAO is not a city of legendary sights and you're unlikely to want to spend more than a few days here. That said, it's a friendly place and a pleasant respite from the mania of big cities in Luzon, especially Manila. It's got some good hotels, bargain shopping – especially for tribal handicrafts – and the fresh seafood sold in many restaurants is almost worth the trip alone. Davao is also the gateway to **Mount Apo**, a magnet for trekkers and climbers. Sun, sand and sea are also on the doorstep at the many islands just off the coast, the biggest and most popular of which is **Samal**.

There's a great deal of cultural diversity in Davao. This immense city – one of the largest in the world in terms of land area – is home to the ethnic Bagobo, Mandaya, Manobo, T'boli, Mansaka and B'laan tribes, animists whose ancestors were first to arrive in Mindanao across land bridges from Malaysia. Other early settlers on the banks of the Davao River were tribes from Cotabato, Zamboanga and Jolo. Conquest by the Spanish failed repeatedly until the mid–nineteenth century, when they were finally able to overrun the Muslim enclaves that had been established by Malay settlers, accomplished sailors who had arrived from across the Sulu Sea.

The city was no stranger to armed struggle, but the **violence** that took place in the 1980s almost brought it to its knees economically. This black decade, marked by violence from the MNLF and the NPA (New People's Army; see

△ Davao and Mount Apo

p.171), earned Davao the notorious title of "Gun Capital of the Philippines" – indeed, it became a haven for the underground movement and a laboratory for urban guerrilla warfare. The emergence of an anti-Communist group known as the Alsa Masa (Rise of the Masses) began in Davao, and eventually this military-backed civilian defence force drove the NPA and MNLF away from the city. Davao today is home to one million people and growing slowly in stature as an investment and tourist destination, held back only by its inevitable association with violence in other areas of Mindanao. Occasionally Davao has been touched by the Mindanao problem: a bomb blast at the airport in 2003 caused a number of fatalities.

Arrival, orientation and information

Davao is well served by air and ferry, from Manila and other key cities. The **airport** lies 11km north of the city centre; the flat fare into the city by taxi is P100. **Ferries** dock 7km to the east at Sasa wharf, from where there are frequent jeepneys and tricycles to the city. **Buses** arrive in Davao at the Ecoland terminal in Quimpo Boulevard, across the Davao River on the southwestern outskirts of the city, a short taxi or jeepney ride into the city centre.

Davao might be a sprawling city, but many key areas are within walking distance of one another on either side of busy **C.M. Recto Avenue**. On the western edge of the city is **San Pedro Street**, linked to Quezon Boulevard, which heads northeast to Magsaysay Park and Santa Ana wharf. From Magsaysay Park, Leon Garcia Street leads northeast out of the city towards the airport. There are two big malls, Gaisano mall and Victoria Plaza, both on J.P. Laurel Avenue. There's also a smaller Gaisano mall near San Pedro Cathedral. All three contain offices for major airlines and ferry companies.

The **tourist information office** (Mon–Sat 8am–6pm; ☏082/222 1956, Ⓦwww.davaotourism.com) is on the second floor of City Hall, San Pedro

DAVAO

▲ ⒷSasa Wharf, T'Boli Weaving Center & Dabaw Museum

ACCOMMODATION

Apo View Hotel	E
Casa Leticia	D
Durian Hotel Davao	A
Hotel Galleria	C
Hotel Maguindanao	I
Marco Polo Davao	G
Park Square Inn	J
Sunny Point Lodge	F
Villa Fontana Inn	H
Waterfront Insular	
Century Hotel Davao	B

RESTAURANTS & BARS

Bistro Rosario	4
Fiesta Dabaw	5
Kibuwi	1
Manukan sa Bacolod	2
Sarung Banggi	3
The Venue	6
Zugba Restaurant	E

N

0 ——— 500 m

ⒶVictoria Plaza Mall & Veloso Street restaurants & bars

Puentespina Tropical Orchids and Plants, Lon Wa Temple, Taoist Temple & Airport

University of the
Southern Philippines

PLDT

Allied Bank

Agdao
Market

WG&A
Office

Sulpicio Office

WG&A
Building

Medical
Mission Hospital

Sta Ana
Wharf

Whitetip
Divers

ⓘ

Immigration
Office

Magsaysay
Park

San Pedro
Hospital

LAPU-LAPU STREET

STA ANA AVENUE

MONTEVERDE STREET

LEON GARCIA STREET

Gaisano
Mall

J.P. LAUREL AVENUE

R. MAGSAYSAY AVENUE

PONCE STREET

QUEZON BOULEVARD

Central
Plaza Mall

Davao City
High School

Central
Bank

TIONKO STREET

F. TORRES STREET

Ateneo de Davao
University

E. JACINTO STREET

ROXAS AVENUE

MABINI STREET

Equitable
Bank

University
Mall

Aldevinco
Shopping
Center

Air
Philippines

PLDT

C. BANGOY STREET

C.M. RECTO STREET

S. DE JESUS STREET

S. PADADA STREET

School

J. CAMUS S.

PALMA GIL STREET

DUTEREL STREET

C

D

E

ⓘ

University
of Mindanao

ANDA STREET

BOLTON STREET

San Pedro
Cathedral

F. IÑIGO STREET

E. QUIRINO AVENUE

SAN PEDRO STREET

PICHON ST (MAGELLANES)

Gaisano
Mall

City Hall

ⓘ

Osmeña
Park

Market

Davao River

▼Ⓑ& Ecoland Bus Terminal

Street, and there's another, smaller tourist office in Magsaysay Park, near Santa Ana wharf (Mon–Fri 8am–noon & 1–5pm; ☎082/221 6955 or 0070); this is the office you need for **permission to climb Mount Apo** (see p.397). A third tourist office (Mon–Sat 8am–6pm; ☎082/221 6798) is next to *Apo View Hotel* in J. Camus Street.

City transport

It's cheap and easy to get around Davao by **taxi**; the flagfall is P25 and after that it's P2 per kilometre, so a cross-city journey will set you back no more than P100. **Jeepneys** run back and forth along all major thoroughfares – it's just a question of flagging one down and hopping on. From C.M. Recto Street there are jeepneys every few minutes heading north, signposted for Gaisano mall or Victoria Plaza. They also run up and down Magsaysay Avenue to and from Santa Ana wharf. **Tricycles** charge P6 per person for trips within the city – this includes Santa Ana wharf, Ecoland bus terminal and north as far as Victoria Plaza.

Accommodation

Davao has a range of good and central **accommodation**, from decent budget hotels to some quality mid-range places and a couple of five-stars.

Apo View Hotel J. Camus St ☎082/221 6430 or 02/893 1288, ⓦwww.apoview.com. The upmarket hotel of choice in Davao, with big, comfortable a/c rooms. You don't always get a view of Mount Apo, although on a clear day you can see it from the top-floor restaurant. The *Pag-asa Piano Bar & Music Lounge* has some entertaining bands in the evening, playing cheesy but fun cover versions of Western pop standards. ❾

Casa Leticia J. Camus St ☎082/224 0501, ⓦwww.casaleticia.com. An attractive mid-range option with rooms ranging from studios and doubles to a smart presidential suite. All rooms are a/c, have private bathrooms and are clean and well appointed. Boasts a reasonable restaurant and a lively music bar, *Toto's*, with jazz, Latin and pop acts every night. ❻

Durian Hotel Davao J.P. Laurel Ave ☎082/221 8216. Large, modern hotel with a good choice of a/c rooms, close to Victoria Plaza in the north of the city. There's a pool on the roof, plus a restaurant, bar and jazz bar with live music every evening. ❼

Hotel Galleria Duterte St ☎082/221 9013. Modest and affordable mid-size hotel in a good location close to the Davao Doctors' Hospital in the west of the city. Rooms are nothing special, but they're well maintained and have a/c and private bathrooms. ❺

Hotel Maguindanao C.M. Recto St ☎082/222 2894. A good combination of reasonable prices and decent rooms, all with a/c and private bathrooms, in a handy location opposite the cathedral. ❺

Marco Polo Davao C.M. Recto St ☎082/221 0888. Perhaps the most popular upmarket hotel in the city, the Marco Polo has 245 comfortable rooms and suites with large bathrooms and extras such as cable TV, fax and broadband Internet. Even standard rooms have views of either the sea or, on a clear day, Mount Apo. ❼

Park Square Inn Quimpo Blvd ☎082/298 0258. Cheap but comfortable short-stay option, a 10min tricycle ride from the city centre on the other side of the Davao River. Rooms are small and spartan, some with shared showers, but this is still a reasonable low-cost, no-frills choice. ❶

Sunny Point Lodge Magellanes St corner Legaspi St ☎082/221 0155. Clean, quiet rooms a short walk west of the city centre near the Davao River. Laundry facilities and free coffee 24hr a day from the café downstairs. ❷

Villa Fontana Inn Bolton St ☎082/222 3797. Good budget option in a convenient location in the centre of town, a few blocks south of the *Marco Polo*. Rooms are ordinary, but well-kept and with simple, clean bathrooms. There's a choice of singles, doubles and family rooms. ❸

Waterfront Insular Century Hotel Davao ☎082/234 3050. Modern, resort-style hotel on the shore, 5km out of town in the Lanang district. Pretty a/c rooms, large outdoor pool and a small beach area. It's the pick of the bunch if you've got the budget and are looking for relaxation and fresh sea breezes. ❽

The City

There are very few notable tourist draws in Davao. It's a less claustrophobic city than many in the Philippines, with wider roads and a few more open spaces, but much of its history was bulldozed in the name of progress in the late twentieth century. The most notable building is the **San Pedro Cathedral** (daily 6am–8pm; free), opposite Osmeña Park; it was built in 1847 under the auspices of the Spanish conquistador Don José Uyanguren, who ruled the city with an iron hand and energetically set about converting the locals to Catholicism. Much of the external structure, though striking, is twentieth century. Inside, however, the original altar and statues of saints are preserved in the beautifully serene eastern wing, with its whitewashed walls and tiled floors.

The influence of the Chinese in Davao is also much in evidence, with two fine temples in the north of the city, easily reached by tricycle. The **Lon Wa Temple** (daily 7am–8pm; free) in Cabaguio Avenue is the biggest in Mindanao and one of the most ornate in the country, with immense carved pillars and two glittering altars. A little to the south along Cabaguio Avenue and signposted down a narrow side street is the **Taoist Temple** (daily 6am–8pm; free) with its red pagoda: ring the bell on the gate and wait for the caretaker to visit. From here you can continue walking south to the **Puentespina Tropical Orchids and Plants** nursery (daily 9am–8pm; P15) in Bolcan Street, which has row upon row of wonderful tropical and sub-tropical orchids, including some fine examples of the rare *waling-waling*, which is endemic to Mindanao.

In the grounds of the *Waterfront Insular Century Hotel Davao* you'll find the **Dabaw Museum** (Tues–Sun 9am–noon & 1–5.30pm; P100), dedicated to the area's cultural minorities such as the Mansaka and the Bogobo and with mannequins dressed in native garb, as well as anthropological and historical exhibitions. From the museum it's a short walk to the **T'boli Weaving Center** (daily 9am–8pm), where you can see weavers at work on looms and buy the hand-woven fabric they produce, with bold geometrical patterns that symbolize tribal beliefs. Colourful wall hangings and table runners cost from P3000.

A major **annual festival** in Davao is the mardi-gras-style **Kadayawan**, a harvest festival held during the third week of August. One of the festival's major components is horse fighting, which pits untrained stallions against each other. There is also street tribal dancing to the sound of drums, and a colourful parade down the Davao River, with gaily decorated boats sailing in convoy.

Eating

F. Torres Street on the western edge of the city centre, close to the Davao City High School, is known as Food Street and, as the name suggests, is home to dozens of **restaurants** specializing in everything from cheap local *merienda* (snacks) to seafood, Chinese, Japanese and even Mongolian cuisine. Davao's malls and the streets around them are also good places to hunt down cheap meals of all descriptions. Also, don't forget to get your fill of stinky **durian** as Davao is the durian capital of the Philippines. This bright green fruit has a pungent smell that has been described as a combination of old cheese, turpentine and onion, but don't let the noxious perfume put you off. Aficionados say the durian's tender white flesh has a taste suggestive of almonds, sherry, custard and ice cream. Durian is available in most restaurants and you can also buy it from street hawkers.

Fiesta Dabaw Tionko St. A popular seafood restaurant with ethnic Muslim seafaring decor and dishes ranging from fresh lapu-lapu to coconut seafood curry and delicious grilled tuna jaw.

Kibuwi F. Torres St. Lively and welcoming native-style restaurant with an extensive menu of fresh seafood; you'll be able to gorge and have a couple of beers for less than P500 per person.

Manukan sa Bacolod F. Torres St. Down-to-earth grill restaurant where the menu revolves mostly around chicken and pork, served with piping hot rice. There are a few vegetable dishes, but this isn't really a place for vegetarians.

Probinsya Veloso St. One of a number of fashionable new restaurants near the Victoria Plaza mall, *Probinsya* (it means provincial) has affordable and busy daily buffets featuring home-style Filipino food such as grilled tuna, pancit and leche flan. In the evenings, free of the buffet hoardes, it's a more relaxed place with an à la carte menu that includes deliciously fresh crab, prawns and lobster.

Sarung Banggi F. Torres St. Fun native-style dining with waiters and waitresses resplendent in various tribal-style outfits. The menu is imaginative and offers much more choice than most of the local grill restaurants. Notable dishes include seafood soup with sour mango and rice, a meat Bicol Express with pork ribs and chilli, and simple grilled tuna or swordfish served with a splash of native lime.

Zugba Restaurant *Apo View Hotel*, J. Camus St. Popular alfresco restaurant that serves tuna jaw, king prawn and grilled lapu-lapu for only a few hundred pesos a head. Choose whatever you fancy from the display and the waiter will give you options for how it can be cooked.

Nightlife

It may not be as avant-garde as Manila, but there's some entertaining laidback **nightlife** on offer in Davao, with cosy live-music venues, karaoke bars and discos. The newest venue for live music is the aptly named *The Venue*, a bustling place close to the Central Bank on Quirino Avenue. It attracts a young, mostly teenage audience, but even if you feel past it, it's fun to wander around and soak up the atmosphere. In Veloso Street you'll find *Passage Bar* and *Studio Onnie*, which both feature regular live bands. Next door to *Studio Onnie* is *Korokan*, where you can rent a private room with friends and let rip with the karaoke.

Listings

Airlines Air Philippines has a ticket office at the Ateneo de Davao University Building in C.M. Recto St, opposite the *Marco Polo Davao Hotel* (℡082/224 6977); Cebu Pacific has one at Summit World on the second floor of Victoria Plaza mall at the northern end of J.P. Laurel Ave (℡082/224 0960).

Banks and exchange There are several banks around University mall, Roxas Ave. Equitable Bank is near the post office on Roxas Ave. For reliable ATMs head to Victoria Plaza or Gaisano mall.

Car rental Avis (℡082/221 6430) *Apo View Hotel;* Nissan Rent-a-Car (℡082/221 0888) lobby of the *Marco Polo Davao.*

Diving Whitetip Divers, PPA Building, Santa Ana wharf (℡082/227 0234), is a good place to stop for information about scuba diving in the area.

Emergencies The city's major hospital is the Davao Doctors' Hospital (℡082/224 0616), E. Quirino Ave, southwest of the city centre. San Pedro Hospital (℡082/224 0616) is on Guerrero St in the city centre.

Ferry offices The main WG&A ticket office is at the eastern end of Santa Ana Ave (℡082/221 1390); you can also book tickets at Aboitiz outlets – there's one on the second floor of Gaisano mall – and at travel agents. The Sulpicio Lines Davao hotline is ℡082/235 2107.

Internet access There are dozens of Internet cafés on the main road outside Victoria Plaza. There are more in the major malls, including Victoria Plaza (top floor) and Gaisano mall, where most are on the third floor.

Phones There's no problem getting a mobile-phone signal in Davao. PLDT has an office on Clara M. Recto Ave, close to the post office, where you can place long-distance calls.

Post The main post office is on Roxas Ave, close to the junction with Clara M. Recto Ave and Magsaysay Ave. Branches of Aboitiz One couriers are in Gaisano mall and SM City mall, which is west of the city centre on the other side of the river in Quimpo Blvd.

Police The main Philippine National Police office is known as Camp Catitipan (℡082/232 5215) and is on Santa Ana Ave. There are dozens of smaller precincts or stations throughout the city, including one opposite the tourist information office in Magsaysay Park.

Shopping For souvenirs and handicrafts, go to the Aldevinco Shopping Center opposite the *Marco Polo Hotel* on C.M. Recto St. It's a maze of small shops selling tribal artefacts and cheap batik clothes from the Philippines, Indonesia and Thailand. With a little hard bargaining, you can grab a sarong for 100

pesos or statues and masks from P400.
Travel agents Major shopping malls are good places to look for travel agents, as are many of the bigger hotels. Amity Travel (℡082/765 3131) is in Gaisano mall and House of Travel (℡082/234 0582) is in the Damosa Complex on J.P. Laurel Ave, 100m south of Gaisano mall.

Around Davao

The countryside surrounding Davao is alluring, with rolling fruit plantations backed by high mountains. The most popular and convenient resort areas are the twin islands of **Samal** and **Talicud**, just off Davao's coast. An easy road trip north of Davao on mainland Mindanao is the **Philippine Eagle Center**, which is at the forefront of conservation work to save the Philippine eagle from extinction, and, further on, stunning **Mount Apo**, accessed from the elevated town of **Kidapan**, whose coolish climate has made it the country's foremost producer of cut flowers.

Samal and Talicud islands

Samal Island – the Island Garden City of Samal to give it its rather grandiose official name – and the smaller island of **Talicud**, lie a stone's throw southeast of Davao in the Gulf of Davao, across the narrow Pakiputan Strait. Both are easy to reach by regular public **bancas** from Sasa wharf. (Jeepneys marked "Sasa" will take you from Davao city centre to within spitting distance of the departure point.) You can also get a more expensive **ferry** from the pier at the *Waterfront Insular Century Hotel Davao*; the *Waterfront* and many travel agents in Davao arrange **day-trips** to Samal for about P1000, including lunch at a resort on the island.

Samal is the better of the two islands to visit, simply because it's larger and there's more to explore. It has some lovely coves and beaches and a number of good areas for scuba diving, with intact coral reefs and a few wrecks; three Japanese wrecks lie next to each other off Pearl Farm Beach on the west coast. You can arrange **diving** trips at many resorts on Samal and also at Whitetip Divers (see opposite). The island also features some immense, deep caves on the east coast that can be reached easily by tricycle or on foot; the cross-island walk is through rolling coconut groves and takes about two hours. **Accommodation** on Samal is mixed. Most reasonably priced resorts are on the northwest coast, facing Davao, south of the village of Caliclic. From where bancas arrive you can walk to these resorts, or hop on a tricycle for the short trip. Like many places, *Paradise Island Beach Resort* (℡082/233 0251; ❹) can get busy at weekends with day-trippers escaping the city, but has good fan and air-conditioned cottages under shady trees in landscaped gardens, a convivial native-style restaurant and scuba diving. Next door to the south is *Costa Marina Resort* (℡082/233 1209; ❹), with twin and double cottages, either fan or air-conditioned. Further south along the west coast is the island's classiest and most expensive resort, *Pearl Farm Resort* (℡082/221 9970, ⓦwww.pearlfarmresort .com; ❽), which has more than seventy native-style cottages either on a hillside overlooking the bay or perched on stilts in the sea. There are also seven luxurious and secluded villas on beautiful little Malipano island, a short hop from the main resort.

Talicud is quieter than Samal and not as touristy, making it a perfect place to escape Davao's crowds for a day or two. On the west coast there's good, easy diving and snorkelling in an area known as Coral Gardens, while there are a couple of more demanding drop-off dives off the north coast. You'll find a couple of modest **resorts** on Talicud: on the east coast *Isla Reta Beach Resort* (❸) has simple wooden cottages, while on the west coast near the barangay of

Bacacay, *Isla Christina Beach Resort* (❷) has concrete air-conditioned rooms sitting on a pretty cove of white sand.

Philippine Eagle Center

The **Philippine Eagle Center** (daily 8am–5pm; adults P50, under 18s P30; ☎082/224 3021, ⓦwww.philippineeagle.org), 35km north of Davao in Malagos, is known for its excellent work breeding the Philippine eagle, or monkey-eating eagle, a majestic creature with a fearsome beak and two-metre wingspan. The birds are extremely elusive, and their existence was documented only in 1896, a century after most other bird species. That first known sighting was by the intrepid British bird collector John Whitehead in Samar, who named the eagle *Pithecophaga jeffryi* after his father, Jeffrey, who financed his expedition. Sadly, the eagle is now officially on the endangered species list, with only a maximum of three hundred believed to be living in the wilds of Mindanao, Samar and Leyte. The centre's captive breeding programme focuses on developing a viable gene pool, the goal being to reintroduce the birds into their natural habitat. Two eagles, named Pag-Asa (Hope) and Pagkakaisa (Unity) were bred in 1992, and since then twelve more have been born. The centre is now home to 32 Philippine eagles, 16 of which were bred in captivity.

The centre is an enjoyable and educational day-trip, but can be uncomfortably busy at weekends, so try to schedule your visit for a weekday when staff are less busy and will sometimes let you handle and feed the birds. **Guided tours** are free, but you should book in advance. It's set in pretty tropical countryside with views of Mount Apo and there are always guides on hand to give you a tour of the many aviaries and displays. Apart from the eagles there are other types of birds, and larger animals such as Philippine deer and warty pigs.

Many hotels and travel agents in Davao offer **day-trips** to the foundation. To get there on your own, take a **bus** (P30) to Calinan (45min) from the Annil transport terminal next to Ateneo de Davao University, from where it's a short tricycle ride.

Kidapawan and Mount Apo

About two hours' drive west of Davao, **KIDAPAWAN** sits on the lower slopes of Mount Apo, and is the best starting point for treks to the summit. Kidapawan's elevated position means it has a refreshingly cool climate, but its proximity to Apo is the only tourist draw; there's really no other reason to be here unless you're passing through on the main road, the National Highway, that runs between Davao and Cotabato. If you haven't already hired a **guide** through the DoT in Davao you can arrange one here at City Hall, next to the police station on the north side of the main plaza, where you can also get permits, but the office isn't always open, so it's best to get one in Davao.

All buses arrive at the terminal on the National Highway, opposite the mosque. There's a Mercury pharmacy next to the mosque and behind it a PT&T office where you can make phone calls. You'll find only two banks in town: PNB at the west end of the National Highway and UCPB in Lapu-Lapu Street, opposite the mosque. Two budget hotels sit on the north side of the National Highway near the plaza, the *Highlander* (❶), which has spartan singles and doubles with a shared bathroom and the *A.J. Hi-Time Hotel* (❶), where there are double rooms with their own shower and toilet. There's better **accommodation** in green surroundings at *Rica's Resort* (❷) in the residential suburb of Magsaysay, ten minutes to the south of town by tricycle. *Kim's Garden & Family Restaurant*, on the National Highway about 200m west of the cathedral, dishes up good, cheap Chinese **food**.

A little further along the National Highway to the west, next to the Iglesa ni Kristo, is the road that leads north to Mount Apo. Jeepneys from Kidapawan will take you to the trail in about 45 minutes.

Climbing Mount Apo

Mount Apo (2954m) overlooks Davao from the north and lords it over the Philippines as the highest mountain in the country: the name Apo means "grandfather of all mountains". Apo is actually a volcano, but is certified inactive and has no recorded eruptions. What it does have is enough flora and fauna to make your head spin – thundering waterfalls, rapids, lakes, geysers, sulphur pillars, primeval trees, endangered plant and animal species and a steaming blue lake. It is the home of the Philippine eagle, the tiny falconet and the Mount Apo mynah. Then there are exotic ferns, carnivorous pitcher plants and the queen of Philippine orchids, the *waling-waling*. The local tribes, the Bagobos, believe the gods Apo and Mandaragan inhabit Apo's upper slopes; they revere it as a sacred mountain, calling it Sandawa or "Mountain of Sulphur".

Recently, Mount Apo has become something of an environmental hot potato and the government is trying to dissuade people from climbing it because of the damage they have done to trails and the litter they have left behind. Small groups of climbers with special interests, such as botany or photography, will still be allowed, but large groups could find they get turned back. The situation is uncertain and changes every year. The best advice is to call the tourist information centre in Magsaysay Park (see p.392) to plead your case. If you have a well-prepared case and some documentation to back it up (a letter from a university or employer explaining why you would like to climb Apo, for instance), there's a good chance you'll get **permission**.

Don't attempt Mount Apo alone: hire a **guide** from one of the tourist offices in Davao, where staff will also help you plan the route and get the necessary permits. Also, make sure you go well prepared. Experienced Apo climbers advise allowing four or five days for the climb, averaging four hours of trekking a day with an average load of 20 kilos to supply you with food and shelter for extreme weather. Towards the peak, temperatures are as low as 5°C, so don't go without a good sleeping bag, warm clothes and a tent. It's a tough trek, but well worth it: the trail is lined with flowers and on the first day you should reach **Mainit Hot Spring**, where you can take a refreshing dip. Day two brings you to the dramatic **Lake Venado**, which looks like a scene from the Jurassic age, with giant trees, vines and a fine fog floating above the lake itself. At the end of the third day you can make camp below the summit and rise at 5am to get to the top in time for sunrise. The views are nothing short of spectacular. This is the highest point in the Philippines, with the whole of Mindanao spread out before you.

General Santos and around

Southwest of Davao on Sarangani Bay, **GENERAL SANTOS** – or "Gensan" – is the Philippines' southernmost city, a dense, noisy metropolis that isn't a significant tourist destination, but is the jump-off point for the agricultural province of Sarangani and idyllic **Lake Sebu**. The vast hinterlands of central Mindanao to the west of General Santos – the provinces of North Cotaboto, Maguindinao, South Cotabato and Sultan Kudarat – are rarely explored by tourists because of occasional violence associated with the fight for Muslim autonomy (see box pp.374–375).

The busy centre of General Santos, sometimes referred to as "Tuna City" because of its profitable tuna-fishing and canning industry, is bounded to the north by the National Highway, to the south by Sarangani Bay and to the west by the Silway River. At the city's heart are two parks – **Freedom Park**, to the east, and **Carlos P. Garcia Park**, to the west – with City Hall between them. From City Hall it's a ten-minute walk north to the National Highway and about the same distance south to P. Acharon Boulevard, which runs along the seafront. As for things to do in General Santos, you can while away a few hours strolling through the two parks before walking south to a third park, Magsaysay, right on the seafront. On the east of this park is a photogenic mosque. For **shopping**, head to Gaisano mall, east of the city along Catolico Avenue.

Practicalities

Tambler **airport** is about twenty minutes by road west of the city, an easy trip by jeepney or tricycle. **Ferries** arrive at Makar wharf, ten minutes west of the airport. There are always plenty of jeepneys, vans and tricycles vying for custom when a ferry arrives, so getting into Gensan itself is no problem. The main terminal for **bus** arrivals is City Terminal near Bulaong Avenue on the western edge of the city near the river. Some buses from Maasin and Cotabato arrive at smaller terminals in Sampaloc Street, but wherever you arrive you can walk or take a tricycle the short distance into town.

There are two **tourist offices**, one in the Department of Trade and Industry building on the National Highway and another in City Hall. Neither has much in the way of maps, but they do have lists of accommodation and useful bus and ferry information. The **post office** is one block north of City Hall. Most **banks** are in a huddle on Pioneer Avenue, which runs south from Carlos P. Garcia Park. There are more on the National Highway, while BPI is on Magsaysay Avenue south of City Hall. For **Internet** access head to the places near Holy Trinity College on Fiscal Gregorio Daprosa Avenue, a few minutes' walk west of Carlos P. Garcia Park. The Aquis Clinic here is open 24 hours a day, while two blocks south at the western end of Atis Street is the **police station**.

Accommodation and eating

The two main areas for **accommodation** are along the National Highway northeast of Freedom Park, and on and around Pioneer Avenue, south of City Hall. Of the two, the City Hall area is marginally better because it's quieter and closer to amenities such as banks and malls.

On National Highway is the ritziest hotel in town, the *East Asia Royale* (☎083/553 4119; ❻), with large air-conditioned rooms, a coffee shop and two restaurants.

In the City Hall area, on Salazar Street, *Clara's Lodge* (☎083/552 3016; ❷) has neat and tidy singles and doubles either with fan or air-conditioning, some with private showers. At the longstanding *Dolores Hotel* (☎083/552 2921; ❸) on Santiago Boulevard – a relatively quiet area a few minutes' walk to the east of City Hall but still close to banks and shops – there's a choice of double or twin rooms either with air-conditioning or fan, but all with private bathrooms.

Next to each other on noisy President Ramon Magsaysay Avenue also east of City Hall you'll find three adequate budget options: *Vince's Pension*, *Phela Grande* and *Zabala Lodge* (all ❶). *757 Inn & Restaurant* on J. Catolico Street, a little east of the city centre (☎083/552 2969 or 3212; ❷), is a modern, comfortable place with well-maintained air-conditioned rooms, all with private bathrooms.

There are lots of functional but **cheap restaurants** in General Santos serving grilled fish – tuna figures prominently on all the menus – and meat, or Filipino dishes such as *sinigang* with rice. At the eastern end of President Sergio Osmena Street, a short walk north of Freedom Park there are a dozen places within a block of each other, including *Tuna Grill*, *Coco Grill* and the friendly *Abi's*, where two people can eat a huge amount for less than 300 pesos. On Pioneer Avenue near the banks is a similar restaurant called *Manokan*, while near the *East Asia Royale* hotel are *Jingling's* and *Fishtahan*.

T'boli and Lake Sebu

To the west of General Santos, the small town of **T'BOLI** sits on the shores of **Lake Sebu**, in a natural bowl surrounded by wooded hills and rolling plantations. This is the ancestral homeland of the T'boli tribe, whose members often wear traditional woven clothes and eye-catching hand-made jewellery. It's a great place to see T'Boli culture at first hand; you can also rent a boat and take a **trip on the lake** itself and shop in the weekly **Saturday market** for brassware, beads and fabric, all at a fraction of the cost of shops in General Santos or Davao. The annual Lem-Lunay T'boli **festival** is held every year on the second Friday of November and concludes with traditional horse fights.

There is some reasonably good **accommodation** around Lake Sebu. The best is *Punta Isla* (❶), a short ride out of town along the lakeshore, which has rudimentary but adequate cottages and a breezy restaurant that serves catch of the day from the lake, usually tilapia. You can get a dorm bed at *Punta Isla* for P75. *Lakeside Tourist Lodge* (❶), near the market where buses and jeepneys arrive, has small, penitential rooms, while *Bao Ba-ay Village Inn* (❷), five minutes' walk north from the marketplace, has marvellous lake views and cottages with balconies.

To reach T'boli, take a **bus** from General Santos to Koronadal, from where jeepneys and air-conditioned mini vans head south to T'boli, a trip of about two hours. Motorcycles are the main form of public transport in T'boli and around the lake itself; a short trip costs P10 and you can negotiate longer journeys around the lake for about P250 for half a day.

Cotabato

On the west coast of Mindanao in the province of Maguindanao, **COTABATO** is at the heart of the Autonomous Region in Muslim Mindanao and, because of the security situation (see box p.374), is not a place many tourists visit. The city itself, which stands on the banks of the Rio Grande (also called the Pulangi River), has been the scene of a number of bombings and kidnappings, while the road heading north to Cotabato from Koronadal has seen several bus hijackings, with passengers robbed at gunpoint. These incidents, however, have been spread out over a number of years, and while many foreign embassies strongly advise against travel to the city and the surrounding area, the authorities in Cotabato itself say it's a safe place, with Muslims, Christians and tribal communities living in relative harmony. Indeed, there have been no high-profile incidents in the province involving tourists in recent years. There have, however, been skirmishes between locals over land rights, and in March 2007 a suspected MILF leader was killed in the area by the military.

The city's **history** is certainly colourful. A settlement sprang up in 1475 near the mouth of Rio Grande, providing a strategic gateway to the resource-rich hinterlands of Mindanao. In 1511 Malay chieftains arrived after Malacca fell into Portuguese hands and various sultans vied for power, resulting in a century of almost constant warfare. Under Spanish rule Cotabato's sphere of influence began to recede as a succession of local rulers signed peace treaties with the colonizers. The peace was shattered in 1886 when an aggrieved sultan led his forces against the Spanish and was forced into a humiliating capitulation that left Muslims simmering. When the Americans arrived in 1900, rule by the sultans was still very much entrenched, with most of them impervious to Jesuit attempts to convert people to "the true religion". An American commander on the gunboat *Panay* wrote of one datu: "His is the very bluest of all the blue Moro blood in this great island. His slaves, in serving him, creep and crouch like dogs, and even the other and lesser Datus bow before him and murmur between their half-closed lips." Because of its position at the geographical and political heart of the ARMM, Cotabato today has become synonymous with the festering Mindanao problem, many of its people fiercely "Maguindanaon" (people of the lake country) and in favour of autonomy, while others are Christians loyal to Manila.

Tourist sights in the city include the **ornate tombs** of Sultan Kudarat and Datu Masturan, opposite the Provincial Capitol building, and **Tamontska Church**, built in 1872 by the Spanish and the oldest church in Cotabato. The eerie **Kutang Bato Caves** are, oddly, right in the middle of the city; they once provided sanctuary for locals hiding from the Spanish. It's worth also taking a look around the ornate **ARMM legislative building** on the northern edge of the city and easy to reach by tricycle. It houses the offices of the rulers of the ARMM and contains a **museum** (Mon–Fri 9am–4pm; free) that charts the area's turbulent history.

Practicalities

Awang **airport**, 10km south of Cotabato, is served by Philippine Airlines from Manila and Seair from Zamboanga and Cebu. From the airport it's a fifteen-minute tricycle ride into the city. **Buses** from Davao, General Santos, Koronadal, Marawi and many north coast towns arrive at the integrated terminal one block east of Cotabato City Hall. **Ferries** from Zamboanga arrive at Polloc pier, 20km north of the city; you can take a jeepney or mini van into town from here. From General Santos and Pagadian, ferries arrive at the wharf right in the centre of town, from where you can walk or take a tricycle to your accommodation. The regional **tourist office** (☎064/421 7804) is in the old Provincial Capitol Building on Piedro Colina Hill, ten minutes inland by tricycle from the city wharf.

Accommodation and eating

The most luxurious **accommodation** in Cotabato is at the *Estosan Garden Hotel* (☎064/421 6777; ❹) on Gutierrez Street, a modern building facing the ARMM legislative building. Rooms are simple and spacious and there's a coffee shop and a restaurant. For something a little cheaper try the boxy *Hotel Filipino* (☎064/421 2307; ❷) on Pendatum Avenue, two blocks inland from the wharf. Its air-conditioned rooms are a little faded, but staff are friendly and the location is central. A few doors away is the *Sanitary Lodging House* (☎064/421 3129; ❶), whose stark rooms almost live up to the hotel's name – there's a choice between fan and air-conditioned and the cheapest rooms have shared bathrooms.

For **eating**, the *Estosan Garden Hotel* has an extensive menu that includes fried or grilled *pigek*, a local fish delicacy. There are three good restaurants near each other in Sinsuat Avenue (close to the Spanish church): *Armando's Steakhouse and Restaurant* specializes in grills; *Las Hermanas* is known for Peking duck; and *Casa Blanca* for steak.

Western Mindanao and Sulu

Western Mindanao and **Sulu** are the parts of the Philippines that set off alarm bells for travellers, with the security situation in a state of flux because of a number of groups agitating for autonomy from Manila. It's an area, though, of huge tourism potential, with jungled mountains, great fluvial plains and a vast finger of land, the **Zamboanga peninsula**, reaching south towards the island of **Basilan**. You can access the western portion of Mindanao through the port town of **Iligan**, one of a number of industrial conurbations in western Mindanao that's useful as a transit point, but doesn't have much else to offer. To the west is another major port, **Ozamis**, jump-off point for the little-explored Mount Malanding National Park. Two of the most pleasant port towns in this area are **Dapitan** and **Dipolog**, but because of their location off the beaten track few visitors see them. Dapitan is especially agreeable, a leafy seaside town associated with national hero José Rizal, who was exiled here. Heading inland you can explore the Muslim city of **Marawi**, which stands on scenic Lake Lanao. In the far south lie **Zamboanga** and the hundreds of islands that make up the spectacular **Sulu archipelago**, including Jolo and Tawi-Tawi.

Iligan to Dipolog

The **northwest coast** of Mindanao stretching from Iligan in the east to Dipolog in the west is mostly rural and undeveloped, but peppered with port towns that make useful places to base yourself if you want to explore this very untouristy area. **Iligan** is the jumping off point for Marawi and Lake Lanao, while along the coast Mount Malindang National Park, reached via **Ozamis**, offers some challenging backwoods trekking and the opportunity to see rare species. From Ozamis the coastal road continues westwards to **Dapitan** – always associated with national hero José Rizal, who was exiled here by the Spanish colonial government – which lies on a picturesque sweeping bay. The next major town along the coast is **Dipolog**, capital of Zamboanga del Norte, and venue for a colourful Cebu-style Sinulog festival every year during the last week of January.

Iligan

A drab industrial port town of little interest to tourists, **ILIGAN** is served by regular ferries from Manila and many other cities, making it a convenient gateway to Mindanao if you're intending to head to Marawi and Lake Lanao. It's primarily a manufacturing city, with vast plants on the outskirts producing steel, caustic soda, tyres and bricks. On September 20 every year there's a **Sinulog festival**, but that's about it in terms of attractions. Around the city are a number of **waterfalls**, the most famous being the Maria Cristina Falls, 9km to the north, the main source of power for the surrounding districts and nearby provinces: 100m high, they plunge into the torrential Agus River. You can reach the falls by taking a jeepney from the pier marked for Agus Bridge; from here, walking the rest of the way takes about half an hour. About 30km north of Iligan is the coastal barangay of Initao, with a wide, white sand **beach** where rickety cottages are available for rent. To get there, take a jeepney from Iligan pier marked for Initao.

Ferries dock on the western edge of the city, from where you can take a jeepney or tricycle into town. **Buses** also arrive here – in Roxas Avenue close to the town centre – from Dapitan and Dipolog to the west, Cagayan de Oro to the east and Marawi to the south. The closest airport is Cagayan de Oro. The **tourist office** is next to City Hall, on the main drag, Quezon Avenue. *Elena's Tower Inn* (℡063/221 5995; ❸), also on Quezon Avenue, provides the best accommodation, with good-value air-conditioned twins and doubles, all with bathroom and cable TV.

Marawi and Lake Lanao

MARAWI, on the shores of Lake Lanao, 25km south of Iligan, was renamed the Islamic City of Marawi on April 15, 1980. The city is the centre of the Islamic religion in the Philippines: 92 percent of the population is Muslim. During the Marcos years, the area around Marawi was where kidnappers were said to hide their victims, but these days the city is generally peaceful, with incidents related to the fight for Muslim autonomy exceedingly rare. Marawi's greatest natural attraction is placid **Lake Lanao**, which sits in a green bowl circled by distant mountains. It's the second largest lake in the Philippines and easy to explore now that authorities have finally completed a circumferential road; you can set out from Marawi early (sunrise over the lake is unforgettable), travel around the shore and return to town in the early evening. The best way to do this is to hire a jeepney or van and driver for the day.

The city's annual festival is the **Kalilang** (April 10–15), which is dominated by Koran-reading competitions and traditional singing and dancing. Marawi is also a terrific place to **shop**. The Palitan (barter centre) is a two-storey building in the heart of the city where you can find virtually any type of clothing, from jeans to traditional tribal garments. Colourful raw cloth and batik products are sold in seemingly endless rows of shops, while other stores stock gold jewellery, exquisite wooden chests and **brassware**, made from raw materials from the province's own mines and manufactured in the nearby barangay of Tugaya – items include serving trays, chests and ceremonial *bolos* (swords). Prices are low (about P800 for a large brass jar) but still don't hesitate to haggle; the shopkeepers are friendly and accommodating. Near the Palitan is the **market** where you can buy local delicacies such as *dudul*, a snack made from coconut milk, ground rice, sugar and durian. There's also *amik*, a native cake made with ground rice, brown sugar and fermented cassava starch.

Marawi has no **tourist office**, but the staff at the *Marawi Resort Hotel* (℡063/520 981; ❸), on the Mindanao State University campus, have good local knowledge. It's also the best place to stay in the area, a quiet establishment surrounded by greenery with a good choice of well-maintained rooms. Also on the campus is the **Aga Kahn Museum**, which has an interesting collection of indigenous art from Mindanao, Sulu and Palawan.

Ozamis and Mount Malindang National Park

The sprawling and somewhat tumbledown port city of **OZAMIS**, sometimes spelled Ozamiz, isn't a major tourist spot, but it's a friendly and laidback place with an old Spanish fortress that's worth a visit. The **fortress**, or cotta (daily 8am–6pm; P12), stands on the seafront and was built in 1765 to guard against Moro pirate raids. It was badly damaged by an earthquake in 1951, but from its crumbling walls there are panoramic views across Panguil Bay. Close to the fortress facing the city plaza is the Immaculate Conception Cathedral, which contains the second biggest pipe organ in the country. The organ was specially built in Germany in the 1960s with the tropical climate in mind; the connections are plated with silver so they won't rot.

Ozamis boasts some adequate budget **accommodation**. *Sky Lodge* (❷) on the main street, Rizal Avenue, is a homely, spick-and-span option with pleasant fan rooms, all with clean showers and toilet. A little west of the city on the Bandero Highway and easy to reach by tricycle, is a gem of a place, *Naomi's Botanical Garden and Tourist Inn* (❷), where pretty fan rooms look out onto a beautiful garden.

Ozamis is also the best place to base yourself for visits to the little-known and little-explored **Mount Malindang National Park**, a densely forested region that offers some tough trekking and the opportunity to see rare species such as the tarsier and flying lemur. You can reach Ozamis by ferry or by regular buses running along the northern coast of Mindanao from Iligan to the east and Dapitan to the west.

There are actually four main peaks in Mount Malindang National Park: North Peak, South Peak, Mount Ampiro and Mount Malindang itself, which is the tallest at 2404m. The area was extensively logged before being declared a national park in 1971, so most of the forest growth today is relatively new.

You need a permit to enter the park, which costs P200 and is available from the protected area office (Mon–Fri 8am–4pm; ☎088/531 2184) in the Provincial Capitol Building in Ozamis. A guide is essential and can be arranged here for P800 a day. From Ozamis you can reach the **park entrance** by taking a jeepney to the barangay of Tangub and from there walking another few kilometres to the tiny sitio of Hoyahoy. There is a good trail from Hoyahoy that leads across steep grasslands to the edge of a huge gorge, at the foot of which is the Labu River, and then upwards along the edge of the gorge and into dense forest. The path peters out and there are no trails to the summits, so you'll have to turn back and return the way you came; this is a tough trek and will take a fit person at least six hours there and back. Even without access to the summits, this is prime trekking country, with frequent sightings of rare birds such as the bleeding heart pigeon and mammals such as the long-tailed macaque. There's a long-established tribal group living in the park, the Subanon, who you may well encounter along some of their logging trails. They consider Mount Malindang their tribal homeland and source of strength.

Dapitan

The scenic and peaceful north coast city of **DAPITAN**, with its red-roofed houses and sweeping ocean bay, has appeal for anyone interested in recent Philippine history, as well as being a good base for exploring the coast of Misamis Occidental, a little-explored province with some remote beaches and friendly fishing villages. The beaches aren't white and endless, but the whole coastline from Ozamis to Dipolog is unspoiled and untouristy and a good area to explore at your leisure.

The main drag in Dapitan is Sunset Boulevard, a romantic seafront promenade where you'll find banks, shops and a number of hotels. Most of the limited tourist attractions are Rizal-related (see box p.404). The **Rizal Shrine** (Tues–

José Rizal in Dapitan

Dapitan's historical significance stems from its status as place of exile for **José Rizal**. The decision to send the irksome revolutionary to Dapitan was taken so he could contemplate his sins against Spain and, according to a letter from the authorities to the friar in Dapitan, "publicly retract his errors concerning religion, and make statements that were clearly pro-Spanish and against revolution." The letter also called on Rizal henceforth to conduct himself in an exemplary manner as a Spanish subject and a man of religion.

He arrived in 1892 and only left shortly before his death in 1896. It was a four-year interregnum that was at first tediously unexciting and later abundantly fruitful. Rizal was initially bored and listless, but soon shed his ennui. He practised medicine, pursued scientific studies, continued his artistic and literary works, widened his knowledge of languages, established a school for boys, promoted community development projects, invented a wooden machine for making bricks and engaged in farming and commerce. Despite his multifarious activities, he maintained an extensive correspondence with his family, relatives, fellow reformists and eminent scientists and scholars in Europe. It was also in Dapitan that he first set eyes on Josephine Bracken, the smouldering Irish beauty who became pregnant by him and bore a stillborn son, buried somewhere in Dapitan in a grave that has never been found. Two hours before Rizal was executed he and Bracken were said to have married in a private ceremony in his cell. After his death Bracken married again in Hong Kong, but died on March 15, 1902, at the age of 26, a victim of tuberculosis. She was buried in the Happy Valley Cemetery in Hong Kong, but her grave, like that of her son, has never been located.

Sun 9am–4pm; P20) on the northern edge of the city in an area known as Talisay is a pleasant parkland area encompassing the grounds where Rizal spent his exile. The park contains faithful reproductions of the simple cottage he lived in, the octagonal schoolroom where he taught, his chicken house and two clinics. The **Rizal Museum** (Tues–Sun 10am–4pm; P10) is also here, and contains memorabilia such as books, notebooks and medical equipment. To get here either take a tricycle from the city centre or walk – it's only ten minutes away on foot across Bagting Bridge with Dapitan Bay on your left. The national hero was nothing if not versatile. He also designed – from memory – a huge grass relief map of Mindanao that still exists today in F. Saguin Street, close to St James's Church where he regularly used to worship.

Practicalities

Dipolog **airport** is only 12km away, with regular buses and mini vans making the journey to Dapitan. WG&A and Supercat **ferries** both arrive at Palauan wharf, half-way between Dapitan and Dipolog (see p.227). Getting into Dapitan from the wharf is no problem: jeepneys cost P10 and minibuses P15. **Buses** arrive at a terminal on the National Highway in the south of the city; there are also regular minibuses back and forth to Dipolog, which terminate in Dapitan at the northern end of Sunset Boulevard, very close to the centre. There's no tourist information office in Dapitan and no major banks.

Accommodation and eating

Top choice in Dapitan for **accommodation** is the *Dapitan City Resort Hotel* (☏065/213 6413; ❸) on Sunset Boulevard. Rooms are plain but comfortable and have air-conditioning, hot showers, TVs and fridges. There's a swimming pool at the front where you can relax with a drink and take in the terrific views across Dapitan Bay. One of the few remaining budget options is the rundown *Aplaya Vida Pension* (❶), also on Sunset Boulevard, where tatty rooms are cheaper than the *Dapitan City Resort Hotel*, but nowhere near as nice.

The *Dapitan City Resort Hotel* has a **restaurant** where the speciality is very reasonably priced seafood. Fast-food restaurants line Sunset Boulevard, and in the city plaza you'll find the venerable old bistro *Corazan de Dapitan*, where corned beef served on hot bread costs P50. *Lab Kamayan* in Bonifacio Street boasts an excellent seafood lunch and dinner buffet (P190) that includes fresh shrimp, king prawns, crab, sweet oysters and grilled fish.

Dipolog

The busy city of **DIPOLOG**, capital of Zamboanga del Norte, lies on the south bank of the Dipolog River on the northwestern coast of Mindanao. Noted for the many rare orchids that grow in the surrounding countryside, Dipolog has few tourist attractions itself, but from here you can explore the undeveloped coast which stretches to Ozamis. During his exile in nearby Dapitan, José Rizal designed the altar in the city's **Holy Rosary Cathedral**, which was built in 1896 and restored during the 1970s. Dipolog has a Cebu-style **Sinulog festival** every year during the last week of January. For picturesque views over both Dipolog and Dapitan, climb the 3003 steps to the top of Linabo Peak in the barangay of Lugdungan, a fifteen-minute tricycle ride east of the city.

Philippine Airlines flies from Manila to Dipolog daily except Saturday. The PAL ticket office (☎065/212 2360) is at the airport, a short tricycle or jeepney ride north of the city centre on the other side of the Dipolog River. Supercat and WG&A both serve Palauan wharf, half-way between Dipolog and Dapitan. The WG&A ticket office (☎065/212 5574) is on Echavez Street at its junction with Quezon Avenue, and the Supercat office sits right next door. Lillian Express and Super 5 Express **buses** arrive at the central market on Quezon Avenue. There's a small **tourist office** (☎065/212 2597) in the Capitol Building in Capitol Avenue on the southeastern edge of the city and another in City Hall (☎065/212 2485), close to the police station at the eastern end of Rizal Avenue. **Banks** and **shops** are either on Quezon Avenue, running north to south, or General Luna Street, which intersects Quezon Avenue from east to west. A small **post office** can be found close to the creek ten minutes' walk south of the city, and there are plenty of Internet cafés, mostly in the area around the *Top Plaza Hotel*.

A number of unexceptional but affordable small **hotels** are located in a relatively small area of the city centre around the central market. The best is *Top Plaza Hotel* (☎065/212 577; ❹) in Quezon Avenue, a reasonably new place with 61 air-conditioned rooms that all have a private bathroom with hot water. A short walk south on the opposite side of the road is the *Arocha Hotel* (☎065/212 2556; ❸), which has small, plain air-conditioned doubles with showers and a coffee shop in the lobby where you can grab noodles and soft drinks, but not much else. There are only a couple of notable **restaurants** in Dipolog. The *Golden Pot* on General Luna Street is a popular Chinese place with functional decor and an extensive menu of soups, rice dishes and fried chicken. *Mickies* in Rizal Avenue is a fast-food burger joint where you can eat for less than 100 pesos.

Zamboanga City

ZAMBOANGA CITY, on the southernmost tip of the Zamboanga peninsula 700km south of Manila, is closer to both Malaysia and Indonesia than it is to the capital of the Philippines, a fact that has contributed to its cosmopolitan makeup. More than seventy percent of the population is Catholic, the rest Muslim, further divided into tribal groups.

This has given Zamboanga City a different atmosphere to the rest of the Philippines: it feels like another country, where different dialects are spoken and Manila is off the radar. Zamboanga's status as a major port, strategically positioned close to the Sulu archipelago, has added to its diverse nature, pulling in immigrants from nearby troublespots such as Basilan. There's no doubt Zamboanga has a reputation as a no-go area for tourists, but locals claim this is only because it has been unfairly tarred by its proximity to the Sulu archipelago, stronghold of Abu Sayyaf. Business has not been helped by the fact that foreign tourists and Christian missionaries have been among the victims of violence. These days, though, Zamboanga is enjoying a modest peace dividend, thanks to an American-supported military campaign against Abu Sayyaf that has seen incidents decrease dramatically. In 2005, the Zamboanga peninsula was the fastest growing region in the Philippines, and in February 2007, a European cruise ship carrying elderly German tourists docked in Zamboanga, the first such vessel to visit since 1998. In the city itself, three new shopping malls are being built. Visitor numbers are unlikely to increase dramatically in the near future, but there are signs Zamboanga could be on the rise. Some people do make it this far, usually on their way to the Sulu archipelago (see p.410).

Arrival and information

Philippine Airlines, Air Philippines and Cebu Pacific all have daily flights from Manila to Zamboanga; Seair flies here from Cotabato, Jolo and Tawi-Tawi. From the **airport** on the northern outskirts of the city it takes about twenty minutes to get to the city centre by taxi; you can take a tricycle for P20 or a jeepney marked for "Canelar". The **ferry** wharf is at the southern end of Lorenzo Street and easy to reach by taxi, jeepney and tricycle. **Buses** arrive at one of two terminals – they're right next to each other – at the northern end of Veterans' Avenue.

The best **tourist office** (Mon–Fri 9am–4pm; ☎062/991 0218) is the DoT's regional office in the *Lantaka Hotel by the Sea*, on the waterfront in Valderosa Street. There's also a city tourism office in Valderosa Street about 200m east of city hall. There's a **travel agent** in the *Lantaka*, Zambo Tours and Travel, where you can book flights and ferries. Another good place for tickets is the Galleria mall on Lorenzo Street, opposite the Plaza Cinema. All ferry companies also have offices right on the city wharf and there's a centralized ferry ticketing office here, but it can be pandemonium. The main city-centre road is Governor Lim Avenue, running from east to west. There are a number of **banks** here, including Landbank, Solid Bank and Bank of Commerce; they all have ATMs and will change US dollars. Mobile phones work in Zamboanga, but there are also a great many public calling offices, including a PLDT office in Jaldon Street, north of Governor Lim Avenue. Good places to look for **Internet** cafés are Alvarez Street near Chong Hua High School and Midreno Citimall a block north of Governor Lim Avenue.

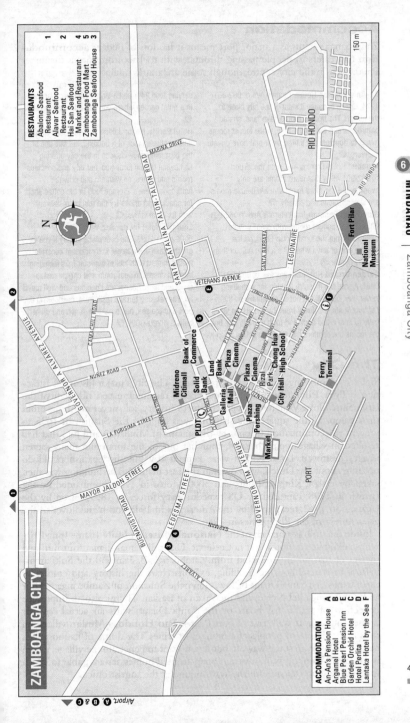

ZAMBOANGA CITY

RESTAURANTS
Abalone Seafood Restaurant	1
Alavar Seafood Restaurant	2
Hai San Seafood Market and Restaurant	4
Zamboanga Food Mart	5
Zamboanga Seafood House	3

0   150 m

N

Airport, A, B & C

MAYOR JALDON STREET

GOVERNOR ALVAREZ AVENUE

BUENAVISTA ROAD

LEDESMA STREET

GOVERNOR A ALVAREZ AVENUE

CAMA CHILI ROAD

SANTA CATALINA TALON-TALON ROAD

MARINA DRIVE

NUÑEZ ROAD

LA PURISIMA STREET

CAMINS STREET

PLDT

Midreno Citimall

Solid Bank

Bank of Commerce

Land Bank

Galleria Mall

Plaza Bank

Plaza Cinema

Plaza Cinema

Plaza Pershing

CORCUERA STREET

Market

GOVERNOR LIM AVENUE

GARMAN

PORT

VETERANS AVENUE

PILAR STREET

MAGALLANES STREET

SEVILLA STREET

TOMAS CLAUDIO STREET

Rizal Park

Chong Hua

City Hall · High School

CORCUERA STREET

VALDEROZA STREET

RIZAL STREET

LEGIONAIRE

SANTA BARBARA

Ferry Terminal

Fort Pilar

National Museum

RIO HONDO

RIO HONDO

ACCOMMODATION
An-An's Pension House	A
Argamel Hotel	B
Blue Pearl Pension Inn	E
Garden Orchid Hotel	C
Hotel Perlita	D
Lantaka Hotel by the Sea	F

Accommodation

Zamboanga's status as a major port means it has lots of budget **accommodation** that caters to people passing through, with rock-bottom rooms for under P500, even in the city centre, though some are a little insalubrious.

An-An's Pension House Camins Ave ☎062/881 4974. Cheap because it's out of the city close to the airport. The budget rooms have fans, shared bathrooms and are a little tatty, while tourist rooms (twins or doubles) are a little airier and have private showers. ❶

Argamel Hotel Camins Ave, near the airport ☎062/991 4974. Standard rooms are only average, but the more expensive a/c deluxe rooms are very spacious and orderly. ❸

Blue Pearl Pension Inn Veterans Ave ☎062/991 2931. Faded budget rooms with small private bathrooms, but the location isn't bad, on the eastern end of town where it's a little quieter than the city centre. ❷

Garden Orchid Hotel Camins Ave ☎062/991 0031. A safe bet if you're looking for something better than budget, but not as expensive as the *Lantaka*. A stone's throw from the airport, so you'll have to take a taxi back and forth into the city, but the rooms are comfortable, there's a coffee shop

serving food 24hr and a large swimming pool set in a quiet garden where you can relax with a drink. ❻

Hotel Perlita Mayor Jaldon St ☎062/993 0990. A dour concrete block of a building, but still one of the best mid-range choices in the city offering somewhat tackily furnished, but tidy and spacious rooms and suites, all with a/c and private bathroom. There's average food in the coffee shop; for snacks and drinks try the rooftop restaurant with its great views. ❹

Lantaka Hotel by the Sea Valderosa St ☎062/991 2033. The best place to stay if you've got the cash. It's a large, fairly modern concrete establishment with lots of five-star frills including Internet access in your room and chi-chi restaurants and bars. Rooms are spacious and well cared for. The relaxing terrace restaurant, overlooking the pool and the sea, has breakfast, lunch and dinner buffets (P220–300). ❾

The City

Sights in Zamboanga are few and far between. The city's major historical attraction is **Fort Pilar** (daily 10am–7pm; P12), a ten-minute taxi ride east of the city centre along Valderosa Street. The fort's history was never anything other than colourful: the squat stone structure was built by the Spanish in 1635 to prevent the continuation of raids by the sultans of Mindanao and Jolo that had resulted in villages being burned, churches put to the torch and many sacred images destroyed. Local raiders were kept at bay, but the Spanish could do nothing about the Dutch, who overran the fort in 1646. The building was then taken by Dalasi, King of Bulig, and 3000 Moros in 1720, bombarded by the British in 1798, captured by US expeditionary forces in 1899, seized by the Japanese in 1942, recaptured by the Americans in 1945 and turned over to the government of the Philippines in 1946.

Inside the walls is a branch of the **National Museum** (daily 10am–4pm; P10), whose exhibits are nothing if not eclectic. Giant dioramas depict four hundred species of marine life collected from Zamboanga, Basilan and the Sulu archipelago. In a neighbouring building, exhibits chart the history and culture of three tribes: the Sama Dilaut of Tawi-Tawi; the Subanon of Zamboanga del Sur and Zamboanga del Norte; and the Yakan of Basilan. There's also an impressive collection of traditional boats of the Sama Dilaut, with an actual *lepa*, or houseboat. A short walk east of Fort Pilar is **Rio Hondo**, a Muslim village on stilts that is home to people of a number of tribes. The dome of its mosque is clearly visible from some way off, but if you want to penetrate the village, which is a maze of bamboo walkways and open-fronted homes, it's advisable to take a local guide who can smooth the way: inquire at the tourist office.

△ Minaret in front of a mosque, near Zamboanga City

Eating and drinking

You can't go wrong ordering **seafood** in Zamboanga. It's always fresh, and P200 will buy you a good meal that could include crab, lobster, lapu-lapu and king prawns. The most popular place among locals is the *Zamboanga Food Mart* at the eastern end of Governor Lim Avenue, where buckets of the day's catch are laid out on ice. It can be grilled with a dash of pepper and lime, or fried in coconut milk with spices. The *Alavar Seafood Restaurant*, ten minutes to the northeast of the city by taxi, is another hot favourite, packed every evening with families sharing huge plates of steamed fish, fried rice and chilli crab. The *Abalone*

Seafood Restaurant is within walking distance of the city centre, a little north on Jaldon Street, while on Ledesma Street towards the airport there are two excellent places close to each other: *Zamboanga Seafood House* and *Hai San Seafood Market and Restaurant*.

The Sulu archipelago

The volcanic **Sulu archipelago** is comprised of about 870 islands off southwest Mindanao between the Sulawesi and Sulu seas, covering an area of 2700 square kilometres from Basilan in the north to Borneo in the south, and home to a surprisingly large population of around twelve million. Access to the Sulu archipelago is either by **ferry** from Zamboanga or on a Seair **flight** to Jolo and Tawi-Tawi.

The tourism potential of these islands is vast. Unfortunately, because of the high-profile activities of a number of groups agitating for Muslim autonomy, among them the notorious Abu Sayyaf, most foreign embassies advise outright against travel here. The situation on the ground is less clear-cut, with contradictory recommendations from travellers who have visited the area. Most of the local people are more than generous, offering accommodation, food and advice about where to go and what to see. Every Filipino you talk to, however, is almost mortified by the thought of a foreigner visiting these islands. Actual incidents are rare, but those that do occur often end in tragedy, and though the Abu Sayyaf is not the force it was a few years ago, it is still active and capable of targeting tourists. Kidnapping is still a lucrative business on the island of Basilan, the northernmost island in the chain, and if any unequivocal recommendation can be given it is that you shouldn't go there.

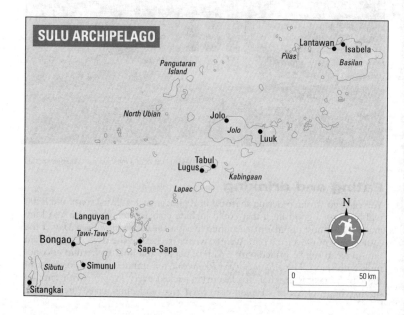

Jolo

Jolo ("ho-*low*"), the largest island in the group, is a risky travel proposition – it's a sometimes lawless outpost where the Philippine military is still conducting operations against fundamentalist Islamic rebels and gangs of terrorists who have made kidnapping something of a cottage industry. It was on Jolo that 21 hostages kidnapped from a Malaysian resort in 2001 were kept captive.

The island's eponymous capital is on the northwest coast and has a population of about 55,000, most of them fisherfolk, farmers and traders. An ancient walled city, **JOLO** was once a pirate base and served as the residence of a sultan until the sultanate was abolished in 1940. The city was almost completely destroyed in 1974 when fighting erupted between government forces and Muslim insurgents who were seeking to establish a secessionist state. Not much remains of the walls today, although you can see four ancient gates which were once used as watchtowers, and a number of graves of Spanish soldiers who died here in the campaign to pacify the Moros. The town boasts a busy **market** where goods are brought – sometimes smuggled – from Malaysia and Indonesia.

There are numerous **ferries** from Zamboanga City to Jolo, arriving at Jolo's main wharf, a short tricycle ride from the town centre. Seair also has daily **flights** from Zamboanga to Jolo. The Seair ticket agent in Jolo can be reached on ☏0916/504 8465.

Tawi-Tawi and around

At the southern end of the peninsula lies the island of **Tawi-Tawi**, whose busy little capital **BONGAO** is a commercial fishing centre, which is slightly smaller than Jolo, but has a cinema, a lively market, banks and a provincial capital building shaped like a mosque. From the **airport** just outside Bongao there are jeepneys into town for P10. There are several pension houses in Bongao, one of the better ones being the *Beachside Inn* (☏068/268 1446; ❷), which has singles, doubles and even a few suites. Their restaurant serves good food – a large bowl of sour fish soup made with fresh lapu-lapu costs P50.

Bongao Peak is a ten-minute walk inland from the town and a fairly easy climb. The peak holds mystical powers for the locals, and villagers take sick people to the top to offer prayers. The colourful plastic ribbons tied to trees each represents a wish and a prayer. Don't forget to buy some bananas at the market

---

Summoning the spirits

The southwestern end of the Sulu archipelago is home to the **Sama Dilaut**, people who generally live in boathouses and depend for their livelihood mainly on the sea, rarely owning or cultivating land. The life of the Sama Dilaut is shaped by his fear of supernatural beings. **Spirit mediums** (*jin*) commune with spirits through dreams and trances. Several times a year, *jin* perform a nightlong public dance, during which participants seek to renew ties with a dead loved one while in a trance. The *jin's* dancing is frenetic and accompanied by rhythmic chanting from various aides; it's the combination of sound and movement that is said to put devotees into the trance, allowing them to speak with the dead. These public dances are held anywhere — in village squares or on basketball courts and there's no problem with tourists turning up to watch. The atmosphere is carnival-like and you'll be welcomed with open arms. The Sama carve grave markers into birds believing that the spirit will be transported into another world, and visit cemeteries to ask for favours from the spirit of the deceased. The markers are vaguely phallic: those for men are tubular and for women flat and triangular with floral patterns.

to take on your hike up the mountain – macaques guard the trail and bananas are your currency with them. From the top, 300m above sea level, you can see Bongao and the surrounding islands. It's also fun to poke around the **market** near the pier, known as the Chinese market, where you can buy herbs, baskets, traditional hats, prayer mats, scarves and batik clothes. Local delicacies on sale here include turtles' eggs and *tarrang bulan*, pancakes sprinkled with peanuts.

From Bongao it's an uncomfortable trip on the dilapidated daily ferry to the island of **Simunul**, but worth it for a vivid glimpse of life on the very margins of the country, both socially and geographically. Simunul lies just 30km from the coast of Sabah and is an impoverished but friendly island, where the inhabitants depend on fishing and trading with Sabah. It has no running water, so locals collect rainwater for drinking. The island is the site of the Sheikh Karimul Makhdum mosque, the first in the Philippines, built in 1380 by Arab missionaries. Sadly, not much of it remains – there's a relatively new mosque on the site now with only four pillars left from the original. Simunul has no hotels, but the tourism office in Bongao (T 0919/775 7287) can arrange homestays. Electricity on the island is from 6pm to midnight and because of the lack of water make sure you take your own, along with enough food.

Travel details

Buses

Balingoan to: Cagayan de Oro (hourly; 1hr).
Bunawan to: Butuan (several daily; 3hr); Davao (several daily; 4hr).
Butuan to: Bunawan (several daily; 3hr); Cagayan de Oro (hourly; 4hr); Davao (daily; 5–6 hr); Surigao (hourly; 2hr).
Cagayan de Oro to: Balingoan (hourly; 1hr); Butuan (hourly; 4hr); Dapitan (2 daily; 6–7hr); Davao (daily; 7hr); Iligan (hourly; 2hr 30min); Malaybalay (3 daily; 4hr); Surigao (2 daily; 6hr).
Cotabato to: Davao (daily; 9hr); General Santos (several daily; 5hr); Kidapawan (several daily; 4hr); Koronodal (several daily; 4hr); Marawi (several daily; 4hr).
Dapitan to: Cagayan de Oro (2 daily; 6–7hr); Dipolog (hourly; 45min); Ozamis (hourly; 2hr).
Davao to: Bunawan (several daily; 4hr); Butuan (daily; 5–6hr); Cagayan de Oro (daily; 7hr); Cotabato (daily; 9hr); General Santos (hourly; 5hr); Kidapawan (hourly; 2hr); Koronodal (hourly; 5hr); Manila (daily; 24hr); Surigao (daily; 8hr).
Dipolog to: Dapitan (hourly; 45min); Ozamis (hourly; 2hr 30min); Zamboanga (2 daily; 7hr).
General Santos to: Cotabato (several daily; 5hr); Davao (hourly; 6hr); Koronodal (hourly; 3hr).
Iligan to: Cagayan de Oro (hourly; 2hr 30min); Dapitan (several daily; 4hr); Dipolog (several daily; 4hr 30min); Marawi (hourly; 2hr); Ozamis (hourly; 2hr); Zamboanga (daily; 7–8hr).

Kidapawan to: Cotabato (several daily; 4hr); Davao (hourly; 2hr).
Koronodal to: Cotobato (several daily; 4hr); Davao (hourly; 5hr); General Santos (hourly; 3hr).
Malaybalay to: Cagayan de Oro (3 daily; 4hr).
Marawi to: Cotabato (several daily; 4hr); Iligan (hourly; 2hr).
Ozamis to: Dapitan (hourly; 2hr); Dipolog (hourly; 2hr 30min); Iligan (hourly; 2hr); Zamboanga (daily; 6hr).
Surigao to: Butuan (hourly; 2hr); Cagayan de Oro (2 daily; 6hr); Davao (daily; 8hr).
Zamboanga to: Dipolog (2 daily; 7hr); Iligan (daily; 7–8hr); Ozamis (daily; 6hr).

Jeepneys and minivans

Balingoan to: Cagayan de Oro (hourly; 1hr).
Benoni to: Mambajao (hourly; 45min).
Cagayan de Oro to: Balingoan (hourly; 1hr).
Dapitan to: Dipolog (every 30min; 1hr).
Dipolog to: Dapitan (every 30min; 1hr).
Koronodal to: T'boli (several daily; 2hr).
Mambajao to: Benoni (hourly; 1hr).
T'boli to: Koronodal (several daily; 2hr).

Ferries

Balingoan to: Benoni (Camiguin; hourly; 1hr 30min).
Benoni to: Balingoan (hourly; 1hr 30min).
Bongao to: Zamboanga (daily; 18hr).
Butuan to: Manila (daily; 42 hr).

Cagayan de Oro to: Manila (daily; 35hr); Iloilo (weekly; 14hr).

Cotabato to: Iloilo (weekly; 16hr).

Davao to: Cebu City (twice weekly; 22hr); General Santos (2 weekly; 7hr); Iloilo (weekly; 18hr); Manila (1–2 daily; 52hr).

Dipolog to: Manila (3 weekly; 36hr).

General Santos to: Davao (2 weekly; 7hr); Manila (daily; 40hr).

Iligan to: Manila (3 weekly; 34hr).

Jolo to: Zamboanga (daily; 12hr).

Ozamis to: Cebu City (3 weekly; 19hr); Manila (daily; 36hr).

Surigao to: Manila (2 weekly; 36hr).

Zamboanga to: Bongao (daily; 18hr); Manila (daily; 27hr); Jolo (daily; 12hr); Sandakan (daily; 18hr).

Plane

Butuan to: Manila (2 daily; 1hr 30min).

Cagayan de Oro to: Cebu (4 weekly; 1hr); Davao (2 weekly; 50min); Manila (8 daily; 1hr 30min).

Camiguin to: Cebu City (2 weekly; 35min).

Cebu City to: Camiguin (2 weekly; 35min); Cotabato (2 weekly; 2hr 15min); Davao (2 daily; 1hr); General Santos (2 daily; 1hr 5min); Zamboanga (3 weekly; 1hr).

Cotabato to: Cebu City (2 weekly; 2hr 15min); Manila (2 daily; 1hr 35min); Zamboanga (3 weekly; 35min).

Davao to: Cagayan de Oro (2 weekly; 50min); Cebu City (2 daily; 1hr); Manila (8 daily; 1hr 45min); Manado (twice weekly; 1hr); Singapore (weekly; 2hr 15min).

Dipolog to: Manila (daily; 1hr 30min).

General Santos to: Cebu City (2 daily; 1hr 5min); Manila (2 daily; 1hr 45min).

Jolo to: Zamboanga (6 weekly; 35min).

Surigao to: Manila (3 weekly; 1hr 50min).

Tawi-Tawi to: Zamboanga (5 weekly; 45min).

Zamboanga to: Cebu City (3 weekly; 1hr); Cotobato (3 weekly; 50min); Jolo (7 weekly; 35min); Manila (4 daily; 1hr 30min); Tawi-Tawi (5 weekly; 45min).

Northern Luzon

CHAPTER 7

Highlights

* **Mount Pinatubo** Trek through valleys of solid lava to the beautiful crater lake at the summit of this active volcano, which erupted catastrophically in 1991. See p.424

* **One Hundred Islands** Find your own private tropical paradise for the day and snorkel on some of the richest reefs in the archipelago. See p.432

* **Surfing in La Union** The sweeping beach at San Juan has big breakers, magical sunsets and some cosy, affordable resorts right on the sand. See p.440

* **Vigan** Atmospheric old Spanish outpost with cobbled streets, horse-drawn carriages and, if you're there at the right time, lively festivals. See p.441

* **Marcos country** In the quaint old villages around Laoag you can see Marcos's birthplace, his palace and his corpse, which lies in an air-conditioned mausoleum in Batac. See p.449

* **Batanes** Enchanting group of little-visited rural islands off the northern tip of Luzon, offering unforgettable scenery and terrific trekking. See p.453

* **Climbing Mount Pulag** Climb the highest peak in Luzon and relax afterwards in the nearby mountain village of Kabayan, home of the mummies. See p.478

* **Sagada** Celebrated mountain Shangri-La with hanging coffins, cave exploration, exceptional trekking and very cheap lodgings. See p.480

* **Trekking around Banaue** Wonderful walks through tribal villages and rice terrace scenery – don't miss the trek to nearby Batad. See p.489

△ Mountain road near Kabayan

7

Northern Luzon

T he island of **Luzon** north of Manila doesn't have the idyllic beaches and lagoons of the Visayas or Palawan, but it does offer immense variety: you can travel in a day from the volcanic landscape around Mount Pinatubo to the numinous tribal villages of the Cordillera mountains. The east coast north of Baler is one of the country's great unexplored wildernesses, while the west coast from the Lingayen Gulf north to the tip of mainland Luzon is taking off as an adventure destination, with terrific surfing and some challenging trekking.

The first significant tourist destination north of Manila is **Clark**, which despite its seedy nightlife makes a good base for adventure sports, including climbing **Mount Arayat** and the active volcano **Mount Pinatubo**, just across the border in Zambales province. A couple of hours southwest of Clark by road sits another former US base, **Subic Bay**, where you can scuba dive on wrecks and explore some of the country's most dense and vibrant rainforest.

In the northwest, the province of La Union offers some reasonable beaches and resorts, with opportunities for surfing, trekking and climbing. Heading north from La Union, the next province you reach is Ilocos Sur, known for the old Spanish city of **Vigan**, the best-preserved city of its kind in the country, with narrow cobblestone streets, aristocratic ancestral homes and horse-drawn carriages. The intriguing capital of Ilocos Norte province, **Laoag**, features a number of sites related to former dictator Ferdinand Marcos, who was born here in the village of Sarrat. About two hours north of Laoag there are excellent beaches around **Pagudpud**, on the northwestern edge of Luzon.

Further north still, **Batanes** province is nothing more than a scattering of small islands, some of which are closer to Taiwan than the Philippines. But they offer some of the best adventure travel in Asia, with exceptional trekking and climbing, and the opportunity to witness a way of life that is quite unlike that found anywhere else in the country.

The northeast of Luzon is one of the archipelago's least explored wildernesses, with miles of beautiful coastline and enormous tracts of tropical rainforest. Those that head this way do so for the excellent surfing on the east coast at **Baler**. Further north is **Palanan**, jump-off point for the barely explored **Northern Sierra Madre Natural Park**.

The mountainous **Cordillera** area is still seen by many lowland Filipinos as a mysterious region populated by primitive tribes and their unfamiliar gods. **Baguio**, the traditional mountain retreat for Manileños during the fierce heat of Easter week, is about as far north as many southerners get. But it's not until you get beyond Baguio that the adventure really begins. Benguet, Ifugao and Mountain provinces are the tribal heartlands of the northern Philippines, settled

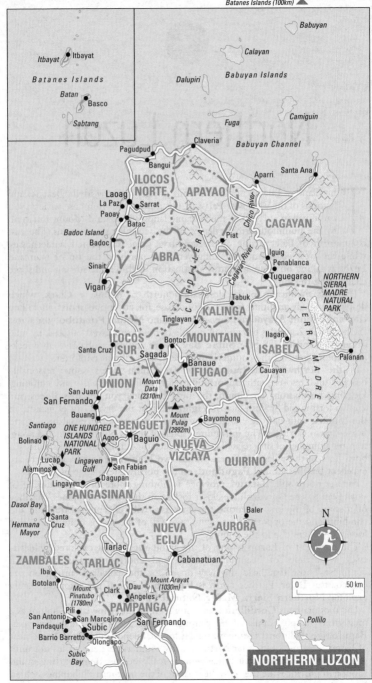

Batanes Islands (100km)

Itbayat
Itbayat

Batanes Islands

Batan
Basco

Sabtang

Babuyan

Calayan

Dalupiri   *Babuyan Islands*

Camiguin

Fuga

Pagudpud   Claveria   *Babuyan Channel*

Bangui

ILOCOS NORTE   **APAYAO**   Aparri   Santa Ana

Laoag
La Paz   Sarrat
Paoay
Batac

Badoc Island
Badoc

Sinait

Vigan

ABRA

Piat

Iguig
Penablanca
Tuguegarao

CAGAYAN

Chico River

Cagayan River

NORTHERN SIERRA MADRE NATURAL PARK

Tabuk

KALINGA

Tinglayan

ILOCOS SUR   Bontoc   **MOUNTAIN**

Santa Cruz   Sagada

LA UNION

Mount Data (2310m)

Banaue

IFUGAO

Kabayan

Ilagan

ISABELA

Cauayan

Palanan

S I E R R A   M A D R E

San Juan
San Fernando
Bauang

Santiago
Bolinao

ONE HUNDRED ISLANDS NATIONAL PARK

Agoo   Baguio

BENGUET

Mount Pulag (2992m)

Bayombong

NUEVA VIZCAYA

QUIRINO

Lucap
Alaminos
Lingayen

Lingayen Gulf   San Fabian
Dagupan

PANGASINAN

Dasol Bay

Hermana Mayor

Santa Cruz

Tarlac

NUEVA ECIJA

AURORA

Baler

N

ZAMBALES   **TARLAC**   Cabanatuan

Iba
Botolan

Mount Pinatubo (1780m)   Clark   Dau
Angeles

Mount Arayat (1030m)

0   50 km

San Antonio
Pandaquit
Barrio Barretto

Pili
San Marcelino
Subic
Olongapo

PAMPANGA

San Fernando

Pollilo

Subic Bay

NORTHERN LUZON

first by indigenous Negritos and then during the Spanish regime by hunter-gatherers from neighbouring areas who were on the move looking for food and water. The area's highlights include the mountain village of **Sagada** with its caves and hanging coffins, and the huge rice terraces at **Banaue** in Ifugao. The Ibaloi village of **Kabayan** in Benguet is where a group of mummies, possibly dating as far back as 2000 BC, were discovered in caves in the early twentieth century. This is an excellent area for walking and climbing, with trails looping through marvellous countryside and a number of challenging peaks including **Mount Pulag**, the highest mountain in Luzon.

The cheapest way to explore the north of the country is by **bus**. There are dozens of services from Manila heading north through Pampanga to Clark and on to La Union and the far north. Bus companies also serve the Cordillera, with regular services to the main hubs of Baguio and Banaue, where you can get onward buses and jeepneys further into the interior. There are also regular buses from Manila to the northeast, with major destinations including Baler and Tuguegarao. In the more remote areas of the north, especially in the mountains beyond Baguio and the Sierra Madre, roads are poor and bus or jeepney trips can be long and rough, with delays and breakdowns always a possibility. You'll have to have patience and a flexible schedule. If time is limited you can **fly** straight to a number of destinations. Airports in the north served from Manila are Clark, Baguio, Laoag, Tuguegarao and Basco in Batanes.

North of Manila

It's a short trip by road north of the capital to **Pampanga**, a largely lowland area known as the country's rice basket because of the paddy fields that cover much of the province. Pampanga's attractions include the gory **crucifixions** every Easter near the provincial capital of **San Fernando** and some terrific adventure activities around the former US air base at **Clark**, starting point for trekking and climbing on Mount Pinatubo. Southwest of Clark at **Subic Bay** is another former US naval base where there's excellent scuba diving on a number of wrecks. Subic is also the gateway to **Zambales** province, an untouristy and rugged area with a spine of jungled mountains on its eastern fringe and a coastal road that winds through gentle barrios with a number of rustic beach resorts. Further up the coast is the **One Hundred Islands National Park**, where you can spend days hopping from one deserted island to the next and snorkelling in limpid water. Immediately north of Pampanga sits the province of **Tarlac**, whose capital Tarlac City is a busy transport hub where buses stop on their way north–south and east–west, making it a good place to change services.

San Fernando

SAN FERNANDO, 50km north of Manila and the capital of Pampanga province, is best known for its controversial **crucifixion of flagellants**. Every year on Good Friday a dozen or so penitents – mostly men but the occasional woman and sometimes even the odd foreigner – are taken to a rice field in the barrio of San Pedro Cutud (often referred to simply as Cutud), 3km west of San Fernando on the main road, and nailed to a cross using two-inch stainless steel nails that have been soaked in alcohol to disinfect them. The penitents are taken down seconds later. Other penitents flagellate themselves using bamboo sticks tied to a rope or shards of glass buried in wooden sticks. The blood is real, but the motivation is questionable to some. The Catholic Church does not approve of the crucifixions and does not endorse them. The media have also turned against the rites, calling them pagan and barbaric, but always managing despite these reservations to allot copious front-page space to photographs of bloodied penitents.

Most **bus** terminals in Manila are closed on Good Friday, so if you want to get a good view of the crucifixions you'll have to travel to San Fernando the night before. Victory Liner buses leave every hour for San Fernando from Pasay (see "Moving on from Manila" box on p.130). Make sure you don't confuse San Fernando in Pampanga with San Fernando in La Union, much further north. From San Fernando there are regular jeepneys to Cutud. There are few good **places to stay** in San Fernando, the best option being *Hotel Grace Lane* (T045/860 1234; ❸), just off the MacArthur Highway, which has simple air-conditioned doubles. Most travellers opt to spend the night in nearby Clark (see below), where there's a much wider choice of rooms. San Fernando's main drag – actually the wide and busy road northwest to Subic Bay and Olongapo – is lined with **fast-food** joints.

Clark and around

Some 70km north of Manila, **CLARK**, formerly the site of an American air base, is popular with trekkers for its proximity to the volcanic mountains of **Pinatubo**, which is active, and **Arayat**, which is not. Clark is a centre for some thrilling adventure sports, including parachuting, microlight flying and off-road motorcycling (see box opposite). A short distance to the south is the undistinguished city of **Angeles**, a useful transport hub.

Clark is one of the Philippines' most notorious sun and sex destinations, with dozens of "girlie bars" catering to high-spending Western males. The name "Clark" is generally used to refer to the tourist area around the former base, particularly along **Fields Avenue** on the south side of the base where most of the bars are – an area also referred to as Balibago. Fields Avenue is a miserable sight, choked with jeepneys and tricycles, its pavements cracked and drains exposed. At night the darkness and the glare from the neon signs hide the rot, but during the day it's a depressing scene. Prostitution is rife in most of these bars, with GROs available to accompany visitors back to their hotel for the price of a few drinks. Newspapers in Manila have carried stories alleging several cases of HIV infection in the area.

In 1991, **Clark Air Base** became the subject of one of the hottest political debates ever to rage in the Philippines. Many Filipinos, enjoying an era of new nationalism in the wake of the downfall of the Marcos regime, saw no reason for the Philippines, however poor, to depend on the world's greatest superpower for its defence. Senators agreed and voted to end the US Air Force's lease on Clark Air Base. America's undignified departure from the Philippines was hastened somewhat by the catastrophic eruption of Mount Pinatubo (see

If you fancy some heart-stopping freefall, head for the long-established Tropical Asia Parachute Center (☎46/431 1419) at 940 Fields Ave, which runs **parachuting** courses for US$240. The centre's headquarters in the base are at the Omni Aviation Hangar about 500m inside Checkpoint gate.

Omni Aviation (☎045/892 6664, ⓦwww.omniaviationcorp.com) also offers 45-minute **flights** over Mount Pinatubo for $55 per person, giving you a stunning view of the crater. The best times for flights are sunrise and sunset. If you're interested, call a day or two in advance to make sure there's a plane available. At Angeles City Flying Club (☎0917/240 1290, ⓦwww.angelesflying.com), about 45 minutes east of Clark by road in Sitio Talimundok, Magalang, you can have a thirty-minute trial **microlight** flight for P1600. The instructor flies you over the lower slopes of Mount Arayat before corkscrewing along the course of the Pampanga River at a speed that seems particularly horrifying when you're sitting on a contraption that looks like it's been made from beach umbrellas and old bicycle parts. To get to the club from Clark you'll either have to hire a taxi or do it in stages by jeepney: first to San Fernando and then east to Magalang, where you can hop on a tricycle to the airfield.

If you prefer to keep your feet closer to the ground, for P500 a half-day you can rent a **motorcycle** from Trent Transport (see p.422), and ride through the fields of lahar, a mass of volcanic debris and water that has solidified into gargantuan cliffs and spires.

p.424), which showered the base in ash. The greatest concern over the withdrawal of 20,000 US Air Force personnel from the area was the potentially devastating effect it might have on the economy. A decision was taken to turn the base – which is roughly as big as Singapore – into a special economic zone with incentives for companies setting up shop there, although so far the results have been mixed. Plans to turn the airport into an international one for tourists have been on the drawing board for many years.

Practicalities

The nearest **bus station** is at **Dau** (pronounced "Da-oo"), served by hourly Victory Liner buses from Manila. From there you can take a tricycle (P50) for the short ride to Fields Avenue or Don Juico Avenue.

Seair **flies** from Manila to Clark twice a week (Wed & Fri) and has a shuttle bus at the airport to take passengers to a number of nearby hotels; if the bus doesn't go right to your hotel you can always do the final stretch in a tricycle or on foot. Seair's Clark office is in the *Tropicana Resort Hotel*, 151 Fields Ave (☎045/323 6713). Seair also has useful flights between Clark and Cebu City, Clark and Busuanga, and Clark and Caticlan (for Boracay).

Another option for getting from Manila to Clark is the Fly-the-Bus service operated by Swagman (☎02/523 8541 or 045/892 0257). The bus leaves the *Swagman Hotel* in A. Flores Street, Ermita, at 11.30am, 3.30pm and 8pm daily and serves a number of hotels in the Clark tourist district.

If you can spend a bit more, it's worth thinking about arranging a special pick-up at Manila airport. *Margarita Station* (☎45/322 0354, ⓦwww.margarita-station.com) – a restaurant, bar and tourist information centre rolled into one – can send a car and driver to meet you for P2100; a van costs P2500, which is good value if there are a few of you splitting the cost.

The Tourist Center is at G/F Al Aide Building, Fields Avenue (☎045/892 5107) near *Margarita Station* and has a branch of Filipino Travel Center inside where you can book flights and enquire about visas. The Tourist Center will change foreign currency, but travellers' cheques can be hard to exchange in Clark because of concerns they may be stolen. *Margarita Station*, for instance, exchanges only American Express travellers' cheques, but at a rate a few pesos lower per dollar than cash; you'll also need to give them a photocopy of your passport and the purchase receipt. Dozens of moneychangers line Fields Avenue and you'll find **banks** on the nearby MacArthur Highway, although the ATMs are unreliable, particularly at weekends when they often run out of cash. A number of **Internet cafés** are dotted around the Fields Avenue area, including one at the back of the *Europhil Hotel* and another at *Margarita Station* that's open 24 hours. Many hotels also have reliable broadband Internet connections for guests with their own laptop.

Amongst the growing number of **adventure-tour companies** in Clark is Trent Transport, 222 Fields Ave (℡045/332 1712); or head for Swagman Travel (℡045/322 2890), whose office is in the Clark City Terminal Building on Don Juico Avenue (near the bar area).

City transport

Three **jeepney stations** can be found in the tourist area, all close to each other near **Checkpoint**, the main gate to the former air base on Fields Avenue. From Checkpoint you can get a jeepney to Dau, Angeles or west along Fields Avenue to the various hotels. Jeepneys up and down Fields Avenue run from Checkpoint to Friendship (another gate) and cost P5, no matter where you get on and off, while tricycles on the same route charge a flat fare of P50 for foreigners.

If you want to go inside the base itself, take a white **taxi** from the car park just outside Checkpoint. The sign at the taxi stand says drivers must use their meter, but they'll almost always try to overcharge. A hotel taxi from the *Holiday Inn* back to the main gate costs P150. Try not to return from Dau to Manila on a Sunday evening, when buses are full of workers heading back to the city. An alternative on a Sunday is to take an **FX van**. A number of FX owners, also returning to the capital for the working week, gather passengers at Dau on a Sunday evening, charging them P90 each for the trip to Manila.

Accommodation

Most of the **hotels** in the area are spread out along Fields Avenue, which runs into Don Juico Avenue. If you want somewhere reasonably quiet, go for a hotel away from the bars. Many hotels in Clark offer discounts for cash or for longer stays, so it's worth comparing a few and doing a little negotiating before you decide.

America Hotel Don Juico Ave ℡045/332 1023. Big, fairly quiet, carpeted establishment with enormous rooms ranging from deluxe doubles to a suite with its own whirlpool bath, though the carpet and the decor is past its best. There's a large indoor pool and a restaurant, but the food is very average. **⑥**

La Casa Pension 511 Tamarind St, Clarkview Subdivision ℡045/322 7984. Clean, quiet rooms, each with bath or shower, in a family home. Food is served at the next-door *Blue Boar Inn*, which is owned by the same couple, a former US Air Force officer and his wife. To get there take a jeepney (P5) to the far end of Don Juico Ave. **❸**

Central Park Hotel 261 Real St ℡045/892 0256, ⓦwww.centralpark-ac.com. Good value mid-range option with simple, comfortable a/c rooms, all with cable TV and in-room Internet connections. Efficient staff can help with travel arrangements, airline tickets and visa extensions, and there's a restaurant, bar, Internet café and small swimming pool. Noisy but convenient location next to *Orchid Inn Resort*. **❸**

Dollhouse Hotel and Cafe 1035 Fields Ave ℡045/892 2720, ⓦwww.dollhousehotel.com. New addition to Fields Avenue, offering comfortable and cool boutique-style rooms, 24-hour room service and Internet. The rooms are seriously over-decorated, but at least they're new, with clean, modern en-suite bathrooms. **❹**

Holiday Inn Resort Clark Field ☏ 045/599 8000. Five-star hotel inside the former US base with swimming pool, restaurants and bars. Rooms have all the usual five-star facilities, but are functional rather than comfortable. Busy at the weekend with overnighters from Manila, so book in advance. **❸**

Oasis Hotel Don Juico Ave ☏ 045/332 3301 to 3305, ⓦ www.oasishotel.com.ph. Well-run establishment with 120 large, clean rooms, a restaurant, a cosy pub and an impressive outdoor pool. Close to the bars, but in a gated community set back from the main road with no tricycles and jeepneys thundering past, which makes it pleasantly quiet. **❹**

Orchid Inn Resort Raymond St ☏ 045/332 0370, ⓦ www.orchid-inn.com. In the busy bar area off the northern end of Fields Avenue and it can therefore be noisy. The pool is lovely, and there's an outdoor restaurant, *La Cantina*, serving a good range of meals and drinks. Rooms are modern (some are in two new extensions), with a/c and private bathrooms. There's free broadband Internet access – if you bring your own laptop. **❻**

Park Chicago Hotel Gloria St ☏ 045/892 0390. Also in the bar area, down a side street off Fields Avenue. Staff are friendly and the a/c is cool and quiet, but as with a number of hotels in Clark, the rooms themselves are a little rundown. **❺**

Woodland Park Resort Kilometer 87, MacArthur Highway, Dau ☏ 045/892 1002, ⓦ www.woodland .ph. A peaceful and secluded garden resort five minutes' tricycle ride from the bus station and the bars, *Woodland* offers the best combination of price and comfort in Clark. Spacious, well-appointed a/c rooms with private bathrooms and cable TV. There's a large swimming pool, restaurant and bar. **❻**

Eating

You don't have to walk far along Fields Avenue or Don Juico Avenue to find affordable and tasty **food**. The American influence is still evident, with a number of restaurants owned by former servicemen who do the cooking themselves and believe in big portions. Inside the base there are a few places close to the *Holiday Inn Resort Clark Field*.

American Legion Don Juico Ave, a ten-minute walk past the *Europhil*. Excellent low-cost food including daily special such as Salisbury steak and spaghetti with meatballs. The hash browns for breakfast are excellent.

Cottage Kitchen Café 352 Don Juico Ave. Pleasant little Creole and Cajun restaurant owned by a friendly former US Air Force officer who plays selections from his impressive collection of jazz and blues CDs. Portions are big and service efficient. The excellent desserts, including pecan pie and ice-cream cake, are home-made.

Dollhouse Hotel and Cafe 1035 Fields Ave. The menu in this newish hotel café seems to have every eventuality covered, with omelettes and pancakes for breakfast, and a lunch and dinner menu that includes Thai, Chinese, Filipino, Italian, and American-style hot dogs and burgers. It's not fine cuisine, but it's filling and hot.

Kokomo's Fields Ave. Mostly sandwiches, burgers and pizzas, but reasonably priced and portions are big. *Kokomo's* is also a meeting place for travellers, offering laundry, ticket reservations, tour bookings, money changing and Internet access.

Margarita Station Fields Ave. A Fields Avenue institution. The windows may be made of chicken wire and the doors of plywood, but *Margarita*

Station serves some of the most consistently reliable and reasonably priced food in Clark, including Western, Filipino and a tempting range of Thai dishes. The Mexican soft-shell tacos stuffed with scrambled egg and sausage are good for breakfast and the chicken teriyaki sandwiches make a great light lunch. The clientele is mostly single, white and male, but the atmosphere's friendly and the staff helpful.

The Red Crab Mahogany Dr, Mimosa Leisure Estate. As the name suggests, this popular native-style restaurant specializes in crab dishes. Walking distance from the *Holiday Inn Resort* inside the base.

Rick's Café Fields Ave. The entrance is nothing more than a modest doorway at the MacArthur Avenue end of Fields, but behind it is a careworn but convivial open-air bar with various big breakfasts for P120 and a good selection of basic home-cooked meals for lunch and dinner. Movies, many recently released, are shown on the big-screen TV from 11am until late.

Salvatore's Fields Ave. Popular Italian restaurant on the first floor above a bar called *Illusions*. The bulk of the menu consists of pizza, but there are also some good pasta dishes and the honey-roast chicken is tangy and delicious.

Angeles

The city of **ANGELES**, a few kilometres north of San Fernando along the MacArthur Highway, is a dense, congested city that has little to recommend it excepting an annual festival called the **Kuliat** held in October. One of the most high-profile Kuliat events is the Battle of the Bands, with judges voting for the best up-and-coming groups in the country.

The city's main historical landmark is the **Holy Rosary Cathedral** in Rizal Street, built during the Spanish era and used as a military hospital by the US Army from 1899 to 1900. From 1896 to 1898, its backyard was an execution grounds for Filipino rebels against the Spanish forces. The **Kamikaze Museum** (daily 9am–5pm; free), at 2 Badjao St in the eastern suburb of Villa Gloria, is an interesting little museum in the home of noted artist Dan Dizon. It rarely gets many visitors, but is well worth the trip for anyone interested in the war years in the Philippines. It showcases Dizon's collections of original kamikaze pilots' uniforms, steel swords given only to kamikaze volunteers and portraits of the first five kamikaze pilots killed in suicide attacks on the Philippines. Dizon claims some 6500 Japanese fighters crashed their aircraft against US warships in kamikaze missions in the Philippines. A tricycle to Badjao Street from the city centre costs P25 and takes ten minutes.

There's a Philippine Rabbit bus terminal at the southern end of Henson Street, close to Mercury Drug Store and PCI Bank, from where **buses** head south to Manila and north to San Fernando in La Union. **Jeepneys**, north to Clark and south to San Fernando, leave from Rizal Street near the market. On Santo Rosario Street opposite Nepo Mall there are a handful of **fast-food restaurants**, including *McDonald's* and *KFC*.

Mount Arayat

Mount Arayat (1030m), an extinct volcano in Arayat, rises from the lowlands of Pampanga in solitary and dramatic fashion, the only mountain for miles around. It is said to be inhabited by Mariang Sinukuan (Maria the Abandoned), and that when Mariang comes down from the mountain and visits the lowlands, her presence can be felt because the air turns fragrant. Some say there is a place on Arayat's wooded slopes where there are many types of fruit, all of which belong to Maria. You can eat as much fruit as you want, but don't take any away from the mountain because an angry Maria will cause you to lose your way.

It takes between seven and nine hours to reach the top of Arayat and get back down, making it just as challenging a **climb** as nearby Pinatubo. Most climbers start out early, around 6am, and come back down the same day, although you can camp overnight near the summit if you want. One of the adventure-tour companies in Clark will arrange a guide and transport for you; see p.422 for details. At the foot of the mountain there's a park with picnic areas and swimming pools. To **get to Mount Arayat** from Manila take a Sierra Madre or Arayat bus company bus from Monumento, EDSA in Caloocan to Arayat (2hr). A taxi from Clark will cost about P100. Direct jeepneys from Clark are rare, but you can take a jeepney south along the MacArthur Highway to San Fernando and then another to Arayat.

Mount Pinatubo

On April 2, 1991, people from the village of Patal Pinto on the lower slopes of **Mount Pinatubo** (1780m) saw small explosions followed by steaming and the smell of rotten eggs coming from the upper slopes of the supposedly dormant volcano, whose last known eruption was 600 years before. The Philippine

Institute of Volcanology and Seismology (PHIVOLCS) immediately installed portable seismometers near the mountain and began recording several hundred earthquakes a day. US Geological Survey personnel arrived in the area on April 23. All signals indicated that magma was rising within the volcano and that an eruption was likely, but no one knew quite how big it would be. On June 12, the first of several major explosions took place. The eruption was so violent that shockwaves could be felt in the Visayas. Nearly 20 million tons of sulphur dioxide gas were blasted into the atmosphere, causing red skies to appear for months after the eruption. A giant ash cloud rose 35km into the sky and red-hot blasts seared the countryside. Ash paralyzed Manila, closing the airport for days and turning the capital's streets into an eerie grey post-apocalyptic landscape. Particles from the eruption landed as far away as the United States. By June 16, when the dust had settled, the top of the volcano was gone, replaced by a two-kilometre-wide caldera containing a lake. Lava deposits had filled valleys, buildings had collapsed, and 350 people were dead.

Pinatubo is quiet once again, except for tourist activity. Regulations require all trekkers to be accompanied by **guides**. The usual tourist **crater trek** begins at your hotel at 5am, when a car picks you up for the drive north to the jump-off point in Santa Juliana, where you must register with the barangay office. You then transfer to a 4x4 jeep that takes you another forty minutes to the start of the climb proper in Crow Valley. It takes three hours of strenuous walking through eerie sunbaked valleys formed by masses of volcanic debris to get to the **crater** and the same to get back down. The effort is more than worth it. When you reach the lip of the crater the sight before you is magnificent, an immense, sparkling blue sulphur lake encircled by precipitous walls of rock and lahar.

Trent Transport (see p.422) charges P3000 per person for the **day package** and around P3500 for an **overnight trip** that includes tents, food, guides and transport. Trekking the lower slopes – without reaching the crater – costs P650 for six hours with a guide. You can book similar tours at Swagman Travel (see p.422), or try one of two local trekking companies: R&J Pinatubo Trek (℡045/602 5231) and Dream Treks (℡0917/955 3409).

Subic Bay and around

Another US base, another US withdrawal. **Subic Bay Naval Base**, also known these days as Subic Bay Freeport Zone, adjoins Olongapo City and is two hours northwest of Clark by road, in Zambales province. It closed down when US forces left in 1992 and is being turned into a playground for the relatively rich, with golf courses, a yacht club, a casino and hotels. The former base area is immense and to get around inside it you'll either have to depend on the regular shuttle buses that have a terminus near the Main Gate and connect hotels in the base to major sights, or rent a car. Avis (℡047/223 3256) and Dollar (℡047/223 2394) have offices in the Subic Sports Plaza on Perimeter Road, Olongapo City. All three offer a car-and-driver package for P300 an hour.

OLONGAPO CITY itself, accessible through Rizal Gate or Magsaysay Gate on the northwestern perimeter of the base, used to be a popular R&R spot for single white males, but when mayor Kate Gordon came to power in 1992, she stopped the go-go dancing and started a citywide clampdown on vice. Olongapo has changed. It's still a busy, concrete sprawl, but littering is a no-no, pavements are clean, and jeepneys must pull over to the side of the road to pick up passengers or risk an immediate on-the-spot fine. There are also some peaceful, clean **beaches** inside the former base, all on its southern fringes

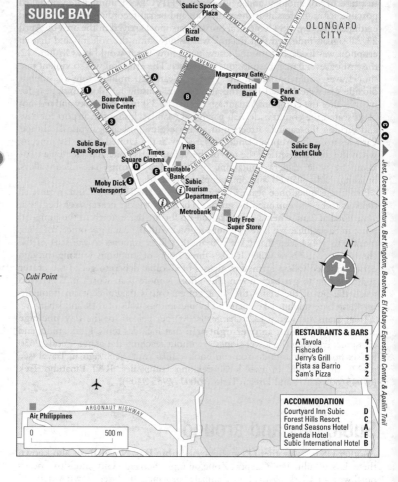

SUBIC BAY

Subic Sports Plaza

Rizal Gate

OLONGAPO CITY

PERIMETER ROAD

MAGSAYSAY DRIVE

RIZAL AVENUE

MANILA AVENUE

DEWEY AVENUE

CANAL ROAD

WATERFRONT ROAD

Magsaysay Gate

Prudential Bank

Park n' Shop

❶
Boardwalk Dive Center

❸

Ⓑ

SANTA RITA ROAD

AGUINALDO STREET

SANTA RAYMUNDO STREET

BURGOS STREET

❷

Subic Bay Yacht Club

Subic Bay Aqua Sports

ROXAS ST.

Times Square Cinema

Ⓓ

PNB

Equitable Bank

Ⓔ

Subic Tourism Department ⓘ

Moby Dick Watersports ❺

SAMPSON ROAD

TAFT STREET

ⓘ

Metrobank

Duty Free Super Store

Cubi Point

N

RESTAURANTS & BARS

A Tavola	4
Fishcado	1
Jerry's Grill	5
Pista sa Barrio	3
Sam's Pizza	2

ACCOMMODATION

Courtyard Inn Subic	D
Forest Hills Resort	C
Grand Seasons Hotel	A
Legenda Hotel	E
Subic International Hotel	B

Air Philippines

ARGONAUT HIGHWAY

0　　　　　500 m

Jest, Ocean Adventure, Bat Kingdom, Beaches, El Kabayo Equestrian Center & Apalin Trail

beyond the airport, so you'll need to take a taxi or hire a car. Hidden Beach, Miracle Beach and Nabasan Beach have good facilities and are calm enough for swimming. Officers Beach and All Hands Beach are behind the airport and were favoured, as the names suggest, by US servicemen.

Bat Kingdom, in the hills above the airport close to the *Legenda Suites* hotel, is a memorable sight at dusk. The "kingdom" is actually an area of rainforest that is home to more than 10,000 fruit bats, one of the largest colonies of its kind in Asia. During the day bats hang from trees asleep, but at dusk they begin to stir. It's a remarkable sight, and sound, as thousands of these giant, harmless creatures take to the air to look for food. They have wingspans as wide as two metres and puppy-like faces. A viewing deck at Bat Kingdom allows you to get quite close: the best time to get there is when the bats begin to wake at around 4pm.

There are plenty of small barrios and beaches outside the base, where rural life goes on pretty much as it has always done. Popular **BARRIO BARRETTO**,

4km north of the base, fronts onto **Baloy Beach**, which is one of the better beaches in Luzon. The barrio was another infamous R&R centre for excitable sailors (it featured briefly in *An Officer and a Gentleman*), but many of the bars have closed down or moved to the town of **SUBIC** proper, 12km to the north along the main coastal road. In Subic, there's some nightlife along the main road – mostly go-go bars – and a few mid-range hotels.

Practicalities

Subic has an **airport**, on the southern edge of the base, but the only scheduled airline which flies there from Manila is Air Philippines, whose Subic ticketing office is Room 153, New Terminal Building, Subic Bay Airport (☎047/252 8173). From the airport there are no jeepneys or tricycles, but a shuttle bus meets flights (P7 to the base's Main Gate). Most **buses** arrive in Olongapo at the terminal on the western edge of the city, a few minutes' walk from Kalaklan Gate on the banks of the Kalaklan River. Victory Liner buses use their own terminal in Rizal Avenue, on the eastern edge of Olongapo, a ten-minute walk from the central area. When you get to Olongapo you can take a blue jeepney for the five-kilometre journey to Barrio Barretto. All the jeepneys in Olongapo are colour-coded. The blue ones run from Kalaklan Gate, near the bus station, through Barrio Baretto and north to the town of Subic.

There's a **tourist office** just north of *Palladium Beach Resort* in Barrio Barretto, and another one in Building 662, Taft Street (☎047/252 4154), inside the base itself. The Subic Tourism Department (☎047/252 4242 or 4123) at Building 662, Dewey Avenue, Subic Bay Freeport Zone, can answer many questions about activities and help you book hotels. Dozens of **banks** are scattered in and around Subic and most have ATMs where you can get a cash advance on your Visa card. Inside Subic, most of the banks are in the Central Business District, which is also where you'll find most hotels, restaurants and shops. Prudential Bank is near the Magsaysay Gate and Metrobank near Chow King in Sampson Road, close to Duty Free Superstore. Equitable Bank and PNB are both behind the Times Square cinema in Santa Rita Road. There's a hospital, the Subic Legend Health and Medical Center (☎047/252 9280 to 9288), inside the base at Cubi Point. Major hotels in Subic have business centres where you can access the **Internet**, but they charge more than the many hole-in-the-wall Internet cafés in Olongapo, most of them along Rizal Avenue and Magsaysay Avenue. In Barrio Barretto popular resorts and restaurants such as *Mango's*, *Barts* and *Johansson's* have reliable Internet.

Accommodation

Visiting the area, you can stay at one of the mid-range **hotels** within the perimeters of the base itself, or look for budget accommodation either in Olongapo City or Barrio Barretto. Most budget travellers go for the bargain beach-side options at **Barrio Barretto**.

The base

There are a number of good but rather expensive hotels inside the **base**, aimed largely at gamblers who fly in on charter flights from Hong Kong and China to try their luck at Subic's casinos.

Courtyard Inn Subic ☎047/252 2366, ⓦwww .courtyardinnsubic.com. Modern hotel, rather soulless, but very clean and with comfortable rooms at mid-level rates. The location is good, close to restaurants in the central business district. ⑤

Forest Hills Resort ☎047/252 1406. Self-catering accommodation in low-rise buildings that used to house naval officers: there are three bedrooms that comfortably sleep six. *Forest Hills* is perched on a hill overlooking Subic, so you'll need to have a car to get around. ⑥

Grand Seasons Hotel Canal Rd ☏ 047/252 2888. The 155 rooms are simple and comfortable, with muted decor and no unnecessary frills. There's a casino, various restaurants and an outdoor pool. ⑧

Legenda Hotel Waterfront Rd ☏ 047/252 1888. The most upmarket hotel in the area, an attractive white low-rise building with almost 200 rooms, mostly standard doubles, but also twins and suites,

some with a sea view. There's a swimming pool, travel agent, health club, shopping arcade, beauty parlour and three restaurants including a ritzy Chinese place dripping with chandeliers. ⑨

Subic International Hotel Rizal Ave ☏ 047/252 2222, ⓦ www.subichotel.com. A good location in a short walk west of Main Gate, *Subic International* used to provide accommodation for forces personnel and has 300 comfortable rooms in three buildings, Alpha, Bravo and Delta. Check for the regular promotional rates, such as P700 per person for four people sharing. ⑨

Olongapo

There's no real reason to stay in **Olongapo City**, but a number of adequate hotels are within walking distance of the Victory Liner bus terminal.

Arlene's Inn Magsaysay Dr ☏ 047/222 2629. Everything you need for a one-night budget stay. Clean a/c rooms with showers and cable TV; some of the rooms are bigger (and cost more) so ask to look at a selection before you choose. *Arlene's Inn II* is a similar place, owned by the same family, across the bridge in Rizal Avenue at the eastern end of town. ②

Kong's 80 Magsaysay Dr ☏ 047/224 1516. Budget option offering a choice of fan or a/c doubles, all with private showers. Take a look at the rooms first because some are in better

condition than others and those at the front are dusty and noisy. ②

Ridgecrest Gardens Hotel 15 Magsaysay Dr ☏ 047/223 7380. The best hotel in Olongapo City, with 31 double rooms, all with a/c and clean showers. ③

Zanzibar Hotel & Restaurant 112 Magsaysay Dr ☏ 047/223 3080. Decent mid-range choice in a good location two blocks east of *Kong's*. The cheapest double rooms are a little cramped, but well maintained, and all have a/c and private showers. ③

Barrio Barretto

A number of laidback resorts are dotted outside the base in **Barrio Barretto**, most of them clearly signposted as you travel along the National Highway. There are also a handful of more rustic resorts at **Baloy Beach**, a fifteen-minute walk north from Barrio Barretto.

Barts Resort Hotel 117C National Highway ☏ 047/223 4148, ⓦ www.bartssubic.com. Comfortable doubles in a grey motel-style building around a small garden and swimming pool, but close to the beach. All rooms have a/c and showers, but *Barts* is a popular nightlife hangout, so can be a little noisy. It's located at the north end of the Barrio Barretto beach, 20min from Olongapo. ⑤

By The Sea 99 National Highway ☏ 047/222 2718, ⓦ www.bythesea.com.ph. Forty comfortable a/c rooms either right on the beach or set back around a quiet garden. Convivial restaurant and bar overlooking the sea and a Mongolian barbecue buffet every evening for P200. ⑥

Playa Papagayo 43 National Highway ☏ 047/222 3825. Hacienda-style development with a choice of new a/c double rooms either on the beach or around a quiet courtyard. It also has a Mexican restaurant. ④

Sheavens Resort Hotel Baloy Beach ☏ 047/223 9430, ⓦ www.sheavens.com. Big but peaceful resort-hotel in an unbeatable location right on the bay. Immaculate rooms, good food (the menu includes European and Thai dishes) and helpful staff who can arrange banca trips and scuba diving. ⑤

Eating and entertainment

Most of the restaurants in **Olongapo City** are on the main drag, Magsaysay Drive. They include the usual range of fast food joints such as *Hard Rock Café*, *Domino's Pizza* and *Chow King*. *Sam's Pizza* in Rizal Avenue offers Italian and European comfort food, but if you want authentic Italian food the undisputed king of restaurants in Subic is *A Tavola*, inside the **base** itself in Palm Street, near the big duty-free stores ten minutes east of Magsaysay Gate along Rizal Avenue and ten minutes from Kalaklan Gate. This gem of a restaurant is owned by an Italian chef and offers home-made pasta dishes and a good selection of affordable wines; two people can eat and drink for about P1000. Also inside the base, *Jerry's Grill* on Waterfront Road is a big, brash restaurant that sells native food in immense portions. Nearby are *Pista sa Barrio* and *Fishcado*, both popular Filipino restaurants offering lots of **seafood**.

In **Barrio Barretto**, *Mango's* beach bar and restaurant is a landmark (look out for the neon sign) serving both Filipino and European cuisine. *Mr Pumpernickel* on Baloy Beach does fine German food. The German owner, Harry, is also the

Subic activities

Subic Bay is a popular **diving** site with nineteen wrecks in still waters, all no more than thirty minutes by boat from the waterfront area. Most wrecks are the remains of World War II vessels, but there are also two Spanish-era hulks, the *El Capitan* and *San Quentin*.

The **USS New York**, though, is the star attraction of Subic's underwater world, a battle cruiser launched in the USA in 1891. She had a long and illustrious career – including time as a fleet flagship in the North Atlantic – and was once the pride of the US fleet in Asia. When World War II broke out, she was virtually retired, and when the Japanese swept the US Marines out of the Philippines, the Americans had no choice but to scuttle her as they departed from Subic in early 1942. The ship now lies on her port side in 27m of water between Alava pier and the northern end of Cubi Point runway. The 120-metre-long hull presents excellent opportunities for what scuba divers call a "swim-through" – an exploration of the inside of the wreck from one end to the other. This is a potentially dangerous exercise and you will need to be an experienced diver to handle it.

The **El Capitan**, lying in a pretty inlet on the east coast of Subic Bay is a much easier wreck dive, suitable for novices. The **San Quentin** is the oldest known wreck in Subic, a wooden gunboat scuttled by the Spanish in 1898 in a futile attempt to block the channel between Grande and Chiquita islands against invading Americans. Other Subic wrecks include the Japanese POW ship *Oryoku Maru* and the *Seian Maru*, a Japanese cargo vessel sunk by the American Navy in 1945.

For **diving trips** try Johan's Adventure Dive Center, right on the shore at Baloy Beach; Moby Dick Watersports (℡047/252 3773) opposite the *Legenda Hotel*; or Subic Bay Aqua Sports (℡047/252 3005 or 7343) on Waterfront Drive. A newer dive outfit, Boardwalk Dive Center (℡047/252 5357), is at Building 664, Waterfront Road, in the same building as the *Boardwalk Inn*.

There are numerous **other activities** at Subic. Inside the base, on the road between the central base area and the airport, you can visit the Jungle Environmental Survival Training Camp (JEST; ℡047/252 4123) and take tours into the area's impressive rainforest with members of the Aeta tribe who trained US Marines here for service in Vietnam. Short trips include lectures and demonstrations on basic jungle survival. Overnight trips involve finding your own potable water and setting traps for food: bat barbecue is a speciality.

Subic has a number of good walking trails, the best of which is the well-marked Apaliin Trail running along the banks of the Apaliin River. At the El Kabayo Equestrian Center, in an area of the base known as Binictican Heights, you can arrange riding lessons or gentle hacks through the rainforest. For reservations, contact the tourist information office in Taft Street (see p.427). Ocean Adventure at Camayan wharf is another one of Subic's major tourist draws, where you can swim with dolphins and whales for P2600 (℡047/252 9000).

liaison officer for Baloy Beach and a good source of information; he can help with guides and tours to Mount Pinatubo. *Johannsson's*, on the National Highway, is a popular hangout for Europeans, with omelettes for breakfast from a bargain P45, and a lunch and dinner menu that includes blue marlin steak, boiled veal with dill sauce, schnitzel, beef stew and an interesting take on *sinigang* using salmon. *Da Mama*, also on the National Highway, is a rustic Italian restaurant with an interesting menu that includes antipasti, vegetable salads, bruschetta, fish, pumpkin and onion soups.

The Zambales coast

Zambales is an undeveloped rural province with a mountainous eastern fringe and a coastline on the west that is still largely undiscovered by tourists, but does boast some scenic beaches and a number of inexpensive resorts. The Zambales coastal road runs from Olongapo in the south to the town of Santa Cruz in the north, then on to the neighbouring province of Pangasinan. A number of towns and barrios are sprinkled along this coast, but none is a major tourist destination in its own right. However, if you hanker to get away from it all and explore a side of the Philippines that visitors rarely see, this is a good place to do it. Nine kilometres to the north of Olongapo, the town of **Subic** has a couple of dive outfits and half-a-dozen sorry looking girlie bars along a busy main road. There's no beach to speak of and nothing to make you want to linger. Further north, **San Antonio** is the departure point for the unspoilt beaches around the barangay of **Pandaquit**, while nearby **Botolan** also has some beaches and a few quiet resorts. Continuing north, the provincial capital of **Iba** is a busy trading and fishing town, but the main attraction is the beach to the west, a quiet and convenient place to break your journey along the coast for a night. Beyond Iba lies the saltworks town of **Santa Cruz**; at nearby Dasol Bay small hotels are ranged along a fine ribbon of sand at Tambobong, from where you can arrange trips to islands in the bay.

Travel along the Zambales coast is easy because of the number of buses running along the main road. Victory Liner has hourly trips in both directions between Olongapo and Alaminos, from where it's only a short hop to the One Hundred Islands (see p.432). There are also dozens of local buses and jeepneys on this route, so it's easy to make short trips from one place to the next.

San Antonio, Pandaquit and Botolan

The first town north of Olongapo is **San Antonio**, which straddles the main north–south road and is about an hour away by bus. San Antonio is a clean and quiet little town with a few general stores and a shady plaza, but there's nothing to see or do there. You can, however, catch a jeepney at the plaza to the fishing village of **PANDAQUIT**, 5km south, which has a long beach with a number of simple resorts offering cheap rooms and fine views of the sunset and the South China Sea. By far the best place to stay is the splendid little *Capones Beach Resort* (☎0918/816 4816; ❷), which is right on the sand at Pandaquit and has clean rooms with fans and showers. Next door to *Capones* is *Nora's Beach Resort* (❸), a basic but clean place with a choice of fan or air-conditioned rooms, all with private bathroom. You can hire bancas on the beach for around P500 for half a day to explore Camera and Capones **islands**, which lie close to each other 45 minutes offshore. These islands don't offer any good snorkelling, but there are a number of quiet coves that make good picnic spots.

About another hour north of San Antonio is **BOTOLAN**, featuring a couple of sleepy but well-run resorts on the wide beach which you can reach by tricycle less than ten minutes from where the bus drops you on the main road. The best is *Rama International Beach Resort* (☏0918/910 1280; ❸), which has clean, rustic cottages on the shore and whose owners can arrange **trips** to Pinatubo, the limestone caves at Santa Cruz, the old hilltop gold-mining town of Acoe or trekking to the top of nearby Mount Binoclutan. The most interesting side trip from here, though, is inland to **Pili**, a barrio partly submerged by water that formed a lake when Pinatubo erupted. You can see the eerie remains of a school and more than six hundred houses whose owners fled to safety when signs of volcanic activity in Pinatubo were first detected. There are also the ruins of a church, with a makeshift altar where residents from nearby barrios still come to pray. Pili sits in a magnificent natural bowl and it's possible to follow the lahar flows from here to Pinatubo itself, but you'll definitely need a guide. You can organize a trip to Pili through *Rama* resort, or do it on your own by taking a jeepney from Botolan. Jeepneys don't go all the way to Pili, but they stop at the nearby barangay of San Marcelino, from where Pili is a pleasant one-hour trek along a narrow, rocky road.

Iba and around

Only thirty minutes by road north of Botolan, the provincial capital of **IBA** was the birthplace in 1907 of popular former president Ramon Magsaysay, who was known as "The Guy". Iba is a busy trading and fishing town, but there's nothing here for tourists. The main attraction is the **beach** to the west, which you can reach in a few minutes by jeepney from the main road where buses arrive. The sand is brown and there's not much in the way of good snorkelling, but it's a pleasant place to break your journey along the coast for a night. There are a number of reasonable **resorts** on the beach, the best of which is *Ocean View Beach House* (☏02/895 3560; ❷) in Balintobog, Amungan, a few kilometres north of Iba at the centre of a gentle crescent beach protected by reefs at both ends. It's a typical concrete barangay home with two bedrooms, a living room and a gate to the beach that you can rent by the day for P3500 at weekends and P1800 during the week. To get there it's an easy tricycle ride from Iba. Five minutes north from Iba by tricycle or jeepney in the barangay of Bantangalinga is *Palmera Garden Beach Resort* (☏047/811 2109; ❸), a big place with concrete air-conditioned rooms and a nice swimming pool set in gardens overlooking the ocean.

About an hour north of Iba lies **Santa Cruz**, with its expansive saltworks and limestone caves. This also marks the southern end of Dasol Bay, where a handful of small hotels have sprung up along beautiful beaches such as **Tambobong**. To get to Tambobong Beach take a jeepney from the plaza in Santa Cruz. There are two islands in **Dasol Bay** that you can reach by hired banca from the small wharf in Santa Cruz: **Hermana Mayor Island**, also known as Miss Universe Island because it was where candidates for the Miss Universe title in 1979 had their photographs taken; and **Hermana Menor Island**, smaller and untouched by development. Neither island has accommodation, but both have some lovely coves of fine white sand and good snorkelling.

The Lingayen Gulf

Most of the beaches dotted along the **Lingayen Gulf**, from Bolinao in the west to Dagupan in the east, are working beaches where people fish in the gulf's rich waters and mend their nets. The sand is generally grey and unappealing and the water likewise. There are a number of resorts along these beaches, but none is anything special. The gulf's primary attraction, reached through the little coastal town of Lucap, is the **One Hundred Islands National Park**, which is worth the trip here alone. At the western end of the gulf around Bolinao you'll find one or two good beaches and some excellent but little-known snorkelling areas.

One Hundred Islands National Park

It's actually 123, but who's counting? These emerald-like tiny islands are part of a **national park** covering almost twenty square kilometres, nestling in the Lingayen Gulf. The park is accessible year-round and there are no opening hours: the only restriction is that you have to register and pay a fee of P50 at the Philippine Tourist Authority **office** in Lucap on the mainland (see below). Some islands have beaches, but many are no more than coral outcrops crowned by scrub. Sadly, much of the underwater coral in the park has been damaged by a devastating combination of cyanide and dynamite fishing, typhoons and the El Niño weather phenomenon. On a positive note, the authorities are going all out to protect what coral is left and help it regenerate, meaning you can only snorkel in approved areas. Marine biologists from the University of the Philippines have been at the forefront of the protection movement, replanting hundreds of *taklobos* (giant clams). The area of the park known as Taklobos Reef, where many of the clams have been planted, has the best snorkelling because of the marine life that they have attracted.

The best place to base yourself for exploring the islands is **Lucap**, which is right on the shore and from where you can island-hop by day (you'll need to take your own food and water), returning to a shower and a comfy bed in the evening. Don't expect Robinson Crusoe solitude, especially at weekends when many of the islands are overrun by day-trippers. You can find your own piece of paradise here, but you'll have to make it clear to the boatman you are not interested in the bigger islands. The only three islands with any form of development are **Governor's Island**, **Children's Island** and **Quezon Island**, where there's basic accommodation.

One of the prettiest little islands is called **Marta**. It's actually two tiny islets connected by a thin strip of bright white sand that almost disappears at high tide. **Marcos Island** has a blowhole and a vertical shaft of rock; you can clamber to the top and then dive into a seawater pool about 20m below. A number of islands, including **Scout Island** and **Quirino Island**, have caves; on **Cuenco Island** there's a cave that goes right through the island to the other side. Some of these dots of land are so small and rocky it's impossible to land on them, while others are big enough to allow for some exploring on foot, with tiny, sandy coves where you can picnic in the shade and swim without anyone disturbing you.

Every year in the last week of February, Lucap stages the **Hundred Islands Festival** to drum up support for the preservation and protection of the islands; highlights include a mardi gras and a river parade.

Practicalities

From bus terminals in Alaminos there are plenty of tricycles and FX taxis for the fifteen-minute ride to Lucap. You can pay your **park entrance fee** and arrange **camping permits** at the small Philippine Tourist Authority **office** (daily 8am–5pm) at the pier in Lucap. From the pier you can also arrange a **boatman** and a boat (P300 for 5hr, P40 every additional hour).

Accommodation and eating

There are three islands where you can **camp** overnight for a small fee, usually P150: Governor's Island, Children's Island and Quezon Island. On Governor's Island there is a **guesthouse** ideal for a family. It has two bedrooms, a living room, dining room, water (four drums), generator lighting and cooking facilities. *Bahay kubos* (wooden houses) on Children's Island are for budget travellers and have screened bedrooms with kerosene lighting and one drum of fresh water. Common areas are provided for dining and cooking as well as for toilet and bath. On Quezon Island, thirty minutes from Lucap at the northern edge of the park, there's a concrete motel-type structure where plain rooms range from doubles to family rooms for up to eight people.

Some of the hotels in **Lucap** itself also have good waterfront restaurants that dish up fresh seafood.

Barny's Lodge & Restaurant ☎075/551 6148 or 0919/430 6589. British-owned and one of the best places near the pier. It's cosy, clean and has a/c rooms with bamboo double beds, private bathrooms and cable TV. Also features a charming native-style restaurant. ❹

Gloria's Cottages ☎075/551 2388. Good location for island-hopping with plain, orderly fan doubles right over the water near the pier. Rooms are basic but good value and all have clean private bathrooms. ❸

Hundred Islands Resort Hotel ☎075/551 5753. Modern establishment in a good location a short walk from the pier with a/c rooms, a café, a grill restaurant and a small, cheesy discotheque. Rooms range from affordable economy doubles to family rooms with five beds. ❺

Kilometer One ☎075/551 2510. The cheapest place in the Lucap area because it's not near the pier, but 2km before it on the main road from Alaminos, which means for island-hopping you'll have to get a tricycle back and forth. The rooms are rudimentary fan doubles and have shared facilities. ❷

Maxine by the Sea ☎075/551 2537. Right on the pier. Plain but clean and adequate doubles with either a/c or fan and private bathrooms. The seafood restaurant here is popular. ❸

Ocean View Lodge ☎075/551 2537. Small home-style guesthouse opposite the pier. Doubles are spacious and come with a choice of a/c or fan, but some of them are windowless and dim. The little restaurant does average local cuisine, but their fish is always fresh. ❸

Vista del Mar ☎075/551 2492. New hotel with a whitewashed exterior and a pleasant coffee shop in the garden, set back from the waterfront about 500m from the pier. Rooms have a/c and mod cons such as refrigerator and cable TV. ❸

Bolinao and around

The landscape around the town of **BOLINAO** is one of cascading waterfalls, rolling hills and white beaches. But the most valuable asset in this small municipality is its 200 square kilometres of coral reefs, which serve as the spawning ground for ninety percent of Bolinao's fish catch. More than 350 species of vertebrates, invertebrates and plants are harvested from the reef and appear in Bolinao's markets each year. The town rose to national prominence in the 1990s, when it was announced that a consortium intended to build a cement factory on the shoreline. Residents protested that this would destroy the ecosystem and the long-term viability of Bonilao's coastal resources. Their protests made the front pages and won national support and, as a result, the plan was shelved.

You can reach Bolinao easily by bus or jeepney from Lucap and Alaminos. There are only a couple of sights in the town itself. The small **Bolinao Museum** (Mon–Sat 9am–4pm; free), on Rizal Street opposite Cape Bolinao High School, contains art, geology, botany and zoology materials collected in the area. The **Church of St James Fortress**, also known as Bolinao Church, is in the main square close to the museum; built by the Augustinians in 1609, it houses rare wooden statues and an antique altar with Aztec masks brought by galleon from Mexico.

The area to the west of town has some pleasant, relaxed beaches and resorts and is a good place to unwind in an unspoilt rural atmosphere, while a 22-kilometre-long **barrier reef** offshore, near **Santiago Island**, offers some wonderful solitary snorkelling. To explore the reef you can rent a banca for the day either at Bolinao wharf (two blocks north of the main road) or at one of the nearby beach resorts.

However, the best beach in the Bolinao area is **Patar Beach**, about thirty minutes west of town, which has fine white sand, good surf and few visitors, especially during the week. You can reach it by jeepney from Rizal Street in Bolinao. Nearby is the old **Cape Bolinao Lighthouse**, constructed in 1905 and the second tallest lighthouse in the country. There's an easy path to the base of the building, and the views across the South China Sea are well worth the climb. Not far offshore lie a number of old Spanish galleons and Chinese junks that local wisdom says contain treasure. Unfortunately there are no accredited dive operators in the area, so your only chance of diving here is to bring your own equipment.

There are a couple of places to stay at Patar Beach: *Bing's Beach Resort* (℡0912/856 1585; ❸) has very simple but adequate and affordable huts on the sand, while *Treasures of Bolinao Beach Resort* (℡0916/372 1979; ❹) features more substantial doubles and a modest restaurant. *Dutch Beach Resort* (℡0912/311 6540; ❸) is a pretty place on the beach about 4km before you reach Patar. Next door is *Tropical Hut Beach Resort* (❸), a modest back-to-nature place with wooden huts and a shared bathroom. In the barangay of Arenda, ten minutes' drive along the road west of Bolinao, sits the *Rock Garden Resort* (℡0912/313 9553 or 075/554 2876; ❸). The beach here is not the best in the area, but *Rock Garden* is a comfortable place to stay, with spick-and-span double rooms and a swimming pool.

Lingayen

The quaint old town of **LINGAYEN**, about an hour by road east of Alaminos, is the capital of Pangasinan province. It dates back to 1611 and contains an atmospheric Spanish square and a small Baroque church. The neighbouring new town, 2km north of the old town on the coast, is a noisy jumble of tricycles, jeepneys and fast-food restaurants. Some travellers end up spending the night here on their way north or south, as it's a convenient place to change buses if you're heading south from La Union or Baguio, then west to Lucap and the One Hundred Islands. There are a few beaches near the town, but none is worth making a special journey for – except perhaps, for historical reasons, Lingayen **Public Beach**, next to the Provincial Capitol Building in the new town. This was where American forces landed on January 9, 1945, paving the way for the liberation of Luzon from Japanese occupation.

There's nowhere to stay in the old town, so if you're looking for a room make sure you get off the bus in the new town, close to the Provincial Capitol Building. *Hotel Consuelo* (℡075/542 8933; ❹) is opposite the Provincial Capitol Building in Alvear Street and has modern a/c rooms and a popular seafood restaurant. The *Lingayen Gulf Resort Hotel* (℡075/542 5871; ❸) is a sprawling government-run **hotel** near the Provincial Capitol Building. Rooms are musty, but all have air-conditioning and good bathrooms with hot water. At P150 a night the dorm beds are some of the cheapest accommodation in the city.

Dagupan

DAGUPAN, less than an hour's drive east of Lingayen, is the Philippines' capital of fish culture. One-fifth of the city's total area consists of fishponds for culturing *bangus* (milkfish), prawns, shrimps, crabs and mussels. This is also where they make much of the nation's *bagoong* (fermented fish paste). In honour of its fishy culture, Dagupan stages the **Bangus Festival** every April, the centrepiece of which is a street party featuring live performances on eight outdoor stages and *bangus* cooked on a giant barbecue grill, said to be the longest in the world; for details call the festival secretariat on ☎075/522 7550. Every Filipino festival has street dancing: in this case participants dress up in *bangus* costumes and perform the intricate steps of traditional dance called Gilon! Gilon!

Dagupan is big, busy and noisy and not a tourist destination. The only notable beach, from a historical point of view at least, is **Roman Blue Beach**, where liberation forces landed on January 9, 1945. Features include the Japanese park and MacArthur Landing Marker, but it is not especially clean for swimming and there are no facilities. To get there take a tricycle (P5) from any of the bus terminals, from outside your hotel or from Rizal Street. **Accommodation** in Dagupan is limited, but you can try the *Folren Hotel* (☎075/522 0666; ❸–❺) in the town centre on Rizal Street. It's in a noisy area, but the a/c rooms are spacious and have cable TV. *Hotel Victoria* (❷–❸) is within walking distance of the Philippine Rabbit bus terminal on A.B. Fernandez Avenue and has some of the cheapest rooms in town. They are slightly rundown but okay for a night.

Tarlac City

Busy, industrial **Tarlac City**, 123km north of Manila, is the halfway point from Manila to the beaches of La Union, the old brick churches and houses of Ilocos and the cool hills of Baguio and the Cordillera – which means that the main road through is nearly always jammed with buses, jeeps, tricycles and all manner of trucks, lorries and juggernauts. It is not a significant tourist destination.

Tarlac City is known to all Filipinos as the birthplace of **Benigno "Ninoy" Aquino**, the anti-Marcos firebrand who was assassinated at Manila airport in 1983. The only notable place of interest in town is the Aquino Center in San Miguel, a ten- to fifteen-minute jeepney ride southeast of the bus stations and the main road, behind the Luisita shopping mall. The centre, an impressive purpose-built glass and steel structure, houses the **Aquino Museum** (Mon, Tues, Thurs & Sat 2–5pm, Wed & Fri 9am–noon; free), as well as an audio-visual room, conference halls, library and ballroom. There are volunteer guides who appreciate a tip, but you can also wander around on your own. It's all there in the museum – young Ninoy Aquino's possessions from his reporting days in Korea, including a Rolleiflex camera, and the medals he received for persuading a notorious Communist rebel to abandon the fight. There is also a replica of Ninoy's cell in Fort Bonifacio, Manila, where he was imprisoned by Marcos during martial law. The cell contains his actual bed, typewriter, exercise equipment and kitchen utensils. Beside the bed is a wooden calendar on which he etched the passing of days with a nail from 1972 to 1979. Also on display are the books that he read while in solitary confinement: *Jesus Rediscovered* by Malcolm Muggeridge, *The Confessions of St Augustine* and Austin Coates's *Rizal: Philippine Nationalist and Martyr*. Even more poignant is the display of belongings Aquino had with him on the day he was assassinated. They include a passport in the name of Marcial Bonifacio, his watch, wedding ring, boots and the bloodstained safari suit he was wearing when he died.

Other than the Aquino connection, Tarlac's significance is as a **transport hub**. Major bus lines going from north to south use it as a rest stop and you might stay here for the night to break a long trip or to wait for a bus. Victory Liner and Dagupan have terminals along the main road (the National Highway) on the busy "V" junction close to the Petron petrol station. The Philippine Rabbit terminal is a few hundred metres further north along the main road, close to *McDonald's*. Dagupan buses from here go west to Olongapo, Lingayen and Dagupan, east to Cabanatuan and south to Manila. Philippine Rabbit and Victory both run north and south between Baguio and Manila. The right fork of the V junction is the main north–south road; the left fork takes you into Tarlac City centre, a short walk, where there are shops, banks and fast-food restaurants around the main square, Ninoy Aquino Plaza. You can also get into the city by walking west along Juan Luna Street, a few minutes north of the Philippine Rabbit terminal.

There are two convenient **hotels** in Tarlac City, both easy to reach by tricycle or on foot from the bus stations. *Asiaten Hotel* (⊤045/982 0355; ❹), at 18 Don Gregorio Ave, is inside a leafy, gated residential area on the west side of the main road behind *King Burger*. Head south from any of the bus stations and it's on your right. The rooms have flouncy bedcovers and fancy curtains, but are comfortable and spacious and boast private bathrooms with hot water. The gardens are pleasant and there's a small pool and a good restaurant. *Grandma's Hotel & Restaurant* (⊤045/982 5142; ❸), a long-standing and well-known mid-range establishment with fifty air-conditioned rooms, swimming pool and restaurant, is on the right-hand side of the highway a little north of the bus stations. Almost opposite the Victory Liner bus terminal near Petron, the *Peking House* restaurant serves solid Chinese **food** such as fried rice, fried chicken, dim sum and sweet and sour pork. A short walk south from here on the opposite side of the road is *St James' Steak House*, where you can get a good carnivorous meal for less than P200.

The northwest and Batanes

The long strip of coastline that stretches from San Fabian to Pagudpud runs through three provinces: La Union, Ilocos Sur and Ilocos Norte. The far northwest is Marcos country, and the late dictator, despite the abominations of his later rule, is held up as quintessential northern stock: wily, prudent and less given to the extravagant showboating of southerners (of whom Imelda, of course, was the dizzy epitome). This does not mean the northwest is humourless or humdrum; the people, like Filipinos generally, are approachable and friendly towards visitors. The landscape is raw and dramatic, characterized by boiling fluvial plains and long ribbons of exposed beach washed by the surf of the South China Sea.

The capital of La Union, **San Fernando**, provides access to nearby beaches and resorts as well as opportunities for trekking and climbing. The beaches here are brown sand, not the dazzling white coves and lagoons of the Visayas, but they are equally beautiful in their own way, with some excellent surfing if you time it right. Heading north from La Union the next province you reach is **Ilocos Sur**, known for the old Spanish settlement of **Vigan**, the best-preserved city of its kind in the country, with narrow cobblestone streets, aristocratic ancestral homes and horse-drawn carriages. Finally there's Ilocos Norte. Its capital **Laoag** has an airport and can be reached by plane in less than an hour from Manila, giving easy access to one of the most fascinating pockets of history in the archipelago, with a number of Marcos-related sites and some atmospheric old Spanish churches. About two hours north of Laoag you'll find excellent beaches around **Pagudpud**, right on the northern tip of Luzon. Two hundred and sixty kilometres beyond the northern Luzon mainland are the idyllic **Batanes** islands that rank as one of the Philippines' greatest treasures: peaceful, undeveloped and visited by few tourists, offering a dazzling landscape of peaks and bays quite unlike anything else in the archipelago.

The **coastal route** north from Manila passes through San Fernando, Vigan and Laoag and is one of the better roads in the Philippines, sealed the whole way and less crowded the further north you get.

San Fabian and around

The town of **SAN FABIAN** on the eastern edge of the Lingayen Gulf is a bustling fishing and trading community with no beaches and little to recommend it. It is, however, the gateway to the northwest coast. The coastal road continues from here all the way up to Laoag and the northernmost tip of the country, making San Fabian a good halfway point to break a journey from Manila. **White Beach**, which runs north from the barangay of **Nibaliw West** to **Mabilao**, is not a patch on its Boracay namesake, but it's clean and quiet, with some decent little resorts dotted along it. It's also where the commander of the Japanese imperial expeditionary forces stepped ashore on December 24, 1941 to begin the bleak years of occupation. San Fabian is on the main road north, the National Highway, and well served by buses heading north from Manila and Dagupan and south from La Union, Ilocos Sur and Ilocos Norte.

Accommodation

There are two main areas for **accommodation**. Nibaliw West is immediately north of San Fabian town proper and is where most of the inexpensive resorts are. It's easy to reach by either tricycle or jeepney from San Fabian. About 3km further north is Bolasi, where there are a couple of more luxurious resorts.

Charissa's Beach Houses Nibaliw West ☏ 075/523 6861. Wooden cottages on the beach, a restaurant and a small swimming pool. The large two-bedroom cottages are good value, sleeping up to six people. ❸

Lazy A Resort Nibaliw West ☏ 075/511 5014. Simple, clean and friendly place with a choice of fan or a/c cottages, all with private shower. You might even get hot water if you're lucky, although it's not guaranteed. The restaurant does cheap, unpretentious food: a Filipino beef and rice breakfast is P80. ❸

San Fabian Beach Resort Bolasi ☏ 075/523 6504. Large and sometimes busy resort on a long

crescent beach. The 29 rooms are all a/c and have showers with hot water. There is also a hostel and a presidential holiday home with two carpeted bedrooms where Ferdinand Marcos used to stay when he was in the area. ❻

Sierra Vista Beach Resort Nibaliw West ☏ 075/511 2030. Pleasant family resort on the beach, with two swimming pools, twenty a/c double rooms and a comfortable restaurant with views. Staff are friendly and it's not as busy as the nearby *San Fabian Beach Resort*. The best place in the area, so it's worth booking ahead. ❼

Agoo

A small and pleasant town on the road north between San Fabian in Pangasinan and San Fernando in La Union, **AGOO** is not a significant tourist destination, but there are a smattering of notable sights; it's worth hopping off the bus here, wandering around for an hour, then continuing your journey north or south.

The most significant building in Agoo is the **Basilica Minore of Our Lady of Charity**, a five-centuries-old Spanish church that has been recently restored with contributions from Italy, Japan and the US. The church, at the back of a leafy plaza on the right-hand side of the main road through Agoo, houses the supposedly miraculous image of Our Lady of Charity; at Easter, thousands of devotees visit Agoo to pay homage to it. Agoo has a reputation among devout Catholics as a place of signs and miracles. In February 1993 a statue of the Virgin Mary here was said to have wept blood and in September 1993 people came from around the country to see an apparition of the Virgin Mary which was predicted to appear by a local boy. It didn't. Opposite the basilica in a fenced garden is the small **Museo Iloko** (Mon–Fri 9am–4pm; P10), beside the Agoo municipal building, which houses religious artefacts, antique furniture, porcelain and miniature dolls.

San Fernando and around

SAN FERNANDO is the capital of La Union province and has few sights itself, but gives access to a number of good **beach resorts**. Most travellers simply get off the bus here and then take a tricycle or jeepney to the beach, spending little time in the city itself, which is congested and not especially attractive. If you have a few hours to spare in San Fernando between bus connections, take a walk up Zigzag Road, past the popular *High Altitude Disco*, to the **Chinese–Filipino Friendship Pagoda**, from where there are great views across the rooftops and out to the South China Sea. A little further up Zigzag Road on top of the hill is the Provincial Capitol Building. Along Quezon Avenue on the northern outskirts of San Fernando sits the impressive **Ma-Cho temple**, testament to the influence of the Chinese in the area, many of whose ancestors arrived before the Spanish did.

There are two areas close to San Fernando with good beaches and a wide range of affordable accommodation. **Bauang** is a short tricycle ride to the south, while **San Juan** is a slightly longer jeepney ride north. The better of the two is San Juan, which is peaceful, sits on a wide fringe of clean beach and has good surfing.

Practicalities

Buses from Manila heading north stop at one of a number of terminals. The Philippine Rabbit terminal is a few kilometres south of the city, while Dominion stops near *McDonald's* just before the city centre and Partas stops on the northern fringe of the city in Quezon Avenue beyond Town Plaza. **Tourist information** is hard to come by in San Fernando, so your best bet is simply to ask at the resorts in Bauang or San Juan, where owners and staff know their way round the province and can offer reliable advice. You can also try *Oasis Country Resort*, a few kilometres south of the city proper, which has a local Department of Tourism office. Swagman Hotels & Travel has an office on the main road from Bauang to San Fernando, opposite the entrance to *Cabana* beach resort. San Fernando City's main drag is Quezon Avenue where there are a number of **banks** with ATMs. The police station is on Quezon Avenue behind La Union Trade Center.

The best **accommodation** in San Fernando is the *Sea and Sky Hotel* (⊤072/242 0465; ❸) at the northern end of town on Quezon Avenue. The rooms at the back look out onto the sea, but those at the front face the road, which is always busy. Centrally located near the noisy Town Plaza is the dingy *Plaza Hotel* (⊤072/888 2996; ❷), offering singles and doubles with air-conditioning and shower. The modern and reasonably efficient *Hotel Mikka* (⊤072/242 5737; ❸) is just beyond the Partas bus terminal on Quezon Avenue, and features 43 comfortable air-conditioned rooms, a restaurant and a bar. There's nothing country about the *Oasis Country Resort* (⊤072/242 5621; ❺) – it's south of the city facing the thundering traffic along the National Highway and has an assortment of business and recreation facilities, including a bowling alley. Good **food** is served up at *Cafe Esperanza*, up a short flight of stairs next to St William Cathedral in the plaza. The dishes are all local and sitting in bowls on the counter, so simply point at whatever takes your fancy. A filling meal here costs less than P100 and there are also some good cakes and snacks. Otherwise the choice is pretty much restricted to fast food: there's a *Chow King* on Governor Luna Street and a *Jollibee* on Quezon Avenue, right opposite the plaza.

Bauang

The long stretch of brown sandy beach north of Bauang town and south of San Fernando doesn't have an official name, but is generally known as **BAUANG** ("ba-whang"). The beach is nice enough for a stroll and swimming, and it's an interesting place to sit and watch the world go by at sunset, but there aren't many activities here and most visitors only stay a day or two on their way north. Bauang is known as a sex tourism centre, and many of the resorts along the beach, though not all, have dreary nightclubs with GROs. Buses from Manila bound for San Fernando, Loaog, Vigan or Abra pass through Bauang town. You can ask the driver to let you off on the main road north of Bauang from where the beach is a short walk. Otherwise, continue to San Fernando and take a tricycle back.

Accommodation

Resorts at Bauang are all dotted along the beach, immediately north of Bauang town. Most have their own restaurants.

Bali Hai Beach Resort ⊤072/242 567, Ⓦ www .balihai.com.ph. Well-managed place in the middle of the beach with a large pool, a restaurant (with vegetarian and children's menus) and a variety of solidly constructed, different sized rooms set around a pleasant tropical garden. If things are quiet you can get twenty-percent discount. ❺
Cabana Beach Resort ⊤072/242 5585. Relaxing family resort on the beach a little south of *Bali Hai*. Twenty-nine a/c rooms ranging from comfortable and affordable singles to spacious twins and deluxe rooms. Large, clean swimming pool and a

casual bar-restaurant that is perfect for sundowners. ❹
China Sea ⊤072/242 6101 or 705 0833, Ⓦ www .chinaseabeachresort.com. Well-maintained and relaxed family resort at the southern end of the beach with swimming pool and spacious a/c cottages on the beach. ❹
🏃 **Coconut Grove Beach Resort** ⊤072/888 4276, Ⓦ www.coco.com.ph. Appealing family option on the southern half of the beach with spacious standard doubles, deluxe doubles and large family rooms. Furnishings are simple, but

everything is clean and the staff friendly. Bar, large swimming pool and bowling green. ❹
Ocean Breeze Resort ☎ 072/888 3530. Inexpensive double rooms have linoleum floors and private showers and are grouped at the back of the main building around a small garden. There's a restaurant fronting the beach and a small nightclub that can be noisy. Good location roughly in the middle of the beach. ❷

Southern Palms ☎ 072/888 5384, ⓦ www.south-ernpalms.com.ph. At the northern end of the beach strip. Clean and comfortable double rooms, plus a bar where there's a good menu of European food. There's a large family room with a kitchen, but *Southern Palms* has its own nightclub and a generally male clientele. Budget rooms a good value for a brief stopover. ❸

San Juan

SAN JUAN, 7km north of San Fernando, is superior to Bauang in every respect. The main beach is north of the little town with its Spanish Baroque church and is a dramatic crescent with big breakers that roll in from the South China Sea. There are a handful of resorts along the sand that are reasonably priced, well managed and quiet. Surfing has become popular here and many of the resorts have surfboards to rent and offer tuition.

Buses from Manila and San Fernando bound for Loaog, Vigan or Abra pass through San Juan; ask the driver to let you off at one of the resorts, which are all signposted along the road. As well as buses, you can catch a jeepney in San Fernando, marked for Bacnotan, from the junction of P. Burgos Street and Quezon Avenue (jeepneys leaving here marked for Lingsat do not go to San Juan). If you are returning to Manila from San Juan either take a jeepney into San Fernando and catch a bus from there, or just stand on the main road outside your resort and flag one down.

Accommodation

Resorts in San Juan do not have nightclubs and are all good for families, right on the beach and with their own restaurants offering very affordable meals.

La Union Surf Resort ☎ 072/242 4544. First resort on your left as you leave San Juan. Basic rooms with fan and cold showers, but a good place to rent surfboards and mingle with the surf crowd. ❶
Puerto de San Juan Resort Hotel ☎ 072/242 2330, ⓦ www.puertodesanjuan.com. Oversized development halfway along the main beach with a range of a/c rooms, all with private bathrooms and hot water, and a large children's playground in front. The big restaurant here has an extensive menu of Chinese, European and Filipino dishes. ❹
Scenic View Tourist Inn ☎ 072/242 2906. A short walk north from *Las Villas*. Three-storey concrete building with a marbled lobby, swimming pool and choice of average a/c rooms. ❷

Sebay Surf Resort & Entertainment Centre ☎ 072/888 4075, ⓦ www.sebay.cjb.net. One of the first resorts as you reach the beach coming from San Fernando with ten spacious native-style a/c rooms, all with cable TV and private shower, although hot water is only available on request. There's a restaurant and bar and surfboards for rent. ❷
🏃 **Sunset German Beach Resort** ☎ 072/888 4719 or 0917/921 2420, ⓦ www.sunsetgermanbeachresort.com. Next to *Scenic View Tourist Inn* and the most northerly of the resorts on the beach. Rooms are spotless, the food in the cosy restaurant is consistently good and there are surfboards and body boards for rent. The choice of rooms includes fan doubles, a/c doubles and dorm beds (P100). ❷

Vigan and around

About 135km north of San Fernando in La Union lies the old Spanish town of **VIGAN**, an essential stop on any swing through the northern provinces. It has become a bit of a cliché to describe Vigan as a living museum, but the town does really justify the description. Vigan is on the UNESCO **World Heritage list** for two reasons: first because it represents a unique fusion of Asian building design and construction with European colonial architecture and planning; and secondly because it is one of the few reasonably intact European trading towns in Southeast Asia.

One of the oldest towns in the Philippines, Vigan lies on the western bank of the Mestizo River and in Spanish times was an important political, military, cultural and religious centre called Nueva Segovia. In the old town, with Plaza Salcedo and Plaza Burgos on the northern edge and Liberation Boulevard to the south, there are streets and pavements of cobble stones and some of the finest old Spanish **colonial architecture** in the country, including some impressive homes that once belonged to friars, merchants and officials. Various governmental and non-governmental organizations have joined forces to preserve the old buildings; many are still lived in, others are used as curio shops, and a few have been converted into museums. Vigan's time-capsule ambience is aided by the decision to close some of the streets to traffic and allow only pedestrians and *calesas* – a ride in one of these makes for a romantic way to tour the town.

Some history

In pre-colonial times, long before Spanish galleons arrived, **Chinese** junks came to Vigan and turned it into a major trading port. They arrived with silk and porcelain, and returned with gold, beeswax and mountain products brought down by natives from the Cordillera. Stories of Vigan's riches spread and before long immigrants from China arrived to settle and trade here, intermarrying with locals and beginning the multicultural bloodline that Biguenos – the people of Vigan – are known for.

The **Spanish** arrived in 1572, General Guido de Lavezares reporting to King Philip that he had sent Captain Juan de Salcedo with seventy or eighty soldiers ashore near the mouth of a river called Bigan. Salcedo conquered Vigan and founded Villa Fernandina de Vigan in honour of King Philip's son, Prince Ferdinand, who died at the age of 4. From Vigan, Salcedo rounded the tip of Luzon and proceeded to pacify Camarines, Albay and Catanduanes. As a reward for his services to the king, Salcedo was awarded the old province of Ylocos, which was then composed of Ilocos Norte, Ilocos Sur, Abra, La Union and some parts of what is now Mountain Province.

In January 1574, Salcedo returned to Vigan, bringing with him **Augustinian missionaries** to begin the important business of evangelization. Salcedo himself set about the task of creating a township his king would be proud of, with grand plazas, municipal buildings and mansions for the governing classes. From Vigan he would control and rule over the surrounding country, collecting tribute from the people and accumulating great wealth on account of the gold trade.

An outbreak of plague caused Vigan temporarily to become something of a hardship posting for the Spanish, but by the middle of the eighteenth century it had risen to become a centre of religious, commercial and social activities. The Chinese settled in a quarter known as **Pariancillo**, from where they exported indigo, lime, jars, tobacco and a type of woven cloth called *abel* to Europe, China, Borneo and Malaysia. Vigan flourished, and the Spanish liked what they saw, continuing to collect tribute and bring the *naturales* to heel in the name of King and God.

One of the potentially incendiary results of Spanish political domination of Vigan was the rise of a *mestizo* masterclass, whose wealth and stature began to cause resentment among landless natives. In 1763 things came to a head when revolutionary **Diego Silang** and his men assaulted and captured Vigan, proclaiming it capital of a free Ilocos. When Silang was cravenly assassinated by two traitors in the pay of the Spanish, his wife, Maria Josefa Gabriela Silang, assumed leadership of the uprising. She was captured and, on September 20, 1763, publicly hanged in the town square.

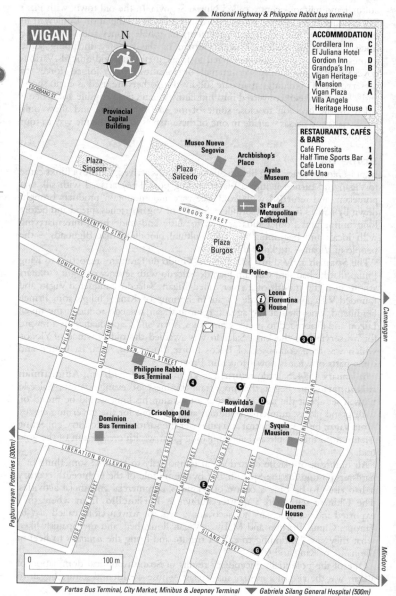

VIGAN

National Highway & Philippine Rabbit bus terminal

N

ACCOMMODATION
Cordillera Inn — C
El Juliana Hotel — F
Gordion Inn — D
Grandpa's Inn — B
Vigan Heritage Mansion — E
Vigan Plaza — A
Villa Angela Heritage House — G

RESTAURANTS, CAFÉS & BARS
Café Floresita — 1
Half Time Sports Bar — 4
Café Leona — 2
Café Una — 3

ESCRIBANO ST

Provincial Capital Building

Plaza Singson

Museo Nueva Segovia

Plaza Salcedo

Archbishop's Place

Ayala Museum

BURGOS STREET

St Paul's Metropolitan Cathedral

FLORENTINO STREET

Plaza Burgos

A 1

BONIFACIO STREET

Police

DEL PILAR STREET

OLEZON AVENUE

Leona Florentina House

i 2

3 B

GEN. LUNA STREET

Philippine Rabbit Bus Terminal

4

C

Rowilda's Hand Loom

D

Dominion Bus Terminal

Crisologo Old House

Syquia Mausion

QUIRINO BOULEVARD

LIBERATION BOULEVARD

JOSE SINGSON STREET

GOVERNOR A. REYES STREET

PLARIDEL STREET

MENA CRISOLOGO STREET

V. DELOS REYES STREET

E

Quema House

SILANG STREET

F

G

0   100 m

Pagburnayan Potteries (300m)

Camanggan

Mindoro

Partas Bus Terminal, City Market, Minibus & Jeepney Terminal

Gabriela Silang General Hospital (500m)

Vigan prospered throughout the nineteenth century, but like Manila suffered the disastrous economic consequences of two World Wars. Unlike Manila, Vigan at least remained structurally relatively unscathed by World War II, the main reason why much of the architecture remains intact today. One of the greatest problems for preservers of Vigan's fine old buildings is the combination of the destructive humidity and the fact that they're primarily built of wood. A number of ancestral houses in the Mestizo district were razed in 1952, 1968 and 1971, never to be replaced. Throughout the twentieth century, many owners left Vigan in favour of a new life in Manila, allowing their ancestral homes to fall into partial ruin, though the town's 1999 inclusion on the World Heritage Site list at least guarantees it some level of protection and funding.

Arrival and information

The Philippine Rabbit **bus terminal** is on the National Highway, on the northern edge of town, a fifteen-minute walk or short tricycle ride from the centre and most hotels. Partas buses arrive at the Partas terminal near the market at the southern end of town, while there's a third terminal, for Dominion buses arriving from Laoag and San Fernando, at the southern end of Quezon Avenue, the main street running south to north.

Vigan is one of the easier Philippine towns to navigate because its streets follow a fairly regular grid pattern. Mena Crisologo Street runs south from Plaza Burgos and is lined with quaint old antique shops and cafés. Running parallel to it is the main thoroughfare, Governor A. Reyes Street. The **tourist office** (Mon–Sat 8am–5pm; ☎077/732 5705) is in Leona Florentina House, near *Café Leona* in Plaza Burgos. You can also get information at the nearby Provincial Capitol Building. There are many **banks**, including branches of Allied Bank, Metro Bank, BPI, Far East Bank and PCI Bank, all close to each other on Quezon Avenue. The **post office** is at the junction of Governor A. Reyes and Bonifacio streets. Also on Governor A. Reyes Street is Powernet, with **Internet** access for P50 an hour. Another option is Click Internet on V. De los Reyes Street, east of Plaza Burgos. Vigan's main **hospital** is the Gabriela Silang General Hospital (☎077/722 2722) on Quirino Boulevard and the **police station** is at the eastern end of Florentino Street.

Accommodation

For such a well-trumpeted tourist destination, most of the **accommodation** in Vigan is what the Department of Tourism refers to as "tourist style", a euphemism for careworn and dusty. Don't have high expectations and you won't be disappointed. At least all the hotels are conveniently situated for the old town and the major attractions.

Cordillera Inn Crisologo St ☎077/722 2727. Ordinary doubles with fan and shared bath or slightly more comfortable doubles with a/c and cramped shower. A hefty breakfast is included – a choice of native sausage, fried beef (tapa) or fish. ❶

El Juliana Hotel Quirino Blvd corner Liberation Blvd ☎077/722 2994. Small a/c or fan rooms come with a toilet and shower. There's a swimming pool, also open to the public. ❷

Gordion Inn 15 Salcedo St ☎077/722 2526. Brightly coloured bed-and-breakfast style place with average a/c rooms that are a little past their best. Redeeming features include the airy brick-walled restaurant, which offers some good vegetarian dishes and serves an excellent breakfast that's included in the price of the room. ❷

Grandpa's Inn 1 Bonifacio St ☎077/722 2118. Rather tired old place on the eastern edge of Bonifacio Street near the river. It's full of curios and has fan singles and doubles with a/c and baths. The location is good and breakfast is included in the price. A good one-night-only budget option. ❶

Vigan Heritage Mansion Liberation Blvd corner Crisologo St ☎077/722 6495, ⓦwww.viganheritage.com. This old-world charm in a restored nineteenth-century mansion belongs to the influential local Singson family (the head of the family is Luis "Chavit" Singson, the local governor who precipitated former president Joseph Estrada's downfall by accusing him of corruption). The a/c rooms are small but atmospheric and there are some beautiful communal areas furnished in the Spanish style, as well as a restaurant specializing in Vigan cuisine. There's a dorm for ten people for P5500, but you can't just have a single bed here; you'll need to find nine others to share with. ⑥

Vigan Plaza Plaza Burgos ☎077/722 8552. Charming mid-range option in an excellent location close to the cathedral and Plaza Burgos. Windows are made of *capiz* shell, floors are hardwood and there's a pretty inner courtyard with a fountain. Rooms are fresh and comfortable, with spotless linen and clean showers. ④

Villa Angela Heritage House 26 Quirino Blvd, a 20-minute walk south from Plaza Burgos. ☎077/722 2914, ⓦwww.villangela.com. The most colonial of all the colonial hotels, this is a beautiful old museum of a place and the billet of choice if you want to wallow in history and don't mind paying a little extra for the privilege. You can ask to be given the room Tom Cruise slept in: he stayed here for a few weeks when *Born on the Fourth of July* was being filmed on the sand dunes near Laoag. Even the dormitory (P150) has Spanish-style wooden bunkbeds and billowing mosquito nets and curtains. ⑥

The City

Most of Vigan's attractions are within reasonable walking distance of one another, although it's easy enough to take a tricycle or a *calesa*, both costing P5 per person. A good way to see all the sights is to start at Plaza Burgos in the north and wander south through the old town. It's worth timing your visit to town to coincide with one of its festivals. The biggest is the **Vigan Town Fiesta**, a week-long celebration consisting of carnivals, parades, musical extravaganzas, beauty and popularity contests and nightly cultural shows. It culminates on January 25 with the celebration of the conversion of St Paul the Apostle, the town's patron saint. The **Viva Vigan Festival of Arts**, held during the first week of May, is a contemporary festival designed to draw attention to Vigan's heritage and the need for conservation. The festival was founded by the Save Vigan Ancestral Homes Association, a non-government organization that has done some great work saving old houses from the wrecking ball or from vulgar modernization by developers. The festival includes a *calesa* parade, religious rituals, a bamboo band playing in front of the Archbishop's Palace, a street-dancing competition in Plaza Burgos and a party in Crisologo Street sponsored by San Miguel Beer. **Holy Week** (before Easter) is also a special time in Vigan, with candlelit processions through the old streets and a *visita iglesia* that sees devotees doing the rounds of churches and cathedrals.

St Paul's Metropolitan Cathedral, the Archbishop's Palace and Museo Nueva Segovia

Built by the Augustinians between 1890 and 1900, **St Paul's Metropolitan Cathedral** (daily 6am–9pm) lacks the organic grandeur of other northern cathedrals such as Paoay, but because of its white walls and frills is nevertheless an attractive sight, like something from a Mexican fairy tale. St Paul's, which stands between Plaza Burgos and Plaza Salcedo on the city's northern edge, is an "earthquake Baroque" church, with thick ramparts and a belfry built 15m away so it stood a chance of surviving if the church itself collapsed. Given Vigan's history, it's not surprising that there's some Chinese influence in the church: note the Fu dogs carved into the facade and the Chinese brass Communion handrails.

Next to the cathedral is the **Archbishop's Palace** (*Arzobizpado*), completed in 1783 and still the official residence of the Archbishop of Nueva Segovia. The only surviving eighteenth-century *arzobizpado* in the country, the palace served as General Emilio Aguinaldo's headquarters in 1898 and was commandeered by the invading American forces under Colonel James Parker in 1899. Inside is the **Museo Nueva Segovia** (Mon–Fri 8.30am–noon & 2–4pm; P15), which showcases ecclesiastical artefacts, antique portraits of bishops and religious paraphernalia from all over Ilcos Sur. The throne-room is impressive, reflecting the power and wealth enjoyed by Spanish-era archbishops. For serious history buffs the palace also contains the archdiocesan archives, documenting life in Ilocus Sur and neighbouring provinces right back to the beginning of Spanish occupation.

Ayala Museum

On the eastern edge of Plaza Burgos, the **Ayala Museum** (Mon–Fri 8.30–11am & 1.30–4.30pm; P10) is in a captivating old colonial house that was once home to one of the town's most famous residents, Padre José Burgos, whose martyrdom in 1872 galvanized the revolutionary movement. It contains Burgos memorabilia including much of his original furniture, his clothes and his diaries, as well as non-Burgos exhibits including fourteen paintings by the artist Villanueva, depicting the violent 1807 Basi Revolt, prompted by a Spanish effort to control the production of *basi* (sugar-cane wine). It also houses a small ethnological collection, period jewellery, costumes and dioramas depicting significant events in the province's history. Next to the museum you can see the remains of the provincial **jail**, which was built in 1657 and where several high-profile dissenters were detained during American rule including Mena Crisologo, Enrique Quema and Estanislao Reyes. Former President Elpidio Quirino was born here in 1890 – his father was warden.

The old town

Vigan's **old town**, once a concentration of *taipans* and *mestizos* who made their fortunes from indigo dye, *abel* fabric, gold and tobacco, is where most of the beautiful ancestral houses are located. The old town area, also known as the Mestizo

△ Vigan street

District and Kasanglayan (where the Chinese live) runs roughly from Plaza Burgos in the north to **Liberation Boulevard** in the south, with most of the interesting architecture along elegant old Crisologo Street, which has been given a makeover and is now closed to traffic, something of a pleasant rarity in the tricycle- and jeepney-plagued Philippines. The houses are made of brick and plaster, with red-tiled roofs, grand staircases and wide *narra* floorboards. Architecturally, the houses are fundamentally Chinese or Mexican, influenced either by the immigrant architects from China's eastern seaboard who prepared the plans, or by ideas picked up by the Spanish in their Mexican colony. But they have flourishes such as sliding *capiz*-shell windows and *ventanillas* (ventilated walls) added by local artisans who took the blueprint and modified it for the earthquake-prone tropics.

There are three ancestral homes open to the public, both offering an intimate view of *ilustrado* life in the exotic east at the turn of the nineteenth and twentieth centuries. The **Crisologo Old House** (daily 10am–5pm; P15) is in Plaridel Street, which runs parallel to Crisologo Street, and houses a small museum and the offices of the Vigan Heritage Commission, where you can get more information about the ancestral houses. **Syquia Mansion** on Quirino Boulevard (Tues–Sat 8.30–11am & 1.30–4.30pm; P10) is the ancestral home of former President Elpidio Quirino, an eye-catching red-brick colonial house that has been restored and furnished in nineteenth-century style and contains a strange collection of presidential memorabilia such as Quirino's hats, neckties and coats. **Quema House** (daily 9am–5pm; P15) is in the southeast of town at the junctions of Liberation Boulevard and Quirino Boulevard and is chock-full of beautiful old polished wood furniture, curios and oil paintings. The *sala* (living area) is especially evocative of the period, with delicate old rocking chairs, marble-topped tables and *capiz* shutters.

Eating, drinking and nightlife

The *Half Time Sports Bar* in A. Reyes Street is one of the few relatively chic places in Vigan, where **nightlife** is otherwise pretty limited and quiet. The food is an average mix of sandwiches and burgers, but the staff are friendly and the beer's cheap. Many of the tables are outdoors, and it's pleasant to sit around in the evening and watch the punters come and go. At *Café Leona,* just south of Plaza Burgos, you can order native **Ilocano dishes**, all for less than P150; try the Special Vigan Sinanglaw, a dish of pork entrails sautéed with ginger, vinegar, fish sauce, onion and pepper. At the pleasant old-world *Café Floresita* near the Ancieto Mansion ancestral home, opposite Plaza Burgos, native *longganisa* (sausage) features in many dishes. Another laidback café is *Café Una* near *Grandpa's Inn*, which serves native dishes with a modern touch such as a tangy *longganisa* pasta.

Another of Vigan's specialities is **empanada**, a type of tortilla stuffed with pork and vegetables that you can pick up for a few pesos from one of the many street stalls around Plaza Burgos. **Street food** in Vigan is affordable and tasty. Try the *pipian*, a soupy combination of pork and chicken cooked with ginger and roasted rice. For **breakfast**, do what the locals do and head out bright and early to the Vigan Slaughterhouse near the barangay of Mindoro, where a bowl of exceptionally fresh *liempo* (beef, innards and onions in broth) costs P10. For a snack, you'll find street vendors selling steaming hot freshly roasted peanuts mixed with garlic.

Shopping

Souvenir-hunters after something more than the usual bulk-produced tourist knick-knacks should head for Rowilda's Hand Loom, on Crisologo Street near the *Cordillera Inn*, which offers the kind of old-style **textiles** that used to be

Philippine Rabbit **buses** leave every hour from the main terminal on the National Highway in Vigan for destinations including Manila and Laoag. Dominion buses leave regularly throughout the day from the terminal at the junction of Quezon Boulevard and Liberation Boulevard for Laoag and San Fernando, with a limited number going all the way to Manila. Florida buses go north to Pagudpud and Tuguegarao (2 daily; 6am & 4pm), leaving from the Caltex Bantay bus terminal, a P10 tricycle ride south from the city centre. From the minibus and jeepney terminal behind the city market on the southern edge of the city at the end of José Singson Street, you can catch air-conditioned **minibuses** north to Laoag. Near the mini-bus and jeepney terminal is a Partas bus terminal for buses north and south along the coastal road.

traded during colonial times. A number of Vigan's small barangays also specialize in textile production. In Mindoro, to the south near the disused airport, you can buy blankets called **binakol**, which have distinctive geometric patterns, while in Camanggaan, to the east, women use old looms to make bedsheets, table mats and runners. Both places can be reached in fifteen minutes by tricycle. Vigan is also known for its **pottery**. The massive wood-fired kilns at the Pagburnayan Potteries in Rizal Street, at the junction with Liberation Boulevard, produce huge jars, known as *burnay*, used by northerners for storing everything from vinegar to fish paste. *Carabao* are used to squash the clay under hoof.

Around Vigan

The coastal road north of Vigan to Laoag is sealed all the way and the journey time between the two towns is about two hours. The road passes through some interesting fishing communities, including Sinait and Badoc, both of which have attractions you may want to break your journey to explore. There's no accommodation in either place, but you can continue your journey the same day because buses on this route are frequent. **SINAIT** is the site of **Sinait Church**, which contains the enshrined image of a Black Nazarene that was found floating in a casket along the coast of Sinait in the seventeenth century. Like many such images it is said to have miraculous properties, and hundreds of devotees flock to pay homage to it every Easter in the belief it will grant their wishes.

About thirty minutes north of Sinait, **BADOC** was the birthplace of the Filipino painter Juan Luna. His reconstructed house, known as the **Juan Luna Historical Landmark** (daily 10am–4pm; donation), stands in a side street close to the seventeenth-century Virgen Milagrosa de Badoc church. The house contains some of his belongings, including clothes and notebooks, as well as some of his early paintings. About a kilometre off the coast of Badoc lies **Badoc Island**, which is gaining a reputation for good surfing and can be reached by hiring a banca from the little wharf in Badoc. It's a marvellous little tropical hideaway, off the beaten track and not known to many visitors. The only accommodation on the island is *Badoc Island Surf Resort* (**●**), which is no more than a few flimsy cottages with a restaurant serving basic food such as sardines and rice.

Laoag and around

In 1818, the province of Ilocos was divided into two and the city of **LAOAG** ("la-wag"), two hours north of Vigan by road, became the capital of Ilocos

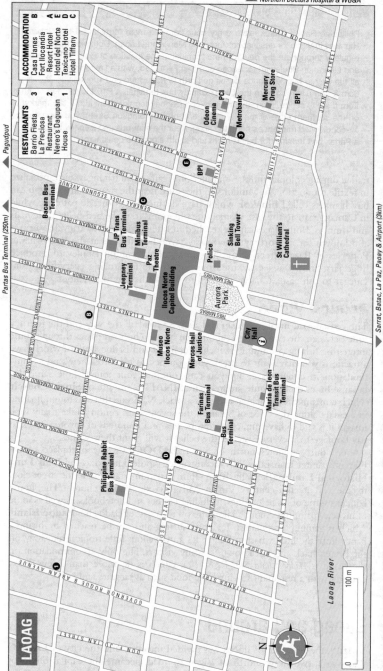

LAOAG

▲ Northern Doctors Hospital & WG&A

ACCOMMODATION
Casa Llanes — B
Fort Ilocandia
Resort Hotel — A
Hotel del Norte — E
Texicano Hotel — D
Hotel Tiffany — C

RESTAURANTS
Barrio Fiesta — 3
La Preciosa
Restaurant — 2
Nereo's Dagupan
House — 1

Pagudpud ◄

Partas Bus Terminal (250m) ◄

◄ Sarrat, Batac, La Paz, Paoay & Airport (3km)

Discolandia (500m), La Paz & A ◄

PCI

Odeon
Cinema

Metrobank

Mercury
Drug Store

BPI

BPI

Bacara Bus
Terminal

JP Trans
Bus Terminal

Minibus
Terminal

Paz
Theatre

Jeepney
Terminal

Ilocos Norte
Capitol Building

Police

Sinking
Bell Tower

St William's
Cathedral

Aurora Park

Museo
Ilocos Norte

Marcos Hall
of Justice

City
Hall

Fariñas
Bus Terminal

Bus
Terminal

Maria de leon
Transit Bus Terminal

Philippine Rabbit
Bus Terminal

Laoag River

N

100 m

0

Norte. Laoag itself is an easygoing city. There are only a handful of things to do and see, but it makes an excellent base for exploring the beautiful coast at nearby **La Paz**, heading north to **Pagudpud**, or touring **Marcos country**. Ilocos Norte is still strongly associated in Filipino minds with former President Ferdinand Marcos. This was very much his patch, and his son Bong-Bong and daughter Imee, both of whom have entered politics, are still popular in these parts: Bong-Bong is governor of Ilocos Norte and Imee is its congresswoman. Many sights around Laoag are associated with the late dictator, who was born south of Laoag in **Sarrat**, while the family seat was 15km southeast of the city in **Batac**, where Marcos lies in a refrigerated glass sarcophagus.

In the city, the main sights are the **Sinking Bell Tower** and **St William's Cathedral**, both close to Aurora Park. The bell tower was built by Augustinian friars with a door big enough for a man on horseback to pass through. The tower has sunk so much that today you can only get through the door by stooping. **St William's Cathedral**, one of the biggest in the Philippines, was built in honour of Laoag's patron saint, William the Hermit. It was originally constructed in 1612, but damaged by typhoon in 1640, earthquake in 1706 and fire in 1843. The structure that stands today has the original foundations, but the rest was added in 1880. The **Marcos Hall of Justice** (daily 9am–4pm; free), the square white building on the west side of Aurora Park, was where a young Ferdinand Marcos was detained in 1939 after being accused of the murder of one of his father's political opponents. Marcos wanted to graduate in law and used his time in detention wisely, swotting for the bar examination and preparing his own defence against a murder charge. In court he wowed the judge with his knowledge of the law and was duly acquitted. He also came top in the bar examinations. Above the room where Marcos was detained hangs a sign that says "Crossroads for a President". The **Ilocos Norte Museum** (Tues–Sat, 9am–noon & 1–4pm; P20) is the best place for a quick but reasonably comprehensive overview of the province's history and culture. Close to the main plaza, it's housed in a restored Spanish-era tobacco warehouse and is nicknamed *Gameng*, from the Ilocano word meaning treasure. Exhibits include vintage costumes, antiques from ancestral houses, farming equipment, Spanish and tribal artefacts.

Practicalities

Laoag has an airport, but at the time of writing it was not served by any scheduled flights from anywhere within the Philippines. The only planes arriving here are charter flights carrying tourists – almost always on gambling holidays to the *Fort Ilocandia Resort Hotel* – from China and Taiwan. Philippine Rabbit, Partas and Farinas **buses** all make the long trip north from Manila, each arriving at a different terminal. The Philippine Rabbit terminal is at the west end of General Antonio Luna Street, the Farinas terminal is in E. Bonifacio Avenue a short walk from Aurora Park, and Partas is on the northern edge of the city in Paco Roman Street. From all these terminals you can easily walk to the city centre or hop on a tricycle.

Laoag City **Tourism Council** (☏077/772 0001) is in the City Hall of Laoag, on the south side of Aurora Park in the city centre, as is the Department of Tourism Information and Assistance Office (☏077/772 0467). There are plenty of banks, convenience stores and pharmacies at the eastern end of Rizal Avenue around the Odeon Cinema. The Philippine National Police Station is on the east side of Aurora Park.

Accommodation, eating and drinking

Laoag isn't a major tourist destination and recommended **hotels** are few and far between, but the *Hotel Tiffany* (☎077/770 3550; ❶), on General Fidel Segundo Avenue, has spacious, candy-coloured rooms, all with private shower. The *Texicano Hotel* (☎077/722 0290; ❷), on Rizal Avenue, has standard singles and double rooms with air-conditioning and cable TV; hotel facilities are basic, but all rooms have a private shower. *Casa Llanes* (☎077/722 0456; ❷), on Governor Primo Lazaro Avenue, is a reasonable budget option in a good location, offering clean, simple singles, doubles and family rooms, all with private showers. *Hotel del Norte* (☎077/722 1697; ❸), on Fonacier Street at the eastern end of town, has affordable singles, doubles and family rooms and a coffee shop serving simple snacks and meals. The most upmarket and ostentatious hotel in the area, perhaps in the country, is *Fort Ilocandia Resort Hotel* (☎077/772 116; ❽) on the seafront in the barangay of Calayab, 3km south of the airport. It was built in 1973 and hastily completed for the wedding reception of Ferdinand and Imelda Marcos's youngest daughter, Irene. Amenities include a government-run casino, a golf course and half a dozen restaurants.

For wholesome Filipino **food**, *Barrio Fiesta* on Manuel Nolasco Street is good value. *La Preciosa Restaurant* on Rizal Avenue opposite the *Texicano Hotel* and *Nereo's Dagupan House* on Governor Primo Lazaro Avenue both specialize in Ilocano dishes such as *pinakbet* (vegetables sautéed in fish paste) and *kare-kare,* and neither costs more than P150 per person, including a couple of San Miguels. Most of Laoag's fast-food restaurants, including *Jollibee* and *Smokey's,* are one block to the east of Aurora Park in Manuel Nolasco Avenue.

For the best of Laoag's **nightlife**, head out to *Discolandia,* a lively bar and club area to the west of the city, beyond the Philippine Rabbit bus terminal, where there are a dozen or more hangouts of varying quality, including late-night clubs such as *Discovery* and *Warehouse,* and more casual bistro-bars such as *Saigon, Café Alfier's* and *Mountainside.*

Batac

In the pretty town of **BATAC**, about 15km south of Laoag, is the **Marcos Mansion** (Mon–Sat 9am–4pm; P25), known as *Balay Ti Ili,* a fascinating nineteenth-century house full of the dictator's belongings. This is where Marcos spent his childhood, before moving to Manila to take up law. Among the items on display are photographs, handwritten speeches and medals. The museum has guides available for tours at no extra charge, although their pro-Marcos sympathies tend to colour their commentary. You can see Marcos's refrigerated corpse in the nearby **mausoleum** (although many believe it's nothing more than a wax model). On a number of occasions the utility company has threatened to cut off the electricity that keeps the corpse cold, alleging that Imelda has not paid the bill. She wants to bury him in the *Libingan ng mga Bayani* (Heroes' Cemetery) in Manila, a proposal that has not found favour with the present government.

From Laoag you can catch a jeepney or minibus to Batac from the minibus terminal behind Paz Theater off General Antonio Luna Street.

Paoay Church and Paoay Lake

A trip to Batac can be combined with a visit to **Paoay Church** and lake, a few kilometres southwest of Batac and served by regular jeepneys from both there and Laoag. Paoay Church, which took ninety years to build, starting in 1804, is included on the World Heritage list. It is perhaps the best-known "earthquake Baroque" church in the Philippines, with 26 immense side buttresses designed to keep it standing. It's an impressive sight, built of thick coral blocks sealed with limestone mortar that was thickened with sugar-cane juice. Nearby is a bell tower dating from 1793.

A couple of kilometres north of the church lies placid **Paoay Lake**, with a circumference of three kilometres. The lake was recently declared a national park in an effort to stop it from being overfished. A trail around the edge makes for a pleasant walk, taking you through lakeside barrios where residents depend on wooden fishtraps in the lake for their main source of food, *tilapia*. Overlooking the lake is the **Malacañang of the North** (Tues–Sun 9am–4pm; P20), an opulent mansion where Marcos stayed during presidential holidays in his home province, set on a vast estate of gentle lawns, with its own golf course (Marcos was an avid golfer). The mansion has seven bedrooms, two living rooms, several studies, kitchens on both floors and a clinic that Marcos made frequent use of when he became ill in later life. You can still see his bed and the oxygen tank and mask next to it. In his main bedroom you can have your photograph taken sitting in his red leather armchair, with a seal on the armrests that says "President of the Republic of the Philippines". Next door is Imelda's boudoir, with its walk-in closets, floor-to-ceiling mirrors and gigantic perfume bottles. You can reach Paoay Lake and the mansion either through Batac or by jeepney from Laoag.

Sarrat

Thirty minutes due east of Laoag by jeepney or FX is the sleepy and pretty village of **SARRAT**, site of one of the area's most intriguing little tourist attractions: the Marcos birthplace and boyhood home, now a **museum** (Tues–Sat 10am–4pm; P15). Marcos was born in this modest old brick and wood house on September 11, 1917. It now houses a number of hagiographic displays that chart Marcos's "brilliant" law career and his ascent to the presidency. Many of his law books are here, together with hand-written speeches, clothes and medals of contested authenticity that he claimed to have won during the war.

A few doors away, in a house that no longer stands, Marcos's lifelong friend, Fabian Ver, was born. Ver became Marcos's most trusted general and is said to have masterminded the assassination of Ninoy Aquino. Sarrat's pretty **Santa Monica Church** was the venue in 1980 for the wedding of Marcos's youngest daughter Irene in a ceremony that cost US$10.3 million. Preparations for the wedding involved thousands of men **remodelling Sarrat** and 3500 contracted employees renovating the 200-year-old church. Large parts of the town were reconstructed, with houses torn down and rebuilt in the old Spanish colonial style. Specially designed carriages were imported from Austria, horses from

Morocco and fresh flowers from Hawaii. Thousands of fake flowers were pinned on those trees that had the audacity not to be in bloom. Dresses for Irene, mum Imelda and sister Imee were designed in Italy and cost US$300,000.

La Paz

La Paz, the beach to the west of Laoag – about fifteen minutes west of the city by tricycle or jeepney – is a sight to behold. More like desert than beach, it measures almost one kilometre across at some points and stretches as far as you can see, fringed by huge sand dunes, some like small hills. This dramatic area of coast, known locally as *Bantay Bimmaboy*, a reference to the pig-like shape of some of the dunes, has become a favourite among Manila film crews who drive north to film love scenes for trashy Tagalog movies in the surf. *Mad Max* and *Born on the Fourth of July* also had segments shot here. There's no accommodation in the area (apart from the expensive *Fort Ilocandia Resort Hotel*; see p.450) and not much shade, so make sure you take drinks, snacks and plenty of sunblock.

Pagudpud and around

From Laoag it's only another couple of hours by bus to **PAGUDPUD** ("Pah-good-pud"), a typical provincial small town with a plaza and a church. The town has little to recommend it to visitors, but it provides access to wonderfully picturesque **Saud Beach**, a few kilometres down a narrow road to the north of town, a beautiful long arch of white sand backed by palm trees. It has also been the backdrop for many a bodice-buster movie, which is how it first came to the attention of Filipino travellers.

The Pagudpud area is deservedly becoming known as a destination that has all the beauty of Boracay, but without the tourists and the nightlife. It's not a place for ravers: just get yourself a cottage and relax for a few days. Saud is the best-known beach, but it's not the only one in the area. A short trip to the west by jeepney or tricycle is **Maira-ira Beach**, if anything better than Saud, hemmed in by mountains and with fine, white sand. There's no accommodation here and few visitors, so whatever the time of day you can almost guarantee having it to yourself. On the eastern side of town, about half an hour from Saud, is the **Blue Lagoon**. The setting here is straight from Robinson Crusoe with a shallow lagoon of dazzling water lapping a sugary crescent of sand. Also east of Pagudpud and accessible by tricycle is the beach at **Ayoyo**. It's not sandy, but it's still beautiful and it rarely sees local visitors, never mind foreign tourists – there's nothing here except palm trees and sea. Bring food and water if you plan on hanging around.

Thirty minutes west of Pagudpud by road is the **Cape Bojeador Lighthouse** (free) at **Burgos**, which makes an excellent half-day trip. From the top of the lighthouse, which was built in 1892 and is the tallest in the country, there are unobstructed views of the coastline and across the South China Sea to the horizon. The lighthouse is still in use and its keeper, Mang Ben – Uncle Ben – will be happy to give you a tour. Ask him to tell you about the ghosts that are said to haunt the place. To get to Burgos from Pagudpud take a jeepney from the main road. Once in Burgos itself, you can take a tricycle to the lighthouse.

Practicalities

The town has no tourist office, but you can get resort and transport details at the Bayan ng Pagudpud (town hall), the little white building on the plaza.

There's a PLDT office next door for long-distance telephone calls and a couple of banks on Rizal Avenue, although neither changes money. **Buses** from all directions arrive on the main road in Pagudpud town, from where plenty of tricycles can take you the rest of the way to Saud Beach.

Accommodation and eating

Resorts on Saud Beach are a little pricier than similar resorts elsewhere, simply because there are so few of them that there's little competition. All the following **resorts** are near the centre of Saud Beach, close to the narrow road leading from Pagudpud town. The best and most expensive of them is *Saud Beach Resort* (☎077/764 1005; ❼). Amenities include a karaoke bar, outdoor sports, a restaurant and boats for rent; rooms are modern and comfortable with air-conditioning and private showers, and there's good food in the restaurant, including fresh fish every day and big Filipino-style breakfasts. *Arinaya White Resort* (☎077/764 1079; ❺) has a range of ordinary doubles and family rooms set back from the beach in a neat garden. At their little wooden restaurant they grill the catch of the day, as long as you give advance notice. *Villa del Mar* (☎077/764 1084; ❺) has less well-maintained doubles, but is worth considering if you're on a budget because you can rent a two-man tent (P700) and camp in the garden. *Evangeline Beach Resort* (☎077/764 1009; ❺) is a friendly family-run place with a choice of five very comfortable concrete cottages and double rooms, owned by the hospitable Romero family. The pleasant restaurant, with terrific views of the sea, serves breakfast (two eggs with garlic rice and spicy native sausage), lunch and dinner. The fresh squid is good, grilled over hot coals and dipped in barbecue sauce.

Batanes

Almost 100km off the northern coast of Luzon, **BATANES** is the smallest, most isolated province in the country: the land that time forgot. There are no cinemas, hotels, supermarkets or fast-food restaurants and hardly any tourists. Cable television arrived a few years ago, causing great excitement, but on some of the ten small islands that make up Batanes electricity is still limited to three or four hours a day. Even on the main island of Batan, the electricity is switched off from midnight until 6am.

This is a memorable place: the scenery is otherworldly, and the people have a prelapsarian grace that comes from a lack of contact with outsiders and their relative contentment with a life lived close to nature. Children get up and take the cows to pasture in the morning before school, *carabaos* are used to plough fields of garlic and yams, and in the evening most people are asleep soon after sundown. High entertainment might consist of a few drinks on the porch or a barbecue on the beach. At times, with their stone cottages and restless seas, the islands are more reminiscent of the Scottish Highlands than the sunny Philippines. The people are different, the language is different, even the weather is different. The coolest months (Dec–Feb) can get chilly with temperatures as low as 7°C, while the hottest months (April–June) are searing.

Batanes is idyllic, but it would be wrong to portray it as a tropical utopia. The realities of life this far away from the rest of the world can sometimes be harsh. Infant mortality is high because of poor access to elementary health care, and petrol and provisions are brought in by ship, which means they cost more. If the seas are rough and the ship can't make it, prices rise further as residents begin to hoard. In the **monsoon** season, when typhoons roar in from the east, boredom can set in. Locals joke that the cargo ship brings 50,000 sacks of rice but 60,000 crates of gin. In fact, this is not such a joke. A government report noted: "Gin has become an almost integral part of an adult's life . . . the primary form of entertainment and vehicle for social interaction." When the wind is howling and the rain covers everything, there isn't much to do except pour yourself a drink and sit it out.

The most economically important islands in the Batanes group are **Batan** – the location of the capital **Basco** – **Sabtang** and **Itbayat**. The people make a living from farming and fishing, but because transport to the mainland is limited, exports are almost nonexistent, which means most of the food grown here is eaten here. The other islands are Dequey, Siayan, Mabudis, Ibuhos, Diago, North Island and Y'Ami, which is closer to Taiwan than it is to the Philippines.

The native inhabitants of Batanes, the **Ivatan**, trace their roots to prehistoric Formosan immigrants and latter-day Spanish conquistadors. Most still make a living from the cultivation of yams and garlic or the raising of goats and cows. Some still wear the *soot*, a raincape made from the stripped leaves of the *vuyavuy* vine. The main dialect, Ivatan, includes some pidgin Spanish: "thank you" is *dios mamajes* and "goodbye" is *dios mavidin*, said only by the person leaving. The person staying behind says *dios machivan*. If you want a detailed account of Ivatan history and culture, go to the library in Basco plaza and buy *The Making of the Ivatans: The Cultural History of Batanes*, by Cesar Hidalgo (P450), which is full of intriguing insights into the way of life on the islands.

Getting to Batanes

The quickest way **to get to Batanes** from Manila is on the Asian Spirit **flight** from Manila to Basco on Mondays, Thursdays and Saturdays. Make sure you book your air tickets well in advance because the chances of getting a peak-season seat at short notice are slim. Flights around Easter are usually fully booked, with a long waiting list of hopefuls.

Chemtrad runs charter flights from Tuguegarao to Basco, but only when it has enough passengers to make the journey worthwhile. It uses small twin-engine aircraft and will usually make the trip if there are eight passengers. This means you can fly from Manila to Tuguegarao with Philippine Airlines and then reserve seats with Chemtrad at Tuguegarao airport (P2450 one way). Two **cargo ships** owned by the Batanes Multi-Purpose Cooperative regularly ply the Manila–Basco sea route, bringing in supplies. The M/V *Queen of Fatima* and the M/V *Don Rudito* both accept passengers, but are not equipped as passenger ships.

Arrival and information

All visitors to the Batanes arrive at the capital Basco. The little **airport** at Basco is in a surreal location, cut into a gentle hillside in the shadow of Mount Iraya. Arriving aircraft are met by a crowd of locals waiting for family, friends and precious cargo from the mainland. There's no public transport into Basco, but someone will always be willing to take you into town for a few pesos. If you haven't got much luggage you can walk, as the town is only 1km down the hill towards the sea.

Basco is built around a rectangular plaza with the municipal buildings and church on the north side and the sea to the south. You can walk from one end of town to the other in five minutes, so there's no need to worry about public transport. Opposite the church is a small police station, although the chances of you having to use it are slim because the crime rate in Batanes is said to be zero. Next to the police station is the **Philippine Information Agency** – affiliated to the government press office – where staff can answer queries about travel and accommodation. Take note of the natural-disaster information board, which details the earthquakes, floods and typhoons that have wreaked havoc on Batanes in the last decade. Another place that can help tourists is the new Batanes Tourism Information Office (℡0981/995067) on the east side of the plaza next to *Mama Lily's*. A day-tour around the island for five people, with transport, guide, lunch and drinks, costs P3510.

Make sure you take **pesos** to Batanes because credit cards are not accepted, even at the airport. You might be able to change US dollars at Landbank in Basco's plaza, but not at a favourable rate. The Laoag International Airways and Chemtrad offices are both at the airport (both daily 7am–5pm), but neither has a telephone so you'll have to go there in person to make reservations.

Making a **telephone call** from Basco became easier with the opening of a Smart Communications Tawag Center (public calling office) in Kaychanarianan Street, also known as Kaycha Street. Calls are made by satellite and cost P16 a minute for national and P40 a minute for international. The public calling office just beyond the National Food Authority Warehouse is cheaper, but the queues are long.

Batan Island

The island of **Batan** is the biggest in the group and site of the tiny capital, **BASCO**. Basco boasts a spectacular location, right on the lower slopes of Mount Iraya, a volcano which has not erupted since the fifteenth century, but is still officially active. The peaceful little town features a plaza on one side, the volcano to the rear, and a small curve of beach where fishing boats come and go. You can walk around the town in half an hour. The only attractions are the crumbling old **Spanish church** on the north side of the plaza and the **Museum of Indigenous People** (daily 9am–4pm; free), which you can reach by walking into the church and out through the doors on the right-hand side; it's small, but provides a quick overview of the Ivatan lifestyle and culture.

Jeepneys connect towns along the coastal road, but this is a quiet place and public transport is limited. The road runs from Basco south through San Vicente and Ivana, then turns north to Songsong and Itbud before cutting across the interior to Dura and back to Basco. If you want to explore the island independently you'll have to be prepared to wait and probably to do some **walking** and **hitching**.

Perhaps the best way to get a quick overall picture of the beauty of Batan is to hire a **jeepney** with driver for the day (P2000) for a grand tour. You can do this through your accommodation. A typical **tour** starts in Basco and runs anticlockwise south along the coastal road to the *Batanes Resort*, turning left up a narrow road to Radar Tukon, an abandoned weather station on top of the hill. From here the whole island is spread at your feet. (The road up to Radar Tukon also makes a wonderful **walk**. It's about 6km and from the top you can continue along a trail that leads down through pastures and farmland to the east coast. If you want to do this walk it's easy enough to take a tricycle from Basco to the starting point near *Batanes Resort*.) An organized tour typically continues south along the coast to the pretty old Spanish village of **Mahatao** and on to **Ivana** with its eye-catching yellow church (this is the departure point for the ferry to Sabtang Island; see p.456).

If anything, the east coast is even more breathtaking than the west, with one blue bay after another. You can drive for miles and hardly see a soul. The road continues, taking you to the village of **Uyugan** before turning north to **Song Song**, where you can see the remains of stone houses that were washed away by a tidal wave. North of Itbud is **Loran Station**, an American communications base used during the Vietnam War, but now abandoned and derelict. Then the road turns inland and uphill through "Marlboro Country", elevated pastures populated by Ivatan bulls and horses, grazing against the backdrop of Mount Iraya and the Pacific Ocean.

The potential for trekking and **camping** on Batan is enticing. There are no campsites, but as long as you respect the landscape no one minds if you pitch a tent for the night near a beach. You might have to give a small consideration to the local barangay captain. Whatever you do, take food and water, because there are few places to get provisions.

Accommodation

Batanes Resort Basco ℡02/927 7293 or Piltel ℡533 3456 or 3444. A government-owned resort with gentle, well-intentioned staff and an absolutely unbeatable location. The six tidy little stone duplex cottages sit on a breezy hillside a couple of kilometres south of Basco, with steps leading down to a marvellous crescent of black sand cove. The food (breakfast P80, lunch P150, dinner P150) is undistinguished, a typical breakfast consisting of oily bright-red hot dogs served with a cold egg and rice, but you don't have to eat at the resort. A jeepney into town for dinner costs P5 and a tricycle back to the resort at night P30. The resort's main problem is water: much of the time you'll have to make do with a bucket of cold water for a shower. ❸

Batanes Seaside Lodge & Restaurant 400m along the National Road from Basco towards Batanes Resort. *Seaside Lodge* may be new, tiled and clean, but the fan and a/c rooms (single, double, family) are relatively expensive and the food and service in the dreary restaurant dismal. There is, however, a pleasant terrace at the rear

with sea views and the upper floors have a wraparound seaview balcony shared by all the guests. ❷

Ivatan Lodge Piltel ℡533 3456 or 3444. Faded yellow building that represents last chance saloon in terms of accommodation in Basco. On the ground floor are various small offices and storerooms, while on the first floor are seven dusty, dilapidated rooms with shared facilities. *Ivatan Lodge* is on the seafront side of the National Road, 200m beyond *Shanedel's* towards the town plaza. ❶

🏃 **Shanedel's Inn & Café** 0669 Kaychanarianan corner National Rd and Abad St, call Piltel ℡533 3456 or 3444. Owned by Shane and Del Millan, this congenial little guesthouse has six rooms with a shared bathroom and offers the best budget accommodation – and the best food – in Basco itself by some way. Grab yourself a cold beer in the terrace restaurant at the rear and watch the sun set over Basco harbour while Del and her daughters rustle you up a dinner of sizzling beef and grilled flying fish. Four people can eat and drink here for less than P500. ❶

Sabtang Island

Don't travel all the way to Batanes and miss the opportunity to spend at least a day exploring **Sabtang**. Even better, bring a tent and some provisions and spend a few days walking around the island. There are no official campsites, but you'll find plenty of open land where you can pitch a tent, with permission from the owner. Sabtang is solitary and peaceful, with some original Ivatan stone villages where life seems to have altered little in a hundred years. Ferries to Sabtang arrive in the port of **SABTANG** on the island's northeast coast, where there's a Spanish church, a school and a few houses. Your best bet for local information and advice is to contact Mrs Ramos, matriarch of one of the island's dynasties. She can offer you food at her little homestead restaurant, 200m along the main street to the left of the pier, and she also has one of the island's few vehicles for hire (P1000). Her driver will take you anti-clockwise around the coast to the stone village of **Sumnanga** and back through Sabtang

Port to Savidog and on to **Chavayan Bay**, where stone houses huddle together against a jungled mountain and the surf pounds in from the Pacific. The road ends here, but there is a cattle path heading further south.

Sabtang lies southwest of Batan, a one-hour journey by small **ferry** (P30) from the pier at Ivana, opposite the big yellow church. Ferries are few and far between but tend to run early in the morning between 6am and 7am. If you get to the pier any later than 7am you could end up waiting until noon, or whenever there are enough passengers to make the trip worthwhile. Avoid the crossing in rough weather: the boats are old and wooden, and have to navigate a six-kilometre-wide channel that is known for its strong currents and big waves. During World War II the Japanese invasion of Sabtang was delayed a number of times because troops were worried about the treacherous crossing.

Itbayat Island

Of the three main islands in the Batanes group, **Itbayat** is the least accessible, but not the least populated; most of the 3500 inhabitants make their living from garlic, fish and cattle. There is no electricity and no accommodation. Itbayat is criss-crossed by trails made by farmers and fishermen, and makes for superb trekking country in good weather. There's no public transport on the island so you'll have to get around either on foot or by asking one of the residents who owns a motorbike to give you a lift. You can stay with the mayor – ask at the town hall in the pretty little capital, **MAYAN** – or ask around for accommodation in someone's home.

A daily **ferry** to Itbayat leaves Basco at either 5am or 6am (4hr; P200) and returns the same day late in the afternoon. It's not a big boat and by no means comfortable. The ferry lands at the west coast harbour of Chinapoliran, from where you can walk or hitch a lift to Mayan. From Mayan you can walk 9km south to **Raele** and from there climb to the top of **Mount Riposed** (231m), from whose summit there are uninterrupted views on all sides. A quicker way to get to Itbayat is to charter a Chemtrad **plane** from Basco for the twenty-minute flight to Raele airport in the southwest of the island. They need eight passengers for each leg of the journey (P700 each way), which means you could be stranded on Itbayat for a while until enough passengers come forward to make the flight possible. Chemtrad has no phone in Basco – its office (daily 7am–5pm) is at the airport.

The northeast

The northeast of the Philippines, comprising the provinces of Nueva Vizcaya, Quirino, Aurora, Isabela and Cagayan, is one of the archipelago's most unexplored wildernesses, with miles of beautiful coastline and enormous tracts of tropical rainforest. The biggest city in the region, **Tuguegarao**, is capital of Cagayan province and, while there's not much to do in the city itself, it's the starting point for trips to the beautiful **Peñablanca Caves** and nearby towns such as **Piat**, site of a Spanish-era church that houses what devotees say is one of the country's most miraculous religious images. Further north still, the area around **Santa Ana** in Cagayan province is largely undiscovered by tourists, but known to Filipinos as the country's best game-fishing area. From Santa Ana it's possible to take the coastal road west into Ilocos Norte and Laoag. This is also the departure point for boat trips to the rugged and isolated **Babuyan Islands**, breeding grounds for humpback whales.

The best-known tourist destination in the whole area is **Baler**, a coastal town six hours northeast of Manila in Aurora province that has become a popular if unrefined surfing destination. North of Baler the whole of the east coast is isolated from the rest of Luzon by the **Sierra Madre** mountains, which are divided into the Northern and Southern Sierra Madre by just one break, which occurs roughly at the half-way point. To travel this coast you either have to take to a banca and do it by sea, or negotiate an unsealed road that north of Baler is often nothing more than rubble.

The next significant settlement beyond Baler is **Palanan**, jump-off point for the barely explored **Northern Sierra Madre Natural Park**, at almost 3600 square kilometres the largest protected area in the Philippines. The climbing and trekking potential here is exciting, but the area is so wild and remote that it's also potentially hazardous, with no communications and forest so dense that in many places it is impenetrable.

There's only one major **airport** for the whole region and that's at Tuguegarao, served by Philippine Airlines from Manila. From Tuguegarao it's possible to take a Chemtrad charter flight to the airstrip at Palanan, but the plane only leaves when it's got enough passengers, so be prepared to wait. Buses run regularly from Manila to Baler via Cabanatuan, about three hours north of the capital. North of Baler the coastal road and public transport are almost nonexistent and you may have to resort to local bancas.

Tuguegarao and around

The capital of Cagayan province, **TUGUEGARAO** ("Too-geg-er-rao") is a busy city of choked streets lined with pawnshops and canteens, offering little of interest for travellers. The best that can be said of it is that from some hotel rooms there are reasonable views of distant hills. The city itself is tatty and chaotic – although not unique in the Philippines in this respect. It is, however, convenient to fly to Tuguegarao if you intend to explore the east coast around the Sierra Madre or the northernmost coast near Santa Ana, or even head west into Kalinga province and its capital Tabuk. Tuguegarao is also the best starting point for a visit to the remarkable cave systems 24km to the east at **Peñablanca**.

Good day-trips from the city include Calvary Hills, an excellent vantage point for views across the Cagayan valley, and **Piat**, where the colourful but solemn annual Sambali festival is held in June.

A number of travel agents in Tuguegarao offer **white-water rafting** trips on the Cagayan River, at 500km the longest in the country. A typical five-day trip begins in the heart of the Sierra Madre and ends more than 150km to the south in Nagtipunan in Quirino province. Day-trips and two-day "discover rafting" trips are also available. For details, call Adventure and Expeditions Philippines (☎078/844 1298).

Practicalities

Philippine Airlines has a **flight** from Manila to Tuguegarao on Monday, Wednesday and Friday. The PAL ticketing office (☎078/846 1050) is at Tuguegarao **airport**, which lies 2km south of the city centre along the National Highway. From the airport you can reach the town centre in twenty minutes by jeepney or tricycle. Autobus, Baliwag Transit and Victory Liner all make the twelve-hour trip from Manila to Tuguegarao passing through Cabanatuan and Ilagan.

The Department of Tourism office (☎078/844 1621 or 2359) is on the second floor of the Supermarket Building in Bonifacio Street. You can ask here about **permits** and **guides** for the caves. This is also the base for the Sierra Madre Outdoor Club, whose members have reliable first-hand information about caving, trekking and climbing. There's a provincial tourist office (☎078/844 0203) in the Expo Building, Capitol Hills, part of the Provincial Capitol complex in the city plaza. Tuguegarao's main drag is Bonifacio Street, where there are plenty of convenience stores and banks, including BPI, which has an ATM.

Accommodation and eating

Most of the **hotels** in Tuguegarao are dreary budget establishments with plain rooms. The newest and cleanest hotel in the city is the *Hotel Ivory and Convention Center* (☎078/844 1278; ❷) on Buntun Highway, ten minutes north of the city centre by tricycle. The hotel's 38 rooms all have air-conditioning, showers, cable TV and telephones, and the 24-hour restaurant features a reasonable menu that includes Filipino breakfast (spicy sausage, egg and rice) for P120. There's also a large and clean swimming pool. In the city centre, *Hotel Roma* (☎078/844 1057; ❶), at the junction of Lun and Abonofacio streets, is an acceptable mid-range option; unappealingly brown and boxy from the outside, but with a clean (fake) marble lobby and simple, well-kept rooms with good showers. *Hotel Lorita* (☎078/844 1390; ❷) within walking distance of the church on Rizal Street has good, affordable doubles, twins and suites, while *Victoria Lodge* (☎078/844 0436; ❶), 11-A Pengue-Ruyu St (one block from the Capitol Building), is a small place with cheap fan singles with their own shower and slightly brighter air-conditioned doubles.

For **eating**, Tuguegarao has the usual fast-food restaurants such as *Shakey's Pizza* and *Jollibee*, most of them along the main drag of Bonifacio Street. For something more authentic, try the *Pampagueña Restaurant* on Rizal Avenue. The menu at this spacious, busy establishment includes **local specialities** such as *gakka* (salted native snails), deep-fried *mori* fish and pickled bamboo shoots. Main courses may include *igado* (pork liver stew with vegetables), *poke-poke* (sautéed slices of eggplant with pork meat) and goat stew, while among the desserts are candy made from buffalo milk and steamed glutinous rice with sweetened mongo and peanuts. The *Ristorante Lorita* in the *Hotel Lorita* does steak, chops, barbecues and Chinese-style seafood. If you're adventurous enough for **street food**, try one of the many *panciterias* – hole-in-the-wall restaurants with plastic furniture serving cheap stir-fried noodles topped with vegetables, chopped liver, ground pork, sliced hotdogs, and the like.

Peñablanca Caves

The major tourist attraction close to Tuguegarao is the marvellous **caves** at Peñablanca, 24km to the east and easy to reach in about an hour by bus or jeepney. This whole area, known as the Peñablanca Protected Area, is riddled with more than 300 cave systems, many of them deep and dangerous, and a good number still largely unexplored. In fact, a mere 75 have been thoroughly documented, starting only in 1977. The easiest cave for tourists to visit is Callao Cave, which has seven immense chambers. The main chamber has a natural skylight and a chapel inside where Mass is celebrated every Sunday. At dusk great flocks of bats leave the cave on their first hunting missions of the night – a sight well worth hanging around to see.

Other accessible caves in the area include Roc, Quibal and San Carlos. Close to the small village of Quibal, Jackpot Cave is for expert cavers only. At 115m, it is the second-deepest cave in the Philippines, with numerous shafts that drop into darkness and a number of streams and pools. The Odessa-Tumbali Cave System, known locally as Abbenditan Cave, is the longest in the country (almost 8km) and another one you shouldn't go near without a guide. This system is said to have at least five other entrances and, when fully explored, could turn out to be 15km longer than has so far been confirmed. It also contains a number of canals and lakes for swimming.

San Carlos Cave is another tough one, with small tunnels that can only be negotiated on hands and knees, and a chamber called the Ice Cream Parlour, with clusters of white stalagmites that resemble scoops of ice cream. San Carlos requires a lot of swimming because of its cold subterranean streams.

Most of the caves are protected, so permission is required for caving and general exploration. Ask at the Department of Tourism office in Tuguegarao (see p.459). A **guide** is essential: contact the caving organization SMOC in Manila (☏02/438 4059) or at the DoT in Tuguegarao, or ask at the *Callao Caves Resort*. Rates for guides are P350–500 per day plus food, depending upon the type of caving. Porters charge P200 a day plus food and carry up to 30kg.

The only **resort** in the Peñablanca Protected Area is the *Callao Caves Resort* (☏078/844 1057; ❶–❸) near Callao Caves, which has a good range of accommodation for any budget, from simple bunk beds in a dorm to two-bedroomed air-conditioned cottages. Staff here also organize guides for caving, and for rafting trips along the Pinacanauan River, which runs through the Peñablanca Protected Area. Jeepneys leave the public market in Tuguegarao for *Callao Caves Resort* every hour or when they are full.

Iguig Calvary Hills and Piat

About 16km to the north of Tuguegarao near the small town of Iguig are **Iguig Calvary Hills**, an excellent vantage point for some epic views across the Cagayan valley and river. There's also a beautiful old church here, a ruined convent and larger-than-life sculptures of the Stations of the Cross, depicting Christ's suffering before his death on Mount Calvary. It's a magical, contemplative place to sit, especially as the sun sets: three large statues right on top of the hill dramatically depict Christ and the two thieves on their crosses.

There are some gentle, wooded walking trails in the area with views across the valley and river, but no accommodation or camping, so you'll have to return to Tuguegarao for the night. To get to Iguig Calvary Hills take a **jeepney** from the public market in Tuguegarao to Iguig, then walk about 2km up the road to the right. To avoid the walk, take a tricycle to Iguig, which will cost P50.

It's possible to combine a trip to Iguig Calvary Hills in one day with a trip to **PIAT**, one hour by road northwest of Iguig; you can catch one of the frequent buses or jeepneys from the main road running through Iguig. The red-brick **Basilica Minore of Our Lady of Piat** in the town of Piat, is an atmospheric Baroque Spanish church dating back to the seventeenth century. It has a gold-plated altar and rare stained-glass windows, but is known throughout the Philippines because it houses the Miraculous Lady of Piat, a 400-year-old image of the Virgin Mary that was brought to the country from Macau in 1604 by Dominican Friars. The annual Sambali festival is held every year during the last week of June in honour of the image. It's a solemn festival, attended by thousands of devotees who pray for miracles. Among the miracles she is already said to have performed are the ending of a drought in 1624, the revival of a mortally sick army officer from nearby Lal-lo in 1738 and the rescue of a stricken boat from the clutches of a terrible storm in 1739.

Piat has a turbulent history, including the massacre in 1600 of dozens of Spanish settlers who were said to have abused the impartial friendship offered them by the Kalingas and Negritos. In 1604 an intrepid missionary dared to return and succeeded in pacifying the belligerent Piatenos. More Spanish followed and the locals welcomed them, their only regret about colonization being that they were ordered to wear hats.

Santa Ana, Palaui Island and the Babuyan Islands

The untouristy fishing town of **SANTA ANA** is about five hours' bus ride north of Tuguegarao on the northeastern tip of Luzon. There's nothing to see or do in the town itself, but the area around it has much to offer if you're a bit adventurous, including some terrific white sand beaches and a number of enticing offshore islands around the barangay of **San Vicente**, fifteen minutes northeast of Santa Ana by road. You can catch a jeepney or tricycle on the main road in Santa Ana, opposite the whitewashed municipal building. The largest of these islands, and the easiest to reach, is **Palaui Island**, which has no roads, limited electricity and no accommodation, although it's not hard to find a room for the night if you ask around among the locals. Don't miss Siwangag Cove on the island's northern coast, a beautiful crescent lagoon watched over by an old Spanish lighthouse. You can reach Palaui Island by banca from either Santa Ana or San Vicente. Bancas also run back and forth to other islands.

Because of the currents that run through the Luzon Strait from the Pacific, all the islands around Santa Ana offer marvellous **game-fishing**. The season is from March to July and for details you can contact the Philippine Game Fishing Foundation, c/o Outdoor Sports, 1320 Quezon Ave, Quezon City (℡02/373 1248 or 0748). They arrange fishing trips to places such as Susay Rock, a steep-sided islet where you can catch barracuda, blue marlin, wahoo, king mackerel and dorado. Camiguin Island is another exceptional fishing destination, but it's four hours offshore in open water washed by strong currents.

The PGFF runs the Don Andres Soriano Sportfishing Camp inside the Philippine Navy headquarters in the barangay of San Vicente, where there are four air-conditioned **rooms** each containing two bunk beds. The only showers are outside and the water is cold. If you've got a tent you can camp in the grounds. This is the only accommodation in the area apart from unofficial homestays with locals: ask at the municipal hall in Santa Ana for details.

From Santa Ana you can rent a private banca for the often rough crossing to the isolated and undeveloped **Babuyan Islands**, a cluster of 24 volcanic and coralline islands 32km off the coast that are breeding grounds for humpback whales. Only five of the islands are inhabited, but even those have no tourist accommodation, limited electricity, no running water and no telephones.

Aparri and around

There's not much to see in the small north coast town of **APARRI**, but its location on the main road heading along the coast makes it a convenient rest stop if you're travelling between Tuguegarao to Laoag. The only **hotel** is the plain *Ars City Hotel* (☏078/822 8744; ●) in the Macanaya area, five minutes by tricycle from where buses and jeepneys stop on the main road through town. Aparri used to have a port with ferries to Laoag and Batanes, but not any more. The only boats you can catch here are rented bancas to take you east along the coast to Santa Ana.

About two hours' bus ride along the coastal road west from Aparri brings you to the town of **CLAVERIA**, a laidback place with a pleasant stretch of white sand beach and a small homestay resort, *Claveria Bayview Inn* (●), a short walk west of town along the shore. You could break your journey with a day or two in this area. There are two gushing **waterfalls**, Macatel and Portabag, where you can swim, and the barely explored **islands** of Fuga, Dalupiri and Calayan, although to reach any of them you'll probably have to hire your own banca because public trips are infrequent.

Palanan and around

The isolated east coast settlement of **PALANAN** is the gateway to the **Northern Sierra Madre Natural Park**. It's difficult to reach and if you are heading here from Manila you will need to allow at least three days to make the trip. If you do reach Palanan, you'll have no regrets. The surrounding Sierra Madre Mountains are one of the country's last great wilderness areas, and the coast is equally remarkable, peppered with some of the most immaculate beaches in the country. Be prepared for some rough travel though. There's no accommodation for hundreds of miles and few places to buy provisions. You can ask the Natural Park office in Cabatuan Road, **Cauayan** in Isabela province for advice on getting to Palanan. There are no hotels or lodges in Palanan, but if you ask at the municipal office or the police station they can point you in the direction of local families who accept guests. The daily charge for board is around P50 with extra for meals.

Palanan has a small **airport**, but it is not served by any scheduled flights. Chemtrad has occasional **charter flights** from Tuguegarao, but the plane only leaves if it is full, so you could be in for a long wait unless you're willing to fork out around US$2000 for the whole charter yourself. And that's only one-way. The only road cutting through the Sierra Madre from west to east begins from just north of Cauayan in Isabela province and ends in Palanan, but landslides mean there's no guarantee a vehicle will make it through. Another place to look for transport across the Sierra Madre is **Ilagan**, about an hour's drive north of Cauayan. You might have to do the trip to Palanan in stages, taking a jeepney part of the way and then walking until you can find another jeepney. The road passes through Benito Soliven and San Marino, two mountain communities where you can ask for a room for the night or rent a private vehicle. The third way of reaching Palanan is by cargo boat from Baler, but this is a long shot. Occasional boats do ply this route and you can ask for a lift, but you might find yourself hanging around for weeks.

Northern Sierra Madre Natural Park

The Sierra Madre comprises a vast and rare swath of wilderness that stretches from the mountains to the ocean. At almost 3600 square kilometres, the **Northern Sierra Madre Natural Park** covers much of the wilderness and remains one of the country's last frontiers, wholly untouched by tourism and so rugged and densely forested that enormous tracts of it remain unmapped. Said by conservationists to be the Philippines' richest protected area in terms of habitat and species, the park is eighty percent land and twenty percent coastal area along a spectacular, cliff-studded seashore. One of the reasons for the health of the park's ecosystems is its inaccessibility from outside. To the east lies the Pacific, which is too rough for boats during part of the year; to the west, no roads cross the park or lead towards the more populated, rice-growing valleys, although there is pressure to build some. In 1992, scientists from around the world converged on the Palanan region and recorded a remarkable range of endemic fauna, including eagles, deer, monkeys, bats and birds. Studies of the park's flora have barely begun.

The park has few wardens and no fences for boundaries, so you can visit any time you want without restriction. Penetrating this wild area can be difficult, but the reward is the sight of a virtually pristine landscape. You can hire a **guide** at the municipal hall in Palanan for a trip down the Palanan River to the village of **Sabang**, from where you can walk through farmland and forest to **Sadsad Falls**, a high cascade that crashes through dense forest into a deep pool. For some of the trip there's no trail, so you'll have to wade upriver through the water. Another memorable trip from Palanan takes you northwards along the coast to the sheltered inlets around Dimalansan and the village of Maconacon. On the isolated beaches here the **Dumagat** people establish their temporary homes (see box below). The Dumagats are nomadic and it's a matter of luck whether you'll see any – if you do the welcome is shy, but friendly.

The Dumagats

The nomadic people known as the **Dumagats** are some of the original inhabitants of the Philippines. They live in small camps on the beaches around Palanan, where they build temporary shelters from bamboo and dried grass, consisting of a sloping panel anchored in the sand to provide protection from the sun and rain. When the group decides to move on the panels are left to rot. The word Dumagat translates roughly as "those who moved to the ocean", and the area around Palanan is the last stronghold of their vanishing culture and way of life. Life for the Dumagats is simple in the extreme: they survive by hunting and gathering, using no modern equipment. The main threats to their continued existence are the commercialization of their homelands, along with exposure to diseases previously unknown to them because of the natural cordon sanitaire of the Sierra Madre. The Dumagats still rely on medicine men who use potions boiled up from leaves and herbs, but these traditional remedies do little for a child afflicted with measles or mumps.

Best beaches in and around Baler

You can **surf** year-round at Baler, although die-hard surfers say the best waves come between October and February, especially early in the morning, diminishing slightly as it gets hotter. You might think the best waves could be had during the typhoon season (June to November), but the wind blows onshore from the Pacific and the waves are fickle, sometimes non-existent. The very hot months of April, May and June bring relatively calm seas with a pleasant breeze, ideal for snorkelling and swimming, but not so good for surfers looking for a big break.

Sabang Beach isn't the only good spot for surfing. **Cemento Beach and Reef** in Cemento barangay sees waves of up to 4m from October to February, making it even more popular among experienced surfers than Sabang. It's also where former president Manuel Quezon built a holiday home; it was destroyed by a typhoon, but you can still see the ruins. To get to Cemento, take a tricycle from Baler town to the river outlet south of Sabang Beach. From there, you can either hire a motorized banca for the ten-minute ride to the reef or make the forty-minute walk. **Ampere Beach** is one hour north of Baler near Dipaculao and can be easily reached by banca from Sabang. Okotan Cave at nearby Bunga Point is used by locals for forecasting the weather; they claim to be able to forecast the intensity of approaching typhoons by listening to the sound the Pacific waves make as they hit the rocks.

Borlongan Beach in Borlongan barangay is another option for surfers, the only difference between this and those closer to Baler being that Borlongan is stony, not sandy. It's an exciting day-trip along the coast from Baler, passing some beautiful coastal scenery and a number of other beaches where you can stop and explore or swim. It takes about two hours to reach from Sabang Beach by banca.

It takes almost six hours in a rented banca to reach **Casiguran Sound** from Baler. This calm and picturesque inlet is protected from onshore winds and waves by a finger of hilly land that stretches south from the mainland, forming a placid body of ocean less than a kilometre wide that's almost totally enclosed except for a narrow gap to the south. There are some exceptional beaches and coves in the area and the calmness of the sound makes it perfect for **swimming**. The area is, however, undeveloped and the only accommodation consists of unofficial homestays in the small town of Casiguran itself, at the enclosed end of the sound.

Baler and around

The east coast town of **BALER**, a laidback trading station at the mouth of the San Luis River, is known for its excellent surfing: it was the location for the surfing scenes in Francis Ford Coppola's *Apocalypse Now*. The shots were filmed at a surfing break known as Charlie's Point, a short walk from the main surfing beach of **Sabang**, easily reached by tricycle from Baler itself. Sabang Beach, a striking ribbon of dark sand and dazzling blue water, is where the local "Baler Boys" hang out, but they aren't territorial and are happy to share waves with visitors. Every year in February this is the venue for the Aurora Cup, which is attracting an increasing number of surfers from overseas. The registration fee is P350, including two dinners, a beach party and a T-shirt.

Practicalities

There are no flights or ferries to Baler, so your only option is the bus: those from Manila and Baguio go via Cabanatuan. Dozens of public **bancas** docked along the San Luis River on the outskirts of Baler town take passengers to various isolated destinations to the north of Baler, including Dipaculao and Casiguran. You can also rent a private banca here for around P500 a day. The **provincial tourist office** (☎042/209 4373) in Baler is in the Provincial Capitol Compound, close to the National Highway and only one block east from where buses terminate.

Accommodation and eating

All the best **accommodation** in Baler is on or around the beach at Sabang. Telephones are a rarity so it's difficult to book in advance. However, apart from during the annual Aurora Cup in February, you won't have any problem finding somewhere to stay.

Arguably the most popular resort among tourists and out-of-town surfers, *Bay's Inn* (②) boasts panoramic views of Baler Bay, the Pacific Ocean and surrounding cliffs and beaches. It has clean doubles with private showers and a popular **restaurant** with views, plus you can rent surfboards for P150 a day. Also right on the beach, the mid-range *Bahia de Baler* (☎042/209 4276; ③) is good value, with a choice of single, double, family and group air-conditioned rooms for half a dozen people or more. *MIA (Make It Aurora) Surf & Sports Resort* (①) has seven single rooms and four doubles that share a common shower, plus five "VIP" rooms with private bathrooms. You can also rent surfing and windsurfing equipment here. *AMCO Beach Resort* (①) is a low-rise colonial-style building and the biggest resort in Sabang. It is not, however, on the beach. Rooms are in good condition with air-conditioning and private hot showers. The restaurant has a modest menu of Filipino and Chinese dishes. The ordinary but friendly *Baler Guesthouse* (①) is on the beach and has seven standard rooms with a shared shower. It's hidden behind *Bay's Inn* and the rooms don't have beach views, but the pretty garden is a nice place to relax and there's a restaurant serving good meals for around P100 per person. The owner, Karen, is always around and happy to dispense advice to travellers.

The Cordillera

To Filipino lowlanders, brought up on sunshine and beaches, the tribal heart-lands of the north and their spiny ridge of inhospitable mountains, **THE CORDILLERA**, are still seen almost as another country, inhabited by myste-rious people who worship primitive gods. Baguio, the traditional mountain retreat for Manileños during the fierce heat of Easter week, is about as far north as many southerners get. But it's not until you get beyond Baguio that the adventure really begins.

The area was first settled by indigenous Negritos and then during the Spanish regime by hunter-gatherers from neighbouring areas who were on the move looking for food and water. Life for many of these tribal people has changed little in hundreds of years, with traditional ways and values still very much in evidence. If anything is likely to erode these traditions and chip away at the insulation it is the coming of tourists: already an increasing number of tribal folk are making more from the sale of handicrafts than they do from the production

Trekking is becoming a serious activity in the Philippines, and although there are few well-marked trails, local guides are always available to show you the way. Because the road network is poor in many parts of the Cordillera, and because there are so many jungled peaks and hidden valleys, trekking is the only way to see some of the region's secrets: burial caves, tribal villages and hidden waterfalls. Gentle day treks are possible, particularly in the main tourist areas of Banaue and Sagada, but there are also plenty of two or three-day treks that take you deep into backwaters where it's easy to get lost. Don't be tempted to wander off into the Cordilleran wilderness on your own: good maps are almost nonexistent and it's easy to become disoriented and lost. Medical facilities and rescue services are few and far between, so if you get into trouble and no one knows where you are, you'll have a long wait for help to arrive.

Most of the challenging trails are around Sagada, Banaue, Bontoc, Tabuk and Tinglayan in the landlocked province of Kalinga. In all of these towns there is a tourist office or municipal hall where someone will be able to help arrange **guides**. In smaller barrios a good place to look for a guide is at the barangay hall. Guides won't have any official certification, but will know the area like the back of their hand. The guide will also carry equipment and supplies, but don't expect him to have any equipment himself. Most guides happily wander through inhospitable landscapes with only flip-flops on their feet. For longer treks, it's useful to take a spare knapsack for equipment and provisions you might want the guide to carry. Food sharing arrangements need to be worked out as well – ask in advance if the guide is expecting you to take food for him. Rates start from around P500 a day, but the guide will expect a tip, even in the form of a few beers and a meal, for getting you home safely.

Don't underestimate the **weather** in the mountains. The Philippines may be tropical, but at altitude it can get within a few degrees of freezing at night and cloud can descend fast, resulting in poor visibility and making it easy to become disoriented. In many places you are likely to be scrambling through difficult terrain. Many trekking clubs in the Philippines ask potential members to take a fitness test first, an indication that walking through this rugged landscape is not a walk in the park.

Some itineraries

Banaue

Banaue-Batad-Cambulo-Pula-Banaue Circular walk best tackled in an anticlockwise direction heading east out of Banaue to Banga-an and then northwards through Cambulo and Pula, returning to Banaue via either the viewpoint on the main

---

of rice. One of the challenges faced by the government is to make the highlands accessible to travellers, without causing the breakup of a social and economic structure that is unique to the region.

The Cordillera, known officially as the Cordillera Autonomous Region or CAR, consists of six provinces: Benguet, Ifugao, Mountain, Kalinga, Abra and Apayao. Many visits to the north start in the city of **Baguio**, gateway to the Cordillera. Any visit to the north should also take in the mountain village of **Sagada** in Mountain province, with its caves and hanging coffins; the riverside town of **Bontoc**, with its magnificent trekking; and the huge rice terraces at **Banaue** in Ifugao. The Ibaloi village of **Kabayan** in Benguet is where a group of mummies, possibly dating as far back as 2000 BC, were discovered in caves in the early twentieth century. Kabayan is a simple, rural village surrounded by impressive Alp-like peaks and reached by a serpentine dirt road that remains impassable for many months a year. It sees few tourists, but is an excellent base

road or the Ifugao village of Bocos. It can take up to ten hours, so if that sounds too daunting for a day-trek try booking accommodation for the night at the *Banga-an Family Inn & Restaurant* (see p.488), which you'll reach after about three hours. If you want to push on a bit further before resting up, there are also some simple guesthouses at Cambulo and Pula; at a steady pace you'll be in Cambulo after five hours and Pula after six. Most of the walk is through marvellous rice terrace scenery, with the section from Cambulo to Pula following a winding river with some cool, deep pools for a refreshing swim. You can cut a few hours of this route by taking a jeepney the first 12km to Batad Junction.

Pula–Mount Amuyao The eight-hour trek – more of a climb in places – from Pula northwards to the 2702-metre summit of Mount Amuyao is a strenuous one; you'll need plenty of provisions and overnight equipment so you can camp en route. Needless to say, a guide is essential. If you're planning on trekking all the way from Banaue and back, allow three days and two nights.

Batad and around The route from Banaue to Batad heads east from Banaue and is reasonably straightforward, passing through the villages of Talop, Kinakin and Dalican before reaching Batad Junction; it's possible to take a jeepney this far. From here you follow a steepish uphill path through rice terraces and into the valleys and mountains; from Batad Junction to Batad itself takes around three hours. There's rustic accommodation in Batad and it's worth staying the night because the next morning you can rise early and penetrate even further into the hinterland, reaching the isolated Ifugao villages of Patpat, Talboc and Guinihon. From Batad you can go back the way you came or continue anti-clockwise through Pula.

Sagada

Sagada–Bomod–Ok Waterfall–Sagada A manageable two-hour hike through rolling countryside to one of the area's best waterfalls, which is terrific for swimming. You can continue walking beyond the falls to Banga-an and then to the barangay of Aguid, a photogenic community of wooden houses set against a backdrop of rice terraces.

Sagada–Mount Ampacao–Sagada. This is a ten-kilometre trek south through valleys and rice terraces to the lower flanks of Mount Ampacao, and another two hours at least to the summit (1889 metres). It's not an especially strenuous climb – and the views are well worth the effort – but for all but the supremely fit it will entail one night of camping along the way, so go prepared. If you don't want to camp, there are a number of trails in the area that can be easily reached during a day-trek that have panoramic views back across the valley to Sagada.

for trekking in the surrounding mountains and for climbing nearby **Mount Pulag**, the highest peak on Luzon.

Access to the Cordillera and the far north is almost always Baguio. Asian Spirit has a daily flight from Manila, and the town is served by numerous buses.

Baguio and around

Filipinos speak of **BAGUIO** with a certain reverence, but for anyone who has seen Europe's mountains or America's national parks, it's something of a disappointment, nothing more than a conveniently placed one-night stop on the way to the mountains beyond. Still, there are some sights in Baguio and at least the nightlife is interesting and cheap. This is a university city, and the student population has given rise to a number of bohemian little cafés, bars and live-music venues.

Also known as City of Pines or City of Flowers, Baguio lies on a plateau 1400m above sea level with mountains on all sides. In the sixteenth century, intrepid **Spanish friars** had started to explore the region, finding a land of fertile valleys, pine-clad hills and mountains, lush vegetation and an abundance of minerals such as copper, gold and ore. Stories about this new discovery spread fast in the capital, and soon more friars, soldiers and fortune-hunters were trekking north to convert the natives to Christianity and profit from the rich natural resources. In the nineteenth century, **colonizing Americans** took over and developed Baguio into a modern city, a showcase recreational and administrative centre, from where they could preside over their precious tropical colony without working up too much of a sweat. In 1944, when American forces landed in Leyte, the head of the Japanese Imperial Army, **General Yamashita**, moved his headquarters to Baguio and helped establish a puppet Philippine government there under President José Laurel. In 1945 the city was destroyed and thousands lost their homes as liberating forces flushed out Yamashita and his army. Yamashita quickly fled north into the interior, leaving a small delaying force to cover his ignominious exit.

The city is also etched on the Filipino consciousness as site of one of the country's worst natural disasters, the **earthquake** of July 16, 1990, which measured 7.7 on the Richter Scale and killed hundreds, mostly in the city's vulnerable shanty towns, many of which cling precariously to the sides of steep valleys.

Baguio's attraction as a spiritual mountain retreat that somehow counteracts the depravity of Manila has faded in recent years. Even the government's tourism secretary was famously moved to refer to Baguio as a "tragedy" when he visited in 2002. The reasons are not hard to divine. The city centre, particularly Session Road, is a tangle of smoke-belching jeepneys and pollution has increased as a result, making a gentle stroll along what should be a picturesque thoroughfare a battle against noise and fumes. Equally disappointing is the lack of good trekking in the hills immediately surrounding the city. You would have thought a city with mountains on every side would have plenty of marked trails through wilderness areas, but there's nothing; just shabby hand-painted banners tied to pine trees advertising college reunions, charismatic prayer meetings and annual corporate conventions.

Arrival and information

Baguio's **airport**, Loakan, lies 7km south of the city beyond Camp John Hay; arriving passengers can get into the city by jeepney. **Buses** from Manila and many towns further north drop passengers on the eastern edge of the city, around the Supreme Court Compound in Upper Session Road.

The **tourist office** (daily 9am–noon & 1–7pm; ☏074/442 6708 or 7014) is in the DoT Complex on Governor Pack Road, a ten-minute walk south of Session Road. They have maps of Baguio, but not much else, and even the maps aren't great. A good place to go for general advice, guided tours and visa extensions is Swagman Travel, 92 Upper General Luna St, Corfu Village, just off Leonard Wood Road (☏074/442 9859). There's a **post office** with a poste restante service at the junction of Session Road and Governor Pack Road. One of the most popular **Internet** cafés is Cyberspace, at the *Mount Crest Hotel* on Legarda Road (daily 8am–1am; P100 an hour with free coffee). In the centre of Baguio head for IWC Inc Internet, on 4/F La Azotea Building on Session

Road (24hr). You can change money at a number of **banks**: PNB is at the northern end of Session Road, while PCI on Magsaysay Avenue will give cash advances on MasterCard or Visa. BPI has a number of branches, including one in Session Road close to the Baden Powell hostel. Be prepared with enough **cash** because ATMs in Baguio often seem to be "off-line". For emergency cash transfers there are two branches of Western Union, one on Session Road down from the post office and the other on Abanao Street. The **police station** is located near City Hall, next to the fire station off Abanao Street, and there's another at the horse-riding area in Wright Park. Baguio Medical Center (℡074/442 4216) is on Governor Pack Road and Baguio General Hospital at the city end of the Marcos Highway.

Accommodation

The choice of **accommodation** in Baguio has improved in recent years with the construction of a number of new hotels that may cost more, but have significantly better facilities than the city's many old lodges. There's a lot of choice around Burnham Park, and many of the newer establishments are found along Legarda Road. If you don't mind being out of the city and taking a taxi everywhere, head for the casual, friendly hotels on Leonard Wood Road around the Botanical Gardens.

Baden Powell International Hostel 26 Governor Pack Rd ℡074/442 5836 or 02/721 7818. Atmospheric old building visible from the bus station end of Session Rd. The lovely sitting room has a fireplace and a piano, but the quality of the rooms varies widely, so look first. Dorm beds P280. ❷

Baguio Aussie Hotel & Pub 92 General Luna St, Corfu Village ℡074/442 5139, ⓦ www.swaggy .com. Latest addition to the Swagman chain in a quiet area on the eastern edge of the city. Twelve deluxe rooms and two family rooms, all with fan, hot water and electric blanket should the nights get chilly. The Swiss-chalet-style restaurant has a cosy atmosphere and fine food, there's a friendly little bar called *Frank's*, and staff can arrange tours, vehicle rental and plane tickets. ❺

Benguet Pine Tourist Inn Chanum St corner Otek St ℡074/442 7325. Popular with travellers, but the rooms are tatty and the inclusive breakfast consists of a runny egg and an oily slice of sweet ham. For P800 you get a double with small shower and lukewarm water. Some rooms are noisy: jeepneys rev their engines outside from before dawn and there's some horrible karaoke at night from nearby beer halls. Close to Burnham Park opposite the Orchidarium. ❸

Concorde Hotel Legarda Rd ℡074/443 2058. One of a number of modern hotels that have sprung up on Legarda Rd, a couple of minutes' walk south of Burnham Park. The *Concorde* is surrounded by trees and has lovely Alpine-style bedrooms with stripped pine furniture, pine floors and eiderdowns on the bed, a real rarity in the tropical Philippines. There's a quaint little brick bar with wagon wheels on the walls, a disco, fitness centre, travel agent, two restaurants and a 24hr café. ❼

El Cielito Inn 50 North Dr ℡072/443 4846, ⓦ www.elcielitoinn.com. Mid-sized hotel with Alpine ambience and a pleasant restaurant, in a good location a ten-minute walk from Session Road. The attractive lobby is wooden with tribal touches, and the rooms are clean and well appointed, if a little on the small side. ❸

Microtels Inns & Suites Upper Session Rd ℡074/619 3333, ⓦ www.microtel-baguio.com. Great value singles, doubles and suites – nothing fancy, but the rooms are well kept and more than adequate as long as you don't mind the rather institutional ambience. Continental breakfast included. ❺

PNKY Home Leonard Wood Rd ℡074/446 7095, ⓦ pnky.allanreyes.com. Wonderfully quiet and cosy bijou bed-and-breakfast accommodation with only four rooms, so book in advance: three of the rooms are for three people and one is big enough for six. The owners are very clued-up and can arrange everything from car rental to massage. Rates include full breakfast in the neighbouring *PNKY Café*. *PNKY* also has a fantastically well-equipped cottage for six people, with two bedrooms, fitted kitchen and open fireplace. ❻

Prime Hotel Session Rd corner Calderon St ℡074/442 7066. Modern place with a/c doubles or twins that have hot water in the bathrooms and cable TV. Central location in the thick of Session Rd, but noisy as a result, so get a room at the back. ❸

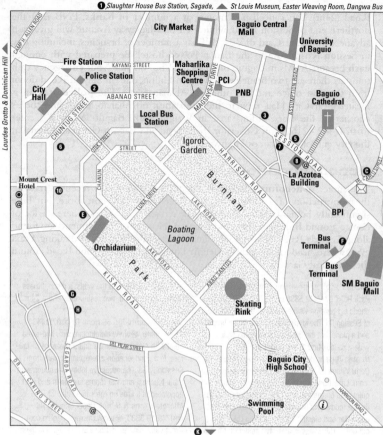

At top of map:

① ,Slaughter House Bus Station, Sagada, ▲ St Louis Museum, Easter Weaving Room, Dangwa Bus

Map labels:

City Market

Baguio Central Mall

University of Baguio

Fire Station   KAYANG STREET

Police Station

City Hall

Maharlika Shopping Centre   PCI

ABANAO STREET

PNB

Baguio Cathedral

Local Bus Station

Igorot Garden

Burnham

La Azotea Building

Mount Crest Hotel

Boating Lagoon

BPI

Orchidarium

Park

Bus Terminal

Bus Terminal

SM Baguio Mall

Skating Rink

DEL PILAR STREET

Baguio City High School

Swimming Pool

Road names: CAMP H ALLEY ROAD, Lourdes Grotto & Dominican Hill, CHUNTUG STREET, OTEK STREET, STREET, CHANUN, LUNA DRIVE, LAKE ROAD, KISAD ROAD, ABAN SANTOS, LEGARDA ROAD, DR J CARINO STREET, MAGSAYSAY DRIVE, HARRISON ROAD, SESSION ROAD, ASSUMPTION ROAD, CARILLE STREET, HARRISON ROAD 2

Prince Palace Hotel Legarda Rd corner Calderon St ☏074/442 7734. Clean and orderly modern, condominium-style hotel with comfortable a/c rooms and some studios with their own kitchenette. ❸

Prince Plaza Hotel Legarda Rd corner Calderon St ☏074/442 5082. Clean and orderly modern, condominium-style hotel with comfortable a/c rooms and some studios with their own kitchenettes. ❸

Villa Romana Ambuklao Rd ☏074/444 7305. Lovely pine lodge with panoramic views, fifteen minutes by jeepney or bus outside Baguio on the road heading north to Ambuklao. Good choice of singles, doubles and family rooms, some with fine views. The views are equally mesmerizing from the restaurant, which serves good breakfasts with strong Benguet coffee. ❶

YMCA Post Office Loop ☏074/442 4766. As the address suggests, it's in a circular side street behind the post office at the top end of Session Rd. Reasonable but institutional accommodation in dorms or shared rooms with shared showers and a school-style canteen. Good location and popular with students. ❶

The City

Baguio's municipal centre – the area around **Burnham Park** – was designed by American architect Daniel Burnham based loosely on Washington DC. The main drag is **Session Road**, which is lined with restaurants and shops, while

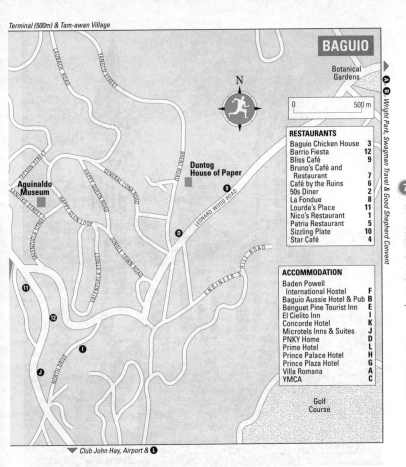

BAGUIO

Botanical Gardens

0   500 m

Duntog
House of Paper

Aguinaldo
Museum

7

NORTHERN LUZON | Baguio and around

RESTAURANTS

Baguio Chicken House	3
Barrio Fiesta	12
Bliss Café	9
Bruno's Café and Restaurant	7
Café by the Ruins	6
50s Diner	2
La Fondue	8
Lourde's Place	11
Nico's Restaurant	1
Patria Restaurant	5
Sizzling Plate	10
Star Café	4

ACCOMMODATION

Baden Powell International Hostel	F
Baguio Aussie Hotel & Pub	B
Benguet Pine Tourist Inn	E
El Cielito Inn	I
Concorde Hotel	K
Microtels Inns & Suites	J
PNKY Home	D
Prime Hotel	L
Prince Palace Hotel	H
Prince Plaza Hotel	G
Villa Romana	A
YMCA	C

Golf
Course

Club John Hay, Airport & L

on a hill above Session Road stands the eye-catching **Baguio Cathedral**. From Session Road and Burnham Park you can easily reach many attractions on foot. If you're going a little further afield, to Camp John Hay, the Botanical Gardens, Mines View or Wright Park and The Mansion, for example, it's easy and cheap to take a taxi.

Burnham Park and Session Road

The city's centrepiece is **Burnham Park**, a hilltop version of Rizal Park in Manila with a manmade boating lake at the centre, a market and rose garden at the northern end and a garden at the southern end that's planted with different species of pine trees from around the world. Burnham Park doesn't possess much grandeur, but it's an interesting place to take a stroll and to watch the people of Baguio at play: there are boats for rent on the lake and tricycles for kids.

Standing imperiously above Session Road, and reached on foot by a flight of a hundred steep steps, **Baguio Cathedral** is a striking example of "wedding cake Gothic", with a rose-pink paint job and twin spires crowned by delicate minarets. The cathedral was consecrated in 1936 and dedicated to Our Lady of Atonement. During World War II it became an evacuation centre and withstood

471

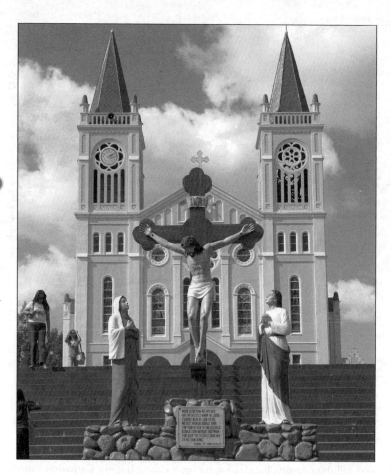

△ Baguio Cathedral

the Japanese carpet-bombing of the city in 1945, saving the lives of thousands who sheltered inside. The stairway to the cathedral from Session Road is lined with vendors selling flowers, balloons, newspapers, sweepstake tickets, candles, rosary beads and other religious paraphernalia. You can also reach the cathedral by taxi, taking the road behind the post office.

The northern end of Session Road leads to Magsaysay Avenue and the **City Market**, one of the liveliest and most colourful in the country, acting as a trading post for farmers and tribes not just from Baguio, but from many of the mountain communities to the north. Bargains include produce such as strawberries, which thrive in the temperate north. There's also peanut brittle, sweet wine, honey, textiles, handicrafts and jewellery.

St Louis University Museum and Aguinaldo Museum

The best museum in Baguio is the **St Louis University Museum of Arts and Culture** (Mon–Sat 9am–4.30pm), near St Louis Hospital on Bonifacio Street, north of Magsaysay Avenue. It displays hundreds of artefacts from the

Cordillera including tribal costumes, weapons and fascinating black and white photographs of sacrifices and other rituals, and is a good place to get a general insight into the history of the north and how it differs from the history of the lowlands and the southern islands. Another small but intriguing little museum is the **Aguinaldo Museum** (Mon–Sat 9am–noon & 1–4pm; P15) in Happy Glen Loop, behind the YMCA. General Aguinaldo, who fought for independence against Spain and America, never actually stayed here, but the museum was established by his daughter to give the people of Baguio a better understanding of the role her father played in the independence struggle. It's more a museum to the man than to the battles he fought or his place in history, containing personal memorabilia, including his uniforms, everyday clothes, weapons, a writing desk and the wheelchair he used when he was injured.

East of Baguio

Travelling out of the city eastwards on Leonard Wood Road for 4km brings you to the **Botanical Gardens** (daily 7am–8pm; P5), also known as the Igorot Village because it contains replica native huts typical of Igorot dwellings in the Cordilleras. The plants and trees are all well labelled and you can wander through thick vegetation along winding concrete pathways. You'll have to get past the fake Igorot tribespeople at the door, who importune tourists to pose with them for a fee.

A little beyond the Botanical Gardens, **Wright Park** is a popular public space where you can hire a sturdy mountain nag for a quick trot around the perimeter. Wright Park is divided in two by Leonard Wood Road. The horses are on the north side and on the south is **The Mansion**, built in 1908 for American governor-generals to the Philippines, damaged in 1945 during the war, and rebuilt in 1947 as a holiday home for Philippine presidents. The Mansion's elaborate main gate is said to be a replica of that at Buckingham Palace in London.

Continuing east from Wright Park along Gibraltar Road you soon come to an area known as **Mines View Park**, a small hillside village where there are a number of souvenir shops including Ibay's, which sells locally made silver jewellery, and Teresita's, which has tribal artefacts and souvenirs. A short walk up the hill from the shops is the **Good Shepherd Convent**, which has a store inside the main gate where you can buy products made by the Good Shepherd nuns, including strawberry, coconut and *ube* jam and cashew and peanut brittle. Most of their products are also sold at the City Market, but are slightly cheaper here. Income generated from sales goes to various charities and the maintenance and upkeep of the convent. The convent is well known to Filipinos, and if you need *pasalubong* – the traditional small gifts given by returning travellers – this is the place to buy them. At the far end of the convent's car park is an observation deck with views across the Cordillera mountains.

Named after American President Theodore Roosevelt's secretary of war, **Camp John Hay**, south of the Botanical Gardens, used to be a rest and recreational facility for employees of the United States military and Department of Defense stationed in the Philippines. During World War II the property was used by the Japanese as a concentration camp for American and British soldiers. In 1991 Camp John Hay was turned over to the Philippine government for development into an upmarket country club, with hotels, golf courses, private mountain lodges (many snapped up by politicians) and sundry restaurants and clubhouses. Development has continued in fits and starts and has been plagued by various allegations of shabby business practices, cronyism and financial mismanagement. However, the expansive, undulating grounds have some nice walks through the pine trees and are also ideal for jogging. A taxi from the city centre costs about P50.

West of Baguio

High on a hill in the western part of the city, off Dominican Hill Road, is **Lourdes Grotto**, a Catholic shrine and place of meditation watched over by an image of Our Lady of Lourdes. To reach the grotto you have to climb 252 steps and when you reach the top it's traditional to light a candle.

Beyond the grotto at the summit of Dominican Hill Road is **Dominican Hill**, from where the views across the city are better than anywhere. Dominican Hill and the derelict building that stands there have a curious history. In 1911 the Dominican Order in the Philippines decided to build a vacation house on the hill, but with a keen eye to business used part of it as a school to take advantage of tax exemptions. During World War II, Dominican Hill was occupied by refugees and the house suffered extensive bomb damage. It was rebuilt in 1947 but the Dominicans had no more need for it and in 1973 it was turned into a hotel managed by a controversial Baguio-based entrepreneur and faith healer whose guests were mostly gravely ill patients from Europe. When the owner died in 1987, allegedly from a hardening of the arteries brought on by his debauched lifestyle, the hotel closed. It still stands, with the white Dominican cross on the roof, but the gates are padlocked and the walls are crumbling. Local residents say that at night they can hear the banging of doors, the clattering of dishes and the screams of Agpaoa's terminally ill guests. Plans have been mooted to build a cable car from Burnham Park to the summit of Dominican Hill, but the funds have never been found. In the meantime, it's possible to take a taxi to the top, or to walk from the grotto, and admire the views.

Tam-awan Village

On the northwest outskirts of Baguio, **Tam-awan Village** (Pinsao Proper, off Tacay Road; ☏074/446 2949, ⊛www.tamawanvillage.com) is a replica tribal village established by well-known Filipino artist Ben Cabrera, also called Bencab. If you want to spend the night in a tribal hut, this is your chance; you can also drink rice wine around a traditional Ifugao *dap-ay*, an outdoor meeting place with a fire at its centre. Food is available from a small coffee shop, work by local artists is on sale in the shop, and staff often perform impromptu ceremonies and dances. There are also regular workshops you can take part in, including basket-weaving and making rice wine. There are eight Ifugao houses and one Kalinga hut. One particular hut, built on stilts like all the rest, is related to fertility – carvings of men with impressive sex organs adorn the walls. Tam-awan is hardly the height of luxury, but well worth an overnight stay for the experience. Small huts for two people cost P550 a night and family huts P800; toilets and showers are shared. Take a jacket because it can get surprisingly cold. On a clear evening, you'll see magnificent China Sea sunsets; hence the name Tam-awan, which means "vantage point". You can reach Tam-awan Village by taxi for less than P100; it's past the Easter Weaving Room on the road to La Trinidad.

Eating, drinking and nightlife

Baguio Chicken House 85 Session Rd. Popular rustic-style place serving just about everything – chicken and steaks, plus Chinese and Filipino food. The set menus are good value and there are some imported wines. Open 24hr.

Barrio Fiesta Session Rd. At the eastern end of Session Rd where it becomes Session Rd 2, this is a big, brash branch of the popular Manila restaurant chain that offers big portions of Filipino home-cooking at very affordable prices. Popular dishes include *kare-kare*, sizzling beef, sour soup and *adobo*.

Bliss Café Leonard Wood Road, located in the *Munsayac Inn* ⊛www.blissnbaguio.com.

Vegetarian café with hippie-chic interiors and a menu that features what must be some of the country's most intriguing food, including pineapple gluten simmered with red bell pepper, a Japanese-style dish of seaweed, tomatoes and ground gluten, and spiral pasta with organic basil, parmesan cheese and olive oil. There are different specials every day and a good wine list.

Bruno's Café and Restaurant Session Rd. Delicious fresh deli-style food from a Swiss expat chef. The irresistible menu includes delights such as liverwurst sandwiches, spaghetti with home-made tomato sauce, and apple pie with cream. Gourmet salads are fresh and tasty, or try the home-made chilli con carne with Swiss lime tart for dessert. On a cool evening try the rich hot chocolate (P27).

Café by the Ruins 25 Chuntug St. Try not to leave Baguio without eating here. It's far and away one of the city's culinary highlights, with excellent organic food prepared with home-grown herbs. There are good vegetarian dishes (Tofu veggieburger P110), or for those with fewer qualms about animal welfare you can try *pinikpikan*, a tribal chicken delicacy that's also known as "killing me softly" because the chicken is beaten slowly to death with a hammer to make the meat bloody and tender. Native rice wine (*tapuy*) P25 a glass or P90 a bottle. Daily 10am–10pm.

50s Diner Abanao St. Ersatz US diner with stainless steel horseshoe bar, neon signs, burgers, pizzas and sandwiches as well as some Asian dishes. Open 7am to midnight.

La Fondue 4/F, La Azoteia Building, Session Rd. Folksy live music and Swiss fondue at P190 for two. San Miguel is P36 and cocktails P55–105. Try for a table on the small balcony overlooking Session Rd.

Lourdes Place Session Rd. They love their country music in these parts and this wonderfully hick little beerhouse is the best place to watch and listen. Great music (most of the time), tasty bar food and cheap local beer.

Nico's Restaurant Slaughterhouse Compound, Santo Niño barangay. One of half-a-dozen cult canteens, close to the slaughterhouse and the Slaughterhouse bus station, where you can test your bravery with a bowl of Soup No. 5. It contains, according to the waitress, "the balls of the cow"; it's cheap too, at P45. Other dishes include what could be the world cheapest T-bone steak (also P45). A cup of coffee will set you back P8.

Patria Restaurant 181 Session Rd ☏074/442 4963. Baguio has a number of good Chinese restaurants, but this is a classic. It's old and dusty, but always busy because the food is excellent and there's a great deal of it. Soup and noodle dishes start from P65, while an enormous mound of fried rice with vegetables is P70.

Sizzling Plate Carino St. As the name implies, *Sizzling Plate* specialises in sizzling steaks, but it's also known for its mouth-watering *sans rival* cake, a sinfully sweet concoction of meringue and creamy butter icing.

Star Café 39 Session Rd. Famous since 1940 for its Chinese cuisine, according to the sign above the door. The portions are immense and it's cheap. A "small" order of Shanghai fried rice and chicken corn soup will set you back P200 and feed three.

Shopping

Baguio now has some of the same gleaming malls you can find in Manila or Cebu – there's a new SM City Baguio at the top end of Session Road – but it also has interesting little cottage-industry outlets where you can rummage for souvenirs and inexpensive home decor. Apart from the City Market and Good Shepherd Convent, one of the most popular shopping pilgrimages is to the **Easter Weaving Room** (daily; ☏074/442 4972 or 443 6724, ⊛www .easterweaving.com) in Easter Street, on the northwestern outskirts of the city. Owned and managed by the Philippine Episcopal Church, the Easter Weaving Room produces hand-woven articles such as rugs, tablemats, wall hangings, textiles, cushion covers and bed linen. You can watch the weavers at work on old hand looms and, if you've got a few weeks to wait, place a personal order. Weaving was first started here in 1909 under the direction of Deaconess Hargreave, who decided to teach young tribal women to weave so they could supplement the family income. You can get to the Easter Weaving Room by jeepney from Kayang Street, at the northern end of Burnham Park, or by taxi for around P50.

Another shop run as a charity is the **Duntog Foundation Handmade Paper Factory** on Ambuklao Road, the main road heading out of Baguio to

For **moving on from Baguio** to Sagada and Bontoc, the best bus terminal is the Dangwa terminal off Magsaysay Avenue behind Baguio Central mall. Lizardo Trans and Dangwa buses leave here hourly for Sagada from 6am. Buses for Kabayan leave from the Slaughterhouse bus terminal in Slaughterhouse Road, a five-minute taxi ride from the city centre. You can also get buses here that go cross-country to Bayombong in the province of Nueva Viscaya. From Baguio to Banaue you've got two choices: either continue north on a clockwise route through Sagada and Bontoc, or take the eastern anti-clockwise route via Bayombong on one of the regular Dangwa buses. Most travellers opt for the former; the eastern route is a long one, about nine hours, and you'll miss out on some of the Cordillera's best sights. Buses for the northwest coast – San Fernando, Vigan and Laoag – all leave from the same terminal in Governor Pack Road outside the *Baden Powell Inn*, near Session Road.

the northeast, beyond Leonard Wood Road, where the unemployed produce a beautiful range of paper, notepads and sketch pads. You can also buy the products made here at **Duntog House of Paper** on Brent Road, off Leonard Wood Road. In Upper Session Road, a short walk from the eastern end of Session Road, **Narda's** manufactures and sells pretty rugs, linen and tablemats, while **Pilak Silver Shop** on Leonard Wood Road near the *Baguio Vacation Hotel* has bargain-basement silver jewellery, hand-made by local silversmiths.

Kabayan and around

The isolated mountain village of **KABAYAN** in Benguet province, 50km or five hours by bus north of Baguio, came to the attention of the outside world in the early twentieth century when a group of mummies was discovered in the surrounding caves. The mummies are believed by some scientists to date back as far as 2000 BC. When the Spanish arrived mummification was discouraged as unhygienic and the practice was thought to have died out, although village elders in Kabayan claimed to remember corpses still being mummified early in the twentieth century. Controversy still surrounds the Kabayan mummies, some of which have "disappeared" to overseas collectors, sold for a quick buck by unscrupulous middlemen. One was said to have been stolen by a Christian pastor in 1920 and wound up as a sideshow in a Manila circus. Some mummies remain, however, and you can see them in their mountaintop caves and also in the small Kabayan branch of the National Museum. Officials know of dozens of other mummies in the area, but will not give their locations for fear of desecration.

Kabayan is a thrilling side trip from Baguio, although because of the rough road you'll need to spend at least one night in the village. It's impossible to get there and back in a day and still have time to actually do anything. Surrounded on all four sides by mountains, Kabayan had no road until 1960 and no electricity until 1978. This extended isolation has left it rural and unspoilt, a good place to involve yourself in the culture of the **mountain people**, who are friendly and helpful, if a little prone to shyness in the company of foreigners (and that means anyone from further afield than Baguio). Time here is counted in seasons, not hours, and every time-related question ("what time's the bus?") is greeted with the curious phrase "by and by", a catchall that appears to mean anything from "soon" or "tomorrow" to "some time next week". Throw away

The last mummy

The last person to be mummified in Kabayan is thought to be the great-grandmother of Florentino Merino, a former mayor of the village. Florentino is an authority on Kabayan history and the **mummies**, a history that is still largely oral and has only been committed to paper in patches.

His great-grandmother, he says, was mummified around 1901. Her body was bathed and dressed, then tied upright to a chair with a low fire burning underneath to start the drying process. A jar was placed under the corpse to catch the body fluids, which are considered sacred, while elders began the process of peeling off the skin and rubbing juices from native leaves into the muscles to aid preservation. Tobacco smoke was blown through the mouth to dry the internal tissues and drive out worms. After two or three days of treatment, the body was inserted into a pine coffin and interred in a cave in the barangay of Duacan, near Kabayan. When Florentino ventured there not too long ago to clean the burial site, he found the cave had been vandalized and the mummified remains of his great-grandmother had gone.

your watch and enjoy it. Kabayan is slow and quiet, but with a faintly supernatural air that makes it never less than fascinating.

Don't miss the small branch of the **National Museum**, at the north end of Kabayan beyond the bridge. The curator is a helpful lady who will give you a personal guided tour of the exhibits, which include the so-called Smiling Mummy and the Laughing Mummy. Admission is free, but donations are appreciated.

It's also peerless trekking country, but you'll need to hire a **guide**; plenty of locals will volunteer. Ask at the museum, *Brookside Café* or the *Kabayan Coop Lodge*. An old trail cut by Spanish missionaries leads out of Kabayan up into the surrounding mountains and to **Timbac Cave**, where you can see a number of mummies. The cave is high on the side of **Timbac Mountain** and a strenuous four- to five-hour climb. Ask your guide to point out the **Tiningshol Burial Rock**, in which niches were carved to inter the mummified dead. There are also a number of **lakes** in the mountains and **rice terraces** where farmers grow *kintoman*, an aromatic red rice that will be served with most of your meals. Many climbers also use the village as their starting point for climbing **Mount Pulag** (see p.478).

Practicalities

Kabayan is best reached through Baguio. Take a Norton Trans **bus** (9am, 11am & noon) from the Slaughterhouse bus station on Slaughterhouse Road, Magsaysay Avenue. The journey, along narrow dirt roads, takes about five hours and is terrifying; there have been a number of accidents involving buses on this road, with fatalities.

There are two **accommodation** options in Kabayan. The *Kabayan Coop Lodge* has very neat, clean rooms with bunk beds for two people (P100 per person) with a shared bath and toilet. It's a friendly place, built mostly of pine, but there's not much hot water so be prepared to shiver in the shower, where you'll have to employ the native technique of tipping water over your head from a bucket – immensely invigorating when the water's petrifyingly cold and it's only a few degrees above zero outside. If the lodge is full, which is unlikely, the Municipal Building up the road has a hall with bunk beds.

There are half-a-dozen sari-sari stores in Kabayan where you can get snacks, but the only place to **eat** is the *Brookside Café*, next to the *Kabayan Coop Lodge*, where the owner can rustle up pork soup and rice (P45), or eggs and bread

(P35). Sugary Benguet coffee (P10) is just the tonic on a cold Cordillera morning. Local officials have banned the sale of alcohol, so if you are likely to want a quick restorative after a long day's hiking, bring your own from Baguio.

Mount Pulag

Standing 2992m above sea level, **Mount Pulag**, also known as Mount Pulog, is the highest mountain in Luzon and classified by the Metropolitan Mountain-eering Society of the Philippines as a Level III strenuous climb, which means, unless you are experienced, don't try it alone. Villagers in Kabayan, where many climbers spend a night before setting off, will tell you it's possible to go without a guide and to get up and down in a day. But their familiarity with these mountains means they tend to overestimate the skill and stamina of visitors. The terrain is steep, there are gorges and ravines, and, in the heat of the valleys below, it's easy to forget it can be bitterly cold and foggy on top. It's also essential to treat the area with respect: a number of indigenous communities including the Ibaloi, Kalanguya, Kankana-eys and Karaos live on Pulag's slopes and regard the mountain as a sacred place. They have a rich folklore about ancestral spirits inhabiting trees, lakes and mountains, and while they're friendly towards climbers you should stick to the trails and not behave in a way that might cause offence. For up-to-date information on which trails are most accessible, contact the **Mount Pulag National Park Office** in Diego Silang Street, Baguio (T074/444 7428), where you can also get a map of the area.

The two best **trails** for first-timers are those that start from Ambangeg and Kabayan. Both are accessible from Baguio on the Norton Trans bus (see opposite). In Ambangeg the trail begins near the police sub-station in the little barangay of **Bokod**. Ask the bus driver to let you off in Ambangeg itself, which is a regular stop on the route north from Baguio. The main ranger station and the Department of Environment and Natural Resources (DENR) office are both a short way along this trail, close to the gate that marks the entrance to Mount Pulag National Park. You must **register** here; it's also the best place to hire a guide, although rangers won't stop you if you haven't got one. There are no lodgings in Bokod, but if you need to rest up for a night the staff at the municipal building will find you a room in the school or a private home. The Kabayan trail, known also as the Akiki or Killer Trail, starts 2km south of Kabayan on the Baguio–Kabayan road. Whichever way you choose to climb Pulag, take a tent and expect to spend the night on top. The next morning wake up early to watch the sun rise and to marvel at the whole of Luzon at your feet.

Bontoc

The capital of Mountain Province, **BONTOC** is the first major town in the north beyond Baguio. It lies on the banks of the Chico River, about an hour east of Sagada by jeepney.

Bontoc is primarily a commercial town used by tourists as a rest stop on the circuit to Banaue. It is, however, gaining a reputation as a good place for **trekking**; one of the best day treks is to the beautiful Maligcong rice terraces. You will need a **guide**, so contact the Bontoc Ecological Tour Guides Associa-tion at the *Pines Kitchenette and Inn*, behind the market in Rizal Plaza. Some of the local tribes can be nervous of foreigners and it would be unwise to approach them without a guide to help smooth the way (P300–500 per day). One local tribe, the Kalingas, have been particularly wary of outsiders, and these days, while not outright unfriendly, are still rather stand-offish.

Don't miss the small but well-run **Bontoc Museum** (Mon–Sat 9.30am–noon & 1–5pm; P20), next to the post office, close to the town plaza. It contains photographs of headhunting victims and of zealous American missionaries trying to persuade incredulous warriors to choose the path of righteousness. Buses and jeepneys go from Bontoc to Sagada and Baguio, and onwards to Banaue.

Practicalities

There are no hotels in Bontoc, so your only **accommodation** options are basic lodges with very simple rooms and food that has to be ordered in advance. *Pines Kitchenette and Inn* (☎074/602 1509; ❶) is a tourist-friendly establishment with reasonable doubles that have their own private shower or cheaper rooms with shared facilities. The restaurant here has a limited menu, but the food is fresh and tasty, including rich beef broth and mixed vegetables. Even cheaper rooms are available at the *Chico Terrace Inn & Restaurant* (☎074/462 3099; ❶) on the main street (the streets in Bontoc have no names) near its junction with the "hospital road". *Lynda's Guesthouse* (☎074/603 1053; ❶) is at the southern end of town behind the departure area for jeepneys to Banaue. *The Village Inn* (☎074/602 1141; ❶), on the main street next to D'Rising Sun bus terminal, is a good place to arrange guides and car rental. There's also the *Churya-a Hotel and Restaurant* (☎074/602 1821; ❶), near the bus station, which has monastic rooms and a canteen serving simple food.

Headhunting and canao

What fascinated everybody about the Igorots in the nineteenth century was their custom of taking **human heads**. They were still doing so in the mid-twentieth century (take a look at the archive photographs in the Bontoc Museum) but the practice has now died out. In the 1850s the French, British and American reading public were titillated by accounts of Igorot bloodlust written by European missionaries. One wrote:

A priest told me how the Igorots cut off a prisoner's head and held it aloft hanging by the hair to lap up the blood which ran down the severed neck, dancing to the sound of their instruments. The officer of our troops tried to take away the head and stop the fiesta, and this caused a brawl. The friar came away from the affair with his habit stained with blood.

Tribal conflict is less common today than it used to be but by no means unknown. Disputes arise over land and water resources and sometimes end in death. The Dalicans and the Fidelisans, two tribes from the Sagada area, once came to blows over water rights until Dalican tribal elders magnanimously proposed a truce, but only because they had run out of bullets. Spats are not resolved these days through headhunting. The usual method of resolving modern tribal "warfare" is for all tribes from the mountains to be present and help mediate between the two factions. After reaching an agreement for a peace pact, the tribes celebrate by having a huge party, known as a **canao**, a ritual feast during which food, rice wine and blood flow freely. A typical *canao* will involve the slaughter of a *carabao*, a pig and half a dozen chickens, whose bladders are "read" for signs of good fortune, in much the same way other cultures read tea leaves. A tribe that breaks a peace pact is obliged to pay compensation in the form of livestock or rice.

Moving on from Bontoc, from the market you can get jeepneys north to Tinglayan, a three-hour trip into the province of Kalinga. Dangwa has buses to Banaue from a small terminal at the southern edge of town and D'Rising Sun bus company has hourly departures for Baguio from next to the *Village Inn*. Jeepneys leave every hour for Sagada from outside *Nellie's Eatery* on the main road.

Sagada

The small town of **SAGADA**, 160km north of Baguio at an altitude of 1500m, has oodles of charm and mystery, much of it derived from the famous hanging coffins, a labyrinth of subterranean caves that were used by the ancients as burial sites. All this helped establish Sagada's reputation as a remote and idyllic hideaway where robust people live a simple life well away from civilization. To a great extent this is still true. Sagada's distance from Manila and the fact that the quickest way to reach it from the capital involves at least one buttock-numbing bus journey on a terrifyingly narrow road mean it has managed to keep at bay the kind of changes tourism has brought to other areas of the country. There are no shops to speak of, the only accommodation is in lodges with only cold water, and most of the locals – Igorots who speak *Kankana-ey* – still exist by farming cabbages, carrots and potatoes, with some rice for household consumption. Sagada's lofty beauty is given added resonance by its very un-Filipino-ness. The landscape is Alpine and the inhabitants are mountain people, their faces shaped not by the sun and sea of the lowlands, but by the thin air and sharp glare of altitude. Many look almost Mongoloid, a long way removed from the soft Spanish features of Manila and Cebu.

To **reach Sagada** from Baguio, take a bus from the Dangwa terminal off Magsaysay Avenue behind Baguio Central mall. These buses are often rudimentary, with uncomfortable seats and no glass in the windows. Take a scarf to cover your mouth because in the dry season dust thrown up by the tyres rolls through the open windows of the bus in clouds, covering everything, and everyone, inside. The road from Baguio to Sagada is the **Halsema Highway** or "Mountain Trail", a narrow, serpentine gash in the side of the Cordillera that is sometimes no more than a rocky track with vertical cliffs on one side and a sheer drop on the other. It's not a trip for those of a nervous disposition: the buses are crowded, uncomfortable and not especially well maintained. About half way into the trip you'll reach the highest point of the Philippine Highway System, 2250m, marked by a sign and a small concrete pagoda. Enjoy the views if you can. They really are marvellous, especially as you ascend out of Baguio beyond La Trinidad and pass through the deep gorges around Mount Data.

Arrival and information

All **buses** and **jeepneys** arriving in Sagada from Baguio and Bontoc terminate

---

Moving on from Sagada

Jeepneys leave for Bontoc every hour (6am to around midday) – or when they are full to the brim. There are no direct buses from Sagada to Banaue, but you can take a jeepney to Bontoc and then another from Bontoc market to Banaue, a two- to three-hour trip over a mountain pass that even in the dry season can be enveloped in mist.

in a small market square opposite the municipal building on the nameless main road. From here you can walk to all the accommodation.

There's a **tourist information centre** in the municipal building on the main road, where all visitors must register with the Sagada Environmental Guides Association (SEGA). You'll also find a **post office** and **police** outpost here, and a branch of the Sagada Rural Bank where you can change US dollars at a reduced rate. There are no other banks for miles around, so it's best to bring enough **cash** with you in pesos. There's one small **hospital**, St Theodore's, on the eastern edge of the village, but facilities are limited. Sagada's attraction lies partly in its lack of infrastructure: communications are unreliable and electricity is fickle. If the lights go out and you haven't got a torch you can rent a kerosene lamp.

Accommodation

Most of the village's restaurants and **guesthouses** are located on the main road, which runs through the town centre past the little market area, the town hall, the police station and the post office. Guesthouses in Sagada are extremely cheap. The town gets packed out at Christmas and Easter, so if you're planning to visit at these times try to book ahead: some guesthouses can be contacted by mobile telephone or by email.

Alfredo's ☎0921/433 6885. Some surprisingly large rooms – they've even got walk-in wardrobes – right opposite the municipal building. Good breakfast includes home-made oatmeal cookies and French bread. ②

Ganduyan Inn & Cafe ☎0921/273 8097 or 0927/434 0212, ✉ganduyan_inn@yahoo.com. Six comfortable rooms in a good central location, 50m from the municipal building. ②

George Guest House About 1km beyond the municipal building ☎0918/548 0406 or 0920/607 0984. Accommodating staff and a good choice of cosy, clean single, double and family rooms; some have private showers with hot water and some have small, private balconies, so ask to see a selection before you choose. Wonderful views from the communal terrace and there's even a resident masseuse for P300 an hour. ②

Greenhouse Four simple but cosy and well-maintained rooms in a private home down a narrow road opposite *Masferré Country Inn*. ②

Igorot Inn ☎0919/809 2448. Bland concrete building a short walk along the main road past the municipal building, on the left. Choice of doubles with or without shower, but a little expensive by Sagada standards. ③

Masferré Country Inn and Restaurant At the far end of Sagada's main street, beyond the town hall. This rustic and charming little lodge is one of the quietest places to stay, with simple, clean rooms and a good restaurant that offers a choice of daily specials such as chicken curry. The proprietress is the widow of the photographer Eduardo Masferré (see p.483), whose beautiful black and white prints are displayed in the dining area. ①

Olahbinan Resthouse ☎0928/406 7647. A ten-minute walk along the main road beyond the municipal building. Inexpensive rooms with shared showers or more comfortable doubles with a private shower. The restaurant has a log fire and there's a balcony upstairs with terrific views. ①

Rock Inn ☎0920/909 5899, ✉rockfarm_sagada@yahoo.com. Fantastic new addition to the growing list of accommodation options in Sagada, with a choice of rooms that ranges from homey singles and doubles to budget attic rooms where you can sleep under duvets on a tatami mat. Delicious meals in the sunny restaurant use vegetables from the gardens. There are areas in the grounds where you can light a bonfire and sit around before bed with a drink or two. The owner, Mr Bang, is a wonderful host and a mine of information. ②

Sagada Guesthouse & Café Central if slightly noisy location above the bus station and the little open-air market. Rooms range from basic singles to average doubles, all with shared showers. ②

St Joseph Resthouse ☎0918/559 5934. On the right-hand side just before you reach Sagada approaching from Bontoc. This convent was converted into Sagada's first guesthouse by St Mary's Mission in the 1970s. It's now managed by the Episcopal Diocese of the northern Philippines. The grounds are the most beautiful in town, with manicured flowers and bushes. Rooms are small and quaint, with shared cold showers, but most have fine views of the mountains. Dorm-style rooms are also available, and amenities include a large restaurant and a gift shop selling local crafts. ❶

Travelers' Inn & Restaurant ☎ 0920/799 2960, ✉ aprilmay_25@yahoo.com or ✉ lopebosaing@yahoo.com. Simple, clean and homey rooms in a central location; the choices include singles, doubles and quads, some without private bathrooms. There's a restaurant downstairs and a cosy, communal lobby area. The friendly owner, Lope, can help arrange trekking and other activities. ❷

The Town and around

Sagada only began to open up as a destination when it got electricity in the early 1970s, and intellectuals – internal refugees from the Marcos dictatorship – flocked here to write and paint. They didn't produce anything of note, perhaps

△ Trekking near Sagada

because they spent, it is said, much of their time drinking the local rice wine, known as *tapuy*. European hippies followed and so did the military, who thought the *turistas* were supplying funds for an insurgency. A 9pm **curfew** remains in place today.

During the day there are plenty of activities, and in the evenings you can settle down by a log fire in one of the quaint little wooden cafés or restaurants. The curfew means you can't drink after 9pm, but by then almost everyone has gone to bed anyway, exhausted after a long day of exploration.

About 500m from the centre of the village heading towards Bontoc is the **Eduardo Masferré Studio** (Mon–Fri 10am–4pm; free), which showcases fascinating old photographs of tribal life in the early twentieth century. Masferré, half-Spanish and half-Filipino, was born in the Cordillera, fathered by a Spanish soldier who converted to the Episcopalian Church and became a missionary. Eduardo began his education in Spain, but returned to the Philippines to become a missionary in Bontoc. After World War II he opened his photographic studio. It wasn't until late in life that he achieved recognition for his photographs of the people of the Cordillera, with an exhibition in Manila in 1982 and others in Copenhagen, Tokyo and Arles. Masferré died in 1995 at the age of 86 and is buried near Echo Valley in Sagada. At nearby **Sagada Weaving** you can buy fabrics and clothes that are produced using traditional tribal designs. A *bahag*, or loincloth, is an exquisitely hand-loomed piece of long cloth wrapped around a man's middle, but increasingly bought by tourists as a throw or table runner. Woven rucksacks cost from P500 and hats are around P300.

Sagada activities

There are dozens of wonderful **treks** around Sagada, for which you'll need to hire a guide from the Sagada Environmental Guides Association in the municipal building (see p.481). A typical five-hour trek for one to four people costs P300 for the group. One of the most popular day-hikes, taking about five hours in all, is to the **hanging coffins** in **Echo Valley**, high on the surrounding limestone cliffs. There are dozens of little paths leading off through deep foliage in this area so it really is essential to go with someone who knows the way.

The area features two prominent **waterfalls**, which make for enjoyable treks. **Bokong Waterfall** is on the eastern edge of Sagada and can be reached in about one hour by taking the steps on the left about 500m beyond Sagada Weaving. Even better is **Bomod-ok Waterfall**, another hour or so beyond Bokong on the road to the barangay of **Banga-an**. The pool at the foot of Bomod-ok is cold, clear and deep: a perfect place for a dip after a long hot walk.

A reasonably gentle 45-minute hike east of town brings you to a scenic area of rice terraces called **Kiltepan**, a name derived from the names of the three barangays the terraces straddle – Kilong, Tetep-an and Antadao. A more adventurous trek takes you south out of Sagada on the road that leads to **Ambasing**. About one hour on foot beyond Ambasing you reach the foothills of **Mount Ampacao** (see box p.467).

Caving in Sagada's deep network of limestone channels and caverns is an exhilarating but potentially risky activity. Many of the caves are slippery and have ravines inside that plunge into the bowels of the earth. A small number of tourists have been killed in these caves, so if you want to explore them you must get a reliable guide from the municipal building. Caves considered too dangerous are occasionally gated and padlocked; while some are dry, many contain pools and underground rivers, a potential hazard if you don't know the area. The best is **Sumaging**, also known as Big Cave, a 45-minute walk south

The Igorots

Filipinos born in the Gran Cordillera Central are generally known as **Igorots**. In the sixteenth century, mountaineers trading gold in Pangasinan, a lowland area to the west of the Cordillera, were called *Ygolotes* – later to be spelled *Igorrotes* – and the word was adopted generically to refer to almost every inhabitant of the mountainous north. Igorots should more accurately be referred to by the names of six different ethno-linguistic groups into which they can be divided – Isneg (from the Apayao area), Kalinga, Bontoc, Ifugao, Kankanay and Ibaloy.

Whatever they are called, historically they all have one thing in common – their ancestors resisted assimilation into the **Spanish Empire** for three centuries. These were the people the Spanish referred to as *indios*, an inaccurate term used for all indigenous populations in the Spanish Empire both in the Americas and the Philippines. In the nineteenth century the Spanish made repeated attempts to pacify the Cordillera and the results were grim. On the positive side they introduced coffee, cacao and citrus fruit, making the Igorot diet less monotonous and adding Vitamin C, but on the negative they seized pigs, chicken and rice, reduced the poor to debt by peonage, burned houses, cut down crops and introduced smallpox.

However, the grimmest result of the discovery and subjugation of the Igorots was subtler, more tragic and longer lasting – the creation of a distinction between highland and lowland Filipinos, which contrasted submission, conversion and civilization on the one hand with "brutish independence", paganism and savagery on the other. The peoples of the Cordillera became minorities in their own country, still struggling today for representation and recognition of a lifestyle that the Spanish tried to discredit as un-Christian and depraved. "So that said pagans will listen, and listen with some effect, try to win their good will with kindness," said an eighteenth-century Spanish missionary handbook. "If these gentle means should not suffice, proceed with prudence to make some threats."

Though some Igorots did convert to Christianity, many are animists and pray to a hierarchy of **anitos**, a catch-all term for any object of worship. *Anitos* include deities that possess shamans and speak to them during seances, spirits that inhabit sacred groves or forests, personified forces of nature and any supernatural apparition. Offerings are made to benevolent *anitos* for fertility, good health, prosperity, fair weather and success in business (or, in the olden days, war). Evil *anitos* are propitiated to avoid illness, crop failure, storms, accident and death. The Igorot world is filled with soul-snatching evil spirits and goblins that must be appeased with elaborate ceremonies. Omens are also carefully observed. A bird, a snake or a lizard seen upon leaving the house might herald sickness. If an omen bird alights on the roof of a house, appropriate ceremonies are conducted to forestall its portent. If the bird returns, the house is abandoned.

of Sagada. The chambers and rock formations inside are eerie and immense, and have all been named after the things they resemble – the Cauliflower, the King's Curtain and the Rice Granary. Guides equipped with lanterns and ropes will take you on a descent to a pool of clear but extremely cold water where you can swim if you're brave enough, and then through a series of tunnels you'll only be able to get through by crawling. Like many caves in town, Sumaging was once a burial cave, although there are no coffins or human remains there now. However, a short walk south of Sagada and then down a steep trail into the valley is **Lumiang Burial Cave**, where around a hundred old coffins are stacked in the entrance, bones and skulls lying scattered around on the floor. Don't point at any of the coffins or skeletons; it's considered the worst kind of bad luck.

Eating

The choice of **food** in Sagada is among the best in the country, largely because fresh produce is available on the doorstep, often straight from the garden or local farmers. The *Log Cabin Café*, up the hill past the *Sagada Guesthouse*, does some of the best in town with steak, pork loin, pasta and vegetarian rice dishes, all prepared by the expatriate French chef. There can't be many places where for the equivalent of a few dollars you can dine on roast pork loin stuffed with Sagada oranges and Sagada mushrooms, accompanied by watercress salad with balsamic vinaigrette and sautéed potatoes. On Saturday evenings there's a popular buffet (P250), with ingredients always bought fresh from the market that morning. You'll need to reserve a table for the buffet a couple of days in advance. The *Yoghurt House*, on the main street past the town hall heading west, is legendary for pancakes and home-made yoghurt. Try the excellent "hiker's breakfast" of banana strawberry pancakes with mounds of yoghurt. The pleasant log-cabin restaurant at *Masferré Country Inn and Restaurant* has a limited menu of daily specials such as curry, *adobo* and rich chicken soup, with the added bonus of pleasant views across the valley to the church. *Café St Joe*, at *St Joseph Resthouse*, offers hefty servings of meat and garden vegetables served with wild rice, and an entire kettle of freshly brewed mountain coffee will set you back P55. At weekends, there are performances by local bands.

Kalinga

The mountains, rice fields and villages in the magical province of **Kalinga** rarely see visitors, never mind foreign tourists. Kalinga is well off the northern tourist trail through Sagada, Bontoc and Banaue, but if you've got time don't miss it – this is real frontier travel, with massive potential for hiking and climbing, hardly any of it yet tapped. The only accommodation is in simple lodges or local homes, the only shops are roadside stores made of tin, and electricity is a rarity, so make sure you bring a good torch. The **Chico River**, which runs through the province roughly from north to south, is slowly being explored by intrepid rafters and kayakers.

The fiercely proud people of Kalinga gained some prominence in 1975 when they launched a successful campaign against construction of a hydroelectric dam, arguing that it would result in the flooding of their rice terraces and sacred burial grounds. The Kalinga, once fierce headhunters, are still called the Peacocks of the North because of their indomitable, fiery spirit and their refusal to ever be colonized. Some men still wear G-strings and a round hat containing tobacco and matches, while the women wear wraparound skirts. Most Kalinga communities live on levelled parts of steep mountain slopes, where a small shrine called a *podayan* guards the entrance to the village.

Tinglayan and Tabuk

The town of **TINGLAYAN**, about half way between Bontoc and Tabuk, is a good place to base yourself if you want to explore Kalinga. From here you can strike out on a number of mountain trails originally carved by the Spanish when they tried, and failed, to bring the Kalinga people into the Catholic fold. There are trails through tribal villages and rice terraces at Ubo and Mangali, and a number of mountain lakes, including Bonnong and Padcharao.

Wherever you go in Kalinga you'll need a **guide**; you can find one by asking at the municipal building on the main road, but be prepared to hang around for

△ Ifugao people

a few hours while staff ask around the town. Law and order in the province still relies very much on tribal pacts brokered by elders. Occasionally there are disputes – over water rights, for instance – that result in violence, and a guide will stop you stumbling into any areas where tensions might be high. **Accommodation** in Tinglayan is almost nonexistent – when you arrive, go to the municipal building where the mayor or one of his staff will offer assistance. From Tinglayan you can either double back to Bontoc or continue on the rough road north through Piat, Kabugao and on to Laoag, a gruelling and slow trip of about ten hours.

The provincial capital of **TABUK**, 50km north of Tinglayan, is the place to sign up for white-water **rafting trips** on the Chico River. Chico River Quest, a well-run company that has high standards of safety, has an office in Tabuk (☏0912/840 1202). You can also make reservations and get details from Rhoda Ceralde in Manila (☏02/434 4121) or the Manila office of Kalinga's congressman (☏02/931 4709).

Tinglayen and Tabuk can both be reached be jeepney heading north from Bontoc, although services in this area are anything but regular and it's a bumpy road, so the trip can take many hours.

Banaue and around

It's a rugged but spectacular trip from Bontoc to **BANAUE** in Ifugao province, along a winding road that leads up into the misty Cordillera and across a

Banaue's stairways to heaven

The **rice terraces** at Banaue are one of the great icons of the Philippines, hewn from the land 2000 years ago by Ifugao tribespeople using primitive tools, an achievement in engineering terms that ranks alongside the building of the pyramids. Called the "Stairway to Heaven" by the Ifugaos, the terraces would stretch 20,000km if laid out end to end. Not only are they an awesome sight, but also an object lesson in **sustainability**. These vast, layered paddies demonstrate that nature need not be destroyed to satisfy man's needs.

The terraces are on the UNESCO **World Heritage list**, a sign that they will not last forever if they are not protected. The walls that link the paddies are beginning to crumble, and there's a shortage of young people to help carry out repairs. Another part of the problem is tourism. People who would otherwise have been working on the terraces are now making a much easier buck flogging reproduction tribal artefacts or rare orchids from the surrounding forests. What's more, rice farming has little allure for the young people of the Cordillera. They are tired of the subsistence livelihood their parents eked from the land and are packing their bags for Manila. The resulting labour shortage means the terraces are producing a mere 35 percent of the area's rice needs when they should be producing a hundred percent.

mountaintop pass. It may only be 300km north of Manila, but Banaue might as well be a world away, 1300m above sea level and far removed in spirit and topography from the beaches and palm trees of the south. This is the heart of **rice terrace** country: the terraces in Banaue itself are some of the most impressive and well known, although there are hundreds of others in valleys and gorges throughout the area, most of which can be reached on foot. Some of the best are at nearby **BATAD**, where there is also rustic accommodation so you can stay overnight and hike back the next morning, and there also wonderful terraces and scenery at **BANGA-AN VILLAGE**, another strenuous day trek from Banaue.

Banaue itself is a small, unimpressive town centred around a marketplace, where there are a few guesthouses and some souvenir shops. The small **Banaue Museum** (daily 8am–5pm; if it's closed ask at the neighbouring *Banaue View Inn* for the key) has old tribal tools, costumes and a collection of photographs of Banaue and its people at the beginning of the twentieth century.

Two kilometres north along the road from the marketplace is the main **lookout point** for the rice terraces. Ifugao elders in traditional costume will ask for a small fee if you want to take their photograph. A handful of souvenir stalls surrounding the lookout sell carved wooden bowls and woven blankets at bargain prices.

Practicalities

All long-distance buses, local buses and jeepneys terminate at the marketplace near the town hall in Banaue, from where it's a short walk to most accommodation. To get trekking maps (P10) of the area and arrange a guide, head to the **tourist office** (Mon–Sat 3–6pm) in the town hall at the end of the road beyond the market and the souvenir shops. Most hotels also have the trekking map. It's not essential for you to hire a **guide** for the treks marked on this map, although they can help you avoid time-consuming mistakes. The usual charge for a guide is P850 a day, plus some snacks and drinks.

There are no banks in Banaue, but most hotels **change money**. If possible, change money before you arrive and make sure you've got enough pesos to last your stay. The **post office** has poste restante, but it's a ten-minute jeepney ride from the marketplace near the *Banaue Hotel and Youth Hostel*. You can make **telephone calls** from the post office. At the *Banaue View Inn* you can access the **Internet** for P120 an hour, but don't depend on the connection always being reliable. There's also a small cybercafé at *Café Jam* (p.489).

Accommodation

Accommodation in Banaue is generally basic, but clean and friendly, and many places have restaurants attached. There are nineteen hotels or lodging houses so finding somewhere without a reservation is not a problem, except at Christmas and Easter.

Banaue Hotel and Youth Hostel A ten-minute journey south from the marketplace by jeepney ☏074/386 4087 or 4088; ☏02/752 0307 or 0308. This rambling and rather eccentric hotel stands on a ledge and has nice grounds, big comfy rooms, a swimming pool and views across the valley to the terraces. In the neighbouring hostel there are dorm beds for P100 a night. The main hotel, with its immense corridors, wide stairways and dusty old carpet, has a decent restaurant. Steep steps lead down from the hotel to Tam-an Village (see opposite), where you can meet Ifugao people and buy handicrafts. Ask for a room with a view across the terraces: these rooms have big balconies, and sunrise over the valley is magical. ❽

Banaue View Inn Next to the Banaue Museum, a few minutes north along the main road from the market area ☏074/386 4078. Big, clean doubles with a shared or private bath. ❶

Banga-an Family Inn & Restaurant About 12km to the east of Banaue near Batad Junction and consequently a great place for a stopover if you're trekking in the area around Batad, Cambulo, Pula and Banga-an (p.487). Comfortable rooms are in a number of stand-alone cottages; showers are cold, but staff will heat a bucket of water for you. There's a rickety restaurant for hot meals, coffee and beer. It's a good idea to book ahead, if only to make sure there'll be fresh food such as chicken at the ready: otherwise it's tinned corned beef and sardines. Call the owner, Erwin Laroco (☏919/880 9308). ❶

Fairview Inn Pinkish stuccoed villa south of town near the *Banaue Hotel* ☏074/386 4002. Clean rooms with basic private bathrooms (not hot water). Make sure you get one of the rooms with a private balcony and a view over the rice terraces. ❷

Greenview Lodge A short walk north of the marketplace on the road to the church ☏074/386 4021. Singles, twins and doubles, some with private showers, and a restaurant offering good coffee and various daily specials for breakfast, lunch and dinner. ❶

Halfway Inn A short walk beyond the market place. ☏074/386 4211. Another popular budget bet with simple singles, doubles and quads, plus bargain basement beds in the dorm for P150 a night. ❷

J&L Pension On the road to the *Banaue Hotel* ☏074/386 4035. Peaceful and quiet, and with a reasonable choice of budget singles, twins and doubles, some with their own bathroom. ❷

People's Lodge and Restaurant Popular budget place just down the road heading towards the church from the market ☏074/386 4014. Cheaper rooms share showers and toilets – but the views from the shared toilets are memorable. More expensive rooms are big with a private shower and, if you're lucky, you'll have excellent views across the valley. Service in the small restaurant is haphazard, but there are other places nearby to eat. ❷

🏃 **Sanafe Lodge** ☏074/386 4085, ⊛www .sanafelodge.com. This is a homey and atmospheric wooden lodge – and if you take a room at the back you'll have marvellous rice terrace views. There's also a huge terrace, ideal for a wake-up cup of coffee or a sunset drink. Rooms are spacious and comfortable, with the choice ranging from doubles to family rooms that can sleep five and beds in the dorm. Downstairs there's also one of Banaue's better restaurants, with European and Filipino food. Well-run by the cheerful and helpful owner, Susan Paredes, the eldest daughter of a former local governor. ❷

🏃 **Spring Village Inn** A few minutes' walk south of the market area on the road to the *Banaue Hotel* ☏074/386 4037. Pleasant, quiet and friendly lodge, with wooden floors throughout and cheery rooms, some with verandas. ❷

Eating and drinking

There's no nightlife scene to speak of in Banaue, just a handful of **restaurants** and small bars that shut down when the last tired trekker heads for bed, usually at around 9pm. The restaurant at the *People's Lodge and Restaurant* does some of the best food in town, mostly Filipino favourites such as soup and *adobo* with hefty portions of piping hot rice. The pancakes are the kind that come from a packet, but with bananas and honey on top they make a tasty breakfast. There's not much for vegetarians, but you can ask for stir-fried vegetables. The "People's Rice" set menu is wild rice with *chop suey* and fried chicken, plus a bowl of asparagus soup and a banana for dessert; a snip at P100. The restaurant at the *Banaue Hotel and Youth Hostel* has an extensive European and Asian menu and there's a buffet every evening (P350). *Café Jam* near the town hall is simple and friendly, with a menu that depends largely on what the owner has managed to buy at the market that day. Typical dishes include *tinola* and curry. At *Tiffany's Diner* on the road to the *Banaue Hotel* (right next to the *Fairview Inn*) you can get basics such as *adobo* and native sausage, while the menu at *Sanafe Lodge* includes Filipino, American, Italian, Korean and Chinese dishes – and if it's not too chilly you can eat on the terrace overlooking the valley.

Tam-an Village

TAM-AN is billed by the tourist authorities as an authentic Ifugao village where a life of bucolic bliss goes on much as it has done for centuries. This isn't quite true. It's actually a rather depressing collection of corrugated tin shacks where children play among the pigs and chickens. This is the other side of provincial life in the developing world – a hard slog to make ends meet and to keep bellies full. There's a sense of desperation here, with women overly keen to sell you tribal knick-knacks they claim are genuine but are clearly reproduction. A small shop about half-way down the steps to Tam-an sells tribal artefacts, some possibly genuine but most not.

There's no need to go on an organized tour to Tam-an. It's right at the back of the *Banaue Hotel and Youth Hostel*, clearly signposted down some steep steps. The hike beyond Tam-an through **POITAN** is much more pleasant, taking you along an ancient irrigation canal through rice terraces and a handful of more traditional villages. From the hotel to Poitan and back will take about four hours.

Batad

The fifteen-kilometre trek east from Banaue to the remote little village of **BATAD** (see box p.467) has become something of a pilgrimage for visitors looking for rural isolation and unforgettable rice terrace scenery. You can shorten the trek by taking a jeepney from the market in Banaue for the first 12km (to Batad Junction – the drivers all know it) before starting a strenuous walk northwards up a steep, marked trail. Batad nestles in a natural amphitheatre, close to the glorious **Tappia Waterfall**, which is 21m high and has a deep, bracing pool for swimming.

Village life in Batad has remained virtually unchanged for centuries, although the development of tourism has seen half-a-dozen primitive **guesthouses** spring up to cater for the influx. Rooms in Batad must be among the cheapest on the planet: P35–50 per head. Choose from the *Foreigner's Inn*, which has a nice balcony restaurant; the wonderful *Hillside Inn*, with its majestic views; and *Simon's Inn*, which has a good cosy café, serving, of all things, pizza. From Batad you can either hike back to Banaue the same way or continue through Cambulo and Pula, a long walk that will mean you staying overnight somewhere along the way (see box p.467).

△ Rice terraces near Batad

Cambulo, Pula and Banga-an

From Batad you can continue trekking north through fields and terraces to the villages of **CAMBULO** and **PULA** (see box p.467), where some of the old thatched homes are well preserved and the residents, especially the children, are friendly and hospitable. There are some unforgettable sights along this route, including waterfalls, steep gorges and a hanging bridge near Cambulo that requires a bit of nerve to cross. From Batad to Cambulo takes about two hours and from Cambulo to Pula another hour. Either camp or spend the night at one of the small **inns** in Pula – nothing more than wooden houses with hard beds – where the owners can brew you strong coffee from their own coffee plants and rustle up some tinned sardines and rice. If you want different food, bring your own. *Cambulo Friends Inn* and *Cambulo Riverside* both charge P50 a night. The path from Pula back to Banaue will bring you out near the Banaue rice terraces viewpoint, from where you can hop on a jeepney back to your hotel. This section of the trek is a long one though – about six hours. You can extend your trekking in the Batad area by backtracking south from Batad to the tiny village of **Banga-an**, which is no more than a few dozen Ifugao homes perched between rice terraces. There are no restaurants and no lodges in Banga-an itself, but it's possible to stay overnight with the villagers for a small fee; they'll also prepare simple meals for you.

Travel details

Buses

Abucay to: Mariveles (hourly; 1hr 15min).
Alaminos to: Bolinao (hourly; 45min); San Fernando, La Union (several daily; 2hr 30min); Manila (hourly; 3hr 30min).

Aparri to: Claveria (several daily; 2hr); Pagudpud (several daily; 3hr); Tuguegarao (hourly; 1hr).
Angeles to: Alaminos (6–8 daily; 3hr); Baguio (6 daily; 6hr); Dagupan (several daily; 2hr); Lingayen (several daily; 2hr); Manila (24 daily; 2–3hr); Olongapo (12 daily; 3hr); San Fernando (La Union; 6 daily; 3hr).

Baguio to: Bayombong (several daily; 5hr); Bokod (2–3 daily; 4hr); Bontoc (hourly; 5–6hr); Kabayan (2–3 daily; 5–6hr); Laoag (several daily; 6hr); Manila (hourly; 7hr); Mount Data (hourly; 3hr); Sagada (hourly; 5–6hr); San Fernando, La Union (hourly; 2hr); Vigan (hourly; 5hr).

Balanga to: Manila (hourly; 4hr); Mariveles (hourly; 1hr); San Fernando, Pampanga (hourly; 2hr).

Baler to: Cabanatuan (several daily; 3hr).

Banaue to: Bontoc; 2–4 daily; 3hr); Cabanatuan (4 daily; 5hr); Cauayan (several daily; 3hr); Manila (several daily; 7hr).

Bolinao to: Alaminos (hourly; 45min).

Bontoc to: Baguio (hourly; 5–6hr); Banaue (2–4 daily; 3hr).

Cabanatuan to: Baler (several daily; 3hr); Dau (several daily; 2hr 45min); Tarlac City (several daily; 2hr 30min).

Dagupan to: Agoo (hourly; 1hr 30min); Bauang (hourly; 2hr); Laoag (hourly; 6hr); Lingayen (hourly; 30min); Manila (hourly; 3hr); San Fabian (hourly; 1hr); San Fernando, La Union (hourly; 1hr 20min); Vigan (hourly; 3–4hr).

Dau to: Alaminos (6–8 daily; 3hr); Baguio (8 daily; 6hr); Cabanatuan (several daily; 2hr 45min); Dagupan (several daily; 2hr); Laoag (2–4 daily; 8–10hr); Lingayen (several daily; 2hr); Manila (24 daily; 2–3hr); Olongapo (hourly; 3hr); San Fernando, La Union (12 daily; 3hr); Vigan (2–4 daily; 6–8hr); Tarlac City (6–8 daily; 3hr).

Iba to: Alaminos (hourly; 2hr); Batolan (hourly; 45min); Dau (hourly; 3hr); San Antonio (hourly; 1hr 3min); Santa Cruz (hourly; 1hr).

Iguig to: Tuguegarao (hourly; 1hr).

Kabayan to: Ambangeg (2–3 daily; 2hr); Baguio (2–3 daily; 5–6hr).

Laoag to: Baguio (several daily; 6hr); Dau (2–4 daily; 6–8hr); Manila (hourly; 10hr); Pagudpud (several daily; 2hr); San Fernando, La Union (hourly; 4hr); Vigan (hourly; 2hr).

Lingayen to: Alaminos (hourly; 1hr); Dagupan (hourly; 30min); Manila (hourly; 3hr); San Fabian (hourly; 1hr 30min); Tarlac City (hourly; 2hr 30min).

Mariveles to: Abucay (hourly; 1hr 15min); Manila (several daily; 4hr); Olongapo (hourly; 2hr).

Olongapo to: Alaminos (hourly; 2–3hr); Batolan (hourly; 2hr); Dau (hourly; 3hr); Iba (hourly; 1–2hr); Manila (hourly; 4hr); San Antonio (hourly; 1hr); Santa Cruz (hourly; 3hr); San Fernando, La Union (several daily; 4hr); Orion (hourly; 1hr 30min).

Orion to: Olongapo (hourly; 1hr 30min).

Pagupud to: Aparri (several daily; 3hr); Laoag (several daily; 2hr); Manila (2–4 daily; 10hr); Vigan (several daily; 4hr).

Peñablanca to: Tuguegarao (hourly; 1hr).

Piat to: Tuguegarao (hourly; 1hr 30min).

Sagada to: Baguio (hourly; 5–6hr); Bontoc (hourly; 1hr); Mount Data (hourly; 3hr).

San Fabian to: Agoo (hourly; 45min); Dagupan (hourly; 1hr); Laoag (hourly; 6hr); Lingayen (hourly; 1hr 30min); Manila (hourly; 4hr); San Fernando, La Union (hourly; 2hr); Vigan (hourly; 3–4hr).

San Fernando (La Union) to: Alaminos (several daily; 2hr 30min); Angeles (6 daily; 3hr); Baguio (hourly; 2hr); Dagupan (hourly; 1hr 20min); Dau (12 daily; 3hr); Laoag (hourly; 5hr); Manila (hourly; 5–6hr); Olongapo (several daily; 4hr); Pagudpud (several daily; 7hr); San Fernando, Pampanga (6 daily; 3hr); San Juan (hourly; 30min); Tarlac City (hourly; 3hr); Vigan (hourly; 3hr).

San Fernando (Pampanga) to: Alaminos (6–8 daily; 3hr); Baguio (6 daily; 6hr); Dagupan (several daily; 2hr); Laoag (2–4 daily; 8–10hr); Lingayen (several daily; 2hr); Manila (24 daily; 2–3hr); Olongapo (12 daily; 3hr); San Fernando, La Union (6 daily; 4hr); Vigan (2–4 daily; 6–8hr).

Santa Ana to: Tuguegarao (hourly; 2hr 45min).

Tuguegarao to: Aparri (hourly; 2hr); Cauayan (hourly; 2hr); Manila (several daily; 10–12hr); Iguig (hourly; 1hr); Peñablanca (hourly; 1hr); Piat (hourly; 1hr 30min); Santa Ana (hourly; 4–5hr).

Vigan to: Badoc (hourly; 1hr); Baguio (several daily; 5hr); Dagupan (hourly; 2–3hr); Dau (2–4 daily; 6–8hr); Laoag (hourly; 2hr); Manila (hourly; 7hr); Pagudpud (several daily; 4hr); San Fabian (hourly; 3–4hr); San Fernando, La Union (hourly; 3hr); Sinait (hourly; 40min).

Jeepneys and FX taxis

Agoo to: Bauang (hourly; 1hr 30min); San Fabian (several daily; 1hr).

Alaminos to: Bolinao (hourly; 1hr); Lucap (every 15mins; 30min).

Angeles to: Dau (every 15min; 30min); San Fernando, Pampanga (every 15 min; 30min); Field's Avenue (Clark; every 15min; 30min).

Arayat to: San Fernando, Pampanga (hourly; 1hr).

Banaue to: Bontoc (hourly; 3hr).

Barrio Barretto to: Olongapo (every 20min; 1hr).

Batac to: Laoag (hourly; 30min); Paoay (hourly; 15min).

Bauang to: San Fernando, La Union (every 20min; 20min).

Bolinao to: Alaminos (hourly; 1hr); Patar Beach (hourly; 45min).

Bontoc to: Banaue (hourly; 3hr); Sagada (hourly; 1hr 30min); Tinglayan (several daily; 2–3hr).

Botolan to: San Marcelino (several daily; 2hr).

Burgos to: Pagudpud (several daily; 1hr).

Dau to: Manila (2–3 daily; 2–3hr).

Iguig to: Tuguegarao (hourly; 1hr 30min).

La Paz to: Laoag (hourly; 15min).

Laoag to: Batac (hourly; 30min); La Paz (hourly; 15min); Pagudpud (hourly; 2hr); Paoay (hourly; 45min); Sarrat (hourly; 30min).

Lucap to: Alaminos (every 15min; 30min).

Olongapo to: Barrio Barretto (every 20min; 1hr); Bagac (several daily; 2hr).

Pagudpud to: Laoag (hourly; 2hr); Burgos (several daily; 1hr).

Pandaquit to: San Antonio (hourly; 45min).

Paoay to: Laoag (hourly; 45min).

Patar Beach to: Bolinao (hourly; 45min).

Peñablanca to: Tuguegarao (hourly; 1hr).

Piat to: Tuguegarao (several daily; 1hr 45min).

Sagada to: Bontoc (hourly; 1hr 30min).

San Antonio to: Pandaquit (hourly; 45min).

San Fabian to: Agoo (several daily; 1hr).

San Fernando (La Union) to: Bauang (every 20min; 20min); San Juan (hourly; 40min).

San Fernando (Pampanga) to: Angeles (every 15 min; 30min); Arayat (hourly; 1–2hr); Cutud (24 daily; 1hr); Fields Avenue (Clark; every 15min; 30min).

San Juan to: San Fernando, La Union (hourly; 40min).

San Marcelino to: Botolan (several daily; 2hr).

Sarrat to: Laoag (hourly; 30min).

Tabuk to: Tinglayan (several daily; 2hr).

Tinglayan to: Bontoc (several daily; 2–3hr); Laoag (irregular; 10hr); Tabuk (several daily; 2hr).

Tuguegarao to: Iguig (hourly; 1hr 30min); Peñablanca (hourly; 1hr); Piat (several daily; 1hr 45min).

Ferries (Batanes)

Batan to: Itbayat (daily; 4hr); Sabtang (2–4 daily; 1hr).

Domestic flights

Baguio to: Manila (daily; 1hr 10min).

Basco to: Manila (3 weekly; 2hr).

Clark to: Manila (6 weekly; 30min).

Laoag to: Manila (daily; 50min).

Tuguegarao to: Manila (3 weekly; 50min).

Contexts

Contexts

History

F ilipinos have sometimes been accused of having no sense of history and of not knowing who they really are, a result of the many diverse influences – Malay, Chinese, European, American – that have collided in the archipelago down the centuries. Historians, at least, have managed to form a general agreement on the five **decisive events** that shaped – and continue to shape – the nation: the beginning of rice cultivation in the northern Cordillera, which led to the construction of the Banaue rice terraces; the Islamization of Sulu and western Mindanao; the arrival of Magellan; the arrival of the founder of Manila, Miguel Lopez de Legazpi; and the Christianization of Luzon.

The pre-colonial period

Human fossil remains found in Palawan suggest that humans first migrated across land bridges from mainland Asia and Borneo during the Ice Age, some 50,000 years ago. Carbon dating of fossilized human remains discovered at Tabon Cave in Palawan indicated so-called "Tabon Man" was living in the cave about 22,000 years ago. Deeper excavations of the cave indicated humans were in the area from 45,000 to 50,000 years ago.

The Aeta or **Negritos**, the country's indigenous people, are said to be descended from these first migrants. But the land bridge theory is disputed by some anthropologists who say human remains found in the Philippines can be dated back two million years, to the time of Java Man, making human settlement in the archipelago coequal to the rest of Southeast Asia. Whatever the truth, successive migrations did populate the islands through the centuries. One of the first of these migrations, about 15,000 years ago, was by Mongoloid tribes driven south from the interior of China by the Han Chinese. Following them came groups from southern China and Vietnam, settling along riverbanks and building houses on stilts to safeguard against floods. They introduced the delicate art of cultivating rice in irrigated fields and domesticated for that purpose the country's ubiquitous beast of burden, the *carabao*. The Ifugaos, who arrived in the influx from China, drifted into northern Luzon, where they constructed one of the world's engineering wonders: the Banaue rice terraces (see box on p.487).

Malays from Indonesia and the Malay peninsula streamed into the islands more than 2000 years ago, sailing through the Sulu Sea and settling first in the Visayas and southwestern Luzon. Their outrigger boats, equipped with lateen sails, each carried a family or clans led by a chief. Once ashore, they remained together in barangays, as their boats were called. (President Marcos, in an effort to revive the past, later decreed that Philippine villages be formally designated barangays.) The bulk of Filipinos today, at least in the Visayas and Mindanao, are descended from these Malay settlers.

Archeological evidence shows a rich pre-colonial culture that included skills in weaving, ship-building, mining and goldsmithing. Contact with Asian neighbours dates back to at least 500 BC in the form of trade with the powerful **Hindu empires** in Java and Sumatra. Trade ties with China were extensive by the tenth century, while contact with Arab traders, which reached its peak in the twelfth century, drew Sufis and missionaries who began the propagation of Islam. In 1380, the Arab scholar Makdam arrived in the Sulu Islands, and in 1475, the Muslim leader Sharif Mohammed Kabungsuwan, from Johore, married a native princess and declared himself the first sultan of Mindanao. By the time the Spanish arrived, **Islam** was well established in Mindanao and had started to influence groups as far north as Luzon, where a great Muslim chief, Suleiman, ruled Manila. There their advance was halted by the Spanish, who dubbed them Moros, after the Moors they had expelled from Spain.

Spanish rule

The country's turbulent modern history began on April 24, 1521 when **Ferdinand Magellan**, a Portuguese seafarer in the service of Spain, arrived in Cebu after sailing for four months across the vast ocean he named the Pacific, the crews on his three ships ravaged by disease and starvation. A few weeks earlier he had sighted the islands, but chose to land in what would later become Cebu because the natives seemed most friendly. Magellan planted a wooden cross to claim the islands for **Spain**. One of the chiefs who was baptized in those early days of Spanish conquest was **Humabon**, who Magellan decided would make a good surrogate in the new colony. He directed the local tribes to pledge allegiance to Humabon, who would represent the Spanish Crown. But Lapu Lapu, a chief on the nearby island of Mactan and Humabon's traditional enemy, resisted. Days later Magellan and his men waded ashore on Mactan to bring Lapu Lapu to heel. Word of the strike had leaked and Lapu Lapu lay in wait with 1500 warriors. When Lapu Lapu's men attacked, unleashing a hail of spears and arrows, most of Magellan's men fled in panic. Magellan was speared through the foot and fell, but was singled out as a target and hacked to death.

Spanish conquistador Ruy Lopez de Villalobos tried once again to claim the islands for Spain in 1543, but was driven out by the natives a year later after naming the Philippines in honour of the future **King Philip II**. King Charles had by then governed Spain for nearly three decades and in 1556 abdicated in favour of his son, Philip, who shared Charles's obsession with the Portuguese and was determined to smash their lucrative trade with the Orient. He chose **Miguel Lopez de Legazpi**, a minor Basque aristocrat, to lead a hazardous expedition to establish a permanent base in the Philippines, which he hoped would act as a wedge between Portugal and China. Legazpi sailed to the Philippines on board the *Capitana*, establishing a colony in Bohol and then moving on to Cebu where he erected the first Spanish fort in the Philippines. But a series of misunderstandings – one involving the gift of a concubine that Legazpi piously refused – made the situation in Cebu perilous, and Legazpi looked for a more solid base.

In 1571 Legazpi's men sighted a small settlement on an immense natural harbour in Luzon, and Legazpi sailed there to appraise it as a possible capital. He and his troops disembarked on May 17, 1571, and the local chieftain, Suleiman, yielded shortly afterwards, allowing a jubilant Legazpi to establish a new Spanish capital – **Manila** – which he formally founded on June 24. The Philippines, originally seen as a springboard for more lucrative ventures elsewhere, was now a permanent Spanish colony – and destined to become the most Westernized country in Asia, as well as the only predominantly Catholic one. Within a decade of the founding of the capital the Spanish controlled the entire country and had converted its people to "the true religion", except for pockets of northern Luzon and Muslim regions of Mindanao. Spanish conquistadors and friars zealously set about propagating **Catholicism**, building churches and bringing rural folk *debajo de las compañas* (under the bells), into organized Spanish *pueblos*, establishing many of the country's towns and cities. They imposed a **feudal system**, concentrating populations under their control into new towns and estates, as a result of which there were numerous small revolts.

Until 1821, the Philippines was administered from **Mexico**, and its Spanish residents, especially those in Manila, grew prosperous and corrupt on the strength of the galleon trade, a venture that involved re-exporting goods from China through Manila to Mexico, taking the route pioneered by Urdaneta. The rural areas, meanwhile, slumbered in seclusion, as remote from Manila as Manila was from much of the outside world. The friars, dreading change, did nothing to improve the subsistence economy, while in the capital, according to an early diarist, "the rich spend ten months of the year with nothing to do."

In theory, Filipinos were to rule themselves under Spain's guidance, but in practice it was the **friars** who ran the show. They derived their power from the enormous influence of the monastic orders, which spanned the world like global corporations. Secular officials came and went, but the clergy stayed. Many friars ignored their vows of celibacy and sired children with local women. They exercised their power through a number of administrative functions, including setting budgets, conducting the parish census, screening recruits for the military and presiding over the police. There were cosmetic local administrations, but they could not act without the friars' consent. The monastic orders were also responsible for the founding of a number of **universities** and **colleges** in Manila, among them Santo Tomas, which dates back to 1601 and still operates. Rural schools, by contrast, were simple affairs run by friars, themselves simple men versed in only a few subjects. They taught the catechism and the lives of the saints by rote, but only in local tongues, on the principal that fluency in Spanish would give the natives ideas above their station.

It wasn't until the late eighteenth century that the ossification brought about by the Spanish regime began to ease, the result of a series of shocks that stimulated an inexorable economic, social and political evolution with dramatic consequences. Attempts by the Dutch, Portuguese and Chinese to establish a presence in the archipelago were repelled. But the **British** managed to occupy Manila for a few months in 1762, raiding it in a sideshow to the Seven Years' War, then being waged by Britain against France and Spain in Europe and America. They handed it back to Spain under the conditions of the Treaty of Paris, signed in 1763, but their easy victory served notice that the Philippines was vulnerable.

With the opening of the Suez Canal in 1869, young Filipinos left their country to study in Europe and returned with liberal ideas and talk of freedom. A small **revolt** in Cavite in 1872 was quickly put down, but the anger and frustration Filipinos felt about colonial rule would not go away. Intellectuals such as Marcelo H. Del Pilar and Juan Luna were the spiritual founders of the independence movement, but it was the writings of a diminutive young doctor from Laguna province, **José Rizal**, that provided the spark for the flame. His novel *Noli Me Tangere* was written while he was studying in Spain, and portrayed colonial rule as a cancer and the Spanish friars as fat, pompous fools. It was promptly banned by the Spanish, but distributed underground along with other inflammatory essays by Rizal and, later, his second novel, *El Filibusterismo*.

In 1892, Rizal returned to Manila and founded the reform movement **Liga Filipina**, which never espoused revolution, only moderate reform. Its members swore oaths and took part in blood rites, and, innocuous as the movement was, the friars smelled sedition. Rizal was arrested and exiled to Dapitan on Mindanao. **Andres Bonifacio** took over the reins by establishing the secret society known as the **Katipunan** or KKK. Its full name was Kataastaasan, Kagalanggalang na Katipunan nang mga Anak ng Bayan, which means "Honorable, respectable sons and daughters of the nation". In August, 1896, the armed struggle for **independence** broke out, and Rizal was accused of master-minding it. Rizal had, in fact, called Bonifacio's revolution "absurd and savage" and had earlier turned down an invitation from Bonifacio to participate in it. His trial lasted a day, one of the seven military judges concluding that Rizal's being a native must be considered "an aggravating factor". Rizal's Spanish military lawyer did little for him so he finally rose to defend himself. "I have sought political liberty," he said, "but never the freedom to rebel." He was duly found guilty and executed by firing squad in Manila in what is now known as Rizal Park on December 30, 1896. The night before he died he wrote *Mi Ultimo Adios*, a farewell poem to the country he loved.

The American imperial adventure

News of Rizal's martyrdom inflamed the uprising ignited by Bonifacio. Spanish officials deluded themselves, blaming it on a few troublemakers, but by now Bonifacio had decided violence was the only option and, with the young firebrand general, **Emilio Aguinaldo**, he called openly for a government "like that of the United States". In 1897, when it became clear they were facing all-out insurrection, the Spanish negotiated a truce with Aguinaldo, who had by now declared himself generalissimo, fallen out with Bonifacio, and had a kangaroo court condemn him to death. The Spanish would pay the rebels 800,000 pesos, half immediately, a quarter when they laid down their arms and the rest after a Te Deum marking the armistice was chanted in Manila Cathedral. In exchange Aguinaldo agreed to go abroad. A cheque in his pocket, he sailed for Hong Kong, disavowing his rebellion and declaring his loyalty to Spain.

As both Aguinaldo and the Spanish expected, peace proved to be temporary. The Filipinos had not abandoned their dream of independence and Spain could not face the prospect of a lost empire, so war resumed. And soon the Filipinos found themselves with an unexpected ally, as the **United States** arrived to taste the glories and perils of imperialism for the first time in its history.

In 1898, as a result of a dispute over Cuba, war broke out between the US and Spain, and as an extension of it the US decided to expel Spain from the Philip-pines. The Spanish fleet was soundly beaten in Manila Bay by ships under the command of George Dewey, who on the morning of April 30, 1898, gave the famous order to his captain, "You may fire when you are ready, Gridley." The Filipinos fought on the side of the US, and when the battle was over General Aguinaldo, now back from Hong Kong having disavowed his disavowal of the rebellion, declared the Philippines independent. The US, however, had other ideas and paid Spain US$20 million for its former possession. Having got rid of one colonizing power, Filipinos were now answerable to another. This was America's first great imperial adventure, and back home it became known as a "splendid little war". **Anti-imperialists**, among them the writer Mark Twain, held that subjugation of foreign peoples violated the basic American precept of government by the consent of the governed, but their sentiments evoked no sympathy in Washington.

In Manila the atmosphere was tense. Filipinos were impatient for independence and their insurrectionist forces were digging in around the city, led by Aguinaldo from his base in Malolos, Bulacan, where he had convened a national assembly with hundreds of delegates. Then, on the evening of February 4, 1899, came the incident that sparked war. US army private William Walter Grayson was on a routine patrol at his Manila base when he surprised and shot three Filipinos. Within minutes Filipino troops fired back from their trenches and the US commander was woken with the words, "The ball has begun." The **Filipino–American War** lasted for three years, although skirmishes continued for another seven years. It resulted in the death of more than 600,000 Filipinos. This little-known conflict has been described as the "first Vietnam". US troops used tactics they would later employ in Vietnam, such as strategic hamleting and scorched-earth, to pacify locals. But crushing the Filipinos was not easy. The US forces, for all their superior firepower, were nagged by relentless heat, torrential rain and pervasive disease. By March 1899, Manila was ablaze as American troops fanned out across the city. Aguinaldo still commanded Filipino forces, but the intensity of the assault shocked him. Malolos, to the north of Manila, the seat of his revolutionary government, was overrun, but by June 1899 the Americans had become bogged down and controlled territory no more than forty kilometres from Manila. The war degenerated into a **manhunt** for Aguinaldo, and when he was finally captured in March 1902 in Palanan on Luzon's east coast, America saw the light at the end of the tunnel.

The war ended officially on July 4, 1902, but the road to independence was a rocky one, with debate raging in Washington and Manila over how best to set a timetable. The Philippines stumbled towards self-rule, with Washington splintered over how much independence its erstwhile charge should be given, what measures would be in place to ensure the protection of US interests there and who would be president.

Benevolent assimilation

When the Filipino–American War ended, the United States set out to chart a new course for the Philippines, part of which was the hasty dispatch of a converted cattle ship, the *Thomas*, carrying American teachers. The teachers fanned out across the country to begin President McKinley's policy of "**benevolent assimilation**", and soon became known as Thomasites, after the ship on which they had arrived. The spread of schools has been applauded by historians as America's single greatest achievement in the Philippines. The Thomasites took to their task with apostolic fervour and Filipinos quickly achieved the highest literacy rate in Southeast Asia. Education, said an American official, would make Filipinos "less likely to be led by political leaders into insurrectionary schemes".

The American administration in the Philippines, guided by Washington, sought to inculcate Filipinos with American ethics, to turn the Philippines into a stable, prosperous, self-confident model of democracy in a developing country. Filipinos learned to behave, dress and eat like Americans, sing American songs and speak Americanized English. American educators decided that teaching Filipinos in their many own languages would require too many textbooks, so American English became the lingua franca of the Philippines. But they weren't American and never became so to the extent that America had wanted. To this day, Filipinos are trying to define their national identity, which is split between the country's multifarious islands and cultures, and further fragmented by the disparate influences of two great colonizing nations.

Meanwhile, the debate was still raging from the end of the Filipino-American War over what form of government the Philippines would have. It wasn't until 1935 that a bill was passed in Washington allowing President Roosevelt to recognize a new Philippine constitution. Presidential elections were held in September of that year and won by **Manuel Quezon**, leading light among a new breed of postwar politicians, who soundly beat Aguinaldo, still spry at the age of 66.

World War II

One of the questions about the new commonwealth was a military one: could it defend itself? Quezon realized how vulnerable the archipelago was and invited the US commander of the country, **General Douglas MacArthur**, to become military adviser to the autonomous regime. MacArthur accepted, demanding US$33,000 a year and an air-conditioned suite in the *Manila Hotel*.

Hostilities broke out in the Philippines within minutes of the attack on **Pearl Harbor**, waves of Mitsubishi bombers targeting military bases in Cavite and at Clark. MacArthur appealed for help from Washington, but it never came. He declared Manila an open city to save its population and prepared for a tactical retreat to Corregidor, the island citadel at the mouth of Manila Bay, from where he would supervise the defence of the strategic Bataan peninsula. Quezon, now increasingly frail from tuberculosis, went with him. Quezon told troops that "America will not abandon us", but as the weeks dragged by without help, his trust in Washington waned.

The Philippines, especially Manila, underwent heavy **bombardment** during World War II and casualties were high. Japanese troops landed on Luzon and conquered Manila on January 2, 1942. MacArthur and Quezon abandoned Corregidor when it became clear the situation was hopeless, but after arriving in Darwin, Australia, MacArthur promised Filipinos, "I have come through and I shall return." Presidential advisers later suggested he revise the wording of his famous statement to "We shall return", so the rest of the army and the White House could bathe in his reflected glory. He refused. MacArthur later said of Corregidor: "It needs no epitaph from me. It has sounded its own story at the mouth of its guns."

When he fled, MacArthur left behind soldiers engaged in a protracted and bloody struggle for **Bataan**. When the peninsula inevitably fell to Japanese forces, Corregidor was next. The Japanese launched an all-out assault on May 5, 1942, and the island, defended by starving and demoralized troops huddled in damp tunnels, capitulated within days. During the notorious Bataan Death March that followed, as many as 10,000 Americans and Filipinos died from disease, malnutrition and wanton brutality. The exact figure is unknown even today.

Two years of **Japanese military rule** followed. Frustrated in their efforts to quell an elusive population and a nascent guerrilla movement, the Japanese turned increasingly to brutality, beheading innocent victims and displaying their bodies as an example. The guerrillas multiplied, however, until their various movements comprised 200,000 men. The strongest force was the People's Anti-Japanese Army, in Tagalog the Hukbalahap or the Huks for short, most of them poor sharecroppers and farm workers looking for any opportunity to improve their abysmal lot. MacArthur, meanwhile, kept his promise to return. On October 19, 1944, with Quezon at his side, he waded ashore at Leyte, forcing a showdown with the Japanese and driving across the island to the port of Ormoc. The Huks later helped the US **liberate Luzon**, acting as guides in the push towards Manila and freeing Americans from Japanese prison camps. No guerrilla exploited his wartime adventures more than an ambitious young lawyer from Ilocos who now had his sights set on entering the political arena in Manila: Ferdinand Marcos.

The Marcos years

The Philippines received full **independence** from the US on July 4, 1946, when Manuel Roxas was sworn in as the first President of the Republic. The postwar period was marked by prevarication in America over what official US policy was towards the archipelago, and by the re-emergence of patronage and corruption in Philippine politics. It was in these rudderless years that **Ferdinand Marcos** came to power, promoting himself as a force for unification and reform.

Marcos (1917–89) was born in Sarrat, Ilocos Norte. A brilliant young lawyer who had successfully defended himself against a murder charge, he was elected to the Philippine House of Representatives in 1949, to the Senate in 1959 and became president in 1965. Marcos's first term as president was innovative and inspirational. He invigorated both populace and bureaucracy, embarking on a huge **infrastructure** programme and unifying scattered islands with a network of roads, bridges, railways and ports. During these early years of the Marcos presidency, before the madness of martial law, First Lady Imelda (see box on p.100) busied herself with social welfare and cultural projects that complemented Marcos's work in economics and foreign affairs. This was the "conjugal autocracy" at the zenith of its power, the Marcos knack for *palabas* (showbusiness style) outshining claims from opposition senators such as Benigo "Ninoy" Aquino that Marcos was intent on establishing a garrison state.

Marcos was the first Filipino president to be re-elected for a **second term**. The country's problems, however, were grave. Poverty, social inequality and rural stagnation were rife. They were made harder to bear by the rising expectations Marcos himself had fostered. Marcos was trapped between the entrenched oligarchy, which controlled Congress, and a rising Communist insurgency that traced its roots back to the Huks, fuelled mostly by landless peasants who had grown disenchanted with the slow speed of reform, but led by the articulate and patriarchal José Marie Sison, who lives today in exile in the Netherlands. The country, chiefly Manila, was roiled by student, labour and peasant unrest, much of it stoked by Communists and their fledgling military wing, the New People's Army. Marcos used the protests, and the spurious excuse of several attempts to liquidate him, to perpetuate his hold on power. On September 21, 1972, he declared **martial law**, arresting Aquino and other opposition leaders. A curfew was imposed and Congress was suspended. Marcos announced he was pioneering a Third World approach to democracy through his "New Society" and his new political party the New Society Movement. His regime became a byword for profligacy, corruption and repression.

The **Mindanao** problem also festered. In 1903 America had implemented the Moro Act, handing over vast tracts of ancestral land to multinational companies looking to establish plantations in America's new colony, among them Dole and Firestone. In 1936 President Quezon took things a step further, passing a law that made all Moro land public and giving much of it to Christian settlers in

Imelda Remedios Visitacion was born on July 2, 1929, in the lovely little town of Tolosa in Leyte. Her youth was troubled, her parents always quarrelling, separating and reconciling, her feckless father unable to hold down a job. To make ends meet they moved to Manila and sponged off relatives, living in a squalid garage. But her father floundered and money ran out, so the family returned to Leyte where Imelda lived until the age of 23, when she returned to Manila with five pesos in her purse, seeking her fortune. Her break came in 1953, when a magazine editor featured her face on his cover; she then entered a beauty contest and won the title of Miss Manila. The jury had actually crowned another woman, but Imelda lodged a tearful personal appeal with the mayor, who arbitrarily awarded her a special prize. Ferdinand later recounted that he saw the magazine picture and told friends, "I'm getting married." He arranged an introduction and, after an eleven-day courtship, proposed.

Following his 1965 election victory, Marcos said of Imelda, "She was worth a million votes." In fact, Imelda had cleverly inveigled tycoon Fernando Lopez into standing as Marcos's vice president, bringing with him his family's immeasurable fortune. Once the election was won, Imelda announced she would be "more than a mere decorative figure" and in 1966 made her international debut when she sang to Lyndon Johnson at a White House dinner. "A blessing not only to her country, but also to the world," gushed a US newspaper columnist.

Imelda believed that nothing succeeds like excess and laid on lavish fiestas for every visiting dignitary, driving the country into hock to defer the bills. She posed as a patron of the arts, flying the dancer Margot Fonteyn and pianist Van Cliburn to Manila. She spent a fortune on a **cultural centre**, a luxury the crippled economy could barely afford, and in 1983 married her youngest daughter in a ceremony in Ilocos that cost a staggering US$10 million. Throughout much of the eighties she went on notoriously profligate **shopping binges** to New York and Los Angeles, spending million of dollars on grotesque art, jewellery and the occasional apartment. In Geneva, another favourite haunt, she spent US$12 million in jewellery in a single day. Back home, her husband had made her governor of Manila with a brief to turn the city into a showpiece. She set about the task with gusto, spending US$31 million on the Coconut Palace (see p.100) and US$21 million on the Manila Film Center (see p.100).

The First Lady – now known as the Iron Butterfly for her thick-skinned bravura – also appointed herself the country's roving envoy, relentlessly roaming the world on jumbo jets "borrowed" from Philippine Airlines to meet Leonid Brezhnev and Fidel Castro, Emperor Hirohito and Chairman Mao, who kissed her hand and called her "Meldy". A prodigious social climber, she pursued Rockefellers and Fords, and dreamed of betrothing her daughter Imee to Prince Charles.

After their downfall, Imelda became deeply upset at reports that three thousand pairs of **shoes** had been found inside Malacañang, claiming she had only accumulated them to promote the Philippine shoe industry in her trips abroad. The shoes became the most potent symbol of her mad spending. Imelda, meanwhile, still lives in Manila. Various corruption cases against her drag painfully through the courts and may never be resolved. Old age has not made a recluse or a wallflower of her; she can sometimes be seen being driven around Makati in her stretch Mercedes sedan, or enjoying lunch with friends at the *Manila Mandarin Hotel*.

exchange for a promise of military service. Muslims were thus marginalized in their homelands and resentment inevitably grew. After the Jabidah Massacre in 1968, when Filipino troops executed 28 Muslim recruits who refused to take part in a hopelessly misconceived invasion of Sabah, Muslims took up arms against the government, forming the Mindanao Independence Movement, a forerunner of the Moro National Liberation Front. Marcos made few real

△ Supporters carry photos of Ferdinand and Imelda Marcos

efforts to quell the insurgency in the south, knowing it would give him another unassailable excuse for martial law. The US became worried that the longer Marcos's excesses continued the faster the Communist insurgency would spread, threatening their military bases in the islands, which had long been of mutual benefit to both the US and the Philippines. They employed more than 70,000 Filipinos and brought in "rent" in the form of American aid. For the US, they were a counterweight to Soviet strength in the region, a concern that had been heightened since defeat in Vietnam.

Marcos would have to be made to reform, but what if he wouldn't? The answer unfolded through the martyrdom of **Ninoy Aquino**, who by the spring of 1980 had been languishing in jail for seven years. Aquino was released from jail on condition he went into exile in the US. In 1983 he decided to return and when he emerged from his plane at Manila airport on August 21, 1983, he was assassinated. The country was outraged. In a snap election called in panic by Marcos on February 7, 1986, the opposition united behind Aquino's widow, **Cory**, and her running mate Salvador Laurel. On February 25, both Marcos and Cory claimed victory and were sworn in at separate ceremonies. Cory became a rallying point for change and was backed by the Catholic Church in the form of Archbishop Cardinal Jaime Sin, who urged people to take to the streets.

When Marcos's key allies saw which way the wind was blowing and deserted him, the game was up. Defence Minister Juan Ponce Enrile and Deputy Chief of Staff of the Armed Forces, General Fidel Ramos, later to become president, announced a coup d'etat. The US prevaricated, but eventually told Marcos to "cut and cut cleanly". Ferdinand and Imelda fled from Malacañang to Clark in helicopters provided by the CIA, and from there into exile in Hawaii, where Ferdinand died in 1989. Conservative estimates of their plunder put the figure at US$10 billion, US$600 million of it spirited into Swiss bank accounts. Back in Manila, the people stormed through the gates of Malacañang.

The return of democracy

The presidency of **Cory Aquino** was plagued by problems because she never managed to bring the powerful feudal families or the armed forces under her control. **Land reform** was eagerly awaited by the country's landless masses, but when Aquino realized reform would also involve her own family's haciendas in Tarlac, she quietly shelved the idea: most of the country's farmers remain beholden to landlords today. Aquino survived seven coup attempts and made little headway in improving life for the majority of Filipinos who were – and still are – living below the poverty line. The Communist New People's Army (NPA) emerged once again as a threat, and human rights abuses continued.

Aquino also had to deal with another thorny issue: the presence of **US military bases** in the country. Clark Air Base and Subic Naval Base were seen by military planners not as outposts, but springboards from which US armed forces could be projected, if the need arose, into Vietnam, China or even the USSR. But public opinion, fuelled by the country's strides towards democracy and greater self-determination, had been turning against the bases for some time, with many seeing them as a colonial imposition. In 1987 Congress voted not to renew the bases treaty and the US withdrawal, set for 1991, was hastened by the portentous eruption of **Mount Pinatubo**, which scattered ash over both Clark and Subic, causing millions of dollars of damage to US aircraft and ships. The pullout made jobless 600,000 Filipinos who had depended on the bases for employment either directly or indirectly.

Ultimately, Aquino's only legacy was that she maintained some semblance of a democracy, which was something for her successor, **Fidel Ramos**, to build on. President Ramos took office on July 1, 1992 and announced plans to create jobs, revitalize the economy and reduce the burdensome foreign debt of US$32 billion. But the first thing he had to do was establish a reliable electricity supply. The country was being paralyzed for hours every day by **power cuts**, and no multinational companies wanted to invest their hard-earned money under such difficult conditions. Ramos's success in breathing new life into the ailing energy sector – at least in Manila and many cities – laid the foundations for a moderate influx of foreign investment, for industrial parks and new manufacturing facilities. The economy picked up, but the problems were still huge. Foreign debt was crippling and tax collection was so lax that the government had nothing in the coffers to fall back on. Infrastructure improved marginally and new roads and transit systems began to take shape. Ramos also liberalized the banking sector and travelled extensively to promote the Philippines abroad. Most Filipinos view his years in office as a success, although when he stepped down at the end of his six-year term in 1998, poverty and crime were still rife.

Erap: scandal and impeachment

Ramos's successor, former vice-president **Joseph Estrada**, was a former tough-guy film actor with pomaded hair and a cowboy swagger who is known universally in the islands as **Erap**, a play on the slang word *pare*, which means friend or buddy. Filipinos joke that Estrada has a poor command of English and often gets his words mixed up. He was once said to have told a reporter, "I learn quickly because I have a pornographic memory." Estrada had a folksy, macho charm that appealed to the masses. He has been more than happy to confirm rumours of his legendary libido by admitting to a string of extra-marital affairs with leading ladies. "Bill Clinton has the sex scandals, I just have the sex," he once said.

Estrada was elected to the presidency against politicians of greater stature on a **pro-poor** platform. His rallying cry was *Erap para sa mahirap*, or "Erap for the poor". He promised food security, jobs, mass housing, education and health for all. The masses – known dismissively among the perfumed elite as the *bakya*, or "low taste" crowd – finally had their man in Malacañang. Needless to say, the business community, the entrenched oligarchy and big investors were worried. They saw Estrada as an economic ignoramus with a louche lifestyle and no understanding of how to instigate the harsh reforms the country so badly needed. There was a sense that the self-styled champion of the poor was out of his intellectual depth and heading for a fall. No one realized quite how dramatic that fall would be, or how soon it would come. Estrada got off to a troubled start in Malacañang, plagued by a series of tawdry scandals that he swept aside. More seriously, accusations surfaced in the media of a lack of direction and a return to the **cronyism** of the Marcos years. Erap bumbled his way from one mismanaged disaster to the next. He accidentally signed papers that secured the release from prison of a notorious cannibal who had killed and eaten a priest. He called a prison warden in Manila to grant a stay of execution for a condemned man, but the line was busy and he couldn't get through, so the convict was put to death. Allegations of Estrada's corruption and great wealth were flying around. The President's candid chief of staff, Aprodicio Laquian, confirmed to the media what had long been suspected: that Erap had an informal midnight cabinet of drinking buddies and sycophants who played cards until the wee hours and made policy to suit themselves. Laquian told a journalist that at four o'clock in the morning he was often the only one sober inside Malacañang. Erap failed to see the funny side and Laquian was promptly dismissed.

The **economy** was floundering and every day there was some new allegation, always denied by Erap with a combative flourish, of cronyism, mismanagement, favours for friends or plain incompetence. In March 2000 Erap realized he had a serious problem and with the help of the Malacañang press office reinvented himself as a diligent, punctilious, morally upright guardian of the nation, going to great pains to show himself in the media as a man of action, a man with a plan.

He seemed to have survived the worse, until two bombshells were dropped in quick succession. The Philippine Center for Investigative Journalism (PCIJ) began its research into Estrada's wealth in the first quarter of 2000. The PCIJ took months to compile its evidence and on July 24, 2000 published a report detailing vast discrepancies between Estrada's declared assets and his actual assets. The report listed seventeen pieces of **real estate** worth P2 billion that had been acquired by Estrada and his various family members since 1998. Some, it was alleged, were for his favourite mistress, former actress Laarni Enriquez.

Bombshell number two exploded in October 2000. Luis Singson, a member of the midnight cabinet and governor of Ilocos Sur, alleged that Estrada had received P500 million in **gambling payoffs** from an illegal numbers game known as *jueteng* (pronounced "wet-eng"). Singson made no bones about his reasons for exposing his close friend. Estrada was about to authorize a legal and potentially profitable government lottery, but had decided to give the licence to run it to another crony, not Singson. Once Singson had gone public with his allegations, opposition congressmen called for the president to be impeached.

Estrada's allies in Congress rallied around him but were outnumbered. On November 13, 2000 Joseph Estrada became the first president of the Philippines to be **impeached**, setting the stage for a trial in the Senate that would hold the nation in its grip for weeks until it reached a dramatic and unexpected conclusion.

The evidence heard during the trial mostly involved testimony from bank officers at a bank where Estrada was said to have opened accounts in fictitious names. These accounts held millions of pesos, allegedly the cash that had been siphoned off from his involvement in *jueteng*. One of the accounts was in the name of José Velarde and was opened with specimen signatures that bore an uncanny resemblance to Estrada's. T-shirts quickly appeared all over Manila bearing the words, "I am the real José Velarde". The bank's vice president, Clarissa Ocampo, testified that she had been to Malacañang and sat next to Estrada as he signed the documents in the name of José Velarde to open the account. Ocampo's bravery in testifying won her many admirers. She was articulate, firm and never wavered even under hectoring interrogation from Estrada's lawyers. She was also photogenic and the press loved her. Her nickname, it turned out, was Kissa.

Then the trial began to unravel. The prosecution claimed it had new evidence, sealed in an envelope, that would prove Estrada's guilt beyond doubt. Estrada's allies in the Senate insisted on a vote to decide whether the new evidence was admissible. The Senate was comprised of eleven pro-Erap senators and ten anti-Erap senators. Not surprisingly, the vote went according to loyalties. The pro-Erap senators voted not to open the envelope and the prosecution walked out in protest. It was a dramatic moment, broadcast live on national television. Anti-Erap senators cried, and the leader of the Senate, his voice breaking, announced his immediate resignation. The trial was over. Erap had survived. Or had he?

The gloomy mood in Manila the next morning was palpable: one of utter disbelief mixed with anger. Filipinos felt robbed of a real chance for truth and justice. The country was in a vacuum with no clear indication in the constitution as to what should happen next. Estrada had been found neither innocent nor guilty. He called for reconciliation, but the calls had a hollow ring about them. People soon began gathering on the streets to demand his resignation. The influential Catholic Church and its leader, the late Cardinal Jaime Sin, also called for Estrada to step down. Half a million people gathered at the EDSA shrine in Ortigas in scenes reminiscent of those before the downfall of Marcos. Fifty thousand militants massed near Malacañang, preparing to kick out the president by force if necessary. On the evening of Friday January 19, 2001, cabinet members saw the cause was lost and began to defect.

Then came the decisive blow. The **military** announced it had withdrawn its support for Estrada. The next morning he was ushered ignominiously from Malacañang and vice-president Gloria Macapagal-Arroyo was promptly sworn in as the fourteenth President of the Republic of the Philippines.

Anti-Erap forces hailed what they deemed a noble moral victory. But a nagging question remained. Estrada had been voted into office by a landslide of 10.7 million people and removed by a predominantly middle-class movement of 500,000 who took to the streets. His impeachment trial had been aborted and he had been found guilty of nothing. The Supreme Court had rubberstamped Macapagal-Arroyo's ascendancy to Malacañang, but given the dubious way power fell into her hands, was she really an elected president? Euphoria quickly gave way to uncertainty.

Macapagal-Arroyo: the politics of the elite

For the general populace, Estrada's eviction from Malacañang was yet another galling example of how an inbred elite pulls all the strings in the Philippines. Estrada may have made things incalculably worse during his two-and-a-half years of misrule, but the country's woes go back a long way – and down a long way too, to the core of political and economic life. Corruption runs unchecked. The gap between the impoverished and a thin layer of super-wealthy grows ever wider. Just sixty of the Philippines' estimated 15 million families control virtually all the nation's wealth, and about 200 run its political life. At the bottom of the pile, the dirt-poor grow in numbers and wretchedness, accounting probably for sixty percent of the population of 76 million. The frustration the poor felt at the humiliation of their hero boiled over shortly after **Macapagal-Arroyo** had taken office. They saw her as another rich kid from a privileged landowning family – her father Diosdado Macapagal had been president in the 1960s.

On May 1, 2001, the consequences of the mob-style street democracy which had swept Macapagal-Arroyo to power almost proved her undoing. Thousands of Erap's supporters marched towards Malacañang where a worried and sleepless Macapagal-Arroyo was holed up inside. By installing two presidents through protests rather than the ballot box, the Philippines seemed to have extended an open invitation for anyone to make a bid for power, provided he or she can draw a big enough crowd. The mobs marching on Malacañang were another sad reminder that the country hasn't grown out of its chaotic political traditions, characterized by poverty, goons, strongmen and street protests.

Macapagal-Arroyo makes great play of her economic prowess and the fact that she's an assiduous administrator, not a flamboyant but empty figurehead. The first year of her presidency was solid if unspectacular, her main priority simply to survive and bring some level of **stability**. Estrada was a festering problem. His supporters said Macapagal-Arroyo had no right to the presidency and that Estrada was legally still in charge. Estrada himself languished in a guarded hospital room, charged with the crime of plunder, which is punishable by death. The House of Representatives and Congress were bitterly divided along pro- and anti-Estrada lines, with the two main parties unable to agree on anything.

Macapagal-Arroyo also had a restless military to deal with, many of whose members, poorly paid and demoralized, were itching for a military regime that would, in their minds, end once and for all the shambolic rule of the politicians. There were rumours of impending coup attempts and, in October 2003, disgruntled soldiers seized control of a hotel and shopping mall in Makati, a small-scale mutiny that was quickly put down, but underlined the fragile nature of Macapagal-Arroyo's position.

In Mindanao and occasionally other areas of the country, Muslim guerrillas were still sowing terror with kidnappings and bombings, and the events of **9/11** had led the US to renew its interest in the Philippines, which was now seen as a haven for terrorists. But the politicians were also divided on whether or not US forces should be asked to help. At Macapagal-Arroyo's behest, the US sent troops to Mindanao to help in the manhunt for members of Abu Sayyaf, who were believed to be receiving funding and training from Al-Qaeda. Even this caused friction, with anti-administration senators arguing that the constitution prevented foreign armies operating on Filipino soil. Macapagal-Arroyo got round the problem by claiming the US was merely in Mindanao to advise, not to fight.

Claiming she was sick of the bickering and self-aggrandizing of the politicians, Macapagal-Arroyo announced that she would free herself of political patronage by not running in the next election in May 2004. The opposition was cynical and, it turned out with justification. One year later Macapagal-Arroyo announced she had decided to run after all. In early 2004, the campaign season for the May elections officially began, pitching Macapagal-Arroyo against four main rivals for the presidency in a race that had a familiar look to it. The main opposition candidate was Fernando Poe Jr, a swarthy action-movie star and close friend of Joseph Estrada's. The elite and the middle classes groaned. But early opinion polls showed Poe – known as "Da King" of Filipino movies for his portrayals of a humble blacksmith who triumphs against injustice – slightly ahead of Macapagal-Arroyo and drawing support from the masses, despite his conspicuous lack of any platform for government.

Throughout the campaign, Macapagal-Arroyo was the epitome of presidential cool, pressing the flesh, charming the media and using the machinery of Malacañang to execute a slick campaign based on the need for experience. Critics said she was using public funds for her campaign, but with FPJ's campaign stumbling because of his apparent lack of political acumen and blundering off-the-cuff comments to the press, none of the accusations stuck.

Critics said Poe was linked to political interest groups, and tried to compare his candidacy to that of his disgraced friend Estrada, who ran on a similar platform, pushing a similar "man of the people" persona. While he was initially seen as frontrunner, Poe's campaign quickly became disorganized and fragmented. It was clear even to many of his most ardent supporters that he didn't have the wherewithal to carry the day. Yet it was still close. Poe received a fraction over nine million votes; Macapagal-Arroyo just over nine-and-a-half million. Perhaps inevitably in a country where votes are bought and sold like cheap stocks, Poe's supporters viewed the election results as flawed and kicked up a persistent stink, fighting their case through the media and then through the courts. The claims were dismissed by the Supreme Court.

Poe seemed chastened by the defeat, embarrassed almost, and faded into the wings. On December 10 2004 he was admitted to hospital in Manila after complaining of feeling unwell at a party. He slipped into a coma while being treated for a brain clot and died on December 14 at the age of 65 without regaining consciousness. His funeral procession drew tens of thousands.

Macapagal-Arroyo's term will end in 2010 and under the constitution she must step down. There was hope that the post Macapagal-Arroyo era would be one that marked the beginning of the end of cronyism, perhaps even the emergence of a new generation of politicians untainted by scandal and patronage. This will not be the case; most of those tipped as successors are familiar names from powerful political dynasties. Perhaps the only exception is the former director-general of the Philippine National Police, Panfilo "Ping" Lacson, who has humble provincial origins, but he is also a highly controversial figure who has been accused down the years of murder, money-laundering and plotting a coup d'etat. He came third in the 2004 elections and it's inconceivable he will not stand again in 2010. For ordinary Filipinos, the country's dirty politics has gone beyond a joke. And there are few candidates for the next presidency who offer any real hope of positive change.

Religion and beliefs

The Philippines is the only **predominantly Catholic** nation in Asia – more than ninety percent of the population is Catholic, with the rest either Protestant or animist. In addition to the Christian majority, there is a Muslim minority of approximately 4.5 million people, concentrated on the southern islands of Mindanao and Sulu. The remainder of the population, largely the indigenous tribes scattered in isolated mountainous regions, worship their own gods and an illustrious company of spirits, some protective, some mischievous and potentially harmful. These indigenous belief systems were the base onto which Christianity and Islam were moulded when they arrived.

Yet to describe the Philippines as a Roman Catholic country is an over-simplification. Elements of tribal belief absorbed into Catholicism have resulted in a form of "folk Catholicism" that manifests itself in various homespun observances – a folk healer might use Catholic liturgy mixed with native rituals, or suited entrepreneurs might be seen scattering rice around their premises to ensure their ventures are profitable. Even the Chinese minority (see p.104) has been influential in colouring Filipino Catholicism with the beliefs and practices of Buddhism, Confucianism and Taoism; many Catholic Filipinos believe in the balance of *yin* and *yang*, and that time is cyclical in nature.

There are other folk beliefs that remain embedded in the national psyche, notably the vivid stories of **beasts and ghouls** that inhabit dark barrios and have the capacity to murder and maim. These might be dismissed by visitors as mere fairy stories, the product of overripe imaginations, but to many Filipinos they are real and serve as a reminder that while the Catholic Church may offer redemption in the next life, there are mysteries in this one that it cannot explain. The religious landscape is complicated further by the emergence of various new Christian sects.

Christianity

Spain introduced **Catholicism** to the Philippines in 1521 with the arrival of Magellan. The Spanish conquered and converted much of the archipelago without military force, instead relying on mendicant missionaries and impressive displays of pomp and circumstance, clerical garb, images, prayers and liturgy. To protect the population from Muslim raiders, the people were resettled from isolated dispersed hamlets and brought *debajo de las compañas* ("under the bells"), into organized Spanish *pueblos*. The church, always situated on the central plaza, became the focus of town life. Masses, confessions, baptisms, funerals and marriages punctuated the tedium of everyday routines and the Church calendar set the pace and rhythm.

During the Spanish period, the Catholic Church was extensively involved in colonial administration, especially in rural areas. Yet its participation in public life was far from successful, with the corruption and greed of the friars resented by many and its great wealth seen as evidence of its corruption and decay. One of the Church's greatest critics was José Rizal, whose classic novel *Noli Me Tangere* (see p.526) portrayed friars as corpulent, lascivious and crooked.

Catholicism was accepted in the Philippines with the emphasis on ceremony, fiesta and the miraculous powers of the many saints. Things are no different today. The **Santo Niño**, whose image appears throughout the archipelago, in churches, on bumper stickers, stuck to the dashboards of taxis and jeepneys, has few rivals in the hierarchy of saints. He is considered the direct link to the Father, the God of all, the Redeemer from infamy, the Absolver of all sins, the Deliverer to a better life. Devotion to the Santo Niño is very much alive. People carry reminders of him as talismans and to ward off the unholy.

Filipinos like to say, half-jokingly, that the reliance on the intercession of the saints in Catholicism suits their lifestyle – at work, Filipinos prefer not to talk directly to the boss but will use someone else to get their message across. Every barangay, town and city has its **patron saint**, for whom grand **fiestas** are held and pious novenas

△ Paouay Church, near Laoag, northern Luzon

recited. In pre-Spanish times some of these events were ancient rites associated with prayers for rain, a good harvest or for the seas to yield bountiful fish. The Spanish were able to adapt some of these rituals by introducing Catholic concepts. Daily life, too, is shot through with Catholic imagery, whether it's government announcements in the press urging people to pray the rosary, or television footage of god-fearing presidential candidates praying for guidance.

Though Church and State have been separate in the Philippines since the American era, the Church continues to carry out a policy of non-interventionist intervention, commenting publicly on government policy without launching into outright criticism. In a country with a chaotic and freewheeling political system, where politicians are known for their profligacy and unscrupulousness, no one is under any illusion that these comments are made merely for their educational value. During the Marcos years the Archbishop of Manila, Cardinal Jaime Sin, who died in 2003 at the age of 77, called for people to take to the streets in peaceful protest, but stopped short of espousing revolution. When President Fidel Ramos – a Protestant – mooted greater use of birth control and even the legalization of abortion, the Church quickly and forcefully restated its objections to both, with the result that Ramos backed off, and when Joseph Estrada was in power, Cardinal Sin coincidentally gave a well-rehearsed series of sermons in Manila Cathedral on the sin of sloth.

The new Christian movements

The supremacy of the Catholic Church is being challenged by a variety of Christian sects. The largest of these is **El Shaddai**, headed by lay preacher Mike Velarde. Known to his followers as Brother Mike, Velarde has captured the imagination of poor Catholics, many of whom feel isolated from the mainstream Church. To make the polarization worse, priests preach in English, a language most barrio folk don't speak well enough to be able to understand a sermon or liturgy. Velarde has bridged this gap by preaching in colloquial and heavily accented Tagalog at huge open-air gatherings every weekend on Roxas Boulevard, overlooking Manila Bay. He wears screamingly loud made-to-measure suits and outrageous bow ties, but his message is straightforward: give to the Lord and He will return it to you tenfold. He now has eight million followers, most of whom suffer from *sakit sa bulsa*, or "ailment of the pocket", but are nevertheless happy to pay ten percent of their income to become card-carrying members of the flock. Brother Mike's relationship with the mainstream Catholic Church is uneasy. His relationship with politicians is not. With so many followers hanging on his every word, Brother Mike is a potent political ally and few candidates for high office are willing to upset him. In the 1998 elections, Brother Mike backed Joseph Estrada, which was a significant factor in the former movie actor's initial success.

One of the candidates in the 2004 elections, Eddie Villanueva, leads another of the Christian groups, the charismatic **Jesus is Lord Church**, which he claims has some seven million members with branches in Asia, Europe and North America. "Brother Eddie" came last out of the five candidates in the elections, but remains a visible opposition figure, calling regularly for Macapagal-Arroyo's resignation on all sorts of grounds ranging from nepotism and election fraud to corruption.

Another well-known group, the **Rizalists**, has only a tenuous connection with standard Christian doctrine. They regard José Rizal (see p.404) as the second son of God and a reincarnation of Christ, and are one of a number of groups who hold Mount Banahaw (see p.161) in Quezon province to be sacred – they believe Christ himself set foot there, and regularly go on pilgrimages to the mountain.

Part of the problem for the Catholic Church is that it suffers from a lack of personnel, putting it at a disadvantage in gaining and maintaining popular support. Most young priests come from the cities and have little interest in serving in the boondocks for a few thousand pesos a month, preferring to get postings overseas or work locally with NGOs. The Church is trying to meet this challenge by drawing more of the clergy from the countryside and by engaging in programmes geared to social action and human rights among the rural and urban poor.

Islam

Islam spread north to the Philippines from Indonesia and Malaysia in the fourteenth century, and by the time the Spanish arrived it was firmly established on Mindanao and Sulu, with outposts on Cebu and Luzon. It was further propagated by Arab merchants and missionaries and by the sixteenth century, Muslim areas had the most highly developed and politically integrated culture in the archipelago. But Miguel Lopez de Legazpi, Spanish conquistador and founder of Manila, wasted no time trying to bring what he saw as a dangerously radical religious group to heel, dispersing Muslims from Luzon and the Visayas. Muslims stood in the way of the Christianization of this great new colony and Legazpi didn't want them around. Yet during three centuries of Spanish rule, dominance over the Muslims of Mindanao and Sulu was never achieved. The Muslim question also plagued the Americans, whose policy was a disastrous one of pacification, paradoxically resulting in the **Moro Wars** of 1901–14.

Islam remains a very dominant influence among Muslims in the southern Philippines, and Muslims have added cultural character to the nation, with Filipino Christians expressing admiration over their warlike defiance of colonization. However, many Muslims feel they have become strangers in their own country, ignored by the Manila-centric government and marginalized by people resettled in Mindanao from Luzon (for more on the Mindanao problem, see box, p.374).

While all Filipino Muslims follow the basic tenets of Islam, their religion has absorbed a number of indigenous elements, such as making offerings to spirits which are known as **diwatas**. A spirit known as **Bal–Bal** is believed in among many Muslim tribes; with the body of a man and the wings of a bird, Bal-Bal is credited with the habit of eating out the livers of unburied bodies. In Jolo and Tawi-Tawi Muslims use mediums to contact the dead, while many Muslim groups trade amulets, wearing them as necklaces to ward off ill fortune. Filipino Muslims also include pre-Islamic customs in their ceremonies marking rites of passage, for example, ascribing guardian "housegods" to teenage boys.

Muslim **women** are freer in the Philippines than in many Islamic countries, and have traditionally played a prominent role in everything from war to ceremonies. "The women of Jolo," wrote a Spanish infantryman in the eighteenth century, "prepare for combat in the same manner as their husbands and brothers and are more desperate and determined than the men. With her child suspended to her breast or slung across her back, the Moro woman enters the fight with the ferocity of a panther."

Tribal beliefs

The number of tribal groups in the Philippines makes the ethnic landscape a confusing one. A number of tribes have only a few hundred members and are Catholic, going about their business in much the same way as any "Westernized" Filipino, wearing the same clothes and probably carrying a mobile phone. There are others, however, whose way of life has remained essentially unchanged: they are nomadic, cultivating fields for a few years before moving on, and their beliefs are **animist**, involving a pantheon of gods, spirits and creatures that guard streams,

The aswang who came to dinner

Heard the one about the pretty young housewife in a remote Visayan village who was possessed by the spirit of a jealous witch and almost died before the village healer saved her? Or the poor woman from a Manila shantytown whose relatives had to restrain her at night because she had taken to flying through the barrio, terrorizing her neighbours? These are news items from the pages of Manila's daily tabloid newspapers, reported as if they actually happened, which many Filipinos think they did – the mayor of Capiz on Panay even had to go to the media to dispel rumours that his town was a haven for witches and devils. Foreign visitors greet news of the latest barrio haunting with healthy cynicism, but when you are lying in your creaking nipa hut in the pitch dark of a moonless evening, miles from civilization and with no electricity to keep the light on, it's not hard to see why so many Filipinos grow up embracing strange stories about creatures that inhabit the night. Even urbane professionals, when returning to the barrio of their childhood for a family get-together or a holiday, can be heard muttering the incantation *tabi tabi lang-po* as they walk through paddy field or forest. Meaning "please let us pass safely", it's a request to the spirits and dwarves that might be lying in wait.

Most Filipino spirits are not the abstract souls of Western folklore who live in a netherworld; they are corporeal entities who live in trees or hang around the jeepney station, waiting to inflict unspeakable horrors on those who offend them. The most feared and widely talked about creature of Philippine folklore is the *aswang* or *manananggal*; hundreds of cheesy films have been made about the havoc they wreak and hundreds of *aswang* sightings have been carried by the tabloid press. By day the *aswang* is a beautiful woman, simply going about her business. The only way to identify an *aswang* is by looking into her eyes at night, when they turn red. The *aswang* kills her victims as they sleep, her modus operandi exploiting the exposed nature of homes in the provinces – she threads her long tongue through the gaps in the nipa floor or walls and inserts it into one of the body's orifices to suck out the internal organs. A variation on the theme has the *aswang* using her tubular tongue to suck the victim's blood, then flying back home before dawn, bloated after her feast, to breastfeed the blood to her children.

Another unpleasant creation of Philippine folklore is the *tiyanak*, said to be the tormented spirit of a baby born from the womb of a woman who dies and is buried while pregnant. The *tiyanak* looks much like any other plump, newborn baby, but lies on a leaf and attracts your attention by crying. If you help it, it will rise and kill you. Others on the bogeyman list include the arboreal *tikbalang*, which has the head of a nag and the body of a man, and specializes in the abduction of virgins. If you see one, you should snatch three hairs from his mane, wind them around your finger and climb on his back: instead of harming you, he'll take you flying. Then there's the *duwende*, an elderly, grizzled dwarf who lurks in the forest and can predict the future, and the *engkanto*, who hides in trees and throws dust in the faces of passers-by, giving them permanently twisted lips.

fields, trees, mountains, forests and houses. The Bagobo of eastern Mindanao, for example, recognize nine heavens, each with its own god. The superior god among many tribes is **Bathala**, who is believed to have created earth and man. Regular sacrifices and prayers are offered to placate the deities and spirits, and additionally some people believe that the souls of their ancestors, if inadequately honoured, punish their living descendants with illness. Tribes of the Cordillera have their own hierarchy of gods, including a multitude of **anitos**, housegods who are the souls of their ancestors and who must be regularly placated with offerings of food.

Anyone reputed to have power over the supernatural and natural is elevated to a position of prominence, and every village has its share of shamans and priests who ply their talents and perform ritual cures. Many achieve some level of fame for their ability to develop **anting-anting**, charms guaranteed to make a person invincible in the face of human enemies and still worn by many Filipinos today. Other sorcerers concoct love potions or produce amulets that are said to make their owners invisible – ideal if you want to exact revenge or make yourself scarce in the face of it. Sorcery is still practised, and celebrated every year at the annual Folk Healing Festival on Siquijor (see p.285), a small Visayan island with a reputation for black magic.

When the Spanish arrived, they found tribal beliefs curious, but had no doubt they could soon supplant them with their own. What terrified them more than native spirits were native social traditions. A Spanish friar, writing in the early nineteenth century about the Igorots of northern Luzon, commented that although they had immense fields of rice and lived comfortably off their labour, they took a horrible pleasure in lying in wait to murder travellers and, without robbing them, "cut off their heads, sip their brains, and adorn the interior of their houses with human skulls". The language may have been ripe, but the facts were essentially correct: **headhunting** was still practised among some northern tribes until the early twentieth century.

Many tribes maintain their own **tribal justice** system today, with punishments typically decided by a twelve-member council and ranging from the payment of restitution to lashes with a bamboo cane. The Tagbanua, who live mostly on Coron Island in Palawan, have asserted their right to punish anyone who violates tribal law inside their domain, while among the Kankanaey of the Cordillera, the **tongtong** is a dialogue held to resolve disputes, with the guilty party ending up paying a penalty.

Music

ny Friday night in Manila, countless **showbands** can be seen in countless hotel lobbies performing accomplished cover versions of Western classics. The line-up and the routine rarely differ: a pretty girl or two, backed by male musicians in wing collars, smile gamely through a repertoire that inevitably features Earth Wind and Fire, KC and the Sunshine Band and, for anyone under 40 in the audience, a smattering of Britney and Kylie. The nation's musical speciality is **mimicry** and when Filipinos mimic they do it exceedingly well. The country's musical culture is largely an appropriated one, assimilated from fifty-odd years of imperial rule by Washington that sought to recreate America in the East and ended up creating a generation of teenagers who thought first Foreigner and then Michael Bolton were cool.

In fact, **indigenous music** does survive. The tribes who were here before the Spanish, have epic folk songs and stories, handed down orally, that are still sung at tribal gatherings and ceremonies. Even today, the pre-eminent means of musical expression of the Bukidnon people in Mindanao is vocal music, with singers usually performing without any accompaniment. The most important of these forms are the epic chants called **ulaging**, which recall the adventures of the hero Agyu and are sung at night, sometimes over several nights. It wasn't until the Spanish introduced religious music and their own instruments, notably the guitar, that indigenous music was partly usurped. Spanish operetta, **zarzuela**, arrived in the late nineteenth century and enjoyed a revival in the 1970s when it was adopted by Tagalog writers. The American colonial period widened the musical influences, exposing Filipinos to forms such as vaudeville, which bore comparison to *zarzuela* and attracted both the elite and the masses.

The postwar period brought Elvis and then the Beatles – after a brief concert tour, the latter were famously forced to withdraw quietly from Manila when they turned down an offer from Imelda Marcos to perform personally for her at Malacañang. America and American culture were everything, with Filipino musicians taking to every new style that emerged. Most Filipino rock bands of the Sixties and Seventies drew exclusively on Americana, even for their appellations, with the Hot Rods and the Hot Dogs big names on the Manila circuit, playing cover versions of songs by Elvis, Carl Perkins and British bands that had cracked America, like the Rolling Stones. One of the most popular Filipino bands of the Seventies was Funk Campaign, who specialized in cover versions of black-consciousness classics from James Brown and Marvin Gaye and played at the *Harlem Club* in Olongapo.

In the 1970s the only truly original artists performing in Manila were folksy beatniks such as singer-songwriters **Joey Ayala** and **Freddie Aguilar**. Ayala was making a name for himself gigging in Manila, playing instruments such as the *hegalong*, a two-stringed guitar from the T'boli tribe of Mindanao, where he was born. Aguilar was on the same small-venue circuit, his acoustic folk, much of it sung in Tagalog, attracting loyal but modest audiences who were as yet unused to contemporary songs sung in any language other than English. Then, in the 1980s something quite unexpected happened.

Revolution

Aguilar had written a popular ballad called "**Anak**" and found himself a fan in First Lady Imelda Marcos who, ever eager to bathe herself in the reflected glory of Manila's celebs, invited him to Malacañang Palace so they could sing the song together at banquets. Aguilar was appalled by the excesses he saw inside the palace and never went back. "Anak", ostensibly about a child that grew up and went astray, came to represent Imelda herself. The more Aguilar played it in the beerhouses of Ermita and Malate, the more people caught on:

You've changed
You've become stubborn
succumbed to vices

For the first time in the Philippines a song had come to represent more than the sum of its parts. As the anti-Marcos movement grew, so did the popularity of "Anak". Aguilar, by now something of a talisman for left-wing groups opposing martial law, took the opportunity to become even more political, recording a heartfelt version of "Bayan Ko" (My Country), a patriotic anthem that now took on extraordinary political significance. Shortly before the Marcoses fled in 1986, in one of the most iconic moments of the revolution, tens of thousands of Cory Aquino's supporters gathered peacefully at Rizal Park and sang "Bayan Ko", led by Cory herself with Freddie Aguilar at her side.

It was also a significant moment for Filipino music, with Aguilar the first major artist to blend success with a serious message. Most of his songs were about uniquely Filipino problems: "Estudyante Blues" was composed as a protest against the penury many students suffer to put themselves through college; "Magdalena" dealt with the plight of Manila's prostitutes; and "Trabaho" (Work) was an agonizing portrayal of the dismal lot of the country's poor.

OPM (Original Pilipino Music)

Aguilar was a profound influence on a new generation of Filipino musicians who had grown tired of ersatz pop and wanted to become more "socially engaged". One of the first among them was **Grace Nono**, who came to public attention when, at an arts festival in Baguio in 1989, she gathered friends and musicians around a ceremonial fire at the *Café by the Ruins* (see p.475) and performed songs taught to her by indigenous tribes near her Mindanao home.

Nono has recorded several successful albums on her own independent record label, **Tao Music**, established because her tribal chanting and native instruments – including a Filipino tribal jew's harp and a reed flute called a *runo* – were considered too radical for any major label. Her repertoire includes "Ader", a Maguindanaoan courtship song from a tribe in western Mindanao, and "Batang Lansangan", a reworking of an Ibaloi children's rhyme with additional lyrics added by Nono about the plight of Filipino street children. With Nono that day in Baguio was Billy Bonnevie, who went on to form the most successful "rock and runo" band in the country today, **Pinikpikan**, their music pushing even further the limits of tribal-pop.

This was **Original Pilipino Music** or Original Pinoy Music (OPM), a phrase that was coined in the late 1980s to accommodate the emergence of music that was considered uniquely Filipino. Nono and her contemporaries proved, albeit on a limited scale, that Filipino music need not be limited to a Filipino audience. Her work received attention outside the country and inspired other Filipinos to make music that was both distinctively from the Philippines and original, and accessible enough to appeal to fans whose main source of music wasn't the beerhouses of Freddie Aguilar's Malate, but MTV Asia. Over the last few years the term OPM, used to signify tribal-pop, has become diluted, and now encompasses the **young stars** of the twenty-first century, most of whom have modelled themselves on Celine Dion and Michael Bublé, not the revolutionary Manila singers of the Marcos years. This new generation includes Nina, Kyla and Erik Santos. Their music is saccharine, resolutely middle-of-the-road and cut for a new generation audience that worships *American Idol* and, after decades of revolutions and attempted revolutions, seems only interested in the security of romance.

Pinoy rock . . . and some folk-pop

OPM in its original form reached the grunge clubs of the Manila student belt, where young Filipino musicians took the concept of traditional music with a Pinoy touch and applied it to the music they were listening to: Kurt Cobain, Pearl Jam and Oasis. And so **Pinoy rock** was born, a genre that sought to channel the Filipino elements pioneered by Nono into something more accessible, with bands giving Western rock a local touch by adding Tagalog lyrics about problems Filipinos could easily relate to. However, Pinoy rock never became the phenomenon many critics thought it would, largely because too many of the bands were still apeing Western acts, thrashing their guitars and screaming cheesy renditions of Led Zeppelin or Nirvana. While the music attracted good crowds to beery late-night hangouts, it floundered on radio because everyone missed the joke – part of the charm of the Pinoy rockers was that they were self-deprecating on stage, but off it the music was nothing new.

There was bound to be a backlash against the calcifying of the Pinoy rock establishment. It came initially from four young men who were to have an extraordinary influence on music in the country: Ely Buendia, Raimund Marasigan, Buddy Zabala and Marcus Adoro – the **Eraserheads**. These four young friends from the University of the Philippines began playing together, with secondhand instruments, because they thought it was the only way they'd ever get girls and were spotted at a university gig. They recorded eight albums between 1993 and 2002 and became the most successful Filipino band ever.

What earned the Eraserheads so many admirers was not just their jaunty but appealingly melodic blend of campus rock and gritty street pop, but also the fact that in a traditionally conservative country, the band thumbed their noses at establishment stars. They appeared on MOR diva Sharon Cuneta's lunchtime TV show apparently half drunk (they weren't, it was a joke) and mimed deliberately badly to a tape when they were told they couldn't play live. The Eraserheads were pandering to no one. What's more, they stood up to critical scrutiny, with lyrics that spoke of the moral bankruptcy of politicians, Manila's urban decay and the problems of being gay in a Catholic country. The spicy ballad "Pare Ko" (My Friend) was censored by radio stations and criticized by politicians because it contained a few expletives, while "Ligaya" (Delight) fused winsome melodies with lyrics of strained relationships and the alienation of young people looking for a future in the big city.

The Eraserheads split up in 2003 (with his usual dry charm, Buendia cited "height differences" as the cause) but not before successful tours of Australia and Malaysia, as well as regular gigs at the Cactus Club in San Francisco. This was about as global as Filipino music had ever got. Buendia has since formed a new band, **Pupil**, with the same manager as the Eraserheads. The three other "heads" have all enjoyed reasonably successful solo careers encompassing playing, producing, writing and the occasional cameo film role.

Other bands saw what they were doing and followed suit, giving rise to a new era of progressive **folk-pop**, as played by the likes of the hugely popular **Rivermaya** (who counted Britpop among their biggest influences) and the Hungry Young Poets, who later became **Barbie's Cradle**, a trio fronted by petite vocalist/guitarist Barbie Almalbis. At the forefront of this movement is Joey Ayala's sister, **Cynthia Alexander**, a bass guitarist and singer whose deeply personal compositions feature resonant violas and cellos, congas, rainsticks and tribal percussion reminiscent of Grace Nono. Her albums *Ripping Yarns* and *Insomnia and Other Lullabyes* both topped the Philippine charts. **Maegan Aguilar**, Freddie's daughter, also graduated from the same folk-pop school, releasing her first album in 1995. While she has never reached her father's heights, she is still going strong on the domestic concert circuit, playing regularly throughout the country on her own and with her dad.

The Eraserheads and those that followed paved the way for musicians to push the boundaries. One of the most talked-about consequences of this was the emergence in the late 1980s of **Filipino hip-hop** or **Pinoy rap** with songs by Dyords Javier and Vincent Dafalong. The genre developed slowly, but hit the mainstream with Francis Magalona's debut album, *Yo!* which included the nationalistic hit "Mga Kababayan" (My Countrymen), a call to political arms that bore the hallmarks of Freddie Aguilar. In 1994, Death Threat released the first Filipino gangsta rap album *Gusto Kong Bumaet* (I Want to be Good). Another Filipino hip-hop artist who achieved prominence in the 1990s was Los Angeles-based Andrew E. who returned to Manila from his family home in Los Angeles to form his own record label and the successful rap group Salbakuta.

Divas and crooners

Despite the proliferation of progressive acts, the populist Philippine music scene has become dominated in recent years by comely solo performers singing plaintive ballads in the style of Whitney Houston or Mariah Carey. Fans of "real music" scoff at the divas and crooners, saying their art is nothing more than glorified karaoke, but the Philippines is in love with them. Ordinary Filipinos see in them a future for themselves, a chance to escape crushing poverty, the only qualification needed being your voice.

In the hierarchy of balladeers, Regine Velasquez and Martin Nievera are at the top. **Regine Velasquez**'s story is the quintessential Tagalog movie script: a beautiful girl from the sticks – she grew up in Leyte – wins a singing contest (with a performance of "You'll Never Walk Alone", in Hong Kong) and heads off to Manila. Her repertoire is typical of the Filipina diva canon, comprising misty-eyed love songs such as "Could It Be?", "What You Are to Me" and "Long For Him". Named most popular Philippine artist in the MTV Asia awards for 2003, Velasquez follows in the tradition of Sharon Cuneta, Pops Fernandez and

Kuh Ledesma, who at one time or another have all been dubbed the country's "concert queen" by the media. Yet Velasquez has the distinction of being among the first Filipina divas whose fame has spread, albeit it a modest fashion, beyond the islands to audiences who otherwise knew nothing about the Philippines. She has collaborated with Paul Anka and Hong Kong's Jacky Cheung, and with Ronan Keating on a version of Boyzone's "When You Say Nothing At All" for her album *Unsolo*.

Martin Nievera puts his success – some twenty years of it now – down to the fact that Filipinos love a good drama. His songs are indeed melodramatic, his album *Forever, Forever* being an open book about his high-profile marital breakup with Pops Fernandez. But like every Filipino musician or singer before him he has yet to make it in the place that matters most, America. In Manila he plays before thousands and is feted by an awestruck media, but while he has made minor inroads into other markets, playing concerts to mostly overseas Filipino communities in Las Vegas, Vancouver and Australia, he still finds time to croon lounge songs in the *Golden Nugget Hotel* in Las Vegas, hoping for that big break into mainstream US showbiz.

Discography

A useful website for general information about Filipino music is ⓦwww.philmusic.com, while ⓦwww.clubdredd.com has good artist profiles. To order these CDs abroad, try ⓦwww.liyra.com.

Freddie Aguilar *Collection* (Ivory). A mixture of studio and live recordings featuring most of the folk hero's greatest songs, including "Trabaho" and a cover version of Joey Ayala's "Mindanao". "Pinoy" is a dark, but melodic exposition of the average Filipino's lot, while the lyrical "Magdalena" was based on conversations Aguilar had with Manila prostitutes, all of whom desperately wanted to escape the life. There's no "Anak", but there are plenty of other Freddie Aguilar collections that feature it.

Cynthia Alexander *Insomnia and Other Lullabyes* (Dypro). Introspective but affecting collection of progressive/tribal ballads from Joey Ayala's talented little sister. The navel-gazing becomes wearisome at times, but there are also some memorable moments, including "No Umbrella", a pleading love song with sonorous strings and plaintive fretless bass.

Joey Ayala *Hubad* (Jeepney Dash). Eleven tracks chosen by Ayala himself for this "Best Of" collection, which is a fine introduction to his unique tribal-influenced folk and rock. Two of the tracks – "1896", about the revolt against Spain, and "Maglakad" (Walk), were recorded live in Japan. The best-known song on the album is "Mindanao", at once a paean to Ayala's birthplace and a haunting appeal for the Manila government to sit up and take notice of the island's problems.

Barbie's Cradle *Music from the Buffet Table* (Warner Music Philippines). Their semi-acoustic sound dominated by the frail but evocative voice of Barbie Almalbis, Barbie's Cradle have injected a new note of realism into OPM songwriting, with lyrics – in both English and Tagalog – that speak not of love and happiness, but of vulnerability and dysfunction. Highlights include "Money for Food", a musical poem about poverty, and "It's Dark and I Am Lonely", a personal and frank assessment of modern life for young people.

Eraserheads *Ultraelectromagneticpop* (BMG Pilipinas). Thoroughly enjoyable debut album featuring spirited Beatles-inspired pop, novelty pieces that poke fun at everyone and everything, and the brilliant "Pare Ko" (My Friend), which had the establishment in a spin because it contained a couple of swear words and gay references. The band matured after this and even got better – their second album, *Circus*, includes the track "Butterscotch" which takes a not so gentle dig at the Catholic Church ("Father Markus said to me/ Just confess and you'll be free/Sit yer down upon me lap/And tell me all yer sins) – but *Ultraelectromagneticpop* will always be special because it blazed a trail.

Martin Nievera *Live with the Philippine Philharmonic Orchestra* (MCA). Two-disc set recorded in Manila that captures some of the energy of Nievera live, when he's a much greater force than on many of his overly sentimental studio recordings. A master of patter and performance, Nievera sings in English, in Tagalog, on his own and with guests including the popular Filipina singing sisters Dessa and Cris Villonco, and his dad, Bert. The highlight is a mammoth montage of Broadway hits from *Carousel*, *West Side Story* and *Evita*, the nadir a self-indulgent spoken preamble to one of his signature songs, "Before You Say Goodbye".

Grace Nono *Isang Buhay* (Tao Music). Quintessential Nono, this is an album of sometimes strident but hypnotic tribal rhythms and original tribal songs blended with additional lyrics drawing attention to the plight of the tribes, the environment and the avarice of the country's rulers. *Isang Buhay* means one house; the title track is Nono's plea for unity.

Pinikpikan *Kaamulan* (Tropical). Psychedelia meets tribal tradition on this, Pinikpikan's third album, released in 2003. The band's influences are eclectic and worn on the sleeve, from the Hindu overtones on "Child" to the flute solos – inspired by the wooden-flute music of the Manobo tribe of Mindanao – on "Butanding", a haunting stream-of-consciousness piece about the endangered whale shark.

Rivermaya *It's Not Easy Being Green* (BMG Pilipinas). Rivermaya's audience is unashamedly middle of the road and so is their music, an amiable blend of guitar-driven pop and laidback love songs for 20-somethings. This album is typical, suffused with British influences ranging from the Beatles to Belle and Sebastian. The highpoint, however, is pure pinoy, the ironic ballad "Grounded ang Girlfriend Ko" (My Girlfriend's Grounded Me), which owes more to the Eraserheads than Britpop.

Regine Velasquez *Unsolo* (Polycosmic). This was the album that marked the beginning of Velasquez's attempts to become an international star, or at least a pan-Asian one, raising her profile with duets featuring the likes of David Hasselhoff – for a syrupy rendition of "More Than Words Can Say" – and Jacky Cheung. There's only one song in Tagalog.

Books

The Philippines hasn't been as well documented in fiction or non-fiction as many of its Asian neighbours. There is, for instance, no classic Western literature set in the country of the kind Somerset Maughan produced as regards Malaya, nor is there much in the way of travel writing taking in the country. There are, however, a number of good **investigative accounts** of two subjects – American involvement in the Philippines and the excesses of the Marcoses.

Some of the books reviewed below are published in the Philippines, and are unlikely to be on sale outside the country, in which case we've listed the publisher in the review. The designation o/p means out of print.

History and politics

Alfonso Aluit *By Sword and Fire: the Destruction of Manila in World War II* (Bookmark). A comprehensive and brutally dispassionate account of a season in hell and man's capacity for pain, revealed not only in the narrative, but also in the many black and white photographs. The scale of the destruction of Manila is horrifying, but it's the stories of ordinary Filipinos woven through the text that really show how much people suffered during the Japanese occupation.

Alan Berlow *Dead Season: A Story of Murder and Revenge*. Prepare to be depressed. This brilliantly atmospheric work of reportage is the story of three murders that took place in the 1970s on the Philippine island of Negros, against the backdrop of Communist guerrilla activity and appeals for land reform. The book is impossible to read without feeling intense despair for a country where humble, peaceful people have too often become the tragic pawns in a seedy game of power and money that is played out around them. Cory Aquino comes out of it badly – the Church asked her to investigate the murders but she refused, fearful that this might entail treading on too many toes.

Raymond Bonner *Waltzing with a Dictator*. Former *New York Times* correspondent Bonner reports on the complex twenty-year US relationship with the Marcos regime and how Washington kept Marcos in power long after his sell-by date: US bases in the country needed a patron and Marcos was the right man. Marcos cleverly played up the threat of a Communist insurgency in the Philippines, making it seem to Washington that he was their only hope of stability.

James Hamilton-Paterson *America's Boy: The Rise and Fall of Ferdinand Marcos and Other Misadventures of US Colonialism in the Philippines*. A controversial narrative history of the US-supported dictatorship that came to define the Philippines. The author makes the very plausible claim that the Marcoses were merely the latest in a long line of corrupt Filipino leaders in a country which had historically been ruled by oligarchies, and gathers firsthand information from senators, cronies, rivals and Marcos family members, including Imelda. Wonderfully written and diligently researched.

Nick Joaquin *Manila, My Manila* (Bookmark). A veteran novelist and poet, the author wrote this paean to the city of his birth at the prodding of the then mayor of Manila, Mel Lopez, who was racking his brains as to how to foster a sense of the city's long and distinguished history among youth who were apparently only interested in Hollywood and the glamour of all things American. Penned in 1988, the result is an eminently readable odyssey through the centuries from the day Rajah Soliman's diminutive kingdom was established on the banks of the Pasig River. Joaquin never quite says exactly what he thinks of contemporary Manila, but reading between the lines it's not hard to feel his dismay; he leaves you with the sense that this is a tribute to the city that was, not the city that exists today.

Stanley Karnow *In Our Image: America's Empire in the Philippines*. This Pulitzer Prize-winning effort is really a book about America, not about the Philippines, says Karnow. The Philippines is the landscape, but the story is of America going abroad for the first time in its history at the turn of the last century and becoming a colonial power. *In Our Image* examines how America has sought to remake the Philippines as a clone of itself, an experiment marked from the outset by blundering, ignorance and mutual misunderstanding. This is also the best book to read if you're looking for a general overview of Philippine history.

Eric Morris *Corregidor*. Intimate account of the defence of the island fortress, based on interviews with more than forty Filipinos and Americans who battled hunger, dysentery and malaria in the run-up to the critical battle with Japanese forces. As the book explains, the poorly equipped Allied troops,

abandoned by General MacArthur and almost forgotten by military strategists in Washington, had little chance of winning, though against all the odds the men on Corregidor held out for six months. Their defeat marked the fall of the Philippines to Japanese occupation.

Beth Day Romulo *Inside the Palace: The Rise and Fall of Ferdinand and Imelda Marcos*. Beth Day Romulo, wife of Ferdinand Marcos's foreign minister Carlos Romulo, was among those who enjoyed the privileges of being a Malacañang insider, something she feels the need to excuse and justify on almost every page. Her book borders on being a Marcos hagiography – she clearly didn't want to upset her old friend Imelda too much – and is gossipy more than investigative, but does nevertheless offer some insight into Imelda's lavish and frivolous lifestyle, and the disintegration of the regime.

William Henry Scott *Barangay: Sixteenth Century Philippine Culture and Society* (Ateneo de Manila University Press; o/p). This lucid account of life in the Philippines during the century the Spanish arrived is the best there is of the period. Yale-educated Scott, an anthropologist and lay missionary, was principal of St. Mary's School in Sagada and taught history at the University of the Philippines for ten years, acquiring an insight into the country that few foreigners have. His love for the Philippines and his deep knowledge of its customs are reflected in this scholarly but accessible investigation into Hispanic-era society, the country's elite, its tribes and their rituals – everything from that most quotidian of rituals, taking a bath, to the once common practice of penis piercing.

Culture and society

Sheila Coronel (ed) *Pork and Other Perks* (Philippine Center for Investigative Journalism). Comprising nine case studies by some of the country's foremost investigative journalists, this pioneering work uncovers the many forms corruption takes in the Philippines and points fingers at those responsible. The book is concerned mainly with what happens to "pork", the budget allocated annually to every senator and congressman. It's thought that much of the money goes towards hiring corrupt contractors who use below-par materials on infrastructure projects, with the politicians themselves benefiting from the discrepancy between the official and actual cost of the projects concerned.

James Hamilton-Paterson *Playing With Water: Passion and Solitude on a Philippine Island*. "No money, no honey," says one of the characters in Hamilton-Paterson's lyrical account of several seasons spent among the impoverished fishermen of a small barrio in Marinduque. It's the kind of refrain you hear time and again in the Philippines, and one that leads large numbers of young men to turn their backs on provincial life to seek fortune in Manila, where they usually end up hawking newspapers, living in shanties and wishing they were back home. This is a rich and original book, which by turns warms you and disturbs you. The author's love of the Philippine landscape and the people – many of whom think he must be related to US actor George Hamilton – is stunningly rendered. The diving accounts will stay with you forever, as will the episode in which H-P discovers he has worms.

Alfredo and Grace Roces *Culture Shock! Philippines.* Entertaining general guide to the world of Philippine social customs and relationships, including pithy and often amusing sections on language, food, festivals and business tips. Directed largely at expats, with detailed sections on house-hunting and employing a maid, but wide enough in scope to provide a useful overview for tourists.

Earl K. Wilkinson *The Philippines: Damaged Culture?* (Book of Dreams). Longtime expat in the Philippines, the late Earl K. Wilkinson exposed in this brave and candid book what he saw as the underlying reasons for the many maladies affecting the country he loved. *Damaged Culture* is never pontificating or presumptuous, but it is sometimes shocking in its revelations of corruption in high places, highlighting a number of travesties of justice which the author campaigned to put right – including spurious charges of molestation against a foreign priest working with street children. Wilkinson deals passionately with the incendiary combination of politics, patronage, corruption and cultural quirks that has retarded economic progress and kept the vast majority of the population mired in poverty. He also offers solutions, arguing that the nation's entrenched elite could start the recovery ball rolling by abandoning its traditional antipathy towards free-market competition.

Art and architecture

Pedro Galende *San Agustin*
(Bookmark). An evocative tribute to
the first Spanish stone church to be
built in the Philippines, San Agustin
in Intramuros. The first part of the
book is a detailed account of the
church's history, while the second is a
walking tour, illustrated with photographs, through the church and the
neighbouring monastery.

Pedro Galende & Rene Javelana
Great Churches of the Philippines
(Bookmark). Coffee-table book full
of beautiful colour photographs of
most of the country's notable
Spanish-era churches. The accompa-
nying text explains the evolution of
the unique "earthquake Baroque"
style developed to protect stone
structures against earthquakes and
which typifies Philippine churches
and provides a reminder that many of

these stunning buildings are in a
perilous state, with little money
available to guarantee their upkeep
and survival.

Maria Elena Paterno *Treasures of
the Philippine National Museum*
(Bookmark). Full-colour coffee-
table book with a simple premise:
to showcase some of the most
notable exhibits in the National
Museum and demonstrate that they
have a significance beyond their
value as artefacts. Among the fifty
exhibits in the book are ancient
Moro weapons from Mindanao and
exquisite pieces of pre-Hispanic
jewellery from northern Luzon, all
superbly photographed from every
conceivable angle, turning them
into dazzling works of art. The
explanatory text is resolutely factual
without being stuffy or academic.

The environment

Robin Broad et al. *Plundering
Paradise: the Struggle for the Environment in the Philippines.* Disturbing but
often inspiring account of short-term
gain for the few at the expense of
long-term loss for everyone. The
book shows how livelihoods and
habitats are disappearing throughout
the Philippines as big business
harvests everything from fish – for
the dinner tables of Hong Kong and
Japan – to trees, turned into
packaging for multi-national
companies and chopsticks for restaurants. The authors travelled through
the Philippines, recording the experi-
ences of people who are fighting
back by working alongside NGOs
and environmental groups to police
the environment and report illegal
logging, poaching and fishing, much

of which is allowed to take place
through the bribing of local officials.

Nigel Hicks *The National Parks and
Other Wild Places of the Philippines.*
Illuminating celebration of the
Philippines' natural heritage, with
terrific photographs. The book
describes all the major protected
areas in the country, as well as a
number of other wild areas that even
Filipinos are largely unaware of.
Some of the practical information is
a little out of date, but there's great
coverage of scenery, wildlife, tribes
and conservation projects.

Gutsy Tuason and Eduardo Cu
Anilao (Bookmark). Winner of the
Palme d'Or at the World Festival of
Underwater Images in Antibes,
France, this stunning coffee-table

collection of colour photographs were all taken around Anilao, Batangas, one of the country's most popular diving areas. What's remarkable about the book is the way it makes you take notice of the small marine life many divers ignore; the images of bobbit worms, ghost pipefish and sea fans are terrific. Anilao is under threat from development and tourism; with these images Tuason and Cu have shown why it must be saved.

Food

Reynaldo Alejandro et al. *The Food of the Philippines*. Proof that there's so much more to Filipino cuisine than *adobo* and rice. The recipes range from classics such as chilli crab simmered in coconut milk to a failsafe method for that trickiest of desserts, leche flan. Every recipe details how to find the right ingredients and what to use as a substitute if you can't. There's also a revealing history of Filipino food.

Glenda Rosales-Barretto *Flavors of the Philippines* (Bookmark). Rosales-Barretto is chief executive officer of the popular *Via Mare* restaurant chain in Manila, and what she doesn't know about Filipino food isn't worth knowing. This lavishly illustrated hardback highlights recipes region by region, from the meat-based cuisine of the northern mountains to the seafood of Palawan and the Visayas. There's a classic Bicol Express, with lots of spices and fish paste, but many of the recipes here are far from standard – instead, modern variations feature, such as fresh vegetarian pancake rolls with peanut sauce and roast chicken with passionfruit.

Fiction

F. Sionil José *Dusk*. By one of the premier novelists in the Philippines (José won the Magsaysay Award, the Asian equivalent of the Nobel for literature, in 1980), this is the fifth book in the author's acclaimed saga of the landowning Rosales family. *Dusk* is set at the end of the nineteenth century, at which time the Filipinos, with the aid of the Americans, finally expelled the Spanish after three centuries of often brutal rule. Of course it wouldn't be a quintessential Filipino novel if it didn't touch on the themes of poverty, corruption, tyranny and love. All are on display here, presented through the tale of one man, a common peasant, and his search for contentment. *Dusk* has been published in the US in paperback, though you can always buy it from the bookshop owned by José himself, Solidaridad at 531 Padre Faura St, Ermita, Manila.

F. Sionil José *Ermita* (Solidaridad). Eminently readable novella that atmospherically evokes the Philippines from World War II until the 1960s and stands as a potent allegory of the nation's ills. The Ermita of the title, apart from being the *mise en scène*, is also a girl, the unwanted child of a rich Filipina raped in her own home by a drunken Japanese soldier. The story follows young Ermita, abandoned in an orphanage, as she tries to trace her mother and then sets about exacting revenge on those she feels have wronged her.

🏃 **José Rizal** *Noli Me Tangere* (Bookmark). Published in 1886 (and promptly banned by the Spanish colonial government), this is a passionate and often elegant exposure of the evils of the friars' rule. It tells the story of barrio boy Crisostomo Ibarra's love for the beautiful Maria

Clara, infusing it with tragedy and significance of almost Shakespearean proportions, documenting the religious fanaticism, the double standards and the rank injustice of colonial rule. The imagery is sometimes overripe, but this will always be a book ahead of its time, having set in motion a chain of events that sparked a revolution; it's still required reading for every Filipino schoolchild.

The Philippines in foreign literature

William Boyd *The Blue Afternoon.* Boyd has never been to the Philippines, but spent hours researching the country from England. Remarkably, he seems to get Manila at the start of the twentieth century just right, infusing it with an oppressive steaminess that makes tragedy for some of the characters seem preordained. In flashbacks, the novel moves from 1930s Hollywood to the exotic, violent world of the Philippines in 1902, recounting a tale of medicine, the murder of American soldiers and the creation of a magical flying machine. This is a brooding, intense book that won't tell you much about the contemporary Philippines, but will put some of the more brutal history into perspective, particularly the war with the US.

Alex Garland *The Tesseract.* Alex Garland has made no secret of his love for the Philippines, so it's hardly surprising that the follow-up to *The Beach* is set there. Garland may get most of his Tagalog wrong (it's *tsismis*, not chismis and *konti* not conte), but his prose captures perfectly the marginal existence of his characters. The story? Well it involves a foreigner abroad, a villainous tycoon called Don Pepe, some urchins and a beautiful girl. The characters may be straight from Cliché Street, but Garland's plot is so intriguing and his

observational powers so keen that it's impossible not to be swept along by the baleful atmosphere the book creates.

Jessica Hagedorn *Dogeaters.* Filipino-American Jessica Tarahata Hagedorn assembles a cast of diverse and dubious characters that comes as close to encapsulating the mania of life in Manila as any writer has ever come. Urchins, pimps, seedy tycoons and corpulent politicos are brought together in a brutal but beautiful narrative that pulls no punches and serves as a jolting reminder of all the country's frailties and woes – *Pulp Fiction* meets Martin Amis in the Third World. Hagedorn also wrote the equally emotive *The Gangster of Love*, about a Filipino immigrant family in America.

🏃 **James Hamilton-Paterson** *Ghosts of Manila.* Filipinos scoffed at it, claiming it did Manila a gross injustice, but their ire seemed more out of pique than reason. Hamilton-Paterson's excoriating novel is haunting, powerful and for the most part alarmingly accurate. Much of it is taken from real life: the extra-judicial "salvagings" (a local word for liquidation) of suspected criminals, the corruption and the abhorrent saga of Imelda Marcos's infamous film centre. From the despair and detritus, the author conjures up a lucid story that is thriller, morality play and documentary in one. Pretty it's not, but if you want Manila dissected, look no further.

Language

Language

Language

T here are more than 150 languages and dialects in the Philippines, nine of which are spoken by almost ninety percent of the population. **Tagalog**, also known as Filipino or Pilipino, is spoken as a first language by seventeen million people – mostly on Luzon, and also in some parts of the Visayas – and was made the national language by the government in 1947. Part of the Malayo-Polynesian family of languages (which also includes Malay, Indonesian, Maori and Fijian), Tagalog is now used to some degree by almost half the population, and is the main language of the street, the tabloid press and informal communication. Officially, English remains the language of instruction in schools and most official business communication is in English. Other major languages include **Cebuano**, spoken by sixteen million people in and around the island of Cebu, and Ilocano, the first language of around eleven million people in northern Luzon. While all Philippine languages and dialects have common roots and certain similarities in sound and grammar, people with limited Tagalog might well find it difficult to communicate if they're from different corners of the country. Add to this linguistic plethora words introduced from Chinese, Spanish and English, and you have something of a communications mess.

   English is widely spoken in the Philippines: most everyday transactions – checking into a hotel, ordering a meal, buying a ferry ticket – can be carried out in English, and most people in the tourism industry speak it reasonably well. Even off the beaten track, many Filipinos understand enough to help with basics such as accommodation and directions, and thus many visitors find they don't need to resort to Tagalog at all, though it doesn't hurt to know a few Tagalog numbers and basic phrases. If you do try to speak Tagalog, however, the reaction is often one of amusement – and the response will come in English. Tagalog, of course, has also been influenced by **Spanish** and has assimilated many Spanish words, such as *mesa* (table) and *cuarto* (bedroom, written *kuwarto* in Tagalog). Few Filipinos actually speak Spanish these days, although some of the wealthy clans who can trace their ancestry back to the Spanish do speak it socially, more as a sign of their heritage and status than because it has any usefulness.

Tagalog

The structure of Tagalog is simple, though the **word order** is different from English; as an example, take "*kumain ng mangga ang bata*", which literally translates as "ate a mango the child". Another key difference between the two languages is the lack of the verb "to be" in Tagalog, which means a simple sentence such as "the woman is kind" is rendered *mabait ang babae*, literally "kind the woman". For **plurals**, the word *mga* is used – hence *bahay/mga bahay* for house/houses – although in many cases Filipinos simply state the actual number of objects or use *marami* (several) before the noun.

Tagalog sounds staccato to the foreign ear, with clipped vowels and consonants. The **p**, **t** and **k** sounds are never aspirated and sound a little gentler than in English. The *g* is always hard, as in **g**et. The letter **c** seldom crops up in Tagalog and where it does – in names such as Boracay and Bulacan, for example – it's pronounced like *k*. The hardest sound to master for most beginners is the **ng** sound as in the English word "si**nging**" (with the *g* gently nazalized, not hard); in Tagalog this sound can occur at the beginning of a word, eg in **ng**ayon (now). The *mg* combination in the word *mga* above looks tricky but is in fact straightforward to pronounce, as *mang*. As for vowels and diphthongs (vowel combinations):

a is pronounced as in **a**pple	iw is a sound that simply doesn't exist in English; it's close to the ieu sound in lieu, but with greater separation between the vowels (almost as in lee-you)
e as in m**e**ss	
i as in d**i**tto, though a little more elongated than in English	
o as in b**o**re	oy as in n**oi**se
u as in p**u**t	uw as in q**ua**rter
ay as in b**uy**	uy produced making the sound **oo** and continuing it to the **i** sound in *ditto*.
aw in m**ou**nt	

Vowels that fall consecutively in a word are always pronounced individually, as is every syllable, adding to the choppy nature of the language; for example, *tao* meaning person or people is pronounced ta-o, while *oo* for yes is pronounced o-o (with each vowel closer to the *o* in *show* than in *bore*).

Unlike some other Southeast Asian languages, Tagalog has no tones, and most words are spoken as they are written, though working out which syllable to **stress** is tricky. In words of two syllables the first syllable tends to be stressed, while in words of three or more syllables the stress is almost always on the final or penultimate syllable; thus Boracay is pronounced Bo-**ra**-kay or sometimes Bo-ra-**kay**, but never **Bo**-ra-kay. Sometimes a change in the stress can drastically alter the meaning: *lalaki*, for instance, can mean "man" if the stress falls on the second syllable, or "to grow big" if the stress falls on the first. In the vocabulary lists that follow, stressed syllables are indicated in **bold** text except where the term in question is obviously an English loan word. Note that English loan words may be rendered a little differently in Tagalog, in line with the rules mentioned above; thus "bus" for instance has the vowel sound of the English word "put".

Tagalog has formal and informal **forms of address**, the formal usually reserved for people who are significantly older. Using the polite form to address someone of a similar age would sound affected and ridiculous, even if you've never met them before. The informal form of "I'm fine" is *mabuti* and the formal *mabuti-po*. The "po" suffix indicates respect and can be added to almost any word or phrase: *o-po* is a respectful "yes" and it's common to hear Filipinos say *sorry-po* for "sorry". Even the lowliest beggar is given esteem by language: the standard reply to beggars is *patawarin-po*, literally, "forgive me, sir." Honorifics are important to Filipinos, with professionals being referred to by their titles in formal situations – for example, Attorney Cruz or Engineer Marcos. In social situations everyone's much more relaxed; first names are fine for people of your own generation; for your elders, use Mr or Mrs (if you know a woman is married) before the surname. It's common to use manong/manang (uncle/aunt) and kuya (brother/sister) to address superiors informally, even if they are not blood relatives (eg manong Jun, kuya Beth).

Though Tagalog is the official language of the Philippines, English still plays a significant role – it is the de facto language of commerce, is used to a degree in parliament and is the only foreign language featuring in all school curricula. The present status of English goes back to 1901, when the US colonial administration decided that teaching Filipinos in their various native tongues would be too complicated and costly; an education system with English at its heart was created instead. Educated Filipinos move seamlessly between English and Tagalog, often in the space of the same sentence, and many English words have been adopted by Filipinos, giving rise to a small canon of patois known affectionately as Taglish: why ask someone to take a photograph when in Visayan you can ask them to do some "kodahan"?

Even Filipinos who speak English with confidence incorporate linguistic oddities that can bamboozle foreigners. Many of these peculiarities stem from the habit of translating something literally from Tagalog, resulting in Filipinos "closing" or "opening" the light, or "getting down" from a taxi. As Tagalog does not indicate gender in the third person, you may well hear a Filipino say something like "Juan has gone to the office because she's very busy." Among those who don't speak English so well, an inability to pronounce the f-sound is common, simply because it doesn't exist in any Philippine tongue. Filipinos are well aware of this trait and often make self-deprecating jokes about it, referring to forks as porks and vice versa. Other ear-catching Taglish phrases include "I'll be the one to" – as in "I'll be the one to buy lunch" instead of "I'll buy lunch" – and "for a while", meaning "wait a moment" or "hang on".

The number of Tagalog **phrasebooks**, **dictionaries** and **coursebooks** outside the Philippines is limited, although with a little effort you should be able to track down any of the titles listed here. *Basic Tagalog for Foreigners and Non-Tagalogs* by Paraluman Aspillera (Tuttle Publishing) is a straightforward coursebook. *Pilipino–English/English–Pilipino Phrasebook and Dictionary* by Jesusa Salvador and Raymond Barrager (Hippocrene Books) is compact enough to carry around and doesn't dwell too much on the complexities of grammar, instead concentrating on useful words and phrases. The *Pocket Filipino Dictionary* (Periplus Editions/Berkeley Books) and the *Concise English–Tagalog Dictionary* (Tuttle) by José Panganiban are both handy references. Once you're in the Philippines, you can find these and other titles at branches of the National Book Store.

Greetings and civilities

hello/how are you?	ka**mus**ta
Fine, thanks	ma**bu**ti, sa**la**mat (*formal*) okay lang (*informal*)
pleased to meet you	ikinalu**lu**god ki**tang** (archaic, but there's no Filipino informal version – most people use English or simply say "kamusta") maki**la**la (*formal*)
goodbye	bye
good morning	magan**dang** u**ma**ga
good afternoon	magan**dang** ha**pon**
good evening/ good night	magan**dang** ga**bi**
please ... (before a request)	**pa**ki ...
excuse me (to say sorry)	ipagpau**man**hin mo **ak**
excuse me (to get past)	makikira**an** lang **po**/pasensiya ka na
sorry	sorry
thank you	sa**la**mat
what's your name?	**a**nong pa**nga**lan mo?
my name is ...	ang pa**nga**lan ko ay ...
do you speak English?	ma**ru**nong ka bang mag-**Ing**les?
I (don't) understand	(hin**di**) ko naiintindi**han**

could you repeat that?	paki-ulit
I/we would like ...	gusto-ko ...
do you have ...?	meron kang ...?
would you like some? (when offering something to eat)	gusto mo?
do you like this?	gusto mo ito?
of course	siyempre
it's okay, go ahead	sige (na)
where are you from?	taga saan ka?
I am from ... (most countries are rendered as in English)	taga ... ako
really?/is that so?	dalaga?
leave it to God; what will be will be	bahala na
I don't know (used to avoid confrontation)	ewan
hang on; wait a minute	sandali lang
okay?/is that okay?	puwede?/puwede ba?
I'll try [to comply with your request]	sisikapan ko (or colloquially say titing nan ko - "I'll see")
[have you] finished?	tapos-na?
[we have] none	wala
Filipino/Filipina	pinoy/pinay (slang)
mate, buddy	pare

honorific used for more senior person: **ma**nong (*m.*) or **ma**nang (*f.*) e.g. manong Jack, kamusta ka?

an expression of mild exasperation, akin to "oh my goodness": ay na**ku**

Common terms

yes	oo
no	hindi
maybe	siguro
good/bad	magaling/masama
big/small	malaki/maliit
easy/difficult	madali/mahirap
open/closed	bukas/sarado
hot/cold	mainit/malamig
cheap/expensive	mura/mahal
a lot/a little	madami/konti
one more/ another...	isa pa ...
beautiful	maganda
hungry	gutom
thirsty	nauuhaw
very ... (followed by adjective)	tunay ...
with/without ...	meron/wala ...
watch out!	ingat!
who?	sino?
what?	ano?
why?	bakit?
when?	kailan?
how?	paano?

Getting around

airport	airport
bus/train station	istasyon ng bus/tren
pier	pier
aeroplane	eroplano
ferry	barco (*for large vessels – "ferry" will also do*)
	banca (*outrigger boat*)
taxi	taxi
bicycle	bisikleta
car	kotse
where do I/we catch the ... to ... ?	saan puwedeng kumuha ng ... papuntang ... ?

when does the ... for ... leave?	kailan aalis ang ... papuntang ...?
when does the next ... leave?	anong oras ho aalis ang ...?
ticket	tiket
can I/we book a seat	puwedeng bumili kaagad ng ticket para i-reserba ang upuan
I'd/we'd like to go to the ... please	gusto naming pumunta sa ...
[I'd like to] pay	bayad po (*to pay your fare to a jeepney or tricycle driver*)

how long does it take?	gaano katagal?
how many kilometres is it to ...?	ilang kilometro papunta sa ...?
please stop here	paki-tigil ditto or para
where is the ...?	saan ang ...?
bank	banko
beach	beach
church	simbahan
cinema	sinehan
filling station	gasolinahan
hotel	hotel
market	palengke
moneychanger	taga-palit ng pera (or just "money-changer")
pharmacy	botika
post office	koreo or post office

restaurant	restoran (see also p.40)
town hall	town hall
left	kaliwa
right	kanan
straight on	derecho/diretso
opposite	katapat ng
in front of	sa harap ng
behind	sa likod ng
near/far	malapit/malayo
north	hilaga
south	timog
east	silangan
west	kanluran
I'm in a hurry	nagmamadali ako
I want to hire a guide	gusto kong kumuha/ magbayad ng guide

Accommodation

do you have any rooms?	meron pa kayong kuwarto?
could I have the bill please?	puwedeng kunin ang check
bathroom	CR (comfort room) or banyo
room with a private bathroom	kuwarto na may sariling banyo
single room	kuwarto para sa isa
double room	kuwarto para sa dalawang tao

clean/dirty	malinis/marumi
air-conditioner	aircon
fan	elektrik fan
key	susi
telephone	telepono
cellphone/mobile phone	cellphone or cell
laundry	labahan
passport	pasaporte

Shopping

money	pera
how much?	magkano?
it's too expensive	masyadong mahal or sobra (too much)
I'll take this one	kukunin ko ito

cigarettes	sigarilyo
matches	posporo
soap	sabon
toilet paper	tisyu

Emergencies

can you help me?	puwede mo akong tulungan?
fire!	sunog
help!	saklolo
there's been an accident	may aksidente

please call a doctor	paki-tawag ng duktor
ill	may sakit
hospital	ospital
police station	istasyon ng pulis

Numbers

0	zero	20	dalawam**pu**
1	i**sa**	21	dalawam**pu**'t i**sa**
2	dala**wa**	22	dalawam**pu**'t dala**wa**
3	tat**lo**	30	tatlum**pu**
4	a**pat**	40	apatna**pu**
5	**lima**	50	limam**pu**
6	a**nim**	60	animna**pu**
7	pi**to**	70	pitum**pu**
8	wa**lo**	80	walam**pu**
9	si**yam**	90	siyamna**pu**
10	sam**pu**	100	sanda**an**
11	la**bing** i**sa**	1000	i**sang** li**bo**
12	la**bing** dala**wa**	1,000,000	i**sang** milyun
13	la**bing** tat**lo**	a half	kala**hati**

Dates and times

what's the time?	**a**nong **o**ras na?	7	siyete
midnight	ha**ting**-ga**bi**	8	otso
morning	u**ma**ga	9	nuwebe
noon	tang**hali**	10	diyes
afternoon	**ha**pon	11	onse
evening/night	ga**bi**	12	dose
minute	mi**nu**to	9 o'clock	alas nuwebe
hour	**o**ras	10.30	alas diyes y media
day	**a**raw	Monday	Lunes
week	ling**go**	Tuesday	Martes
month	**bu**wan	Wednesday	Miyerkoles
year	ta**on**	Thursday	Huwebes
today/now	nga**yon**	Friday	Biyernes
tomorrow	**bu**kas	Saturday	Sabado
yesterday	ka**ha**pon	Sunday	Linggo
		January	Enero

Note that when telling the time, Filipinos often resort to Spanish numbers. Likewise, days of the week and months of the year are mostly derived from Spanish. For reference we give details here, using the local spelling.

		February	Pebrero
		March	Marso
		April	Abril
		May	Mayo
		June	Hunyo
1	uno	July	Hulyo
2	dos	August	Agosto
3	tres	September	Setyembre
4	kuwatro	October	Oktubre
5	singko	November	Nobyembre
6	seis	December	Disyembre

Food and drink terms

Most menus in the Philippines are in English, although in places that specialize in Filipino cuisine you'll see Tagalog on the menu, usually with an explanation in English below. For foods that arrived in the Philippines comparatively recently there often isn't an equivalent Filipino word, so to have cake, for example, you ask for cake. Even in the provinces waiters and waitresses tend to speak enough English to understand what you're after.

When the time comes to get your **check** ("bill" is rarely used) make a rectangular shape in the air with your thumb and forefinger. If you want to catch the waiter's attention, it's okay to raise your hand or, if he's within earshot, quietly call "waiter". For the waitress, use "miss".

General terms and ingredients

bread	tinapay	can I see the menu?	patingin ng menu?
bread rolls	pan de sal	I would like ...	gusto ko ...
butter	mantikilya	delicious	sarap
jam	no precise equivalent, though palaman is used for anything spread on bread	hot (spicy)	maanghang
		can I have the bill please?	puwede kunin ang check
cheese	keso	to go Dutch	KKB (from kanya-kanyang bayad, literally "each his own pays")
egg	itlog		
salt	asin		
pepper	paminta		
soy sauce	toyo	restaurant	restoran; or carinderia for a canteen-style place where you choose from dishes placed on the counter; or ihaw-ihaw for a grill restaurant
sugar	asukal		
coconut milk	gata		
fermented fish/ shrimp paste	bagoong		
fish sauce	patis		
rice	bigas (the uncooked grain) or kanin (cooked rice)	breakfast	almusal
		lunch	tanghalian
salted egg	itlog na maalat (hard to miss in supermarkets because the shells are bright purple)	dinner	hapunan (rare) or dinner
		fork	tinidor
		glass	baso
		knife	kutsilyo
I'm vegetarian	vegetarian ako or gulay lang ang kinakain ko (literally "I only eat vegetables")	plate	plato
		spoon	kutsara

Food preparation

adobong	*adobo*-style, stewed in soy sauce and vinegar, with pepper and garlic
binuro	covered in salt and cooked slowly, often sealed in leaves or foil
dinaing	(of fish) cut open like a butterfly and fried or grilled
ginataan	cooked in coconut milk
gisa/ginsa/gisado	sautéed
inadobo	sautéed in vinegar and soy sauce
inasinan	salted
inihaw	grilled over charcoal
kinilaw	marinated in vinegar and spices
pinais	wrapped in leaves and steamed
pinaksiw	(of fish) cooked with vinegar and spices
prito	fried
rellenong	stuffed, often with sausage, egg, cheese and raisins
sinigang	cooked with tamarind to make a sour soup or stew

Meat (*karne*) and poultry

atay	liver
baboy	pork
baka	beef
kambing	goat
kordero/karnero	lamb
lengua	tongue
manok	chicken
pata	pig's knuckle (trotters)
pato	duck
pugo	quail
tenga ng baboy	pig's ears

Common dishes

adobo	chicken and/or pork simmered in soy sauce and vinegar with pepper and garlic
beef tapa	beef marinated in vinegar, sugar and garlic, then dried in the sun and fried
Bicol Express	fiery dish of pork ribs cooked in coconut milk, soy sauce, vinegar, *bagoong* and hot chillies
bistek tagalog	beef tenderloin with calamansi and onion
bulalo	beef shank in onion broth
dinuguan	pork cubes simmered in pig's blood with garlic, onion and laurel leaves

ginisang monggo	any combination of pork, vegetables or shrimp sautéed with mung beans
kaldereta	spicy mutton stew
kare-kare	rich oxtail stew with eggplant, peanut and *puso ng saging* (see under "Vegetables")
lechon (de leche)	roast whole (suckling) pig, dipped in a liver paste sauce
longganisa/ longganiza	small beef or pork sausages, with a lot of garlic
longsilog	longganisa with garlic rice and fried egg
mechado	braised beef
pochero	boiled beef and vegetables
sisig	fried chopped pork, liver and onions
tapsilog	beef tapa with garlic rice and fried egg
tinola	tangy soup with chicken, papaya and ginger
tocino	marinated fried pork
tosilog	marinated fried pork with garlic rice and fried egg

Fish (*isda*) and seafood

alimango	crab
bangus	milkfish
galunggong	round scad
hipon	shrimps
hito	catfish
lapu-lapu	grouper
panga ng tuna	tuna jaw
pusit	squid
sugpo	prawns
tahong	mussels
talaba	oysters
tanguingue	popular and affordable sea fish, not unlike tuna in flavour

Common dishes

daing na bangus	*bangus* marinated in vinegar and spices, then fried
gambas	shrimps sautéed in chilli and garlic sauce
pinaksiw na lapu-lapu	lapu-lapu marinated in vinegar and spices, served cold
rellenong bangus	stuffed *bangus*

Vegetables (*gulay*)

abong bamboo	bamboo shoots
alogbati	red-stemmed plant with heart-shaped leaves, added to salads and stews
ampalaya	bitter melon or bitter gourd, a rough-skinned vegetable used to add a slightly bitter taste to stews; the leaves are used, steamed, in salads, and medicinally
bawang	garlic
camote/kamote	sweet potato
dahon ng sili	chilli pepper leaves, added to soups and stews
gabi	taro, a versatile root crop whose leaves, stalks and tuber can all be cooked and eaten
kabute	oyster mushroom
kamatis	tomato
kangkong	convolvulus leaves; also called swamp cabbage or water spinach
labanos	white radish, added to soups or in a tangy salad with tomato, vinegar, olive oil and sugar
luya	ginger
monggo beans	mung beans
puso ng saging	banana heart, the rust-coloured pod that forms on the banana tree and contains the flowers; it's chopped up and added to dishes such as Bicol Express
sibuyas	onion
sili	chillies
sitaw	string beans
talong	eggplant/aubergine
taogue	beansprouts (pronounced *ta-o-gay*)
ube	purple yam
upo	winter melon or gourd

Common dishes

adobong kangkong	*kangkong* cooked *adobo*-style, in vinegar and soy, with lots of garlic
Bicol Express	vegetables cooked with coconut milk, soy sauce, vinegar, hot chilli and a dash of *bagoong*
ginataang ng puso ng saging	banana heart cooked in coconut milk, sometimes with shrimp or fish added
laing	taro leaves cooked in coconut milk
pechay	Chinese cabbage, sometimes spelled *petsay* or *pitsay*; also known as *bok choi* or *pak choy*

| pinakbet | vegetable stew with *bagoong*, cooked in broth, often with | | small pieces of meat added |

Noodles and miscellaneous dishes

kilawing puso ng saging	noodles fried with ground beef or pork and banana heart	pancit	noodles
		pancit bihon	thin vermicelli rice noodles with shrimp and vegetable
lumpia	egg rolls, filled with vegetables and sometimes meat	pancit canton	thick rice noodles with shrimp and vegetable
lumpia ubod	egg rolls filled with hearts of palm	sotanghon	thin translucent rice noodles
mami	noodle soup	torta (de cangrejo)	(crab) omelette

Snacks (merienda) and street food

adidas	chicken's feet; named after the sports-shoe manufacturer, they're served on a stick with a choice of sauces for dipping		served with a cup of vinegar for dipping
arroz caldo	rice porridge with chicken	lugaw	plain rice porridge, traditionally thought of as food for the convalescent; it can be enriched with boiled tripe, green onions, fried garlic and egg
balut	raw, half-formed duck embryo		
camote	sweet potato fried with brown sugar, or boiled and served with a pat of butter		
		mais	steamed corn-on-the-cob
chicharon	fried pork skin, served with a vinegar dip	pugo	hard-boiled quail's eggs, sold in packets of fifteen to twenty
dilis	dried anchovies, eaten whole and dipped in vinegar as a bar snack or added to vegetable stews	puto	rice muffins, available in a range of funky colours, including puce, green and baby pink
		siopao	Chinese buns filled with spicy pork
ensaimada	sweet cheese rolls	sorbetes	ice cream; the term is used mainly of the home-made varieties sold from colourful handcarts
fish balls, squid balls	mashed fish or squid blended with wheat flour and deep fried; served on a stick with a sweet sauce		
		sumsumon	pig's ear
goto	rice porridge containing almost anything, including tripe, entrails, ears and pieces of snout; the fried garlic floating on top is delicious and a splash of calamansi adds some tang	taho	mushy confection of mashed bean curd, caramel and tapioca; a popular breakfast on-the-move, it's sold by vendors who carry it in canisters over their shoulders
isaw	grilled chicken or pig's intestines dyed a funky orange to make even more appetizing; it's	tokneneng	hard-boiled *balut* covered in orange dough and deep-fried while you wait

Fruit (*fruitas*)

atis	custard apple
balimbing	starfruit (aka carambola)
bayabas	guava
buko	coconut
calamansi	lime
chico	sapodilla (roughly the size of an egg with brown skin and sticky, soft flesh)
guayabano	soursop (large, oval fruit with knobbly spines outside and fragrant flesh inside)
kaimito	star apple (plum-coloured and round, about the size of a tennis ball, with leathery skin and soft white pulp inside)
langka	jackfruit
lanzones	outside the size and colour of a small potato; inside there's sweet, translucent flesh with a bitter seed
mangga	mango (available in sweet and sour varieties)
mangosteen	round, with a shiny dark purple skin and soft white flesh inside
pakwan	watermelon
papaya	papaya
piña	pineapple
saging	banana (there are dozens of varieties, from the cooking banana *sabo* to finger-like *senoritas* and red-skinned *morado*)

Desserts

bibingka	cake made of ground rice, sugar and coconut milk, baked in a clay stove and served hot with fresh, salted duck's eggs on top
bilo-bilo	glutinous rice and small pieces of tapioca in coconut milk
brazos	meringues, often with cashew-nut filling
cassava cake	sticky, dark cake with a fudge-like consistency
champorado	chocolate rice pudding
guinatan	chocolate pudding served with lashings of coconut cream
halo-halo	sweet concoction made from ice cream, shaved ice, jelly, beans and tinned milk; the name literally means "mix-mix"
kutsinta	brown rice cake with coconut shavings
leche flan	caramel custard
maja blanca	blancmange of corn and coconut cream
polvoron	sweets made from butter, sugar and toasted flour, pale in colour with a crumbly texture
puto bumbong	glutinous rice steamed in a bamboo tube, infusing it with a delicate, woody taste; lilac colouring gives it a distinctive purple sheen
sago at nata de coco	blend of sago and coconut served cold in a glass
suman	sweet and sticky rice cake served inside a banana leaf

Drinks (inumin)

merong/walang yelo/asukal	with/without ice/sugar
alak	wine (in practice, everyone just says "wine")
beer	beer
buko juice	coconut water
calamansi juice/soda	calamansi juice made into a cold drink by adding soda or a hot one with boiled water and a touch of honey
chocolate-eh	thick hot chocolate
gatas	milk
ginebra	gin
juice	juice
kape	coffee

lambanog alcoholic drink made from fermented fruit and available in a range of flavours

mineral mineral water

rum rum (the cheap, popular Tanduay has become almost synonymous with rum, so you could just ask for Tanduay and Coke)

tapuy rice wine

tsa tea

tubig water

tubo juice sugar-cane juice

Glossary

amihan the northwest monsoon from November to April (dry season)

bahay house

bahay kubo wooden house

bahay na bato house built of stone

bahay na tisa house with a roof of terracotta tiles and decorative tiles around the windows

banca boat carved from wood, with stabilizing outriggers made from bamboo; the so-called "big bancas" are used as ferries and often feature cabins

barangay the smallest political voting unit, whose residents elect "barangay captains" to represent their views to the mayor; barangays take different forms, ranging from part of a village through a whole village to a district of a town or city

barong or barong tagalog formal shirt worn by men, woven from fine fabric such as *piña* and worn hanging outside the pants

barrio village

bulol rice god carved from wood, used by many northern hill tribes in religious rituals and as talismans

buri type of palm used to make mats and rugs

butanding whale shark

calesas/kalesas horse-drawn carriages, still seen in some areas including Chinatown in Manila and Vigan

capiz a white seashell that's almost translucent when flattened and is used to make windows and screens

carabao water buffalo

carinderia canteen where food is presented in pots on a counter-top

carozza ornate carriage used in religious processions to transport statues of saints or holy relics

chinito a Filipino/Filipina who looks Chinese

cogon/kogon wild grass that is often used as thatch on provincial homes and beach cottages

CR toilet (= "comfort room")

derecho/diretso straight ahead; sign used to indicate a bus is going to make few stops

DoT Department of Tourism

earthquake Baroque style of church architecture typical of Spanish churches in the Philippines, which were built with thick buttresses to protect them from earthquakes and a separate bell tower that wouldn't hit the main church if the tower collapsed

estero drainage canal

GRO guest relations officer; waitress or hostess in a bar who receives a cut of the payment for the drinks a customer buys her; often a euphemism for sex worker

habagat southwest monsoon from May to October (wet season)

ilustrado the wealthy elite

isla island

kalye street

kundiman genre of music combining elements of tribal music with contemporary lyrics to produce epic songs of love and loss

kuweba cave

malong tube-like woven garment worn by many Muslims in Mindanao, similar to a sarong

Moro Muslim

narra the national tree, whose wood is considered best for furniture

nido edible birds' nests, harvested in Palawan

nipa short, sturdy palm that is dried and used for building houses

nito native vine woven into hats, mats and decorative items such as lampshades

OPM Original Pilipino Music, acronym used to describe pop and rock performed by Filipino artists

Pilipino Filipino; also means Tagalog

pinay/pinoy slang for Filipina/Filipino

piña fibre taken from the outside of the pineapple and woven into fine, shiny cloth

poblacion town centre

sabong cockfighting

sala living room

sampaguita member of the jasmine family with delicate white petals and fine perfume, considered the national flower

santo saint; also small statues of the saints found in churches and sold in antique shops

Santo Niño the Christ Child; patron of many communities, revered by Christian Filipinos

sari-sari store small store, often no more than a hut, selling essentials such as matches, snacks, shampoo and toothpaste

sikat native grass woven into various items, especially rugs

sitio small village or outpost, often consisting of no more than a few houses

tabo scoop, commonly used to bathe with in the provinces

tamaraw dwarf water buffalo, an endangered species found only on Mindoro

terno classic Filipino formal gown popularized by Imelda Marcos, with high butterfly sleeves and low, square-cut neckline

tinikling folk dance in which participants hop adeptly between heavy bamboo poles as they are struck together at shin-height, at increasing speed

zarzuela style of light opera introduced to the Philippines from Spain at the end of the nineteenth century

Travel
store

ROUGH GUIDES Complete Listing

ROUGH GUIDES

Visit us online
www.roughguides.com
Information on over 25,000 destinations around the world

- **Read** Rough Guides' trusted travel info
- **Access** exclusive articles from Rough Guides authors
- **Update** yourself on new books, maps, CDs and other products
- **Enter** our competitions and win travel prizes
- **Share** ideas, journals, photos & travel advice with other users
- **Earn** points every time you contribute to the Rough Guide community and get rewards

ROUGH GUIDES BROADEN YOUR HORIZONS

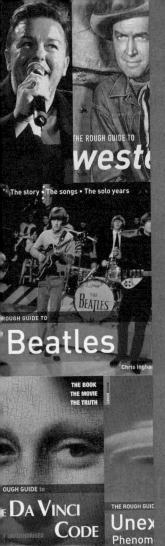

In some countries,
the children
are the tourist
attraction.

IF YOU SEE IT ▸

child sex tourism

prostituted children

sexual offences against children

REPORT IT

www.reportchildsex.com

For more information:

www.ecpat.org.nz

www.childprotection.org.ph

ecpat.nz

"every child's right... freedom from sexual exploitation"

Small print and
Index

A Rough Guide to Rough Guides

Published in 1982, the first Rough Guide – to Greece – was a student scheme that became a publishing phenomenon. Mark Ellingham, a recent graduate in English from Bristol University, had been travelling in Greece the previous summer and couldn't find the right guidebook. With a small group of friends he wrote his own guide, combining a highly contemporary, journalistic style with a thoroughly practical approach to travellers' needs.

The immediate success of the book spawned a series that rapidly covered dozens of destinations. And, in addition to impecunious backpackers, Rough Guides soon acquired a much broader and older readership that relished the guides' wit and inquisitiveness as much as their enthusiastic, critical approach and value-for-money ethos.

These days, Rough Guides include recommendations from shoestring to luxury and cover more than 200 destinations around the globe, including almost every country in the Americas and Europe, more than half of Africa and most of Asia and Australasia. Our ever-growing team of authors and photographers is spread all over the world, particularly in Europe, the USA and Australia.

In the early 1990s, Rough Guides branched out of travel, with the publication of Rough Guides to World Music, Classical Music and the Internet. All three have become benchmark titles in their fields, spearheading the publication of a wide range of books under the Rough Guide name.

Including the travel series, Rough Guides now number more than 350 titles, covering: phrasebooks, waterproof maps, music guides from Opera to Heavy Metal, reference works as diverse as Conspiracy Theories and Shakespeare, and popular culture books from iPods to Poker. Rough Guides also produce a series of more than 120 World Music CDs in partnership with World Music Network.

Visit www.roughguides.com to see our latest publications.

Rough Guide travel images are available for commercial licensing at www.roughguidespictures.com

Rough Guide credits

Text editor: Nikki Birrell and Alice Park
Layout: Dan May
Cartography: Rajesh Chhiber
Picture editor: Jj Luck
Production: Aimee Hampson
Proofreader: Anne Burgat
Cover design: Chloë Roberts
Photographer: Simon Bracken
Editorial: London Kate Berens, Claire
Saunders, Ruth Blackmore, Polly Thomas,
Alison Murchie, Karoline Densley, Andy Turner,
Keith Drew, Edward Aves, Sarah Eno, Lucy
White, Jo Kirby, Samantha Cook, James Smart,
Natasha Foges, Roísín Cameron, Emma Traynor,
Emma Gibbs, Joe Staines, Duncan Clark, Peter
Buckley, Matthew Milton, Tracy Hopkins, Ruth
Tidbull; **New York** Andrew Rosenberg, Steven
Horak, AnneLise Sorensen, Amy Hegarty, April
Isaacs, Ella Steim, Anna Owens, Joseph Petta,
Sean Mahoney; **Delhi** Madhavi Singh, Karen
D'Souza
Design & Pictures: London Scott Stickland,
Dan May, Diana Jarvis, Mark Thomas, Jj Luck,
Chloë Roberts, Nicole Newman, Sarah Cummins;
Delhi Umesh Aggarwal, Ajay Verma, Jessica

Subramanian, Ankur Guha, Pradeep Thapliyal,
Sachin Tanwar, Anita Singh
Production: Aimee Hampson, Vicky Baldwin
Cartography: London Maxine Repath, Ed
Wright, Katie Lloyd-Jones; **Delhi** Jai Prakash
Mishra, Rajesh Chhibber, Ashutosh Bharti, Rajesh
Mishra, Animesh Pathak, Jasbir Sandhu, Karobi
Gogoi, Amod Singh, Alakananda Bhattacharya,
Swati Handoo
Online: New York Jennifer Gold, Kristin
Mingrone; **Delhi** Manik Chauhan, Narender
Kumar, Rakesh Kumar, Amit Kumar, Amit Verma,
Rahul Kumar, Ganesh Sharma, Debojit Borah
Marketing & Publicity: London Liz Statham,
Niki Hanmer, Louise Maher, Jess Carter, Vanessa
Godden, Vivienne Watton, Anna Paynton, Rachel
Sprackett; **New York** Geoff Colquitt, Megan
Kennedy, Katy Ball; **Delhi** Reem Khokhar
Manager India: Punita Singh
Series Editor: Mark Ellingham
Reference Director: Andrew Lockett
Publishing Coordinator: Helen Phillips
Publishing Director: Martin Dunford
Commercial Manager: Gino Magnotta
Managing Director: John Duhigg

Publishing information

This second edition published September 2007 by
Rough Guides Ltd,
80 Strand, London WC2R 0RL
345 Hudson St, 4th Floor,
New York, NY 10014, USA
14 Local Shopping Centre, Panchsheel Park,
New Delhi 110017, India
Distributed by the Penguin Group
Penguin Books Ltd,
80 Strand, London WC2R 0RL
Penguin Group (USA)
375 Hudson Street, NY 10014, USA
Penguin Group (Australia)
250 Camberwell Road, Camberwell,
Victoria 3124, Australia
Penguin Books Canada Ltd,
10 Alcorn Avenue, Toronto, Ontario,
Canada M4V 1E4
Penguin Group (NZ)
67 Apollo Drive, Mairangi Bay, Auckland 1310,
New Zealand

Cover concept by Peter Dyer.
Typeset in Bembo and Helvetica to an original
design by Henry Iles.
Printed and bound in China
© Rough Guides 2007
No part of this book may be reproduced in any
form without permission from the publisher except
for the quotation of brief passages in reviews.
576pp includes index
A catalogue record for this book is available from
the British Library
ISBN: 978-1-84353-806-6
The publishers and authors have done their
best to ensure the accuracy and currency of
all the information in **The Rough Guide to
the Philippines**, however, they can accept no
responsibility for any loss, injury, or inconvenience
sustained by any traveller as a result of
information or advice contained in the guide.

3   5   7   9   8   6   4

Help us update

We've gone to a lot of effort to ensure that the
second edition of **The Rough Guide to the
Philippines** is accurate and up to date. However,
things change – places get "discovered", opening
hours are notoriously fickle, restaurants and
rooms raise prices or lower standards. If you
feel we've got it wrong or left something out,
we'd like to know, and if you can remember the
address, the price, the time, the phone number,
so much the better.
We'll credit all contributions, and send a copy of
the next edition (or any other Rough Guide if you

prefer) for the best letters. Everyone who writes
to us and isn't already a subscriber will receive
a copy of our full-colour thrice-yearly newsletter.
Please mark letters: **"Rough Guide Philippines
Update"** and send to: Rough Guides, 80 Strand,
London WC2R 0RL, or Rough Guides, 345
Hudson St, 4th Floor, New York, NY 10014. Or
send an email to **mail@roughguides.com**
Have your questions answered and tell others
about your trip at
www.roughguides.atinfopop.com

Acknowledgements

The clichés are true, the Philippines is a hospitable country, and there were many who went out of their way to help when they didn't have to. Among them were Lynne Palma and Vicky Aldaba in Manila, Cristina and Noel Matta in Palawan, and Liok Minola in Cebu. Old friends David Wheeler and Sam Dixon were enthusiastic guides to nightlife. Monica de Leon and the staff at Seair's Inflight magazine pointed me in the right direction many times and helped with logistics. Geselle Javison kindly checked and re-checked the language section. Thanks as always to Giselle and Bridget.

SMALL PRINT

Readers' letters

Thanks to all the readers who have taken the time to write in with comments and suggestions (and apologies if we've inadvertently omitted or misspelt anyone's name):

Rick Asher, Arden Bashforth, Polly Bay, Jun Canta, Sam Dixon, Macy Espaldon, Susan Flores, Jonathan Gabel, Fernando Gomez, Geselle Javison, Kalle Kalitta, Alisa Mandel, Matt Othman, Harold Otness, Sam Ryder, Ed Scott, John Shepherd, Michael Tan, Team DiveZone, Arjun Tyagi, David Wheeler, Mike White.

Photo credits

All photos © Rough Guides except the following:

Index

Map entries are in colour.

INDEX

Map symbols

maps are listed in the full index using coloured text

▪▫▪▫▪	Province boundary	✈	Airport
▪▪▪▪	International boundary	◉	Accommodation
─ ─ ─	Chapter division boundary	▣	Restaurant/café/bar
═══	Major road	⊞	Hospital/medical centre
═══	Minor road	ⓘ	Tourist office
▬▬▬	Motorway	⊠	Post office
▥▥▥	Steps	ⓒ	Phone office
───	Unpaved road	E	Embassy/consulate
-----	Path	�	Museum
─┼─┼─	Railway	⊙	Statue/memorial
─ ─ ─	Ferry route	⚑	Golf course
─Ⓜ─	Metro line & station	@	Internet access
───	River	★	Bus stop
───	Wall	∴	Ruins
⊠	Gate	✝	Church (regional maps)
)(	Bridge	⛪	Monastery
⋀⋁	Spring/spa	☪	Mosque
▲	Mountain peak	☐	Market
⋀⋀	Mountain range	▦	Building
/⋀	Volcano	⊞	Church (town maps)
⫛	Waterfall	⬭	Stadium
⸰⸰⸰⸰	Reef	⊞	Cemetery
⫯⫯⫯	Cliff	▦	Park
♦	Point of interest	▦	Beach
⋎	Viewpoint	⬓	Swamp
ⵠ	Lighthouse	▦	Forest
⌂	Cave	◹	Dense/Impenetrable area

MAP SYMBOLS

I